January 13–14, 2015
Mumbai, India

Association for
Computing Machinery

Advancing Computing as a Science & Profession

PEPM'15

Proceedings of the 2015 ACM SIGPLAN Workshop on

Partial Evaluation and Program Manipulation

Sponsored by:

ACM SIGPLAN

Co-located with:

POPL'15

Association for
Computing Machinery

Advancing Computing as a Science & Profession

The Association for Computing Machinery
2 Penn Plaza, Suite 701
New York, New York 10121-0701

ISBN: 978-1-4503-3297-2

Additional copies may be ordered prepaid from:

ACM Order Department
PO Box 30777
New York, NY 10087-0777, USA

Phone: 1-800-342-6626 (USA and Canada)
+1-212-626-0500 (Global)
Fax: +1-212-944-1318
E-mail: acmhelp@acm.org
Hours of Operation: 8:30 am – 4:30 pm ET

Printed in the USA

Foreword

It is our great pleasure to welcome you to the *ACM SIGPLAN 2015 Workshop on Partial Evaluation and Program Manipulation – PEPM'15*, taking place in Mumbai, India, on the 13th and 14th of January 2015. The PEPM series aims to bring together researchers and practitioners working in the broad area of program transformation, an area which spans from refactoring, partial evaluation, super-compilation, staged programming, fusion and other meta-programming to model-driven development, program analyses including termination, inductive programming, program generation and applications of machine learning and probabilistic search.

In response to the call for papers, 27 abstracts were submitted, from which 20 materialized as paper submissions. Their topics covered theory and applications of various analysis and program manipulation techniques. The program committee decided to accept 14 of them, ten as full papers, three as short papers and one as a brief announcement. Few submissions got three reviews, the majority got four, and the remaining ones five. Afterwards the PC voted to select the best paper accepted for *PEPM'15*. We are delighted to announce that the award for the best paper submitted goes to

Constraint Specialisation in Horn Clause Verification

by **Bishoksan Kafle** and **John P. Gallagher**

This volume also includes the abstract of the invited talk by Shriram Krishnamurthi.

Putting together *PEPM'15* was a team effort. First of all, we would like to thank the authors of all submitted papers, not only for writing up their technical work for PEPM, but also for their prompt submission of the final copy for these proceedings. Without the Program Committee, we would have had no programme either, and we are very grateful to the PC members for their hard work, particularly since they conducted the reviewing and sometimes shepherding duties quite thoroughly under tight deadlines. A number of Additional Reviewers also contributed to the reviewing process, and we and the PC would like to acknowledge their help and effort.

Shortly after the acceptance notification deadline of *PEPM'15* and while preparing these proceedings, we got informed that Germán Puebla passed away after a long fight with cancer. Germán has published a considerable number of papers at previous PEPMs, was an invited speaker of *PEPM'03* and served as program co-chair of *PEPM'09*. On behalf of the PEPM community we would like to dedicate these proceedings to Germán's memory. He will be missed.

The PEPM Steering Committee, and particularly its chair, Oleg Kiselyov, have given us support, advice and encouragement throughout the process. Sriram Rajamani and David Van Horn, the General Chair and the Workshops Chair for *POPL'15*, eased the burden of making local and organizational arrangements, as well as assisting us in finalizing the production timetable. The staff at Sheridan Communications has assisted us in getting the proceedings together. Finally, we would like to thank our sponsor, ACM SIGPLAN, for their continued support of the PEPM series.

We hope that you will find these proceedings interesting and thought provoking and that the symposium will provide you with a valuable opportunity to share ideas with other researchers and practitioners from institutions around the world.

Kenichi Asai
PEPM'15 Program Co-Chair
Ochanomizu University, Japan

Konstantinos Sagonas
PEPM'15 Program Co-Chair
Uppsala University, Sweden / NTUA, Greece

Table of Contents

Session: Analysis

PEPM 2015 Workshop Organization

Program Chairs: Kenichi Asai *(Ochanomizu University, Japan)*
Kostis Sagonas *(Uppsala University, Sweden / NTUA, Greece)*

POPL'15 Workshop Chair: David van Horn *(University of Maryland, USA)*

Steering Committee Chair: Oleg Kiselyov *(University of Tsukuba, Japan)*

Steering Committee: Elvira Albert *(Complutense University of Madrid, Spain)*
Wei-Ngan Chin *(National University of Singapore, Singapore)*
Jurriaan Hage *(Utrecht University, Netherlands)*
Shin-Cheng Mu *(Academia Sinica, Taiwan)*
Simon Thompson *(University of Kent, UK)*

Program Committee: Andreas Abel *(Gothenburg University, Sweden)*
Elvira Albert *(Complutense University of Madrid, Spain)*
Małgorzata Biernacka *(University of Wrocław, Poland)*
Matthias Blume *(Google, USA)*
Cristiano Calcagno *(Facebook, UK)*
Jacques Carette *(McMaster University, Canada)*
Jeremy Gibbons *(University of Oxford, UK)*
Nao Hirokawa *(JAIST, Japan)*
Atsushi Igarashi *(Kyoto University, Japan)*
Andrei Klimov *(Keldysh Institute of Applied Mathematics, Russia)*
Michael Leuschel *(University of Düsseldorf, Germany)*
Sam Lindley *(University of Edinburgh, UK)*
Michał Moskal *(Microsoft Research, USA)*
Keiko Nakata *(Institute of Cybernetics, Estonia)*
Jeremy Siek *(Indiana University, USA)*
Peter Thiemann *(University of Freiburg, Germany)*
Janis Voigtländer *(University of Bonn, Germany)*
Kwangkeun Yi *(Seoul National University, Korea)*
Tetsuo Yokoyama *(Nanzan University, Japan)*

Additional reviewers:

Miltiadis Allamanis
Meital Ben-Sinai
Richard Bubel
Witold Charatonik
Avik Chaudhuri
Yuki Chiba
Jesús Correas Fernández
Samir Genaim
Miguel Gomez-Zamalloa
Thomas Jensen
Marek Materzok
Manuel Montenegro
Hakjoo Oh
Roly Perera
Sukyoung Ryu
Filip Sieczkowski
Josef Svenningsson
Vesal Vojdani
Eran Yahav

Sponsor: acm SIGPLAN

Co-located with: POPL 2015
Mumbai, India
January 12-18

Desugaring in Practice: Opportunities and Challenges

Shriram Krishnamurthi
Brown University
sk@cs.brown.edu

Abstract

Desugaring, a key form of program manipulation, is a vital tool in the practical study of programming languages. Its use enables pragmatic solutions to the messy problems of dealing with real languages, but it also introduces problems that need addressing. By listing some of these challenges, this paper and talk aim to serve as a call to arms to the community to give the topic more attention.

Categories and Subject Descriptors D.3.4 [*Programming Languages*]: Processors

Keywords Desugaring; Resugaring; Semantics; Optimization

The Need for Desugaring

Concise core languages have a venerable place in the study of programming languages. By providing a means to reduce languages to an essence, they help us focus on important details and eschew ones irrelevant to the purpose of study. Furthermore, the difficulty of reducing some features may point to places where the language suffers from design flaws.

The use of core languages is not only of theoretical value. Practical systems also benefit from having a smaller number of features to work with: interpreters, compilers, type-checkers, program analyses, model checkers, and so on. Indeed, lurking inside every one of these systems is usually a smaller core fit for that purpose.

Unfortunately, the *process* of reducing a language to a core—which we loosely dub *desugaring*—has not received the attention it deserves, perhaps because it is not usually considered of theoretical interest.[1] As programming language research is increasingly applied to large languages (usually of industrial importance), the need to shrink languages—and hence for desugaring—has increased significantly, and with it the challenges faced.

[1] I use the term "loosely" for the following reason. In principle, a close reading of the term "desugaring" implies that the core language is a *strict subset* of the source. In practice, it is often useful for the "core" to be a slightly different language, better suited to the task at hand: for instance, for semantic analysis, we might map some object languages to a λ-calculus. In such cases, the desugarer is technically a compiler. However, it is rarely a general-purpose compiler, and the term "desugar" better evokes its intended purpose. This justifies our abuse of language.

PEPM '15, Jan 13–14 2015, Mumbai, India.

ACM 978-1-4503-3297-2/15/01.
http://dx.doi.org/10.1145/2678015.2678016

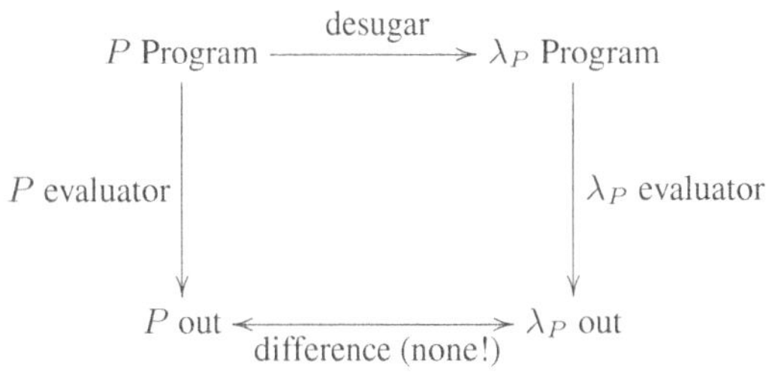

Figure 1. Testing Strategy for λ_P

Desugaring in Semantic Specifications

Figure 1 illustrates a process that is now used for many real-world languages such as JavaScript and Python. For the language P, researchers define a core language, λ_P. Does λ_P really captures the essence of P: i.e., cover all of P and when translated, with the same behavior? It is usually easy to produce an evaluator for λ_P, while P evaluators are already available. Using test suites, programs found in the wild, etc., we can check for this conformance.

Once a suitable λ_P and desugaring pair have been found, the result is of practical value. Writing tools for λ_P is much easier than dealing with the full details of P itself. Therefore, even research groups with limited resources can—with the help of desugaring—try to apply their tools to real programs, thereby improving the utility of their research and the quality of their evaluation.

Challenges

While this picture is attractive in theory, there are many practical problems that confront the widespread use of desugaring. While some research has made progress on many of these fronts, general solutions that apply widely remain out of reach and are therefore ripe areas for future investigation. Some of these are described below, arranged in the order I conjecture to be the simplest to the most sophisticated.

Shrinking output in a semantics-preserving way The first and most persistent problem a user of any desugaring output confronts is the often large size of the output. Even simple examples can produce very large output: for instance, in the JavaScript semantics S5 [2], `console.log("Hello world")` produces the output shown in Figure 2. This code blow-up can frustate attempts to understand the output and to subsequently debug programs that process it.

Two main factors result in this blow-up: the inherent complexity of the source language, and the consequence of using a context-insensitive recursive-descent code generation process. The former is essential complexity from the perspective of preserving the language's behavior. We believe the latter can be addressed

```
{let
 (%context = %nonstrictContext)
 {%defineGlobalAccessors(%context,
                         "console");
  {let
   (#strict = false)
   {let
    (%obj1 = %context["console" , {[#proto: null,
                                    #class: "Object",
                                    #extensible: true,]}])
     {let
      (%fun2 = %ToObject(%obj1)["log" , {[#proto: null,
                                          #class: "Object",
                                          #extensible: true,]}])
      {let
       (%ftype3 = prim("typeof", %fun2))
       if (prim("!", prim("stx=", %ftype3 , "function")))
          {%TypeError("Not a function")}
          else
          {%fun2(%ToObject(%obj1),
                 %mkArgsObj({[#proto: null,
                              #class: "Object",
                              #extensible: true,]
                             '0' : {#value ("hello world") ,
                                    #writable true ,
                                    #configurable true}}))}}}}}}}
```

Figure 2. Desugaring of `console.log("hello world")`

by various program optimization techniques that can usefully shrink this output without altering its semantics. However, techniques designed for source programs can often perform weakly on generated code and vice versa. We are experimenting with the viability of different techniques for this purpose.

Shrinking output by altering semantics It is both worthwhile and uncontroversial to apply semantics-preserving optimizations. A more controversial idea is to engage in semantics-*altering* transformations.

A fully semantics-preserving desugaring must contain code that handles every possible corner case; the more complex the language, the more cases there are. This will include cases that are being disregarded in the current application. For instance, most static analyses assume away the presence of dynamic features like `eval` or reflective ones like Python's `locals`. By removing support for some features, we can have a noticeable effect on the size of desugared output. Furthermore, this interacts with semantics-preserving optimizations by exposing new opportunities for reduction.

Resugaring Desugared programs can be hard to work with. By having control over the desugaring process, it should be possible to at least partially "reverse" the desugaring process—in effect, to "resugar" programs. This becomes especially interesting in the presence of black-box transformations such as evaluation, optimization, and so on: to still present the new program in terms of the source that the author wrote. While there have been many ad hoc proposals to do this (e.g., for debugging optimized code), there are relatively few approaches that formally specify the properties expected of the resugaring process.

Relating multiple desugarings Desugaring is always relative to some purpose. In practice, different purposes often rely on different desugarings. For instance, a type-checker will want algebraic datatype definitions preserved; a type-inference system might want a `let`-like construct to also be preserved to perform polymorphic generalization; while an interpreter might want all these eliminated. Therefore, there is rarely *the* core of a language, but rather many cores.

Because all these desugarings correspond to the same surface language, it would be ideal to relate them to one another. While a testing approach (as in Figure 1) offers one way to relate them, it would be helpful to also do so formally, especially by focusing on the differences between them and identifying how these differences are semantics-preserving.

Learning desugaring from examples Finally, it is worth asking how much the process of generating a desugaring can be automated. In our experience, creating a semantics—with most of the time spent on desugaring—can be enormously time-consuming: from 6 to 28 person-months of highly-trained labor. This level of effort makes it infeasible to tackle the semantics of the large number of languages and systems in widespread use.

However, as Figure 1 suggests, we can think of this as a learning problem where, because of the presence of the evaluators acting as ground truth, we can generate new examples to improve the quality of learning. We have tried to apply a variety of machine learning techniques to this task, with distinctly mixed results so far. Nevertheless, it seems necessary to work on this if we are to have the Next 700 Semantics.

Impact on Reproducible Research

Desugaring has a valuable role in presenting research in a reproducible way. When researchers attempt to tackle large, industrial languages, they rarely ever tackle the language as a whole. Rather, it is common to pick some strict subset of the language. Unfortunately, the precise parameters of this subset are usually left loosely specified—or even unspecified—and need to be reconstructed from a paper presentation. This makes accurate comparison of competing work difficult, giving too much credit to some work and not enough to others.

Having a family of related desugarings, and semantics-altering desugarings that formally restrict the language, offers a way out of this dilemma. By picking and publishing a formally restricted desugaring, authors can effectively advertise precisely what sublanguage they are actually working with. Because this is a computational artifact, other authors can use it in their comparisons, making it easier for authors, program committees, and third-party researchers to arrive at a much more accurate understanding of how different projects compare.

Desguaring in the Language

Finally, the Lisp family has a venerable tradition of providing desguaring features in the language itself. Recently, languages like Racket have taken this to new heights, enabling the definition of entirely new languages [1]. Though the challenges above have been written in terms of desugaring for semantics, many of them apply equally well to desugaring in the language, such as shrinking the output in semantics-preserving and even semantics-altering ways (for comprehension, debugging, and perhaps even performance), resugaring, and applying different desugarings in different contexts. As this powerful idea ripples (in various guises) through many other language families—from C++ to Scala to Haskell—the need for research to tackle these problems will only increase.

Acknowledgments

The work reported here was primarily done in collaboration with Arjun Guha, Joe Gibbs Politz, Ben Lerner, and Justin Pombrio. I thank them for forming and shaping my perspective. I have also benefited greatly by working with Claudiu Saftoiu, Junsong Li, and my other co-authors. This work is partially supported by the NSF and Google.

References

[1] M. Flatt and PLT. Reference: Racket. Technical Report PLT-TR2010-1, PLT Inc., June 2010. `http://racket-lang.org/tr1/`.

[2] J. G. Politz, M. Carroll, B. S. Lerner, J. Pombrio, and S. Krishnamurthi. A tested semantics for Getters, Setters, and Eval in JavaScript. In *Dynamic Languages Symposium*, 2012.

Imperative Polymorphism by Store-Based Types as Abstract Interpretations

Casper Bach Poulsen Peter D. Mosses Paolo Torrini

Swansea University

{cscbp,p.d.mosses,p.torrini}@swansea.ac.uk

Abstract

Dealing with polymorphism in the presence of imperative features is a long-standing open problem for Hindley-Milner type systems. A widely adopted approach is the value restriction, which inhibits polymorphic generalisation and unfairly rejects various programs that cannot go wrong. We consider abstract interpretation as a tool for constructing safe and precise type systems, and investigate how to derive store-based types by abstract interpretation. We propose store-based types as a type discipline that holds potential for interesting and flexible alternatives to the value restriction.

Categories and Subject Descriptors D.3.1 [*PROGRAMMING LANGUAGES*]: Formal Definitions and Theory—semantics

Keywords type systems; operational semantics; references; polymorphism; abstract interpretation; store-based typing

1. Introduction

The Hindley-Milner type discipline is elegant and flexible for functional languages, but extending it to deal soundly with imperative features can be challenging. In particular, adding ML-style reference types to this discipline, without introducing appropriate constraints on generalisation, is well-known to break type safety [21]. Consider the program:

$$\begin{array}{l}\texttt{let}\ c\ \texttt{=}\ \texttt{ref}\ (\lambda x.x)\\ \texttt{in}\ c\ \texttt{:=}\ (\lambda x.1+x);\\ \quad(\texttt{!}c)\,\texttt{true}\end{array}$$

Assuming generalisation is unconstrained, line 1 sets `c` equal to a reference of type $\forall\alpha.\ (\alpha \to \alpha)$ `ref`. Line 2 makes an assignment which appears to be valid, since the type `int` $\to$ `int` of the expression is an instance of $\forall\alpha.\ (\alpha \to \alpha)$. Line 3 leads to a run-time type error, attempting to evaluate $1 +$ `true`. However, the static analyser does not detect the update in the store, and gives this program type `bool`, since `bool` $\to$ `bool` is an instance of $\forall\alpha.\ \alpha \to \alpha$, too.

Several techniques have been proposed to deal with this problem (see section 4.2), which may result in a serious obstacle to refactoring, hindering type-directed replacement of functional code by imperative code. The solution that has been widely adopted in practice, mainly due to its simplicity, is the so-called *value restriction* proposed by Wright [23]: generalisation of type parameters is only allowed for let-expressions where the expression being bound is a value. This turns out to be liberal enough in most cases, since unevaluated expressions can be lifted to values by η-expansion. However, this can be problematic when we are interested in program behaviour rather than merely the input-output relation, since η-lifting may force radical changes in the order of evaluation.

In this paper, we propose a novel approach to relaxing the value restriction, that we call *store-based typing*, and that we have developed using a transformational technique. The contributions we are making fall into two categories:

- Technical: we use a novel combination of techniques, including a variant of coinductive big-step semantics [11] and abstract interpretation [6] to guide the transformation of a dynamic operational semantics into a type semantics that is safe by construction.
- Practical: a novel approach to type inference with promising potential for more flexible typing disciplines for imperative polymorphism.

The rest of this paper is structured as follows: we first introduce a coinductive big-step semantics for the call-by-value λ-calculus without references in Sect. 2. The big-step semantics forms the basis for deriving safe base, mono- and polytype systems in Sect. 3, which is largely based on Cousot's work on types as abstract interpretations [5], but using an operational, rather than denotational, approach. Extending our language with references in Sect. 4, we propose a store-based polytype semantics for imperative let-polymorphism. Section 5 recalls related work and outlines future directions.

2. A Novel Style of Coinductive Semantics

Consider the following grammar for the λ-calculus with integer constants $i \in \mathbb{Z}$ and variables $x \in Var$.

$$Expr \ni e ::= \lambda x.e \mid e\ e \mid x \mid i$$

Using ordinary big-step semantics, also known as *natural semantics* [10], the *inductive* interpretation of the following rules defines the judgment $\rho \vdash e \Rightarrow v$ to hold just when left to right, eager evaluation of e in environment ρ terminates with value v.

$$\frac{}{\rho \vdash \lambda x.e \Rightarrow \langle x, e, \rho\rangle} \qquad \frac{\rho(x) = v}{\rho \vdash x \Rightarrow v} \qquad \frac{}{\rho \vdash i \Rightarrow i}$$

$$\frac{\rho \vdash e_1 \Rightarrow \langle x, e, \rho'\rangle \quad \rho \vdash e_2 \Rightarrow v_2 \quad \rho'[x \mapsto v_2] \vdash e \Rightarrow v}{\rho \vdash e_1\ e_2 \Rightarrow v}$$

PEPM '15, January 13–14, 2015, Mumbai, India.

ACM 978-1-4503-3297-2/15/01...$15.00.
http://dx.doi.org/10.1145/2678015.2682545

Here, environments $\rho \in Env \triangleq Var \xrightarrow{\text{fin}} Val$, and values $v \in Val$ include integers i and closures $\langle x, e, \rho \rangle$.

The above semantics does not distinguish between expressions whose evaluation diverges (e.g., $\omega \triangleq (\lambda x.x\, x)(\lambda x.x\, x)$) and those whose evaluation gets stuck (e.g., $0\,0$). Leroy and Grall [11] show that the *coinductive* interpretation of such big-step rules lets some diverging expressions have values, but not all. For example, $\rho \vdash \omega \Rightarrow v$ for all ρ, v, but not $\rho \vdash \omega\,(0\,0) \Rightarrow v$, since the premises of the application rule require a value for the stuck term

To detect divergence one can follow Cousot [7] as well as Leroy and Grall, and define a divergence predicate $\Rightarrow^\infty$ coinductively:

$$\frac{\rho \vdash e_1 \Rightarrow^\infty}{\rho \vdash e_1\, e_2 \Rightarrow^\infty} \qquad \frac{\rho \vdash e_1 \Rightarrow \langle x, e, \rho' \rangle \quad \rho \vdash e_2 \Rightarrow^\infty}{\rho \vdash e_1\, e_2 \Rightarrow^\infty}$$

$$\frac{\rho \vdash e_1 \Rightarrow \langle x, e, \rho' \rangle \quad \rho \vdash e_2 \Rightarrow v_2 \quad \rho'[x \mapsto v_2] \vdash e \Rightarrow^\infty}{\rho \vdash e_1\, e_2 \Rightarrow^\infty}$$

This gives $\rho \vdash \omega\,(0\,0) \Rightarrow^\infty$. There are two pragmatic problems: (i) the need for extra rules and premises, known as the *duplication problem* [3, 4]; (ii) to prove a property of our semantics may involve *both* $\Rightarrow$ and $\Rightarrow^\infty$. The alternative of merely adding a $\perp$ element to the semantics still involves a significant number of extra rules and premises that also clutter the reasoning steps involved in proofs.

Here, we propose a new way of encoding divergence that subsumes both the ordinary $\rho \vdash e \Rightarrow v$ relation and the $\rho \vdash e \Rightarrow^\infty$ predicate. We introduce a 'divergence flag':

$$Div \ni \delta ::= \downarrow \mid \uparrow$$

A change from $\downarrow$ to $\uparrow$ corresponds to divergence arising. Augmenting our relation with this flag, the judgment becomes $\rho \vdash e_{/\delta} \Rightarrow v_{/\delta'}$, saying that evaluating e in divergence state δ gives the outcome v in divergence state δ'. Figure 1 gives the rules for our augmented relation. The crucial rule that allows us to propagate divergence between premises is the divergence rule DIV. The intuition is that, if we are diverging, no value is produced, so we may choose any value v. The other rules are obtained from the original big-step rules systematically, reflecting the intended order of evaluation.

$$\frac{}{\rho \vdash i_{/\downarrow} \Rightarrow i_{/\downarrow}}\ (\text{INT}) \qquad \frac{}{\rho \vdash e_{/\uparrow} \Rightarrow v_{/\uparrow}}\ (\text{DIV})$$

$$\frac{\rho(x) = v}{\rho \vdash x_{/\downarrow} \Rightarrow v_{/\downarrow}}\ (\text{VAR}) \qquad \frac{}{\rho \vdash \lambda x.e_{/\downarrow} \Rightarrow \langle x, e, \rho \rangle_{/\downarrow}}\ (\text{ABS})$$

$$\frac{\rho \vdash e_{1/\downarrow} \Rightarrow \langle x, e, \rho' \rangle_{/\delta} \quad \rho \vdash e_{2/\delta} \Rightarrow v_{2/\delta'} \quad \rho'[x \mapsto v_2] \vdash e_{/\delta'} \Rightarrow v_{/\delta''}}{\rho \vdash e_1\, e_{2/\downarrow} \Rightarrow v_{/\delta''}}\ (\text{APP})$$

Figure 1. Coinductive evaluation rules using a divergence flag

It is worth spelling out the relationship between the rules with the divergence flag and Leroy and Grall's big-step semantics. The rules corresponding to the $\Rightarrow^\infty$ relation can be obtained by unfolding the premises of the big-step rules relative to the DIV rule. The judgment $\rho \vdash e_{/\downarrow} \Rightarrow v_{/\uparrow}$ is not derivable under an inductive interpretation of our rules (ensured by insisting that the conclusion and first premise start in a converging state for all rules, except DIV). Therefore, if we can derive it using coinduction, it must be a diverging computation. It is, however, possible to prove $\rho \vdash e_{/\downarrow} \Rightarrow v_{/\downarrow}$ for some diverging computations (e.g., $\rho \vdash \omega_{/\downarrow} \Rightarrow v_{/\downarrow}$ for any v).

In summary, a proof that something coevaluates to $\downarrow$ does not imply that it is in the inductive relation. In contrast, a proof that something coevaluates to $\uparrow$ implies that it is a diverging computation, and thus not in the inductive relation. The lack of distinction between some converging and diverging computations in the coinductive relation is not important for the purpose of this paper. The important point is that we have obtained a concisely defined relation containing all converging and diverging computations.

3. Deriving Church/Curry Polytypes

The abstract interpretation framework [6] provides a systematic method for constructing safe approximations of the semantics of programs. We follow [5] in abstracting type systems from the so-called collecting semantics, but start from coinductive big-step operational semantics instead of denotational semantics.

We first define an abstraction to *base types* (obtained by replacing types for ground values in expressions) as in [13, 14]. Subsequently, we introduce an abstraction of base types (after extending the language with a let construct) to Hindley-Milner polytypes. Polytypes can be further abstracted to monotypes, following [5].

3.1 Collecting Semantics

Let $\mathbb{S} \triangleq Env \to \wp(Val \times Div)$. With reference to the coinductive interpretation of the rules in Fig. 1, let $\mathbf{S}[\![\bullet]\!] \in Expr \to \mathbb{S}$ be defined by $\mathbf{S}[\![e]\!] \triangleq \Lambda\rho.\ \{\langle v, \delta \rangle \mid \rho \vdash e_{/\downarrow} \Rightarrow v_{/\delta}\}$, where Λ is meta-level function abstraction (following [5]).

A *property* of an expression is a subset of $\mathbb{S}$, i.e., an element of $\mathbb{C} \triangleq \wp(\mathbb{S})$. We are interested in the programs that do not get stuck. However, this property is undecidable. It can be approximated by introducing a notion of type. The *collecting semantics* $\mathbf{C}[\![\bullet]\!] \in Expr \to \mathbb{C}$, defined by $\mathbf{C}[\![e]\!] \triangleq \{\mathbf{S}[\![e]\!]\}$, is the property that gives the most precise information on a program. Abstract interpretation gives us a method for constructing approximations of well-behaved programs as type systems, starting from the collecting semantics, by using abstractions that ensure type soundness by definition. The notion of type soundness we are interested in here is the usual one, adapted to our big-step semantics:

$$\Gamma \vdash e : t \Longrightarrow \vdash \rho : \Gamma \Longrightarrow \exists v, \delta.\ \vdash v : t \wedge \rho \vdash e_{/\downarrow} \Rightarrow v_{/\delta}$$

where Γ is a typing environment and t a type.

Given two partially ordered sets $\langle \mathbb{P}, \sqsubseteq^{\mathbb{P}} \rangle$, $\langle \mathbb{Q}, \sqsubseteq^{\mathbb{Q}} \rangle$, a Galois connection $\langle \mathbb{P} \sqsubseteq^{\mathbb{P}} \rangle \underset{\alpha}{\overset{\gamma}{\leftrightarrows}} \langle \mathbb{Q}, \sqsubseteq^{\mathbb{Q}} \rangle$ arises for total functions $\alpha \in \mathbb{P} \to \mathbb{Q}$ (*abstraction*) and $\gamma \in \mathbb{Q} \to \mathbb{P}$ (*concretisation*) whenever $\alpha(p) \sqsubseteq^{\mathbb{Q}} q \iff p \sqsubseteq^{\mathbb{P}} \gamma(q)$ for all $p \in \mathbb{P}$ and $q \in \mathbb{Q}$. The progression we establish can be depicted:[1]

$$\langle \mathbb{C}, \subseteq^{\mathbb{C}} \rangle \underset{\alpha^b}{\overset{\gamma^b}{\leftrightarrows}} \langle \mathbb{B}, \supseteq^{\mathbb{B}} \rangle \underset{\alpha^p}{\overset{\gamma^p}{\leftrightarrows}} \langle \mathbb{P}, \supseteq^{\mathbb{P}} \rangle \underset{\alpha^m}{\overset{\gamma^m}{\leftrightarrows}} \langle \mathbb{M}, \supseteq^{\mathbb{M}} \rangle$$

where $\mathbb{C}$ is the domain for the collecting semantics, $\mathbb{B}$ for the base type semantics, $\mathbb{P}$ for the polytype semantics, and $\mathbb{M}$ for the monotype semantics. At each step, abstraction is defined so as to induce a typing relation as an abstract derivation that is sound with respect to the concrete one. The Galois connections arising by composition, from $\alpha^p \circ \alpha^b$ and $\alpha^m \circ \alpha^p \circ \alpha^b$ respectively, ensure that type soundness holds for polytypes and monotypes.

3.2 Base Type Abstraction

The idea is to replace the set of integers by an `int` type and preserve the structure of all other constructs. We proceed in three steps: defining the domain, describing the Galois connection, and using this to infer the structure of the type semantics.

Domain definitions. We are interested in the type of values that a program returns when it terminates. For this reason, we do not need the *Div* flag in the definition of the base type domain:

$$BType \ni b ::= \texttt{int} \mid \langle x, e, \rho^b \rangle$$

$$\rho^b \in BEnv \triangleq Var \xrightarrow{\text{fin}} BType \qquad \mathbb{B} \triangleq \wp(BEnv \times BType)$$

[1] The double headed arrow represents *Galois insertions*, meaning that the mapping is surjective.

Galois connection. We define the abstraction α^b of the collecting semantics in terms of an abstraction α^b_s of the denotations, which in turn is defined in terms of α^b_v which abstracts values, and α^b_ρ which abstracts environments by pointwise application of α^b_v.

$$\alpha^b \in \mathbb{C} \to \mathbb{B} \qquad \alpha^b_s \in \mathbb{S} \to \mathbb{B}$$
$$\alpha^b_v \in \mathit{Val} \to \mathit{BType} \qquad \alpha^b_\rho \in \mathit{Env} \to \mathit{BEnv}$$
$$\alpha^b_v(i) \triangleq \texttt{int} \qquad \alpha^b_v(\langle x, e, \rho\rangle) \triangleq \langle x, e, \alpha^b_\rho(\rho)\rangle$$
$$\alpha^b_s(S) \triangleq \{\langle \rho^b, b\rangle \mid \forall \rho.\ \rho^b = \alpha^b_\rho(\rho) \Longrightarrow$$
$$\exists v.\ b = \alpha^b_v(v) \wedge \langle v, \downarrow\rangle \in S(\rho)\}$$
$$\alpha^b_\rho(\rho) \triangleq \Lambda x.\ \alpha^b_v(\rho(x)) \qquad \alpha^b(C) \triangleq \bigcap_{S \in C}^{\mathbb{B}} \alpha^b_s(S)$$

The definition of α^b_s is designed to match our soundness schema. However, here it is convenient to strengthen it by restricting typeability to terminating programs, in order to derive the typing relation as an inductive one. Notice that from this particular definition of α^b_s, it follows that diverging and stuck programs have no type.

For all $\Delta \subseteq \mathbb{C}$, the following property holds:

$$\alpha^b(\bigcup^{\mathbb{C}} \Delta) = \bigcap_{C \in \Delta}^{\mathbb{B}} \alpha^b(C)$$

since:

$$\alpha^b(\bigcup^{\mathbb{C}} \Delta) = \bigcap_{S \in \bigcup \Delta}^{\mathbb{B}} \alpha^b_s(S) = \bigcap_{C \in \Delta, S \in C}^{\mathbb{B}} \alpha^b_s(S) = \bigcap_{C \in \Delta}^{\mathbb{B}} \alpha^b(C)$$

which suffices to establish the Galois connection:

$$\langle \mathbb{C}, \subseteq^{\mathbb{C}} \rangle \underset{\alpha^b}{\overset{\gamma^b}{\longleftrightarrow}} \langle \mathbb{B}, \supseteq^{\mathbb{B}} \rangle$$

Type semantics. Given the abstract specification of the desired typing semantics $\mathbf{B}[\![\bullet]\!] \in \mathit{Expr} \to \mathbb{B}$:

$$\mathbf{B}[\![e]\!] \triangleq \{\langle \rho^b, b\rangle \mid \rho^b \vdash e \Rightarrow^b b\}$$

the Galois connection provides a guideline for inferring its structural definition. The guiding constraint is the following:

$$\alpha^b(\mathbf{C}[\![e]\!]) \supseteq^{\mathbb{B}} \mathbf{B}[\![e]\!]$$

and therefore:

$$\alpha^b_s(\mathbf{S}[\![e]\!]) \supseteq^{\mathbb{B}} \mathbf{B}[\![e]\!]$$

Unfolding the definitions of $\mathbf{B}[\![\bullet]\!]$, $\mathbf{S}[\![\bullet]\!]$, and α^b_s, we obtain:

$$\rho^b \vdash e \Rightarrow^b b \Longrightarrow \rho^b = \alpha^b_\rho(\rho) \Longrightarrow$$
$$\exists v.\ b = \alpha^b_v(v) \wedge \rho \vdash e_{/\downarrow} \Rightarrow v_{/\downarrow}$$

Reasoning on the structure of the $\Rightarrow$ relation, a definition of $\Rightarrow^b$ can be found, by choosing it so that the proof goes through by induction on $\Rightarrow^b$. The simplest relation that admits such a structural induction proof is the one given by the following rules:

$$\frac{}{\rho^b \vdash i \Rightarrow^b \texttt{int}}\ (\text{B-INT}) \qquad \frac{\rho^b(x) = b}{\rho^b \vdash x \Rightarrow^b b}\ (\text{B-VAR})$$

$$\frac{}{\rho^b \vdash \lambda x.e \Rightarrow^b \langle x, e, \rho^b\rangle}\ (\text{B-ABS})$$

$$\frac{\rho^b \vdash e_1 \Rightarrow^b \langle x, e, \rho^b\rangle \quad \rho^b \vdash e_2 \Rightarrow^b b_2 \quad \rho^b[x \mapsto b_2] \vdash e \Rightarrow^b b_1}{\rho^b \vdash e_1\, e_2 \Rightarrow^b b_1}\ (\text{B-APP})$$

3.3 Hindley-Milner Polymorphism

Determining the base type of an expression essentially involves evaluating the expression, hence base types are rather useless as a type system. However, they can be useful as an intermediate abstraction [14]. Notice that base types have an implicitly polymorphic character (closure types can be informally understood to be polymorphic). For this reason, they provide an optimal starting point to define abstractions to proper polymorphic types.

Here we are interested in Hindley-Milner polymorphism, which has a well-known syntactic characterisation with good computational properties [8]. Also known as let-polymorphism, it is syntactically an extension of typed λ-calculus with type variables, allowing for type schemes (i.e., type expressions with variables), and it does not require any explicit use of quantification. Semantically, we characterise types as monotypes, and explain type schemes away in terms of sets of monotypes, that for us are the polytypes.

Hindley-Milner polymorphism is more restrictive than the unconstrained syntactic polymorphism of system F, but is more liberal than so-called weak polymorphism [17]. Weak polymorphism does not allow instantiation of type variables with polytypes (*predicative* restriction), nor functions to have polytype arguments (*prenex* restriction). Hindley-Milner polymorphism is obtained by relaxing the prenex restriction in let-expressions, whose evaluation is characterised by the following rule:

$$\frac{\rho \vdash e_{2/\downarrow} \Rightarrow v_{2/\delta} \qquad \rho[x \mapsto v_2] \vdash e_{1/\delta} \Rightarrow v_{1/\delta'}}{\rho \vdash (\texttt{let}\ x\ \texttt{=}\ e_2\ \texttt{in}\ e_1)_{/\downarrow} \Rightarrow v_{1/\delta'}}\ (\text{LET})$$

Domain definitions. We can abstractly specify the polytype domain as follows, on top of a minimal monotype syntax.

$$\mathit{MType} \ni m ::= \texttt{int} \mid m \to m$$
$$p \in \mathit{PType} \triangleq \wp(\mathit{MType})$$
$$\rho^p \in \mathit{PEnv} \triangleq \mathit{Var} \xrightarrow{\text{fin}} \mathit{PType} \qquad \mathbb{P} \triangleq \wp(\mathit{PEnv} \times \mathit{MType})$$

Galois connection. Value and environment abstraction give us naturally sets (comparable to the general types in [14]). Such sets may not be computable, but this does not prevent us from specifying type soundness by abstraction.

$$\alpha^p \in \mathbb{B} \to \mathbb{P} \qquad \alpha^p_\rho \in \mathit{BEnv} \to \wp(\mathit{PEnv})$$
$$\alpha^p_b \in \mathit{BType} \to \mathit{PType}$$
$$\alpha^p_b(\texttt{int}) \triangleq \{\texttt{int}\}$$
$$\alpha^p_b(\langle x, e, \rho^b\rangle) \triangleq \{m_2 \to m_1 \mid \forall b_2.\ m_2 \in \alpha^p_b(b_2) \Longrightarrow$$
$$\exists b_1.\ m_1 \in \alpha^p_b(b_1) \wedge \rho^b[x \mapsto b_2] \vdash e \Rightarrow^b b_1\}$$
$$\alpha^p_\rho(\rho^b) \triangleq \{\rho^p \mid \forall x.\ \rho^p(x) \subseteq \alpha^p_b(\rho^b(x))\}$$
$$\alpha^p(B) \triangleq \{\langle \rho^p, m\rangle \mid \forall \rho^b.\ \rho^p \in \alpha^p_\rho(\rho^b) \Longrightarrow$$
$$\exists b.\ m \in \alpha^p_b(b) \wedge \langle \rho^b, b\rangle \in B\}$$

The following Galois connection holds between base types and polytypes:

$$\langle \mathbb{B}, \supseteq^{\mathbb{B}} \rangle \underset{\alpha^p}{\overset{\gamma^p}{\longleftrightarrow}} \langle \mathbb{P}, \supseteq^{\mathbb{P}} \rangle$$

Type semantics. The specification of the semantics is:

$$\mathbf{P}[\![\bullet]\!] \in \mathit{Expr} \to \mathbb{P}$$
$$\mathbf{P}[\![e]\!] \triangleq \{\langle \rho^p, m\rangle \mid \rho^p \vdash e \Rightarrow^p m\}$$

Since Hindley-Milner polymorphism has principal types [8], we expect principality to be provable along the lines of [5, Sect. 12].

The guiding constraint provided by the Galois connection to define $\Rightarrow^p$ is the following:

$$\alpha^p(\mathbf{B}[\![e]\!]) \supseteq^{\mathbb{B}} \mathbf{P}[\![e]\!]$$

and therefore:

$$\forall m \in p.\ \rho^p \vdash e \Rightarrow^p m \Longrightarrow \rho^p \in \alpha^p_\rho(\rho^b) \Longrightarrow$$
$$\exists b.\ p \subseteq \alpha^p_b(b) \wedge \rho^b \vdash e \Rightarrow^b b$$

The expected definition of $\Rightarrow^p$ can be found by reasoning on the structure of e in order to make the proof go through by induction on $\Rightarrow^p$. Rules P-INT and P-VAR are similar to B-INT and B-VAR. The rule for $\rightarrow$ introduction:

$$\frac{\rho^p[x \mapsto \{m_2\}] \vdash e \Rightarrow^p m_1}{\rho^p \vdash \lambda x.e \Rightarrow^p m_2 \rightarrow m_1} \quad \text{(P-ABS)}$$

is basically built into the definition of α^p_b. Notice that x has to be typed by m_2 in this rule as b_2 can vary arbitrarily in that definition. The restriction of the polytype of x to a singleton here corresponds to the fact that the prenex restriction applies to non-let-expressions. The rule for $\rightarrow$ elimination:

$$\frac{\rho^p \vdash e_1 \Rightarrow^p m_2 \rightarrow m_1 \qquad \rho^p \vdash e_2 \Rightarrow^p m_2}{\rho^p \vdash e_1\ e_2 \Rightarrow^p m_1} \quad \text{(P-APP)}$$

can be inferred from the case of $e = e_1\, e_2$ of the proof. In fact, it is the simplest rule such that the premises of the B-APP instance needed to get the statement conclusion can be obtained via the induction hypothesis: given $\rho^p \in \alpha^p_\rho(\rho^b)$, from $\rho^p \vdash e_2 \Rightarrow^p m_2$ it follows $m_2 \in \alpha^p_b(b') \wedge \rho^b \vdash e_2 \Rightarrow^b b'$ for some b'; from $\rho^p \vdash e_1 \Rightarrow^p m_2 \rightarrow m_1$ it follows $(m_2 \rightarrow m_1) \in \alpha^p_b(\langle x, e', \rho^b\rangle) \wedge \rho^b \vdash e_1 \Rightarrow^b \langle x, e', \rho^b\rangle$ for some e', and thus, by definition of α^p_b, also $m_1 \in \alpha^p_b(b) \wedge \rho^b[x \mapsto b'] \vdash e' \Rightarrow^b b$ for some b. The rule for let:

$$\frac{p \neq \emptyset \qquad \begin{array}{l}\forall m_2 \in p.\ \rho^p \vdash e_2 \Rightarrow^p m_2 \\ \rho^p[x \mapsto p] \vdash e_1 \Rightarrow^p m_1\end{array}}{\rho^p \vdash \texttt{let}\ x\ \texttt{=}\ e_2\ \texttt{in}\ e_1 \Rightarrow^p m_1} \quad \text{(P-LET)}$$

can be inferred from the case $e = \texttt{let}\ x\ \texttt{=}\ e_2\ \texttt{in}\ e_1$. First we need to extend the base type abstraction to LET. This gives us:

$$\frac{\rho^b \vdash e_2 \Rightarrow^b b_2 \qquad \rho^b[x \mapsto b_2] \vdash e_1 \Rightarrow^b b_1}{\rho^b \vdash \texttt{let}\ x\ \texttt{=}\ e_2\ \texttt{in}\ e_1 \Rightarrow^b b_1} \quad \text{(B-LET)}$$

Rule P-LET can then be justified as the rule needed for the B-LET case: from the first premise of P-LET it follows there is a b_2 such that $p \subseteq \alpha^p_b(b_2) \wedge \rho^b \vdash e_2 \Rightarrow^b b_2$; from $\rho^p[x \mapsto p] \vdash e_1 \Rightarrow^p m_1$ it follows $m_1 \in \alpha^p_b(b_1) \wedge \rho^b[x \mapsto b_2] \vdash e' \Rightarrow^b b_1$.

3.4 Church/Curry Monotype Abstraction

Following Cousot [5], we can specify the monotype domain:

$$\rho^m \in \mathit{MEnv} \triangleq \mathit{Var} \xrightarrow{\text{fin}} \mathit{MType} \qquad \mathbb{M} \triangleq \wp(\mathit{MEnv} \times \mathit{MType})$$

and define a Galois insertion between polytypes and monotypes:

$$\langle \mathbb{P}, \supseteq^{\mathbb{P}} \rangle \underset{\alpha^m}{\overset{\gamma^m}{\leftrightarrows}} \langle \mathbb{M}, \supseteq^{\mathbb{M}} \rangle$$

$$\alpha^m(P) \triangleq \{\langle \rho^m, m\rangle \mid (\Lambda x.\{\rho^m(x)\}, m) \in P\}$$
$$\gamma^m(M) \triangleq \{(\Lambda x.\{\rho^m(x)\}, m) \mid \langle \rho^m, m\rangle \in M\}$$

The surjectivity of α^m ensures γ^m is injective, but α^m involves a loss of information [5, Sect. 7]. The monotype semantics is:

$$\mathbf{M}[\![\bullet]\!] \in \mathit{Expr} \rightarrow \mathbb{M}$$
$$\mathbf{M}[\![e]\!] \triangleq \{\langle \rho^m, m\rangle \mid \rho^m \vdash e \Rightarrow^m m\}$$

By following the constraint:

$$\alpha^m(\mathbf{P}[\![e]\!]) \supseteq^{\mathbb{B}} \mathbf{M}[\![e]\!]$$

it is not difficult to see that the definition of $\Rightarrow^m$ simply involves replacing polytype environments with monotype ones in the $\Rightarrow^p$ rules, leaving the rest unchanged. Notice that $\texttt{let}\ x\ \texttt{=}\ e_2\ \texttt{in}\ e_1$ and $(\lambda x.e_1)\, e_2$ here become equivalent.

4. Store-Based Types

In this section we propose a novel approach to imperative polymorphism. It is straightforward to extend the language considered in the previous section with ML-style references, and to add locations and stores to its coinductive big-step evaluation rules. When using abstract interpretation to define type systems for the extended language, however, we need to choose how to approximate the locations and stores.

Here, we give a polymorphic type system that results from retaining exact information about allocation and updates, while approximating all values other than locations by types (as in the previous section). This system allows so-called *strong updates* [2] where assignment can change the type of value stored at a location. We give examples of programs that have types in our system, but not with previous approaches. Further exploration of our approach is needed to establish its potential usefulness and safety.

4.1 Store-Based Types

Adding stores to the call-by-value λ-calculus, the grammar from Sect. 2 is extended as follows:

$$\mathit{Expr} \ni e ::= \ldots \mid \texttt{ref}\ e \mid \texttt{!}e \mid e\ \texttt{:=}\ e$$

Values $v \in \mathit{Val}$ now include locations $l \in \mathit{Loc}$. The rules in Fig. 2 give the dynamic semantics of our extended language, which defines the judgment $\rho \vdash e_{/\sigma|\delta} \Rightarrow v_{/\sigma'|\delta'}$ to hold when left to right evaluation of expression e in environment ρ, store σ, and divergence state δ, gives the outcome consisting of value v, result store σ', and divergence state δ'. Here, stores $\sigma \in \mathit{Loc} \rightarrow \mathit{Val}$ denote possibly-infinite maps. In addition to the rules R-REF, R-DREF, and R-ASGN, we have added the rule R-STO-WK. The latter rule is used to allow coinductive reasoning about diverging computations that produce infinite stores [16] (for example, it provides a means of proving that $(\lambda x.x\,x)(\lambda x.\texttt{let}\ r\ \texttt{=}\ \texttt{ref}\ 1\ \texttt{in}\ x\,x)$ diverges; without it, a coinductive hypothesis will not match).

A *store-based type* is a pair consisting of a type and a type store. The syntax of types is:

$$\mathit{MType}^\varsigma \ni M ::= \texttt{int} \mid l \mid \langle M, \varsigma\rangle \rightarrow \langle M, \varsigma\rangle$$

Here, $\varsigma \in \mathit{Loc} \xrightarrow{\text{fin}} \mathit{MType}^\varsigma$ is a type store.[2] Store-based types depart from the usual approach to store typing [17]: we introduce the notion of type store as the type level abstraction of a store, in which locations are treated as types themselves. Store-based function types $\langle M, \varsigma\rangle \rightarrow \langle M', \varsigma'\rangle$ record an argument type store ς and a return type store ς'. The rules in Fig. 3 define the judgment $\Gamma^P \vdash e_{/\varsigma} \Rightarrow^S M_{/\varsigma'}$ to hold when expression e in the polytype environment $\Gamma^P \in \mathit{Var} \xrightarrow{\text{fin}} \wp(\mathit{MType}^\varsigma)$ and type store ς has type M in type store ς'.

We highlight rules that differ from traditional ML typing rules:

S-ABS. The function type records the inferred argument type M_2, argument type store ς_0 under which the function body evaluates, the result type M_1, and the updated type store ς_Δ resulting from function body evaluation.

S-APP. Applying a store-based abstraction involves checking that the current store ς is compatible with the function argument type store ς_0, using the $\preceq^\varsigma$ relation. When both type store and argument type are compatible with the function type, the type store ς'' is updated relative to the function return type store ς_Δ, using the $\oslash$ operation, which shadows mappings in ς'' by ς_Δ, and creates fresh locations for newly allocated references between ς'' and ς_Δ.

[2] Whereas dynamic stores are potentially infinite, type stores are finite. Typing restricts stores to those that are finitely typeable.

$$\frac{}{\rho \vdash i_{/\sigma|\downarrow} \Rightarrow i_{/\sigma|\downarrow}}\ (\text{R-INT}) \qquad \frac{}{\rho \vdash e_{/\sigma|\uparrow} \Rightarrow v_{/\sigma'|\uparrow}}\ (\text{R-DIV})$$

$$\frac{\rho(x) = v}{\rho \vdash x_{/\sigma|\downarrow} \Rightarrow v_{/\sigma|\downarrow}}\ (\text{R-VAR})$$

$$\frac{\rho \vdash e_{/\sigma|\delta} \Rightarrow v_{/\sigma'|\delta'} \quad l \notin (\text{dom}(\sigma) \cup \text{dom}(\sigma'))}{\rho \vdash e_{/\sigma[l\mapsto v']|\delta} \Rightarrow v_{/\sigma'[l \mapsto v']|\delta'}}\ (\text{R-STO-WK})$$

$$\frac{}{\rho \vdash \lambda x.e_{/\sigma|\downarrow} \Rightarrow \langle x, e, \rho\rangle_{/\sigma|\downarrow}}\ (\text{R-ABS})$$

$$\frac{\rho \vdash e_{1/\sigma|\downarrow} \Rightarrow \langle x, e, \rho'\rangle_{/\sigma'|\delta} \quad \rho \vdash e_{2/\sigma'|\delta} \Rightarrow v_{2/\sigma''|\delta'} \quad \rho'[x \mapsto v_2] \vdash e_{/\sigma''|\delta'} \Rightarrow v_{/\sigma'''|\delta''}}{\rho \vdash e_1\ e_{2/\sigma|\downarrow} \Rightarrow v_{/\sigma'''|\delta''}}\ (\text{R-APP})$$

$$\frac{\rho \vdash e_{2/\downarrow|\sigma} \Rightarrow v_{2/\delta|\sigma'} \quad \rho[x \mapsto v_2] \vdash e_{/\delta|\sigma'} \Rightarrow v_{/\delta'|\sigma''}}{\rho \vdash \texttt{let}\ x\ \texttt{=}\ e_2\ \texttt{in}\ e_{1/\downarrow|\sigma} \Rightarrow v_{/\delta'|\sigma''}}\ (\text{R-LET})$$

$$\frac{\rho \vdash e_{/\sigma|\downarrow} \Rightarrow v_{/\sigma'|\delta} \quad l \notin \text{dom}(\sigma')}{\rho \vdash \texttt{ref}\ e_{/\sigma|\downarrow} \Rightarrow l_{/\sigma'[l\mapsto v]|\delta}}\ (\text{R-REF})$$

$$\frac{\rho \vdash e_{/\sigma|\downarrow} \Rightarrow l_{/\sigma'|\delta}}{\rho \vdash \texttt{!}e_{/\sigma|\downarrow} \Rightarrow \sigma'(l)_{/\sigma'|\delta}}\ (\text{R-DREF})$$

$$\frac{\rho \vdash e_{1/\sigma|\downarrow} \Rightarrow l_{/\sigma'|\delta} \quad l \in \text{dom}(\sigma') \quad \rho \vdash e_{2/\sigma'|\delta} \Rightarrow v_{2/\sigma''|\delta'}}{\rho \vdash e_1\ \texttt{:=}\ e_{2/\sigma|\downarrow} \Rightarrow v_{2/\sigma''[l\mapsto v_2]|\delta'}}\ (\text{R-ASGN})$$

Figure 2. Coinductive big-step rules for call-by-value λ-calculus with references

$$\frac{}{\Gamma^P \vdash i_{/\varsigma} \Rightarrow^S \texttt{int}_{/\varsigma}}\ (\text{S-INT})$$

$$\frac{\Gamma^P(x) = P \quad M \in P}{\Gamma^P \vdash x_{/\varsigma} \Rightarrow^S M_{/\varsigma}}\ (\text{S-VAR})$$

$$\frac{\Gamma^P[x \mapsto \{M_2\}] \vdash e_{/\varsigma_0} \Rightarrow^S M_{1/\varsigma_\Delta}}{\Gamma^P \vdash \lambda x.e_{/\varsigma} \Rightarrow^S \langle M_2, \varsigma_0\rangle \to \langle M_1, \varsigma_\Delta\rangle_{/\varsigma}}\ (\text{S-ABS})$$

$$\frac{\Gamma^P \vdash e_{1/\varsigma} \Rightarrow^S \langle M_2, \varsigma_0\rangle \to \langle M_1, \varsigma_\Delta\rangle_{/\varsigma'} \quad \Gamma^P \vdash e_{2/\varsigma'} \Rightarrow^S M_{2/\varsigma''} \quad \varsigma_0 \preceq \varsigma''}{\Gamma^P \vdash e_1\ e_{2/\varsigma} \Rightarrow^S M_{1/\varsigma'' \oslash \varsigma_\Delta}}\ (\text{S-APP})$$

$$\frac{P \neq \emptyset \quad \forall M_2 \in P.\, \Gamma^P \vdash e_{2/\varsigma} \Rightarrow^S M_{2/\varsigma'} \quad \Gamma^P[x \mapsto P] \vdash e_{1/\varsigma'} \Rightarrow^S M_{1/\varsigma''}}{\Gamma^P \vdash \texttt{let}\ x\ \texttt{=}\ e_2\ \texttt{in}\ e_{1/\varsigma} \Rightarrow^S M_{1/\varsigma''}}\ (\text{S-LET})$$

$$\frac{\Gamma^P \vdash e_{/\varsigma} \Rightarrow^S M_{/\varsigma'} \quad l \notin \text{dom}(\varsigma')}{\Gamma^P \vdash \texttt{ref}\ e_{/\varsigma} \Rightarrow^S l_{/\varsigma'[l\mapsto M]}}\ (\text{S-REF})$$

$$\frac{\Gamma^P \vdash e_{/\varsigma} \Rightarrow^S l_{/\varsigma'}}{\Gamma^P \vdash \texttt{!}e_{/\varsigma} \Rightarrow^S \varsigma'(l)_{/\varsigma'}}\ (\text{S-DREF})$$

$$\frac{\Gamma^P \vdash e_{1/\varsigma} \Rightarrow^S l_{/\varsigma'} \quad l \in \text{dom}(\varsigma') \quad \Gamma^P \vdash e_{2/\varsigma'} \Rightarrow^S M_{2/\varsigma''}}{\Gamma^P \vdash e_1\ \texttt{:=}\ e_{2/\varsigma} \Rightarrow^S M_{2/\varsigma''[l\mapsto M_2]}}\ (\text{S-ASGN})$$

$$\begin{aligned}\varsigma_1 \oslash \varsigma_2 \triangleq\ & \{(l \mapsto \varsigma_1(l)) \mid l \notin \text{dom}(\varsigma_2)\} \\ & \cup \{(l \mapsto \varsigma_2(l)) \mid l \in (\text{dom}(\varsigma_1) \cap \text{dom}(\varsigma_2))\} \\ & \cup \{(l_{\mathit{fresh}} \mapsto \varsigma_2(l)) \mid \exists l.\, l \notin \text{dom}(\varsigma_1) \wedge l \in \text{dom}(\varsigma_2) \wedge \\ & \qquad l_{\mathit{fresh}} \notin (\text{dom}(\varsigma_1) \cup \text{dom}(\varsigma_2))\}\end{aligned}$$

$$\frac{\forall l \in \text{dom}(\varsigma_1).\, \varsigma_1(l) \preceq^M \varsigma_2(l)}{\varsigma_1 \preceq^\varsigma \varsigma_2} \qquad \frac{}{M \preceq^M M}$$

$$\frac{M_1 \preceq^M M_2 \quad M_1' \preceq^M M_2' \quad \varsigma_1 \preceq^\varsigma \varsigma_2 \quad \varsigma_1' \preceq^\varsigma \varsigma_2'}{\langle M_1, \varsigma_1\rangle \to \langle M_1', \varsigma_1'\rangle \preceq^M \langle M_2, \varsigma_2\rangle \to \langle M_2', \varsigma_2'\rangle}$$

Figure 3. Inductive rules for store-based typing with strong updates

S-REF **and** S-DREF. Locations are reflected at the type-level. Dereferencing a location via S-DREF produces the type stored at the corresponding location in a type store ς.

S-ASGN. Assignment supports strong updates: the type being assigned to a location is not checked against the type assigned to the location in the type store before the update.

4.2 Store-Based Types for Imperative Polymorphic Type Inference

We consider examples of how store-based types allow for Hindley-Milner polymorphism. Using the rules in Fig. 3, $\lambda x.\texttt{ref}\ x$ can be assigned a type in the set $\{\langle M, \cdot\rangle \to \langle l, (l \mapsto M)\rangle \mid M \in \mathit{MType}^\varsigma \wedge l \in \mathit{Loc}\}$, where $\cdot$ is an empty map. Extending our language with sequencing and booleans it follows that:

$$\mathit{mkref} \triangleq \texttt{let}\ m\ \texttt{=}\ (\lambda x.\texttt{ref}\ x)\ \texttt{in}\ m\, 1\texttt{;}\ m\,\texttt{true}$$

$$\cdot \vdash \mathit{mkref}_{/\cdot} \Rightarrow^S l_{/(l\mapsto\texttt{bool})}$$

The following expression which adds an application of the identity function inside the bound let-expression produces the same type and type store as *mkref*:

$$\mathit{mkref}' \triangleq \texttt{let}\ m\ \texttt{=}\ (\lambda y.y)\,(\lambda x.\texttt{ref}\ x)\ \texttt{in}\ m\,1\texttt{;}\ m\,\texttt{true}$$

Consider the following somewhat contrived expression from [22]:

$$\begin{aligned}\mathit{effect}\ \triangleq\ & \lambda z.\texttt{let}\ \mathit{id}\ \texttt{=}\ (\lambda x.\texttt{if true then}\ z \\ & \qquad\qquad \texttt{else}\ (\lambda y.\texttt{ref}\ x\texttt{;}\ y)\texttt{;}\ x) \\ & \texttt{in}\ \mathit{id}\,1\texttt{;}\ \mathit{id}\,\texttt{true}\end{aligned}$$

If we further extend our language with conditionals, the judgment $\cdot \vdash \mathit{effect}_{/\cdot} \Rightarrow^S \texttt{bool}_{/\cdot}$ holds. Since our type system supports strong updates, $\cdot \vdash \mathit{strong}_{/\cdot} \Rightarrow^S \texttt{bool}_{/(l\mapsto\texttt{bool})}$ holds, where:

$$\mathit{strong} \triangleq \texttt{let}\ x\ \texttt{=}\ \texttt{ref}\ 1\ \texttt{in}\ x\ \texttt{:=}\ \texttt{true}$$

	T [21]	L&W [12]	W [23]	T&J [20]	G [9]	SB
mkref	✓	✓	✓	✓	✓	✓
mkref′	—	✓	✓	✓	—	✓
effect	✓	—	—	—	✓	✓
strong	—	—	—	—	—	✓

Table 1. Comparing existing approaches and store-based typing

Table 1 summarises which expressions we are able to type check using store-based typing (SB) compared to existing approaches to imperative polymorphism in the literature.

5. Concluding Remarks

Using a novel approach to coinduction in big-step operational semantics, we have presented a method to deriving type systems that are safe by construction from big-step operational semantics, by treating types as abstract interpretations. We propose store-based typing as an interesting avenue for further research.

5.1 Related Work

Our suggestion for dealing with divergence in Sect. 2 is closely related to the traditional approach using an $\Rightarrow^{\infty}$ predicate, which typically requires classical reasoning in proofs. Nakata and Uustalu [16] provide a constructive alternative using coinductive trace-based big-step semantics. In their approach, finite and infinite traces are distinguishable in the coinductive trace-based big-step relation. Abel and Chapman [1] encode divergence using the delay monad by wrapping computations in a coinductive type which produces a potentially infinitely-delayed value. Our encoding of divergence in a stateful way suggests that it could lend itself to implementation as a monad too.

Wright [23] provides an overview of previous approaches to Hindley-Milner polymorphism in ML-like languages. Not covered by Wright is Garrigue's more recent work [9], which uses a subtyping based approach to relax the value restriction by generalising type variables that occur only at covariant positions.

Separation logic [18] is concerned with reasoning about imperative programs and mutable data structures. Our proposed type stores reflects the runtime store. Ideas from separation logic may conceivably carry over to allow for more sophisticated store-based type analysis. Our reflection of the runtime store is also analogous to Morrisett's typed assembly language [15] which tracks the state of registers. In our system with strong updates, we expect safety to hold by the compatibility check of type stores in applications. Smith et al.'s alias types [19] instead uses linear types to track aliasing to allow for strong updates.

Ahmed [2] describes a logical relations approach to deriving type systems that are safe by construction. Like our work, she starts from an object language and derives type systems. She proves that the semantic model she uses for her derivation, based on logical relations, implies type safety. Using abstract interpretation, the appropriate definition of a Galois connection can give us a safety principle for free – an aspect explicitly mentioned by Cousot [5] in connection with the relationship between abstract interpretation and logical relations.

5.2 Future Directions

Store-based types were conceived by thinking of types as abstract interpretations, but the safety of the rules in Fig. 3 remains to be rigorously checked using the approach described in Sect. 3. From initial experiments with a Prolog prototype implementation of store-based types, we conjecture that the rules in Fig. 3 are safe.[3]

It is straightforward to restrict store-based typing to *invariant updates* such that locations in stores never change type. This would allow function types to be simplified to only contain locations that are subterms of the argument type. This may be a first step towards constructing a mapping from function monotypes with ML-style reference types into corresponding store-based type counterparts.

Abstract interpretation provides a guiding principle for constructing safe type systems. As Sect. 3 shows, it is also useful for relating type systems. An interesting line of research is to compare the expressiveness of different approaches to imperative polymorphism in the literature to our proposal.

Acknowledgments

Thanks to the referees and Neil Sculthorpe for exceptionally helpful suggestions for improving the paper. This work was supported by an EPSRC grant (EP/I032495/1) to Swansea University in connection with the *PLanCompS* project (`www.plancomps.org`).

[3] The Prolog prototype is available at: `http://www.plancomps.org/pepm2015`.

References

[1] A. Abel and J. Chapman. Normalization by evaluation in the delay monad: A case study for coinduction via copatterns and sized types. In *MSFP'14*, volume 153 of *EPTCS*, pages 51–67, 2014.

[2] A. J. Ahmed. *Semantics of Types for Mutable State*. PhD thesis, Princeton University, 2004.

[3] C. Bach Poulsen and P. D. Mosses. Deriving pretty-big-step semantics from small-step semantics. In *ESOP'14*, volume 8410 of *LNCS*, pages 270–289. Springer, 2014.

[4] A. Charguéraud. Pretty-big-step semantics. In *ESOP'13*, volume 7792 of *LNCS*, pages 41–60. Springer, 2013.

[5] P. Cousot. Types as abstract interpretations. In *POPL'97*, pages 316–331. ACM, 1997.

[6] P. Cousot and R. Cousot. Systematic design of program analysis frameworks. In *POPL'79*, pages 269–282. ACM, 1979.

[7] P. Cousot and R. Cousot. Inductive definitions, semantics and abstract interpretations. In *POPL'92*, pages 83–94. ACM, 1992.

[8] L. Damas and R. Milner. Principal type-schemes for functional programs. In R. A. DeMillo, editor, *POPL'82*, pages 207–212. ACM, 1982.

[9] J. Garrigue. Relaxing the value restriction. In *FLOPS'04*, volume 2998 of *LNCS*, pages 196–213. Springer, 2004.

[10] G. Kahn. Natural semantics. In *STACS'87*, volume 247 of *LNCS*, pages 22–39. Springer, 1987.

[11] X. Leroy and H. Grall. Coinductive big-step operational semantics. *Inf. Comput.*, 207:284–304, 2009.

[12] X. Leroy and P. Weis. Polymorphic type inference and assignment. In *POPL'91*, pages 291–302. ACM, 1991.

[13] B. Monsuez. Polymorphic typing by abstract interpretation. In *FSTTCS'92*, volume 652 of *LNCS*, pages 217–228. Springer, 1992.

[14] B. Monsuez. System F and abstract interpretation. In *SAS'95*, volume 983 of *LNCS*, pages 279–295. Springer, 1995.

[15] G. Morrisett. Typed assembly language. In B. C. Pierce, editor, *Advanced Topics in Types and Programming Languages*. The MIT Press, 2004.

[16] K. Nakata and T. Uustalu. Trace-based coinductive operational semantics for while. In *TPHOLs'09*, volume 5674 of *LNCS*, pages 375–390. Springer, 2009.

[17] B. C. Pierce. *Types and programming languages*. MIT Press, 2002.

[18] J. C. Reynolds. Separation logic: A logic for shared mutable data structures. In *LICS'02*, pages 55–74. IEEE, 2002.

[19] F. Smith, D. Walker, and G. Morrisett. Alias types. In *ESOP'00*, volume 1782 of *LNCS*, pages 366–381. Springer, 2000.

[20] J.-P. Talpin and P. Jouvelot. The type and effect discipline. *Inf. Comput.*, 111(2):245–296, 1994.

[21] M. Tofte. Type inference for polymorphic references. *Inf. Comput.*, 89(1):1–34, Sept. 1990.

[22] A. K. Wright. Typing references by effect inference. In *ESOP'92*, volume 582 of *LNCS*, pages 473–491. Springer, 1992.

[23] A. K. Wright. Simple imperative polymorphism. *Lisp Symb. Comput.*, 8(4):343–355, Dec. 1995.

Object-sensitive Type Analysis of PHP

Henk Erik van der Hoek Jurriaan Hage

Department of Computing and Information Sciences
Utrecht University
mail@henkerikvanderhoek.nl,J.Hage@@uu.nl

Abstract

In this paper we develop an object-sensitive type analysis for PHP, based on an extension of the notion of monotone frameworks to deal with the dynamic aspects of PHP, and following the framework of Smaragdakis et al. for object-sensitive analysis.

We consider a number of instantiations of the framework to see how the choices affect the running cost of the analysis, and the precision of the outcome. In this setting we have not been able to reproduce the major gains reported by Smaragdakis et al., but do find that abstract garbage collection substantially increases the scalability of our analyses.

Categories and Subject Descriptors D.3.2 [*Software*]: Language Classifications—Object-oriented languages; F.3.2 [*Logics and Meanings of Programs*]: Semantics of Programming Languages—Program analysis; D.3.4 [*Programming Languages*]: Processors – *soft typing, PHP*

General Terms Languages, Theory, Verification

Keywords static analysis, monotone frameworks, PHP, object-sensitivity, abstract garbage collection, cost and precision

1. Introduction

Statically typed languages perform type checking at compile time, allowing type errors to be caught at the earliest possible stage, and enabling compilers to perform optimizations. However, since the type checker runs at compile time it must be conservative and reject programs that may execute correctly. Also, programming in a language with explicit type checking is sometimes perceived as more difficult.

In dynamically typed languages type checking is performed at run-time. This implies that type errors are only caught at run-time, which means that programs only fail if a type error does show up. Moreover, in many dynamic languages, apparent type inconsistencies are often resolved by silently coercing values to another type. This may easily lead to actual errors remaining undetected. Moreover, to perform run-time type checking, every value must be tagged in some way by a description of its type, which leads to substantial overheads. For example, type analysis plays an important role in reducing run-time overhead in HipHop, a PHP compiler developed by Facebook [23], and has later led to the Hack language that seamlessly integrates with PHP and adds type annotations [22]. Moreover, type information can improve features like on-the-fly auto-completion, and type related error detection.

```
1  class Value {
2    function evaluate () {
3      $v = $this->v;
4      return $v;
5    }
6  }
7
8  class Multiply {
9    function evaluate () {
10     $l = $this->l;
11     $x = $l->evaluate ();
12     $r = $this->r;
13     $y = $r->evaluate ();
14     $z = $x * $y;
15     return $z;
16   }
17 }
18 $x = new Value ();
19 $v = 10;
20 $x->v = $v;
21 $y = new Value ();
22 $v = false;
23 $y->v = $v;
24 $z = new Multiply ();
25 $z->l = $x;
26 $z->r = $y;
27 $r = $z->evaluate ();
```

Figure 1. A lowered expression evaluator in PHP

Researchers have tried to overcome the problems of dynamically typed languages and gain the advantages of static typing by performing a form of (soft) type inference at compile time, including [3, 4, 6, 8, 10, 19]. Type analysis determines *for each program point, which types each variable may have at the exit of that point.* To illustrate the analysis, consider the simple expression evaluator in Figure 1 after it has been lowered to the core syntax that our analysis supports. The type analysis should for example determine that the variable $\$l$ on line 10 is an object of type `Value` and that the variable $\$x$ on line 11 is an integer while variable $\$y$ on line 13 is a Boolean. Note that in order to determine the receiver method of the method call on line 11, line 13 and line 27, the type of the receiver object has to be known. This behaviour, known as dynamic method dispatching, results in a mutual dependency between the control flow and the propagated type information.

Type analysis for dynamic languages is ofted phrased as a dataflow analysis for which standard solutions such as monotone frameworks exist [16]; much of what we do is based on this stan-

PEPM'15, January 13-14 2015, Mumbai, India.

http://dx.doi.org/10.1145/2678015.2682535

dard work on static analyses. Often, context-sensitivity is employed to increase precision, in the form of call-site sensitivity: the analysis results for different calls are separated with the help of call strings or contours that describe an abstraction of the call stack that led to the given program point. In [15], a different approach to context is described that uses the creation points of objects instead of the labels of call strings; this is called object sensitivity. We use the framework of [20] as our starting point, to investigate how well different instances of their framework do within the context of type analysis for PHP. In this paper, we

- specify an object-sensitive type analysis for PHP as an instance of a monotone framework that supports dynamic control flow edges discovery (see Section 4),
- specify several analysis variations of the analysis (see Section 5), and
- implement a prototype of the type analysis, and report on an experimental evaluation of its precision and performance for different analysis variations (see Section 6).

2. Preliminaries

To pave the way for later sections, we shortly discuss the variant of monotone frameworks that we employed in our work. PHP is a dynamic language that supports a number of features (higher-order functions, dynamically added methods (to objects and classes), and subtyping) for which pre-computing a static call graph is not reasonable. For this reason we employ a variation of the embellished monotone frameworks as described in [16]. It allows us to discover new control flow edges on-the-fly, comparable to [10] and [8]. Intuitively, it discovers new flow edges in the same way as implementations of embellished monotone frameworks discover sensible context values (for a given program point). For reasons of space we omit a detailed discussion of this aspect of our work, and refer instead to [21] for a further discussion. We only reiterate here what is necessary to understand what follows.

A particular choice we made in our formulation of monotone frameworks is what is exactly an "item of work" to be stored in the worklist algorithm that is employed by our variant of the maximal fixed point algorithm [16, Chapter 2]. In our case such an item describes that execution can reach a particular program point under a given context: $(l, \delta) \in \mathbf{Point} = \mathbf{Label} \times \mathbf{Context}$.

The language PHP

When dealing with an actual programming language, it typically does not pay to deal with the complete syntax of the language, but only those aspects that are of interest, for example because other language constructs can be desugared into these; this is also the approach we take here. This is not problematic since we are primarily interested in the sets of types computed for the variables in the program, not in providing feedback about these sets to the programmer. A pleasant side effect is that it also allows us to phrase our analysis more concisely. We do note that there are aspects of PHP that our analysis does not cover: string coercion (by calling `__toString`), object cloning (using `clone`), namespaces, treating strings as arrays of characters, anonymous functions, references, `eval`, include files with non-literal file names, object destructors, and parts of the Standard PHP Library (in particular, `ArrayAccess`, `Clonable` and `Iterator`).

3. Control Flow Graphs for PHP

We shall specify the type analysis over an intermediate representation (IR). The intermediate representation captures the key operations which are necessary to perform an object sensitive typing analysis. For example, various looping constructs are rewritten to an equivalent `while` loop and composite expressions, e.g., $a = b * 2 + c;$ are lowered to a sequence of simple statements, $tmp1 = b{*}2; a = tmp1{+}c$. Furthermore, since class and function identifiers are case insensitive in PHP all class and function identifiers are rewritten to their lowercase form. In addition to rewriting, the translation to the intermediate representation also takes care of including files. Note that these simplifications do not change the expressiveness of the language. A subset of the IR that we call core IR will be formally specified below. It includes features like class definitions, object allocations, method invocations and field reads and writes. A formal description of our type analysis on the core IR is given in Section 4. For additional constructs such as native functions, exceptions and arrays we refer to [21].

$$
\begin{array}{lll}
\mathrm{P} & ::= & \mathrm{C\ S} \\
\mathrm{C} & ::= & \textbf{class}\ \mathrm{c\ M} \mid \textbf{class}\ \mathrm{c}\ \textbf{extends}\ \mathrm{c\ M} \mid \mathrm{C\ C} \\
\mathrm{M} & ::= & [\textbf{function}\ \mathrm{m}\ (\vec{p})]^{l_n}_{l_x}\ \mathrm{S} \mid \mathrm{M\ M} \\
\mathrm{S} & ::= & [\mathrm{v = L}]^l \mid [\mathrm{v = v}]^l \mid [\mathrm{v = v\ op\ v}]^l \mid \mid \mathrm{S}_1\ \mathbf{;}\ \mathrm{S}_2 \mid [\textbf{skip}]^l \\
 & \mid & \textbf{if}\ [\mathrm{v}]^l\ \textbf{then}\ \mathrm{S}_1\ \textbf{else}\ \mathrm{S}_2 \\
 & \mid & \textbf{while (true)}\ \mathrm{S} \mid [\textbf{break}]^l \mid [\textbf{continue}]^l \\
 & \mid & [\textbf{new}\ \mathrm{c}]^l \mid [\mathrm{v.f = v}]^l \mid [\mathrm{v = v.f}]^l \mid [\mathrm{v = v.m}\ (\vec{p})]^{l_c}_{l_r} \\
 & \mid & [\textbf{return}\ \mathrm{v}]^l \\
\mathrm{L} & ::= & \textbf{true} \mid \textbf{false} \mid \textbf{null} \mid \mathrm{n}
\end{array}
$$

Figure 2. The syntax of the core language of PHP

We assume the following syntactic categories:

n	$\in$ **Num**	Integers
x, y	$\in$ **Var**	Variables
c	$\in$ **ClassName**	Class names
f	$\in$ **FieldName**	Field names
m	$\in$ **MethodName**	Method names
op	$\in$ **Operators**	Binary operators

A syntax for IR Core is given in Figure 2, describing the syntax of programs (P), classes (C), statements (S) and literals (L) respectively. We adopt terminology from [16], e.g., everything between square brackets is called an *elementary block*. We assume each elementary block is annotated with a distinct label, e.g., l.

We write **Method** for **ClassName** $\times$ **MethodName**, Figure 3 contains a number of auxiliary functions to be used by our analysis (following [16], when we write, e.g., $init_*$ to refer to $init$ for the progam under analysis).

4. The type analysis

Type analysis determines *for each program point, which types each variable may have at the exit of that point.* To compute an approximation of the types for variables in a given program, we first lower a PHP application to the syntax given in the previous section. We can then perform a type analysis, in tandem with a *points-to* analysis. A points-to analysis computes a static approximation of all the heap objects that a pointer variable can refer to at run-time. PHP lacks a syntactic difference between pointer variables (which point to heap allocated objects) and regular variables. Not knowing whether a variable may be a pointer variable our type analysis computes a static approximation of all the values that a variable may point to at run-time. This approach is similar to the approach taken in [10] to perform type analysis of JavaScript programs.

Type analysis and control flow information are mutually dependent: suppose class `A` and `B` both support (different) methods called `foo`, and we can establish by means of our type analysis that the variable `x` may be of type `A`, but not `B`. Then we can conclude that the call to `x.foo()` can only pass control to the `foo` of `A` and not

$init$: **Program** $\rightarrow$ $\mathcal{P}$(**Label**) returns the initial labels of the program.
$flow$: **Program** $\rightarrow$ **Flow** returns the intraprocedural flow graph; interprocedural edges will be added on-the-fly during fixed point iteration.
$entry$: **Program** $\times$ **Method** $\rightarrow$ **Label** returns the exit label l_n of a method.
$exit$: **Program** $\times$ **Method** $\rightarrow$ **Label** returns the exit label l_x of a method.
$return$: **Program** $\times$ **Label** $\rightarrow$ **Label** returns the return label l_r corresponding to a given call label l_c.
$resolve$: **Program** $\times$ **Method** $\rightarrow$ **Method** resolves a dynamic method call by traversing the inheritance hierarchy, until the method looked for is encountered.
$className$: **Program** $\times$ **Label** $\rightarrow$ **ClassName** returns the class name of the allocated object given an allocation site label.

Figure 3. Auxiliary functions for retrieving information about programs

the `foo` of `B`. Since the body of `B.foo` is not analyzed at this point, this may in turn lead to smaller points-to/type sets.

To deal with the dynamic method dispatching of PHP (that it shares with other object-oriented languages), also the flow of abstract state information and call graph information are mutually dependent. This is why we employ a variation of Embellished Monotone Frameworks to deal with this dynamic aspect of the language (as shortly discussed in Section 2).

4.1 The type lattice

We model our abstract value as a 4-tuple. Each component of the tuple contains an abstraction for a specific type: integers, booleans, objects, and null values. One can therefore view our type analysis as an extension of a points-to analysis since the tuple component for objects contains the points-to information.

The abstract representation of sets of integer values is by means of sign sets, $\mathcal{P}(\textbf{Sign})$ where $\textbf{Sign} = \{\texttt{-}, \texttt{0}, \texttt{+}\}$, which form a complete lattice under set inclusion. The function

$$fromInteger : \textbf{N} \rightarrow \textbf{Sign}$$

abstracts in the usual way integers to signs. In our implementation we provide abstract operators like $\hat{+}$ to compute precisely with abstract values.

The abstract Booleans are elements of the set $\mathcal{P}(\textbf{Bool})$ where $\textbf{Bool} = \{\texttt{true}, \texttt{false}\}$. In this case, the abstraction is just the identity function, and the abstract operators are the concrete operators extended to sets of booleans element-wise.

A variable may refer to heap allocated data. Every time an object is allocated, the $record$ function is used to create a heap context (see Section 5). The analysis will keep track of an abstract object for each heap context, which thus play the role of abstract addresses. Formally abstract addresses are $\mathcal{P}(\textbf{HContext})$ where **HContext** depends on the chosen analysis variation (see Section 5). We require the existence of a total function $label$: **HContext** $\rightarrow$ **Label** from heap context to allocation site label. Theoretically, this reduces the freedom one has in choosing the $record$ (and $merge$) functions. Practically, this choice does not prevent us from specifying all of the common analysis variations.

An abstract value is then a tuple where each component describes a different type of (abstract) value:

$$v \in \textbf{Value} = \mathcal{P}(\textbf{HContext}) \times \mathcal{P}(\textbf{Bool}) \times \mathcal{P}(\textbf{Sign}) \times \textbf{Null}$$

where the abstract values for representing null values **Null** are $\{\top, \bot\}$, where $\top$ represents $null$. For example, $(\bot, \bot, \{+\}, \top)$ represents concrete values that are either a positive integer, or the $null$ value.

We assume the definition of a family of auxiliary functions for injecting individual components, into the lattice, e.g.,

$$inject_{\mathcal{P}(\textbf{Sign})} : \mathcal{P}(\textbf{Sign}) \rightarrow \textbf{Value}$$
$$inject_{\mathcal{P}(\textbf{Sign})}(l) = (\bot, \bot, l, \bot)$$

Vice versa, PHP silently coerces any value into a value of a suitable type when needed, and our type analysis must mimic this behaviour. Therefore we need a family of $coerce$ functions. The $coerce$ function takes an abstract value and coerces it into a value of a particular type (but taking into account all its abstract components). For example, to coerce an abstract value to a set of signs we employ

$$
\begin{aligned}
& coerce_{\mathcal{P}(\textbf{Sign})} : \textbf{Value} \rightarrow \mathcal{P}(\textbf{Sign}) \\
& coerce_{\mathcal{P}(\textbf{Sign})}(\gamma s, bs, ss, n) = \\
& \quad \textbf{let } boolToSign(\texttt{true}) = \texttt{+} \\
& \quad \phantom{\textbf{let }} boolToSign(\texttt{false}) = \texttt{0} \\
& \quad \phantom{\textbf{let }} nullToSign(\top) = \{\texttt{0}\} \\
& \quad \phantom{\textbf{let }} nullToSign(\bot) = \emptyset \\
& \quad \textbf{in } \{ \texttt{+} \mid \gamma \in \gamma s \} \cup \{ boolToSign(b) \mid b \in bs \} \\
& \quad \phantom{\textbf{in }} \cup\, ss \cup nullTosign(u)
\end{aligned}
$$

which tells us, for example, that `true` and abstract addresses are interpreted as positive integers, and $null$ and `false` as `0`. We omit all other injection and coercion functions.

Abstract values can be mapped to a *set* of types by the function

$$
\begin{aligned}
& type : \textbf{Value} \rightarrow \mathcal{P}(\textbf{Type}) \\
& type\ (\gamma s, bs, ss, n) = \\
& \quad \textbf{let } type_{\textbf{Address}}\ (\gamma s) = \{ className_*(label(\gamma)) \mid \gamma \in \gamma s \} \\
& \quad \phantom{\textbf{let }} type_{\textbf{Boolean}}\ (bs) = \{ \text{Boolean} \mid b \in bs \} \\
& \quad \phantom{\textbf{let }} type_{\textbf{Sign}}\ (ss) = \{ \text{Integer} \mid s \in ss \} \\
& \quad \phantom{\textbf{let }} type_{\textbf{Null}}\ (\top) = \{ \text{Null} \} \\
& \quad \phantom{\textbf{let }} type_{\textbf{Null}}\ (\bot) = \emptyset \\
& \quad \textbf{in } \bigcup \{ type_{\textbf{Address}}(\gamma s),\ type_{\textbf{Boolean}}(bs), \\
& \quad \phantom{\textbf{in } \bigcup \{} type_{\textbf{Sign}}(ss),\ type_{\textbf{Null}}(n) \}
\end{aligned}
$$

where $\textbf{Type} = \textbf{ClassName}_* \cup \{ \text{Integer}, \text{Boolean}, \text{Null} \}$, and the $className_*$ and $label$ functions are used to translate a heap context to a class name. The $label$ function depends on the chosen analysis variation (see later in this paper). Consider the abstract value $v = (\bot, \{\texttt{true}\}, \{\texttt{+}\}, \bot)$ which signifies that the corresponding concrete value is either a positive integer or a Boolean true value. Applying the $type$ function to this value results in a union type: { Boolean, Integer }.

The analysis operates on abstract states consisting of an abstract stack and an abstract heap, formalized as follows:

$$
\begin{aligned}
& \sigma \in \textbf{State} = \textbf{Stack} \times \textbf{Heap} \\
& H \in \textbf{Heap} = (\textbf{HContext} \times \textbf{FieldName}_*) \mapsto \textbf{Value} \\
& H ::= [\,] \mid H[(\gamma, f) \mapsto v] \\
& S \in \textbf{Stack} = \textbf{Ident} \mapsto \textbf{Value} \\
& S ::= [\,] \mid S[z \mapsto v] \\
& z \in \textbf{Ident} = \textbf{Var}_* \cup \textbf{Z} \cup \{\mathbb{R}, \mathbb{T}\}
\end{aligned}
$$

The value $\mathbb{R}$ is a placeholder for the return value of a method invocation, and $\mathbb{T}$ for the receiver object. We use elements of **Z** for representing the values associated with actual parameters in a method call, and which are mapped later to formal parameters. Since the maximum number of parameters in bounded in a given program, the set **Ident** remains finite. Although, formally, S is a list we take the liberty to view it as a finite mapping whenever convenient. We extend **State** to $\textbf{State}_\bot$ with a least element $\bot$ to represent unreachable code.

The transfer functions that make up the dynamic part of our analysis operate on abstract states using eleven state manipulation primitives which act as an interface. The first seven ($empty$, $read$, $write$, $writeHeap$, $readHeap$, $readField$ and $writeField$) are used for the intraprocedural transfer functions while $toParameters$, $toVariables$, $clearStack$ and $clearHeap$ are used for the interprocedural transfer functions. We provide only type signatures for the primitives in Figure 4 [21].

The $read$ function reads an abstract value from the abstract stack given an identifier. The $readField$ function returns an abstract value given an identifier and a field name. First an abstract value is read from the stack, given the identifier. This abstract value may refer to multiple heap context elements. For each heap context element an abstract value is read from the heap using the auxiliary function $readHeap$. The return value of the $readField$ function is obtained by joining these abstract values. Following PHP semantics, all read functions return an abstract $null$ if a binding cannot be found. The $write$, $writeField$ and $writeHeap$ are analogous to the versions for reading. In the case of $writeField$ it is important to note that multiple heap context elements on the abstract heap may be updated (because the abstract value read for z may refer to multiple heap context elements). In the case of $writeHeap$, if the heap already contains a value for the given pair (γ, f) the previous and the new value are joined together.

The $toParameters$ function translates the variables to parameter positions. For each variable in $\vec{p}$ a new binding is created between the parameter position and the value of p_i in the abstract stack. The $toVariables$ function translates parameter positions to variables. For each variable in $\vec{p}$ a new binding is created between the variable p_i and the value corresponding to the parameter position i in the abstract stack. Additionally, the special $this$ identifier $\mathbb{T}$ is propagated. The $clearStack$ and the $clearHeap$ functions clear the stack and heap components of the abstract state.

4.2 The analysis itself

We specify the analysis as an instance of the Extended Monotone Framework (as described in detail in [21]). It is a 7-tuple

$$(\textbf{State}_\bot, \mathcal{F}_{State}, init(P_*), \iota^{TA}, f_{l,\delta}^{TA}, \phi_{l,\delta}^{TA}, next_{l,\delta}^{TA}),$$

of which the first five components (the lattice, the function space for transfer functions, the extremal labels, the extremal value, and the transfer functions, respectively), are also part of the Embellished Monotone Frameworks. The components $\phi_{l,\delta}^{TA}$ and $next_{l,\delta}^{TA}$ are specific to our framework, and describe the mutually recursive relationship between intraprocedural and interprocedural flow. They allow us to discover new edges during fix point iteration, and add them to the control flow graph (both intra and inter).

For reasons of space, we focus on what is different with respect to [16, Section 2.5]. As usual, with every program point (l, δ) we associate two values $A_\circ(l, \delta)$ and $A_\bullet(l, \delta)$. The former collects all the information flowing in from statements that precede it (in the analysis flow direction, forward in this case), and the latter describes what holds after the elementary block l has been executed. The formulas for $A_\circ(l, \delta)$ are those of [16].

The *extremal value* ι^{TA} denotes that the extremal program points are reachable: $\iota^{TA} = empty$ (recall that $empty$ is one of our primitives).

The major differences with our Extended Monotone Frameworks is that as part of the analysis we also iteratively compute the intraprocedural F and interprocedural IF flow edges. The formulas are as follows:

$$\begin{aligned} F &\in \textbf{Flow} = \mathcal{P}(\textbf{Point} \times \textbf{Point}) \\ F &= \{\, next_{e,\Lambda}^{TA}(\emptyset) \mid e \in E\} \cup \\ &\quad \{\, next_{l',\delta'}^{TA}(IF) \mid ((l,\delta),(l',\delta')) \in F \,\} \end{aligned}$$

$$\begin{aligned} IF &\in \textbf{InterFlow} = \mathcal{P}(\textbf{Point} \times \textbf{Point} \times \textbf{Point} \times \textbf{Point}) \\ IF &= \phi_{l,\delta}^{TA}(A_\bullet(l,\delta)) \cup IF \text{ for all}(l,\delta) \text{ in } F \end{aligned}$$

In the remainder of the section we shall provide the remaining pieces of the puzzle: the extremal value ι^{TA}, the transfer functions $f_{l,\delta}^{TA}$ and f_{l_c,l_r}^{TA}, the dynamic intraprocedural flow function $next_{l,\delta}^{TA}$ and the dynamic interprocedural flow function $\phi_{l,\delta}$.

A transfer function $f_{l,\delta}^{TA} : \textbf{State}_\bot \to \textbf{State}_\bot$ specifies how flow and context sensitive type information flows from the entry to the exit of an elementary block. Data flow information should only be propagated if the elementary block is reachable, so we define

$$f_{l,\delta}^{TA}(\sigma) = \begin{cases} \bot & \text{if } \sigma = \bot \\ \psi_{l,\delta}(\sigma) & \text{otherwise} \end{cases}$$

that delegates the actual work to the function $\psi_{l,\delta} : \textbf{State} \to \textbf{State}$. Procedure return is exceptional in that we need to combine two flows. Therefore we need a binary transfer function $f_{l_c,l_r}^{TA} : \textbf{State}_\bot \to \textbf{State}_\bot \to \textbf{State}_\bot$. The first parameter describes the data flow information before the method call and the second parameter describes the data flow information at the exit of the method body. It is defined similarly to the unary version:

$$f_{l_c,l_r}^{TA}(\sigma, \sigma') = \begin{cases} \bot & \text{if } \sigma = \bot \text{ or } \sigma' = \bot \\ \psi_{l_c,l_r}(\sigma, \sigma') & \text{otherwise} \end{cases}$$

For each kind of elementary block we define the necessary ψ functions in Figures 5 and 6. Most of these should be self evident, but some remarks may be useful in understanding: In the rules for booleans and numbers, we have to apply the correct function to inject the value into the state. In the rule for binary operators, we apply the lifted operator $\widetilde{\odot}$ that "simulates" $\odot$ in the abstract domain. Neither $skip$, boolean tests and method exits affect the state, so we use the identity function there. In the case of a new statement we invoke the $record$ function that creates a new heap context. We will describe several variations in Section 5.

The transfer function for a method call (the first case in Figure 6) implements a part of the parameter passing semantics. The transfer function for a method call translates the identifiers corresponding to actual parameters to parameter position by means of the $toParameters$ function. Subsequently, the transfer function for a method entry translates the parameter positions to the formal parameter identifiers using the $toVariables$ function. The special $this$ identifier, $\mathbb{T}$, is used to make the receiver object available in the callee. The transfer function for a method entry implements the second half of the parameter passing semantics by translating the parameter positions to the formal parameters. The transfer function for $return$ propagates the abstract value stored in the identifier v to the special return identifier $\mathbb{R}$. The only binary transfer function ψ_{l_c,l_r} for return, reads the return value, stores it, and ensures the new state combines the stack component of the caller with the heap components of the callee.

Upon each method call new edges may be added to the interprocedural flow, IF. Each edge in the interprocedural flow represents a method invocation which may occur in the program under analysis. Each interprocedural flow edge is specified by a tuple consisting of four program points: the call position of the caller, the entry of the callee, the exit of the callee and the return position of the caller. For a given method invocation $[v = v'.m\ (\vec{p})]^{l_c}$, the $\phi_{l_c,\delta}^{TA}$ function

$empty$: **State**
$read$: **Ident** × **State** → **Value**
$write$: **Ident** × **Value** × **State** → **State**
$readField$: **Ident** × **FieldName** × **State** → **Value**
$readHeap$: **HContext** × **FieldName** × **Heap** → **Value**
$writeField$: **Ident** × **FieldName** × **Value** × **State** → **State**
$writeHeap$: **HContext** × **FieldName** × **Value** × **Heap** → **Heap**
$toParameters$: $\mathcal{P}$(**Var**$_*$) × **State** → **State**
$toVariables$: $\mathcal{P}$(**Var**$_*$) × **State** → **State**
$clearStack$: **State** → **State**
$clearHeap$: **State** → **State**

Figure 4. The signatures of the eleven manipulation primitives

$$
\begin{array}{lll}
[skip]^l & : \psi_{l,\delta}(\sigma) = & \sigma \\
[b]^l & : \psi_{l,\delta}(\sigma) = & \sigma \\
[v = b]^l & : \psi_{l,\delta}(\sigma) = & write(v, inject_{\mathcal{P}(\mathbf{Bool})}(\{b\}), \sigma) \\
[v = n]^l & : \psi_{l,\delta}(\sigma) = & write(v, inject_{\mathcal{P}(\mathbf{Sign})}(fromInteger(n)), \sigma) \\
[v = v']^l & : \psi_{l,\delta}(\sigma) = & write(v, read(v', \sigma), \sigma) \\
[v = v' \odot v'']^l & : \psi_{l,\delta}(\sigma) = & write(v, read(v', \sigma) \mathbin{\tilde{\odot}} read(v'', \sigma), \sigma) \\
[v = \mathsf{new}\ C]^l & : \psi_{l,\delta}(\sigma) = & \mathbf{let}\ \gamma = record(l, \delta) \\
 & & \quad value = inject_{\mathcal{P}(\mathbf{HContext})}(\{\gamma\}) \\
 & & \mathbf{in}\ write(v, value, \sigma) \\
[v.f = v']^l & : \psi_{l,\delta}(\sigma) = & writeField(v, f, read(v', \sigma), \sigma) \\
[v = v'.f]^l & : \psi_{l,\delta}(\sigma) = & write(v, readField(v', f, \sigma), \sigma)
\end{array}
$$

Figure 5. Intraprocedural transfer functions

$$
\begin{array}{lll}
[v = v'.method(\vec{p})]^{l_c} & : \psi_{l_c,\delta}(\sigma) = & \mathbf{let}\ value = read(v', \sigma) \\
 & & \quad \sigma' = toParameters(\vec{p}, \sigma) \\
 & & \mathbf{in}\ write(\mathbb{T}, value, \sigma') \\
[C.method(\vec{p})]^{l_n} & : \psi_{l_n,\delta}(\sigma) = & toVariables(\vec{p}, \sigma) \\
[\mathsf{return}\ v]^l & : \psi_{l,\delta}(\sigma) = & \mathbf{let}\ value = read(v, \sigma) \\
 & & \mathbf{in}\ write(\mathbb{R}, value, \sigma) \\
[C.method(\vec{p})]^{l_x} & : \psi_{l_x,\delta}(\sigma) = & \sigma \\
[v = v'.method(\vec{p})]^{l_r} & : \psi_{l_c,l_r}(\sigma, \sigma') = & \mathbf{let}\ value = read(\mathbb{R}, \sigma') \\
 & & \quad \sigma'' = clearHeap(\sigma) \sqcup clearStack(\sigma') \\
 & & \mathbf{in}\ write(v, value, \sigma'')
\end{array}
$$

Figure 6. The interprocedural transfer functions

retrieves the set of heap context elements to which the identifier v' may point. An edge will be added to the interprocedural flow for each heap context element. Dynamic dispatch is resolved at runtime, so depending on the heap context element different method definitions may be called. The $resolve_*$ function is used to traverse the inheritance hierarchy and locate the targeted method definition. The $merge$ function (see Section 5) combines the call label l_c, a heap context element γ and the current analysis context δ and returns the context under which the callee will be analyzed (for all other elementary blocks $\phi_{l\delta}^{TA}(\sigma) = \emptyset$), see Figure 7).

Adding new intraprocedural edges with $next_{l,\delta}^{TA}$

Whenever a new interprocedural edge to some method is added, it may well be necessary to add additional interprocedural edges. This is the role of the $next_{l,\delta}^{TA}$ function. We need to distinguish three cases.

For a method invocation $[v = v'.method(\vec{p})]^{l_c}$, information needs to propagate from the caller to the entry of the callee. The interprocedural flow, IF, tells us to which callee and to which context the data flow information needs to propagate.

$$
\begin{array}{l}
next_{l_c,\delta}(IF) = \\
\quad \{((l_c,\delta),(l_n,\delta')) \mid ((l_c,\delta),(l_n,\delta'),(l_x,\delta'),(l_r,\delta)) \in IF\} \\
\quad \cup \\
\quad \{((l_x,\delta'),(l_r,\delta)) \mid ((l_c,\delta),(l_n,\delta'),(l_x,\delta'),(l_r,\delta)) \in IF\}
\end{array}
$$

In the case of $[end^{l_x}]$, information needs to propagate back to the caller at the end of a method body. To avoid poisoning information should only flow back to the original context under which the caller was being analyzed:

$$
\begin{array}{l}
next_{l_x,\delta}(IF) = \\
\quad \{((l_x,\delta),(l_r,\delta')) \mid ((l_c,\delta'),(l_n,\delta),(l_x,\delta),(l_r,\delta')) \in IF\}
\end{array}
$$

Finally, if l corresponds to any other elementary block the information will be propagated following the standard intraprocedural

$$
\begin{array}{rcl}
\phi^{TA}_{l_c,\delta}(\sigma) = \textbf{let } \gamma s & = & coerce_{\mathcal{P}(\textbf{HContext})}(read(v',\sigma)) \\
edge(\gamma) & = & \textbf{let } \delta' = merge(l_c,\gamma,\delta) \\
 & & \quad \tau = className_*(label(\gamma)) \\
 & & \quad m_r = resolve_*((\tau,m)) \\
 & & \quad l_r = return_*(l_c) \\
 & & \textbf{in}((l_c,\delta),(entry_*(m_r),\delta'),(exit_*(m_r),\delta'),(l_r,\delta)) \\
\textbf{in } \{\, edge(\gamma) \mid \gamma \in \gamma s \,\} & &
\end{array}
$$

Figure 7. The function $\phi^{TA}_{l_c,\delta}$

flow, under the same context:

$$next_{l,\delta}(IF) = \{((l,\delta),(l',\delta)) \mid (l,l') \in flow_* \}$$

On soundness

Since there is no formal specification of PHP, the soundness of our implementation can only be established by comparing the inferred types of our type analysis to the observed types while running the program. To cover all execution paths a set of unit tests was written. The inferred type set is obtained by running the type analysis and transforming the calculated abstract values to type sets (using $type$, see Section 4).

The run-time type sets are obtained by instrumenting the original source code of the programs listed in Section 6. On each assignment the run-time type of the assigned variable is obtained by means of the $gettype$ function. If the resulting type constitutes an object or a resource the type is further refined by calling get_class and $get\_resource\_type$ respectively. This results in a run-time type set since each assignment may be executed multiple times with possibly different values. Hence different types may be observed.

We then compared the observed run-time types with the inferred type sets by our implementation. We found that for all assignments in each program the types we observed formed a subset of the inferred type sets. In other words, the type analysis was able to infer all types observed at run-time, providing an empirical approximation to soundness. Note, though that it is as good as the unit tests we have written. As we shall see later (see Figure 12), for many of the assignments we *inferred* the exact same set of types as we *observed dynamically*.

5. Object-sensitive type analysis

Object-sensitivity is particularly well suited context abstraction for analysing object-oriented programs. However, an object-sensitive analysis has many degrees of freedom relating to which context elements are selected upon each method invocation or object allocation. In this paper we use the framework of [20] to describe various forms of object-sensitivity, borrowing their terminology of full-object-sensitivity, plain-object-sensitivity and type-sensitivity. Their framework offers a clean model to design and reason about different analysis variations. An analysis variation is given by defining the two context manipulation functions:

$$record : \textbf{Label} \times \textbf{Context} \rightarrow \textbf{HContext}$$
$$merge : \textbf{Label} \times \textbf{HContext} \times \textbf{Context} \rightarrow \textbf{Context}$$

Every time an object is allocated, the $record$ function is used to create a heap context. The heap context is stored and used as an abstraction of the allocated object. The $merge$ function is used on every method invocation. The call site label, the heap context of the receiver object and the current context are merged to obtain the context in which the invoked method will be executed. The type analysis described in Section 4 uses these two context manipulation functions in some of its transfer functions ($record$ is used for the new block, and the $merge$ and $label$ functions are employed by $\phi^{TA}_{l_c,\delta}$). The $label$ function is not a context manipulation function but rather an artefact of our type analysis which requires the existence of a total function from heap context to allocation site label.

A *full-object-sensitive* analysis will analyze every dispatched method under the heap context associated with the receiver object. Since the heap context consists of multiple allocation site labels, the hope is that these labels split the data flow facts into separate sets of facts that are widely different. Milanova et al. [15] was the first to use allocation site labels for this purpose. We can specify a concrete full-object-sensitive analysis by defining the $record$, $merge$ and $label$ functions as follow:

$$\textbf{Context} = \textbf{Label}^n$$
$$\textbf{HContext} = \textbf{Label}^m$$
$$record(l,\delta) = first_m(cons(l,\delta))$$
$$merge(l,\gamma,\delta) = first_n(\gamma)$$
$$label(\gamma) = car(\gamma)$$

The context under which a method will be analyzed depends on the heap context of the receiver object. The heap context of the receiver object depends on (1) its allocation site label and (2) the context under which the receiver object was allocated. So, the context under which a method is analyzed depends on the allocation site label of the receiver, the allocation site label of the object that allocated the receiver, the allocation site label of the object that allocated the object that allocated the receiver, and so on.

We follow [20] in naming the common analysis variations: for a full-object-sensitive analysis with a regular context depth of n and a heap context depth of $m+1$ we write $n$full+mH. In order to make the set of heap contexts finite we limit the number of allocation site labels in a context element to a fixed number (in practice 2). Hence, 1full, 1full+1H and 2full+1H are of particular interest.

Plain-object-sensitivity

In contrast to full-object-sensitivity, a plain-object-sensitive analysis combines both the heap context of the receiver object and the regular context of the caller:

$$\textbf{Context} = \textbf{Label}^n$$
$$\textbf{HContext} = \textbf{Label}^m$$
$$record(l,\delta) = first_m(cons(l,\delta))$$
$$merge(l,\gamma,\delta) = first_n(cons(car(\gamma),\delta))$$
$$label(\gamma) = car(\gamma)$$

Both full-object-sensitive and plain-object-sensitive analyses store allocation site labels as context elements using the $record$ function. The distinction lies in the $merge$ function. The $merge$ function decides which elements to keep when a method is invoked: only keep the heap context elements of the receiver object (as in full-object-sensitivity) or merge the heap context of the receiver object with the regular context of the caller (as in plain-object-sensitivity). Paddle [13], for example, uses plain-object-sensitivity.

Smaragdakis et al. [20] found that full-object-sensitivity outperforms plain-object-sensitivity. The explanation they provide is that with plain-object-sensitivity it is more likely that when merging the allocation site label of the receiver object with the allocation site label of the caller object the two labels are more likely to be correlated. For example the receiver and the caller object are exactly the same if an object calls a method on itself. And if they are correlated they will do a worse job at separating the data flow facts.

For a plain-object sensitive analysis with a regular context depth of n and a heap context depth of $m + 1$ we shall write $n$plain+mH. Note that 1plain and 1plain+1H coincides with respectively 1full and 1full+1H, so we shall simply denote these analysis variations with 1obj and 1obj+1H.

Type Sensitivity

Generally speaking, the precision of an analysis is improved by separating data flow information depending on the calling context. To achieve termination, we abstract the possibly infinite set of calling contexts to a finite set of abstract contexts δ. But finite is not necessarily small: any given program may have many allocation sites. To overcome the combinatorial explosion of abstract contexts, [20] introduced a type-sensitive analysis is to improve scalability by using a coarser approximation of objects: instead of allocation site labels we approximate an object by its type. Hence a type sensitive analysis is similar to an object sensitive analysis: whereas an object sensitive analysis uses allocation site labels as context elements, a type sensitive analysis uses types as context elements. In the remainder of the section we shall describe two variations on this theme.

A 2-type-sensitive analysis employs a regular context which consists of two types. This reduces the number of possible context elements as the number of types in a program is typically much smaller than the number of allocation sites. For a 2type+1H analysis we define the following context manipulation functions:

$$\begin{aligned} \textbf{Context} &= \textbf{ClassName}^2 \\ \textbf{HContext} &= \textbf{Label} \times \textbf{ClassName} \\ record(l, \delta = [C_1, C_2]) &= [l, C_1] \\ merge(l, \gamma = [l', C], \delta) &= [\mathcal{T}(l'), C] \\ label(\gamma = [l, C]) &= l \end{aligned}$$

One may notice that the merge function only uses the heap context of the receiver object and ignores the context of the caller object. In this sense the 2type $+ 1H$ analysis is a variation of the 2full $+ 1H$ analysis, and not of the 2plain $+ 1H$ analysis.

Consider a statement $obj = [newA]^l$ inside a class C. Following [20], the function $\mathcal{T}$: **Label** $\rightarrow$ **ClassName** returns the upper bound C on the dynamic type of the allocator object.

Another choice of context is to replace only one allocation site label with a type. This leads to a 1type1obj $+ 1H$ analysis:

$$\begin{aligned} \textbf{Context} &= \textbf{Label} \times \textbf{ClassName} \\ \textbf{HContext} &= \textbf{Label}^2 \\ record(l, \delta = [l', C_2]) &= [l, l'] \\ merge(l, \gamma = [l_1, l_2], \delta) &= [l_1, \mathcal{T}(l_2)] \\ label(\gamma = [l_1, l_2]) &= l_1 \end{aligned}$$

This choice of context is interesting, because we expect the number of context elements to be in between that of a 2full $+ 1H$ analysis and a 2type $+ 1H$ analysis.

6. Evaluation

We have implemented and evaluated several of the analysis variations, as described in Section 5, up to a context depth of 2. Our implementation consists of two distinct phases. In the first phase, an intermediate representation is obtained by parsing the original PHP program using PHC [1]. In a pipeline of sequential transformations PHC lowers the original AST to various intermediate forms, in our case to an intermediate representation called Higher Internal Representation (HIR). This is the last phase in which the result of the transformation is still a valid PHP program. In the second phase the HIR is read by the type inferencer which is written in Haskell and the UU Attribute Grammar system.

Project	Description	LoC
Ray Tracer	A PHP implementation of a ray tracer. Ray tracing is a technique to generate an image of a 3D scene by tracing a ray of light through the image plane and simulating the effects of each object it intersects.	915
Gaufrette	Gaufrette is a file system abstraction layer, which allows an application developer to develop an application without knowing where the files are stored and how. Gaufrette offers support for various file systems like Amazon S3 and Dropbox.	2974
PHPGeo	PHPGeo provides an abstraction to different geographical coordinate systems and allows an application developer to calculate distances between different coordinates.	1634
MIME	A MIME library which allows an application developer to compose and send email messages according to the MIME standard [2].	486
MVC	A framework which implements the model-view-controller pattern for web application.	2583
Dijkstra	An implementation of Dijkstra's algorithm [5] using adjacency lists to represent a graph structure.	4854
Floyd	An implementation of the Floyd-Warshall algorithm [7] using an adjacency matrix to represent a graph structure.	5742
Interpreter	An object-oriented implementation of a small expression language, including a parser.	843

Figure 8. List of projects in the test suite

The PHP programs in the test suite are shown in Figure 8. It was necessary to make small modifications to the original programs on some occasions due to the use of unsupported language features (see Section 2). These modifications are documented in a file called `modifications.txt`, which is present in the directory of each project.

The source code (in Haskell) and the test suite are publicly available from
`http://www.github.com/henkerik/objectsensitivetyping/`.
The experiments were performed on a machine with a Intel Core 2 Duo 3.0Ghz processor with 3.2GiB of internal memory running Ubuntu 12.04.

Results

We shall compare the precision of plain-object sensitivity to full-object sensitivity. Theoretically, we expect that a full object sensitive analysis shall give a better precision for the same context depth. We included the results of a context-insensitive, a 1obj sensitive and a 1obj+1H sensitive analysis for comparison. For each analysis variation we collected the following set of precision and performance metrics:

- **# of union types** shows the number of assignments for which the type analysis could not infer a single type. Note that due to the dynamic nature of PHP it is not always possible to infer a single type.
- **# of union types collapsed** shows the number of assignments for which the type analysis could infer a single type after collapsing object types with a common ancestor. Moreover, the $Null$ type is ignored if the remaining type set only contains class names.
- **# of polymorphic call sites** shows the number of method call sites for which the type analysis could not infer a unique receiver method.
- **# of call graph edges** shows the number of call graph edges.
- **average var points-to** shows the average number of allocation sites to which a variable can refer.
- **execution time** shows the average running time for 20 executions of the implementation. We used Criterion [1] to obtain the execution time.

We shall illustrate the concept of collapsing types with a common ancestor. Consider a program with two classes named `Add` and `Minus` with a common parent class `Expr`. The following table shows various type sets and their collapsed counter parts:

Un-collapsed Types	Collapsed Types
{ Boolean, Integer }	{ Boolean, Integer }
{ Boolean, Null }	{ Boolean, Null }
{ Add, Minus }	{ Expr }
{ Add, Null }	{ Add }

Table 1. Collapsing types

In Figure 9 and 10 we provide the main results of our experiments. All metrics in these tables are end-user (i.e. context-insensitive) metrics. This means that the analysis result for different contexts are joined together for the same program label.

We shortly summarise our findings. In terms of precision, 2plain $+ 1H$ and 2full $+ 1H$ do not differ at all, except for `raytracer` where 2full $+ 1H$ analysis achieves better precision. We expect these small differences to be due to the relatively small size of the programs. In terms of performance, 2full $+ 1H$ always either outperforms the 2plain $+ 1H$ analysis or both analyses end up taking a similar amount of time. Interestingly, increasing the context depth does not necessarily result in a performance penalty. For example, the context insensitive analysis (which only uses one context Λ) performs significantly worse than the more complicated 2full $+ 1H$ analysis for 6 of the 8 test programs. This difference is most striking in the case of the *phpgeo* test program where the context insensitive analysis is more than 7 $\times$ slower than the 2full$+1H$ analysis. We suspect the main reason is that the higher precision enables the analysis to exclude a broader range of target methods while resolving a method call.

[1] http://hackage.haskell.org/package/criterion

In terms of performance, 2type $+ 1H$ only outperforms the 2full $+ 1H$ analysis for 3 of 8 test programs. Compared to the 2full $+ 1H$ analysis, the 1type1obj+1H analysis does not perform better for a single test program. Contrary to our expectations the type sensitive analysis often performs worse than a full object sensitive analysis of the same context depth.

If we increase the context depth of an analysis, the execution time is influenced by two opposing forces. On the one hand a deeper context depth may result in each data flow fact being analyzed more often, leading to an increase in the execution time. On the other hand, a deeper context may avoid poisoning of the analysis results. This prevents the propagation of data flow facts because the analysis is able to infer statically that some program paths are impossible, leading to a decrease in the execution time.

The relative strength of these two forces depends strongly on the specific implementation decisions. We suspect that our implementation differs in this regard with that used in [20], leading to different experimental observations. Consider for example the extreme case of an context insensitive analysis, which employs only one context Λ. The context insensitive analysis performs worse in terms of performance than the 2full $+ 1H$ analysis for 6 out of the 8 test programs in our experiments. However, the context insensitive analysis performs better in terms of performance than the 2full $+ 1H$ analysis for all test programs in the experiments described in [20].

Since the number of contexts of a type sensitive analysis lies in between the number of contexts of a context insensitive analysis (only one context) and a 2full $+ 1H$ analysis (theoretically $\mathcal{O}(n^2)$ number of contexts, where n is the number of allocation sites in a program) one may expect a performance increase using the implementation of Smaragdakis et al. while a performance decrease is expected using our implementation.

In terms of precision, 2type $+ 1H$ performs worse than 2full+1 for 3 out of 8 test programs. Only for the *raytracer* test program the 1type1obj+1H analysis performs worse in terms of precision, for the others results are identical.

Abstract Garbage Collection

Our experiments show that the type analysis only terminates within a reasonable amount of time if abstract garbage collection [14] is enabled. Abstract garbage collection prevents the propagation of abstract objects which are known to be unreachable. Table 11 shows the execution time of the analysis with and without abstract garbage collection. We ran this experiment only on a subset of the test suite. Programs excluded for this experiment ran out of memory when abstract garbage collection was disabled.

	GC Enabled (s)	GC Disabled (s)
mime	0.40	0.59
raytracer	6.48	13.56
interpreter	2.33	5.36

Figure 11. Performance Metrics of Abstract Garbage Collection

Exact inferred type sets

Consider the table in Figure 12. It provides for each program, and for each analysis variation, the number of assignments reachable in the program (RA), and the number of assignments among those for which our the analysis variant inferred exactly the same set of types as those observed in our unit tests (PM = precise match), and the relative portion of the assignments for which this is the case. For example, for *raytracer*, the insensitive variant discovered 730 reachable assignments, and inferred for 360 (i.e, 49 percent) type sets that exactly matched the dynamically observed types for that

		insensitive	1obj	1obj+1H	2plain+1H	2full+1H
raytracer	# of union types	324	-84	0	-6	-12
	# of union types coll.	213	-28	0	-6	-12
	# of poly. call sites	26	-22	0	0	0
	# of callgraph edges	155	-28	0	0	0
	average var points-to	11.24	1.47	1.47	1.47	1.47
	execution time (s)	8.81	5.43	7.43	7.00	6.02
gaufrette	# of union types	141	-12	4	0	0
	# of union types coll.	69	-7	4	0	0
	# of poly. call sites	8	-1	0	0	0
	# of callgraph edges	234	-1	0	0	0
	average var points-to	3.43	2.36	2.36	2.36	2.36
	execution time (s)	4.22	2.97	3.44	3.45	3.09
phpgeo	# of union types	164	-22	0	0	0
	# of union types coll.	119	-25	0	0	0
	# of poly. call sites	52	-52	0	0	0
	# of callgraph edges	244	-108	0	0	0
	average var points-to	14.60	1.69	1.69	1.69	1.69
	execution time (s)	14.74	3.65	4.74	1.94	1.94
mime	# of union types	62	0	-5	0	0
	# of union types coll.	28	0	-5	0	0
	# of poly. call sites	2	0	0	0	0
	# of callgraph edges	49	0	0	0	0
	average var points-to	2.47	1.12	1.07	1.07	1.07
	execution time (s)	0.45	0.43	0.43	0.51	0.51
mvc	# of union types	179	-47	1	0	0
	# of union types coll.	110	-57	0	0	0
	# of poly. call sites	36	-27	0	0	0
	# of callgraph edges	301	-143	0	0	0
	average var points-to	8.16	1.44	1.09	1.09	1.09
	execution time (s)	12.59	4.60	5.81	5.70	5.20
dijkstra	# of union types	128	-1	-8	0	0
	# of union types coll.	61	-2	-36	0	0
	# of poly. call sites	3	0	-2	0	0
	# of callgraph edges	144	0	-12	0	0
	average var points-to	3.74	2.05	1.31	1.31	1.31
	execution time (s)	12.15	6.75	4.47	3.84	3.36
floyd	# of union types	150	1	-4	0	0
	# of union types coll.	42	0	-15	0	0
	# of poly. call sites	9	0	-2	0	0
	# of callgraph edges	176	0	-9	0	0
	average var points-to	5.15	1.75	1.51	1.50	1.50
	execution time (s)	18.87	13.17	13.73	12.90	11.80
interpreter	# of union types	241	-12	0	0	0
	# of union types coll.	92	-2	0	0	0
	# of poly. call sites	59	0	0	0	0
	# of callgraph edges	495	0	0	0	0
	average var points-to	5.05	3.90	3.90	3.90	3.90
	execution time (s)	2.03	2.05	2.10	2.95	2.09

Figure 9. Comparison of plain and full object sensitivity

		1obj+1H	2type+1H	1type1obj+1H	2full+1H
raytracer	# of union types	240	56	-56	-18
	# of union types coll.	185	6	-6	-18
	# of poly. call sites	4	14	-14	0
	# of callgraph edges	127	14	-14	0
	average var points-to	1.47	3.86	1.47	1.47
	execution time (s)	7.43	7.29	7.65	6.02
gaufrette	# of union types	133	4	-4	0
	# of union types coll.	66	0	0	0
	# of poly. call sites	7	0	0	0
	# of callgraph edges	233	0	0	0
	average var points-to	2.36	2.84	2.36	2.36
	execution time (s)	3.44	4.00	3.39	3.09
phpgeo	# of union types	142	4	-4	0
	# of union types coll.	94	0	0	0
	# of poly. call sites	0	40	-40	0
	# of callgraph edges	136	96	-96	0
	average var points-to	1.69	4.26	1.69	1.69
	execution time (s)	4.74	4.56	2.22	1.94
mime	# of union types	57	0	0	0
	# of union types coll.	23	0	0	0
	# of poly. call sites	2	0	0	0
	# of callgraph edges	49	0	0	0
	average var points-to	1.07	1.88	1.07	1.07
	execution time (s)	0.43	0.45	0.52	0.51
mvc	# of union types	133	27	-27	0
	# of union types coll.	53	25	-25	0
	# of poly. call sites	9	13	-13	0
	# of callgraph edges	158	26	-26	0
	average var points-to	1.09	2.54	1.09	1.09
	execution time (s)	5.81	4.06	5.49	5.20
dijkstra	# of union types	119	0	0	0
	# of union types coll.	23	0	0	0
	# of poly. call sites	1	0	0	0
	# of callgraph edges	132	0	0	0
	average var points-to	1.31	1.77	1.31	1.31
	execution time (s)	4.47	4.82	4.45	3.36
floyd	# of union types	147	0	0	0
	# of union types coll.	27	0	0	0
	# of poly. call sites	7	0	0	0
	# of callgraph edges	167	0	0	0
	average var points-to	1.51	4.31	1.51	1.50
	execution time (s)	13.73	16.44	13.57	11.80
interpreter	# of union types	229	0	0	0
	# of union types coll.	90	0	0	0
	# of poly. call sites	59	0	0	0
	# of callgraph edges	495	0	0	0
	average var points-to	3.90	4.70	3.90	3.90
	execution time (s)	2.10	1.90	2.10	2.09

Figure 10. Comparison of type sensitivity and object sensitivity

assignment (by running the program on a number of unit tests, as described at the end of Section 4). For the $2\text{full} + 1H$ case, one fewer assignment was found to be reachable, and the percentage improved to 63 percent.

If we assume our analysis to be sound, the assignments that have a precise match cannot be improved upon. Although the variation between the ratio's for a given program are never very high, and for some programs they are almost identical across different variations, it does show that the more precise variants can sometimes give substantially better numbers, and that on the whole the percentages are not bad at all.

7. Related Work

The concept of soft typing was introduced in [4]. A soft type system accepts all programs in a dynamically typed language and inserts dynamic checks in places where it cannot statically infer provably correct types. Flanagan introduces hybrid type checking, which is a synthesis of static typing and dynamic contract checking [6]. Gradual typing, see, e.g., [19] allows mixing static and dynamic typing within one program: type annotated program elements are checked statically, others dynamically.

There is quite a bit of work on soft typing for particular languages, including PHP, Python, and JavaScript. Due to reasons of space we can only provide details for a few of these. The works discussed here provide additional pointers to related work. Jensen et al. [10] presents a static program analysis to infer detailed and sound type information for Javascript programs by means of abstract interpretation. Their analysis is both flow and context sensitive and supports the full language, as defined in the ECMAScript standard, including its prototypical object model, exceptions and first-class functions. The analysis results are used to detect programming errors and to produce type information for program comprehension. The precision of the analysis is improved by employing a technique called recency abstraction. This enables the analysis to perform strong updates on this object, keeping the abstraction as precise as possible.

Fritz et al. [8] performs type analysis for Python programs, focusing on balancing precision and cost by controlling a widening operator that is employed during fix point iteration. The proposed analysis is based on data flow and is both flow and context sensitive. The analysis supports first class functions and Python's dynamic class system. Both [8] and [10] employ an extension to embellished monotone frameworks that is similar to ours.

Camphuijsen et al. [3] presents a type analysis for PHP as part of a tool to detect suspicious code. The analysis is flow and context sensitive and the type system is based on union types, but also support user-provided polymorphic types for functions. First-class functions and object-oriented programming constructs are not supported by the analysis. A widening operator is used to force termination in the presence of infinitely nested array structures.

Context-sensitivity has a pretty long history, see, e.g., [18] and [17]. Object-sensitivity as a particular form of context-sensitivity was introduced by Milanova et al. [15]. Smaragdakis et al. [20] describe a framework in which it is possible to describe different variations of object sensitivity. Their abstract semantics is parametrized by two functions which manipulate contexts, $record$ and $merge$ that we also employ in our work. They then specify many variations of object-sensitivity by choosing different $record$ and $merge$ functions. They also introduced the concept of type sensitivity as an approximation of object sensitivity. Their work shows that type sensitivity preserves much of the precision of object sensitivity at considerably lower cost.

8. Conclusion and Future Work

In this paper we described an object sensitive type analysis for PHP. The presence of dynamic method dispatching in PHP implies that control flow and data flow information are mutually dependent: propagation of points-to information may make additional methods reachable, which may in turn increase the propagated points-to information.

We specified the type analysis as an extension of a points-to analysis. In addition, we presented a novel method to capture the coercion rules of PHP by means of the $coerce$ and $reject$ functions. We considered multiple variations of an object sensitive analysis, and gave the results of an experimental evaluation of our implementation on eight PHP applications. We did not succeed in achieving gains similar to those in [20]. We did find that abstract garbage collection is essential to decrease memory consumption to an acceptable level.

We do not yet support first class functions and closures that require an even more elaborate lattice to model the abstract state. Following [8], it seems we should be able to base such an extension on monotone frameworks we used in this work. Extensions to improve the precision of our analysis is to employ recency abstraction [10], or path-sensitivity [9].

In [11], the authors observes that most client analyses do not care about the specific exception objects, rather they care about the impact of exceptions on the control flow of a program. This leads to the question whether our type analysis can also benefit from a coarsening of exception objects. Because PHP is also used as a procedural (not object-oriented) language, it also makes sense to apply the hybrid approach of [12] that combines call-site sensitivity with object sensitivity. Finally, we wonder whether the Datalog query language used in the DOOP framework employed by Smaragdakis is expressive enough to describe the coercion rules of PHP.

We shall also report on our extension to embellished monotone frameworks for dealing with the dynamic aspects of PHP, and comparing it with other work in this area in another paper.

References

[1] P. Biggar, E. de Vries, and D. Gregg. A practical solution for scripting language compilers. In *Proceedings of the 2009 ACM symposium on Applied Computing*, SAC '09, pages 1916–1923, New York, NY, USA, 2009. ACM.

[2] N. Borenstein and N. Freed. MIME (Multipurpose Internet Mail Extensions): Mechanisms for Specifying and Describing the Format of Internet Message Bodies. RFC 1341 (Proposed Standard), June 1992. Obsoleted by RFC 1521.

[3] P. Camphuijsen, J. Hage, and S. Holdermans. Soft typing php. Technical Report UU-CS-2009-004, Department of Information and Computing Sciences, Utrecht University, 2009.

[4] R. Cartwright and M. Fagan. Soft typing. *PLDI '91: 1991 Conference on Programming Language Design and Implementation*, pages 278–292, Jun 1991.

[5] E. W. Dijkstra. A note on two problems in connexion with graphs. *Numerische mathematik*, 1(1):269–271, 1959.

[6] C. Flanagan. Hybrid type checking. In *POPL '06: Conference record of the 33rd ACM symposium on Principles of programming languages*, pages 245–256, New York, USA, 2006. ACM.

[7] R. W. Floyd. Algorithm 97: Shortest path. *Commun. ACM*, 5(6):345–, June 1962.

[8] L. Fritz and J. Hage. Cost versus precision for approximate typing for python. Technical Report UU-CS-2014-017, Department of Information and Computing Sciences, Utrecht University, 2014.

[9] H. Hampapuram, Y. Yang, and M. Das. Symbolic path simulation in path-sensitive dataflow analysis. In *ACM SIGSOFT Software Engineering Notes*, volume 31, pages 52–58. ACM, 2005.

	insensitive			1obj			1obj+1H			2plain + $1H$			2full + $1H$		
	RA	PM	%	RA	PM	%	RA	PM	%	RA	PM	%	RA	PM	%
raytracer	730	360	49 %	729	441	60 %	729	441	60 %	729	447	61 %	729	459	63 %
gaufrette	672	432	64 %	671	436	65 %	671	432	64 %	671	432	64 %	671	432	64 %
phpgeo	699	518	74 %	699	538	77 %	699	538	77 %	699	538	77 %	699	538	77 %
mime	320	211	66 %	320	211	66 %	320	213	67 %	320	213	67 %	320	213	67 %
mvc	566	173	31 %	561	213	38 %	561	221	39 %	561	221	39 %	561	221	39 %
dijkstra	575	321	56 %	575	323	56 %	522	323	62 %	522	323	62 %	522	323	62 %
floyd	798	556	70 %	798	557	70 %	761	559	73 %	761	559	73 %	761	559	73 %
interpreter	555	265	48 %	555	267	48 %	555	267	48 %	555	267	48 %	555	267	48 %

Figure 12. How often does what we statically infer correspond exactly to what is dynamically observed?

[10] S. H. Jensen, A. Møller, and P. Thiemann. Type analysis for JavaScript. In *Proc. 16th International Static Analysis Symposium (SAS)*, volume 5673 of *LNCS*. Springer-Verlag, August 2009.

[11] G. Kastrinis and Y. Smaragdakis. Efficient and effective handling of exceptions in java points-to analysis. In *Compiler Construction*, pages 41–60. Springer, 2013.

[12] G. Kastrinis and Y. Smaragdakis. Hybrid context-sensitivity for points-to analysis. In *Proceedings of the 34th ACM SIGPLAN Conference on Programming Language Design and Implementation*, PLDI '13, pages 423–434, New York, NY, USA, 2013. ACM.

[13] O. Lhoták. *Program analysis using binary decision diagrams*. PhD thesis, McGill University, 2006.

[14] M. Might and O. Shivers. Improving flow analyses via γcfa: abstract garbage collection and counting. *ACM SIGPLAN Notices*, 41(9):13–25, 2006.

[15] A. Milanova, A. Rountev, and B. Ryder. Parameterized object sensitivity for points-to analysis for Java. *ACM Transactions on Software Engineering and Methodology (TOSEM)*, 14(1):1–41, 2005.

[16] F. Nielson, H. R. Nielson, and C. Hankin. *Principles of Program Analysis*. Springer-Verlag New York, Inc., Secaucus, NJ, USA, 1999.

[17] M. Pnueli. Two approaches to interprocedural data flow analysis. *Program flow analysis: theory and applications*, pages 189–234, 1981.

[18] O. Shivers. Control flow analysis in scheme. In *PLDI '88: Proceedings of the ACM SIGPLAN 1988 conference on Programming Language design and Implementation*, pages 164–174, New York, NY, USA, 1988. ACM.

[19] J. Siek and W. Taha. Gradual typing for objects. *ECOOP '07: 21st European Conference on Object-Oriented Programming*, Jul 2007.

[20] Y. Smaragdakis, M. Bravenboer, and O. Lhoták. Pick your contexts well: understanding object-sensitivity. In *Proceedings of the 38th annual ACM SIGPLAN-SIGACT symposium on Principles of programming languages*, POPL '11, pages 17–30, New York, NY, USA, 2011. ACM.

[21] H. E. van der Hoek. Object sensitive type analysis for PHP, 2013. `http://www.cs.uu.nl/people/jur/msctheses/henkerikvanderhoek-msc.pdf`.

[22] J. Verlaguet, J. Beales, E. Letuchy, G. Levi, J. Marcey, E. Meijer, A. Menghrajani, B. O'Sullivan, D. Paroski, J. Pearce, J. Pobar, and J. Van Dyke Watzman. The Hack language. `http://hacklang.org`, consulted Oct. 2014.

[23] H. Zhao, I. Proctor, M. Yang, X. Qi, M. Williams, Q. Gao, G. Ottoni, A. Paroski, S. MacVicar, J. Evans, and S. Tu. The HipHop compiler for PHP. In *Proceedings of the ACM International Conference on Object Oriented Programming Systems Languages and Applications*, OOPSLA '12, pages 575–586, New York, NY, USA, 2012. ACM.

Structurally Heterogeneous Source Code Examples from Unstructured Knowledge Sources

Venkatesh Vinayakarao Rahul Purandare
Indraprastha Institute of Information Technology, Delhi
{venkateshv,purandare}@iiitd.ac.in

Aditya V. Nori
Microsoft Research
adityan@microsoft.com

Abstract

Software developers rarely write code from scratch. With the existence of Wikipedia, discussion forums, books and blogs, it is hard to imagine a software developer not looking up these sites for sample code while building any non-trivial software system. While researchers have proposed approaches to retrieve relevant posts and code snippets, the need for finding variant implementations of functionally similar code snippets has been ignored. In this work, we propose an approach to automatically create a repository of structurally heterogeneous but functionally similar source code examples from unstructured sources. We evaluate the approach on stackoverflow[1], a discussion forum that has approximately 19 million posts. The results of our evaluation indicates that the approach extracts structurally different snippets with a precision of 83%. A repository of such heterogeneous source code examples will be useful to programmers in learning different implementation strategies and for researchers working on problems such as program comprehension, semantic clones and code search.

Categories and Subject Descriptors H.3.3 [*Information Search and Retrieval*]: Retrieval models; D.3.3 [*Language Constructs and Features*]: Control structures

General Terms Code Search, Programs, Examples, Mining, Knowledge Representation, Similarity

Keywords Example Retrieval

1. Introduction

Structural heterogeneity is very commonly observed in functionally similar source code written in high level programming languages such as Java. For example, *factorial* can be implemented either using recursion or loops or programming constructs such as BigInteger. Listings 1, 2 and 3 show examples for different implementations of a simple factorial program.

Unstructured sources such as discussion forums contain several examples in the form of partial program snippets that implement functionality relevant to the topic discussed. We propose an

[1] http://stackoverflow.com/

PEPM '15, January 13–14, 2015, Mumbai, India.
Copyright © 2015 ACM 978-1-4503-3297-2/15/01...$15.00.
http://dx.doi.org/10.1145/2678015.2682537

```
public static int factorial(int n) {
    int fact = 1;
    for (int i = 1; i <= n; i++) {
        fact *= i;
    }
    return fact;
}
```

Listing 1: Factorial using loop

```
public static long calc(long n){
    if (n <= 1)
        return 1;
    else
        return n * calc(n-1);
}
```

Listing 2: Factorial using recursion

```
public static void main(string[] args) {
    BigInteger fact = BigInteger.valueof(1);
    for (int i = 1; i <= 8785856; i++)
        fact = fact.multiply(BigInteger.valueof(i));
    system.out.println(fact);
}
```

Listing 3: Factorial using BigInteger

approach to extract such code examples. Henceforth, we refer to such examples that are well discussed as *familiar code*. We refer to a short text that describes the familiar code as a *topic*. Listing 3 shows a familiar code for the topic, "factorial". Knowledge of variant implementations plays a significant role in several research areas such as program comprehension, semantic clone detection and code search.

Familiar code snippets frequently occur in massive code repositories. For example, Apache commons' BrentOptimizer.java[2] uses Brent's algorithm. As Sridhara et al. [17] claim, spotting such familiar code in massive code bases reduces the amount of code to read, and thus supports program comprehension. Knowing just one implementation or a few structurally similar implementations limits the amount of familiar code that we can spot. Therefore, we believe, an approach to mine structurally heterogeneous code examples will help program comprehension.

Structurally different code examples that exhibit same or similar behavior are candidates for semantic clones. For a given topic, we find structurally different and functionally relevant source code. Thus, our approach directly supports semantic clone detection. The

[2] https://commons.apache.org/proper/commons-math/apidocs/org/apache/commons/math3/optimization/univariate/BrentOptimizer.html

Table 1: Comparison of Discussion Forum characteristics with Code Repository.

#	Discussion Forum	Code Repository
1	Coding concerns common to several projects.	Project specific concerns.
2	Language How-tos.	Domain How-tos.
3	Partial Code.	Compilable Code.
4	Discussions on snippets.	Code & few comments.
5	Alternate approaches discussed.	Single approach & mostly missing reasoning.
6	Captures popularity and correctness of discussions explicitly in the form of responses, comments and ratings.	There is no way to know how many people have read or used a specific snippet from a specific repository.
7	Multilingual Connections. For example, gives Java version of C code.	No connection or references to other language implementations.

output of our approach is a set of semantic clones exemplifying the given topic.

Code search tools need to deal with elimination of duplicate or near-duplicate results. Those tools that search over unstructured sources typically retrieve familiar code. They can improve their results by leveraging techniques to identify structural heterogeneity or just by using a repository of familiar code snippets.

In this work, we discuss the challenges and propose an approach to extract structurally heterogeneous familiar code examples for a given topic from an unstructured source. We implement a prototype using data from a popular discussion forum for a list of 12 topics. We use light-weight program analysis and information retrieval techniques so that partial programs can be effectively retrieved from large scale data sources. Finally, we evaluate the approach and show that structural complexity of familiar code can be used to further refine the results.

2. Mining Familiar Code Snippets

Many researchers have worked on code search over code repositories [2, 3, 10, 13]. Discussion forums have very different characteristics when compared to code repositories. We highlight some key observations that came out of our study in Table 1. Due to these fundamental differences, the approaches used to search a code repository cannot be used to search discussion forum. Also, we believe, due to these differences, use of discussion forum for extracting sample code should not be overlooked.

We take stackoverflow posts that contain a Java code snippet. We could have used any other high level programming language since our methods can easily be modified to work with any language. We extract code snippets and tokens (keywords from the natural language discussion around the snippet) from such relevant posts. We rank code snippets based on vocabulary similarity. Here, we also include the vocabulary elements from code snippet such as identifier and method names. We transform the snippet into a form that captures the structural information. For each code snippet, we check if a snippet's structure differs from its predecessors and thus remove snippets that are structurally duplicates. Further, we use structural complexity to detect and remove outliers. Figure 1 outlines this approach to mine familiar code snippets. The result of this approach is a set of structurally heterogeneous and functionally similar source code samples.

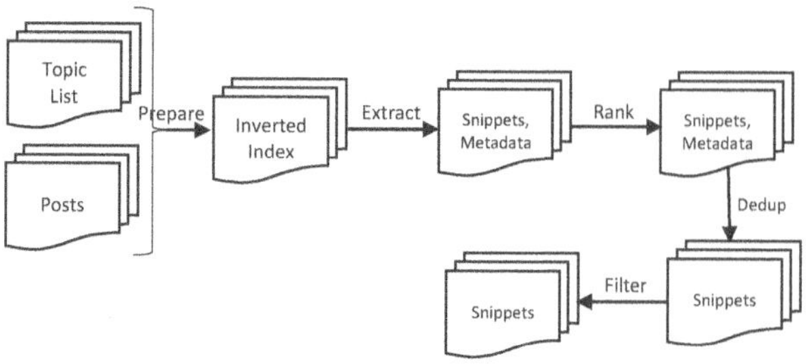

Figure 1: Steps showing the mining of sample code for a topic list from stackoverflow.

2.1 Identifying Posts with Java Snippets

Posts in stackoverflow are typically short text with code embedded in between. The convention in stackoverflow is to place code snippets inside *<code>... </code>* xml blocks. We retrieve such blocks that have at least one *code* element. Posts may contain partial programs i.e., the code snippet may refer to anything between uncompilable statements to fully compilable classes. Moreover, the embedded code could be of any programming language and not necessarily Java.

Research shows that method definitions play a major role in code search [15]. In this work, we limit our analysis to Java methods. We look for *public* or *private* keywords in the code snippet to identify methods. We wrap methods into a custom class template so that we can use Eclipse JDT[3] to parse them into an Abstract Syntax Tree (AST). If Eclipse JDT is able to parse it, we consider that the code snippet we have is indeed a Java code snippet. Several code samples exist without these keywords and our approach drops them. These may sound restrictive but we still ended up with 29,299 code snippets to analyze which is sufficient to pull distinct examples.

Code snippets that are not method definitions could still be useful and are acceptable as mined examples. Static analysis on partial programs [6] could help us identify partial Java code that do not have these modifiers (public or private) and thus enable us mine more examples. This is left for future work.

2.2 Collecting Keywords

Firstly, we tokenize text in the post with the objective of extracting representative terms. We use TF-IDF technique [1] to derive such terms. For this, we had to compute a set of unique terms in the post and the number of posts that they appeared in. In our case, since the text is very short, term frequency (TF) does not have any impact. Hence, it is reasonable to use the inverse document frequency (IDF) value to find the representative terms for a post. For any term t in the entire corpus of posts P, *idf* is given by the following formula where N is the total number of posts.

$$idf(t, P) = \log \frac{N}{|\{p \in P : t \in p\}|} \quad (1)$$

Secondly, we capture terms from the vocabulary used in the code snippet. From the ASTs, we capture vocabulary in the form of method name and variable names. There are variables that do not carry much semantic value such as the loop index variables. In this context, by semantic value, we refer to the natural language expressiveness of the variable. We observe that these variables are usually left as a single character such as i or j. There are cases where variables of length less than three carry semantic value. For

[3] http://www.eclipse.org/jdt/

Table 2: Precision before and after the use of sequence information.

#	Case	Method#1	Method#2
1	Convert int to String	50	75
2	Factorial	100	100

instance, n typically refers to "number of ..." or "count", and sd refers to "standard deviation". For this work, we ignore such short variables. Without loss of generality, we chose to drop all terms that had any non-alphabetic character. This step of filtration does not impact our approach or results. Leveraging state of the art vocabulary manipulation techniques such as Normalize [21] can help us improve our work.

2.3 Relevance and Ranking

Now that we have a collection of code snippets and associated metadata in the form of keywords, our next task is to rank them based on relevance to topic. We tokenize the stackoverflow post title. We also grab the variable names and method name from the code snippet. We compare the topic with these data (tokenized title and elements from code snippet) and quantify the relevance.

Firstly, we study the snippets ranked based on term frequency (TF) score. We observe three major issues:

1. **Favoring long posts**: Long posts tend to have more terms with high frequency and hence such long posts are preferred over shorter posts.
2. **Sequence information is ignored**: Sequence of terms in topic is important for retrieving relevant results.
3. **Specialization problem**: There are terms such as *Array* and *Array List* that require different results even though they contain some terms in common.

Research on quality of example programs [4] shows that users prefer shorter examples. Term Frequency has the disadvantage of bias towards longer documents [20]. To address this concern, we use augmented term frequency $tf(t,p)$ computed as follows:

$$tf(t,p) = \frac{f(t,p)}{1 + max\{f(t,p)\}} \tag{2}$$

where $f(t,p)$ represents the raw frequency of term t in post p.

Consider the topic *convert int to string*. This is not same as *convert string to int*. If we go with just the term frequency, results relevant to either of these queries will score the same. To avoid this, we compute longest common subsequence metric for each result. The intuition is that if the terms "convert", "int" and "string" appear in the same order in the result as well, the result scores higher. Table 2 shows the precision for two topics before and after the application of this method. Note that while this approach does not impact *factorial*, it had a positive impact on *convert int to string* topic.

Our ranking model is as follows. Let $w_1, w_2..., w_n$ denote any vector of terms that represents a post p. Let $t_1, t_2, ..., t_k$ be the topic vector representing a topic T. The distance function ϕ is defined as follows:

$$\phi(p,T) = \lambda \sum_{i=1}^{k-1}((loc(t_{i+1},p) - loc(t_i,p)) \tag{3}$$

The function $loc(t,p)$ refers to the location (or index) of term t in post p. λ denotes heuristically derived weight. For a match in title, we believe the post should be more relevant and hence have a higher $\lambda = 6$ and for code snippet match, we keep λ as 3. We add up the scores computed for title and code snippet to get the final score for a post p as:

$$\phi(p,T) = \phi_{title}(p,T) + \phi_{snippet}(p,T) \tag{4}$$

Binary Search is not the same as *Binary Search Tree*. Similarly, *Array* is not same as *Array List*. We observe that TF based approach is unable to differentiate these kinds of results. Judges did not like the results of *sort array* since they saw results relevant to *sort array list*. We refer to this non-trivial problem as a specialization problem and leave this as future work.

Table 3: Structural information extracted from source code.

Code	Structure
`public static int factorial(int n) {`	`<algo>`
`int fact = 1;`	`<loop>`
`for (int i=1; i<=n; i++) {`	`<=`
`fact *= i;`	`*=`
`}`	`</loop>`
`return fact;`	`</algo>`
`}`	

2.4 De-duplication

Our assumption is that several short code snippets are heavily reused. Thus, snippets of same structure are expected to show up as the result. Current research [3] has used structural similarity to predict functional similarity. We have the reverse objective. Out of all the structurally similar examples, we wish to retain only one result.

To compute structural similarity, we flatten the structure into term-like items. Sridhara et al. [17] group structural elements into three significant categories: return, conditionals and loops. We use conditionals and loops. We leave *return* for future work. Table 3 illustrates one sample run of structure generation. Each code snippet C_i is transformed into a vector of structural terms c_j. Structural similarity $similarity(C_1, C_2)$ between two code snippets C_1 and C_2 is computed as follows:

$$similarity(C_1, C_2) = \frac{|C1 \cap C2|}{max\{|C1|, |C2|\}} \tag{5}$$

Note that for any pair of identical factorial code snippets, we arrive at the maximum possible similarity score (of one). A recursive version of factorial when compared with the iterator based version will have very few common structures, thereby resulting in a smaller similarity score.

2.5 Structural Complexity

Our intuition is that the snippets that are functionally similar would have programming constructs that are similar in terms of their structural complexity even though they may differ considerably in their structures.

We observe the structural elements in familiar code and learn how they contribute to structural complexity. For instance, loops do not change the structural complexity irrespective of which form they take such as *while* or *for*. Our approach to approximate both of them to a generic *loop* as shown in Table 3 helps us to take advantage of this similarity. However, several such structural patterns exist in source code that could be leveraged to compute structural complexity. For instance, loops can be flattened to *switch* or *if* statements especially for small index values of loops. There are many familiar code examples that have a recursive equivalent of loop form.

We compute structural complexity in terms of Structural Lines of Code (LOC_{ST}). Here, we compute the number of statements in the flattened version of the source code (referred as structure

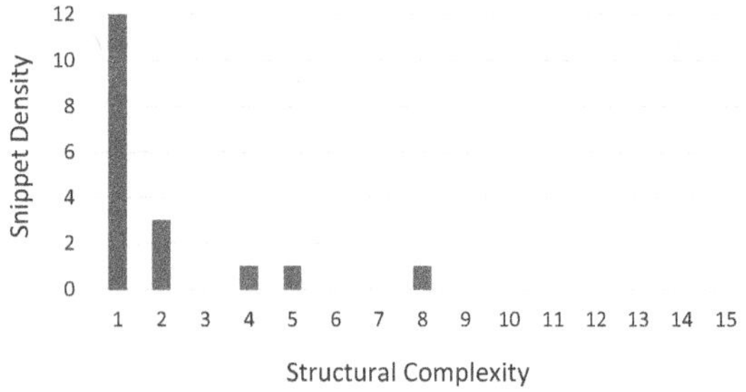

(a) Factorial: Most examples are of low structural complexity.

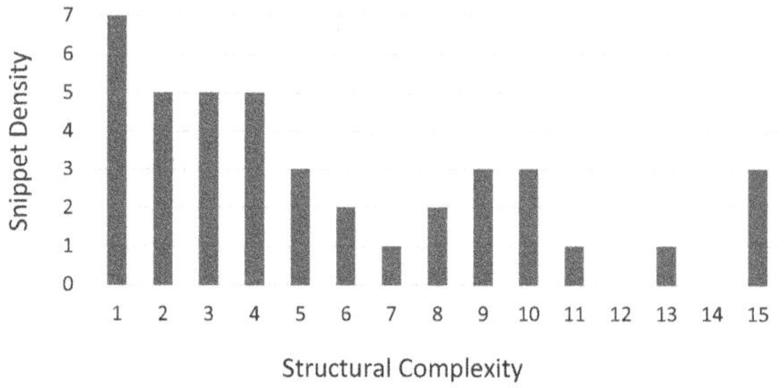

(b) Binary Search: Widespread structural complexity values.

Figure 2: Structural complexity characterizes the topics. Note that, in general, *Factorial* is less complicated structurally than *Binary Search*. Factorial code samples in the LOC_{ST} buckets of 4 and above are most probably irrelevant and can be treated as outliers. For *Binary Search*, the outliers are likely to be in the first LOC_{ST} bucket since there are sufficiently large number of samples in high-complexity buckets.

in Table 3). We categorize statements as Loop(l), Assignment (a), Declaration(d), Call(c), Recursive Call(rc), Return(r) and Expression(e) and assign a weight of $l = 5, a = 2, d = 2, c = 3, rc = 4$ and $r = 0$. These weights are manually derived by observing several code examples. We observe that complexity of expressions is directly proportional to the number of operators used in the expression. Hence we assign e to the number of operators. A simple coarse grained model with such weights works for us. For a code snippet C that has statements $< c_1, c_2, c_3, ...c_n >$ with corresponding type dependent weight $< w_1, w_2, w_3...w_n >$, LOC_{ST} is computed as follows:

$$LOC_{ST}(C) = \sum_{i=1}^{n} w_i \tag{6}$$

We compute structural complexity as discussed above on all the code snippets mined so far. Our intuition is that, in-spite of being structurally heterogeneous, the structural complexity of the code snippets (relevant to a specific topic) should not vary significantly. So, irrespective of whether recursion or loops are used, factorial code is simple by structural complexity when compared with implementations of binary search. Figure 2a suggests that most of the relevant code snippets for factorial have very low structural complexity. We learn from Figure 2b that code snippets that implement binary search tend to be more complex than those that implement factorial. At the same time, we also see several very simple implementations grouped in the first bucket of structural complexity, for binary search. These turned out to be simple snippets such as node and tree definitions that are relevant to binary search tree discussions. As we strengthen our methods to find more and more relevant code snippets, we will see concentrated regions in the structural complexity charts. We observe that the structural complexity gives a reasonable metric to detect outliers. Outliers are typically code samples that are either too simple such as empty methods, or extremely long and complicated methods. These become candidates because of high vocabulary similarity. We treat examples that lie in the sparse regions away from the skyscrapers as outliers. So, for factorial, any example with LOC_{ST} of 4 and above are considered to be outliers.

3. Experimental Setup

We asked 13 graduate students working in the computer science department with at least 6 years of exposure to programming, to give us one query for a typically searched code snippet and one recently searched query, thereby leaving us with 26 queries. We dropped some of the responses which we believe would not have Java implementations. For example, "sort a python dictionary by value" was dropped. This resulted in 12 topics. We mine code examples for these from stackoverflow's XML dump of all posts. On this data dump, we apply the steps detailed in Section 2 i.e., preparation, keyword collection, ranking, de-duplication and structural complexity based filtering. We analyzed over 19 million posts, found 29,299 code snippets that were Java methods. We mined 523 implementations in total for the 12 topics that we started with.

4. Evaluation

Our evaluation criteria consist of two parts. Firstly, we check the relevance:

- The code snippet must show how to implement the given topic in Java. Sometimes, an API call to existing library will also be sufficient and hence it is considered as a good solution.
- A code snippet may not be implementing the given topic alone. For a query like *file reading*, a code snippet that shows how to print numbers from a file is considered as a good example.
- Example retrieved may partly implement the topic. For instance, there are several options while opening a file in Java. Example need not be exhaustive to be relevant. However, just the first two lines of file reading is not considered to be a relevant and good example.
- Code snippets that neither demonstrate the use nor exhibit an implementation of given topic should be marked as irrelevant.

Next, we ensure that the results are structurally diverse.

- Example retrieved should not be similar to an already retrieved example. Two examples should be marked as being structurally similar using the following guidelines:
  - if we rename the variables and remove white spaces and change the indentation, the examples become the same.
  - irrelevant code inserted or deleted in between is not considered as a variant example.
  - use of different api should be considered as a variant example.

Three graduate students evaluated all the results and marked them on a binary scale as relevant/irrelevant. We used this data to compute precision. Firstly, we checked the precision we get if we do not use any technique apart from string match of topic name in stackoverflow post vocabulary. The precision varied from 17% (convert integer to string) to 93% (for factorial) with a mean of 63% and standard deviation of 22%. Hence, the topic set has no bias towards the potential for string match.

Table 4: We are able to extract variant implementations with a precision of 83.3%. Count column shows the number of example snippets retrieved. Precision demands both functional relevance and structural heterogeneity.

#	Topic	Count	Precision
1	Binary Search	7	100
2	Check file exists	4	50
3	Compare objects	7	75
4	Convert integer to string	2	75
5	Deep copy	3	100
6	Factorial	5	100
7	File reading bufferedreader	2	50
8	Keyboard input	3	100
9	Merge sort	2	100
10	Palindrome	5	100
11	Reverse string	9	100
12	Sorting array	3	50

5. Results

We have extracted structurally heterogeneous and semantically similar code snippets for 12 topics with a precision of 83.3% with a mean and median of approximately four examples for each topic. Table 4 shows the number of structurally diverse results obtained from our approach and its corresponding precision, for each topic. From these results, we are convinced that the availability of multiple examples allows us to leverage dominant structures, variables and words (from post body) and score each snippet. We find stackoverflow to be a rich source for demonstrating an approach to mine heterogeneous examples. We also observe that structural complexity characterizes the topics and therefore can be used to filter outliers as shown in Figure 2 and discussed in Section 2.5.

Lexicons play a major role in identifying APIs that are frequently used to do key functions. For example, BigInteger is typically used in factorial computation in Java. Our method found that BigInteger is popular in the context of factorial and retrieved it (shown in Listing 3) as an example. When multiple people refer to a BigInteger based factorial implementation, an understanding of technicalities behind BigInteger is not required to believe that the API plays a role in factorial computation. This goes well with the natural way humans comprehend software.

Lack of context is a key challenge. Our topic *check file exists* has ambiguous context. It may refer to file on local disk or file on remote server. Most of the judges felt that former was the need and judged the latter implementations as irrelevant.

We also observe the issue of picking a heavily correlated wrong example from the post. For instance, file reader and file writer are discussed together and they end up getting similar score.

Threats to Validity Our current evaluation uses 12 topics. We have showed that our topics have no bias from the context of vocabulary matches. It is still possible that we get a lower precision when we increase the number of topics. Moreover, the way the topics are worded could impact the results. Topics need to support search. We assume that users can try out a few queries to quickly get to good results. We have used a single discussion forum as our source to mine snippets. A different discussion forum might impact results. As long as the forum is large and if it reflects the same properties as listed in Table 1, we believe the results should not be very different. Our assumption that the variables of length one or two does not hold semantic value does not hold in all cases. If the topics are such that the relevant code samples use several abbreviations of length one or two, our approach may result in poor precision.

6. Related Work

Prompter [12] and SeaHawk [11] use stackoverflow to help developers (through an IDE extension) with relevant posts using the current code context. They construct queries based on terms in current context. They use several attributes such as textual similarity, code similarity and user reputation to suggest relevant post. However, their work stops at retrieving API names and code-like words. Rigby et al. [14] extract elements of code from informal discussions. Cordeiro et al. [5] extract relevant posts based on stack trace of exceptions. Instead of posts and code-like elements, we extract heterogeneous source code examples for given topics and thus our problem, method and techniques are different.

Sourcerer [2] is a code search engine that collects open source projects, and uses vocabulary and structural information to search for code. Holmes et al. [9] extract examples from source code repositories. Holmes and Murphy [8] use program context to find relevant source code from existing repository using structural information. They work with fully compilable code and use call hierarchy based API usage information. Their techniques cannot be used on code fragments available on discussion forums. Discussion forums have partial yet re-usable code that is better for learning when compared with examples extracted from source repositories since they have discussions associated with them. We leverage these discussions to find source code examples for a given topic.

AlgorithmSeer's [18] algorithm search works on the intuition that the algorithms discussed in scholarly documents are related. A similar idea has been applied on source code using Latent Semantic Indexing and Structural Semantic Indexing [3]. Gulwani et al.'s [7] Programming by Example (PBE) attempts algorithm discovery for automating repetitive tasks. While this uses text as input/output, they have also applied similar idea to automatically suggest corrections to student assignments which are essentially source code [16]. However, this approach works with a large example set of submitted solutions and compares with other solutions. Since the assignment is same, structural similarity serves as a good measure to solve this problem. In contrast, we look at structural dissimilarity to pull up distinct examples for the same topic. We are particularly inspired by the Zhang et al.'s [19] idea of algorithmic comparison. In our work, missing call hierarchy information makes construction of value dependency graphs, impossible. Further, we do not use input/output values or even execute the code samples. Our approach leverages light weight information retrieval and program analysis techniques. Thus, we are able to process several thousand code samples within a few seconds.

7. Conclusion and Future Work

Our initial contribution yields a reasonably accurate approach to mine structurally heterogeneous and functionally similar code snippets from heterogeneous sources. We exploit information retrieval and partial program analysis techniques to arrive at a repository of such code samples. We show that it is possible to retrieve such samples from unstructured sources and discuss the challenges. We have used stackoverflow posts for our research. The same approach can be applied on wikipedia, blogs and books as well.

Understanding the fundamental elements of programming from the perspective of variants of implementations and the way they show up in code opens up new ways to solve problems such as semantic clones. The ability to spot familiar code in massive code bases can not only add value directly to program comprehension but also have several other useful applications. We find the resultant code samples to demonstrate a very high educative and illustrative value. This can be used in designing programming language course texts.

We plan to conduct a study comparing our results against the benchmarks for code retrieval tools such as ohloh[4] and post retrieval tools such as Prompter [12]. We have left the following as future work:

1. Application of information retrieval techniques to address issues such as specialization problem and support non-alphabetic terms in vocabulary. We will also benefit from a vocabulary normalization algorithm such as Normalize [21].
2. Application of partial program analysis techniques towards detecting code and better extraction of structural elements.
3. Structural complexity computation should support program constructs beyond Java method definitions.
4. Examples lie in contexts. For instance, *reading a file* is not same as *reading an integer list from a file* while the latter might still be acceptable as an example of the former.
5. We use a static topic list. To increase the scale, we will need a long list which could be a result of another automated approach.
6. Concepts such as *greedy algorithm* are context specific. For example, the idea of greedy algorithm can be applied on Huffman tree construction during Huffman coding. Retrieving samples for such topics require domain knowledge.

Classic program analysis approaches fail to capture semantics at scale and thus makes a good case to apply information retrieval techniques. Our approach should scale very well to extract code examples in a language independent fashion. While precision seems to be good, recall is still an issue. State of the art program analysis and information retrieval techniques can further help to improve recall. We will need to show that ideas from information retrieval around context extraction can be extended to source code.

Acknowledgments

This work is supported by Confederation of Indian Industries (CII) and Microsoft Research. We thank Dr. Matthew Dwyer and Dr. Sebastian Elbaum for their suggestions to improve this work.

References

[1] R. A. Baeza-Yates and B. Ribeiro-Neto. *Modern Information Retrieval*. Addison-Wesley Longman Publishing Co., Inc., Boston, MA, USA, 1999.

[2] Sushil Bajracharya, Trung Ngo, Erik Linstead, Yimeng Dou, Paul Rigor, Pierre Baldi, and Cristina Lopes. Sourcerer: A search engine for open source code supporting structure-based search. In *Companion to the 21st ACM SIGPLAN Symposium on Object-oriented Programming Systems, Languages, and Applications*, OOPSLA '06, pages 681–682, New York, NY, USA, 2006. ACM.

[3] S. K. Bajracharya, J. Ossher, and C. V. Lopes. Leveraging usage similarity for effective retrieval of examples in code repositories. In *Proceedings of the Eighteenth ACM SIGSOFT International Symposium on Foundations of Software Engineering*, FSE '10, pages 157–166, New York, NY, USA, 2010. ACM.

[4] J. Börstler, M. S. Hall, M. Nordström, J. H. Paterson, K. Sanders, C. Schulte, and L. Thomas. An evaluation of object oriented example programs in introductory programming textbooks. *SIGCSE Bull.*, 41(4):126–143, Jan. 2010.

[5] J. Cordeiro, B. Antunes, and P. Gomes. Context-based recommendation to support problem solving in software development. In *Recommendation Systems for Software Engineering (RSSE), 2012 Third International Workshop on*, pages 85–89, June 2012.

[6] B. Dagenais and L. Hendren. Enabling static analysis for partial java programs. In *Proceedings of the 23rd ACM SIGPLAN Conference on Object-oriented Programming Systems Languages and Applications*, OOPSLA '08, pages 313–328, New York, NY, USA, 2008. ACM.

[7] S. Gulwani. Automating string processing in spreadsheets using input-output examples. In *Proceedings of the 38th Annual ACM SIGPLAN-SIGACT Symposium on Principles of Programming Languages*, POPL '11, pages 317–330, New York, NY, USA, 2011. ACM.

[8] R. Holmes and G. C. Murphy. Using structural context to recommend source code examples. In *Proceedings of the 27th International Conference on Software Engineering*, ICSE '05, pages 117–125, New York, NY, USA, 2005. ACM.

[9] R. Holmes, R. J. Walker, and G. C. Murphy. Strathcona example recommendation tool. In *Proceedings of the 10th European Software Engineering Conference Held Jointly with 13th ACM SIGSOFT International Symposium on Foundations of Software Engineering*, ESEC/FSE-13, pages 237–240, New York, NY, USA, 2005. ACM.

[10] C. McMillan, M. Grechanik, D. Poshyvanyk, Q. Xie, and C. Fu. Portfolio: Finding relevant functions and their usage. In *Proceedings of the 33rd International Conference on Software Engineering*, ICSE '11, pages 111–120, New York, NY, USA, 2011. ACM.

[11] L. Ponzanelli, A. Bacchelli, and M. Lanza. Leveraging crowd knowledge for software comprehension and development. In *Software Maintenance and Reengineering (CSMR), 2013 17th European Conference on*, pages 57–66, March 2013.

[12] L. Ponzanelli, G. Bavota, M. Di Penta, R. Oliveto, and M. Lanza. Mining stackoverflow to turn the IDE into a self-confident programming prompter. In *Proceedings of the 11th Working Conference on Mining Software Repositories*, MSR 2014, pages 102–111, New York, NY, USA, 2014. ACM.

[13] S. P. Reiss. Semantics-based code search. In *Proceedings of the 31st International Conference on Software Engineering*, ICSE '09, pages 243–253, Washington, DC, USA, 2009. IEEE Computer Society.

[14] P. C. Rigby and M. P. Robillard. Discovering essential code elements in informal documentation. In *Proceedings of the 2013 International Conference on Software Engineering*, ICSE '13, pages 832–841, Piscataway, NJ, USA, 2013. IEEE Press.

[15] S. Sim, C. Clarke, and R. Holt. Archetypal source code searches: a survey of software developers and maintainers. In *Program Comprehension, 1998. IWPC '98. Proceedings., 6th International Workshop on*, pages 180–187, Jun 1998.

[16] R. Singh, S. Gulwani, and A. Solar-Lezama. Automated feedback generation for introductory programming assignments. In *Proceedings of the 34th ACM SIGPLAN Conference on Programming Language Design and Implementation*, PLDI '13, pages 15–26, New York, NY, USA, 2013. ACM.

[17] G. Sridhara, L. Pollock, and K. Vijay-Shanker. Automatically detecting and describing high level actions within methods. In *Proceedings of the 33rd International Conference on Software Engineering*, ICSE '11, pages 101–110, New York, NY, USA, 2011. ACM.

[18] S. Tuarob, P. Mitra, and C. L. Giles. "Building a Search Engine for Algorithms" by Suppawong Tuarob, Prasenjit Mitra, and C. Lee Giles with Martin Vesely As Coordinator *SIGWEB Newsl.*, (Winter):5:1–5:9, Jan. 2014.

[19] F. Zhang, Y.-C. Jhi, D. Wu, P. Liu, and S. Zhu. A first step towards algorithm plagiarism detection. In *Proceedings of the 2012 International Symposium on Software Testing and Analysis*, ISSTA 2012, pages 111–121, New York, NY, USA, 2012. ACM.

[20] A. Singhal, C. Buckley, and M. Mitra. Pivoted document length normalization. In *Proceedings of the 19th Annual International ACM SIGIR Conference on Research and Development in Information Retrieval*, SIGIR '96, pages 21–29, New York, NY, USA, 1996. ACM.

[21] D. Lawrie, D. Binkley, and C. Morrell. Normalizing source code vocabulary. In *Reverse Engineering (WCRE), 2010 17th Working Conference on*, pages 3–12, Oct 2010.

[4] https://code.ohloh.net/

Generalising Tree Traversals to DAGs

Exploiting Sharing without the Pain

Patrick Bahr

Department of Computer Science
University of Copenhagen
paba@di.ku.dk

Emil Axelsson

Department of Computer Science and Engineering
Chalmers University of Technology
emax@chalmers.se

Abstract

We present a recursion scheme based on attribute grammars that can be transparently applied to trees and acyclic graphs. Our recursion scheme allows the programmer to implement a tree traversal and then apply it to compact graph representations of trees instead. The resulting graph traversals avoid recomputation of intermediate results for shared nodes – even if intermediate results are used in different contexts. Consequently, this approach leads to asymptotic speedup proportional to the compression provided by the graph representation. In general, however, this sharing of intermediate results is not sound. Therefore, we complement our implementation of the recursion scheme with a number of correspondence theorems that ensure soundness for various classes of traversals. We illustrate the practical applicability of the implementation as well as the complementing theory with a number of examples.

Categories and Subject Descriptors D.1.1 [*Programming Techniques*]: Applicative (Functional) Programming; F.3.3 [*Logics and Meanings of Programs*]: Studies of Program Constructs—Program and Recursion Schemes

Keywords attribute grammars, sharing, graph traversal, Haskell

1. Introduction

Functional programming languages such as Haskell excel at manipulating tree-structured data. Using algebraic data types, we can define functions over trees in a natural way by means of pattern matching and recursion. As an example, we take the following definition of binary trees with integer leaves, and a function to find the set of leaves at and below a given depth in the tree:

$$\mathbf{data}\ \mathit{IntTree} = \mathit{Leaf}\ \mathit{Int} \mid \mathit{Node}\ \mathit{IntTree}\ \mathit{IntTree}$$

$$\begin{aligned}&\mathit{leavesBelow} :: \mathit{Int} \to \mathit{IntTree} \to \mathit{Set}\ \mathit{Int}\\ &\mathit{leavesBelow}\ d\ (\mathit{Leaf}\ i)\\ &\quad \mid d \leqslant 0 \qquad\qquad = \mathit{Set.singleton}\ i\\ &\quad \mid \mathit{otherwise} \qquad = \mathit{Set.empty}\\ &\mathit{leavesBelow}\ d\ (\mathit{Node}\ t_1\ t_2) =\\ &\quad \mathit{leavesBelow}\ (d-1)\ t_1\ \cup\ \mathit{leavesBelow}\ (d-1)\ t_2\end{aligned}$$

PEPM '15, January 13–14, 2015, Mumbai, India.

ACM 978-1-4503-3297-2/15/01...$15.00.
http://dx.doi.org/10.1145/2678015.2682539

One shortcoming of tree structures is that they are unable to represent sharing of common subtrees, which occur, for example, when a compiler substitutes a shared variable by its definition. The following tree has a shared node a that appears twice:

$$\begin{aligned}t = \mathbf{let}\ &a = \mathit{Node}\ (\mathit{Node}\ (\mathit{Leaf}\ 2)\ (\mathit{Leaf}\ 3))\ (\mathit{Leaf}\ 4)\\ \mathbf{in}\ &\mathit{Node}\ a\ a\end{aligned}$$

Unfortunately, a function like *leavesBelow* is unable to observe this sharing, and thus needs to traverse the shared subtree in t twice.

In order to represent and take advantage of sharing, one could instead use a directed graph representation, such as the structured graphs of Oliveira and Cook [32]. However, such a change of representation would force us to express *leavesBelow* by traversing the graph structure instead of by plain recursion over the *Node* constructors. If we are only interested in graphs as a compact representation of trees, this is quite a high price to pay. In an ideal world, one should be able to leave the definition of *leavesBelow* as it is, and be able to run it on both trees and graphs.

Oliveira and Cook [32] define a fold operation for structured graphs which makes it possible to define structurally recursive functions as algebras that can be applied to both trees and graphs. However, *leavesBelow* is a context-dependent function that passes the depth parameter down the recursive calls. Therefore, an implementation as a fold – namely by computing a function from context to result – would not be able to exploit the sharing present in the graph: intermediate results for shared nodes still have to be recomputed for each context in which they are used. Moreover, it is not possible to use folds to transform a graph without losing sharing.

This paper presents a method for running tree traversals on directed acyclic graphs (DAGs), taking full account of the sharing structure. The traversals are expressed as attribute grammars (AGs) using Bahr's representation of tree automata in Haskell [5]. The underlying DAG structure is completely transparent to the AGs, which means that the same AG can be run on both trees and DAGs. The main complication arises for algorithms that pass an accumulating parameter down the tree. In a DAG this may lead to a shared node receiving conflicting values for the accumulating parameter. Our approach is to resolve such conflicts using a separate user-provided function. For example, in *leavesBelow*, the resolution function for the depth parameter would be *min*, since we only need to consider the deepest occurrence of each shared subtree. As we will show, this simple insight extends to many tree traversals of practical relevance.

The paper makes the following contributions:

- We present an implementation of AGs in Haskell that allows us to write tree traversals such that they can be applied to compact DAG representations of trees as well.
- We extend AGs with rewrite functions to implement tree transformations that preserve sharing if applied to DAGs.

- We prove a number of general correspondence theorems that relate the semantics of AGs on trees to their semantics on corresponding DAG representations. These correspondence results allow us to prove the soundness of our approach for various classes of traversals.
- Our implementation and the accompanying theory covers an important class of algorithms, where an inherited attribute maintains a variable environment. This makes our method suitable for certain syntactic analyses, for instance in a compiler. We demonstrate this fact on a type inference implementation.

The rest of the paper is organised as follows: Section 2 presents embedded domain-specific languages, which are an important motivation for this work. Section 3 introduces recursion schemes based on AGs, and section 4 shows how to run AGs on DAGs. Section 5 gives the semantics and theoretical results for reasoning about AGs on trees and DAGs. Some proofs were elided or abridged to save space. The full proofs are presented in the accompanying technical report [6]. Likewise, the exact implementation of the recursion schemes is omitted. It is instead available in an accompanying repository: `https://github.com/emilaxelsson/ag-graph`.

2. Running Example

To illustrate the ideas in this paper, we will use the following simple expression language:

```
data Exp = LitB Bool                -- Boolean literal
         | LitI Int                 -- Integer literal
         | Eq Exp Exp               -- Equality
         | Add Exp Exp              -- Addition
         | If Exp Exp Exp           -- Condition
         | Var Name                 -- Variable
         | Iter Name Exp Exp Exp    -- Iteration

type Name = String
```

Most constructs in *Exp* have a straightforward meaning. For example, the following is a conditional expression that corresponds to the Haskell expression **if** $x \equiv 0$ **then** 1 **else** 2:

```
If (Eq (Var "x") (LitI 0)) (LitI 1) (LitI 2)
```

However, *Iter* requires some explanation. This is a looping construct that corresponds to the following Haskell function:

```
iter :: Int → s → (s → s) → s
iter 0 s b = s
iter n s b = iter (n − 1) (b s) b
```

The expression *iter n s b* applies the *b* function *n* times starting in state *s*. The corresponding expression *Iter* "x" *n s b* (where n, s, b :: *Exp*) works in the same way. However, since we do not have functions in the *Exp* language, the first argument of *Iter* is a variable name, and this name is bound in the the body *b*. For example, the Haskell expression *iter* 5 1 ($\lambda s \rightarrow s + 2$) is represented as

```
Iter "s" (LitI 5) (LitI 1) (Add (Var "s") (LitI 2))
```

2.1 Type Inference

A typical example of a function over expressions that has an interesting flow of information is simple type inference, defined in Figure 1. The first argument is the environment – a mapping from bound variables to their types. Most of the cases just check the types of the children and return the appropriate type. The environment is passed unchanged to the recursive calls, except in the *Iter* case, where the bound variable is added to the environment. The only case where the environment is used is in the *Var* case, where the type of the variable is obtained by looking it up in the environment.

```
data Type = BoolType | IntType deriving (Eq)
type Env  = Map Name Type

typeInf :: Env → Exp → Maybe Type
typeInf env (LitB _)                      = Just BoolType
typeInf env (LitI _)                      = Just IntType
typeInf env (Eq a b)
  | Just ta         ← typeInf env a
  , Just tb         ← typeInf env b
  , ta ≡ tb                               = Just BoolType
typeInf env (Add a b)
  | Just IntType    ← typeInf env a
  , Just IntType    ← typeInf env b       = Just IntType
typeInf env (If c t f)
  | Just BoolType   ← typeInf env c
  , Just tt         ← typeInf env t
  , Just tf         ← typeInf env f
  , tt ≡ tf                               = Just tt
typeInf env (Var v)                       = lookEnv v env
typeInf env (Iter v n i b)
  | Just IntType    ← typeInf env n
  , ti'@(Just ti)   ← typeInf env i
  , Just tb         ← typeInf (insertEnv v ti' env) b
  , ti ≡ tb                               = Just tb
typeInf _ _                               = Nothing

insertEnv :: Name → Maybe Type → Env → Env
insertEnv v Nothing env = env
insertEnv v (Just t) env = Map.insert v t env

lookEnv :: Name → Env → Maybe Type
lookEnv = Map.lookup
```

Figure 1: Type inference for example EDSL.

Note that *typeInf* has many similarities with *leavesBelow* from the introduction: It is defined using recursion over the tree constructors; it passes an accumulating parameter down the recursive calls; it synthesises a result from the results of the recursive calls. Naturally, it also has the same problems as *leavesBelow* when applied to an expression with shared sub-expressions: It will repeatedly infer types for shared sub-expressions each time they occur.

This issue can be resolved by adding a *let binding* construct to *Exp* in order to explicitly represent shared sub-expressions. The type inference algorithm can then be extended to make use of this sharing information. However, let bindings tend to get in the way of syntactic simplifications, which is why optimising compilers often try to inline let bindings in order to increase the opportunities for simplification. In general, it is not possible to inline all let bindings, as this can lead to unmanageably large ASTs. This leaves the compiler with the tricky problem of inlining enough to trigger the right simplifications, but not more than necessary so that the AST does not explode.

Ideally, one would like to program syntactic analyses and transformations without having to worry about sharing, especially if the sharing is only used to manage the size of the AST. The method proposed in this paper makes it possible to traverse expressions *as if all sharing was inlined*, yet one does not have to pay the price

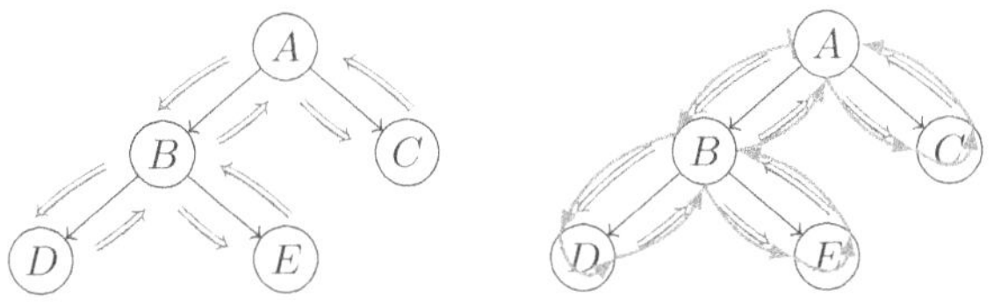

(a) Attribute propagation. (b) Tree traversal.

Figure 2: Propagation of attribute values by an attribute grammar.

of duplicated sub-expressions, since the internal representation of expressions is an acyclic graph.

3. Attribute Grammars

In this section we describe the representation and implementation of attribute grammars in Haskell. The focus of our approach is put on a simple representation of this recursion scheme that at the same time allows us to easily move from tree-structured data to graph-structured data. To this end, we represent tree-structured data as fixed points of functors:

```
data Tree f = In (f (Tree f))
```

For instance, to represent the type *Exp*, we define a corresponding functor *ExpF* below, which gives us the type *Tree ExpF* isomorphic to *Exp* (modulo non-strictness):

```
data ExpF a = LitB Bool | LitI Int   | Var Name
            | Eq a a    | Add a a    | If a a a
            | Iter Name a a a
```

Apart from requiring functors such as *ExpF* to be instances of *Functor*, we also require them to be instances of the *Traversable* type class. This will keep the representation of our recursion scheme on trees simple and is indeed necessary in order to implement it on DAGs. Haskell is able to provide such instances automatically via its **deriving** clause.

An attribute grammar (AG) consists of a number of *attributes* and a collection of *semantic functions* that compute these attributes for each node of the tree. One typically distinguishes between *inherited attributes*, which are computed top-down, and *synthesised attributes*, which are computed bottom-up. For instance, if we were to express the type inference algorithm *typeInf* as an AG, it would consist of an inherited attribute that is the environment and a synthesised attribute that is the inferred type.

Figure 2a illustrates the propagation of attribute values of an AG in a tree. The arrows facing upwards and downwards represent the propagation of synthesised and inherited attributes, respectively. Due to this propagation, the semantic functions that compute the attribute values for each node n have access to the attribute values in the corresponding neighbourhood of n. For example, to compute the inherited attribute value that is passed down from B to D, the semantic function may use the inherited attributes from A and the synthesised attributes from D and E. This scheme allows for complex interdependencies between attributes. Provided that there are no cyclic dependencies, a traversal through the tree that computes all attribute values of each node can be executed as illustrated in Figure 2b.

3.1 Synthesised Attributes

We defer the formal treatment of AGs until section 5 and focus on the implementation in Haskell for now. We start with the simpler case, namely synthesised attributes. The computation of synthesised attributes follows essentially the same structure as a fold, i.e. the following recursion scheme:

```
type Algebra f c = f c → c

fold :: Functor f ⇒ Algebra f c → Tree f → c
fold alg (In t) = alg (fmap (fold alg) t)
```

The algebra of a fold describes how the value of type c for a node in the tree is computed given that it has already been computed for its children.

AGs go beyond this recursion scheme: they allow us to use not only values of the attribute of type c being defined but also other attributes, which are computed by other semantic functions. To express that an attribute of type c is part of a larger collection of attributes, we use the following type class

```
class c ∈ as where
  pr :: as → c
```

Intuitively, $c \in as$ means that c is a component of as, and gives the corresponding projection function. We can give instance declarations accordingly, which gives us for example that $a \in (a, b)$ with the projection function $pr = fst$. Using closed type families [13], the type class $\in$ can be defined such that it works on arbitrarily nested product types, but disallows ambiguous instances such as $Int \in (Int, (Bool, Int))$ for which multiple projections exist. But there are also simpler implementations of $\in$ that only use type classes [5].

We can thus represent the semantic function for a synthesised attribute of type s as follows:

```
type Syn f as s = (s ∈ as) ⇒ as → f as → s
```

To compute the attribute of type s we can draw from the complete set of attributes of type as at the current node as well as its children.

For example, the following excerpt gives one case for the synthesised type attribute of type inference (cf. the reference implementation in Figure 1):

```
typeInf_S :: Syn ExpF as (Maybe Type)
typeInf_S _ (Add a b)
  | Just IntType ← pr a
  , Just IntType ← pr b = Just IntType
  ...
```

However, instead of the above *Syn* type, we shall use a more indirect representation, which will turn out to be beneficial for the representation of inherited attributes, and later for rewrite functions. It is based on the isomorphism below, which follows from the Yoneda Lemma for all functors f and types as, s:

$$(\forall a.(a \to as) \to (f\ a \to s)) \cong f\ as \to s$$

It allows us to define the type $Syn\ f\ as\ s$ alternatively as follows:

$$\forall\, a.(s \in as) \Rightarrow as \to (a \to as) \to f\ a \to s$$

We further transform this type by turning the first two arguments of type as and $a \to as$ into implicit parameters [29], which provides an interface closer to that of AG systems:

```
type Syn f as s = ∀ a.(?below :: a → as, ?above :: as,
                       s ∈ as) ⇒ f a → s
```

Combining the implicit parameters with projection gives us two convenient helper functions for writing semantic functions:

```
above :: (?above :: as, i ∈ as) ⇒ i
above = pr (?above)

below :: (?below :: a → as, s ∈ as) ⇒ a → s
below a = pr (?below a)
```

The complete definition of the synthesised type attribute for type inference is given in Figure 3. The function $typeInf_I$ is the semantic function for the inherited environment attribute. It will

```
typeInf_S :: (Env ∈ as) ⇒ Syn ExpF as (Maybe Type)
typeInf_S (LitB _)                    = Just BoolType
typeInf_S (LitI _)                    = Just IntType
typeInf_S (Eq a b)
  | Just ta        ← typeOf a
  , Just tb        ← typeOf b
  , ta ≡ tb                           = Just BoolType
typeInf_S (Add a b)
  | Just IntType   ← typeOf a
  , Just IntType   ← typeOf b         = Just IntType
typeInf_S (If c t f)
  | Just BoolType  ← typeOf c
  , Just tt        ← typeOf t
  , Just tf        ← typeOf f
  , tt ≡ tf                           = Just tt
typeInf_S (Var v)                     = lookEnv v above
typeInf_S (Iter v n i b)
  | Just IntType   ← typeOf n
  , Just ti        ← typeOf i
  , Just tb        ← typeOf b
  , ti ≡ tb                           = Just tb
typeInf_S _                           = Nothing

typeInf_I :: (Maybe Type ∈ as) ⇒ Inh ExpF as Env
typeInf_I (Iter v n i b) = b ↦ insertEnv v ti above
                           where ti = typeOf i
typeInf_I _              = ∅
```

Figure 3: Semantic functions for synthesised and inherited attributes of type inference.

be explained in the following subsection. The code uses a convenient helper function for querying the synthesised type of a sub-expression:

```
typeOf :: (?below :: a → as, Maybe Type ∈ as) ⇒
    a → Maybe Type
typeOf = below
```

3.2 Inherited Attributes

The representation of semantic functions defining inherited attributes is slightly more complicated, which is to say that there is no representation that is both elegant and convenient to use. We need to represent a mapping that assigns attribute values to the children of a node. The most convenient way to represent such mappings in Haskell is in the form of a finite mapping provided by the type constructor *Map*.

Thus, given a node of type $f\ a$, where type a represents child positions of the node, we assign inherited attribute values of type i to each child node by providing a mapping of type $Map\ a\ i$. This gives us the following representation of semantic functions for inherited attributes:

```
type Inh f as i = ∀ a.(?below :: a → as, ?above :: as,
                       i ∈ as, Ord a) ⇒ f a → Map a i
```

Note that we have to add the constraint $Ord\ a$, since the operations to construct finite mappings require this.

The above type does not ensure that the returned mapping is complete, i.e. that each child is assigned a value. However, this situation provides the opportunity to allow so-called *copy rules*. Such copy rules are a common convenience feature in AG systems and state when inherited attributes are simply propagated to a child. In our case, we copy an inherited attribute value to a child if no assignment is made in the mapping of the semantic function.

To make it convenient to construct mappings as the result of semantic functions for inherited attributes, we define infix operators $\mapsto$ and $\&$, which allow us to construct singleton mappings $x \mapsto y$ and take the union $m \ \&\ n$ of two mappings. Moreover, we use $\emptyset$ to denote the empty mapping.

The semantic function for the inherited environment attribute of type inference is given by $typeInf_I$ in Figure 3. The only interesting case is *Iter*, in which the local variable is inserted into the environment. The environment is only updated for the sub-expression b (because it only scopes over the body of the loop). Hence, the other sub-expressions (n and i) will get an unchanged environment by the abovementioned copy rule. Similarly, for all other constructs in the EDSL, the environment is copied unchanged.

3.3 Combining Semantic Functions to Attribute Grammars

Now that we have Haskell representations for semantic functions, we need combinators that allow us to combine them to form complete AGs.

At first, we define combinators that combine two semantic functions to obtain a semantic function that computes the attributes of both of them. For synthesised attributes, this construction is simple:

```
(⊗) :: Syn f as s1 → Syn f as s2 → Syn f as (s1, s2)
(sp ⊗ sq) t = (sp t, sq t)
```

The implementation for inherited attributes is more difficult as we have to honour the copy rule. That is, given two semantic functions i and j, where i assigns an attribute value for a given child node but j does not, the product of i and j must assign an attribute value consisting of the value given by i and a copy for the second attribute. We elide the details of the implementation and instead give only the type of the corresponding combinator:

```
(⊛) :: Functor f ⇒
    Inh f as i1 → Inh f as i2 → Inh f as (i1, i2)
```

Finally, a complete AG is given by a semantic function of type $Syn\ f\ (s,i)\ s$ and another one of type $Inh\ f\ (s,i)\ i$. That is, taken together the two semantic functions define the full attribute space (s,i). Moreover, we have to provide an initial value of the inherited attribute of type i in order to run the AG on an input tree of type $Tree\ f$. In general, the initial value of the inherited attributes does not have to be fixed but may depend on (some of) the synthesised attributes. These constraints are summarised in the type of the function that implements the run of an AG:

```
runAG :: Traversable f ⇒ Syn f (s, i) s →
            Inh f (s, i) i → (s → i) → Tree f → s
```

We are now able to define type inference as a run of the AG defined in Figure 3:

```
typeInf :: Env → Tree ExpF → Maybe Type
typeInf env = runAG typeInf_S typeInf_I (λ_ → env)
```

In this example, the initialisation function for the inherited attribute is simply a constant function that returns the environment. In the next section, we shall see an example that uses the full power of the initialisation function.

3.4 Example: Richard Bird's *repmin*

A classic example of a tree traversal with interesting information flow is Bird's *repmin* problem [8]. The problem is as follows: given a tree with integer leaves, compute a new tree of the same shape but where all leaves have been replaced by the minimal leaf in the original tree. Bird shows how this can be achieved by a single traversal in a lazy functional language.

To code *repmin* as an AG, we first define a functor corresponding to the tree type from section 1:

$$\textbf{data}\ \mathit{IntTreeF}\ a = \mathit{Leaf}\ \mathit{Int} \mid \mathit{Node}\ a\ a$$

Next, we introduce two attributes:

$$\textbf{newtype}\ \mathit{Min}_S = \mathit{Min}_S\ \mathit{Int}\ \textbf{deriving}\ (\mathit{Eq}, \mathit{Ord})$$
$$\textbf{newtype}\ \mathit{Min}_I = \mathit{Min}_I\ \mathit{Int}$$

Min_S is the synthesised attribute representing the smallest integer in a subtree, and Min_I is the inherited attribute which is going to be the smallest integer in the whole tree. We also define a convenience function for accessing the Min_I attribute:

$$\mathit{globMin} :: (?\mathit{above} :: as, \mathit{Min}_I \in as) \Rightarrow \mathit{Int}$$
$$\mathit{globMin} = \textbf{let}\ \mathit{Min}_I\ i = \mathit{above}\ \textbf{in}\ i$$

The semantic function for the Min_S attribute is as follows:

$$\mathit{min}_S :: \mathit{Syn}\ \mathit{IntTreeF}\ as\ \mathit{Min}_S$$
$$\mathit{min}_S\ (\mathit{Leaf}\ i) \quad = \mathit{Min}_S\ i$$
$$\mathit{min}_S\ (\mathit{Node}\ a\ b) = \mathit{min}\ (\mathit{below}\ a)\ (\mathit{below}\ b)$$

The Min_I attribute should be the same throughout the whole tree, so we define a function that just copies the inherited attribute:

$$\mathit{min}_I :: \mathit{Inh}\ \mathit{IntTreeF}\ as\ \mathit{Min}_I$$
$$\mathit{min}_I\ \_ = \emptyset$$

Finally, we need to be able to synthesise a new tree that depends on the globally smallest integer available from the Min_I attribute:

$$\mathit{rep} :: (\mathit{Min}_I \in as) \Rightarrow \mathit{Syn}\ \mathit{IntTreeF}\ as\ (\mathit{Tree}\ \mathit{IntTreeF})$$
$$\mathit{rep}\ (\mathit{Leaf}\ i) \quad = \mathit{In}\ (\mathit{Leaf}\ \mathit{globMin})$$
$$\mathit{rep}\ (\mathit{Node}\ a\ b) = \mathit{In}\ (\mathit{Node}\ (\mathit{below}\ a)\ (\mathit{below}\ b))$$

Now we have all the parts needed to define *repmin*:

$$\mathit{repmin} :: \mathit{Tree}\ \mathit{IntTreeF} \to \mathit{Tree}\ \mathit{IntTreeF}$$
$$\mathit{repmin} = \mathit{snd} \circ \mathit{runAG}\ (\mathit{min}_S \otimes \mathit{rep})\ \mathit{min}_I\ \mathit{init}$$
$$\quad \textbf{where}\ \mathit{init}\ (\mathit{Min}_S\ i, \_) = \mathit{Min}_I\ i$$

The *init* function uses the synthesised smallest integer as the initial inherited attribute value.

3.5 Informal Semantics

Instead of reproducing the implementation of runAG here, we shall informally describe the semantics of an AG and describe in which way runAG implements this semantics. The formal semantics is given in section 5.

The semantic functions of an AG describe how to compute the value of an attribute at a node n using the attributes in the "neighbourhood" of n. For synthesised attributes, this neighbourhood consists of n itself and its children, whereas for inherited attributes, it consists of n, its siblings, and its parent. Running the AG on a tree t amounts to computing, for each attribute a, the mapping $\rho_a : N \to D_a$ from the set of nodes of t to the set of values of a. In other words, the tree is decorated with the computed attribute values. We call the collection of all these mappings ρ_a a *run* of the AG on t. In general, there may not be a unique run (including no run at all), since there can be a cyclic dependency between the attributes. However, if there is no such cyclic dependency, runAG will effectively construct the unique run of the AG on the input tree, and return the product of all synthesised attribute values at the root of the tree.

Figure 2b illustrates how runAG may compute the run of a given AG by a traversal through the tree. Such a traversal is, however, not statically scheduled in advance but rather dynamically exploiting Haskell's lazy semantics.

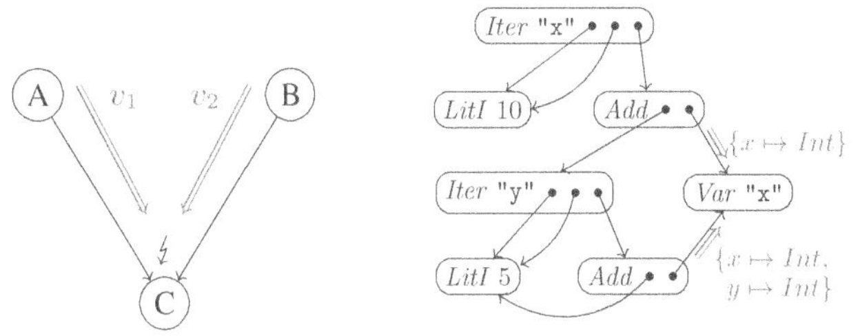

(a) Abstract problem. (b) Example: type inference.

Figure 4: Confluence of inherited attributes.

4. Attribute Grammars on DAGs

Our goal is to apply algorithms intended to work on trees without or with only little change to DAGs such that we can exploit the sharing for performance gains. The key observation that allows us to do this is the fact that AGs are unaware of the underlying representation they are working on. Semantic functions simply compute attributes of a node using attribute values in the neighbourhood of the node. The informal semantics of AGs on trees given in section 3.5 is equally applicable to DAGs.

This straightforward translation of the semantics to DAGs, however, will rarely yield a well-defined run. The problem is that in the presence of sharing – i.e. there is a node with more than one incoming edge – the semantic function for an inherited attribute may overlap: it assigns potentially different values to the same attribute at the same node. Figure 4a illustrates the problem: the semantic function for the inherited attribute computes for each of the two nodes A and B the value v_1 resp. v_2 of the inherited attribute that should be passed down to the child node of A resp. B. However, A and B share the same child, C, which therefore receives both values for the inherited attribute.

The easiest way to deal with this situation is to traverse the sub-DAG reachable from C multiple times – once for each of the conflicting attribute values v_1 and v_2. This is what happens if we would implement traversals as folds in the style of Oliveira and Cook [32]. But our goal is to avoid such recomputation.

A simple special case is if we know that v_1 and v_2 are always the same. That happens, for example, if inherited attributes are only copied downwards as in the repmin example from section 3.4. However, for the type inference AG, this is clearly not the case. One example that shows the problem is the DAG in Figure 4b, where the shared variable `"x"` is used in two different environments.

Nonetheless, for type inference, as for many other AGs of interest, we can still extend the semantics to DAGs in a meaningful way by providing a commutative, associative operator $\oplus$ on inherited attributes that combines confluent attribute values. In the illustration in Figure 4a, the inherited attribute at C is then assigned the value $v_1 \oplus v_2$. For the type inference AG, a (provably) sensible choice for $\oplus$ is the intersection of environments (cf. section 4.3). In Figure 4b, intersecting the environments of the node Var `"x"` yields the environment $\{x \mapsto \mathit{Int}\}$.

This observation allows us to efficiently run AGs on DAGs. Our implementation provides a corresponding variant of runAG:

$$\mathit{runAGDag} :: \mathit{Traversable}\ f \Rightarrow (i \to i \to i) \to$$
$$\quad \mathit{Syn}\ f\ (s,i)\ s \to \mathit{Inh}\ f\ (s,i)\ i \to (s \to i) \to \mathit{Dag}\ f \to s$$

The interface differs in two points from runAG: (1) it takes DAGs as input and (2) it takes a binary operator of type $i \to i \to i$, which is to be used to combine confluent attributes as described above.

For instance, we may use the type inference AG to implement type inference on DAGs as follows:

$typeInf_G :: Env \to Dag\ ExpF \to Maybe\ Type$
$typeInf_G\ env = runAGDag\ intersection$
$\quad typeInf_S\ typeInf_I\ (\lambda\_ \to env)$

We will not go into the details of the implementation of $runAGDag$. Instead we refer to the informal semantics that we have given above as well as the formal semantics given in section 5

But we shall briefly explain how DAGs of type $Dag\ f$ are represented. We represent DAGs with explicit nodes and edges, with nodes represented by integers:

type $Node = Int$

Edges are represented as finite mappings from $Node$ into $f\ Node$. In this way, each node is mapped to all its children, but also its labelling. In addition, each node has a designated root node. This gives the following definition of Dag as a record type:

data $Dag\ f = Dag\ \{root :: Node,$
$\quad edges :: IntMap\ (f\ Node)\}$

Note that acyclicity is not explicitly encoded in this definition of DAGs. Instead, we rely on the combinators to construct such DAGs to ensure or check for acyclicity.

Following Gill [20], we provide a function that observes the implicit sharing of a tree of type $Tree\ f$ and turns it into a DAG of type $Dag\ f$:

$reifyDag :: Traversable\ f \Rightarrow Tree\ f \to IO\ (Dag\ f)$

As a final example, we turn the $repmin$ function from section 3.4 into a function $repmin_G$ that works on DAGs.

$repmin_G :: Dag\ IntTreeF \to Tree\ IntTreeF$
$repmin_G = snd \circ runAGDag\ const\ (mins_S \otimes rep)\ min_I\ init$
$\quad$ **where** $init\ (Min_S\ i, \_) = Min_I\ i$

The only additional definition we have to provide is the function to combine inherited attribute values, for which we choose $const$, i.e. we arbitrarily pick one of the values. The rationale behind this choice is that the value of inherited attribute – computed by min_I – is globally the same since it is copied. The formal justification for this choice is given in section 4.1 below.

The type of $repmin_G$ indicates that it is not quite the function we had hoped for: it returns a tree rather than a DAG. We defer addressing this issue until section 4.5.

4.1 Trees vs. DAGs

The most important feature of our approach is that we can express the semantics of an AG on DAGs in terms of the semantics on trees. This is achieved by two correspondence theorems that relate the semantics of AGs on DAGs to the semantics on trees. The theorems are discussed and proved in section 5. But we present them here informally and illustrate their applicability to the examples that we have seen so far.

To bridge the gap between the tree and the DAG semantics of AGs, we use the notion of *unravelling* (or *unsharing*) of a DAG g to a tree $\mathcal{U}(g)$, which is the uniquely determined tree $\mathcal{U}(g)$ that is bisimilar to g. Since we only consider finite acyclic graphs g, the unravelling $\mathcal{U}(g)$ is always a finite tree. The correspondence theorems relate the result of running an AG on a DAG g to the result of running it on the unravelling of g. The practical relevance of these theorems stems from the fact that $reifyDag$ turns a tree t into a DAG g that unravels to t.

The first and simplest correspondence result is applicable to all so-called *copying* AGs, which are AGs that copy all their inherited attributes. That is, in concrete terms, the semantic function of each inherited attribute returns the empty mapping $\emptyset$. Such AGs are by no means trivial, since inherited attributes may still be initialised as a function on the synthesised attributes. The repmin AG is, for

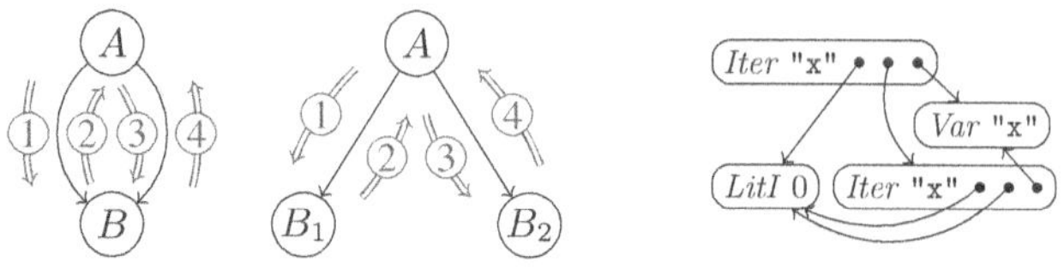

(a) A DAG g. (b) Unravelling of g. (c) Example DAG.

Figure 5: Cyclic dependency in non-circular AG on DAGs.

example, copying. The following correspondence theorem is thus applicable to repmin:

Theorem 1 (sketch). *Given a copying AG G, a binary operator $\oplus$ on inherited attributes with $x \oplus y \in \{x, y\}$ for all x, y, and a DAG g, we have that G terminates on $\mathcal{U}(g)$ with result r iff $(G, \oplus)$ terminates on g with result r.*

The above theorem is immediately applicable to the repmin AG. We obtain that $repmin_G$ applied to a DAG g yields the same result as $repmin$ applied to $\mathcal{U}(g)$. That is, we get the same result for $repmin\ t$ and $fmap\ repmin_G\ (reifyDag\ t)$.

Before we discuss the second correspondence theorem we have to consider the termination behaviour of AGs on trees vs. DAGs.

4.2 Termination of Attribute Grammars

While AGs are quite flexible in the interdependency between attributes they permit – which in general may lead to cyclic dependencies and thus non-termination – they come with a tool set to check for circular dependencies. Already when Knuth [25, 26] introduced AGs, he gave an algorithm to check for circular dependencies and proved that absent such circularity AGs terminate.

This result also applies to our AGs. And the example AGs we have considered this far are indeed non-circular – $runAG$ will terminate for them (given any finite tree as input). Somewhat surprisingly this property does not carry over to acyclic graphs.

The essence of the phenomenon that causes this problem is illustrated in Figure 5. Figure 5a shows a simple DAG consisting of two nodes, and Figure 5b its unravelling to a tree. The double arrows illustrate the flow of information from a run of an AG. The numbers indicate the order in which the information flows: we first pass information from A to B_1 (via the inherited attribute) then from B_1 back to A (via the synthesised attribute) and then similarly to and from B_2. This is a common situation, which one e.g. finds in type inference. The underlying AG is non-circular, and the numbering indicates the order in which attributes are computed and then propagated.

However, in a DAG the two children of A may very well be shared, i.e. represented by a single node B. This causes a cyclic dependency, which can be observed in Figure 5a: information flow (2) can only occur after (1) and (3), as only then all the information coming to B has been collected. But (3) itself depends on (2).

Cyclic dependencies can easily occur with the type inference AG. In the DAG in Figure 5c the lower *Iter* loop computes the initial state of the upper *Iter* loop, and both loops use the variable `"x"` for the state. The variable node inherits two environments – one from each of the *Iter* nodes – which are resolved by intersection. Thus, the type of the variable depends on the environment from the upper loop, which depends on the type of the lower loop, which in turn depends on the type of the variable.

Semantically, the non-termination manifests itself in the lack of a unique run. While the type inference AG has a unique run on the unravelling of this DAG, there are exactly two distinct runs on the DAG itself: one in which the *Var* `"x"` node is given the synthesised attribute value *Nothing* and another one in which it is given the

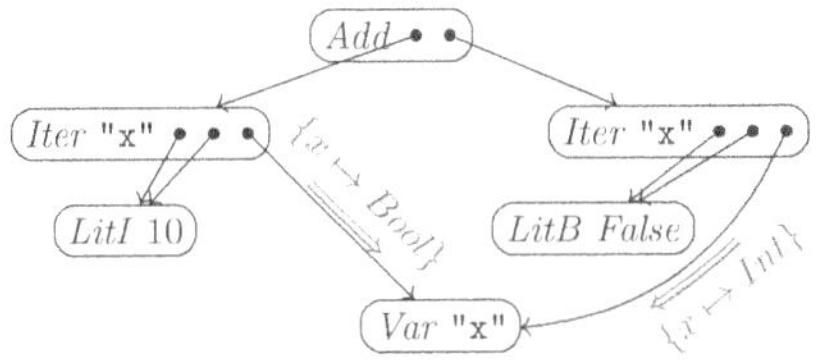

Figure 6: DAG that is not well-scoped.

value *Just IntType*. We discuss how to resolve this issue in the next section.

Note that this issue cannot occur for the repmin example. The repmin AG is non-circular and thus terminates on trees. By virtue of Theorem 1, it thus terminates on DAGs as well.

4.3 Correspondence by Monotonicity

Relating the semantics of the type inference AG on trees to its semantics on DAGs is much more difficult – even if the issue of termination is sorted out. In general, for these kinds of AGs, we do not have a simple equality relation as we have for copying AGs. In fact, it should be expected that type inference on a DAG is more restrictive than on its unravelling: a node that is shared in a DAG can only be assigned a single type, whereas its corresponding copies in the unravelling may have different types.

However, we can prove the following property: if the type inference AG infers a type t for a DAG g, then it infers the same type t for $\mathcal{U}(g)$. This soundness property follows immediately from a more general *monotonicity* correspondence theorem.

In order to apply this theorem, we have to find, for each attribute a, a quasi-order $\lesssim$ on the values of attribute a, such that each semantic function f is monotone w.r.t. these quasi-orders. That is, given two sets of inputs A and B, with B bigger than A, also the result of f applied to B is bigger than f applied to A. We say that an AG is monotone w.r.t. $\lesssim$, if each semantic function is. Moreover, we require the binary operator $\oplus$ on inherited attributes be *decreasing* w.r.t. the order $\lesssim$, i.e. $x \oplus y \lesssim x, y$.

Theorem 2 (sketch). *Let G be a non-circular AG, $\oplus$ an associative, commutative operator on inherited attributes, and $\lesssim$ such that G is monotone and $\oplus$ is decreasing w.r.t. $\lesssim$. If $(G, \oplus)$ terminates on a DAG g with result r, then G terminates on $\mathcal{U}(g)$ with result r' such that $r \lesssim r'$.*

Note that due to the symmetry of Theorem 2, we also know that if $\oplus$ is increasing, i.e. $x, y \lesssim x \oplus y$, then we have that $r' \lesssim r$. We obtain this corollary by simply considering the inverse of $\lesssim$.

Let's see how the above theorem applies to the type inference AG. The order $\lesssim$ on Env is the usual order on partial mappings (i.e. the subset order on the DAG of partial mappings); $\lesssim$ on *Maybe Type* is the least quasi-order with $Nothing \lesssim t$ for all t :: *Maybe Type*; and $\lesssim$ on *Set Name* is the subset order. With these orders all semantic functions are monotone, and the operator $\oplus = intersection$ is decreasing. We thus get the soundness property by applying Theorem 2: if type inference on a DAG g returns r then it returns r' on $\mathcal{U}(g)$ with $r \lesssim r'$. In particular, if $r = Just\ t$ then also $r' = Just\ t$.

The DAG in Figure 6 is an example where $r = Nothing$ and $r' = Just\ t$. The problem is that the variable "x" is shared between two contexts in which it has different types. That is, intersecting the environments yields the empty environment. However, the above phenomenon as well as non-termination can only occur if the DAG is not *well-scoped* in the following sense: a DAG is well-scoped if no variable node is shared among different binders, or shared between a bound and free occurrence. This restriction rules out the DAG in Figure 6 as well as the one in Figure 5c.

Given this well-scopedness property, we can show that type inference on a well-scoped DAG g produces the same result as on its unravelling $\mathcal{U}(g)$ – provided it terminates. It only remains to be shown that whenever the result r on g is $Nothing$, then also the result r' on $\mathcal{U}(g)$ is $Nothing$. The full version of Theorem 2, as we will see in section 5.4, is much stronger than stated above: we have the relation $\lesssim$ between a run on a DAG and a run on its unravelling not only for the final results r and r' but for each node and each attribute. That means if we get a type t for a sub-DAG of g, then we also get the type t for the corresponding subtree of $\mathcal{U}(g)$. Consequently, if we got a type for $\mathcal{U}(g)$ but not for g itself, then the reason could not be a type mismatch. It can only be because a variable was not found in the environment. That, however, can never happen because of well-scopedness. Hence, also $r' = Nothing$.

We still have to deal with the issue of termination, though. Semantically, non-termination means that there may be either no run or multiple different runs on DAGs. While monotonicity does not prove termination in general, it can help us to at least establish the existence of runs:

Proposition 1 (sketch). *Given G, $\oplus$, and $\lesssim$ as in Theorem 2 such that $\lesssim$ is well-founded on inherited attributes, then $(G, \oplus)$ has a run on any DAG.*

Proposition 1 immediately applies to the type inference AG. Thus it remains to be shown that runs are unique. As we have seen in Figure 5c, this is not true in general. However, restricted to well-scoped DAGs it is: if there were two distinct runs on a DAG g, then the runs can only differ on shared nodes, since runs on $\mathcal{U}(g)$ are unique. Moreover, the type attribute depends only on type attributes of child nodes, except in the case of variables. Hence, there must be a variable node to which the two runs assign different types. However, well-scopedness makes this impossible.

Thus, we can conclude that $typeInf_G$ on a well-scoped DAG g behaves as $typeInf$ on its unravelling $\mathcal{U}(g)$.

It is always possible to make a DAG well-scoped by means of alpha-renaming. However, note that renaming on a DAG may lead to duplication. For example, renaming one of the loops in Figure 6 would require introducing a new variable node. As a safe approximation, in particular when using *reifyDag*, making sure that all binders introduce distinct variable names guarantees that the DAG is well-scoped.[1]

Finally, it is important to note that monotonicity is not an intrinsic property of AGs, but depends on the choice of $\lesssim$.[2] In particular, we may choose one order $\lesssim$ for using Theorem 2 and another one for proving termination using Proposition 1.

4.4 Observing the Sharing

In this paper, we have only looked at AGs for which we want to get the same result when running on a DAG and running on its unravelling. That is, we have only cared about DAGs as a compact representation of trees, and we want to get the same result regardless of how the tree is represented.

However, there are cases where we actually want to give meaning to the sharing in the DAG. One such case is when estimating signal delays in digital circuits. The time it takes for an output of a logic gate to switch depends on how many other gates are connected to it – i.e. its *load*. A higher load leads to slower switching.

As a simple example, let us for a while assume that the *IntTreeF* functor defined in section 3.4 represents digital circuits. *Leaf* can represent inputs and *Node* can be a NAND gate (any n-ary Boolean function can be computed by a network of NAND gates).

[1] See `Rename.hs` in the accompanying repository.

[2] For example, any AG is monotone w.r.t the full relation.

$$\textbf{type } \mathit{Circuit} = \mathit{Dag}\ \mathit{IntTreeF}$$

To implement delay analysis as an AG, we start by defining attributes for delay and load:

$$\textbf{newtype } \mathit{Delay} = \mathit{Delay}\ \mathit{Int}\ \textbf{deriving}\ (\mathit{Eq}, \mathit{Ord}, \mathit{Num})$$
$$\textbf{newtype } \mathit{Load}\ = \mathit{Load}\ \ \mathit{Int}\ \textbf{deriving}\ (\mathit{Eq}, \mathit{Ord}, \mathit{Num})$$

The delay attribute can be computed by summing the maximum input delay, some intrinsic gate delay and a load-dependent term:

$$\begin{aligned}
&\mathit{gateDelay} :: (\mathit{Load} \in \mathit{as}) \Rightarrow \mathit{Syn}\ \mathit{IntTreeF}\ \mathit{as}\ \mathit{Delay} \\
&\mathit{gateDelay}\ (\mathit{Leaf}\ _) \quad = \mathit{Delay}\ 0 \\
&\mathit{gateDelay}\ (\mathit{Node}\ a\ b) = \mathit{max}\ (\mathit{below}\ a)\ (\mathit{below}\ b) \\
&\qquad\qquad\qquad\qquad + \mathit{Delay}\ 10 + \mathit{Delay}\ l \\
&\quad \textbf{where } \mathit{Load}\ l = \mathit{above}
\end{aligned}$$

In this simplified delay analysis, we interpret load as the number of connected gates, so the load attribute that is propagated down is 1 for both inputs:

$$\begin{aligned}
&\mathit{gateLoad} :: \mathit{Inh}\ \mathit{IntTreeF}\ \mathit{as}\ \mathit{Load} \\
&\mathit{gateLoad}\ (\mathit{Node}\ a\ b) = a \mapsto 1\ \&\ b \mapsto 1 \\
&\mathit{gateLoad}\ _ \qquad\quad\ \ = \emptyset
\end{aligned}$$

The delay analysis is completed by running the AG on a circuit DAG using $(+)$ as the resolution function:

$$\begin{aligned}
&\mathit{delay} :: \mathit{Load} \to \mathit{Circuit} \to \mathit{Delay} \\
&\mathit{delay}\ l = \mathit{runAGDag}\ (+)\ \mathit{gateDelay}\ \mathit{gateLoad}\ (\lambda_ \to l)
\end{aligned}$$

Note that the semantic function for the load attribute does not do any interesting computation. Instead, it is the resolution function that "counts" the number of connected gates for each node.

Since the above AG is monotone and $+$ is increasing w.r.t. the natural order on integers, Theorem 2 gives us the expected result that the delay of a circuit DAG is greater than or equal to the delay of its unravelling.

The circuit description system Wired [4] implements analyses on circuit DAGs using a generic traversal scheme and semantic functions similar to the ones above. It should be possible to give a more principled implementation of these analyses in terms of AGs using monotonicity as a proof principle.

4.5 Transforming and Constructing DAGs

The definition of repmin_G from the beginning of section 4 uses $\mathit{runAGDag}$ to run the repmin AG on DAGs. While repmin_G does take DAGs as input, it produces trees as output. The reason for this is that while the AG is oblivious to whether it runs on a DAG or a tree, it does explicitly construct a tree as its output.

However, there is no reason why it should do so. The only assumption that is made in constructing the synthesised tree attribute is that its values can be combined using the constructors of the underlying functor $\mathit{IntTreeF}$. However, this assumption is true for both the type $\mathit{Tree}\ \mathit{IntTreeF}$ and $\mathit{Dag}\ \mathit{IntTreeF}$. Indeed, by drawing ideas from macro tree transducers [7, 15] our AG recursion scheme can be generalised to preserve sharing in the result of an AG computation. That is, if applied to trees the AG constructs trees and if applied to a DAG the AG constructs DAGs in its attributes. An important property of this generalised recursion scheme, which we call *parametric AGs*, is that both Theorem 1 and Theorem 2 carry over to this generalisation.

For the sake of demonstration we shall only consider a simple instance of this generalised recursion scheme. For more details we refer the reader to the technical report [6]. The instance of parametric AGs that we consider consists of an ordinary AG together with a simple "rewrite" function, which is used to transform the input DAG. This intuition is encoded in the following type that can be seen as a specialisation of Syn:

$$\begin{aligned}
&\textbf{type } \mathit{Rewrite}\ f\ \mathit{as}\ g = \forall\ a.(?\mathit{below} :: a \to \mathit{as}, ?\mathit{above} :: \mathit{as}) \\
&\qquad\qquad\qquad\qquad\qquad \Rightarrow f\ a \to g\ a
\end{aligned}$$

The semantic function rep, which defines the repmin transformation, has to be modified only superficially to fit this type:

$$\begin{aligned}
&\mathit{rep}' :: (\mathit{Min}_I \in \mathit{as}) \Rightarrow \mathit{Rewrite}\ \mathit{IntTreeF}\ \mathit{as}\ \mathit{IntTreeF} \\
&\mathit{rep}'\ (\mathit{Leaf}\ i) \quad\ \ = \mathit{Leaf}\ \mathit{globMin} \\
&\mathit{rep}'\ (\mathit{Node}\ a\ b) = \mathit{Node}\ a\ b
\end{aligned}$$

Note that the parametric polymorphism of the type $\mathit{Rewrite}$ allows us to instantiate the construction performed by rep' to both trees and DAGs. Apart from this polymorphism, functions of this type are no different from semantic functions for synthesised attributes. Therefore, we can extend the function runAG such that it takes a rewrite function as an additional semantic function:

$$\begin{aligned}
&\mathit{runRewrite} :: (\mathit{Traversable}\ f, \mathit{Functor}\ g) \Rightarrow \\
&\quad \mathit{Syn}\ f\ (s,i)\ s \to \mathit{Inh}\ f\ (s,i)\ i \to \mathit{Rewrite}\ f\ (s,i)\ g \to \\
&\quad (s \to i) \to \mathit{Tree}\ f \to \mathit{Tree}\ g
\end{aligned}$$

The definition of repmin can thus be reformulated as follows:

$$\begin{aligned}
&\mathit{repmin} :: \mathit{Tree}\ \mathit{IntTreeF} \to \mathit{Tree}\ \mathit{IntTreeF} \\
&\mathit{repmin} = \mathit{runRewrite}\ \mathit{min}_S\ \mathit{min}_I\ \mathit{rep}'\ \mathit{init} \\
&\quad \textbf{where } \mathit{init}\ (\mathit{Min}_S\ i) = \mathit{Min}_I\ i
\end{aligned}$$

The corresponding variant for DAGs, not only takes DAGs as input but also returns DAGs:

$$\begin{aligned}
&\mathit{runRewriteDag} :: (\mathit{Traversable}\ f, \mathit{Functor}\ g) \Rightarrow \\
&\quad (i \to i \to i) \to \mathit{Syn}\ f\ (s,i)\ s \to \mathit{Inh}\ f\ (s,i)\ i \to \\
&\quad \mathit{Rewrite}\ f\ (s,i)\ g \to (s \to i) \to \mathit{Dag}\ f \to \mathit{Dag}\ g
\end{aligned}$$

The definition of repmin_G is adjusted accordingly:

$$\begin{aligned}
&\mathit{repmin}_G :: \mathit{Dag}\ \mathit{IntTreeF} \to \mathit{Dag}\ \mathit{IntTreeF} \\
&\mathit{repmin}_G = \mathit{runRewriteDag}\ \mathit{const}\ \mathit{min}_S\ \mathit{min}_I\ \mathit{rep}'\ \mathit{init} \\
&\quad \textbf{where } \mathit{init}\ (\mathit{Min}_S\ i) = \mathit{Min}_I\ i
\end{aligned}$$

Now repmin_G has the desired type – and the implementation of $\mathit{runRewriteDag}$ has the expected property that sharing of the input DAG is preserved. However, repmin_G does not produce the same result for a DAG g as repmin does for $\mathcal{U}\ (g)$. But it does produce a DAG that unravels to the result of repmin, i.e. both are equivalent modulo unravelling. This is an immediate consequence of the corresponding variant of Theorem 1 for AGs with rewrite functions [6]:

Theorem 3 (sketch). *Given a copying rewriting attribute grammar G, a binary operator $\oplus$ on inherited attributes with $x \oplus y \in \{x, y\}$ for all x, y, and a DAG g, we have that G terminates on $\mathcal{U}\ (g)$ with result t iff $(G, \oplus)$ terminates on g with result h such that $\mathcal{U}\ (h) = t$.*

The type of $\mathit{Rewrite}$ as given above is unnecessarily restrictive, since it requires that each constructor from the input functor f is replaced by a single constructor from the target functor g. In general, a rewrite function may produce arbitrary layers built from g. This generalisation can be expressed as follows, where $\mathit{Free}\ g$ is the free monad of g:

$$\begin{aligned}
&\textbf{type } \mathit{Rewrite}'\ f\ \mathit{as}\ g = \forall\ a.(?\mathit{below} :: a \to \mathit{as}, ?\mathit{above} :: \mathit{as}) \\
&\qquad\qquad\qquad\qquad\qquad \Rightarrow f\ a \to \mathit{Free}\ g\ a
\end{aligned}$$

5. Semantics

We present the semantics of AGs on trees and DAGs. To keep the presentation simple, we restrict ourselves to a set theoretic semantics. For a formal treatment of parametric AGs as discussed in section 4.5, we refer the reader to the technical report [6].

To give the semantics on DAGs, we have to restrict ourselves to functors that are representable by finitary containers [1]. In the

Haskell implementation, this assumption corresponds to the restriction to functors that are instances of the *Traversable* type class. Traversable functors (that satisfy the appropriate associated laws) are known to be exactly representable by finitary containers [9].

Definition 1. A *finitary container* F is a pair $(\mathsf{Sh}, \mathsf{ar})$ consisting of a set Sh of *shapes*, and an *arity* function $\mathsf{ar}\colon \mathsf{Sh} \to \mathbb{N}$. Each finitary container F gives rise to a functor $\mathsf{Ext}(F)\colon \mathsf{Set} \to \mathsf{Set}$, called the *extension* of F, that maps each set X to the set of (dependent) pairs $(s, \overline{x})$, where $s \in \mathsf{Sh}$ and $\overline{x} \in X^{\mathsf{ar}(s)}$. By abuse of notation we also write F for the functor $\mathsf{Ext}(F)$.

5.1 Trees and DAGs

Analogously to the way trees and DAGs are parametrised by a functor in our Haskell implementation, we parametrise the corresponding semantic notions by a finitary container. In the following, we use the shorthand notation $(s_i)_{i<l}$ for a tuple $(s_0, \ldots, s_{l-1}) \in \Pi_{i<l} S_i$.

Definition 2. The set of trees $\mathsf{Tree}(F)$ over a finitary container F is the least fixed point of $\mathsf{Ext}(F)$. That is, each tree t is of the form $(s, (t_i)_{i<l})$ with $t_i \in \mathsf{Tree}(F)$ for all $i < l$. The set $\mathcal{P}(t)$ of *positions* of t is the least set of finite sequences over $\mathbb{N}$ such that $\langle\rangle \in \mathcal{P}(t)$ and if $p \in \mathcal{P}(t_j)$, then $\langle j\rangle \cdot p \in \mathcal{P}(s, (t_i)_{i<l})$. Given a position $p \in \mathcal{P}(t)$, we define the subtree $t|_p$ of t at p as follows: $t|_{\langle\rangle} = t$ and $(s, (t_i)_{i<l})|_{\langle j\rangle \cdot p} = t_j|_p$ for all $j < l$.

For DAGs, we use a representation similar to the Haskell implementation, viz. a mapping from nodes to their child nodes.

Definition 3. A *graph* $g = (N, E, r)$ over a finitary container F is given by a finite set N of nodes, an *edge* function $E\colon N \to F(N)$, and a root node $r \in N$. A graph g induces a *reachability* relation $\xrightarrow{g}$, which is the least transitive relation $\xrightarrow{g}$ such that $n \xrightarrow{g} n_j$, whenever $E(n) = (s, (n_i)_{i<l})$. We write $\xleftarrow{g}$ for the inverse of $\xrightarrow{g}$. A graph $g = (N, E, r)$ is called a *DAG* if (a) each node $n \in N$ is reachable from r, i.e. $r \xrightarrow{g} n$, and (b) g is *acyclic*, i.e. $\xleftarrow{g}$ is well-founded. The set of all DAGs over F is denoted $\mathsf{DAG}(F)$. Given a DAG $g = (N, E, r)$ and a node $n \in N$, the *sub-DAG* of g rooted in n, denoted $g|_n$, is the DAG (N', E', n), where $N' = \{m \in N | n \xrightarrow{g} m\}$ is the set of nodes reachable from n in g, and E' is the restriction of E to N'.

Note that as DAGs are finite, $\xrightarrow{g}$ is well-founded iff $\xleftarrow{g}$ is well-founded. Moreover, each tree $t \in \mathsf{Tree}(F)$ gives rise to a DAG $\mathcal{G}(t) = (\mathcal{P}(t), E, \langle\rangle) \in \mathsf{DAG}(F)$, where

$$E(p) = (s, (p \cdot \langle i\rangle)_{i<l}) \quad \text{if} \quad t|_p = (s, (t_i)_{i<l}).$$

Conversely, each DAG $g = (N, E, r)$ gives rise to a tree $\mathcal{U}(g)$, called the *unravelling* of g, as follows:

$$\mathcal{U}(g) = (s, (\mathcal{U}(g|_{n_i}))_{i<l}) \quad \text{if} \quad E(r) = (s, (n_i)_{i<l})$$

The mapping $\mathcal{U}(\cdot) : \mathsf{DAG}(F) \to \mathsf{Tree}(F)$ is well-defined by the principle of well-founded recursion with the well-founded relation $<$ given by: $g < h$ iff $g = h|_n$ with n a node in h that is not the root. Well-foundedness of $<$ follows from the well-foundedness of the reachability relation $\xleftarrow{g}$ for each DAG $g \in \mathsf{DAG}(F)$.

Similarly to positions in trees, we define *paths* in a DAG. Given a DAG $g = (N, V, r)$ and node $n \in N$, the set $\mathcal{P}_g(n)$ of paths to n in g is inductively defined as the least set with (a) $\langle\rangle \in \mathcal{P}_g(r)$, and (b) if $p \in \mathcal{P}_g(n)$ and $E(n) = (s, (n_i)_{i<l})$, then $p \cdot \langle i\rangle \in \mathcal{P}_g(n_i)$ for all $i < l$. The set of all paths in a DAG g, denoted $\mathcal{P}(g)$, is then simply the union $\bigcup_{n \in N} \mathcal{P}_g(n)$. This union is a disjoint union, i.e. for each path $p \in \mathcal{P}(g)$, there is a unique node $n \in N$ such that $p \in \mathcal{P}_g(n)$. We denote this unique node n as $g[p]$. We can observe the close relationship between paths and positions in the unravelling of DAGs: we have that $\mathcal{P}(g) = \mathcal{P}(\mathcal{U}(g))$.

5.2 Attribute Grammars and Their Semantics

In the following we will work with families $(D_a)_{a \in I}$ of sets and families $(f_a)_{a \in I}$ of functions $f_a\colon X \to D_a$ defined on them. To work with them conveniently, we make use of the notation D_A, with $A \subseteq I$, for the set $\Pi_{a \in A} D_a$ and f_A for the function of type $X \to D_A$ that maps each $x \in X$ to $(f_a(x))_{a \in A}$.

Definition 4. An *attribute grammar (AG)* $G = (S, I, D, \alpha, \delta)$ over a finitary container $F = (\mathsf{Sh}, \mathsf{ar})$ consists of:

- finite, disjoint sets S, I of *synthesised* resp. *inherited* attributes,
- a family $D = (D_a)_{a \in S \cup I}$ of *attribute domains*,
- a family $\alpha = (\alpha_a\colon D_S \to D_a)_{a \in I}$ of *initialisation functions*,
- a family $\delta = (\delta_a)_{a \in S \cup I}$ of *semantic functions*, where

$$\delta_a\colon F(D_S) \times D_I \to D_a \quad \text{if } a \in S$$
$$\delta_a : \Pi_{((s,\overline{d}),d) \in F(D_S) \times D_I} D_a^{\mathsf{ar}(s)} \quad \text{if } a \in I$$

In other words, δ_a maps each $((s, \overline{d}), d) \in F(D_S) \times D_I$ to some $e \in D_a$ if $a \in S$ and to some $\overline{e} \in D_a^{\mathsf{ar}(s)}$ if $a \in I$.

The semantics of an AG is defined in terms of runs on a tree or a DAG. A run is simply a decoration of all nodes in the tree/DAG with elements of the attribute domains that is consistent with the semantic and initialisation functions.

Definition 5. Let $G = (S, I, D, \delta, \alpha)$ be an AG on F and $t \in \mathsf{Tree}(F)$. A family $\rho = (\rho_a)_{a \in S \cup I}$ of mappings $\rho_a\colon \mathcal{P}(t) \to D_a$ is called a *run* of G on t if the following conditions are met:

- $\alpha_a(\rho_S(\langle\rangle)) = \rho_a(\langle\rangle)$ for all $a \in I$
- For each $p \in \mathcal{P}(t)$ with $t|_p = (s, (t_i)_{i<l})$, we have that

$$\delta_a((s, (\rho_S(p \cdot \langle i\rangle))_{i<l}), \rho_I(p)) = \begin{cases} \rho_a(p) & \text{if } a \in S \\ (\rho_a(p \cdot \langle i\rangle))_{i<l} & \text{if } a \in I \end{cases}$$

If there is a unique run ρ, we obtain the result $\rho_S(\langle\rangle) \in D_S$, which we denote by $[\![G]\!](t)$.

For the semantic function δ_a of an inherited attribute a, we use the notation $\delta_{a,j}$ for the function that returns the j-th component of the result of δ_a. For example, we can reformulate the condition on ρ_a from the above definition as follows:

$$\delta_{a,j}((s, (\rho_S(p \cdot \langle i\rangle))_{i<l}), \rho_I(p)) = \rho_a(p \cdot \langle j\rangle) \quad \text{for all } j < l$$

In general an AG may have multiple runs or no run at all. However, we can give sufficient conditions on AGs that ensure that a given AG has exactly one run on any tree. One such condition is that the semantic functions have no cyclic dependencies, which is known as *non-circularity* in the literature on AGs.

We will not go into the details of deciding non-circularity and instead refer to the algorithm of Knuth [25, 26]. An important consequence of non-circularity is that we can schedule the construction of the unique run of the AG on an input tree. In particular, given a tree $t \in \mathsf{Tree}(F)$ and AG $G = (S, I, D, \delta, \alpha)$ on F, there is a well-founded order $<$ on the set $(S \cup I) \times \mathcal{P}(t)$, which describes in which order the run of G on t can be constructed. In the following, when we say that an AG is non-circular, we assume that such a well-founded order exists for any input tree.

The definition of a run on DAGs is more difficult as a node in a DAG may have multiple parents, which leads to the situation depicted in Figure 4, where a node may receive several inherited attribute values. Our approach in this paper is to assume, for each inherited attribute a, a binary operator $\oplus_a$ that combines attribute values. In order to obtain well-defined notion of a run, we must in general assume that $\oplus_a$ is associative and commutative, i.e. it does not matter in which order inherited attributes are combined:

Definition 6. Let $G = (S, I, D, \alpha, \delta)$ be an AG on F, $\oplus = (\oplus_a \colon D_a \times D_a \to D_a)_{a \in I}$ a family of associative and commutative binary operators, and $g = (N, E, r) \in \mathsf{DAG}(F)$. A family $\rho = (\rho_a)_{a \in S \cup I}$ of mappings $\rho_a \colon N \to D_a$ is called a *run* of G modulo $\oplus$ on g if the following conditions are met:

- $\rho_a(r) = \alpha_a(\rho_S(r))$ for all $a \in I$
- For all $n \in N$ with $E(n) = (s, (n_i)_{i<l})$ and $a \in S$, we have
$$\rho_a(n) = \delta_a((s, (\rho_S(n_i))_{i<l}), \rho_I(n))$$
- For all $n \in N$ and $a \in I$, we have
$$\rho_a(n) = \bigoplus_{(m,j,s,(n_i)_{i<l}) \in M} \delta_{a,j}((s, (\rho_S(n_i))_{i<l}), \rho_I(m))$$
– where M is the set of all tuples $(m, j, s, (n_i)_{i<l})$ such that $E(m) = (s, (n_i)_{i<l})$ and $n_j = n$, and the sum is w.r.t. $\oplus_a$.

If there is a unique run ρ, we obtain the result $\rho_S(r) \in D_S$, which we denote by $(\!|G, \oplus|\!)(g)$.

Note that the definition of runs on DAGs generalises the definition of runs on trees in the sense that a run on a tree t is also a run on the corresponding DAG $\mathcal{G}(t)$ and vice versa.

In the following three sections, we shall formally state and prove the correspondence theorems that we used in section 4.

5.3 Copying Attribute Grammars

At first we consider the case of copying AGs, i.e. AGs whose semantic functions for all inherited attributes simply copy the value of the attribute from each node to all its child nodes:

Definition 7. An AG $G = (S, I, D, \alpha, \delta)$ over F is called *copying*, if $\delta_{a,j}((s, \bar{d}), (e_b)_{b \in I}) = e_a$ for all $a \in I$, $(s, \bar{d}) \in F(D_S)$, $j < \mathsf{ar}(s)$ and $(e_b)_{b \in I} \in D_I$. A family $(\oplus_a \colon D_a \times D_a \to D_a)_{a \in I}$ of binary operators is called *copying* if $d \oplus_a e \in \{d, e\}$ for all $a \in I$ and $d, e \in D_a$.

Given such a setting as described above, we can show that, for each run of an AG on a DAG g, we find an equivalent run of the AG on $\mathcal{U}(g)$, and vice versa. Equivalence of runs is defined as follows: given an AG $G = (S, I, D, \alpha, \delta)$ over F, we say that a run ρ of G on a DAG $g \in \mathsf{DAG}(F)$ and a run ρ' of G on $\mathcal{U}(g)$ are *equivalent* if $\rho'_a(p) = \rho_a(g[p])$ for all $a \in S \cup I$ and $p \in \mathcal{P}(g)$.

Theorem 1. *Given a copying AG $G = (S, I, D, \alpha, \delta)$ over F, a copying $\oplus = (\oplus_a \colon D_a \times D_a \to D_a)_{a \in I}$, and a DAG $g = (N, E, r) \in \mathsf{DAG}(F)$, we have that for each run of G modulo $\oplus$ on g there is an equivalent run of G on $\mathcal{U}(g)$, and vice versa.*

Proof sketch. Given a run ρ on g, we construct ρ' on $\mathcal{U}(g)$ by setting $\rho'_a(p) = \rho_a(g[p])$. Conversely, given a run ρ on $\mathcal{U}(g)$, we construct a run ρ' on g by setting $\rho'_a(n) = \rho_a(p)$ for some $p \in \mathcal{P}_g(n)$. This is well-defined since ρ_a is constant for $a \in I$, and for $a \in S$, we have $\rho_a(p) = \rho_a(q)$ whenever $\mathcal{U}(g)|_p = \mathcal{U}(g)|_q$. □

Corollary 1. *Given G, $\oplus$, and g as in Theorem 1 such that G is non-circular, we have that $(\!|G, \oplus|\!)(g) = [\![G]\!](\mathcal{U}(g))$.*

Note that for copying AGs we do not need $\oplus$ to be commutative and associative to obtain a well-defined semantics on DAGs – as long as $\oplus$ is copying, too.

5.4 Correspondence by Monotonicity

Next we show that if the attribute domains D_a of an AG G are quasi-ordered such that the semantic and initialisation functions are monotone and $\oplus_a$ are decreasing, then the result of any run of G on a DAG g is less than or equal to the result of the run of G on $\mathcal{U}(g)$. We start by making the preconditions of this theorem explicit:

Definition 8. A family of binary operators $(\oplus_a \colon D_a \times D_a \to D_a)_{a \in A}$ on a family of quasi-ordered sets $(D_a, \lesssim_a)_{a \in A}$ is called *decreasing* if $d_1 \oplus_a d_2 \lesssim d_1, d_2$ for all $a \in A$ and $d_1, d_2 \in D_a$. A function $f \colon S \to T$ between two quasi-ordered sets $(S, \lesssim_S)$ and $(T, \lesssim_T)$ is called *monotone* if $s_1 \lesssim_S s_2$ implies $f(s_1) \lesssim_T f(s_2)$ for all $s_1, s_2 \in S$. An AG $G = (S, I, D, \alpha, \delta)$ equipped with a quasi-order $\lesssim_a$ on D_a for each $a \in S \cup I$, is called *monotone* if each α_a and δ_a is monotone, where the orders on D_S, $F(D_S) \times D_I$ and D_S^n are defined pointwise according to $(\lesssim_a)_{a \in S \cup I}$. That is, e.g. $\lesssim_A$ on D_A is defined by $(d_a)_{a \in A} \lesssim_A (e_a)_{a \in A}$ iff $d_a \lesssim_a e_a$ for all $a \in A$, and $\lesssim$ on $F(D_S) \times D_I$ is defined by $((s, (d_i)_{i<k}), d) \lesssim ((t, (e_i)_{i<l}), e)$ iff $s = t$, $d_i \lesssim_S e_i$ for all $i < l$ and $d \lesssim_I e$.

Theorem 2. *Let $G = (S, I, D, \alpha, \delta)$ be a non-circular AG, $\oplus = (\oplus_a \colon D_a \times D_a \to D_a)_{a \in S \cup I}$ associative and commutative operators, and $(\lesssim_a)_{a \in S \cup I}$ quasi-orders such that G is monotone and $\oplus$ is decreasing w.r.t. $(\lesssim_a)_{a \in S \cup I}$. Given a run ρ of G modulo $\oplus$ on a DAG $g = (N, E, r)$ and the run ρ' of G on $\mathcal{U}(g)$, we have $\rho_a(g[p]) \lesssim_a \rho'_a(p)$ for all $a \in S \cup I$ and $p \in \mathcal{P}(g)$.*

Proof sketch. Since G is non-circular, there is a well-founded order $<$ on $(S \cup I) \times \mathcal{P}(\mathcal{U}(g))$ compatible with G. The above inequation can then be shown by well-founded induction using $<$. □

Corollary 2. *Given G, $\oplus$, $(\lesssim_a)_{a \in S \cup I}$, and g as in Theorem 2, and given that $(\!|G, \oplus|\!)(g)$ is defined, then $(\!|G, \oplus|\!)(g) \lesssim_S [\![G]\!](\mathcal{U}(g))$.*

Note that while we assume non-circularity of the AG – as in Corollary 1 – $(\!|G, \oplus|\!)(g)$ may not be defined – unlike in Corollary 1. Nonetheless, for the proof of Theorem 2 the assumption of non-circularity is essential since it is the basis of the induction argument. The issue of non-termination of AGs on DAGs was discussed in section 4.2 exemplified with the DAG depicted in Figure 6.

Nevertheless, in case the AG is monotone w.r.t. well-founded orders, we can at least prove the existence of runs on DAGs:

Proposition 1. *Given G, $\oplus$, and $(\lesssim_a)_{a \in S \cup I}$ as in Theorem 2 such that $\lesssim_a$ is well-founded for every $a \in I$, then, on any DAG there is a run of G modulo $\oplus$.*

6. Related Work

Graph Representations The immediate practical applicability of our recursion schemes is based on Gill's idea of turning the implicit sharing information in a Haskell expression into an explicit graph representation [20]; thus making sharing visible. The twist of our work is, however, that we provide recursion schemes that are – from the outside – oblivious to sharing but – under the hood – exploit the sharing information for efficiency.

Oliveira and Cook [32] introduced a purely functional representation of graphs, called *structured graphs*, using Chlipala's *parametric higher-order abstract syntax* [12]. The recursion scheme that Oliveira and Cook use is a fold generalised to (cyclic) graphs. For a number of specialised instances, e.g. *map* on binary trees and *fold* on streams, the authors provide laws for equational reasoning. Oliveira and Löh [33] generalised structured graphs to indexed data structures with particular focus on EDSLs. While AGs could be implemented as a fold on structured graphs, doing so would incur a performance penalty due to recomputation as soon as inherited attributes are used. Moreover, the indirect representation of sharing in structured graphs hinders a direct efficient implementation of AGs.

The Lightweight Modular Staging framework, by Rompf and Odersky [36], allows its internal graph representation to be traversed through a tree-like interface, and the implementation takes care of the administration of avoiding duplication in the generated code for shared nodes. However, as far as we can tell, there is no support for using the tree interface to write algorithms such as our type inference, which avoids duplicated computations when shared nodes are used in different contexts.

Buneman et al. [10] introduce a language UnQL for querying graph-structured data. Queries are based on structural recursion, which means that the user can view the data as a tree, regardless of the underlying representation (which can even be cyclic). The motivation behind UnQL is similar to ours; however, UnQL does not appear to support propagation and merging of accumulating parameters (inherited attributes) in recursive functions.

Tree and Graph Automata There is a strong relationship between tree automata and attribute grammars, where bottom-up acceptors correspond to synthesised attributes and top-down acceptors correspond to inherited attributes. The difference is that automata are used to characterise tree languages and devise decision procedures, i.e. the automaton itself is the object of interest rather than the results of its computations. Our notion of rewriting attribute grammars is derived from tree transducers [19], i.e. tree automata that characterise tree transformations, and our representation of them in Haskell is based on Hasuo et al. [21]. Our representation of AGs in Haskell is directly taken from Bahr's *modular tree automata* [5], which are in turn derived from representations of tree automata based on the work of Hasuo et al. [21].

While a number of generalisations of tree automata to graphs have been studied, a unified notion of graph automata remains elusive [35]. There are only specialised notions of graph automata for particular applications, and our notion of AGs on DAGs falls into this category as well. There are some automata models that come close to our approach. However, they either cause recomputation in case of conflicting top-down state (instead of providing a resolution operator $\oplus$) [18, 30], restrict themselves to bottom-up state propagation only [3, 11, 16], or assume that the in-degree of nodes is fixed for each node label [23, 34]. Either approach is too restrictive for the application we have demonstrated in this paper. Moreover, none of these automata models allow for interdependency between bottom-up and top-down state.

Kobayashi et al. [27] consider a much more general form of compact tree representations than just DAGs: programs that produce trees. The authors study and implement tree transducers on such compact tree representations. To this end, they consider generalised finite state transformations (GFSTs) [14], which subsume both bottom-up and top-down transducers. However, GFSTs only provide top-down state propagation. Bottom-up state propagation has to be encoded inefficiently and is restricted to finite state spaces.

Attribute Grammars Viera et al. [39] were the first to give an embedding of AGs in Haskell that allows the programmer to combine semantic functions to construct AGs in a modular fashion. They do not rely on a specific representation of trees as we do, but instead make heavy use of Template Haskell in order to derive the necessary infrastructure. As a result, their approach is applicable to a wider variety of data types. At the same time, however, this approach excludes transparent execution of thus defined AGs on graph structures.

The idea to utilise the structure of attributes that happen to be tree-structured – as our parametric AGs from section 4.5 do – also appears in the literature on AGs, albeit with a different motivation: so-called *higher-order attribute grammars* [40] permit the execution of the AG nested within those tree-structured attributes. By composing parametric AGs sequentially similarly to the composition of tree transducers [19], we can achieve the same effect.

Higher-order attribute grammars implicitly introduce sharing when duplicating higher-order attributes. Saraiva et al. [38] exploit this sharing for their implementation of incremental attribute evaluation. Their goal, however, is different from ours: the sharing structure makes equality tests, which are necessary for incremental evaluation, cheaper and increases cache hits.

Data Flow Analysis Despite the difference in their application, there is some similarity between our correspondence theorems for simple AGs and the soundness results for data flow analysis (DFA) [2]. In particular, variants of Theorem 2 also appear in the literature on DFA. In the context of DFA, these soundness results are formulated as follows: the maximum fixpoint (MFP) is bounded by the meet over all paths (MOP). The MFP roughly corresponds to the run of an AG on a DAG, whereas the individual paths in the MOP correspond to the run of an AG on a tree. However, there are a number of differences.

First of all we only consider acyclic graphs, whereas DFA typically considers cyclic graphs. As a consequence, there are stronger requirements for DFA, in particular, the ordering has to have finite height. Secondly, AGs perform bidirectional computations, whereas DFA typically only considers unidirectional problems, i.e. either forward or backwards analyses. There are DFA frameworks that do support bidirectional analyses, however, they come with additional restrictions, e.g. separability [24].

The differences become more pronounced if we consider the parametric AGs outlined in section 4.5, which allow us to implement sharing-preserving graph transformations. The closest analogue in the DFA literature is an approach that interleaves unidirectional DFA with transformation steps [28]. However, we are not aware of a DFA framework that combines bidirectional analyses with graph transformations.

7. Discussion and Future Work

We have presented a technique that allows us to represent trees as compact DAGs, yet process them as if they were trees. The distinguishing feature of our approach is that it avoids recomputation for shared nodes even in the case of interdependent bottom-up and top-down propagation of information. This approach is supported by complementing correspondence theorems to prove the soundness of the shift from trees to DAGs. In particular, correspondence by monotonicity (Theorem 2) provides a widely applicable proof principle since it is parametric in the quasi-order. We have presented three examples for which correspondence by monotonicity gives useful results: $leavesBelow$ (cf. [6]), $typeInf$ and $gateDelay$. The $typeInf$ algorithm follows a general pattern for simple syntax-directed analyses for which monotonicity gives strong correspondence properties. Another similar example, size inference, is given in the file `Size.hs` in the accompanying repository.

A difficult obstacle in this endeavour is ensuring termination of the resulting graph traversals. As we have shown, for some instances, such as type inference, termination can only be guaranteed if further assumptions are made on the structure of the input DAG. A priority for future work is to find more general principles that allow us to reason about termination on a higher level analogous to the correspondence theorems we presented. We already made some progress in this direction as Theorem 1, Theorem 3 and, to a limited degree, Proposition 1 allowed us to infer termination of graph traversals. A potential direction for improvement is a stricter notion of non-circularity that guarantees termination of AGs on DAGs. A simple approximation of this could be for example a coarser notion of dependency: if an attribute a depends on attribute b, then b may not depend on a. The resulting notion of non-circularity would for example prove that the AG corresponding to $leavesBelow$ from the introduction terminates on DAGs.

Another direction for future work is to extend the expressive power of our recursion scheme:

- Extend AGs with fixpoint iteration [17, 31, 37] to deal with cyclic graphs and to implement analyses based on abstract interpretation.
- Support a wider class of data types, e.g. mutually recursive data types and GADTs. Both should be possible using well-known techniques from the literature [22, 41].
- Support deep pattern matching in AGs. This can be done by extending the AG and $Rewrite$ type with a parameter that can partially uncover nested subtrees. Deep patterns would make it easier to express e.g. rewrite rules in a compiler.

The motivation behind this work is to make traversals over trees with sharing more efficient. In the accompanying technical report [6] we present results from our measurements on a set of benchmarks. In summary, the benchmarks show that running algorithms on DAGs is asymptotically more efficient than running on trees when the DAG has a lot of sharing. They also show that the overhead of running on DAGs when there is no sharing is less than $2\times$ for trees of size 2^{16}, both for AGs and the generalised AGs presented in section 4.5. To achieve this, our implementation works on a more efficient representation of DAGs that uses explicit pointers only if necessary, i.e. only for sharing. The essential idea is to replace f inside the definition of Dag with $Free\ f$, where $Free$ is the free monad construction. That is, we interleave the tree and the graph representation. As a consequence, the representation of DAGs without sharing is essentially a tree. This fact can be exploited by using the tree implementation of AGs for DAGs without sharing. The upshot of this implementation is that there is no overhead of running AGs on DAGs without sharing.

Acknowledgements The first author is funded by the Danish Council for Independent Research, Grant 12-132365. The second author is funded by the Swedish Foundation for Strategic Research, under grant RAWFP.

References

[1] M. Abbott, T. Altenkirch, and N. Ghani. Categories of containers. In *FoSSaCS*, 2003.

[2] A. V. Aho, R. Sethi, and J. D. Ullman. *Compilers: principles, techniques, and tools*. Addison-Wesley Longman Publishing Co., Inc., Boston, MA, USA, 1986. ISBN 0-201-10088-6.

[3] S. Anantharaman, P. Narendran, and M. Rusinowitch. Closure properties and decision problems of dag automata. *Inf. Process. Lett.*, 94(5): 231 - 240, 2005.

[4] E. Axelsson. *Functional Programming Enabling Flexible Hardware Design at Low Levels of Abstraction*. PhD thesis, Chalmers University of Technology, 2008.

[5] P. Bahr. Modular tree automata. In *MPC*, 2012.

[6] P. Bahr and E. Axelsson. Generalising Tree Traversals to DAGs: Exploiting Sharing without the Pain. Available from authors' web site, 2014. Technical report with full proofs.

[7] P. Bahr and L. E. Day. Programming macro tree transducers. In *WGP*, 2013.

[8] R. Bird. Using circular programs to eliminate multiple traversals of data. *Acta Inform.*, 21(3):239–250, 1984.

[9] R. Bird, J. Gibbons, S. Mehner, J. Voigtländer, and T. Schrijvers. Understanding idiomatic traversals backwards and forwards. In *Haskell*, 2013.

[10] P. Buneman, M. Fernandez, and D. Suciu. UnQL: a query language and algebra for semistructured data based on structural recursion. *The VLDB Journal*, 9(1):76–110, 2000.

[11] W. Charatonik. Automata on DAG representations of finite trees. Research report, Max-Planck-Institut für Informatik, March 1999.

[12] A. Chlipala. Parametric higher-order abstract syntax for mechanized semantics. In *ICFP*, 2008.

[13] R. A. Eisenberg, D. Vytiniotis, S. Peyton Jones, and S. Weirich. Closed type families with overlapping equations. In *POPL*, 2014.

[14] J. Engelfriet. Bottom-up and top-down tree transformations — a comparison. *Mathematical systems theory*, 9(2):198–231, 1975.

[15] J. Engelfriet and H. Vogler. Macro tree transducers. *J. Comput. System Sci.*, 31(1):71–146, 1985.

[16] B. Fila and S. Anantharaman. Running tree automata on trees and/or dags. Technical report, LIFO, 2006.

[17] J. Fokker and S. D. Swierstra. Abstract interpretation of functional programs using an attribute grammar system. In *LDTA*, 2009.

[18] A. Fujiyoshi. Recognition of directed acyclic graphs by spanning tree automata. *Theor. Comput. Sci.*, 411(38–39):3493 - 3506, 2010.

[19] Z. Fülöp and H. Vogler. *Syntax-Directed Semantics: Formal Models Based on Tree Transducers*. Springer-Verlag New York, Inc., 1998.

[20] A. Gill. Type-safe observable sharing in Haskell. In *Haskell*, 2009.

[21] I. Hasuo, B. Jacobs, and T. Uustalu. Categorical views on computations on trees (extended abstract). In *ICALP*, 2007.

[22] P. Johann and N. Ghani. Foundations for structured programming with GADTs. In *POPL*, 2008.

[23] T. Kamimura and G. Slutzki. Transductions of dags and trees. *Math. Syst. Theory*, 15(1):225–249, 1981.

[24] U. P. Khedker and D. M. Dhamdhere. A generalized theory of bit vector data flow analysis. *ACM Trans. Program. Lang. Syst.*, 16(5): 1472–1511, 1994.

[25] D. Knuth. Semantics of context-free languages: Correction. *Math. Syst. Theory*, 5(2):95–96, 1971.

[26] D. E. Knuth. Semantics of context-free languages. *Theory Comput. Syst.*, 2(2):127–145, 1968.

[27] N. Kobayashi, K. Matsuda, A. Shinohara, and K. Yaguchi. Functional programs as compressed data. *Higher-Order and Symbolic Computation*, pages 1–46, 2013.

[28] S. Lerner, D. Grove, and C. Chambers. Composing dataflow analyses and transformations. In *POPL*, pages 270–282, 2002.

[29] J. R. Lewis, J. Launchbury, E. Meijer, and M. B. Shields. Implicit parameters: dynamic scoping with static types. In *POPL*, 2000.

[30] M. Lohrey and S. Maneth. Tree automata and XPath on compressed trees. In *CIAA*, 2006.

[31] A. Middelkoop. *Inference with Attribute Grammars*. PhD thesis, Universiteit Utrecht, Feb. 2012.

[32] B. C. Oliveira and W. R. Cook. Functional programming with structured graphs. In *ICFP*, 2012.

[33] B. C. d. S. Oliveira and A. Löh. Abstract syntax graphs for domain specific languages. In *PEPM*, 2013.

[34] D. Quernheim and K. Knight. Dagger: A toolkit for automata on directed acyclic graphs. In *FSMNLP*, 2012.

[35] J.-C. Raoult. Problem #70: Design a notion of automata for graphs, 2005. URL `http://rtaloop.mancoosi.univ-paris-diderot.fr/problems/70.html`. The RTA list of open problems.

[36] T. Rompf and M. Odersky. Lightweight modular staging: A pragmatic approach to runtime code generation and compiled DSLs. In *GPCE*, 2010.

[37] M. Rosendahl. Abstract interpretation using attribute grammars. In *WAGA*, 1990.

[38] J. Saraiva, D. Swierstra, and M. Kuiper. Functional incremental attribute evaluation. In *Compiler Construction*, 2000.

[39] M. Viera, S. D. Swierstra, and W. Swierstra. Attribute grammars fly first-class. In *ICFP*, 2009.

[40] H. H. Vogt, S. D. Swierstra, and M. F. Kuiper. Higher order attribute grammars. In *PLDI*, 1989.

[41] A. R. Yakushev, S. Holdermans, A. Löh, and J. Jeuring. Generic programming with fixed points for mutually recursive datatypes. In *ICFP*, 2009.

Incremental Evaluation of Higher Order Attributes

Jeroen Bransen Atze Dijkstra S. Doaitse Swierstra
Utrecht University, The Netherlands
{J.Bransen,atze,doaitse}@uu.nl

Abstract

Compilers, amongst other programs, often work with data that (slowly) changes over time. When the changes between subsequent runs of the compiler are small, one would hope the compiler to incrementally update its results, resulting in much lower running times. However, the manual construction of an incremental compiler is very hard and error prone and therefore usually not an option.

Attribute grammars provide an attractive way of constructing compilers, as they are compositional in nature and allow for aspect oriented programming. In this work we extend previous work on the automatic generation of incremental attribute grammar evaluators, with the purpose of (semi-)automatically generating an incremental compiler from the regular attribute grammar definition, by adding support for incremental evaluation of higher order attributes, a well known extension to the classical attribute grammars that is used in many ways in compiler construction, for example to model different compiler phases.

Categories and Subject Descriptors D.3.4 [*Programming Languages*]: Processors—Incremental compilers

General Terms Algorithms, Languages, Theory

Keywords incremental evaluation, attribute grammars, change propagation, program transformation, type inference

1. Introduction

Attribute grammars (Knuth 1968) are known to be well-suited for the implementation of the semantics of programming languages. There exist several attribute grammar compilers including UUAGC (Swierstra et al. 1998), JastAdd (Hedin and Magnusson 2003) and Silver (Van Wyk et al. 2010), using which many attribute grammar based compilers have been implemented. The motivating example for this paper is the *Utrecht Haskell Compiler* (Dijkstra et al. 2009). The implementation of the UHC consists of attribute grammar code combined with Haskell expressions (Peyton Jones 2003), which is compiled by the UUAGC to a Haskell program, which is then compiled by the Glasgow Haskell Compiler (GHC) to an executable. In this paper we therefore use Haskell as the basis for the implementation of our techniques.

PEPM '15, January 13–14, 2015, Mumbai, India.

ACM 978-1-4503-3297-2/15/01...$15.00.
http://dx.doi.org/10.1145/2678015.2682541

The typical usage of a compiler like the UHC is as follows. The programmer works on a project containing many lines of source code, and compiles and runs the code in order to test. The programmer then changes some lines of code, and compiles and runs the code again. This changing code, compiling and running repeats itself until the project is finished. A potential problem with a traditional compiler is that when the project grows, the compilation time increases, even though the changes to the compiled program are minimal between consecutive runs. To solve that problem we aim to build an *incremental compiler*, that uses results of the previous compilation to efficiently update the results based on the small changes made to its input.

Incremental compilation is not a new idea, but the problem is that building such compilers is very hard and error-prone. In our work we therefore aim to *(semi-)automatically generate* an incremental compiler from the attribute grammar definition of the regular compiler. Because data dependencies are explicit in attribute grammar definitions, we hope to statically use this dependency information to generate attribute grammar evaluators that incrementally update their output based on (small) changes to the input.

In this paper, building upon our earlier work (Bransen et al. 2014), we extend our techniques to support higher order attributes (Vogt et al. 1989). A higher order attribute is an attribute value which itself is a tree structure over which attributes can be computed. Higher order attributes are heavily used in the UHC and support for this in the context of incremental evaluation of attribute grammars is therefore essential to reach our goal. A theoretical limitation is that we rely on attribute grammars to be *linearly ordered* (Engelfriet and Filè 1982); we have reasons to believe that all practical attribute grammars fall in that class (Van Binsbergen et al. 2015).

The outline of the paper is as follows. In Section 2 we informally introduce attribute grammars together with a running example that we use in the rest of the paper to explain our technique. We then give a high-level overview of our approach in Section 3 before describing the details. Section 4 introduces earlier work on the representation of changes made to the input, and in Section 5 we describe the techniques for incremental attribute grammar evaluation without higher order attributes. This is similar to our earlier work (Bransen et al. 2014) but adapted to support the main contribution of this paper in Section 6 where the support for higher order attributes is added. In Section 7 we evaluate the results with a benchmark and we discuss some shortcomings in Section 8. Finally, we describe related work (Section 9) and conclude (Section 10).

2. Attribute grammars and running example

To illustrate the techniques described in this paper we use a simple running example that we introduce in this section. Alongside the example we informally introduce some core attribute grammar concepts and show some syntax from the *Utrecht University Attribute Grammar Compiler* (Swierstra et al. 1998). Although the

UUAGC syntax is not important for the techniques described in this paper, we believe that it might help the reader in understanding the usefulness of attribute grammars.

2.1 Running example

As running example for this paper we look at the very simple task of pretty printing expressions of the untyped lambda calculus, containing variables, lambda abstractions and applications. To illustrate the use of inherited attributes, we make the example slightly less trivial by printing no parentheses around variables or around the child expression of a lambda abstraction. Concretely, a certain term is pretty printed as follows.

```
\f.\x.(\y.y) ((f x) x)
```

This results in a string which can be parsed back unambiguously to the AST from which it was pretty printed, but not necessarily with the minimum number of parentheses: in the above example the parentheses around `f x` could have been left out.

2.2 Attribute grammars

Attribute grammars as introduced by (Knuth 1968) consist of a *context-free grammar*, a set of attribute definitions per nonterminal, and for each attribute defined at a production a semantic rule defining the value of the attribute in terms of other attributes. Attributes can be *inherited*, meaning that the value is passed from parent to child nodes in the derivation tree ("defined from above"), or *synthesized*, meaning that the value is passed from the child node to the parent node ("defined from below").

The UUAGC implements attribute grammars in a slightly different way, by letting the user specify an *abstract syntax tree* (AST) instead of a context-free grammar describing the concrete syntax. As the default back-end of UUAGC is Haskell, the AST corresponds to an algebraic data type with notation similar to that of Haskell, except that the children of a constructor are named.

Data types In UUAGC syntax the data type for representing expressions of the untyped lambda calculus is defined as follows.

```
data TopLam
  | Top e :: Lam
data Lam
  | Var x  :: String
  | Lam x  :: String
        e  :: Lam
  | App e1 :: Lam
        e2 :: Lam
```

The *TopLam* type is convenient as top level wrapper in later stages, but not strictly necessary. Such a wrapper is for example used to initialise an attribute with an empty environment.

Although we do not use the context-free grammars from the original definition (Knuth 1968) in this paper, we stick to the original terminology. Therefore, when talking about a *nonterminal* we refer to an algebraic type and a *production* refers to a constructor of that data type. For example, *App* is a production of *Lam* and has two nonterminal children. The *Var* production has only a terminal child, since *String* is a built-in Haskell type and has not been defined as a nonterminal in the attribute grammar.

Attribute definitions For the pretty printing of the example we introduce two attributes: a synthesized attribute *pp* that contains the result of the computation, and an inherited attribute *needp* indicating whether or not parentheses are necessary. This is defined as follows.

```
attr Lam
  inh needp :: Bool
  syn pp    :: String
```

Note that both *Bool* and *String* are plain Haskell types.

Semantic rules The computation of the value of the attributes is specified by means of semantic rules. In our system the semantic rules can be arbitrary Haskell expressions, in which we may refer to other attributes. The attributes that can be referred to are the inherited attributes of the production itself (coming from the parent) and the synthesized attributes of children (defined within the children). The attributes for which a value needs to be defined are the synthesized attributes of the production and the inherited attributes of the children.

A semantic rule has the form $c.a = e$, where c is the name of the corresponding child or the special name **lhs**[1] to refer to the parent, a is the name of the attribute, and e is an arbitrary Haskell expression. To refer to other attributes in the expression the notation $@c.a$ is used; $@c$ refers to a terminal value.

For our example we define the semantic rules as follows.

```
sem Lam
  | Var lhs.pp  = @x
  | Lam lhs.pp  = pParens @lhs.needp $
                    "\\" ++ @x ++ "." ++ @e.pp
        e.needp = False
  | App lhs.pp  = pParens @lhs.needp $
                    @e1.pp ++ " " ++ @e2.pp
        e1.needp = True
        e2.needp = True
```

We use the following (Haskell) helper function for conditionally placing parentheses around an expression.

```
pParens :: Bool → String → String
pParens True s = "(" ++ s ++ ")"
pParens False s = s
```

At the top level we set the value of *needp* to *False*, because parentheses are not needed around the whole expression. To do this we use a wrapper *TopLam*, in which we give *needp* its initial value and return the pretty printed expression as the only result.

```
attr TopLam
  syn pp :: String
sem TopLam
  | Top e.needp = False
        lhs.pp  = @e.pp
```

Trivial attribute equations like the last line can be omitted. The UUAGC will add such equation using default rules, in this case a *copy rule* for simply propagating an attribute value.

2.3 Standard evaluation

The standard non-incremental evaluation of attribute grammars in the UUAGC is done by generating Haskell code that performs the evaluation. The data types are a straightforward translation except that the constructor names are prefixed with the nonterminal name in order to avoid name clashes (note that UUAGC does not require production names to be unique, whereas in Haskell constructor names have to). This results in the following data type to be generated:

```
data Lam = LamVar String
         | LamLam String Lam
         | LamApp Lam    Lam
```

[1] Left-hand side, terminology coming from context-free grammars

The most straightforward way of generating the actual evaluation code is to build a function that takes a tuple of all inherited attributes as argument and returns a tuple of all synthesized attribute for each nonterminal. Because some inherited attributes may depend on synthesized attributes of that same nonterminal, this relies on Haskell's lazy evaluation to compute the result, and may even loop for cyclic attribute grammars.

In order to get static guarantees about non-cyclicity and to generate code that can also be evaluated in a strict way, we rely on linearly ordered attribute grammars (Engelfriet and Filè 1982). In a linearly ordered attribute grammar the attributes are split up into a linear sequence of *visits*, where each visit takes some inherited attributes as input and produces the values of some synthesized attributes, with the restriction that synthesized attributes can only depend on the inherited attributes from visits up to the visit they are computed in. Although the class of absolutely non-circular attributes is larger than the class of linearly ordered attribute grammar, experience has shown that all practical attribute grammars fall in the latter class. There exist many algorithms for automatically finding such a linear order from the attribute grammar definition.

In the rest of the paper we talk about linearly ordered attribute grammars when we mention attribute grammars, and the techniques described here work for linearly ordered attribute grammars with an arbitrary number of visits. However, because our example contains only a single inherited and a single synthesized attribute, we can simplify some details in the explanation.

The generated function evaluating the attributes for the *Lam* production of our example is:

```
semLamLam :: String → (Bool → String)
                → Bool → String
semLamLam _x _e _lhsIneedp =
  let _eOneedp  :: Bool
      _eOneedp  = False
      _eIpp     :: String
      _eIpp     = _e _eOneedp
      _lhsOpp   :: String
      _lhsOpp   = pParens _lhsIneedp $
                    "\\" ++ _x ++ "." ++ _eIpp
  in _lhsOpp
```

Note that the argument for the child is not the type of the child, but the type of the *evaluator* of the child, which can be invoked to compute the attributes for the child. At top level we construct the complete evaluator with the function *semLam*.

```
semLam :: Lam → Bool → String
semLam (LamVar x)     = semLamVar x
semLam (LamLam x e)   = semLamLam x (semLam e)
semLam (LamApp e1 e2) = semLamApp (semLam e1)
                                  (semLam e2)
```

For the other nonterminals and productions similar functions are generated.

3. High-level overview

Attribute grammar evaluators can be thought of as tree-walk evaluators '*walking*' up and down the AST. A visit may occur when the values of some further inherited attributes of a node have become available and the evaluator is guaranteed to be able to compute the values of some further synthesized attributes of that node.

One of the steps the evaluator can perform is to directly compute a synthesized attribute, for example when its value is constant or it depends only on available inherited attributes. In many cases other attributes are needed for which the evaluator should first compute some inherited attributes of children of the node, and then recursively visit some of the children before being able to compute some synthesized attributes and returning to the calling node. So, in the overall evaluation of the attributes of the top level node, the evaluator can be thought as walking up and down the tree, possibly visiting subtrees multiple times (multiple visits), before finally returning all synthesized attributes at the top level. In the context of a compiler this is typically a representation of the executable that is generated.

Now when the AST changes, for example in a compiler due to a change in the input source code, we would like to efficiently recompute the changed attribute values. One approach to incremental computation is to use *change propagation* to propagate the changed values through the tree and only evaluate expressions that have changed inputs (Reps et al. 1983). In other words, the evaluator only visits nodes in which something changed, either due to a direct change to that subtree or to a change in the attribute values. However, in many cases there are large parts of the AST in which nothing has changed, so the evaluator needs to perform much fewer steps to compute a new consistent attributed tree.

Implementation wise there are several aspects that need to be addressed. First of all the identification of changes to the AST. In this work we describe how to represent such changes using paths to locations in the AST and inserted values, assume values of this data type are constructed by some external process like a diff tool or a structure editor. Given such a value the incremental evaluation is performed by invalidating the visit results on the path from the root of the AST to the changed subtree. For every visit to a node that has already been evaluated before, it is checked whether the inherited attributes are changed and whether the visit was invalidated. If both are not the case the previous result is returned and thus the whole subtree does not need to be visited for that visit.

To implement this all in a strongly-typed fashion in Haskell we use several advanced Haskell features. For the representation of a node we use the *record syntax*, which produces a standard data type with constructors with named getters and setters for its fields. To carry around type information about the type of children we use *Generalized Algebraic Data Types* (Cheney and Hinze 2003; Xi et al. 2003). In order to associate derived types to their original types we use *type families*. Finally, we use higher-ranked types to pass generic functions as arguments to higher-order functions. Note that our implementation uses only pure functions, even though we like to think about updating the internal state of nodes as a side-effect.

4. Representation of changes

When talking about incremental evaluation in the context of attribute grammars, we assume that our input AST changes slowly over time, and we hope to efficiently recompute the attribute values after a change. In this paper we start from a description of the change to the AST produced by some external tool, for example an structure editor or some diff algorithm keeping track of changes to the source code files.

In this section we describe how to represent these changes, which is described in (Bransen and Magalhães 2013) in more detail. The representation that we describe here is not only used as an external value to alter the original AST, but also inside the evaluation to keep track of changes to constructed values, as described in Section 6.

Informally, we represent a change to the AST by a path describing the location and a new tree that is to be inserted in that location. However, instead of always replacing the full subtree, we allow the newly inserted tree to refer in some places to values of the original tree, thereby reusing existing parts. In that way an insertion of a value v into a list can for example be modelled by a path p and a *Cons* v (*Ref* p), indicating that the value at location p should be replaced by the *Cons* constructor with a value v and as its tail the value that was originally at location p.

Paths Because ASTs usually consist of a family of mutually recursive data types, we need to carry around some type information in the paths. We therefore use the generalized algebraic data type *Path f t* to represent a path in a tree of type *f* pointing to a node of type t. The constructors of this type are the *End* constructor for the empty path, and a constructor for each nonterminal child for each production. For our example this leads to:

```
data Path f t where
  End      :: Path f f
  LamPLam  :: Path Lam t → Path Lam t
  LamPAppL :: Path Lam t → Path Lam t
  LamPAppR :: Path Lam t → Path Lam t
  TopLamP  :: Path Lam t → Path TopLam t
```

Replacement The values that can be inserted into the tree to replace a subtree, are similar to the the original data for that nonterminal. However, we extend it with a constructor that represents re-usage of existing values, by means of a path. Because this path is relative to the top of the tree which depends on the context, we parametrize over the type of the top level. For our *Lam* nonterminal we can therefore represent the replacement values as follows.

```
data TopLamR top = TopLamRTop (LamR top)
                 | TopLamR (Path top TopLam)
data LamR top = LamRVar String
              | LamRLam String (LamR top)
              | LamRApp (LamR top) (LamR top)
              | LamR (Path top Lam)
```

Full change Using the paths and replacement values, we can represent a change by a pair of those values. However, as the type of the replacement depends on the type of the node that the path points to, we can not directly specify it as a pair. Instead, we use a *type family* to map each nonterminal type to its corresponding replacement type as follows.

```
type family   ReplType a      :: * → *
type instance ReplType TopLam = TopLamR
type instance ReplType Lam    = LamR
```

Using this type we can finally represent changes, which are also parametrized over the type of the top level node.

```
type Change top t = (Path top t, ReplType t top)
```

5. Incremental evaluation

In this section we describe how to write attribute evaluators that can efficiently respond to changes in the AST. Although this section forms an important part of the final solution, the techniques described here do not work as expected for higher order attributes. We postpone the discussion on higher order attributes to Section 6.

The basic idea of our incremental evaluation technique is quite simple: we store the previous input and output of a visit, and whenever the inputs are unchanged the previous output is returned without recomputation. Because visit computations can invoke visits of the children, this can lead to superlinear speedups. However, because the AST can change, we also need to keep track of changes to child nodes for deciding when to recompute, complicating matters a bit.

5.1 Representation

In order to store all information we create a data type for evaluators with a constructor for each production. For the *Lam* production of the example this data type, written using Haskell record notation, looks as follows.

```
data TLam top = TLamVar {...} | TLamLam {
  tlam_eval     :: ∀ t. TLam top → Path Lam t
                   → SemType t top,
  tlam_change   :: ∀ r. TLam top
                   → (∀ t. Path top t → SemType t top)
                   → Path Lam r
                   → ReplType r top → TLam top,
  tlam_v0       :: TLam top → Bool
                   → (String, TLam top),
  tlam_v0_dirty :: Bool,
  tlam_e        :: TLam top
  } | TLamApp {...}
```

This data type contains a record for each production representing the state of the evaluator for that node, and has the following fields:

- An *eval* function to retrieve the evaluator for the node at a given location, which is used when a subtree is inserted in a different part of the AST.
- A *change* function for pushing a change to the current subtree.
- A vX function for each visit X.
- A *dirty* flag for each visit function indicating whether or not that visit is *dirty*, i.e. some state changed since last evaluation and the visit should be re-evaluated because it may return a different result.
- A field for the state of the evaluator of each child. These are the only fields that can differ for different productions of the same nonterminal.

The type *SemType* appearing in the type of the *change* function is again a type family mapping the nonterminal types to the corresponding evaluator types.

```
type family   SemType t      :: * → *
type instance SemType TopLam = TTopLam
type instance SemType Lam    = TLam
```

It is important to notice that *change* and all visit functions take the current state of the evaluator as argument and return the new state of the evaluator, because the state can be updated. We use this pattern because we work in a purely functional language without global state, which means that all state of an evaluator for a subtree is stored inside the evaluator type of that subtree. The advantage of this is that we do not need any global cache purging strategies but just rely on Haskell's garbage collection for cleaning up unused values, and that whenever a subtree is duplicated and used in multiple places, the states of those subtrees are not shared but diverge from the point when they were split up.

In the next section we introduce the implementation of all these functions and explain how they are used, by showing the implementation of the example.

5.2 Implementation

The semantic functions return an instance of such data type, in which the computation is "remembered". Let us illustrate this with the *Lam* constructor of the example. The basic function is implemented as follows, with *eval*, *change* and v_0 bound in the where-clause:

```
semLamLam :: String → TLam top → TLam top
semLamLam x_ e_ = TLamLam {
  tlam_v0       = v0,
  tlam_eval     = eval,
```

```
    tlam_change   = change,
    tlam_v0_dirty = True,
    tlam_e        = e_
  } where
    ...
```

The actual visit code is implemented as follows, where each visit takes the state of the children and the inherited attributes, and returns the synthesized attributes and the new state of the children. These functions are then wrapped to support incremental evaluation in case nothing has changed.

```
realv0 :: TLam top → Bool → (String, TLam top)
realv0 e0 _lhsIneedp = (_lhsOpp, e1) where
  _eOneedp   = False
  (_eIpp, e1) = tlam_v0 e0 e0 _eOneedp
  _lhsOpp    = pParens _lhsIneedp $
               "\\" ++ x_ ++ "." ++ _eIpp
```

There are several things to notice here. The evaluation order is made explicit in the source code, so computations only depend on values that were defined in earlier bindings. For the computation of the pp value of the child e the visit v_0 of the child is invoked, taking the current state of the child as argument (next to the first occurrence of e_0 used to retrieve the visit function from that current state) and returning the new state of the child. Finally, together with the pp value for the current node the new state of the child is returned.

The wrapping code for a visit is then as follows. The visit is performed as usual by calling the $realv_0$ function. However, then the visit function in the evaluator is replaced by a memoizing version that directly returns the synthesized attributes in case nothing has changed.

```
v0 :: TLam top → Bool → (String, TLam top)
v0 cur inh = (syn, res) where
  (syn, e') = realv0 (tlam_e cur) inh
  res = update $ cur {
    tlam_v0       = memv0,
    tlam_v0_dirty = False,
    tlam_e        = e'}
  memv0 cur' inh' = if    inh ≡ inh'
                       ∧ ¬ (tlam_v0_dirty cur')
                    then (syn, cur')
                    else  v0 cur' inh'
```

The *update* function is a helper function that is used to update the *dirty* flags after some evaluation has happened. This is where the static dependency graph is represented.

```
update cur = cur {
  tlam_v0_dirty = tlam_v0_dirty cur
                  ∨ tlam_v0_dirty (tlam_e cur)
}
```

To get the evaluator residing at a given path the eval function is used. This function is implemented by simply propagating the request to the given path and then returning the evaluator. Note that on the type level the target type t of the path is already present, so at the end of the path we can return the current evaluator since the *End* constructor is the witness to the fact that $t{\sim}Lam$ in this case.

```
eval :: TLam top → Path Lam t → SemType t top
eval cur End          = cur
eval cur (LamPLam p) = tlam_eval (tlam_e cur)
                                 (tlam_e cur) p
```

The change function is used to propagate a change to the evaluator. When the current evaluator is changed we replace the full evaluator with the new one, and otherwise we propagate the change to the corresponding child. After propagating the type we update the *dirty* flags.

```
change :: TLam top
       → (∀ t.Path top t → SemType t top)
       → Path Lam r
       → ReplType r top
       → TLam top
change cur lu End            repl = semLamR lu repl
change cur lu (LamPLam p) repl = update_e p $
  cur {tlam_e = tlam_change (tlam_e cur)
                (tlam_e cur) lu p repl}
```

The updating of the dirty flags is slightly less trivial; one could think that we need to invalidate all visits in which the child e is used because somewhere in that subtree something has definitely changed. However, it could be the case that no information from that changed node is ever used. Therefore, we adopt the following strategy: whenever the child of a node is replaced all visits in which that child is used are invalidated, and otherwise we use the *update* function to propagate changes. This is implemented as follows.

```
update_e End cur = cur {tlam_v0_dirty = True}
update_e _   cur = update cur
```

Finally, for the changed child the new evaluators should be constructed or reused. This is done using the following function which is very similar to the *semLam* function except that is takes a lookup function as first argument to retrieve the evaluators for the reused nodes.

```
semLamR :: (∀ t.Path top t → SemType t top)
        → LamR top
        → TLam top
semLamR lu (LamR p)         = lu p
semLamR _  (LamRVar x)      = semLamVar x
semLamR lu (LamRLam x e)    = semLamLam x
                                (semLamR lu e)
semLamR lu (LamRApp e1 e2) = semLamApp
                                (semLamR lu e1)
                                (semLamR lu e2)
```

5.3 Example invocation

The example lambda term as shown in Section 2.1 is represented as follows.

```
term = LamLam "f" (LamLam "x" (LamApp
         (LamLam "y" (LamVar "y"))
         (LamApp
           (LamApp (LamVar "f") (LamVar "x"))
           (LamVar "x"))))
```

To perform the initial evaluation of the attributes the semantic wrapper function needs to be invoked. This returns the evaluator for which the top level visit can be invoked to retrieve the result and the new state of the evaluator.

```
st1 = semTopLam (TopLamTop term)
(str, st2) = ttoplam_v0 st1 st1
```

The value of *str* is `\f.\x.(\y.y) ((f x) x)` as expected.

Let us imagine we would like to add a lambda abstraction to the term to let it be `\f.\x.\y.(\y.y) ((f x) x)`. We represent that change by a path and a replacement value. The path needs to point to the subterm under the outermost two lambda abstractions and can thus be represented as follows.

```
path = TopLamP (LamPLam (LamPLam End))
```

The replacement needs to be of type *LamR* and is a lambda abstraction. However, its body is the value which was at the location of *path*, so we represent the inserted value by the following.

$$repl = LamRLam \text{ "y" } (LamR\ path)$$

To push this change to our evaluator we call the *change* function as follows.

$$st_3 = ttoplam\_change\ st_2\ st_2 \\ \quad (ttoplam\_eval\ st_2\ st_2)\ path\ repl$$

Finally, we can retrieve the result again by calling the top level visit function.

$$(str_2, st_4) = ttoplam\_v_0\ st_3\ st_3$$

The result is that str_2 has the desired value, but for computing this value the pretty printing result of the shared subtree has been reused.

5.4 Intra-visit attributes

One difficulty that does not occur in the running example of this paper is that of so called *intra-visit* attributes. In linearly ordered attribute grammars the computation of the synthesized attributes may depend on inherited attributes of that visit or earlier visits. However, with the implementation that we propose the inherited attributes of previous visits are not in scope and need to be explicitly passed to the visit in which the inherited attribute is used.

For the standard non-incremental evaluation the *visit-tree* approach (Saraiva et al. 2000) is used by the UUAGC. There it is statically computed which attributes from the first visit are used in subsequent visits, and these are passed as extra arguments to the second visit. For the second visit the attributes used in later visits are passed on to the third visit, and so on.

However, in our implementation we can do better. Since we are already explicitly encoding the current state of a node, the attributes used in later stages can be stored inside this record. Whenever such attribute value is updated due to the recomputation of the visit in which the attribute was declared, the visits in which the attribute is used can be invalidated by setting the *dirty* flag to *True*. The result of this is that only visits that really use the intra-visit attribute are recomputed, and no intermediate visits that only pass on the value to the subsequent visit.

6. Higher order attributes

An important extension to attribute grammars is that of higher order attribute grammars (Vogt et al. 1989). In a typical attribute grammar the attribute values themselves can be trees, and the idea of a higher order attribute grammar is to decorate those trees again with attributes. In the UUAGC this is implemented by allowing the user to give an expression, which can refer to attributes as usual, constructing a new child of the current node for which attributes are also evaluated.

The use of higher order attributes is especially useful in the context of building a compiler, where the result of one compiler phase is again a tree, over which attributes are computed in the next phase. Another use of higher order attributes is to abstract over common patterns like generation of fresh variables.

The problem with the incremental evaluation as discussed in the previous section is that whenever a change to the AST occurs, the value of the higher order attribute changes and therefore the attributes of the corresponding higher order child have to be recomputed. However, when a small change to AST happens, we also expect only a small change the higher order child, and we want to have the same incremental speedups for changes to the higher order child as we have in the case of a change to the AST. In this section we extend the example with a higher order child and show how our technique can be extended to obtain the desired behaviour.

6.1 Extended example

We now extend the running example in the following way. Imagine that our input AST is not a term in the lambda calculus as discussed previously, but in a language that also contains let-bindings. The AST of such language is represented as follows.

```
data Sug
  | Var x  :: String
  | Lam x  :: String
        e  :: Sug
  | App e1 :: Sug
        e2 :: Sug
  | Let x  :: String
        e1 :: Sug
        e2 :: Sug
```

What usually happens in a compiler is *desugaring*, by rewriting the AST with a rich syntax to an AST containing only simpler constructions. In this case we desugar the *Sug* data type to the *Lam* data type by translation an expression like **let** $x = y$ **in** z to the expression $(\lambda x.z)\ y$. In UUAGC syntax this can be written as follows.

```
attr Sug
  syn desug :: Lam
sem Sug
  | Var lhs.desug = LamVar @x
  | Lam lhs.desug = LamLam @x @e.desug
  | App lhs.desug = LamApp @e1.desug @e2.desug
  | Let lhs.desug = LamApp
                      (LamLam @x @e2.desug)
                      @e1.desug
```

At top level, for which we have also added a *TopSug* nonterminal as convenient wrapper, we now need to *instantiate* the result of the desugaring as new child. We can then get the result of the pretty printing by simply referring to the *pp* attribute of the higher order child. For this we use the **inst** syntax that defines the higher order child and instantiates it.

```
attr TopSug
  syn pp :: String
sem TopSug
  | Top inst.des :: TopLam
        inst.des =  TopLamTop @e.desug
        lhs.pp   =  @des.pp
```

As before, the last rule could be omitted because it is a copy rule that can be automatically generated by the UUAGC, but for clarity we have included it here.

Of course one could also get the same behaviour by directly returning a pretty printed version of the *Sug* language by pretty printing the let-case in the correct way, but that leads to code duplication and is therefore undesired.

6.2 Improved evaluation

The instantiation of the higher order child is evaluated by constructing the value of the higher order child and then calling the *semTopLam* on it as follows.

```
semTopSugTop = ... where
  ...
  realv0 :: TSug top -> (String, TSug top)
  realv0 e0 = (_lhsOpp, e1) where
```

$$
\begin{array}{ll}
(\_eIdesug, e_1) & = tsug\_v_0\ e_0\ e_0 \\
des\_val\_ & = TopLamTop\ \_eIdesug \\
des\_inst\_ & = semTopLam\ des\_val\_ \\
(\_lhsOpp, \_) & = ttoplam\_v_0\ des\_inst\_\ des\_inst\_
\end{array}
$$

However, although $des\_inst\_$ itself is also an AST that implements the incremental behaviour, we do not represent changes to that AST and construct a new one every time a (small) change happens to the $TSug$ AST.

To retain incremental behaviour for higher order attributes, we add a new synthesized attribute to $TSug$ that is computed in in a similar fashion as the $desug$ attributes. Such attribute is a representation of the change to the higher order attribute compared to the previous evaluation which we call *derived change*. Whenever a change happens to the $TSug$ AST and a memoized value is used for the $desug$ attribute, a reference is used as value for the derived change.

In order to fill the path in the references of this derived change, we need information about the location where the current value of the tree ends up when it is instantiated. To propagate that information we also add an inherited attribute to $TSug$ containing that information. This path can then be stored when a reference is returned.

To implement this, the type of $tsug\_v_0$ is changed to the following.

$$
\begin{array}{l}
tsug\_v_0 :: TSug\ top \\
\quad \rightarrow (\forall\ t.Path\ Lam\ t \rightarrow Path\ TopLam\ t) \\
\quad \rightarrow (Lam, LamR\ TopLam, TSug\ top),
\end{array}
$$

The second argument is the path where the Lam value ends up when it is instantiated, but instead of (inefficiently) appending to the end of a path, we use the trick of *difference lists*. As a synthesized attribute the $LamR\ TopLam$ is added, which represents the change to the Lam relative to the previous evaluation, in some top level structure $TopLam$ (when the higher order child is instantiated).

The visit function for $semSugApp$ is then changed as follows.

$$
\begin{array}{l}
semSugApp = \ldots\ \mathbf{where} \\
\quad \ldots \\
\quad v_0 :: TSug\ top \\
\qquad \rightarrow (\forall\ t.Path\ Lam\ t \rightarrow Path\ TopLam\ t) \\
\qquad \rightarrow (Lam, LamR\ TopLam, TSug\ top) \\
\quad v_0\ cur\ p = (syn, synr, res)\ \mathbf{where} \\
\qquad (syn, synr, (e_1', e_2')) = realv_0\ (tsug\_e_1\ cur, \\
\qquad\qquad\qquad\qquad\qquad tsug\_e_2\ cur)\ p \\
\qquad res = update\ \$\ cur\ \{ \\
\qquad\quad tsug\_v_0 \qquad = memv_0, \\
\qquad\quad tsug\_v_0\_dirty = False, \\
\qquad\quad tsug\_e_1 \qquad = e_1', \\
\qquad\quad tsug\_e_2 \qquad = e_2'\} \\
\qquad memv_0 :: TSug\ top \\
\qquad\quad \rightarrow (\forall\ t.Path\ Lam\ t \rightarrow Path\ TopLam\ t) \\
\qquad\quad \rightarrow (Lam, LamR\ TopLam, TSug\ top) \\
\qquad memv_0\ cur'\ p' = \mathbf{if}\ \ \neg\ (tsug\_v_0\_dirty\ cur') \\
\qquad\qquad \mathbf{then}\ (syn, LamR\ (p\ End), cur') \\
\qquad\qquad \mathbf{else}\ \ v_0\ cur'\ p'
\end{array}
$$

Note the in $memv_0$ the $synr$ attribute is replaced by a reference to the path p, which is completed by passing the End constructor. Due to the smart use of a higher-ranked type together with GADTs and type families this is all strongly typed and also works for families of mutually recursive data types.

In the $realv_0$ function of $semSugApp$ the paths are altered by function composition to construct the correct path for each of the children. Note that these paths do not correspond to constructors of the $TSug$ AST over which these attributes are computed, but are relative to the $desug$ attribute in which the different parts end up.

$$
\begin{array}{l}
realv_0 :: (TSug\ top, TSug\ top) \\
\qquad \rightarrow (\forall\ t.Path\ Lam\ t \rightarrow Path\ TopLam\ t) \\
\qquad \rightarrow (Lam, LamR\ TopLam, TSug\ top, TSug\ top) \\
realv_0\ (e_{10}, e_{20})\ p = (\_lhsOdesug, \_lhsOdesugR, e_{11}, e_{21}) \\
\quad \mathbf{where} \\
\qquad (\_e_1Idesug, \_e_1IdesugR, e_{11}) = tsug\_v_0\ e_{10}\ e_{10} \\
\qquad\qquad\qquad\qquad (p \circ LamPAppL) \\
\qquad (\_e_2Idesug, \_e_2IdesugR, e_{21}) = tsug\_v_0\ e_{20}\ e_{20} \\
\qquad\qquad\qquad\qquad (p \circ LamPAppR) \\
\qquad \_lhsOdesug \ \ = LamApp\ \ \_e_1Idesug\ \ \_e_2Idesug \\
\qquad \_lhsOdesugR = LamRApp\ \_e_1IdesugR\ \_e_2IdesugR
\end{array}
$$

Finally, at top level the higher order child is instantiated only the first time. The field des_0 is of type $Maybe\ (TLam\ top)$ and is initially set to $Nothing$. In subsequent evaluations in $semTopSugTop$ that field is used for updating the existing evaluator as follows.

$$
\begin{array}{l}
realv_0 :: TSug\ top \rightarrow Maybe\ (TTopLam\ TopLam) \\
\qquad \rightarrow (String, TSug\ top, TTopLam\ TopLam) \\
realv_0\ e_0\ des_0 = (\_lhsOpp, e_1, des_1)\ \mathbf{where} \\
\quad (\_eIdesug, \_eIdesugR, e_1) = tsug\_v_0\ e_0\ e_0\ TopLamP \\
\quad des\_val\_ \ \ = TopLamTop\ \ \_eIdesug \\
\quad des\_valR\_ = TopLamRTop\ \_eIdesugR \\
\quad des\_inst\_ \ = \mathbf{case}\ des_0\ \mathbf{of} \\
\qquad Nothing \rightarrow semTopLam\ des\_val\_ \\
\qquad Just\ v \ \ \rightarrow ttoplam\_change\ v\ v\ (ttoplam\_eval\ v\ v) \\
\qquad\qquad\qquad End\ des\_valR\_ \\
\quad (\_lhsOpp, des_1) = ttoplam\_v_0\ des\_inst\_\ des\_inst\_
\end{array}
$$

With this transformation in place, we now have restored the incremental behaviour of our code when higher order attributes are used.

7. Evaluation

We have implemented the techniques described into a simple compiler[2]. To simplify the implementation the compiler takes a linearly ordered attribute grammar as input and generates the code as described in the previous sections.

To evaluate the effectiveness of our approach we have implemented a constraint-based type inference algorithm (Heeren et al. 2002) for the lambda calculus with let bindings and let polymorphism. Furthermore, we have added a desugaring step to the algorithm as with the running example in this paper and used a higher order attribute to infer types for the desugared version of the AST. This is exactly the case where our previous work falls short because of the use of the higher order attributes. Furthermore, it is a typical use case in compiler construction with attribute grammars.

7.1 Implementation details

For the inference of the types we use bottom-up type rules as shown in Figure 1 which gather constraints used elsewhere by a constraint solver. Type judgements are of the form $\mathcal{M}, \mathcal{A}, \mathcal{C} \vdash e : \tau$ where e is the expression being typed, τ is the type, $\mathcal{M}$ is a set of monomorphic type variables, $\mathcal{A}$ is a set of assumptions and $\mathcal{C}$ is a list of constraints. It is important to notice that in the corresponding implementation $\mathcal{M}$ is a value that is passed top-down and $\mathcal{A}$, $\mathcal{C}$ and τ are passed bottom-up. In contrast to the well-known algorithm $\mathcal{W}$ (Damas and Milner 1982), the bottom-up constraint based type inference algorithm has a bottom-up behaviour that makes it suitable for incremental evaluation.

[2] The code can be found at:
`http://www.staff.science.uu.nl/~brans106/iehoa.zip`

$$\frac{\beta \text{ fresh}}{\mathcal{M}, \{x : \beta\}, [\,] \vdash x : \beta} \text{ VAR}$$

$$\frac{\begin{array}{c}\beta \text{ fresh} \\ \mathcal{M}, \mathcal{A}_1, \mathcal{C}_1 \vdash e_1 : \tau_1 \\ \mathcal{M}, \mathcal{A}_2, \mathcal{C}_2 \vdash e_2 : \tau_2 \\ \mathcal{C}_{new} = [\tau_1 \equiv \tau_2 \rightarrow \beta]\end{array}}{\mathcal{M}, \mathcal{A}_1 \cup \mathcal{A}_2, \mathcal{C}_1 +\!\!+ \mathcal{C}_2 +\!\!+ \mathcal{C}_{new} \vdash e_1\ e_2 : \beta} \text{ APP}$$

$$\frac{\begin{array}{c}\beta_1, \beta_2 \text{ fresh} \\ \mathcal{M} \cup \{\beta_1\}, \mathcal{A}, \mathcal{C} \vdash e : \tau \\ \mathcal{C}_{new} = [\beta_2 \equiv \beta_1 \rightarrow \tau] +\!\!+ [\beta_1 \equiv \tau' \mid x : \tau' \in \mathcal{A}]\end{array}}{\mathcal{M}, \mathcal{A} \backslash x, \mathcal{C}_{new} +\!\!+ \mathcal{C} \vdash \lambda x \rightarrow e : \beta_2} \text{ ABS}$$

$$\frac{\begin{array}{c}\beta \text{ fresh} \\ \mathcal{M}, \mathcal{A}_1, \mathcal{C}_1 \vdash e_1 : \tau_1 \\ \mathcal{M}, \mathcal{A}_2, \mathcal{C}_2 \vdash e_2 : \tau_2 \\ \mathcal{C}_{new} = [\beta \equiv \tau_2] +\!\!+ [\tau' \leqslant_{\mathcal{M}} \tau_1 \mid x : \tau' \in \mathcal{A}_2]\end{array}}{\mathcal{M}, \mathcal{A}_1 \cup \mathcal{A}_2 \backslash x, \mathcal{C}_1 +\!\!+ \mathcal{C}_{new} +\!\!+ \mathcal{C}_2 \vdash \textbf{let } x = e_1 \textbf{ in } e_2 : \beta} \text{ LET}$$

Figure 1. Bottom-up type rules

The type rules can be translated to AGs in an almost straightforward way. We use one inherited attribute for $\mathcal{M}$, and three synthesized attributes corresponding to $\mathcal{A}$, $\mathcal{C}$ and τ. There are however two implementation details that do not follow directly from the type rules.

Fresh variable generation The generation of fresh variables is usually implemented in AGs using a *threaded* attribute, which is both synthesized and inherited. Such an attribute is a simple counter which is increased every time a fresh variable is needed. As described in our previous work (Bransen et al. 2014), such threaded attributes are bad for the effectiveness of the incremental evaluation. In previous work we have suggested several solutions for this, which could also be applied here, but to simplify the toy implementation we have chosen to implement fresh variable generation with a global mutable state instead.

Intermediate constraint solving In the constraint based type inference most time is spent in solving the constraints, not constructing the constraints. The incremental AG machinery is used for making the constraint generation phase more efficient after changes in the AST. With constraint solving being done only at top level we still spend most time there, since the constraint solving is completely redone even after a simple change.

However, many of the generated constraints are equivalent to the constraints generated earlier, so the result of the constraint solving should also be stored. There is a certain order in which constraints should be solved, so it is not possible to solve all constraints as soon as they are generated. For a closed expression, in which no free variables appear, it is possible to solve all constraints and immediately apply all resulting substitutions. In the constraint generation the expression is closed if and only if $\mathcal{A}$ is empty. Based on this observation we have defined our code in such way that whenever $\mathcal{A}$ is empty, all constraints generated so far are solved and the substitutions are applied to τ; no more constraints remain.

7.2 Benchmarking

At first we have run the code on some hand-crafted cases to validate correctness and do preliminary measures. We have measured large speedups (100x) in specific artificial cases, and overall the overhead seemed within acceptable bounds.

To more thoroughly evaluate the effectiveness and measure the overhead of our approach we have run several benchmarks. For the time measurement we used *Criterion* (O'Sullivan 2009) which is a framework for measuring the performance of Haskell programs. It takes care of running benchmarks multiple times for more accurate results, forcing evaluation of the benchmark results, avoiding undesired sharing between runs and generating statistics. In our case we have directed Criterion to use 100 runs for each benchmark.

In order to generate arbitrary sugared lambda expressions and changes to the AST we used *QuickCheck* (Claessen and Hughes 2000) which is a tool for formulating and testing properties of Haskell programs. As a part of this tool there is a set of functions for generating arbitrary instances of data types, which we use to generate the data for our benchmarks.

7.3 Results

In Figure 2 we show the benchmark results. In each sub figure two bar charts are shown: *Base* is the standard evaluation as described in Section 2 and *Incr* is the incremental evaluation as described in Section 6. For all different test cases we have used a set of 100 randomly generated well-typed lambda terms, and five different types of changes for each of them. The unit of measure on the y-axis is in milliseconds, and notice that that last two sub figures have a y-axis spanning twice as much time.

The initial run for both approaches is shown in Figure 2a. The overhead of the incremental evaluation is a 9.3% time increase on average. Figure 2b and Figure 2c show are the corner cases in which the expression is only changed at top level by adding an unused let binding or application of the identity function respectively. Even though it is to be expected that in these cases the code would benefit maximally from incremental evaluation, the speedups are only 28.2% and 32.3%.

Two cases where we would expect speedups but have measured decrease in runtime are the deletion of an arbitrary subtree (Figure 2d) and doing an arbitrary (valid) change (Figure 2e). The increase in runtime is 8.9% and 15.5% respectively. Finally in Figure 2f we show the worst case for incremental computation in which the full AST is replaced by another one, such that no information can be reused. Here the overhead is also 15.5%, which we believe is reasonable if large speedups would be achieved on other cases.

8. Discussion

Benchmarks We have been able to achieve large speedups (100x) in hand-crafted test cases, but we have not measured any speedups in the larger benchmarks. One of the reasons is that the generation of arbitrary well-typed lambda terms is not easy, and our solution is ad-hoc. As a result of this, the types of the generated lambda terms are quite large and evaluating those could take up large parts of the overall computation time.

To improve upon this better benchmarks need to be constructed, for example by generating the lambda terms in a uniformly distributed way (Claessen et al. 2014). Furthermore, the types of changes presented in our benchmarks should be closer to real use, for example by taking data from a structure editor or the revision history of some project.

Overhead One common problem of incremental evaluation is that there is always overhead involved. In our case the initial evaluation is slower because of the extra state that is built up next to the actual evaluation, and in the case of the example the overhead can actually be larger than the actual computation. It is therefore not desirable to apply this technique to all attribute grammars.

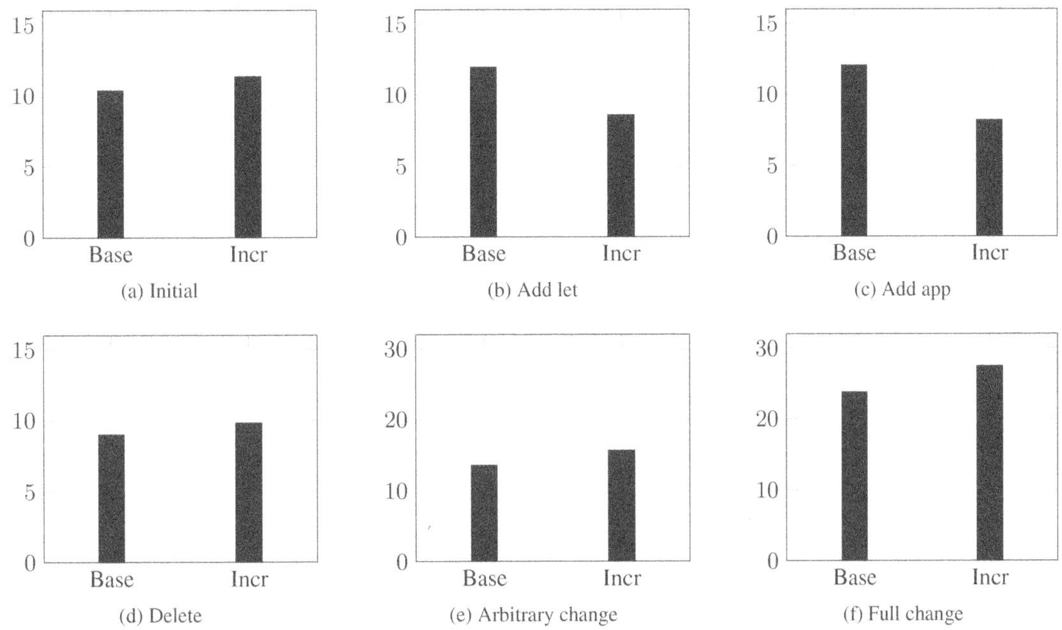

Figure 2. Benchmark results of constraint based type inference

A possible solution for this problem is to rely on Haskell's lazy evaluation mechanism to perform the extra work to achieve incremental speedups at the moment that the incremental step happens, resulting in practically no extra runtime in the first evaluation. In our previous work we found promising results in that direction, but in order to support higher order attributes we need to do more work and evaluate some part of the state in a slightly stricter way.

The reason our current approach does not perform so well on our benchmark is probably because it is too fine-grained. For the type inference example in many nodes only some constraints are gathered, and only in some nodes the constraints are solved. With our incremental evaluation of attributes we check for equality of inherited nodes and propagate the dirty flags for every node, which may take more time than the actual constraint gathering. For our technique to be usable in practice we therefore intend to run the checks only in certain nodes, for example only on nodes where constraints are solved. Although this leads to more actual attribute evaluation, it can be much faster in practice.

Non-observable construction An important limitation of our technique is that it requires knowledge of the construction of the higher order attribute. In particular, when a higher order attribute a is used to construct a new value of a higher order attribute, a path needs to be constructed to indicate in which part of the new AST a ends up. However, because our expressions can be arbitrary Haskell, we can write attribute grammars for which we can not (automatically) find out this information.

In order for our technique to work we therefore require the construction of higher order attributes to be of a restricted form in which only constructors, attribute references, and constants are used. In particular, pattern matching is not allowed as it would highly complicate dependency analysis.

However, in practice there are of course cases where more complicated code is written to construct the higher order tree. Another possibility is to mix observable and non-observable construction of higher order attributes and only get good incremental behaviour when enough attributes can be observed. A concrete example of this could for example be type inference, where the AST describes expressions of the untyped lambda calculus and the result is a term in the typed lambda calculus. In that case, the spine of the result, so the expression itself, can be constructed in an observable way for which incremental behaviour is retained, but the types themselves are considered *black boxes* for which all information is lost after they are reconstructed.

9. Related work

Dynamic dependencies One of the recent developments in incremental computing is that of so-called self-adjusting computation (Chen et al. 2014). In self-adjusting computation all data is labelled with either static or changeable, and special constructs are added to the language in order to handle changeable data in such a way that changes can be efficiently propagated. Based on the types, these special constructs can even be automatically inferred by the compiler.

The important difference to our approach is that in self-adjusting computation all dependencies are gathered dynamically in the first run. While evaluating in the first run a dependency graph is built, and that graph is used in subsequent runs to propagate the changes. Although in essence our technique is doing the same thing, in the attribute grammar world all dependencies are known statically and can therefore be used to generate incremental evaluators that have no runtime dependency tracking overhead.

Function caching Another technique for the incremental evaluation of higher order attribute grammars is to use function caching or memoization (Vogt et al. 1991; Saraiva et al. 2000). Because the subtree and inherited attributes together are used as key for the memoization table, this technique also works for higher order attributes. However, the problem is that such technique requires a global cache which needs to be purged to avoid running out of memory, since otherwise the cache could infinitely grow. However, no purging strategy can perfectly predict future calls to the function, so it can result both in recomputations due to wrong cache items being purged and in cache items that are stored and take up memory but are never used.

In our approach the cache is (implicitly) stored inside the AST, such that the subtree itself is not a parameter of the cache lookup. This does not only make sure that our caches stores exactly the values that are needed, but also can result in faster lookups. In our approach we do however only store one cache item per visit per node, with the immediate previous values, so when a tree is changed to another tree and then is changed back, some recomputation can happen.

Incremental higher order evaluation The work of (Cai et al. 2014) discusses automatically generating incremental evaluators for higher-order languages, by statically constructing derivatives of functions that can handle changes efficiently. However, to get actual incremental speedups the work assumes the existence of certain user-defined change structures that specify for all base-types how changes can be constructed and represented.

Our support for higher order attributes is similar to the construction of derivatives for higher order functions. However, in our case the basic incremental attribute grammar forms the basic change structure, and therefore there is no need for the user to specify any extra information to get incremental speedups. Our work on the other hand only works for the class of attribute grammars, which is of course much more limited than higher order languages in general.

Profiling based caching (Söderberg and Hedin 2011) describe the incremental evaluation of reference attribute grammars based on caching in an imperative setting. However, to improve caching behaviour they use a selective caching mechanism based on profiling, thereby optimising the caching to specific use cases. To avoid cases like our running example where the actual computation time is in some cases smaller than the overhead, such an approach could be viable in our setting too.

10. Conclusion

We have presented a technique for the incremental evaluation of higher order attribute grammars. Our technique is based on earlier work and uses static dependency information to generate efficient evaluators. We have created a toy implementation of our tool and verified that the resulting code is strongly typed and returns correct results. We have measured large runtime speedups on some handcrafted cases indicating that our technique can be effective, but it is future work to evaluate the techniques on a wider scale to find out in which cases attribute grammars can benefit from incremental evaluation.

References

van Binsbergen, L. T., Bransen, J., and Dijkstra, A. (2015). Linearly ordered attribute grammars - with augmenting dependency selection. In *Proceedings of the ACM SIGPLAN 2015 Workshop on Partial Evaluation and Program Manipulation*, PEPM '15, New York, NY, USA. ACM.

Bransen, J., Dijkstra, A., and Swierstra, S. D. (2014). Lazy stateless incremental evaluation machinery for attribute grammars. In *Proceedings of the ACM SIGPLAN 2014 Workshop on Partial Evaluation and Program Manipulation*, PEPM '14, pages 145–156, New York, NY, USA. ACM.

Bransen, J. and Magalhães, J. P. (2013). Generic representations of tree transformations. In *Proceedings of the the 9th ACM SIGPLAN Workshop on Generic Programming (WGP'13)*, WGP '13.

Cai, Y., Giarrusso, P. G., Rendel, T., and Ostermann, K. (2014). A theory of changes for higher-order languages: Incrementalizing λ-calculi by static differentiation. In *Proceedings of the 35th ACM SIGPLAN Conference on Programming Language Design and Implementation*, PLDI '14, pages 145–155, New York, NY, USA. ACM.

Chen, Y., Acar, U. A., and Tangwongsan, K. (2014). Functional programming for dynamic and large data with self-adjusting computation. In *Proceedings of the 19th ACM SIGPLAN International Conference on Functional Programming*, ICFP '14, pages 227–240, New York, NY, USA. ACM.

Cheney, J. and Hinze, R. (2003). First-class phantom types. Technical report, Cornell University.

Claessen, K., Duregård, J., and Pałka, M. (2014). Generating constrained random data with uniform distribution. In Codish, M. and Sumii, E., editors, *Functional and Logic Programming*, volume 8475 of *Lecture Notes in Computer Science*, pages 18–34. Springer International Publishing.

Claessen, K. and Hughes, J. (2000). QuickCheck: a lightweight tool for random testing of Haskell programs. *SIGPLAN Not.*, 35(9):268–279.

Damas, L. and Milner, R. (1982). Principal type-schemes for functional programs. In *Proceedings of the 9th ACM SIGPLAN-SIGACT symposium on Principles of programming languages*, POPL '82, pages 207–212, New York, NY, USA. ACM.

Dijkstra, A., Fokker, J., and Swierstra, S. D. (2009). The architecture of the Utrecht Haskell Compiler. In *Proceedings of the 2nd ACM SIGPLAN symposium on Haskell*, Haskell '09, pages 93–104, New York, NY, USA. ACM.

Engelfriet, J. and Filè, G. (1982). Simple multi-visit attribute grammars. *Journal of computer and system sciences*, 24(3):283–314.

Hedin, G. and Magnusson, E. (2003). Jastadd: An aspect-oriented compiler construction system. *Sci. Comput. Program.*, 47(1):37–58.

Heeren, B., Hage, J., and Swierstra, S. D. (2002). Generalizing Hindley-Milner type inference algorithms. Technical Report UU-CS-2002-031, Department of Information and Computing Sciences, Utrecht University.

Knuth, D. E. (1968). Semantics of context-free languages. *Theory of Computing Systems*, 2(2):127–145.

O'Sullivan, B. (2009). Criterion: Robust, reliable performance measurement and analysis. `http://hackage.haskell.org/package/criterion`.

Peyton Jones, S. L. (2003). *Haskell 98, Language and Libraries. The Revised Report.* Cambridge University Press. Journal of Functional Programming Special Issue 13(1).

Reps, T., Teitelbaum, T., and Demers, A. (1983). Incremental context-dependent analysis for language-based editors. *ACM Trans. Program. Lang. Syst.*, 5:449–477.

Saraiva, J., Swierstra, S. D., and Kuiper, M. F. (2000). Functional incremental attribute evaluation. In *Proceedings of the 9th International Conference on Compiler Construction*, CC '00, pages 279–294, London, UK. Springer-Verlag.

Söderberg, E. and Hedin, G. (2011). Automated selective caching for reference attribute grammars. In Malloy, B., Staab, S., and van den Brand, M., editors, *Software Language Engineering*, volume 6563 of *Lecture Notes in Computer Science*, pages 2–21. Springer Berlin / Heidelberg.

Swierstra, S. D., Alcocer, P. R. A., and Saraiva, J. (1998). Designing and Implementing Combinator Languages. In *Advanced Functional Programming*, pages 150–206.

Van Wyk, E., Bodin, D., Gao, J., and Krishnan, L. (2010). Silver: An extensible attribute grammar system. *Science of Computer Programming*, 75(1–2):39 – 54. Special Issue on ETAPS 2006 and 2007 Workshops on Language Descriptions, Tools, and Applications (LDTA '06 and '07).

Vogt, H. H., Swierstra, S. D., and Kuiper, M. F. (1989). Higher order attribute grammars. In *Proceedings of the ACM SIGPLAN 1989 Conference on Programming language design and implementation*, volume 24 of *PLDI '89*, pages 131–145, New York, NY, USA. ACM.

Vogt, H. H., Swierstra, S. D., and Kuiper, M. F. (1991). Efficient incremental evaluation of higher order attribute grammars. In *PLILP*, pages 231–242.

Xi, H., Chen, C., and Chen, G. (2003). Guarded recursive datatype constructors. In *Proceedings of the 30th ACM SIGPLAN-SIGACT Symposium on Principles of Programming Languages*, POPL '03, pages 224–235, New York, NY, USA. ACM.

Linearly Ordered Attribute Grammars

with Automatic Augmenting Dependency Selection

L. Thomas van Binsbergen
Royal Holloway, University of London
ltvanbinsbergen@acm.org

Jeroen Bransen
Utrecht University
j.bransen@uu.nl

Atze Dijkstra
Utrecht University
atze@uu.nl

Abstract

Attribute Grammars (AGs) extend Context-Free Grammars with attributes: information gathered on the syntax tree that adds semantics to the syntax. AGs are very well suited for describing static analyses, code-generation and other phases incorporated in a compiler.

AGs are divided into classes based on the nature of the dependencies between the attributes. In this paper we examine the class of Linearly Ordered Attribute Grammars (LOAGs), for which strict, bounded size evaluators can be generated. Deciding whether an Attribute Grammar is linearly ordered is an NP-hard problem. The Ordered Attribute Grammars form a subclass of LOAG for which membership is tested in polynomial time by Kastens' algorithm (1980). On top of this algorithm we apply an augmenting dependency selection algorithm, allowing it to determine membership for the class LOAG. Although the worst-case complexity of our algorithm is exponential, the algorithm turns out to be efficient for practical full-sized AGs. As a result, we can compile the main AG of the Utrecht Haskell Compiler without the manual addition of augmenting dependencies.

The reader is provided with insight in the difficulty of deciding whether an AG is linearly ordered, what optimistic choice is made by Kastens' algorithm and how augmenting dependencies can resolve these difficulties.

Categories and Subject Descriptors D.3.1 [*Programming Languages*]: semantics; D.3.4 [*Programming Languages*]: compilers, code generation; F.3.1 [*Logics and meanings of programs*]: mechanical verification

Keywords attribute grammars; ordered attribute grammars; linearly ordered attribute grammars; Kastens' algorithm; augmenting dependencies; compilers; semantics; Utrecht Haskell Compiler

1. Introduction

Attribute Grammars (AGs) extend Context-Free Grammars (CFGs) with attributes at each non-terminal [11]. Attribute definitions describe computations, in terms of other attributes and terminal symbols, that gather information on (parts of) the abstract syntax tree associated with the grammar. These computations are useful to perform different kinds of static analyses and code-generation. Besides being suitable for implementing compilers, programming with AGs provides some general advantages [6]:

- AGs can be seen as a domain-specific language for tree-based computations.
- AGs relieve the programmer of the task of efficiently combining multiple computations on the same tree[1].
- Descriptions of separate computations are easily divided into coherent code-fragments, increasing the maintainability and reusability of the source code.
- Most of the trivial pieces of code can be generated, allowing the programmer to focus on exactly those pieces that require creativity and expertise.
- AGs enable declarative programming in imperative settings.

Among other tools and compilers, the Utrecht University Attribute Grammar Compiler (UUAGC)[2] and the Utrecht Haskell Compiler (UHC)[3] have been largely implemented using AGs. In both cases, the UUAGC is used to compile the AGs, generating Haskell code as output.

The UUAGC generates folds and algebras for executing the semantics of an AG from its description (source text) [16]. In case the attribute definitions are cyclic, the UUAGC relies on Haskell's lazy evaluation to remain executable, potentially leading to loops at runtime. The UUAGC can also generate *strict evaluators* for AGs that are non-circular [3, 10]. For some non-circular AGs we can determine an evaluation order statically. AGs for which this is possible form the class of *Linearly Ordered Attribute Grammars* (LOAGs). The approach of finding a static evaluation order has been introduced by Kastens in 1980 [8]. It allows the generation of evaluators that are strict, efficient and require little memory. These properties are desirable especially for large scale projects such as the UHC. However, finding a linear order for the attributes of an AG is an NP-complete problem [7].

The polynomial runtime algorithm given by Kastens orders only a subset of the LOAGs, making some optimistic choices. These choices are guided by the *dependencies* between attributes. LOAGs of considerable size are likely to contain combinations of dependencies that prevent Kastens' algorithm from finding an evaluation order. The main AG in the UHC is an example of such an AG. *Augmenting dependencies* can be used to help Kastens' algorithm

PEPM '15, January 13–14, 2015, Mumbai, India.

ACM 978-1-4503-3297-2/15/01...$15.00.
http://dx.doi.org/10.1145/2678015.2682543

[1] A computation can be efficient in multiple regards, e.g. time and space complexity. This topic is briefly discussed in the future work section of this paper.

[2] http://www.cs.uu.nl/wiki/HUT/AttributeGrammarManual

[3] http://www.cs.uu.nl/wiki/UHC

finding the order. This approach was successfully employed in the development of the UHC and in other large AG projects found in literature [12, 14]. Finding the right combination of augmenting dependencies is not only tedious work, it also demands insight in the produced evaluation order, where knowledge on this matter is otherwise unnecessary. This paper deals with this problem, making the following contributions:

- We explain the required constructions for ordering LOAGs.
- We show why Kastens' algorithm is only suitable for a subset of LOAG.
- We show how augmenting dependencies can be found automatically.
- We present an algorithm capable of ordering all LOAGs by selecting augmenting dependencies automatically with a backtracking strategy. Although the algorithm is exponential in theory, we argue that backtracking is rare for practical AGs.

Section 2 introduces the running example of this paper and introduces AGs informally. A formal definition of AGs is given in Section 3. LOAGs are defined and examined in Section 4. In Section 5 we show why Kastens' algorithm can not find a static evaluation order for all LOAGs. Section 6 explains how augmenting dependencies are selected automatically. The most important Haskell functions of our algorithm for ordering all LOAGs with automatic augmenting dependency selection are given in Section 7.

2. Running Example

We introduce Attribute Grammars informally using a running example. Every AG consists of three constructs that we introduce one at a time: abstract syntax, attributes and semantic functions.

As a running example we consider a simplistic module system IMODULE that declares modules similarly to Haskell. Each module consists of a header and a body. The header declares the functions that constitute the interface of the module, identifying which functions the module exports. The function declarations in the header are written as type signatures. The body of the module contains the required function definitions, datatype definitions and optional unexported helper definitions. Figure 1 gives an example.

```
module BinIntTrees
  flatten :: Tree → [Int]
where
  data Tree = Bin Tree Tree
            | Leaf Int
  flatten (Leaf i)  = [i]
  flatten (Bin l r) = flatten l ++ flatten r
```

Figure 1. A simple module defined with IMODULE.

The goal of the running example is to verify that the module's body implements the interface of the module, while gathering the exported definitions. Additionally, we wish to verify that all the type signatures and datatype definitions rely only on types that are available to them. Attribute Grammars are used to define the abstract syntax of this system, gather the exported definitions and perform the static analyses for determining whether the module is valid.

2.1 Abstract Syntax

In the pipeline common to most compilers (parsing → validating → generating) AGs are typically used in the second and third phase. The *abstract syntax tree*, of which instances are generated by a parser in the form of *parse trees*, forms the basis of an AG description. The abstract syntax of a language is a context-free grammar describing the syntax without literals or keywords as terminal symbols. For example, the concrete syntax displayed in Figure 1 contains keywords **module**, **where** and **data** that are irrelevant to the *semantics* of the language. In Figure 2 a description of the abstract syntax of IMODULE is given in notation accepted by the UUAGC[4]. The constructor functions of a datatype (non-terminal Dat) are represented by a list of types for every constructor. We allow ourselves to simplify the representation of datatypes because a precise representation would not add to the purpose of the example.

```
data Module | Module h  : [TySig] b    : Body
data Body   | Body   ds : [Dat]   fs   : [Fun]
data TySig  | TySig  id : FunId   ty   : [TyId]
data Dat    | Dat    id : TyId    cons : [[TyId]]
data Fun    | Fun    id : FunId   def  : FunDef
```

Figure 2. Description of the abstract syntax of IMODULE.

The abstract syntax consists of non-terminals Module, Body, TySig, Dat and Fun, each with a single, equally named production. Each production has a set of child nodes that are either terminal (e.g. *TyId*) or non-terminal. Non-terminal Module has two children, the module's header and its body, identified by h and b respectively. We say that h and b are *non-terminal occurrences* of type [TySig] and Body respectively. In a parse tree every node is an *instance* of one of the non-terminals and is *derived* by one of the production rules of that non-terminal. Declarations for lists of non-terminals, e.g. [TySig], are missing. The required non-terminals and productions for lists are generated by the UUAGC and shown in Figure 3.

```
data [TySig] | Nil
             | Cons hd : TySig tl : [TySig]
data [Fun]   | Nil
             | Cons hd : Fun   tl : [Fun]
data [Dat]   | Nil
             | Cons hd : Dat   tl : [Dat]
```

Figure 3. Generated abstract syntax of IMODULE.

2.2 Attributes

The next step is to add *attributes* to the grammar. Attributes are associated with non-terminals and defined at production level. For every attribute a of non-terminal X there is one *attribute occurrence* at every occurrence of X. Similarly, we speak of *attribute instances* at the level of parse trees.

Synthesized attributes (top-down) are used to gather information and can be viewed as results of computations. *Inherited* attributes (bottom-up) are used to share information and can be viewed as parameters of a computation. Figure 4 shows the attribute declarations we use for IMODULE.

An attribute is not uniquely identified by its name. Instead, it is identified by the combination of a non-terminal, a name and a direction (inh or syn), e.g. Module.$err(syn)$. In the same way, an attribute occurrence is identified by the combination of a production, a node, a name and a direction, e.g. *Module*.b.$err(syn)$.

[4] The UUAGC uses datatypes and constructors to define abstract syntax. Throughout this paper we use formal language terminology and speak of non-terminals and production rules instead.

```
                      -- Types from other modules
attr Module inh ts   : [TyId]
                      -- The exported function definitions
            syn ex   : [(FunId, FunDef)]
                      -- Whether the module is invalid
            syn err : Bool
                      -- All types defined by the module
            syn ts   : [TyId]

                      -- Functions declared in the header
attr Body   inh ss   : [FunId]
                      -- Types from other modules
            inh ts   : [TyId]
                      -- The exported function definitions
            syn ex   : [(FunId, FunDef)]
                      -- Whether the body is invalid
            syn err : Bool
                      -- All types defined by the module
            syn ts   : [TyId]
attr [TySig] TySig   -- Declaration for two non-terminals
            inh ts   : [TyId]
            syn ss   : [FunId]
            syn err : Bool
attr [Dat] Dat
            inh ts   : [TyId]
            syn ts   : [TyId]
            syn err : Bool
attr [Fun] Fun
            inh ss   : [FunId]
            syn ex   : [(FunId, FunDef)]
```

Figure 4. Attribute declarations for IMODULE.

2.3 Semantic functions

With the attributes in place, it is now possible to define the semantics of IMODULE. *Semantic function definitions* describe for every attribute occurrence how it is computed in terms of other attribute occurrences and terminal symbols.

The flow of information from attribute to attribute is shown in graphs. In the *dependency graphs* we use throughout this paper, an arrow $a \rightarrow b$ implies that a is used to calculate b and thus that b depends on a. In other words, our graphs are actually data flow graphs rather than dependency graphs, but the latter can be obtained by reversing all edges so we speak about dependency graphs in the rest of this paper.

Figures 8 and 9 show dependency graphs for productions ***Module*** and ***Body***. The parent node of a production, identified by lhs, is positioned above its children. Each non-terminal occurrence is connected with its attribute occurrences: synthesized attributes at its right and inherited attributes at its left.

There are two types of dependencies: dependencies that appear between parent and child nodes (black) and the dependencies that appear above parent nodes or below child nodes (gray). The black dependencies are *direct dependencies*, extracted directly from the semantic functions. The gray dependencies are *induced dependencies*, i.e. dependencies between *those* attributes at some *other* production. The productions that induce the dependencies between occurrences of children h, ds, and fs are not shown.

2.3.1 Semantics

This section explains how the attributes are used to describe the semantics of IMODULE on a high-level. The explanation follows the order shown in Figure 5.

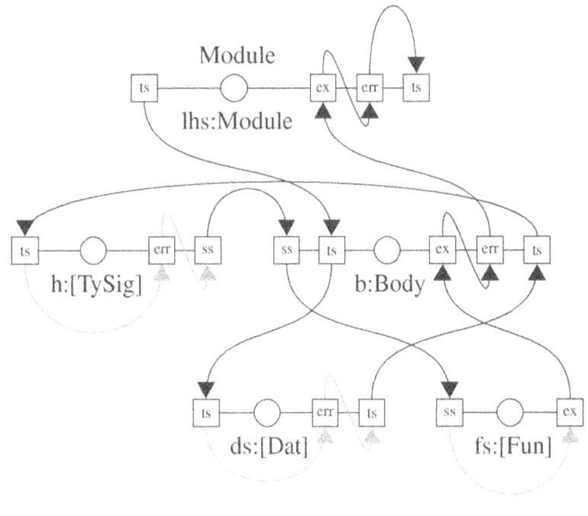

Figure 5. A linear order for evaluating the attributes of IMODULE. The order is not complete, the gray arrows represent parts that have not been fully specified. Note that this graph is not a dependency graph.

Recall that our goals are verifying that only available types are used, verifying that the module's body implements the interface and gathering the definitions of the exported functions.

First we verify that all the type signatures and datatype definitions use only available types. Types are made available by other modules ($\texttt{lhs}.ts(inh) \rightarrow \texttt{b}.ts(inh)$), e.g. Int from Prelude, or through datatype definitions in the module's body ($\texttt{b}.ts(syn)$). Child ds in ***Body*** uses the types arriving from other modules to verify whether its datatype declarations use only available types ($\texttt{ds}.ts(inh) \rightarrow \texttt{ds}.err(syn)$) and appends the newly constructed types to the received set, passing the new set upwards ($\texttt{ds}.ts(syn) \rightarrow \texttt{b}.ts(syn)$). The new set of types is presented to the module's header ($\texttt{b}.ts(syn) \rightarrow \texttt{h}.ts(inh)$), enabling the header to verify whether its type signatures are valid ($\texttt{h}.ts(inh) \rightarrow \texttt{h}.err(syn)$).

Secondly, we construct the list of exported definitions and test whether this list is complete. The signatures produced by the header are passed downwards into the body of the module ($\texttt{h}.ss(syn) \rightarrow \texttt{b}.ss(inh)$). ***Body***'s child `fs` (function definitions) uses the signatures arriving from the header to produce a list of exports ($\texttt{fs}.ss(inh) \rightarrow \texttt{fs}.ex(syn)$), by returning only the definitions that are required according to the module's interface. The exports are passed upwards to the module declaration ($\texttt{fs}.ex(syn) \rightarrow \texttt{b}.ex(syn)$). The exported function definitions ($\texttt{lhs}.ex$) and exported types ($\texttt{lhs}.ts$) are directly copied from the body. The module reports an error ($\texttt{lhs}.err$) when the lists of exports is incomplete ($\texttt{b}.ex(syn)$ is compared with $\texttt{h}.ss(syn)$) or when b or h report an error.

2.3.2 Definitions

Dependency graphs are useful as visual aids. It might therefore be a design choice to draw these graphs before giving the actual AG description. To fully describe an AG, every dependency needs to be reflected in some semantic function definition. Some dependencies represent the flow of information from one attribute to another without modification (e.g. ***Body***.$\texttt{lhs}.ts(inh) \rightarrow$ ***Body***.$\texttt{ds}.ts(inh)$ and ***Module***.$\texttt{b}.ex(syn) \rightarrow$ ***Module***.$\texttt{lhs}.ex(syn)$). The semantic function definitions for such dependencies can be generated by the UUAGC based on the attribute's name and direction.

The semantic function definitions for the attributes of non-terminal lists are also generated by the UUAGC. For example, the equation for [Dat].lhs.$ts(syn)$, of type $[\mathit{TyId}]$, is generated using (++) to combine results from individual Dat-elements with [] as a base element (corresponding to Haskell's monoid instance for lists). The UUAGC allows the user to specify which union function and which base element to use for an attribute. The generated semantic function definitions are shown in Figure 7. Figure 6 appends the manual semantic function definitions to IMODULE. Occurrences of attributes and terminals are referenced using the @-symbol in the right-hand side of the equations.

```
sem Module | Module
  lhs.err = ¬ (all (∈ (map fst @b.ex)) @h.ss)
               ∨ @h.err ∨ @b.err
  h.ts    = @b.ts
  b.ss    = @h.ss
sem TySig | TySig
  lhs.ss  = [@id]
  lhs.err = ¬ (all (∈ @lhs.ts) @ty)
sem Dat | Dat
  lhs.ts  = @id : @lhs.ts
  lhs.err = ¬ (all (all (∈ @lhs.ts)) @cons)
sem [Dat] | Cons
  lhs.ts  = @tl.ts
  tl.ts   = @hd.ts
sem Fun | Fun
  lhs.ex  = if (@id ∈ @lhs.ss)
              then [(@id, @def)]
              else []
```

Figure 6. The manual semantic function definitions for the semantics of IMODULE.

2.3.3 Reflection

We have described semantics, useful in the second phase of a compiler for IMODULE, in a small number of simple steps. The AG computing the semantics of our system is orderable, while Kastens' algorithm is not able to recognise it as such, as we shall see in Section 5. Section 6 explains the use of augmenting dependencies and shows which augmenting dependency successfully hints at the order proposed in Figure 5 and how the augmenting dependency is found.

3. Attribute Grammars

This section formalises AGs and other concepts required in subsequent sections.

Definition 1. *An* Attribute Grammar *(AG) is a triple* $\langle G, A, E\rangle$, *where* $G = \langle V = \Sigma \cup N, P, S\rangle$ *is a context-free grammar.* V *is partitioned into a set of terminal symbols* Σ *and a set of non-terminal symbols* N. P *is a non-empty set of* productions, *with* $p \in P$ *of the form* $p : X_{p,0} \rightarrow \alpha_1 X_{p,1}, \alpha_2 X_{p,2}, \ldots, \alpha_{|p|} X_{p,|p|} \alpha_{|p|+1}$, *with* $\alpha_i \in \Sigma^*$ *and* non-terminal occurrences $X_{p,i}$. *A non-terminal occurrence* $X_{p,i}$ *is an occurrence of non-terminal* $X \in N$ *iff* $\mathcal{T}(X_{p,i}) = X$. $S \in N$ *is the start symbol of the grammar.* A *is a set of* attributes $(X \cdot a)$, *with* $X \in N$ *and* a *an* attribute identifier. A *is divided into sets of inherited and synthesized attributes for every* $X \in N$, *i.e.* $A_{inh}(X)$ *and* $A_{syn}(X)$ *respectively.* $(X \cdot a)$ *denotes that the attribute identified by* a *is associated with non-terminal* X. E *is the set of* semantic function definitions, *with* $(X_{p,i} \cdot a, \lambda) \in E$ *denoting that* λ *is the definition for the* attribute occurrence $(X_{p,i} \cdot a)$.

```
sem Module  | Module b.ts   = @lhs.ts
                     lhs.ts = @b.ts
                     lhs.ex = @b.ex
sem Body    | Body   ds.ts  = @lhs.ts
                     fs.ss  = @lhs.ss
                     lhs.ex = @fs.ex
                     lhs.ts = @ds.ts
                     lhs.err = @ds.err
sem [TySig] | Nil    lhs.err = False
                     lhs.ss = []
            | Cons   lhs.err = @hd.err ∨ @tl.err
                     lhs.ss = @hd.ss ++ @tl.ss
                     hd.ts  = @lhs.ts
                     tl.ts  = @lhs.ts
sem [Dat]   | Nil    lhs.err = False
                     lhs.ts = @lhs.ts
            | Cons   lhs.err = @hd.err ∨ @tl.err
                     hd.ts  = @lhs.ts
sem [Fun]   | Nil    lhs.ex = []
            | Cons   lhs.ex = @hd.ex ++ @tl.ex
                     hd.ss  = @lhs.ss
                     tl.ss  = @lhs.ss
```

Figure 7. The generated semantic function definitions for the semantics of IMODULE.

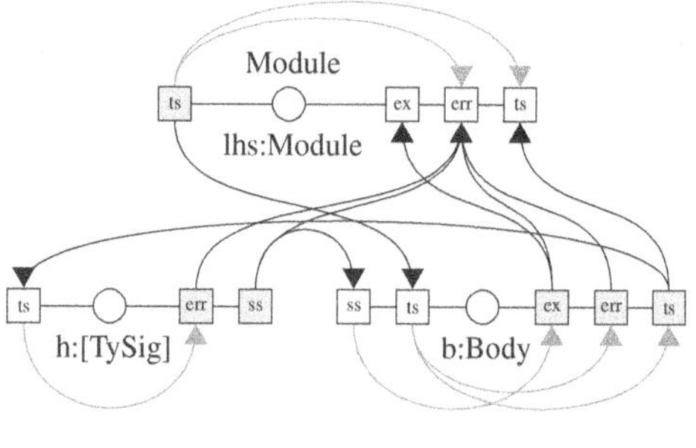

Figure 8. Induced dependency graph for production *Module*. Direct dependencies are black, induced dependencies are gray.

3.1 Input and output dependencies

The attribute occurrences of production $p \in P$ are divided into *input* and *output* occurrences. The input occurrences of p, denoted with $O_{inp}(p)$, are the occurrences made *available* to p by the context of p. Output occurrences of p, denoted with $O_{out}(p)$, are the occurrences that the semantic functions of p *deliver* to the context of p [13, 15].

$$O_{inp}(p) = \{\, X_{p,0} \cdot a \mid (X \cdot a) \in A_{inh}(\mathcal{T}(X_{p,0})) \,\} \cup \{\, X_{p,i} \cdot a \mid i > 0,\ (X \cdot a) \in A_{syn}(\mathcal{T}(X_{p,i})) \,\} \quad (1)$$

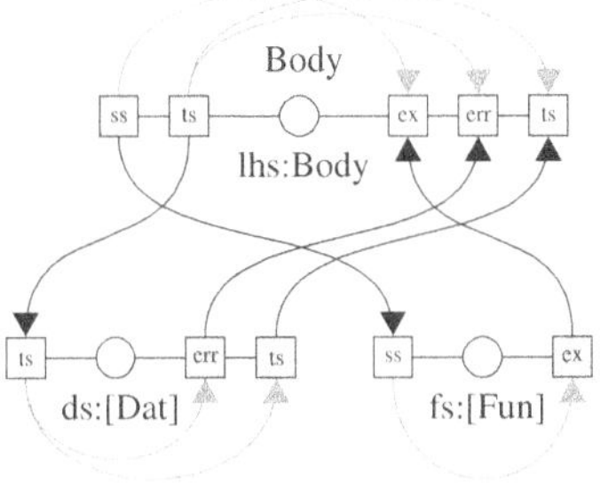

Figure 9. Induced dependency graph for production *Body*. Direct dependencies are black, induced dependencies are gray.

$$O_{out}(p) = \{\ X_{p,0} \cdot a \mid (X \cdot a) \in A_{syn}(\mathcal{T}(X_{p,0}))\ \} \cup \{\ X_{p,i} \cdot a \mid i > 0,\ (X \cdot a) \in A_{inh}(\mathcal{T}(X_{p,i}))\ \} \tag{2}$$

The dependency graphs in this paper show input occurrences with gray backgrounds and output occurrences with white backgrounds.

In this paper we consider AGs that are *normalised*: only input occurrences of a production can be used in the right-hand side of semantic function definitions for that production and only output occurrences of a production are considered to have semantic function definitions. The class of AGs we consider is therefore a subset of the class of AGs written in Bochmann Normal Form as only the first of the two restrictions is used to define this class [2].

3.2 Direct dependencies

From the semantic functions we extract the *direct dependencies*. We define the set $SF_P(b)$ to be the occurrences referenced in the right-hand side of the semantic function of b. Using SF_P we formalise the *direct dependency graph* of production p:

$$\begin{aligned} D_P(p) = \{\ & (X_{p,i} \cdot a \to X_{p,j} \cdot b) \\ \mid\ & (X_{p,j} \cdot b \in O_{out}(p)) \\ ,\ & (X_{p,i} \cdot a \in SF_P(X_{p,j} \cdot b))\ \} \end{aligned} \tag{3}$$

4. Linearly Ordered Attribute Grammars

We are interested in finding an evaluation order of an AG's attributes statically, as the order can be used to generate simple and efficient evaluators. The Linearly Ordered Attribute Grammars form the largest class of AGs for which this is possible [7, 15].

Definition 2. *An AG* $= \langle G, A, D \rangle$, *with context-free grammar* $G = \langle \Sigma \cup N, P, S \rangle$, *is a* Linearly Ordered Attribute Grammar *or* LOAG, *if there exist linear orders* $LO(p)$ *for all* $p \in P$ *such that:*

- *Every linear order* $LO(p)$ *respects the direct dependencies, i.e. if* $(X_{p,i} \cdot a \to X_{p,j} \cdot b) \in D_P(p)$ *then* $(X_{p,i} \cdot a < X_{p,j} \cdot b) \in LO(p)$.
- *The relative ordering of the attributes is the same for all occurrences of a non-terminal, i.e. if* $(X_{p,i} \cdot a < X_{p,i} \cdot b) \in LO(p)$ *then* $(X_{q,j} \cdot a < X_{q,j} \cdot b) \in LO(q)$ *for all p, q, i and j with* $\mathcal{T}(X_{p,i}) = \mathcal{T}(X_{q,j})$.

From the linear orders on productions we can obtain a linear order $LO(\delta)$ for any valid parse tree δ of the input AG. A strict evaluator can be generated that evaluates all attribute instances of δ in the order specified by $LO(\delta)$. Since we are interested in finding the linear order statically we can only argue about non-terminals, attributes, productions and attribute occurrences.

LOAGs have been a popular subject in AG literature, although defined slightly differently in several instances [1, 7, 13, 15]. The subclass OAG, for which Kastens' algorithm can generate evaluators in polynomial runtime, has been more popular in practical implementations due to the complexity of generating evaluators for LOAGs. This paper shows that LOAGs are useful in practice too, by giving an algorithm that is efficient for practical LOAGs. The definition of LOAGs given here supports this purpose and allows simple comparison with Kastens' OAG.

4.1 LOAG preconditions

A linear order that respects all direct dependencies can only exist if there are no dependency cycles. An acyclic direct dependency graph is a precondition for LOAGs.

Every parse tree is the product of 'gluing' multiple production rules together [11]. We therefore also have to test for any dependency cycles produced by 'gluing' productions together. For that purpose we introduce the notion of an *induced dependency graph*. An acyclic induced dependency graph is a second precondition for LOAGs.

4.2 Induced dependencies

If there is a path between two attribute occurrences $(X_{p,i} \cdot a)$ and $(X_{p,i} \cdot b)$ then there has to be a dependency $(X_{q,j} \cdot a \to X_{q,j} \cdot b)$, for all $X_{q,j}$ with $\mathcal{T}(X_{q,j}) = \mathcal{T}(X_{p,i})$, in order to take all possible ways in which production rules can be 'glued' together into account. We have to be pessimistic and consider all such *induced dependencies*.

Adding induced dependencies might result in new paths between two attributes of a non-terminal occurrence and hence to more induced dependencies. See Figure 10 for an example of how induced dependencies are propagated.

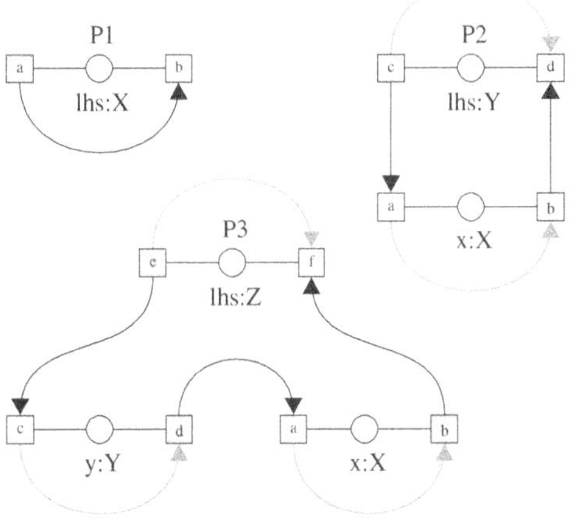

Figure 10. Dependency $(a \to b)$ in P1 induces a dependency $(a \to b)$ in P2 and P3, which causes a path from c to d in P2 and thus an induced dependency $(c \to d)$ in P2 and P3. The new path from e to f in P3 induces a dependency $(e \to f)$ in P3.

In any induced dependency graph all the occurrences of the same non-terminal (e.g. `Body` in productions ***Module*** and ***Body*** of Figures 8 and 9) display the same dependencies between its attributes. These shared dependencies are collected at non-terminal level in the graph ID_S (left-hand side of Figure 17)[5]. To recognise paths of dependencies we use ID_P^+, the transitive closure of ID_P.

[5] Kastens introduces ID_S as the induced dependency graph for symbols (hence the S), although only non-terminal symbols have attributes.

$$IDP(p) = DP(p) \cup \{ (X_{p,i} \cdot a \rightarrow X_{p,i} \cdot b) \mid q \in P , (X_{q,j} \cdot a \rightarrow X_{q,j} \cdot b) \in ID_P^{+}(q) , (\mathcal{T}(X_{p,i}) = \mathcal{T}(X_{q,j})) \} \quad (4)$$

$$IDS(X) = \{ (X \cdot a \rightarrow X \cdot b) \mid p \in P, (X_{p,i} \cdot a \rightarrow X_{p,i} \cdot b) \in IDP(p), X = \mathcal{T}(X_{p,i}) \} \quad (5)$$

4.3 Interfaces and visit-sequences

To find a linear order on attribute instances of any parse tree, we first determine in which order the generated evaluator will examine the nodes of any parse tree. We do so by deciding for every non-terminal which *visits* are made to it and in which order. Every visit is a pair of inherited and synthesized attributes that can be seen as a function that receives the inherited attributes as parameters and returns the synthesized attributes as a result.

Definition 3. *An* interface $I_f(X)$ *for non-terminal* X *is a sequence of* n *visits, i.e.* $I_f(X) = (v_i)_{i=1}^{n}$, *where every visit* v_i *is a pair* (I_i, S_i), *with* $I_i \subseteq A_{inh}(X)$ *and* $S_i \subseteq A_{syn}(X)$. *The interface must be complete and the visits disjoint:*

$$\bigcup_{(I_i,S_i)\in I_f(X)} I_i = A_{inh}(X) \qquad \bigcup_{(I_i,S_i)\in I_f(x)} S_i = A_{syn}(X) \quad (6)$$

$$\forall((I_i,S_i) \in I_f(X), (I_j,S_j) \in I_f(X), i \neq j)\ (I_i \cap I_j = \emptyset)$$
$$\forall((I_i,S_i) \in I_f(X), (I_j,S_j) \in I_f(X), i \neq j)\ (S_i \cap S_j = \emptyset) \quad (7)$$

Reflecting on Figure 5 we see that all nodes are visited once by the linear order we proposed, except node b of type Body which is visited twice. The first visit to b is $(\{ts\}, \{ts\})$ and the second is $(\{ss\}, \{ex, err\})$. These visits make up the interface for non-terminal Body shown in Figure 11.

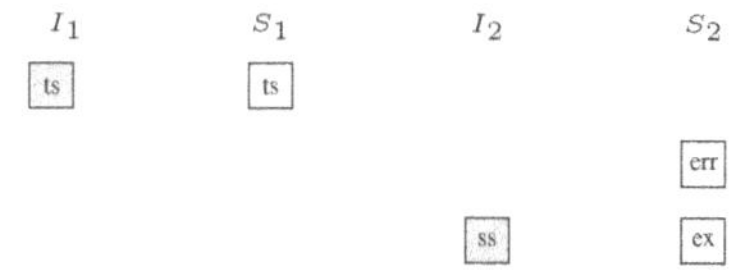

Figure 11. A possible interface for non-terminal Body.

Visits are connected by *visit-sequences*. For every non-terminal X and for every visit $v_i \in I_f(X)$, we show how every production of X *implements* visit v_i with a visit-sequence. A visit-sequence is a sequence of eval- and visit-instructions. The generated evaluator executes these instructions in the order specified by the visit-sequence. Every eval-instruction is associated with an attribute occurrence and tells the evaluator to execute the semantic function definition of that attribute occurrence. Every visit-instruction is associated with a non-terminal occurrence K and a visit number i, and tells the evaluator to execute the visit-sequences implementing the i-th visit to K. For every visit-sequence s in a valid set of visit-sequences - with s implementing visit $v_i = (I_i, S_i)$ to an occurrence K of non-terminal X, derived by production p - the following conditions must hold:

1. Before s is executed, every j-th visit to K, with $j < i$, must be executed.
2. Before s is executed, every occurrence of attributes I_i at K must be evaluated.
3. Every occurrence of attributes S_i at the parent of p must be evaluated in s.
4. If occurrence b, depending on a, is evaluated in s:
   (a) Then a must be evaluated in s before b,
   (b) or there must be a visit-instruction in s, before b is evaluated, of which the corresponding visit-sequence evaluates a.

Figures 12 and 13 show visit-sequences for productions ***Module*** and ***Body*** that encode the linear order proposed in Figure 5. The first three conditions on a valid set of visit-sequences can easily be checked using these figures:

1. There is no visit-sequence in which there is a **visit** 2 before a **visit** 1.
2. Every **visit** is preceded by the evaluation of the inherited attributes of that visit (the parameters of that computation).
3. Every visit-sequence evaluates the synthesized attributes of the implemented visit (the results of that computation).

1 : **eval** b.*ts*
2 : **visit** 1 b
3 : **eval** h.*ts*
4 : **visit** 1 h
5 : **eval** b.*ss*
6 : **visit** 2 b
7 : **eval** lhs.*ex*
8 : **eval** lhs.*err*
9 : **eval** lhs.*ts*

Figure 12. A visit-sequence for the production ***Module*** of non-terminal Module that implements visit $(\{ts\}, \{ex, err, ts\})$.

1 : **eval** ds.*ts*
2 : **visit** 1 ds
3 : **eval** lhs.*ts*

1 : **eval** fs.*ss*
2 : **visit** 1 fs
3 : **eval** lhs.*ex*
4 : **eval** lhs.*err*

Figure 13. Two visit-sequences for production ***Body*** of non-terminal Body separated by a line break. The top visit-sequence implements visit $(\{ts\}, \{ts\})$ and the bottom visit-sequence implements visit $(\{ss\}, \{ex, err\})$.

The fourth condition can be checked by looking at the individual linear orders that the visit-sequences encode: no dependency in the induced dependency graphs given in Figures 8 and 9 is contradicted by the linear orders shown in Figures 14 and 15.

Similarly to the way production rules are 'glued' together to form a valid parse tree δ of the input grammar, the linear orders encoded by visit-sequences can be 'glued' together to form a linear order on δ [13]. Such 'gluing' is only possible if all visit-sequences rely on the same set of interfaces, one for every non-terminal. This explains the need for constructing interfaces and the second requirement of Definition 2. Figure 16 shows how the orders of Figures 12 and 13 are 'glued' together. The result is the same order as the one shown in Figure 5.

We can now describe a high-level algorithm for LOAGs:

- Test the two preconditions for LOAGs.
- Only if they hold:

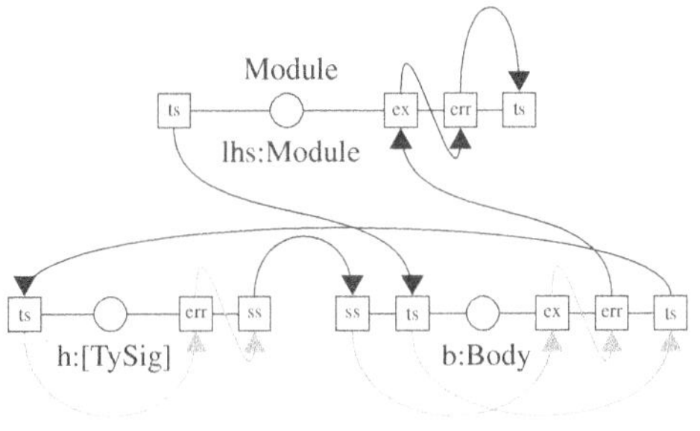

Figure 14. The linear order encoded by the visit-sequence of Figure 12. The gray arrows represent the linear orders of other visit-sequences.

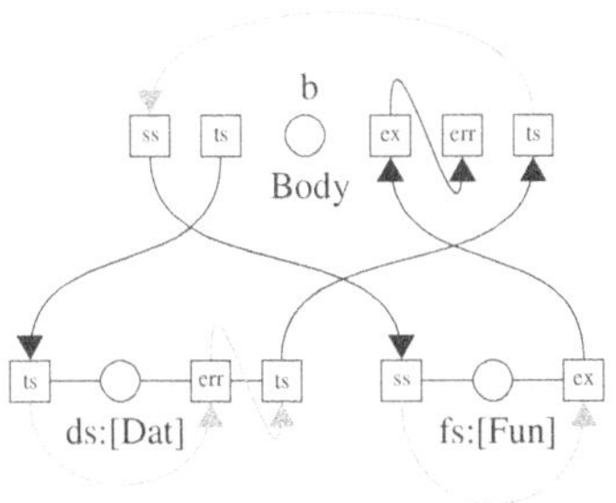

Figure 15. The linear order encoded by the visit-sequences of Figure 13. The gray arrows represent the linear orders of other visit-sequences.

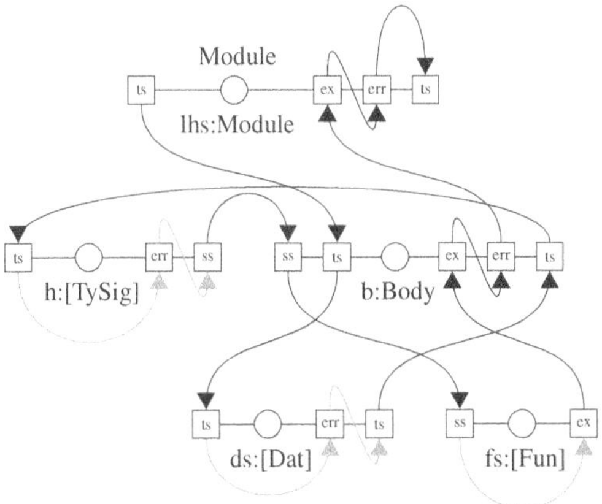

Figure 16. Linear orders encoded by visit-sequences can be 'glued' together if the visit-sequences adhere the same interfaces for their shared non-terminals. Note that the gray arrows around node `b` of type `Body` in Figures 14 and 15 have been replaced by paths.

- Use graph IDs to find interfaces for all non-terminals.
- Use the interfaces and graph ID_P to implement all visits of the interfaces using visit-sequences.

Kastens' algorithm is an implementation of this high-level algorithm. The next section shows how Kastens' algorithm finds the interfaces and why this method does not suffice for all LOAGs.

5. Kastens' algorithm

In his 1980 paper, Kastens presents a polynomial algorithm for deciding whether an AG is an *Ordered Attribute Grammar* (OAG), a subclass of LOAG [8]. OAG is a proper subclass of LOAG[6], hence every OAG is an LOAG but there exist LOAGs that are not an OAG [3, 12].

5.1 Constructing interfaces

Kastens' algorithm constructs $I_f(X)$ from $ID_S(X)$ by partitioning the attributes of X in disjoint sets P_i, with $i \geqslant 1$, as follows:

- Assign all synthesized attributes that have no outgoing dependencies to P_1.
- Assign all inherited attributes that have no outgoing dependencies to P_2.
- Assign all synthesized attributes a to the set P_i if i is odd, all the inherited attributes that depend on a are assigned to P_j with $j < i$ and all synthesized attributes that depend on a are assigned to P_k with $k \leqslant i$.
- Assign all inherited attributes a to the set P_i if i is even, all the synthesized attributes that depend on a are assigned to P_j with $j < i$ and all inherited attributes that depend on a are assigned to P_k with $k \leqslant i$.

Note that the set partitioning constructed by the above procedure is almost of the same shape as our interfaces, except that we pair P_i with P_{i-1} to form a visit (if i is even) and our indices are ascending with respect to the dependencies: if attributes a and b are in different visits and $(a \rightarrow b) \in ID_S$ then a is assigned to a visit with lower index then b.

Interfaces are thus constructed from the partitioning as follows: If m is the highest even index with $P_m \cup P_{m-1} \neq \emptyset$, then $v = m/2$ is the number of visits in $I_f(X)$. $I_f(X)$ is formed by saying (P_m, P_{m-1}) is the first visit, (P_{m-2}, P_{m-3}) is the second visit, up until the v-th visit (P_2, P_1).

Figure 17 shows the interfaces calculated by Kastens' algorithm for non-terminals `[TySig]` and `Body` of IMODULE. The right-hand side of the figure shows the first (and only) visit (I_1, S_1) of the interfaces for both non-terminals. The induced dependencies from ID_S have been added to the picture (solid gray). It shows that ID_S can be split into connected components that we call *threads* (T_1 and T_2).

Interfaces must satisfy the requirement that the induced dependencies do not point 'in the wrong direction' (westwards in our figures). Interfaces that do not satisfy this requirement do not allow visit-sequences that satisfy condition 4 of the conditions on visit-sequences (Section 4.3).

Kastens' method for creating interfaces ensures that no dependency points westwards; however, there is still freedom in splitting visits and moving attributes across visits in the interface. For example, the attributes of T_2 are assigned to the same visit as the attributes of T_1, although the induced dependencies do not enforce this. If we split the visit of non-terminal `Body` such that the attributes `Body`.$ts(inh)$ and `Body`.$ts(syn)$ are in an earlier visit, we would get another interface (the one from Figure 11), in which no induced dependency will point westward as well. As we shall see later, the combination of the interfaces from Figure 17 is invalid and it is impossible to discover this by looking at the individual interfaces.

Deciding which interfaces to select is a combinatorial problem and constitutes the NP-hardness of finding a linear order. When the

[6] The removal of the adverb linearly suggests that the ordered attribute grammars form a greater class even though they form a strict subclass. We decide to stick with the established terminology however.

interface contains multiple threads with multiple visits, many different interfaces without arrows pointing westwards are possible. Kastens' algorithm optimistically decides to construct the interface containing the smallest number of visits. The next section shows that this choice is not always correct.

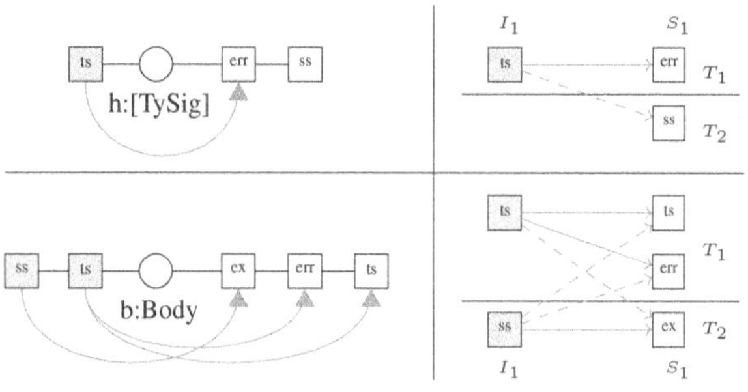

Figure 17. Graphs IDs_S (left) and interfaces (right) with induced intra-visit dependencies (gray) and non-induced intra-visit dependencies (dashed gray) for `[TySig]` (top) and `Body` (bottom).

5.2 Intra-visit dependencies

By fixing the interfaces we introduce a third type of dependency, the *intra-visit dependency*, that has to be taken into account at condition 4 of the conditions on valid sets of visit-sequences (Section 4.3). From condition 2 it follows that every synthesized attribute of a visit v_i depends on all inherited attributes of v_i. From condition 1 it follows that all attributes of v_i depend on all attributes of visit v_j when $j < i$. Given $I_f(X)$, the interface of X, we gather the intra-visit dependencies of X in the set $IVD(X)$:

$$\begin{aligned} IVD(X) = \{\ & X \cdot a \to X \cdot b \mid (I_i, S_i) \in I_f(X), \\ & X \cdot a \in I_i,\ X \cdot b \in S_i\ \} \\ & \cup \\ \{\ & X \cdot a \to X \cdot b \mid (I_{i-1}, S_{i-1}) \in I_f(X), \\ & (I_i, S_i) \in I_f(X), \\ & X \cdot a \in S_{i-1},\ X \cdot b \in I_i\ \} \end{aligned} \tag{8}$$

All induced dependencies are represented by the intra-visit dependencies, i.e. $IDs_S(X) \subseteq IVD^+(X)$. However, some intra-visit dependencies might not be induced (dashed gray in Figure 17).

The intra-visit dependencies imposed by the interfaces might produce cycles together with the direct dependencies at production level, making it impossible to construct a set of valid visit-sequences. Selecting a combination of interfaces for all nonterminals simultaneously such that no cycles occur is a combinatorial problem as fixing one interface might impose restrictions on the other interfaces.

5.3 Ordered Attribute Grammars

An AG is an LOAG if there exist interfaces whose intra-visit dependencies do not lead to cycles with the direct dependencies. An AG is an OAG if Kastens' algorithm finds these interfaces.

Definition 4. *An AG is an* Ordered Attribute Grammar *or* OAG *iff the graph ED_P is acyclic with $IVD(X)$ based on $I_f(X)$ calculated by Kastens' algorithm.*

$$\begin{aligned} ED_P(p) = & D_P(p) \cup \\ & \{\ (X_{p,i} \cdot a \to X_{p,i} \cdot b) \\ & \mid\ (X \cdot a \to X \cdot b) \in IVD(X),\ X = \mathcal{T}(X_{p,i})\ \} \end{aligned} \tag{9}$$

It is important to note that the definition above would be a definition for LOAGs if it had not stated that the interfaces are calculated by Kastens' algorithm (shown in Section 5).

The interfaces of Figure 17 are the ones constructed by Kastens' algorithm. These interfaces impose the intra-visit dependencies (`Body`.$ss(inh)$ $\to$ `Body`.$ts(syn)$) and (`[TySig]`.$ts(inh)$ $\to$ `[TySig]`.$ss(syn)$) (among others). Together with the direct dependencies (`h`.ss $\to$ `b`.ss) and (`b`.ts $\to$ `h`.ts) of production ***Module*** these intra-visit dependencies generate the cycle (`h`.ts $\to$ `h`.ss $\to$ `b`.ss $\to$ `b`.ts $\to$ `h`.ts) shown in Figure 18. The AG description given for IMODULE is therefore *not* an OAG. However, if the interface of `Body` is split into two visits there is no dependency cycle. We have given this interface in Figure 11. Figure 14 shows that there is no dependency cycle using this interface.

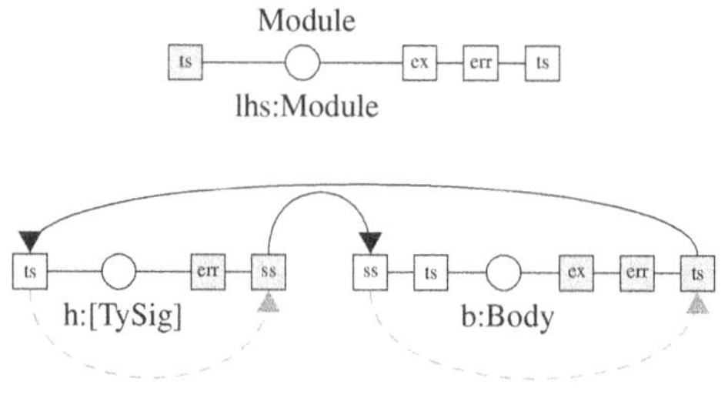

Figure 18. The intra-visit dependencies imposed by the interfaces calculated by Kastens' algorithm form a cycle with the direct dependencies in production ***Module***.

In the next section we show that Kastens' algorithm can be forced to find this interface by adding an augmenting dependency.

6. Augmenting Dependencies

In his 1980 paper, Kastens introduces another class that trivially equals LOAG.

Definition 5. *An AG is an* Arranged Orderly Attribute Grammar (AOAG) *if it is recognised as an OAG by extending the set of direct dependencies with a set of* augmenting dependencies *called ADS.*

Every AOAG is an LOAG because the AOAG is recognised as an OAG with the right set of augmenting dependencies (proving we can construct the required linear orders). Every LOAG is an AOAG because for the LOAG there exists a set of interfaces that impose a set of intra-visit dependencies that cause no cycles. These intra-visit dependencies can be taken as augmenting dependencies and added to the AG description to recognise the LOAG as an OAG. Therefore the classes are equal.

6.1 Manually adding augmenting dependencies

A reference to an attribute can be added to the right-hand side of a semantic function definition, without changing the semantics of that expression, using conditional expressions. Add the attribute a of the augmenting dependency $(a \to b)$ to the semantic function definition of b as the **else**-branch of an **if-then-else** expression with a guard that is always `True`. The **then**-branch contains the old semantic function definition. This method is being used frequently in practice, for example in [3, 12, 14]. A difficulty of this approach is that the resulting AG may not be well-typed.

Augmenting dependencies can also be made explicit by adding syntax to the AG compiler (as has been done in the UUAGC) for the special purpose of extending D_P to contain the set of augmenting dependencies. This way the types of the attributes are no longer a concern and arbitrary augmenting dependencies can be added.

$$D'_P(p) = D_P(p) \cup \{ (X_{p,i} \cdot a \to X_{p,i} \cdot b) \mid (X \cdot a \to X \cdot b) \in ADS), X = \mathcal{T}(X_{p,i}) \} \quad (10)$$

Adding augmenting dependencies by hand is only a solution for small AGs that are not likely to be changed. Although the method has been used to compile the UHC, it requires a great deal of trial-and-error to find the right augmenting dependencies for such a large AG description. Moreover, adding (and also removing) static analyses often requires a revision of the set of augmenting dependencies.

6.2 Automatically adding augmenting dependencies

We consider the following problem: "*given an AG that is not an OAG* (there is at least one dependency cycle) *that does satisfy the LOAG preconditions* (there are no direct or induced dependency cycles), *find a set of augmenting dependencies that show the AG is an AOAG*".

If there is a dependency cycle while the LOAG preconditions hold, that dependency cycle must contain some intra-visit dependencies that are not part of ID_S (or there was a cycle containing only direct or induced dependencies). We can prevent this dependency cycle by selecting the reverse of one of these intra-visit dependencies as an augmenting dependency.

In our example, Kastens' algorithm can be forced to generate the interface shown in Figure 11 for non-terminal Body by adding the augmenting dependency b.$ts(syn)$ $\to$ b.$ss(inh)$. Figure 19 shows how the augmenting dependency is used to force a different relative ordering for the threads of non-terminal Body. Recall that in the figures depicting interfaces no dependencies may point westward.

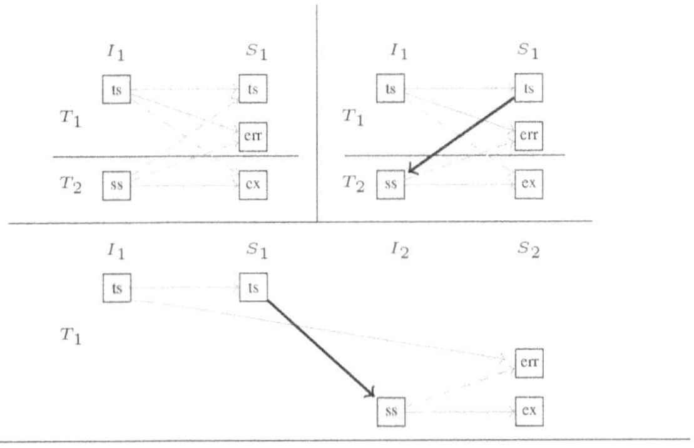

Figure 19. Choosing the augmenting dependency $ts(syn) \to ss(inh)$ results in a different interface for non-terminal Body. Top-left: the old interface. Top-right: the old interface with the augmenting dependency highlighted. Bottom: the new interface.

6.2.1 Selecting augmenting dependencies

The goal of an augmenting dependency is to impose a new dependency between attributes of the same non-terminal, such that the threads calculated for that non-terminal are different, leading to a different interface and a different set of imposed intra-visit dependencies.

We argue that if there exists some set of augmenting dependencies that prove an AG is ordered, then we can prove that the AG is ordered using only intra-visit dependencies not in ID_S. We find the set with a backtracking algorithm. As *candidates* to our selection procedure we only consider the reverses of non-induced intra-visit dependencies (the dashed gray dependencies). Moreover, these intra-visit dependencies should be part of a dependency cycle.

Since the problem is NP-hard, our set of candidates can not always be perfect: it may contain dependencies that, by adding them to the direct dependencies, lead to a cyclic ID_P (the preconditions for LOAGs no longer hold). Let ID_P be the induced dependency graph before adding $(a \to b)$ as an augmenting dependency and ID'_P afterwards. We examine which dependencies in ID_P will lead to cycles in ID'_P:

1. A dependency $(b \to a) \in ID_P$.
2. A dependency $(b' \to a') \in ID_P$ causing a cycle with $(a' \to b') \in ID'_P$ that is imposed as an induced dependency from the new dependency $(a \to b)$.
3. A dependency $(c \to d) \in ID_P$ causing a cycle with $(d \to c) \in ID'_P$ that is imposed as an induced dependency, through a series of steps, by the new dependency $(a \to b)$.
4. Both $(c \to d) \in ID'_P$ and $(d \to c) \in ID'_P$ are induced by $(a \to b)$.

In the first three cases, the augmenting dependency is not a candidate. In the fourth case, the augmenting dependency must induce a dependency, and its reverse, simultaneously.

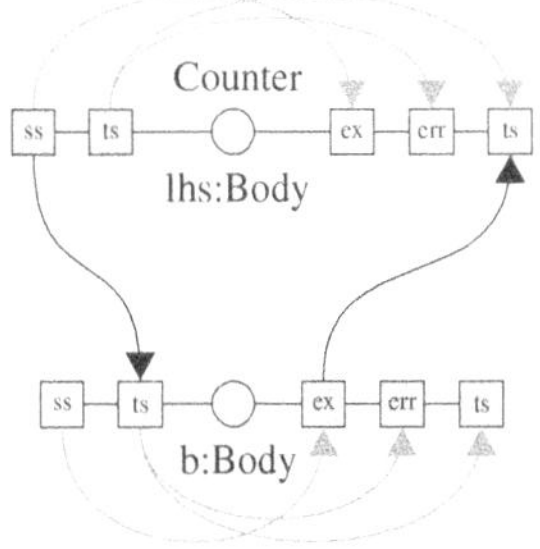

Figure 20. The choice of (Body.b.ts(syn) $\to$ Body.b.ss(inh)) as an augmenting dependency results in a cycle in production ***Counter*** that is unresolvable, as it induces both the dependency (***Counter***.lhs.ts(inh) $\to$ ***Counter***.lhs.ex(syn)) and the dependency (***Counter***.b.ex(syn) $\to$ ***Counter***.b.ts(inh)).

From the cycle in Figure 18 we extract candidates (b.$ts(syn)$ $\to$ b.$ss(inh)$) and (h.$ss(syn)$ $\to$ h.$ts(inh)$) which both successfully alter the interfaces such that IMODULE is recognised as an OAG. If we add production ***Counter*** (shown in Figure 20) to the AG description, we observe that selecting candidate (b.$ts(syn)$ $\to$ b.$ss(inh)$) induces both (b.$ex(syn)$ $\to$ b.$ts(inh)$) and (lhs.$ts(inh)$ $\to$ lhs.$ex(syn)$) in ***Counter***. Graph ID_P becomes cyclic and backtracking is required for the algorithm to choose (h.ss $\to$ h.ts) as an augmenting dependency instead. This counter-example to our selection procedure is both contrived and type incorrect. Any AG which forces our algorithm to backtrack will contain constructions similar to the one described and we expect that such dependency combinations are rare in practical AGs. Our claim is supported by the tests we ran as no backtracking was required for any of the UHC's AG descriptions (more about this in Section 8).

7. AOAG Algorithm

We have written the functions using our own $AOAG$ monad built on top of Haskell's ST monad. The code given in this section is a pseudo version of our actual implementation in the UUAGC.

7.1 Calculating interfaces

Function *aoag* is the main function of the AOAG algorithm[7] and is given in Figure 21.

```
-- receives direct dependency graph D_P
aoag   :: Graph s → AOAG s (Maybe (Graph s))
aoag dp = do
    -- induced dependencies, Section 4.2
  m_ids ← induced dp
  case m_ids of
    Nothing  → return Nothing  -- cycle in ID_P
    (idp, ids) → do
        -- construct set partitioning, Figure 22
        -- by calling partition on all non-terminals
      itfs             ← partition_nts ids
        -- all ivds and non-induced ivds, Section 5.2
      (ivds, ni_ivds) ← intras itfs
      mc               ← oagtest dp ivds
      case mc of   -- did oagtest find a cycle in ED_P?
          -- no, it is an OAG and we return the interfaces
        Nothing → return (Just itfs)
          -- yes, start backtracking algorithm
        Just c → explore c dp idp ids itfs ni_ivds
```

Figure 21. The main function of the AOAG algorithm

The function returns a set of interfaces which can be used together with function *intras* and D_P to calculate ED_P from Definition 4 (not shown). Graph ED_P is used to calculate the visit-sequences exactly as in Kastens' algorithm and Pennings [8, 13]. Note that we do not convert the set partitionings to interfaces and use the set partitionings directly (even though we refer to them as interfaces).

The dependency graphs (of type *Graph s*) are *STRef*s that point to the graph hidden in state behind the usual graph operations. Since we use pointers, we have to make copies of ID_P and the interfaces to allow backtracking.

Function *partition* in Figure 22 calculates the interfaces according to Kastens' algorithm by assigning every attribute a to a set partition P_i (see Section 5) based on the successors of a according to $ID_S(X)$.

7.2 Backtracking algorithm

Backtracking is performed by function *explore*, given in Figure 23. It uses function *insertCandidate* that inserts a dependency a to the induced dependency graph in such a way that all the effects of choosing a as a candidate are propagated through ID_P and ID_S. If a cycle is encountered *Nothing* is returned, otherwise all the new induced dependencies imposed by a are returned. The new induced dependencies may demand a rectification of the interfaces. The interfaces are rectified by increasing the partition index of certain attributes until no more dependencies are pointing 'in the wrong direction'. An example of rectification is shown in Figure 19 and the function *reschedule* is shown in Figure 24. Function *depOccs* (of type *Edge* → [*Edge*]) transforms dependencies from non-terminal level to production level by generating all the occurrences of the given dependency.

[7] We have named the algorithm after the class AOAG because the algorithm adds augmenting dependencies to the direct dependencies of the input AG. In the future work section we discuss an algorithm that solves the problem more directly and refer to this algorithm as the LOAG algorithm.

```
partition :: Graph s → Nonterminal → AOAG s ()
partition ids x = do
  as ← attributes x          -- A(X)
  forM_ as (assign ids)   -- attempt to assign all
 where
  assign :: Graph s → Vertex → AOAG s ()
  assign ids a = do
    dir        ← direction a   -- synthesized or inherited
    mnr        ← partition_ix a   -- has a been assigned?
    when (isNothing mnr) $ do   -- only if not:
          succs ← successors ids a
          case succs of   -- has no successors
            []  → let  part   | dir ≡ Syn = 1
                              | dir ≡ Inh = 2
                   in  wrap_up a part   -- assign
            ss  → do
                 -- returns the highest partition index to
                 -- which an successors has been
                 -- assigned, or Nothing if not all
                 -- successors have been assigned yet
              mmax_part ← max_partition ss
                 -- can we assign a yet?
              case mmax_part of
                Nothing → return ()   -- no
                  -- attribute b, partition index mx
                Just (b, mx) →          -- yes
                    -- rules of Section 5.1
                  let dir_b | even mx = Inh
                            | odd mx  = Syn
                      part  | dir_b ≡ dir = mx
                            | dir_b ≢ dir = mx + 1
                  in wrap_up a part   -- assign
     where wrap_up a part = do   -- actual assignment
            assign_partition a part
            preds  ← predecessors ids a
              -- some preds might now be assignable
            forM_ preds (assign ids)
```

Figure 22. Function *partition* assigns every attribute to a partition for constructing interfaces.

7.3 Extending implementations of Kastens' algorithm

In this section we have given an outline of a Haskell implementation of the AOAG algorithm together with the definition of some of its most important functions. Existing implementations of Kastens' algorithm can easily be extended and turned into an algorithm for scheduling LOAGs with a small number of changes.

Kastens' algorithm can detect three types of cycles depending on the graph in which it is encountered: D_P, ID_P or ED_P. The first change is to obtain the non-induced intra-visit dependencies (candidates) from the interfaces. The second change is to ensure that the main function of the algorithm returns failure when it discovers a cycle in D_P or ID_P. The third change is to add the set of augmenting dependencies (ADS) as an additional parameter to the main function. The augmenting dependencies are then added to D_P (as shown in Section 6.1).

The main function can now call itself recursively and use ADS as an accumulating parameter. If the initial call (with an empty ADS) encounters a cycle in D_P or ID_P then the input AG is not LOAG. If it encounters a cycle in ED_P then the input AG is not

```
-- try candidates one-by-one until the first result
explore  :: [Vertex]    → Graph s → Graph s
           → Graph s → Graph s → [Edge]
           → AOAG s (Maybe (Graph s))
explore c dp idp ids itfs =
    -- candidates are swapped ivds and part of the cycle
  explore' ∘ filter (∈ [(f, t) | f ← c, t ← c])
           ∘ concatMap (depOccs ∘ swap)
where
  explore' :: [Edge] → AOAG s (Maybe (Graph s))
  explore' [] = return Nothing   -- no more candidates
  explore' (a : as) = do
    idpC  ← copy idp
    idsC  ← copy ids
    ifC   ← copy itfs
    let backtrack = explore c dp idpC idsC ifC as
    mEs ← insertCandidate a idp   -- see Section 7.2
    case mEs of   -- is ID_P cyclic?
      Nothing  → backtrack    -- yes
      Just es  → do           -- no
        reschedule ids es   -- rectify interfaces
        (ivds, ni_ivds) ← intras itfs
        mc              ← oagtest dp ivds
        case mc of    -- is there another cycle in ED_P?
          Nothing → return (Just itfs)   -- no
          Just c  → do    -- yes, select candidates
            mres ← explore c dp idp ids itfs ni_ivds
            case mres of   -- did the candidates help?
              Nothing → backtrack              -- no
              Just res → return (Just res)   -- yes
```

Figure 23. Function *explore* executes the backtracking algorithm for automatically selecting augmenting dependencies.

OAG but we can try to find augmenting dependencies that prove it is AOAG/LOAG. Whenever a cycle is encountered in a call to the main function, the main function should behave as follows:

- If the cycle is in D_P or ID_P it returns failure.
- If the cycle is in ED_P we use the candidates obtained from the interfaces. We extend ADS with one of the candidates to get ADS' and use it as an argument in a recursive call. If this call returns failure we add another candidate to ADS instead (backtracking step). If failure is returned while there are no more candidates to try, we return failure as well. If the call returns a result (for example graph ED_P), we return this result. In this case ADS' proves that the input AG is an AOAG/LOAG and visit-sequences can be constructed from the (non-cyclic) ED_P constructed by the successful call.

Calling the main function recursively is very inefficient as the graphs D_P and ID_P are recalculated at every call with only a relatively small number of extra edges. That is why we have chosen to propagate the changes in graph ID_P directly using *insertCandidate* and adjust the interfaces accordingly using *reschedule* as shown in the definition of *explore* in Figure 23.

```
reschedule :: Graph s → [Edge] → AOAG s ()
reschedule ids es = forM_ es fix_edge
where fix_edge :: Edge → AOAG s ()
      fix_edge (f, t) = do
        Just oldf ← partition_ix f
        Just oldt ← partition_ix t
        dirf      ← direction f
        dirt      ← direction t
        let newf | oldf < oldt = oldt + dist
                 | otherwise   = oldf
            dist | dirf ≢ dirt = 1
                 | otherwise   = 0
        unless (oldf ≡ newf) $ do
            -- replace the previous assignment
          reassign_partition f newf
          preds ← predecessors f
            -- some predecessors might need to be fixed
          forM_ (map (flip (,) f) preds) fix_edge
```

Figure 24. Function *reschedule* makes sure that all edges are pointing in the right direction, given a list of edges that are the result of adding a certain fake dependency.

8. Discussion

8.1 Theoretical contributions

This paper presents an algorithm of exponential complexity for finding a static evaluation order of any LOAG, where others have given algorithms of polynomial complexity for recognising a subset of the LOAGs [8, 12, 13]. We argue that backtracking is rare for practical AGs and that our algorithm is therefore efficient in practice.

This paper explains why Kastens' algorithm is incomplete: it does not solve the combinatorial problem of finding the right sets of visits for every interface simultaneously.

AGs that are not in LOAG form a class that can be divided into two based on whether these AGs satisfy the LOAG preconditions. The preconditions can be tested in polynomial time, thus AGs that do not satisfy the preconditions are efficiently recognised. AGs that are not in LOAG but do satisfy the LOAG preconditions can be constructed. This is shown by Natori et al. [12]. These AGs will force our algorithm to perform an exhaustive search of all candidates. We have not encountered any real-world examples of such AGs to test our algorithm with. It is interesting to see if we can generate large examples, either from scratch or by altering existing AGs, to examine the runtime of our algorithm further.

8.2 Practical contributions

The build process of the Utrecht Haskell Compiler compiles many AGs, some of which, including the main AG, require augmenting dependencies to be added in the source code to find a static evaluation order. Adding the right augmenting dependencies is tedious work, demanding insight in the scheduling process and the occasional trial-and-error. We have tested the AOAG algorithm on the AGs encountered in the UHC and compiled them successfully, in runtimes comparable with the original implementation of Kastens' algorithm. The AOAG algorithm compiles the main AG in 13 seconds, automatically selecting 10 augmenting dependencies, while our old implementation of Kastens' algorithm takes 17 seconds with 24 augmenting dependencies that were manually added to the source code while the UHC was developed. Using the same 24 augmenting dependencies the AOAG algorithm takes 6 seconds to compile, showing that roughly 7 seconds are required to evaluate the effects of the automatically selected augmenting dependencies.

The following numbers give an indication of the size of UHC's main AG. It consist of:

- 30 non-terminals.
- 134 productions.
- 1332 attributes (44.4 per non-terminal!).
- 9766 direct dependencies.

Even though the main AG contains many complicated dependency patterns, none of these patterns form a counter-example to our augmenting dependency selection mechanism and no backtracking is required.

We have tested our algorithm on all AGs contained in the UHC, AGs of other projects within Utrecht University and simple examples encountered in literature. We would have liked to test with more real-world AGs. Unfortunately there is no default syntax for writing AGs and we currently cannot easily test examples that have not been written in syntax that the UUAGC accepts.

The AOAG algorithm can be used as a complete compiler for LOAGs and as a tool for finding augmenting dependencies. These augmenting dependencies can be added to the source code manually. It has been implemented as a replacement for Kastens' algorithm in the latest version of the UUAGC and can be found on Hackage[8].

8.3 Future and relevant work

Other alternatives to Kastens' algorithm are found in literature. For example, Natori et al. introduce class OAG* [12] with an alternative way of constructing the interfaces. The Eli system contains a variant of Kastens' algorithm for recognising a superclass of OAG [9]. Pennings describes an algorithm for chained scheduling, relying on alternative induced dependency graphs [13]. These approaches lead to polynomial runtime algorithms for detecting membership of a subclass of LOAG (and a superclass of OAG). We have not implemented these approaches to compare them with the AOAG algorithm, although it would be interesting to see whether these algorithms are sufficient to compile the UHC without augmenting dependencies.

Adding an augmenting dependency might lead to a cycle that can only be solved by yet another augmenting dependency, influencing the runtime of the algorithm. AGs can be constructed that require an arbitrary number of augmenting dependencies, while a different choice in the first step works immediately. We have not investigated whether taking this into account can improve the runtime of the algorithm for large AG descriptions.

A common approach for solving NP hard problems is the use of a so-called SAT solver. The SAT problem is the standard NP complete problem [5] and even though no polynomial time algorithms for solving the problem are known, there exist many heuristic solvers that work well in many practical cases [4]. In future work we encode the LOAG scheduling problem as a SAT problem and use an existing SAT solver to solve the scheduling problem. Such approach may not only lead to a solution that works better in practice, but also allows for extra constraints to be put on the resulting schedule. Such extra constraints may be used to optimise the schedule even further.

Pennings' chained scheduling algorithm finds an order that is better suited for evaluators generated in purely functional programming languages. In an AG compiler generating both imperative and purely functional code, it is beneficial to have multiple options available. We have been able to express constraints in our SAT formulation for minimising the number of visits in the interfaces. It would be interesting to find other optimisations that we can express with constraints, and to investigate what the effects of these optimisations are on the time and space efficiency of the generated evaluators.

[8] http://hackage.haskell.org/package/uuagc

8.4 Conclusion

Finding a static evaluation order for AGs is hard. We have shown that we can find an order for all LOAGs, by automatically selecting augmenting dependencies from a set of candidates with a backtracking algorithm. Although the algorithm we presented is exponential in theory, experiments with the Utrecht Haskell Compiler show that it is efficient for practical full-sized AG descriptions and does not require backtracking.

References

[1] H. Alblas. Attribute evaluation methods. In *Attribute Grammars, Applications and Systems*, volume 545 of *Lecture Notes in Computer Science*, pages 48–113. Springer Berlin / Heidelberg, 1991. ISBN 978-3-540-54572-9.

[2] G. V. Bochmann. Semantic evaluation from left to right. *Communications of the ACM*, 19(2):55–62, Feb. 1976.

[3] J. Bransen, A. Middelkoop, A. Dijkstra, and S. D. Swierstra. The Kennedy-Warren algorithm revisited: ordering Attribute Grammars. In C. Russo and N.-F. Zhou, editors, *Practical Aspects of Declarative Languages*, volume 7149 of *Lecture Notes in Computer Science*, pages 183–197. Springer Berlin / Heidelberg, 2012.

[4] K. Claessen, N. Een, M. Sheeran, N. Sörensson, A. Voronov, and K. Åkesson. Sat-solving in practice. *Discrete Event Dynamic Systems*, 19(4):495–524, Dec. 2009. ISSN 0924-6703.

[5] S. A. Cook. The complexity of theorem-proving procedures. In *Proceedings of the Third Annual ACM Symposium on Theory of Computing*, STOC '71, pages 151–158, New York, NY, USA, 1971. ACM.

[6] A. Dijkstra. *Stepping Through Haskell*. PhD thesis, Utrecht University, 2005.

[7] J. Engelfriet and G. Filè. Simple multi-visit attribute grammars. *Journal of computer and system sciences*, 24(3):283–314, 1982.

[8] U. Kastens. Ordered attributed grammars. *Acta Informatica*, 13:229–256, 1980.

[9] U. Kastens, P. Pfahler, and M. T. Jung. The eli system. In *Proceedings of the 7th International Conference on Compiler Construction*, CC '98, pages 294–297, London, UK, UK, 1998. Springer Berlin / Heidelberg.

[10] K. Kennedy and S. K. Warren. Automatic generation of efficient evaluators for attribute grammars. In *Proceedings of the 3rd ACM SIGACT-SIGPLAN symposium on Principles on programming languages*, POPL '76, pages 32–49, New York, NY, USA, 1976. ACM.

[11] D. E. Knuth. Semantics of context-free languages. *Mathematical systems theory*, 2(2):127–145, June 1968.

[12] S. Natori, K. Gondow, T. Imaizumi, T. Hagiwara, and T. Katayama. On eliminating type 3 circularities of ordered attribute grammars. In D. Parigot and M. Mernik, editors, *Second Workshop on Attribute Grammars and their Applications, WAGA'99*, pages 93–112, Amsterdam, The Netherlands, March 1999. INRIA rocquencourt.

[13] M. C. Pennings. *Generating Incremental Attribute Evaluators*. Ph.D. thesis, Computer Science, Utrecht University, November 1994.

[14] T. W. Reps and T. Teitelbaum. *The Synthesizer Generator Reference Manual*. Texts and monographs in computer science. Springer Berlin / Heidelberg, 3rd edition, 1989. ISBN 978-3-540-96910-5.

[15] J. Saraiva. *Purely Functional Implementation of Attribute Grammars*. PhD thesis, Utrecht University, 1999.

[16] S. D. Swierstra, P. R. A. Alcocer, and J. Saraiva. Designing and implementing combinator languages. In *Advanced Functional Programming*, volume 1608 of *Lecture Notes in Computer Science*, pages 150–206. Springer Berlin / Heidelberg, 1999.

Verifying Relational Properties of Functional Programs by First-Order Refinement

Kazuyuki Asada Ryosuke Sato Naoki Kobayashi
University of Tokyo
{asada,ryosuke,koba}@kb.is.s.u-tokyo.ac.jp

Abstract

Much progress has been made recently on fully automated verification of higher-order functional programs, based on refinement types and higher-order model checking. Most of those verification techniques are, however, based on *first-order* refinement types, hence unable to verify certain properties of functions (such as the equality of two recursive functions and the monotonicity of a function, which we call *relational properties*). To relax this limitation, we introduce a restricted form of higher-order refinement types where refinement predicates can refer to functions, and formalize a systematic program transformation to reduce type checking/inference for higher-order refinement types to that for first-order refinement types, so that the latter can be automatically solved by using an existing software model checker. We also prove the soundness of the transformation, and report on preliminary implementation and experiments.

Categories and Subject Descriptors D.2.4 [*Software Engineering*]: Software/Program Verification

Keywords Automated verification, Higher-order functional language, Refinement types

1. Introduction

There has been much progress in automated verification techniques for higher-order functional programs [11–14, 17, 18, 20].[1] Most of those techniques abstract programs by using *first-order* predicates on base values (such as integers), due to the limitation of underlying theorem provers and predicate discovery procedures. For example, consider the program:

```
  let rec sum n =
    if n<0 then 0 else n+sum(n-1).
```

Using the existing techniques [11, 13, 17, 18], one can verify that sum has the first-order refinement type: $(n : \mathbf{int}) \rightarrow \{m : \mathbf{int} \mid m \geq n\}$, which means that sum n returns a value no less than n. Here, $\{m : \mathbf{int} \mid P(m)\}$ is the (refinement) type of integers m that satisfy $P(m)$.

Due to the restriction to the first-order predicates, however, it is difficult to reason about what we call *relational properties*, such as the relationship between two functions, and the relationship between two invocations of a function. For example, consider another version of the sum function:

```
let rec sumacc n m =
  if n<0 then m else sumacc (n-1) (m+n)
and sum2 n = sumacc n 0
```

Suppose we wish to check that $\mathtt{sum2}(n)$ equals $\mathtt{sum}(n)$ for every integer n. With general refinement types [8], that would amount to checking that sumacc and sum2 have the following types:[2]

$$\mathtt{sumacc} : (n : \mathbf{int}) \rightarrow (m : \mathbf{int}) \rightarrow \{r : \mathbf{int} \mid r = m + \mathtt{sum}(n)\}$$
$$\mathtt{sum2} : (n : \mathbf{int}) \rightarrow \{r : \mathbf{int} \mid r = \mathtt{sum}(n)\}$$

The type of sum2 means that sum2 takes an integer as an argument and returns an integer r that equals the value of $\mathtt{sum}(n)$. With the first-order refinement types, however, sum cannot be used in predicates, so the only way to prove that $\mathtt{sum2}(n)$ equals $\mathtt{sum}(n)$ would be to verify precise input/output behaviors of the functions:

$$\mathtt{sum}, \mathtt{sum2} : (n : \mathbf{int}) \rightarrow \{r : \mathbf{int} \mid (n \geq 0 \wedge r = n(n+1)/2) \vee (n < 0 \wedge r = 0)\}.$$

Since this involves non-linear and disjunctive predicates, automated verification (which involves automated synthesis of the predicates above) is difficult. In fact, most of the recent automated verification tools do not deal with non-linear arithmetic.

Actually, with the first-order refinement types, there is a difficulty even with the "trivial" property that sum satisfies $\mathtt{sum}\ x = x + \mathtt{sum}\ (x-1)$ for every $x \geq 0$. This is almost the definition of the sum function, and it can be expressed and verified using the general refinement type:

$$\mathtt{sum} : \{f : \mathbf{int} \rightarrow \mathbf{int} \mid \forall x.\, x \geq 0 \Rightarrow f(x) = x + f(x-1)\}.$$

Yet, with the restriction to first-order refinement types, one would need to infer the precise input/output behavior of sum (i.e., that $\mathtt{sum}(x)$ returns $x(x+1)/2$).[3]

We face even more difficulties when dealing with higher-order functions. Consider the program in Figure 1. Here, a list is encoded as a function that maps each index to the corresponding element

[1] In the present paper, by *automated* verification, we mean (almost) fully automated one, where a tool can automatically verify a given program satisfies a given specification (expressed either in the form of assertions or refinement type declarations), without requiring invariant annotations (such as pre/post conditions for each function). It should be contrasted with refinement type checkers [5, 21] where a user must declare refinement types for *all* recursive functions including auxiliary functions. Some of the automated verification techniques above require a hint [20], however.

[2] As defined later, a formula $t_1 = t_2$ in a refinement type means that *if both t_1 and t_2 evaluate to (base) values*, then the values are equivalent.

[3] Another way would be to use uninterpreted function symbols, but for that purpose, one would first need to check that sum is total.

PEPM '15, January 13–14, 2015, Mumbai, India.

ACM 978-1-4503-3297-2/15/01...$15.00.
http://dx.doi.org/10.1145/2678015.2682546

```
let nil i = None in
let tl xs = fun i-> xs(i+1) in
let cons x xs =
 fun i -> if i=0 then Some(x) else xs(i-1) in
let rec append xs ys =
 match xs(0) with None -> ys
   | Some(x) -> let xs' = tl xs in
                cons x (append xs' ys)
```

Figure 1. Append function for functional encoding of lists

(or None if the index is out of bounds) [14], and the append function is defined. Suppose that we wish to verify that append xs nil = xs. With general refinement types, the property would be expressed by:

$$\begin{aligned}\texttt{append} : (x : \textbf{int} \to \textbf{int option}) \to \\ \{y : \textbf{int} \to \textbf{int option} \mid y(0) = \texttt{None}\} \to \\ \{r : \textbf{int} \to \textbf{int option} \mid r = x\}\end{aligned}$$

(where $r = x$ means the extensional equality of functions r and x) but one cannot directly express and verify the same property using first-order refinement types.

To overcome the problems above, we allow[4] programmers to specify (a restricted form of) general refinement types in source programs. For example, they can declare

$$\begin{aligned}&\texttt{sum2}: (n : \textbf{int}) \to \{r : \textbf{int} \mid r = \texttt{sum}(n)\}\\ &\texttt{append}: (x : \textbf{int} \to \textbf{int option}) \to\\ &\qquad \{y : \textbf{int} \to \textbf{int option} \mid y(0) = \texttt{None}\} \to\\ &\qquad \{r : \textbf{int} \to \textbf{int option} \mid \forall i. r(i) = x(i)\}.\end{aligned}$$

To take advantage of the recent advance of verification techniques based on first-order refinement types, however, we employ automated program transformation, so that the resulting program can be verified by using only first-order refinement types. The key idea of the transformation is to apply a kind of tupling transformation [6] to capture the relationship between two (or more) function calls at the level of first-order refinement. For example, for the sum program above, one can apply the standard tupling transformation (to combine two functions sum and sumacc into one) and obtain:

```
let rec sum_sumacc (n, m) =
  if n<0 then (0,m) else
  let (r1,r2)=sum_sumacc (n-1, m+n) in
    (r1+n, r2)
```

Checking the equivalence of sum and sum2 then amounts to checking that sum_sumacc has the following first-order refinement type:

$$((n, m) : \textbf{int} \times \textbf{int}) \to \{(r_1, r_2) : \textbf{int} \times \textbf{int} \mid r_2 = r_1 + m\}.$$

The transformation for append is more involved: because the return type of the append function refers to the first argument, the append function is modified so that it returns a pair consisting of *the first argument and* the result:

```
let append2 xs ys = (xs, append xs ys).
```

Then, append2 is further transformed to append3 below, obtained by replacing (xs, append xs ys) with its tupled version.

```
let append3 xs ys (i,j) =
                (xs(i), append xs ys j).
```

[4] But programmers are not obliged to specify types for all functions. In fact, for the example of sum2, no declaration is required for the function sum.

The required property append xs nil = xs is then verified by checking that append3 has the following first-order refinement type $\tau_{\texttt{append3}}$:

$$\begin{aligned}&(x : \textbf{int} \to \textbf{int option}) \to\\ &(y : ((x : \textbf{int}) \to \{r : \textbf{int option} \mid x = 0 \Rightarrow r = \texttt{None}\})) \to\\ &((i, j) : \textbf{int} \times \textbf{int}) \to \{(r_1, r_2) : \textbf{int} \times \textbf{int} \mid i = j \Rightarrow r_1 = r_2\}.\end{aligned}$$

The transformation sketched above has allowed us to express the *external* behavior of the append function by using first-order refinement types. With the transformation alone, however, the first-order refinement type checking does not succeed: For reasoning about the *internal* behavior of append, we need information about the relation between the two function calls xs(i) and append xs ys j, which cannot be expressed by first order refinement types. As already mentioned, with the restriction to first-order refinement types, the relationship between the return values of the two calls can only be obtained by relating the input/output relations of functions xs and append. To avoid that limitation, we further transform the program, by inlining append and tupling the two calls of the body of append3:

```
let append4 xs ys (i,j) =
   match xs(0) with None -> nil2 (i,j)
     | Some(x) ->
       let xs' = tl xs in
       let xszs' = append4 xs' ys in
       let xszs'' = cons2 x x xszs' in
         xszs'' (i,j)
```

Here, nil2 and cons2 x x xszs' are respectively tupled versions of (nil,nil) and (cons x xs', cons x zs'), where xszs' is a tupled one of xs' and zs'.

At last, it can automatically be proved that append4 has type $\tau_{\texttt{append3}}$. (To clarify the ideas, we have over-simplified the transformation above. The actual output of the automatic transformation formalized later is more complicated.)

We formalize the idea sketched above and prove the soundness of the transformation. We also report on a prototype implementation of the approach as an extension to the software model checker MoCHi [11, 14] for a subset of OCaml. The implementation takes a program and its specification (in the form of refinement types) as input, and verifies them automatically (without invariant annotations for auxiliary functions) by applying the above transformations and calling MoCHi as a backend.

The rest of the paper is organized as follows. Section 2 introduces the source language. Section 3 presents the basic transformation for reducing the (restricted form of) general refinement type checking problem to the first-order refinement type checking problem. Roughly, this transformation corresponds to the one from append to append3 above. As mentioned above, the basic transformation alone is not sufficient for automated verification via first-order refinement types; we therefore improve the transformation in Section 4 (which roughly corresponds to the transformation from append3 to append4 above). Section 5 reports on experiments and Section 6 discusses related work. We conclude the paper in Section 7. For the space restriction, proofs and some definitions are omitted, which are available in a full version [3].

2. Source Language

This section formalizes the source language and the verification problem.

2.1 Source Language

The source language, used as the target of our verification method, is a simply-typed, call-by-value, higher-order functional language

$$
\begin{aligned}
&V \text{ (value)} \quad ::= n \mid \mathbf{fix}(f, \lambda x.\, t) \mid (V_1, \ldots, V_n)\\
&A \text{ (answer)} \quad ::= V \mid \mathit{fail}\\
&E \text{ (eval. ctx.)} ::= [\,] \mid \mathsf{op}(\widetilde{V}, E, \widetilde{t}) \mid \mathbf{if}\ E\ \mathbf{then}\ t_1\ \mathbf{else}\ t_2\\
&\qquad \mid E\,t \mid V\,E \mid (\widetilde{V}, E, \widetilde{t}) \mid \mathbf{pr}_i E
\end{aligned}
$$

$$
\begin{aligned}
&E[\mathsf{op}(n_1, \ldots, n_k)] \longrightarrow E[[\![\mathsf{op}]\!](n_1, \ldots, n_k)]\\
&E[\mathbf{fail}] \longrightarrow \mathit{fail}\\
&E[\mathbf{if\ true\ then}\ t_1\ \mathbf{else}\ t_2] \longrightarrow E[t_1]\\
&E[\mathbf{if}\ V\ \mathbf{then}\ t_1\ \mathbf{else}\ t_2] \longrightarrow E[t_2] (V \neq \mathbf{true})\\
&E[\mathbf{fix}(f, \lambda x.\, t)V] \longrightarrow E[t[f \mapsto \mathbf{fix}(f, \lambda x.\, t)][x \mapsto V]]\\
&E[\mathbf{pr}_i(V_1, \ldots, V_n)] \longrightarrow E[V_i]
\end{aligned}
$$

Figure 2. Operational semantics of the source language

with recursion. The syntax of *terms* is given by:

$$
\begin{aligned}
t \text{ (terms)} ::= &\ x \mid n \mid \mathsf{op}(t_1, \ldots, t_n) \mid \mathbf{if}\ t\ \mathbf{then}\ t_1\ \mathbf{else}\ t_2\\
&\mid \mathbf{fix}(f, \lambda x.\, t) \mid t_1\, t_2 \mid (t_1, \ldots, t_n) \mid \mathbf{pr}_i t \mid \mathbf{fail}
\end{aligned}
$$

We use meta-variables $x, y, z, \ldots, f, g, h, \ldots$, and ν for variables. We have only integers as base values, which are denoted by the meta-variable n. The term $\mathsf{op}(\widetilde{t})$ (where $\widetilde{t}$ denotes a sequence of expressions) applies the primitive operation op on integers to $\widetilde{t}$. We assume that we have the equality operator $=$ as a primitive operation. We express Booleans by integers, and write **true** for 1, and **false** for 0. The term $\mathbf{fix}(f, \lambda x.\, t)$ denotes the recursive function defined by $f = \lambda x.t$. When f does not occur in t, we write $\lambda x.t$ for $\mathbf{fix}(f, \lambda x.\, t)$. The term $t_1 t_2$ applies the function t_1 to t_2. We write $\mathbf{let}\ x = t\ \mathbf{in}\ t'$ for $(\lambda x.t')t$, and write also $t; t'$ for it when x does not occur in t'. The terms $(t_1, \ldots, t_n)$ and $\mathbf{pr}_i t$ respectively construct and destruct tuples. The special term **fail** aborts the execution. It is typically used to express assertions; $\mathbf{assert}(t)$, which asserts that t should evaluate to **true**, is expressed by $\mathbf{if}\ t\ \mathbf{then\ true\ else\ fail}$. We call a closed term a *program*. We often write $\widetilde{t}$ for a sequence $t_1, \ldots, t_n$.

For the sake of simplicity, we assume that tuple constructors occur only in the outermost position or in the argument positions of function calls in source programs. We also assume that all the programs are simply-typed below (where **fail** can have every type).

The small-step semantics is shown in Figure 2. In the figure, $[\![\mathsf{op}]\!]$ is the integer operation denoted by op. We write $\longrightarrow^*$ for the reflexive and transitive closure of $\longrightarrow$, and $t \longrightarrow^k t'$ if t is reduced to t' in k steps. We write $t \uparrow$ if there is an infinite reduction sequence $t \longrightarrow t_1 \longrightarrow t_2 \longrightarrow \cdots$. By the assumption that a program is simply-typed, for every program t, either t evaluates to an answer (i.e., $t \longrightarrow^* V$ or $t \longrightarrow^* \mathit{fail}$) or diverges (i.e., $t \uparrow$).

We express the specification of a program by using refinement types. The syntax of refinement types is given by:

$$
\begin{aligned}
&\tau \text{ (types)} ::= \rho \mid \{\nu : \textstyle\prod_{i=1}^n (x_i : \rho_i) \mid P\}\\
&\rho \text{ (non-tuple types)} ::= \{\nu : \mathbf{int} \mid P\} \mid \{\nu : (x : \tau_1) \to \tau_2 \mid P\}\\
&P \text{ (predicates)} ::= t \mid P \wedge P \mid \forall x.P
\end{aligned}
$$

where we have used a notational convention $\prod_{i=1}^n (x_i : \rho_i)$ to denote $(x_1 : \rho_1) \times \cdots \times (x_{n-1} : \rho_{n-1}) \times \rho_n$ (thus, the variable x_n actually does not occur). The type $(x : \rho_1) \times \rho_2$ is a dependent sum type, where x may occur in ρ_2, and $(x : \tau_1) \to \tau_2$ is a dependent product type, where x may occur in τ_2. We use a metavariable σ to denote $\mathbf{int}$, $(x : \tau_1) \to \tau_2$, or $\prod_{i=1}^n (x_i : \rho_i)$. Intuitively, a *refinement type* $\{\nu : \sigma \mid P\}$ describes a value ν of type σ that satisfies the *refinement predicate* P. For example, $\{\nu : \mathbf{int} \mid \nu > 0\}$ describes a positive integer. The type $\{f : \mathbf{int} \to \mathbf{int} \mid \forall x, y.\ x \leq y \Rightarrow f(x) \leq f(y)\}$ describes a monotonic function on integers.

(Predicate) $\models_{\mathrm{p}}^n\ \subseteq \{P : \text{closed}\}$

- $\models_{\mathrm{p}}^n \forall x.\, P \stackrel{\text{def}}{\Longleftrightarrow} \models_{\mathrm{p}}^n P[x \mapsto m]$ for all integers m
- $\models_{\mathrm{p}}^n P_1 \wedge P_2 \stackrel{\text{def}}{\Longleftrightarrow} \models_{\mathrm{p}}^n P_1$ and $\models_{\mathrm{p}}^n P_1$
- $\models_{\mathrm{p}}^n t \stackrel{\text{def}}{\Longleftrightarrow} A = \mathbf{true}$ for all A and $k \leq n$ s.t. $t \longrightarrow^k A$

(Value) $\models_{\mathrm{v}}^n, \models_{\mathrm{v}}\ \subseteq \{V : \text{closed}\} \times \{\tau : \text{closed}\}$

- $\models_{\mathrm{v}}^n V : \{\nu : \sigma \mid P\} \stackrel{\text{def}}{\Longleftrightarrow} \models_{\mathrm{v}}^n V : \sigma$ and $\models_{\mathrm{p}}^n P[\nu \mapsto V]$
- $\models_{\mathrm{v}}^n V : \mathbf{int} \stackrel{\text{def}}{\Longleftrightarrow} V = m$ for some integer m
- $\models_{\mathrm{v}}^n V : (x_1 : \tau_1) \to \tau_2 \stackrel{\text{def}}{\Longleftrightarrow}$ for all $n' \leq n$ and V_1, $\models_{\mathrm{v}}^{n'} V_1 : \tau_1$ implies $\models_{\mathrm{c}}^{n'} V V_1 : \tau_2[x_1 \mapsto V_1]$
- $\models_{\mathrm{v}}^n (V_1, \ldots, V_n) : \prod_{i=1}^n (x_i : \rho_i) \stackrel{\text{def}}{\Longleftrightarrow}$ $\models_{\mathrm{v}}^n V_i : \rho_i[x_1 \mapsto V_1, \ldots, x_{i-1} \mapsto V_{i-1}]$ for all $i \leq n$
- $\models_{\mathrm{v}} V : \tau \stackrel{\text{def}}{\Longleftrightarrow} \models_{\mathrm{v}}^n V : \tau$ for all n

(Term) $\models_{\mathrm{c}}, \models_{\mathrm{c}}^n\ \subseteq \{t : \text{closed}\} \times \{\tau : \text{closed}\}$

- $\models_{\mathrm{c}}^n t : \tau \stackrel{\text{def}}{\Longleftrightarrow} \models_{\mathrm{v}}^{n-k} A : \tau$ for all A and $k \leq n$ s.t. $t \longrightarrow^k A$
- $\models t : \tau \stackrel{\text{def}}{\Longleftrightarrow} \models_{\mathrm{c}}^n t : \tau$ for all n
  ($\Longleftrightarrow \models_{\mathrm{v}} A : \tau$ for all A s.t. $t \longrightarrow^* A$)

Figure 3. Semantics of types

A refinement predicate P can be constructed from expressions and top-level logical connectives $\forall x$ and $\wedge$, where x ranges over integers. The other logical connectives can be expressed by using expression-level Boolean primitives, but their semantics is subtle due to the presence of effects (non-termination and abort) of expressions, as discussed later in Section 2.2.

We often write just σ for $\{x : \sigma \mid \mathbf{true}\}$; $\tau_1 \to \tau_2$ for $(x : \tau_1) \to \tau_2$, and $\rho_1 \times \rho_2$ for $(x : \rho_1) \times \rho_2$ if x is not important; τ^m for $\tau \times \cdots \times \tau$ (the m-th power); $\{(\nu_i)_{i \in n} : \prod_{i=1}^n (x_i : \rho_i) \mid P\}$ for $\{\nu : \prod_{i=1}^n (x_i : \rho_i) \mid P[\nu_1 \mapsto \mathbf{pr}_1 \nu, \ldots, \nu_n \mapsto \mathbf{pr}_n \nu]\}$; and $\forall \widetilde{x}.P$ for $\forall x_1, \ldots, x_n.P$.

For a type τ we define the *simple type* $\mathtt{ST}(\tau)$ *of* τ as follows:

$$
\begin{aligned}
&\mathtt{ST}(\{\nu : \sigma \mid P\}) = \mathtt{ST}(\sigma) \qquad \mathtt{ST}(\mathbf{int}) = \mathbf{int}\\
&\mathtt{ST}((x : \tau_1) \to \tau_2) = \mathtt{ST}(\tau_1) \to \mathtt{ST}(\tau_2)\\
&\mathtt{ST}((x : \tau_1) \times \tau_2) = \mathtt{ST}(\tau_1) \times \mathtt{ST}(\tau_2)
\end{aligned}
$$

Also, we define the *order of* τ by:

$$
\begin{aligned}
&\mathit{order}(\{\nu : \sigma \mid P\}) = \mathit{order}(\sigma) \qquad \mathit{order}(\mathbf{int}) = 0\\
&\mathit{order}((x : \tau_1) \to \tau_2) = \max(\mathit{order}(\tau_1) + 1, \mathit{order}(\tau_2))\\
&\mathit{order}((x : \tau_1) \times \tau_2) = \max(\mathit{order}(\tau_1), \mathit{order}(\tau_2)).
\end{aligned}
$$

The syntax of types is subject to the usual scope rule; in $(x : \rho_1) \times \rho_2$ and $(x : \tau_1) \to \tau_2$, the scope of x is ρ_2 and τ_2 respectively. Furthermore, we require that every refinement predicate is well-typed and have type **int**. (See the full version of this paper [3] for the details.) To enable the reduction to first-order refinement type checking, we shall further restrict the syntax of types later in Section 2.3.

2.2 Semantics of Refinement Types

The semantics of types is defined in Figure 3, using step-indexed logical relations [1, 2, 7]. Roughly speaking, $\models_{\mathrm{c}}^n t : \tau$ means that t behaves like a term of type τ within n steps computation. For example, $\models_{\mathrm{c}}^n t : \mathbf{int}$ means that if t evaluates to an answer within

n steps, then the answer is not *fail* but an integer, (otherwise if t needs more than n steps to evaluate, t may diverge or fail). Also, the condition $\models^n_c t : \mathbf{int} \to \mathbf{int}$ means that if t evaluates to an answer A within n steps, say at k-step ($k \leq n$), then A must be a function, and $\models^{n-k}_c A\, m : \mathbf{int}$ must hold for every integer m, i.e., if $A\, m$ converges to an answer within $n-k$ steps, then the answer is not *fail* but an integer. The connectives $\forall$ and $\wedge$ have genuine logical meaning, and especially they are commutative, so we often use the prenex normal form.

Notice that, by the definition, $\models^n_p t$ holds for every n if t diverges. We write & and || for (expression-level) Boolean conjunction and disjunction. Notice that the semantics of $t_1 \wedge t_2$ and t_1 & t_2 are different. For example, let Ω be a divergent term. Then $\models 1 : \{x : \mathbf{int} \mid \Omega \wedge x = 0\}$ does NOT hold, but $\models 1 : \{x : \mathbf{int} \mid \Omega \,\&\, x = 0\}$ DOES hold, since $\Omega \,\&\, x = 0$ diverges.

The goal of our verification is to check whether $\models t : \tau$ holds, given a program t and a type τ. Since the verification problem is undecidable, we aim to develop a sound but incomplete method below. As explained in Section 1, our approach is to use program transformation to reduce the (semantic) type checking problem $\models t : \tau$ to the first-order refinement type checking problem $\models t' : \tau'$ where τ' does not contain any function variables in refinement predicates, and to check $\models t' : \tau'$ using an automated verification tool such as MoCHi [11, 14, 19], which combines higher-order model checking [10] and predicate abstraction.

2.3 Restriction on Refinement Types

To enable the reduction of the refinement type checking problem $\models t : \tau$ to the first-order one $\models t' : \tau'$, we have to impose some restrictions on the type τ. The most important restriction is that only first-order function variables (i.e., functions whose simple types are of the form $\mathbf{int} \times \cdots \times \mathbf{int} \to \mathbf{int} \times \cdots \times \mathbf{int}$) may be used in refinement predicates. The other restrictions are rather technical. We describe below the details of the restrictions, but they may be skipped for the first reading.

1. We assume that every closed type τ satisfies the well-formedness condition $\emptyset \vdash_{\mathtt{WF}} \tau$ defined in Figure 4. In the figure, $\mathtt{ElimHO}_n(\Gamma)$ filters out all the bindings of types whose *depth* are greater than n, where the depth of a type is defined by:

$$\begin{array}{c} depth(\{\nu : \sigma \mid P\}) = depth(\sigma) \qquad depth(\mathbf{int}) = 0 \\ depth((x : \tau_1) \to \tau_2) = 1 + \max\{depth(\tau_1), depth(\tau_2)\} \\ depth((x : \tau_1) \times \tau_2) = \max\{depth(\tau_1), depth(\tau_2)\}. \end{array}$$

In addition to the usual scope rules and well-typedness conditions of refinement predicates (that have been explained already in Section 2.1), the rules ensure that (i) only depth-1 function variables (i.e., variables of types whose depth is 1) may occur in refinement predicates, (ii) in a type of the form $(x : \tau_1) \to \{\nu : \sigma \mid P\}$ where τ_1 is a depth-1 function type, x may occur in P but not in σ (there is no such restriction if τ_1 is a depth-0 type), and (iii) in a type of the form $(f_1 : \tau_1) \times \{f_2 : \sigma_2 \mid P_2\} \times \cdots \times \{f_n : \sigma_n \mid P_n\}$, f_1 may occur in $P_2, \ldots, P_n$ but not in $\sigma_2, \ldots, \sigma_n$.

2. In a refinement predicate $\forall x_1, \ldots, x_n.\ \wedge_j t_j$, for every t_j, if x_i occurs in t_j, there must be an occurrence of application of the form $f(\ldots, x_i, \ldots)$. Also, for every t_j, if a function variable f occurs, every occurrence must be as an application ft.

3. The special primitive **fail** must not occur in any refinement predicate. Also, in every application $t_1 t_2$ in a refinement predicate, t_2 must not contain function applications nor **fail**. (In other words, t_2 must be *effect-free*, in the sense that it neither diverges nor fail.)

4. Abstractions (i.e., $\mathbf{fix}(f, \lambda x. t)$) must not occur in refinement predicates, except in the form $\mathbf{let}\ x = t\ \mathbf{in}\ t'$.

5. In refinement predicates, usual if-expressions are not allowed; instead we allow "branch-strict" if-expression $\mathbf{ifs}\ t\ \mathbf{then}\ t_1\ \mathbf{else}\ t_2$ where t_1 and t_2 are both evaluated before the evaluation of t. This is equivalent to $t_1; t_2; \mathbf{if}\ t\ \mathbf{then}\ t_1\ \mathbf{else}\ t_2$; hence, in other words, we allow if-expressions only in this form.

$$\frac{\Gamma \mid \emptyset \vdash_{\mathtt{WF}} P}{\Gamma \vdash_{\mathtt{WF}} P}\ (\text{WF-PREDINIT}) \qquad \frac{\Gamma \mid \emptyset \vdash_{\mathtt{WF}} \tau}{\Gamma \vdash_{\mathtt{WF}} \tau}\ (\text{WF-INIT})$$

$$\frac{\mathtt{ST}(\mathtt{ElimHO}_0(\Gamma), \mathtt{ElimHO}_1(\Delta)) \vdash_{\mathtt{S}} t : \mathbf{int}}{\Gamma \mid \Delta \vdash_{\mathtt{WF}} t}\ (\text{WF-PREDTERM})$$

$$\frac{\Gamma \mid \Delta \vdash_{\mathtt{WF}} P_1 \qquad \Gamma \mid \Delta \vdash_{\mathtt{WF}} P_2}{\Gamma \mid \Delta \vdash_{\mathtt{WF}} P_1 \wedge P_2}\ (\text{WF-PREDAND})$$

$$\frac{\Gamma \mid \Delta, y_1 : \mathbf{int}, \ldots, y_n : \mathbf{int} \vdash_{\mathtt{WF}} P}{\Gamma \mid \Delta \vdash_{\mathtt{WF}} \forall y_1, \ldots, y_n. P}\ (\text{WF-PREDFORALL})$$

$$\frac{\Gamma, \Delta \mid \emptyset \vdash_{\mathtt{WF}} \sigma \qquad \Gamma \mid \Delta, x : \sigma \vdash_{\mathtt{WF}} P}{\Gamma \mid \Delta \vdash_{\mathtt{WF}} \{x : \sigma \mid P\}}\ (\text{WF-REFINE}) \qquad \frac{}{\Gamma \mid \Delta \vdash_{\mathtt{WF}} \mathbf{int}}\ (\text{WF-INT})$$

$$\frac{\Gamma, \Delta \mid \emptyset \vdash_{\mathtt{WF}} \tau_1 \qquad \Gamma, \Delta \mid x : \tau_1 \vdash_{\mathtt{WF}} \tau_2}{\Gamma \mid \Delta \vdash_{\mathtt{WF}} (x : \tau_1) \to \tau_2}\ (\text{WF-FUN})$$

$$\frac{\Gamma \mid \Delta \vdash_{\mathtt{WF}} \tau_1 \qquad \Gamma \mid \Delta, x : \tau_1 \vdash_{\mathtt{WF}} \tau_2}{\Gamma \mid \Delta \vdash_{\mathtt{WF}} (x : \tau_1) \times \tau_2}\ (\text{WF-PAIR})$$

$$\frac{}{\vdash_{\mathtt{WF}} \emptyset}\ (\text{WF-ENIL}) \qquad \frac{\vdash_{\mathtt{WF}} \Gamma \qquad \Gamma \vdash_{\mathtt{WF}} \tau \qquad (x : \_) \notin \Gamma}{\vdash_{\mathtt{WF}} \Gamma, x : \tau}\ (\text{WF-ECONS})$$

$$\mathtt{ElimHO}_n(\Gamma) \stackrel{\text{def}}{=} \{(x : \tau) \in \Gamma \mid depth(\tau) <= n\}$$

$$\Gamma, \Delta ::= \emptyset \mid \Gamma, x : \tau$$

Figure 4. Well-formedness of types

Please note that the above restrictions are essential only for the refinement predicates that occur in σ of a given type checking problem $\stackrel{?}{\models} t : \{\nu : \sigma \mid P\}$ rather than the top level refinement P; since given

$$\stackrel{?}{\models} t : \{\nu : \sigma \mid \forall \widetilde{x}.\ \wedge_i\, t_i\}$$

where $\forall \widetilde{x}.\ \wedge_i\, t_i$ does not satisfy the restrictions above, we can replace it by an equivalent problem

$$\stackrel{?}{\models} \mathbf{let}\ \nu = t\ \mathbf{in}\ (\nu, (\lambda \widetilde{x}. t_i)_i) : \sigma \times \prod_i (\mathbf{int}^n \to \{r : \mathbf{int} \mid r\}).$$

Remark 1. As in the case above, there is often a way to avoid the restrictions 1–5 listed above. A more fundamental restriction (besides the restriction that only first-order function variables may be used in refinement predicates), which is imposed by the syntax of refinement predicates defined in Section 2.1, is that existential quantifiers cannot be used. Due to the restriction, we cannot express the type:

$$\begin{array}{l} n : \mathbf{int} \to \{f : \mathbf{int} \to \mathbf{int} \mid \exists x. 1 \leq x \leq n \wedge f(x) = 0\} \\ \quad \to \{\nu : \mathbf{int} \mid \nu = 1\}, \end{array}$$

which describes a higher-order function that takes an integer n and a function f, and returns 1 if there exists a value x such that $1 \leq x \leq n \wedge f(x) = 0$. This is a typical specification for a search function.

3. Encoding Functional Refinement

In this section, we present a transformation $(-)^\sharp$ for reducing a general refinement type checking problem to the first-order refinement type checking problem. In the rest of the paper, we use the assumptions explained in Section 2.1.

We first explain the ideas of the transformation $(-)^\sharp$ informally in Section 3.1. We give the formal definition of the transformation in Section 3.2. Finally in Section 3.3, we show the soundness of our verification method that uses $(-)^\sharp$.

3.1 Idea of the Transformation

The transformation $(-)^\sharp$ is in fact the composition of four transformations: $((((-)^{\sharp_1})^{\sharp_2})^{\sharp_3})^{\sharp_4}$. We explain the idea of each transformation from $(-)^{\sharp_4}$ to $(-)^{\sharp_1}$ in the reverse order of the applications, since $(-)^{\sharp_4}$ is the key step and the other ones perform preprocessing to enable the transformation $(-)^{\sharp_4}$.

$\sharp_4$: *Elimination of universal quantifiers and function symbols from a refinement predicate*

We first discuss a simple case, where there occur only one universal quantifier and one function symbol in a refinement predicate. Consider a refinement type of the form

$$\{f : \mathbf{int} \to \mathbf{int} \mid \forall x.\ P[f\,x]\}$$

where $P[f\,x]$ contains just one occurrence of $f\,x$ and no other occurrences of function variables. It can be encoded into the first-order refinement type

$$(x : \mathbf{int}) \to \{r : \mathbf{int} \mid P[r]\}.$$

By the semantics of types, the latter type means that, *for all argument* x, its "return value" r (i.e., $f x$) satisfies $P[r]$. The application $f\,x$ in the former type is expressed by the refinement variable r of the return value type, and the original quantifier $\forall x$ is encoded by the function type, or more precisely, "for all" in the semantics of the function type.

Now, let us consider a more general case where multiple function symbols occur. Given the type checking problem

$$\overset{?}{\models} (t_1, t_2)\ :\ \{(f, g) : (\tau_1 \to \tau_1') \times (\tau_2 \to \tau_2') \mid \forall x_1, x_2.\ P[f\,x_1, g\,x_2]\}$$

where each of the two different function variables occurs once in $P[f\,x_1, g\,x_2]$, we can transform it to:

$$\mathbf{let}\ f = t_1\ \mathbf{in}\ \mathbf{let}\ g = t_2\ \mathbf{in}\ \lambda(x_1, x_2).\, (f\,x_1, g\,x_2)\ :\ ((x_1, x_2) : \tau_1 \times \tau_2) \to \{(r_1, r_2) : \tau_1' \times \tau_2' \mid P[r_1, r_2]\}.$$

As in the case above for a single function occurrence, the transformation preserves the validity of the judgment.

To apply the transformation above, the following conditions on the refinement predicate (the part $\forall x_1, x_2.\ P[f\,x_1, g\,x_2]$ above) are required. (i) all the occurrences of function variables (f and g) are distinct from each other (ii) function arguments (x_1 and x_2 above) are variables rather than arbitrary terms, and they are distinct from each other, and universally quantified (iii) function variables f and g in a predicate P in $\{\nu : \sigma \mid P\}$ are declared at the position of ν. Those conditions are achieved by the preprocessing $(-)^{\sharp_3}$, $(-)^{\sharp_2}$, and $(-)^{\sharp_1}$ explained below.

$\sharp_3$ *Replication of functions*

If a function variable occurs n (> 1) times in a refinement predicate, we replicate the function and make a tuple consisting of n copies of the function. For example, for a typing

$$t : \{f : \mathbf{int} \to \mathbf{int} \mid P[f\,x, f\,y]\}$$

where f occurs exactly twice, we transform this to

$$\mathbf{let}\ f = t\ \mathbf{in}\ (f, f) :\ \{(f_1, f_2) : (\mathbf{int} \to \mathbf{int})^2 \mid P[f_1\,x, f_2\,y]\},$$

so that each of the function variables f_1 and f_2 now occurs just once in the refinement predicate.

$\sharp_2$ *Normalization of function arguments in refinement predicates*

In this step, we ensure that all the function arguments in refinement predicates are variables, different from each other, and quantified universally.

Given a type of the form:

$$\{f : \mathbf{int} \to \mathbf{int} \mid \forall \widetilde{x}.\ P[f\,t]\}$$

where $P[-]$ is a context with one occurrence of the hole $[\,]$ and t is either a non-variable, or a quantified variable $x_i \in \{\widetilde{x}\}$ but there is another occurrence of x_i, we transform this to

$$\{f : \mathbf{int} \to \mathbf{int} \mid \forall \widetilde{x}, y.\ y = t \texttt{ => } P[f\,y]\}$$

where y is a fresh variable.

Recall that => is an expression-level Boolean primitive. Thus, the transformation above preserves the semantics of types only if t is effect-free; this is guaranteed by Assumption (iv) in Section 2.3.

$\sharp_1$ *Removal of dependencies between functional arguments and return types*

In Step $\sharp_4$ above, we assumed "(iii) function variables ... in a predicate P in $\{\nu : \sigma \mid P\}$ are declared at the position of ν"; this can be relaxed so that a function variable in P may be bound at the position of f in $(f\!:\tau) \to \{\nu : \sigma \mid P\}$ as described below. A judgment

$$\overset{?}{\models} t : (f : \tau_1 \to \tau_2) \to \{\nu : \tau \mid P\}$$

can be transformed to

$$\overset{?}{\models} \mathbf{let}\ g = t\ \mathbf{in}\ \lambda f'.\, (f', g\,f') :\ (f\!:\tau_1 \!\to\! \tau_2) \to \{(f', \nu) \!: (f'\!:\tau_1 \to \tau_2) \times \tau \mid P[f \mapsto f']\}$$

where the function variable f' is fresh. Here, the function argument has been copied and attached to the return value, so that P may refer to the original argument.

In Section 1, $(-)^{\sharp_1}$ has been used for the example of `append2`. We now demonstrate uses of $(-)^{\sharp_2}$ and $(-)^{\sharp_4}$ with the other example in Section 1:

$$\overset{?}{\models} \texttt{(sum, sum2)}\ :\ (f : \mathbf{int} \to \mathbf{int}) \times \{g : \mathbf{int} \to \mathbf{int} \mid \forall n.\, g(n) = f(n)\}.$$

The refinement predicate is transformed by $(-)^{\sharp_2}$ to

$$\forall n, n_1, n_2.\ n_1 = n \texttt{ => } n_2 = n \texttt{ => } g(n_1) = f(n_2),$$

which is equivalent to

$$\forall n_1, n_2.\ n_1 = n_2 \texttt{ => } g(n_1) = f(n_2).$$

By $(-)^{\sharp_4}$, the above type checking problem is reduced to the following one:

$$\overset{?}{\models} \lambda(n_1, n_2).\, (\texttt{sum}\,n_1, \texttt{sum2}\,n_2)\ :\ ((n_1, n_2) : \mathbf{int}^2) \to \{(r_1, r_2) : \mathbf{int}^2 \mid n_1 = n_2 \texttt{ => } r_2 = r_1\}.$$

One may notice that the result of the transformation above is different from that of `sum` and `sumacc` in Section 1, which is obtained by applying a further transformation explained in Section 4.

3.2 Transformations

We give formal definitions of the transformations $(-)^{\sharp_1}$, $(-)^{\sharp_2}$, $(-)^{\sharp_3}$, and $(-)^{\sharp_4}$ in this order.

$$\left(\left\{ \nu : \prod_{i=1}^{n} x_i\colon \mathbf{int} \times \prod_{j=1}^{m} f_j\colon ((y_j{:}\tau_j) \to \tau'_j) \,\middle|\, P \right\}\right)^{\sharp_1} \stackrel{\text{def}}{=}$$

$$\left\{\nu : \prod_{i=1}^{n} x_i\colon \mathbf{int} \times \prod_{j=1}^{m} (f_j\colon (y_j{:}\tau_j) \to \tau'_j)^{\sharp_1} \,\middle|\, P\right\}$$

$$(((y_k)_k{:}\tau) \to \tau')^{\sharp_1} \stackrel{\text{def}}{=}$$

$$\left((y_k)_k\colon (\tau)^{\sharp_1}\right) \to \left((y'_k)_{k\in D(1)} : \tau^{(1)}\right) \times \left((\tau')^{\sharp_1} [y_k \mapsto y'_k]_{k\in D(1)}\right)$$

where, for the type $\tau = \left\{(y_k)_k : \prod_k (y_k\colon \rho_k) \mid P\right\}$,

$$D(1) \stackrel{\text{def}}{=} \{k \mid \rho_k \text{ is depth-1}\}$$

$$\tau^{(1)} \stackrel{\text{def}}{=} \left\{(y_k)_{k\in D(1)} : \prod_{k\in D(1)} (y_k\colon \rho_k) \,\middle|\, P\right\}$$

Note that $(\tau)^{\sharp_1} = \tau$ if τ is at most order-1; hence we have the obvious projection $\mathbf{pr}^{(1)} : (\tau)^{\sharp_1} \to \tau^{(1)}$, which is used below.

$$(\mathbf{fix}(f, \lambda x.\, t))^{\sharp_1} \stackrel{\text{def}}{=} \mathbf{fix}(f, \lambda x.\, (\mathbf{pr}^{(1)} x, (t)^{\sharp_1}))$$

$$(t_1\, t_2)^{\sharp_1} \stackrel{\text{def}}{=} \mathbf{pr}_2((t_1)^{\sharp_1}\, (t_2)^{\sharp_1})$$

Figure 5. Returning Input Functions $(-)^{\sharp_1}$

$$\left(\left\{ \nu\colon \prod_{i=1}^{n} (x_i{:}\mathbf{int}) \times \prod_{j=1}^{m} (f_j\colon (y_j{:}\tau_j) \to \tau'_j) \,\middle|\, P \right\}\right)^{\sharp_2} \stackrel{\text{def}}{=}$$

$$\left\{ \nu\colon \prod_{i=1}^{n} (x_i{:}\mathbf{int}) \times \prod_{j=1}^{m} \left(f_j\colon \left(y_j\colon (\tau_j)^{\sharp_2}\right) \to (\tau'_j)^{\sharp_2}\right) \,\middle|\, (P)^{\sharp_2} \right\}$$

$$(\forall x_1, \ldots, x_n.\, \wedge_k\, t_k)^{\sharp_2}$$

$$\stackrel{\text{def}}{=} \texttt{eOQ}\left(\forall \widetilde{x_i}.\forall \widetilde{z_{k,l}} \wedge_k \left(\texttt{argEq}(\texttt{app}(t_k)) \Rightarrow \texttt{sArg}(t_k)\right)\right)$$

$$\stackrel{\text{def}}{=} \forall \widetilde{z_{k,l}} \wedge_k \left(\left(\texttt{argEq}(\texttt{app}(t_k)) \Rightarrow \texttt{sArg}(t_k)\right)[x_i \mapsto z_k^i]\right)$$

where $\texttt{sArg}$ and $\texttt{argEq}$ are defined as below, and the variables $z_{k,1}, \ldots, z_{k,m_k}$ are all the elements of $\{\, z^{\langle (f\,t)^i \rangle} \mid (f\,t)^i \in \texttt{app}(t_k) \,\}$.

$$\texttt{sArg}((f\,t)^i) \stackrel{\text{def}}{=} f\, z^{\langle (f\,t)^i \rangle}$$

$\texttt{sArg}(t^i)$ is defined compositionally when t is not an application

$$\texttt{argEq}(\{a_1, \ldots, a_m\}) \stackrel{\text{def}}{=} \texttt{argEq}(\{a_1\}) \,\&\, \cdots \,\&\, \texttt{argEq}(\{a_m\})$$

$$\texttt{argEq}(\{(f\,t)^i\}) \stackrel{\text{def}}{=} (z^{\langle (f\,t)^i \rangle} = \texttt{sArg}(t))$$

Figure 6. Normalization of function arguments $(-)^{\sharp_2}$

For the sake of simplicity, w.l.o.g., we assume that every term has a type of the following form:

$$\tau ::= \left\{ \nu : \prod_{i=1}^{n} x_i\colon \mathbf{int} \times \prod_{j=1}^{m} (f_j\colon (y_j\colon \tau_j) \to \tau'_j) \,\middle|\, P \right\}.$$

In fact, any type (and accordingly terms of that type) can be transformed to the above form: e.g.,

$$\{(f, x) : (f\colon \{f : \tau{\to}\tau' \mid P_1\}) \times \{x : \mathbf{int} \mid P_2\} \mid P\}$$

can be transformed to

$$\{(x, f) : \mathbf{int} \times (\tau{\to}\tau') \mid P_1 \wedge P_2 \wedge P\}.$$

(The logical connective $\wedge$ was introduced as a primitive in Section 2 for this purpose.) For an expression t of the above type, we write $\mathbf{pr}_i^{\mathbf{int}}(t)$ to refer to the i-th integer (i.e., x_i), and $\mathbf{pr}_j^{\to}(t)$ to refer to the j-th function (i.e., f_j). The operators $\mathbf{pr}_i^{\mathbf{int}}$ and $\mathbf{pr}_j^{\to}$ can be expressed by compositions of the primitive $\mathbf{pr}_i$ in Section 2.1. Inside the refinement predicate P above, we sometimes write x_i and f_j to denote $\mathbf{pr}_i^{\mathbf{int}}\nu$ and $\mathbf{pr}_j^{\to}\nu$ respectively.

$\sharp_1$: Removal of Dependencies between Functional Arguments and Return Types

Figure 5 shows the key cases of the definition of the transformation $(-)^{\sharp_1}$ for types and terms. For types, $(-)^{\sharp_1}$ copies (the depth-1 components of) the argument type of a function type to the return type. For example, a refinement type of the form

$$((x, f)\colon \mathbf{int}{\times}(\mathbf{int}{\to}\mathbf{int})) \to \{r\colon \sigma \mid P(r, x, f)\}$$

is transformed to a type of the form

$$((x, f)\colon \mathbf{int}{\times}(\mathbf{int}{\to}\mathbf{int})){\to}(f'\colon (\mathbf{int}{\to}\mathbf{int})){\times}\{r\colon \sigma \mid P(r, x, f')\}.$$

Note that the return type no longer depends on the argument f.

As for the term transformation, in the rule for $\mathbf{fix}(f, \lambda x.\, t)$, (the depth-1 components of) the argument x is added to the return value. $t_1 t_2$, $(t_1)^{\sharp_1}\,(t_2)^{\sharp_1}$ returns a pair of (the depth-1 components of) the value of t_2 and the value of $t_1 t_2$; therefore, we extract such the value of $t_1 t_2$ by applying the projection. For example, the term $\mathbf{fix}(f, \lambda x.\, f\, x)$ is transformed to $\mathbf{fix}(f, \lambda x.\, (\mathbf{pr}^{(1)} x, \mathbf{pr}_2(f\, x)))$.

After the transformation $(-)^{\sharp_1}$, the type of the program satisfies a more restricted well-formedness condition, obtained by replacing all judgments $\Gamma \mid \Delta \vdash_{\texttt{WF}} P$ in Figure 4 with $\Gamma, \Delta \mid\ \vdash_{\texttt{WF}} P$.

$\sharp_2$: Normalization of Function Arguments in Refinement Predicates

Figure 6 defines the transformation $(-)^{\sharp_2}$. In the figure, $\&$ is an expression-level Boolean conjunction, and $\wedge_k\, t_k$ abbreviates $t_1 \wedge \cdots \wedge t_k$. For each occurrence of application $(f\,t')^i$ in P (where i denotes its position in P, used to discriminate between multiple occurrences of the same term $f\,t'$; i is omitted if it is clear), we prepare a fresh variable $z^{\langle (f\,t')^i \rangle}$; for an occurrence of a term t^i in P, $\texttt{app}(t^i)$ is the set of occurrences of applications in t^i; $\texttt{sArg}(t^i)$ is the term obtained by replacing the argument t' of each $(f\,t')^i \in \texttt{app}(t^i)$ with $z^{\langle (f\,t')^i \rangle}$; and $\texttt{argEq}(-)$ equates such t' and $z^{\langle (f\,t')^i \rangle}$. In the figure, $\texttt{eOQ}(-)$ eliminates the original quantifiers $\forall \widetilde{x_i}$ as follows: by the assumption 2 in Section 2.3, for each i and k, if x_i occurs in t_k, then x_i occurs at least once as the argument of an application, and so there is some z_k^i such that $(z_k^i = x_i) \in \texttt{argEq}(t_k)$; hence $\forall x_i$ can be eliminated by substituting z_k^i for x_i.

For example, consider the type

$$\{(f, g)\colon (\mathbf{int} \to \mathbf{int})^2 \mid \forall x.\, f\,x = g\,x\}.$$

Let t be $(f\,x = g\,x)$ and P be $\forall x.\, t$, then

$$\texttt{app}(t) = \{f\,x, g\,x\},$$

$$\begin{aligned}\texttt{argEq}(\texttt{app}(t)) &= \texttt{argEq}(f\,x) \,\&\, \texttt{argEq}(g\,x)\\ &= (z^{\langle fx \rangle} = \texttt{sArg}(x)) \,\&\, (z^{\langle gx \rangle} = \texttt{sArg}(x))\\ &= (z^{\langle fx \rangle} = x) \,\&\, (z^{\langle gx \rangle} = x),\end{aligned}$$

$$\texttt{sArg}(f\,x = g\,x) = (f\,z^{\langle fx \rangle} = g\,z^{\langle gx \rangle}),$$

and the transformed predicate before $\texttt{eOQ}(-)$ is

$$\forall x, z^{\langle fx \rangle}, z^{\langle gx \rangle}.\ z^{\langle fx \rangle} = x \ \&\ z^{\langle gx \rangle} = x \ \texttt{=>}\ f\,z^{\langle fx \rangle} = g\,z^{\langle gx \rangle}.$$

By applying $\texttt{eOQ}(-)$, we obtain:

$$\forall z^{\langle fx \rangle}, z^{\langle gx \rangle}.\ z^{\langle fx \rangle} = z^{\langle fx \rangle} \ \&\ z^{\langle gx \rangle} = z^{\langle fx \rangle} \ \texttt{=>}\ f\,z^{\langle fx \rangle} = g\,z^{\langle gx \rangle},$$

$$\left(\left\{\nu : \prod_{i=1}^{n}(x_i\colon \mathbf{int}) \times \prod_{j=1}^{m}(f_j\colon \tau_j \to \tau'_j) \;\middle|\; P\right\}\right)_{\phi}^{\sharp_3} \stackrel{\text{def}}{=}$$

$$\left\{\nu : \prod_{i=1}^{n}(x_i\colon \mathbf{int}) \times \prod_{j=1}^{m}\prod_{l=1}^{m_j}(f_{j,l}\colon (\tau_j)_{\phi_j}^{\sharp_3} \to (\tau'_j)_{\phi'_j}^{\sharp_3})) \;\middle|\; P'\right\}$$

where, $\phi = \{\prod_{i=1}^{n}\mathbf{int} \times \prod_{j=1}^{m}(\phi_j \to \phi'_j) \mid M\}$; $m_j = M(j)$; let $a_{j,1}, \ldots, a_{j,m'_j}$ be all the occurrences of applications of f_j occurring in P and let m'_j be $mul(P, j)$ ($m'_j \leq m_j$ since $\tau \leq_{mul} \phi$); and

$$P' \stackrel{\text{def}}{=} P[a_{j,l} \mapsto f_{j,l}\, t_{j,l}]_{j\in\{1,\ldots,m\},l\in\{1,\ldots,m'_j\}}$$

(where $a_{j,l} = f_j\, t_{j,l}$)

$$(\mathbf{fix}(f, \lambda x.\, t))_T^{\sharp_3} \stackrel{\text{def}}{=} \overrightarrow{\mathbf{fix}(f, \lambda x.\, (t)_T^{\sharp_3}\,[f \mapsto \overrightarrow{f}^{m}])}^{m}$$

$(m = T(\mathbf{fix}(f, \lambda x.\, t))$ and $\overrightarrow{t}^{m} = \underbrace{(t, \ldots, t)}_{m}$ for a term t)

$$(t_1\, t_2)_T^{\sharp_3} \stackrel{\text{def}}{=} \left(\mathbf{pr}_1 (t_1)_T^{\sharp_3}\right) (t_2)_T^{\sharp_3}$$

Figure 7. Replication of functions $(-)^{\sharp_3}$

which may be simplified further to

$$\forall z^{\langle fx\rangle}, z^{\langle gx\rangle}.\ z^{\langle fx\rangle} = z^{\langle gx\rangle} \Rightarrow f\, z^{\langle fx\rangle} = g\, z^{\langle gx\rangle}.$$

$\sharp_3$: Replication of Functions

As explained in Section 3.1, $(-)^{\sharp_3}$ replicates a function f_j according to the number m_j of occurrences of f_j in the predicate P of a refinement type $\tau = \left\{\nu : \prod_{i=1}^{n}\mathbf{int} \times \prod_{j=1}^{\ell}(f_j\colon \tau_j \to \tau'_j) \;\middle|\; P\right\}$; we call m_j *the multiplicity of* f_j and write $mul(\tau, j)$ or $mul(P, j)$. We call the sequence $(m_j)_j = m_1 \cdots m_\ell$ *the multiplicity of* τ.

The transformation $(t)^{\sharp_3}$ is parameterized by a *multiplicity type* ϕ for types, and a *multiplicity annotation* T for terms. The multiplicity types are defined by the following grammar:

$$\phi ::= \{\prod_{i=1}^{n}\mathbf{int} \times \prod_{j=1}^{m}(\phi_j \to \phi'_j) \mid M\}$$

Here, M is a function from $\{1, \ldots, m\}$ to positive integers such that $M(j) = 1$ if $\phi_j \to \phi'_j$ is not depth-1. Intuitively, $M(j)$ denotes how many copies should be prepared for the j-th function (of type $\phi_j \to \phi'_j$). For a refinement type $\tau = \left\{\nu : \prod_{i=1}^{n}(x_i\colon \mathbf{int}) \times \prod_{j=1}^{m}(f_j\colon \tau_j \to \tau'_j) \;\middle|\; P\right\}$ and a multiplicity type $\phi = \{\prod_{i=1}^{n}\mathbf{int} \times \prod_{j=1}^{m}(\phi_j \to \phi'_j) \mid M\}$, we write $\tau \leq_{mul} \phi$ if all the multiplicities in τ are pointwise less than or equal to those in ϕ, i.e., if $\leq M(j)$, $\tau_j \leq_{mul} \phi_j$, and $\tau'_j \leq_{mul} \phi'_j$ for all j. Intuitively, $\tau \leq_{mul} \phi$ means that copying functions according to ϕ is sufficient for keeping track of the correlations between functions expressed by τ. Thus, in the transformation rule for types in Figure 7, we assume that $\tau \leq_{mul} \phi$, and replicate each function type according to ϕ.

The multiplicity annotation T used in the transformation of terms maps each (occurrence of) subterm to its *multiplicity*. Here, if a subterm has simple type $\mathbf{int}^n \times \prod_{j=1}^{\ell}(\tau_j \to \tau'_j)$, then its *multiplicity* is a sequence $m_1 \cdots m_\ell$ of positive integers. In the case for abstractions, as explained in Section 3.1, a function $\mathbf{fix}(f, \lambda x.\, t)$ is copied to an m-tupled function where m is the multiplicity of $\mathbf{fix}(f, \lambda x.\, t)$. In the case for applications, correspondingly to the case for abstractions, after that we have to insert projection $\mathbf{pr}_1$ for matching types correctly.

$$\left(\left\{\nu : \prod_{i=1}^{n}(x_i\colon \mathbf{int}) \times \prod_{j=1}^{m}(f_j\colon (y_j\colon \tau_j) \to \tau'_j) \mid P\right\}\right)^{\sharp_4} \stackrel{\text{def}}{=}$$

$$\prod_{i=1}^{n}(x_i\colon \mathbf{int}) \times \left(\begin{array}{l} \left((y_j)_j\colon \prod_{j=1}^{m}\left((\tau_j)^{\sharp_4}\right)_\perp\right) \\ \to \left\{(r_j)_j\colon \prod_{j=1}^{m}\left((\tau'_j)^{\sharp_4}\right)_\perp \;\middle|\; (P)^{\sharp_4}\right\} \end{array}\right)$$

where, let $a_1, \ldots, a_{m'}$ be all the occurrences of applications in P, then, for $P = \forall z_1, \ldots, z_{m'}.\, \wedge_k t_k$,

$$(P)^{\sharp_4} \stackrel{\text{def}}{=} ((\wedge_k t_k)[a_l \mapsto r_{\hat{j}(a_l)}]_{l\in m'})[\hat{z}^{(a_l)} \mapsto y_{\hat{j}(a_l)}]_{l\in m'}.$$

$$((t_1, \ldots, t_n, t'_1, \ldots, t'_m))^{\sharp_4} \stackrel{\text{def}}{=}$$

$$\mathbf{let}\ x_1 = (t_1)^{\sharp_4}\ \mathbf{in} \cdots \mathbf{let}\ x_n = (t_n)^{\sharp_4}\ \mathbf{in}$$

$$\mathbf{let}\ f_1 = (t'_1)^{\sharp_4}\ \mathbf{in} \cdots \mathbf{let}\ f_m = (t'_m)^{\sharp_4}\ \mathbf{in}$$

$$(x_1, \ldots, x_n, \lambda y.\, (f_1\,(\mathbf{pr}_1 y), \ldots, f_m\,(\mathbf{pr}_m y)))$$

where t_i are integers and t'_i are functions.

$$\left(\mathbf{pr}_i^{\mathbf{int}} t\right)^{\sharp_4} \stackrel{\text{def}}{=} \mathbf{pr}_i\,(t)^{\sharp_4}$$

$$(\mathbf{pr}_j^{\to} t)^{\sharp_4} \stackrel{\text{def}}{=} \mathbf{let}\ w = (t)^{\sharp_4}\ \mathbf{in}\ t'$$

$$\text{where } t' \stackrel{\text{def}}{=} \lambda y.\, \mathbf{pr}_j((\mathbf{pr}_{n+1} w)(\underbrace{\overbrace{\perp, \ldots, \perp}^{j-1}, y, \perp, \ldots, \perp}_{m}))$$

and n and m are the numbers of the integer components and the function type components in the simple type of t, respectively.

Figure 8. Elimination of universal quantifiers and function symbols from a refinement predicate $(-)^{\sharp_4}$

Given a type checking problem $\overset{?}{\models} t : \tau$, we infer ϕ and T *automatically* (so that the transformation $(-)^{\sharp_3}$ is fully automatic). For multiplicity types, we can choose the least ϕ such that $\tau \leq_{mul} \phi$, and determine $T(t)$ according to ϕ. For some subterms, however, their multiplicity annotations are not determined by τ; for example, if $t = t_1 t_2$, then the multiplicity of t_2 depends on the refinement type of t_2 used for concluding $\models t_1\, t_2 : \tau$. For such a subterm t', we just infer the value of $T(t')$. Fortunately, as long as ϕ and T satisfy a certain consistency condition (for example, in **if** t_0 **then** t_1 **else** t_2, it should be the case that $T(t_1) = T(t_2)$), the transformation is sound (see Section 3.3). Since larger ϕ and T are more costly but allow us to keep track of the relationship among a larger number of more function calls (for example, if $T(f) = 2$, then we can keep track of the relationship between two function calls of f; that is sufficient for reasoning about the monotonicity of f), in the actual verification algorithm, we start with minimal consistent ϕ and T, and gradually increase them until the verification succeeds.

$\sharp_4$: Elimination of Universal Quantifier and Function Symbols

Figure 8 defines the transformation $(-)^{\sharp_4}$. For a type τ, we write $(\tau)_\perp$ for the *option type* $\tau + 1$; we explain this later.

For the transformation of refinement predicates, we use the functions $\hat{j}(-)$ and $\hat{z}^{(-)}$ defined as follows. For an input type $\{((x_i)_{i\leq n}, (f_j)_{j\leq m}) : \ldots \mid P\}$ of $(-)^{\sharp_4}$, we can assume that by $(-)^{\sharp_1}$, function symbols occurring in a refinement predicate are in $\{f_j \mid j \leq m\}$; and that by $(-)^{\sharp_2}$ and $(-)^{\sharp_3}$, all application occurrences in P have distinct function variables, and have distinct argument variables that quantified universally. Thus, there is an injection $\hat{\jmath}(-)$ from the set X of occurrences of applications in P to $\{j \mid j \leq m\}$ such that for any application occurrence ft, $f = f_{\hat{\jmath}(ft)}$; and also there is a bijection $\hat{z}^{(-)}$ from the same set X to the set of the variables that are universally in P.

For example, let us continue the example used for $\sharp_2$:

$$\{ (f, g) \colon (\mathbf{int} \to \mathbf{int})^2 \mid \forall z^{\langle fx \rangle}, z^{\langle gx \rangle}.\ z^{\langle fx \rangle} = z^{\langle gx \rangle} \Rightarrow f\, z^{\langle fx \rangle} = g\, z^{\langle gx \rangle} \}.$$

The transformed type is of the form

$$((y_1, y_2) \colon (\mathbf{int})^2_\bot) \to \left\{(r_1, r_2) \colon (\mathbf{int})^2_\bot \mid (\ldots)^{\sharp_4}\right\}.$$

The occurrences of applications are:

$$a_1 = f\, z^{\langle fx \rangle}, \quad a_2 = g\, z^{\langle gx \rangle},$$

and

$$\hat{z}^{(f\, z^{\langle fx \rangle})} = z^{\langle fx \rangle}, \quad \hat{z}^{(g\, z^{\langle gx \rangle})} = z^{\langle gx \rangle}.$$

Since the functions f and g are declared in this order,

$$\hat{\jmath}(f\, z^{\langle fx \rangle}) = 1, \quad \hat{\jmath}(g\, z^{\langle gx \rangle}) = 2.$$

Hence, the predicate $(\ldots)^{\sharp_4}$ is $y_1 = y_2 \Rightarrow r_1 = r_2$ and the transformed type is

$$((y_1, y_2) \colon (\mathbf{int})^2_\bot) \to \{(r_1, r_2) \colon (\mathbf{int})^2_\bot \mid y_1 = y_2 \Rightarrow r_1 = r_2\}.$$

The transformation of terms follows the ideas described in Section 3.1 except that option types have been introduced. For example, the term $(\lambda x.\, t_1, \lambda y.\, t_2)$ is transformed into the term

$$\lambda(x, y).\, \mathbf{let}\ r_1 = \mathbf{if}\ x = \bot\ \mathbf{then}\ \bot\ \mathbf{else}\ (t_1)^{\sharp_4}\ \mathbf{in}$$
$$\mathbf{let}\ r_2 = \mathbf{if}\ y = \bot\ \mathbf{then}\ \bot\ \mathbf{else}\ (t_2)^{\sharp_4}\ \mathbf{in}\ (r_1, r_2).$$

Here, $\bot$ is the exception of option types (i.e. `None` in OCaml or `Nothing` in Haskell), and we have omitted a projection from $(\tau)_\bot$ to τ above. The option type (and the conditional branch **if** $x = \bot$ **then** $\ldots$), is used to preserve the side effect (divergence or failure). For example, consider the following program:

```
let rec f x = ... and g y = g y in
let main n = assert (f n > 0)
```

This program defines functions `f` and `g` but does not use `g`. The body of the main function is transformed to `fst(fg(n,⊥))>0`, where `fg` is a (naïvely) tupled version of `(f,g)`, which simulates calls of `f` and `g` simultaneously. Without the option type, the simulation of a call of `g` would diverge.

As for the transformation of tuples in Figure 8, tuples of functions are transformed to functions on tuples as described in Section 3.1. Tuples of integers are just transformed in a compositional manner. In the case for projections, we can assume that $(t)^{\sharp_4}$ $(= x)$ is a tuple consisting of integers and a single function. If $\mathbf{pr}_i t$ is a function, $\mathbf{pr}_{i-n}(x\, (\bot, \ldots, \bot, w, \bot, \ldots, \bot))$ should correspond to $(\mathbf{pr}_i t)\, w$. Hence, the output of the transformation is $\lambda w.\, \mathbf{pr}_{i-n}(x\, (\bot, \ldots, \bot, w, \bot, \ldots, \bot))$. Otherwise, $\mathbf{pr}_i t$ is just transformed in a compositional manner.

Finally, we define $(-)^\sharp_T$ as the composition of the transformations:

$$(t)^\sharp_T = ((((t)^{\sharp_1})^{\sharp_2})^{\sharp_3}_T)^{\sharp_4}.$$

3.3 Soundness of the Transformation

The transformation $(-)^\sharp$ reduces type checking of general refinement types (with the assumptions in Section 2.3) into that of first-order refinement types, and its soundness is ensured by Theorem 1 below.

In the theorem, for a given typing judgment $\overset{?}{\models} t : \tau$, we assume a condition called *consistency* on multiplicity annotation T and multiplicity type ϕ. We give its formal definition in the full version of this paper [3]; intuitively, T and ϕ are consistent (with respect to t and τ) if it makes consistent assumptions on each subterm, so that the result of the transformation is simply-typed.

Theorem 1 (Soundness of Verification by the Transformation)**.** *Let t be a term and τ be a type of at most order-2.. Let T and ϕ be a multiplicity annotation and a multiplicity type for $((t)^{\sharp_1})^{\sharp_2}$ and $((\tau)^{\sharp_1})^{\sharp_2}$ and suppose that they are consistent and $\tau \leq_{mul} \phi$. Then,*

$$\models (t)^\sharp_T : (\tau)^\sharp_\phi \qquad \textit{implies} \qquad \models t : \tau.$$

Proof. See the full version [3]. □

As explained in Section 3.2, ϕ and T above are automatically inferred, and gradually increased until the verification succeeds. Thus, the transformation is automatic as a whole. The converse of Theorem 1, completeness, holds for order-1 types, but not for order-2: see Section 4.2.

4. Transformations for Enabling First-Order Refinement Type Checking

The transformation $(-)^\sharp$ in the previous section allowed us to reduce the refinement type checking $\overset{?}{\models} t : \tau$ to the first-order refinement type checking $\overset{?}{\models} (t)^\sharp : (\tau)^\sharp$, but it does not necessarily enable us to prove the latter by using the existing automated verification tools [11, 13, 14, 17, 18, 20]. This is due to the incompleteness of the tools for proving $\models (t)^\sharp : (\tau)^\sharp$. They are either based on (variations of) the first-order refinement type system [21] (see Appendix B for such a refinement type system), or higher-order model checking [10, 11], whose verification power is also equivalent to a first-order refinement type system (with intersection types). In these systems, the proof of $\models t : \tau$ (where τ is a first-order refinement type) must be compositional: if $t = t_1 t_2$, then τ' such that $\models t_1 : \tau' \to \tau$ and $\models t_2 : \tau'$ is (somehow automatically) found, from which $\models t_1 t_2 : \tau$ is derived. The compositionality itself is fine, but the problem is that τ' must also be a first-order refinement type, and furthermore, most of the actual tools can only deal with linear arithmetic in refinement predicates. To see why this is a problem, recall the example of proving `sum` and `sum2` in Section 1. It is expressed as the following refinement type checking problem:

$$\overset{?}{\models} (\mathtt{sum}, \mathtt{sum2}) :$$
$$(\mathtt{sum} : \mathbf{int} \to \mathbf{int}) \times ((n : \mathbf{int}) \to \{r : \mathbf{int} \mid r = \mathtt{sum}(n)\}).$$

It can be translated to the following first-order refinement type checking problem:

$$\overset{?}{\models} \lambda(x, y).(\mathtt{sum}\, x, \mathtt{sum2}\, y) :$$
$$((x, y) : \mathbf{int}^2) \to \{(r_1, r_2) : \mathbf{int}^2 \mid x = y \Rightarrow r_1 = r_2\}.$$

However, for proving the latter in a compositional manner using only first-order refinement types, one would have to infer the following non-linear refinement types for `sum` and `sum2`:

$$(x : \mathbf{int}) \to$$
$$\{r : \mathbf{int} \mid (x \leq 0 \Rightarrow r = 0) \wedge (x > 0 \Rightarrow r = x(x+1)/2)\}.$$

To deal with the problem above, we further refine the transformation $(-)^\sharp$ by (i) tupling of recursive functions [6] and (ii) insertion of assumptions.

4.1 Tupling of Recursion

The idea is that when a tuple of function calls is introduced by $(-)^{\sharp_4}$ ($(f_1\, (\mathbf{pr}_1 y)), \ldots, f_m\, (\mathbf{pr}_m y))$ in Figure 8 and $(\mathtt{sum}\, x, \mathtt{sum2}\, y)$ in the example above), we introduce a new recursive function for computing those calls simultaneously. For the example above, we introduce a new recursive function sum_sum2 defined by:

```
let rec sum_sum2 (x,y) = sum_sumacc(x,y,0)
and sum_sumacc(x,y,m) =
      if x<0 then if y<0 then (0,0) else ...
```

More generally, we combine simple recursive functions as follows. Consider the program:

$$\textbf{let } f = \textbf{fix}(f, \lambda x.\textbf{ if } t_{11} \textbf{ then } t_{12} \textbf{ else } E_1[f\,t_1]) \textbf{ in}$$
$$\textbf{let } g = \textbf{fix}(g, \lambda y.\textbf{ if } t_{21} \textbf{ then } t_{22} \textbf{ else } E_2[g\,t_2]) \textbf{ in} \dots (f, g) \dots$$

where E_1 and E_2 are evaluation contexts, and t_{ij}, E_i, and t_i have no occurrence of f nor g. Then, we replace $\lambda(x,y).\,(f\,x, g\,y)$ in $(-)^{\sharp_4}$ with the following tupled version:

$$\begin{array}{l}\lambda(x',y').\textbf{ let } \_ = f\,x' \textbf{ in}\\ \quad \textbf{fix}\big(h,\ \lambda(x,y).\\ \qquad \textbf{if } t_{11} \textbf{then if } t_{21} \textbf{ then } (t_{12}, t_{22}) \textbf{ else } (t_{12}, E_2[g\,t_2])\\ \qquad \textbf{else if } t_{21} \textbf{then } (E_1[f\,t_1], t_{22})\\ \qquad \textbf{else let } (r_1, r_2) = h\,(t_1, t_2) \textbf{ in } (E_1[r_1], E_2[r_2])\ \big)(x',y').\end{array}$$

The first application $f\,x'$ is inserted to preserve side effects (i.e., divergence and failure *fail*). To see why it is necessary, consider the case where $t_{11} = \textbf{true}$, $t_{12} = \textbf{fail}$ and $t_{21} = \Omega$. The call to the original function fails, but without $\textbf{let } \_ = f\,x' \textbf{ in} \cdots$, the call to the tupled version would diverge.

The function sum_sumacc shown in Section 1 can be obtained by the above tupling (with some simplifications).

4.2 Insertion of Assume Expressions

The above refinement of $(-)^{\sharp_4}$ alone is often insufficient. For example, consider the problem of proving that the function:

```
let diff (f,g) = fun x -> f x - g x
```

has the type

$$\begin{array}{rcl}\tau & \stackrel{\text{def}}{=} & \{(f,g) : (\textbf{int} \to \textbf{int})^2 \mid \forall x.\, f\,x > g\,x\}\\ & \to & \{h : \textbf{int} \to \textbf{int} \mid \forall x.\, h\,x > 0\}.\end{array}$$

The function is transformed to the following one by $(-)^{\sharp_4}$:

```
let diff fg = fun x ->
   let r1,r2 = fg (x, ⊥) in
   let r1',r2' = fg (⊥, x) in r1 - r2'
```

and the type τ is transformed to

$$\begin{array}{l}\big(\,((x_1,x_2) : \textbf{int}^2) \to \{(r_1,r_2)\colon \textbf{int}^2 \mid x_1 = x_2 \Rightarrow r_1 > r_2\}\big)\\ \quad \to \quad (\textbf{int} \to \{r\colon \textbf{int} \mid r > 0\}).\end{array}$$

Here, $\bot$ is used as a dummy argument as explained in Section 3.2-$\sharp_4$. We cannot conclude that $\texttt{r1} - \texttt{r2'}$ has type $\{r\colon \textbf{int} \mid r > 0\}$ because there is no information about the correlation between r1 and r2': from the refinement type of fg, we can infer that $x = \bot \Rightarrow r_1 > r_2$ and $\bot = x \Rightarrow r_1' > r_2'$, but $r1 > r2'$ cannot be derived.[5] In fact, $\models (\texttt{diff})^\sharp : (\tau)^\sharp$ does not hold,[6] which is a counterexample of the converse of Theorem 1.

[5] One may think that we can just combine the two calls of fg as

```
let diff fg =
fun x -> let r1,r2 = fg(x,x) in r1-r2'
```

This is certainly possible for the example above, but it is in general difficult if the occurrences of the two calls of fg are apart.

[6] To see this, apply $(\texttt{diff})^\sharp$ to

$$\lambda(x_1,x_2).\textbf{ if } x_1 = x_2 \textbf{ then } (1,0) \textbf{ else } (0,0)$$

and apply the returned value to, say, 0.

Table 1. Results of preliminary experiments

program	size (before $\sharp'$)	size (after $\sharp'$)	pred.	time[sec]
sum-acc	56	282	0	0.54
sum-simpl	40	270	0	0.75
sum-mono	27	279	0	0.45
mult-acc	63	347	0	0.38
a-max-gen	112	476	1	0.29
append-xs-nil	72	1364	0	45.57
append-nil-xs	63	725	0	16.43
rev	128	1868	0	176.24
insert	32	6262	0	52.49

To overcome the problem, we insert the following assertion just after the second call:

```
assume(let (r1'',r2'') = fg(x,x) in
          r1=r1'' & r2'=r2'')
```

Here, assume(t) is a shorthand for **if** t **then true else** loop() where loop() is an infinite loop. From fg(x,x), we obtain $\texttt{r1''} > \texttt{r2''}$ by using the refinement type of fg. We can then use the assumed condition to conclude that $\texttt{r1} > \texttt{r2'}$. In general, whenever there are two calls

```
let r1,r2 = fg (x, ⊥) in
C[let r1',r2' = fg (⊥, y) in ...]
```

(where C is some context), we insert an assume statement as in

```
let r1,r2 = fg (x, ⊥) in
C[let r1',r2' = fg (⊥, y) in
   assume(let (r1'',r2'') = fg(x,y)
               in r1=r1'' & r2'=r2''); ...]
```

We write $(-)^{\sharp'}$ for the above assume-inserted version of $(-)^\sharp$. The formal definition of $(-)^{\sharp'}$ is described in the full version of this paper [3]. In the target language, **fail** is treated as an exception, and we define **assume** (t) as a shorthand for:

$$\textbf{if } (\textbf{try } t \textbf{ with fail} \to \textbf{false}) \textbf{ then true else } \texttt{loop}().$$

Note that our backend model checker MoCHi [11, 14] supports exceptions. After replacing $(-)^\sharp$ with $(-)^{\sharp'}$, Theorem 1 is still valid:

$$\models (t)^{\sharp'}_{T} : (\tau)^{\sharp'}_{\phi} \qquad \text{implies} \qquad \models t : \tau.$$

See the full version [3] for the details of the proof.

5. Implementation and Experiments

We have implemented a prototype, automated verifier for higher-order functional programs as an extension to a software model checker MoCHi [11, 14] for a subset of OCaml.

Table 1 shows the results of the experiments. The columns "size" show the size of the programs before and after the transformations described in Section 4, where the size is measured by word counts.[7] The column "pred." shows the number of predicates manually given as hints for the backend model checker MoCHi. The experiment was conducted on Intel Core i7-3930K CPU and 16 GB memory. The implementation and benchmark programs are available at http://www-kb.is.s.u-tokyo.ac.jp/~ryosuke/mochi_rel/.

The programs used in the experiments are as follows. The programs "sum-acc", "sum-simpl", and "append-xs-nil" are those

[7] Because the transformation is automatic, we consider the number of words is a more appropriate measure (at least for the output of the transformation) than the number of lines.

given in Section 1. The program "mult-acc" is similar to "sum-acc" but calculates the multiplication. The program "sum-mono" asserts that the function sum is monotonic, i.e., $\forall m, n.\ m \leq n \Rightarrow$ $\mathtt{sum}(m) \leq \mathtt{sum}(n)$. The program "a-max-gen" finds the max of a functional array; the checked specification is that "a-max-gen" returns an upper bound. Here is the main part of the code of "a-max-gen".

```
let rec array_max i n array =
  if i >= n then 0 else
  let x = array i in
  let m' = array_max (i+1) n array in
    if x > m' then x else m'
let main i n =
  let array = make_array n in
  let m = array_max 0 n array in
    if i < n then assert (array i <= m)
```

The program "append-nil-xs" asserts that append nil xs = xs. The program "rev" asserts that two list reversal functions are the same, the one uses snoc function and the other one uses an accumulation parameter. The program "insert" asserts that insert x xs is sorted for a sorted list xs. Note that, for all the programs, invariant annotations were not supplied, except the specification being checked. For example, for "a-max-gen" above, the specification is that the main has type **int** → **int** → **unit**, which just means that the assertion assert (array i <= m) never fails; no type declaration for array_max was supplied. For the "append-xs-nil", as described in Section 1, the verifier checks that append has the type

$$xs\colon \tau \to (\{ys\colon \tau \mid ys(0) = \mathtt{None}\}) \to \{rs\colon \tau \mid \forall i. xs(i) = rs(i)\}$$

where $\tau \stackrel{\text{def}}{=}$ **int** → (**int option**). (See Appendix A for more details.)

In the table, one may notice that the program size is significantly increased by the transformation. This has been mainly caused by the tupling transformation for recursive functions. Since the size increase incurs a burden for the backend model checker, we plan to refine the transformation to suppress the size increase. Most of the time for verification has been spent by the backend model checker, not the transformation.

The programs above have been verified fully automatically except "a-max-gen", for which we had to provide one predicate by hand as a hint (for predicate abstraction) for the underlying model checker MoCHi. This is a limitation of the current implementation of MoCHi, rather than that of our approach. We have not been able to experiment with larger programs due to the limitation of MoCHi. We expect that with a further improvement of automated refinement type checkers, our verifier works for larger and more complex programs. Despite the limitation of the size of the experiments, we are not aware of any other verification tools that can verify all the above programs with the same degree of automation.

6. Related Work

Knowles and Flanagan [8, 9] gave a general refinement type system where refinement predicates can refer to functions. Their verification method is however a combination of static and dynamic checking, which delegates type constraints that could not be statically discharged to dynamic checking. The dynamic checking will miss potential bugs, depending on given arguments. On the other hand, our method is static and fully automatic.

Some of the recent work on (semi-)automated[8] refinement type checking [13, 24] supports the use of uninterpreted function symbols in refinement predicates. Uninterpreted functions can be used only for total functions. Furthermore, their method cannot be used to prove relational properties like the ones given in Section 1, since their method cannot refer to the definitions of the uninterpreted functions.

Unno et al. [19] have proposed another approach to increase the power of automated verification based on first-order refinement types. To overcome the limitation that refinement predicates cannot refer to functions, they added an extra integer parameter for each higher-order argument so that the extra parameter captures the behavior of the higher-order argument, and the dependency between the higher-order argument and the return value can be captured indirectly through the extra parameter. They have shown that the resulting first-order refinement type system is *in theory* relatively complete (in the same sense as Hoare logic is). With such an approach, however, a complex encoding of the information about a higher-order argument (essentially Gödel encoding) into the extra parameter would be required to properly reason about dependencies between functions, hence *in practice* (where only theorem provers for a restricted logic such as Presburger arithmetic is available), the verification of relational properties often fails. In fact, none of the examples used in the experiments of Section 5 (with encoding into the reachability verification problem considered in [19]) can be verified with their approach.

Suter et al. [15, 16] proposed a method for verifying correctness of first-order functional programs that manipulate recursive data structures. Their method is similar to our method in the sense that recursive functions can be used in a program specification. For example, the example programs "sum-simpl" and "append-nil-xs" can be verified by their method (if lists are not encoded as functions). Their method however can deal only with specifications which does not include partial functions. For this reason, if we rewrite the definition of sum as:

```
let rec sum n = if n=0 then 0 else n+sum(n-1)
```

their method cannot verify "sum-simpl" correctly, while our method can.

There are less automated approaches to refinement type checking, where programmers supply invariant annotations (in the form of refinement types) for all recursive functions [4, 5], and then verification conditions are generated and discharged by SMT solvers. Xu's method [22, 23] for contract checking also requires that contracts must be declared for all recursive functions. In contrast, in our method, a refinement type is used only for specifying the property to be verified, and no declaration is required for auxiliary functions.

There are several studies of interactive theorem provers (Coq, Agda, etc.) that can deal with general refinement types. These systems aim to support the verification, not to verify automatically. Therefore, one must give a complete proof of the correctness by hand. Moreover, these systems cannot deal directly with terminating programs and the proof of the termination is also required.

7. Conclusion and Future Work

We have proposed an automated method for verification of relational properties of functional programs, by reduction to the first-order refinement type checking. We have confirmed the effectiveness of the method using a prototype implementation. Future work includes a proof of the relative completeness of our verification method (with respect to a general refinement type system) and an extension of the method to deal with more expressive refinement types. As described in Section 2, we restrict refinement predicates to top-level quantifiers over the base type and first-order function variables. Relaxing this limitation is also left for future work.

[8] Not fully automated in the sense that a user must supply hints on predicates.

Acknowledgment

We would like to thank Naohiko Hoshino and anonymous referees for useful comments. This work was supported by Kakenhi 23220001.

References

[1] A. Ahmed. Step-indexed syntactic logical relations for recursive and quantified types. In *ESOP '06*, pages 69–83, 2006.

[2] A. W. Appel and D. McAllester. An indexed model of recursive types for foundational proof-carrying code. *TOPLAS*, 23(5):657–683, Sept. 2001.

[3] K. Asada, R. Sato, and N. Kobayashi. Verifying relational properties of functional programs by first-order refinement. An extended version, available from `http://www-kb.is.s.u-tokyo.ac.jp/~ryosuke/pepm2015.pdf`, 2014.

[4] G. Barthe, C. Fournet, B. Grégoire, P.-Y. Strub, N. Swamy, and S. Zanella-Béguelin. Probabilistic relational verification for cryptographic implementations. In *POPL '14*, volume 49, pages 193–205, 2014.

[5] J. Bengtson, K. Bhargavan, C. Fournet, A. D. Gordon, and S. Maffeis. Refinement types for secure implementations. *TOPLAS*, 33(2):8, Jan. 2011.

[6] W.-N. Chin. Towards an automated tupling strategy. In *PEPM 1993*, pages 119–132, 1993.

[7] D. Dreyer, A. Ahmed, and L. Birkedal. Logical step-indexed logical relations. In *LICS '09*, pages 71–80, 2009.

[8] K. Knowles and C. Flanagan. Type reconstruction for general refinement types. In *ESOP '07*, pages 505–519, 2007.

[9] K. L. Knowles and C. Flanagan. Hybrid type checking. *TOPLAS*, 32 (2), Jan. 2010.

[10] N. Kobayashi. Model checking higher-order programs. *J. ACM*, 60 (3):20, 2013.

[11] N. Kobayashi, R. Sato, and H. Unno. Predicate abstraction and CEGAR for higher-order model checking. In *PLDI '11*, pages 222–233, 2011.

[12] C.-H. L. Ong and S. J. Ramsay. Verifying higher-order functional programs with pattern-matching algebraic data types. In *POPL '11*, pages 587–598, 2011.

[13] P. M. Rondon, M. Kawaguchi, and R. Jhala. Liquid types. In *PLDI '08*, pages 159–169, 2008.

[14] R. Sato, H. Unno, and N. Kobayashi. Towards a scalable software model checker for higher-order programs. In *PEPM '13*, pages 53–62, 2013.

[15] P. Suter, M. Dotta, and V. Kuncak. Decision procedures for algebraic data types with abstractions. In *POPL '10*, volume 45, page 199, 2010.

[16] P. Suter, A. S. Köksal, and V. Kuncak. Satisfiability modulo recursive programs. In *SAS '11*, pages 298–315, 2011.

[17] T. Terauchi. Dependent types from counterexamples. In *POPL '10*, pages 119–130, 2010.

[18] H. Unno and N. Kobayashi. Dependent type inference with interpolants. In *PPDP '09*, pages 277–288, 2009.

[19] H. Unno, T. Terauchi, and N. Kobayashi. Automating relatively complete verification of higher-order functional programs. In *POPL '13*, page 75, 2013.

[20] N. Vazou, P. M. Rondon, and R. Jhala. Abstract refinement types. In *ESOP '13*, 2013.

[21] H. Xi and F. Pfenning. Dependent types in practical programming. In *POPL '99*, pages 214–227, 1999.

[22] D. N. Xu. Hybrid contract checking via symbolic simplification. In *PEPM '12*, pages 107–116, 2012.

[23] D. N. Xu, S. Peyton Jones, and K. Claessen. Static contract checking for Haskell. In *Workshop on Haskell*, pages 41–52, 2009.

[24] H. Zhu and S. Jagannathan. Compositional and lightweight dependent type inference for ML. In *VMCAI '13*, 2013.

A. Verification of "append-xs-nil"

We show that how our verifier transforms and verifies the program "append-xs-nil". The whole program is shown below:

```
let rec make_list n =
  if n < 0 then []
  else Random.int 10 :: make_list (n-1)
let rec append xs ys =
  match xs with
    [] -> ys
  | x::xs' -> x :: append xs' ys
let main n i =
  let xs = make_list n in
  let rs = append xs [] in
  assert (List.nth rs i = List.nth xs i)
```

The goal is to verify that the main function has type **int** $\rightarrow$ **int** $\rightarrow$ **unit**, which means that the assertion never fails. As mentioned in Section 5, only the program above is given to the verifier, without any annotations.

The verifier first encodes lists as functions. We use notations for lists and functions interchangeably below. The verifier next guesses a multiplicity annotation T by a heuristics. For this program, the verifier guesses that all the multiplicities are 1.

Then, the transformation $(-)^{\sharp 1}$ is applied to the program, and the following program is obtained.

```
let rec make_list n =
  if n < 0 then []
  else Random.int 10 :: make_list (n-1)
let rec append xs ys =
  match xs with [] -> [],ys,ys
  | x::xs' ->
      let xs'',ys',rs = append xs' ys in
      x::xs'', ys', x::rs
let main n i =
  let xs = make_list n in
  let xs',ys',rs = append xs [] in
  assert (List.nth rs i = List.nth xs' i)
```

The new `append` returns copies of its arguments `xs` and `ys`, and `xs'`, the copy of `xs`, is used in the assertion instead of `xs`.

The transformations $(-)^{\sharp 2}$ and $(-)^{\sharp 3}$ have no effect in this case. By applying the transformation $(-)^{\sharp 4}$, the following program is obtained:

```
let rec make_list n =
  if n < 0 then []
  else Random.int 10 :: make_list (n-1)
let rec append xs ys (i,j,k) =
  match xs with
    [] -> let r1,r2,r3 = None, ys j, ys k in
          assume (j=k => r2=r3); r1, r2, r3
  | x::xs' ->
      let xs''ys'rs = append xs' ys in
      if i = 0 & k = 0 then
        let _,r2,_ = xs''ys'rs(None,j,None) in
        x, r2, x
      else if i = 0 & k <> 0 then
        let _,r2,r3 = xs''ys'rs(None,j,k-1) in
        x, r2, r3
      else if k = 0 then
```

```
        let r1,r2,_ = xs''ys'rs(i-1,j,None) in
        r1, r2, x
      else
        xs''ys'rs(i-1,j,k-1)
let main n i =
  let xs = make_list n in
  let xs'_nil_rs = append xs [] in
  let xs'rs (i,j) =
    let r1,r2,r3 = xs'_nil_rs (i, None, j) in
    r1, r3
  in
  let r1,r2 = xs'rs (i,i) in
  assert (r2 = r1)
```

Here, we omit some constructors and pattern-matchings of option types.

The existing model checker MoCHi infers that the transformed `append` has the following first-order refinement type:

$$(\mathbf{int} \to \mathbf{int}) \to$$
$$((j : \mathbf{int}) \to \{y : \mathbf{int} \mid j = 0 \Rightarrow y = \mathtt{None}\}) \to$$
$$((i, j, k) : \mathbf{int}^3) \to \{(r_1, r_2, r_3) : \mathbf{int}^3 \mid i = j \Rightarrow r_1 = r_2\}$$

From the result of MoCHi, the verifier reports that the original program is safe.

B. A Refinement Type System

This section gives a sound type system for proving $\models t : \tau$. Here we do not assume the restrictions in Section 2.3. We obtain also *first-order refinement type system* by restricting the type system so that function variables are disallowed to occur in predicates in all the refinement types. Various *automatic* verification methods [11, 13, 14, 17, 18, 20] are available for the first-order refinement types.

The type judgment used in the type system is of the form $\Gamma \vdash^{\mathcal{L}}_{\mathrm{t}} t : \tau$, where Γ, called a type environment, is a sequence of type bindings of the form $x : \tau$, and $\mathcal{L}$ is (the name of) the underlying logic for deciding the validity of predicates, which we keep abstract through the paper. Below, we use general well-formedness $\vdash_{\mathtt{GWF}}$ (defined in the full version of this paper [3]), which represents usual scope rules of dependent types.

We define *value environments* as mappings from variables to closed values and use a meta variable η for them. For a value environment η and an environment Γ such that $\vdash_{\mathtt{GWF}} \Gamma$, we define $\eta \models^n_{\mathrm{e}} \Gamma$ as follows:

$$\emptyset \models^n_{\mathrm{e}} \emptyset \overset{\mathrm{def}}{\iff} \text{true}$$

$$\eta \cup \{x \mapsto V\} \models^n_{\mathrm{e}} \Gamma, x : \tau \overset{\mathrm{def}}{\iff} \eta \models^n_{\mathrm{e}} \Gamma \text{ and } \models^n_{\mathrm{v}} V : \tau[\eta]$$

The type judgment $\Gamma \vdash^{\mathcal{L}}_{\mathrm{t}} t : \tau$ semantically means that for any n and η, if $\eta \models^n_{\mathrm{e}} \Gamma$, then $\models^n_{\mathrm{v}} t[\eta] : \tau[\eta]$.

The *general refinement type system* is given in Figures 9 and 10. The judgment $\Gamma \mid P \vdash^{\mathcal{L}} P'$ means that, in $\mathcal{L}$, P implies P' under the type environment Γ. We assume that the logic $\mathcal{L}$ satisfies that, if $\Gamma \mid P \vdash^{\mathcal{L}} P'$, then for any n and η such that $\eta \models^n_{\mathrm{e}} \Gamma$ holds, $\models^n_{\mathrm{p}} P[\eta]$ implies $\models^n_{\mathrm{p}} P'[\eta]$. In Figure 9, we define $t'(\!|x \leftarrow t|\!)$ as **let** $x = t$ **in** t', and extend it to the operations $P(\!|x \leftarrow t|\!)$ and $\sigma(\!|x \leftarrow t|\!)$ compositionally. For example, $(\forall y.t_1 \wedge t_2)(\!|x \leftarrow t|\!) = \forall y.(t_1(\!|x \leftarrow t|\!)) \wedge (t_2(\!|x \leftarrow t|\!))$. We define $t(\!|x_1 \leftarrow t_1, \ldots, x_n \leftarrow t_n|\!)$ as $((t(\!|x_n \leftarrow t_n|\!)) \cdots)(\!|x_1 \leftarrow t_1|\!)$.

The type system is sound with respect to the semantics of types. A proof is given in the full version of this paper [3].

Theorem 2 (Soundness of the Type System). *$\vdash^{\mathcal{L}}_{\mathrm{t}} t : \tau$ implies $\models t : \tau$.*

$$\frac{\Gamma(x) = \tau \qquad \Gamma \vdash_{\mathtt{GWF}} \tau}{\Gamma \vdash^{\mathcal{L}}_{\mathrm{t}} x : \tau}\ (\text{T-VAR}) \qquad \frac{}{\Gamma \vdash^{\mathcal{L}}_{\mathrm{t}} n : \mathbf{int}}\ (\text{T-CONST})$$

$$\frac{\begin{array}{c}\Gamma \vdash^{\mathcal{L}}_{\mathrm{t}} t : \{\nu : \mathbf{int} \mid P\} \\ \Gamma, x : \{\nu : \mathbf{int} \mid P \wedge \nu = \mathbf{true}\} \vdash^{\mathcal{L}}_{\mathrm{t}} t_1 : \tau \\ \Gamma, x : \{\nu : \mathbf{int} \mid P \wedge \nu \neq \mathbf{true}\} \vdash^{\mathcal{L}}_{\mathrm{t}} t_2 : \tau \\ (x \notin FV(t_1) \cup FV(t_2))\end{array}}{\Gamma \vdash^{\mathcal{L}}_{\mathrm{t}} \mathbf{if}\ t\ \mathbf{then}\ t_1\ \mathbf{else}\ t_2 : \tau(\!|x \leftarrow t|\!)}\ (\text{T-IF})$$

$$\frac{\text{The arity of } [\![\mathsf{op}]\!] \text{ is } n \qquad \Gamma \vdash^{\mathcal{L}}_{\mathrm{t}} t_i : \mathbf{int}}{\Gamma \vdash^{\mathcal{L}}_{\mathrm{t}} \mathsf{op}(t_1, \ldots, t_n) : \mathbf{int}}\ (\text{T-OP})$$

$$\frac{\Gamma, f : (x_1 {:} \tau_1) \to \tau_2, x_1 : \tau_1 \vdash^{\mathcal{L}}_{\mathrm{t}} t : \tau_2 \quad (f \notin FV(\tau_1) \cup FV(\tau_2))}{\Gamma \vdash^{\mathcal{L}}_{\mathrm{t}} \mathbf{fix}(f, \lambda x_1.t) : (x_1 {:} \tau_1) \to \tau_2}\ (\text{T-FIX})$$

$$\frac{\Gamma \vdash^{\mathcal{L}}_{\mathrm{t}} t : \{\nu : (x_1 {:} \tau_1) \to \tau_2 \mid P\} \qquad \Gamma \vdash^{\mathcal{L}}_{\mathrm{t}} t_1 : \tau_1}{\Gamma \vdash^{\mathcal{L}}_{\mathrm{t}} t t_1 : \tau_2(\!|x_1 \leftarrow t_1|\!)}\ (\text{T-APP})$$

$$\frac{\Gamma \vdash^{\mathcal{L}}_{\mathrm{t}} t_i : \rho_i(\!|x_1 \leftarrow t_1, \ldots, x_{i-1} \leftarrow t_{i-1}|\!) \quad \text{for all } i \leq n}{\Gamma \vdash^{\mathcal{L}}_{\mathrm{t}} (t_1, \ldots, t_n) : \prod_{i=1}^n (x_i {:} \rho_i)}\ (\text{T-TUPLE})$$

$$\frac{\Gamma \vdash^{\mathcal{L}}_{\mathrm{t}} t : \{\nu : \prod_{i=1}^n (x_i {:} \rho_i) \mid P\} \qquad \rho_i = \{\nu_i : \sigma_i \mid P_i\}}{\Gamma \vdash^{\mathcal{L}}_{\mathrm{t}} \mathbf{pr}_i t : \{\nu_i : \sigma_i \mid P_i\}(\!|x_1 \leftarrow \mathbf{pr}_1 t, \ldots, x_{i-1} \leftarrow \mathbf{pr}_{i-1} t|\!)}\ (\text{T-PROJ})$$

$$\frac{}{\Gamma, x : \{\nu : \sigma \mid \mathbf{false}\} \vdash^{\mathcal{L}}_{\mathrm{t}} \mathbf{fail} : \tau}\ (\text{T-FAIL})$$

$$\frac{\vdash^{\mathcal{L}}_{\mathrm{es}} \Gamma' <: \Gamma \qquad \Gamma \vdash^{\mathcal{L}}_{\mathrm{t}} t : \tau \qquad \Gamma' \vdash^{\mathcal{L}}_{\mathrm{s}} \tau <: \tau'}{\Gamma' \vdash^{\mathcal{L}}_{\mathrm{t}} t : \tau'}\ (\text{T-SUB})$$

$$\frac{\Gamma \vdash^{\mathcal{L}}_{\mathrm{t}} t : \{\nu : \sigma \mid P(\!|\nu \leftarrow t|\!)\}}{\Gamma \vdash^{\mathcal{L}}_{\mathrm{t}} t : \{\nu : \sigma \mid P\}}\ (\text{T-SUBST})$$

$$\frac{\Gamma \vdash^{\mathcal{L}}_{\mathrm{t}} t : \{\nu : \sigma \mid P\} \qquad \Gamma \vdash^{\mathcal{L}}_{\mathrm{t}} t : \{\nu : \sigma \mid P'\}}{\Gamma \vdash^{\mathcal{L}}_{\mathrm{t}} t : \{\nu : \sigma \mid P \wedge P'\}}\ (\text{T-CONJ})$$

Figure 9. Typing rules

$$\frac{\Gamma \vdash^{\mathcal{L}}_{\mathrm{s}} \sigma <: \sigma' \qquad \Gamma, \nu : \sigma \mid P \vdash^{\mathcal{L}} P'}{\Gamma \vdash^{\mathcal{L}}_{\mathrm{s}} \{\nu : \sigma \mid P\} <: \{\nu : \sigma' \mid P'\}}\ (\text{SUB-REFINE})$$

$$\frac{}{\Gamma \vdash^{\mathcal{L}}_{\mathrm{s}} \mathbf{int} <: \mathbf{int}}\ (\text{SUB-INT}) \qquad \frac{\Gamma \vdash^{\mathcal{L}}_{\mathrm{s}} \tau_1' <: \tau_1 \qquad \Gamma, x_1 : \tau_1' \vdash^{\mathcal{L}}_{\mathrm{s}} \tau_2 <: \tau_2'}{\Gamma \vdash^{\mathcal{L}}_{\mathrm{s}} (x_1 : \tau_1) \to \tau_2 <: (x_1 : \tau_1') \to \tau_2'}\ (\text{SUB-FUN})$$

$$\frac{\Gamma, x_1 : \rho_1, \ldots, x_{i-1} : \rho_{i-1} \vdash^{\mathcal{L}}_{\mathrm{s}} \rho_i <: \rho_i' \quad \text{for all } i \leq n}{\Gamma \vdash^{\mathcal{L}}_{\mathrm{s}} \prod_{i=1}^n (x_i {:} \rho_i) <: \prod_{i=1}^n (x_i {:} \rho_i')}\ (\text{SUB-TUPLE})$$

$$\frac{}{\vdash^{\mathcal{L}}_{\mathrm{es}} \emptyset <: \emptyset}\ (\text{ENVSUB-NIL}) \qquad \frac{\vdash^{\mathcal{L}}_{\mathrm{es}} \Gamma <: \Gamma' \qquad \Gamma \vdash^{\mathcal{L}}_{\mathrm{s}} \tau <: \tau'}{\vdash^{\mathcal{L}}_{\mathrm{es}} \Gamma, x : \tau <: \Gamma', x : \tau'}\ (\text{ENVSUB-CONS})$$

Figure 10. Subtyping rules

Threads as Resource for Concurrency Verification

Duy-Khanh Le Wei-Ngan Chin Yong Meng Teo

Department of Computer Science, National University of Singapore

{leduykha,chinwn,teoym}@comp.nus.edu.sg

Abstract

In mainstream languages, threads are first-class in that they can be dynamically created, stored in data structures, passed as parameters, and returned from procedures. However, existing verification systems support reasoning about threads in a restricted way: threads are often represented by unique tokens that can neither be split nor shared.

In this paper, we propose "*threads as resource*" to enable more expressive treatment of first-class threads. Our approach allows the ownership of a thread (and its resource) to be flexibly split, combined, and (partially) transferred across procedure and thread boundaries. We illustrate the utility of our approach in handling three problems. First, we use "threads as resource" to verify the *multi-join pattern*, i.e. threads can be shared among concurrent threads and joined multiple times in different threads. Second, using inductive predicates, we show how our approach naturally captures the *threadpool idiom* where threads are stored in data structures. Lastly, we present how thread liveness can be precisely tracked. To demonstrate the feasibility of our approach, we implemented it in a tool, called THREADHIP, on top of an existing PARAHIP verifier. Experimental results show that THREADHIP is more expressive than PARAHIP while achieving comparable verification performance.

Categories and Subject Descriptors D.1.3 [*Concurrent Programming*]: Parallel programming; F.3.1 [Logics and Meanings of Programs]: Specifying and Verifying and Reasoning about Programs

General Terms Languages, Verification

Keywords Threads as Resource; Concurrency Verification; First-class Threads; Separation Logic

1. Introduction

Threads are considered as first-class in mainstream languages such as Java, C#, and C/C++ in that threads can be treated like objects of any other type: they can be dynamically created, stored in data structures, shared among different threads, passed as parameters, and returned from procedures. Hence, it is desirable for verification systems to support reasoning about first-class threads.

PEPM '15, January 13–14, 2015, Mumbai, India.

http://dx.doi.org/10.1145/2678015.2682540

One of the most popular techniques for reasoning about concurrent programs is separation logic [21, 23]. Originally, separation logic was used to verify heap-manipulating sequential programs, with the ability to express non-aliasing in the heap [23]. Separation logic was extended to verify shared-memory concurrent programs, e.g. concurrent separation logic [21], where ownerships of heap objects are considered as *resource*, which can be shared and transferred among concurrent threads. Using fractional permissions [2], one can express full ownerships for exclusive write accesses and partial ownerships for concurrent read accesses. Ownerships of stack variables can also be considered as resource and treated in the same way as heap objects [1].

Separation logic was traditionally extended to verify concurrent programs with parallel composition [21]. Recent works also extended separation logic to handle dynamically-created threads [12, 14, 15, 18, 19]. Hobor [14] allows threads to be dynamically created using fork but does not support join. Gotsman et al. [12] use thread handles to represent threads, while CHALICE [19] uses tokens, VERIFAST [15] uses thread permissions, and PARAHIP [18] uses **and**-conjuncts for the same purpose. A fork operation returns a unique handle/token/**and**-conjunct/permission (collectively referred to as thread token) and a join operation on a thread token causes the joining thread (joiner) to wait for the completion of the thread corresponding to the token (joinee). However, existing works [12, 14, 15, 18, 19] support reasoning about threads in a limited way: unique tokens (representing threads) are not allowed to be split and shared among different threads. As such, existing works do not fully consider threads as first-class.

Reasoning about first-class threads is challenging because threads are dynamic and non-lexically-scoped in nature. A thread can be dynamically created in a procedure (or a thread), but shared and joined in other procedures (or threads). In this paper, we propose an expressive treatment of first-class threads, called "*threads as resource*". Our approach enables threads' ownerships to be reasoned about in a similar way to other types of resource. A thread's ownership is created when it is forked, and destroyed when it is joined. In contrast to ownership of a normal heap object which specifies values of its fields, ownership of a thread carries resource that can be obtained by the joiner when the thread is joined. This is to cater for the intuition that when a joiner joins with a joinee, the joiner expects to obtain (in order to later read or write) certain resource transferred from the joinee. As threads in fork/join programs are typically non-lexically-scoped, we allow threads' ownerships to be soundly split, combined, and (possibly partially) transferred among procedures and threads.

Our approach elegantly solves at least three verification problems that were not properly supported. First, threads can now be passed as arguments, shared, and joined by different threads. This enables verification of intricate fork/join behaviors such as *multi-join pattern* where a thread is shared and joined in multiple threads. Using our approach, the ownership of the joinee (and its resource) can be split and transferred (or shared) among the multiple joiners, so that they can respectively join with the joinee and get their corresponding portions of the joinee's resource. Second, by treating threads in a similar way to heap objects, we can apply current advances in separation logic for heap objects to threads. For example, by combining "threads as resource" with inductive predicates, we can naturally capture a programming idiom called threadpool where threads are stored in data structures. Lastly, we can formally reason about the "liveness" of a thread. We achieve this by adding a special predicate that explicitly indicates when a thread is dead (i.e. after it is joined). Our approach has been implemented in a tool, called THREADHIP, on top of the PARAHIP verifier [18]. Experimental results show that our new tool THREADHIP is more expressive than PARAHIP, whilst achieving comparable verification performance.

The rest of this paper is organized as follows. Section 2 motivates our idea of "threads as resource". Section 3 introduces our core programming language and specification language, with a focus on modeling threads as resource. Section 4 presents our approach in details. Section 5 discusses three main applications of our approach. Section 6 presents our prototype implementation and experimental results. Section 7 summarizes related work. Section 8 concludes our paper.

2. A Motivating Example

This section illustrates our treatment of "threads as resource" for reasoning about programs with first-class threads. Fig. 1 shows a C-like program posing challenges to existing verification systems. In

```
1  data cell { int val; }
2
3  void thread1(cell x, cell y)
4    requires x↦cell(vx) * y↦cell(vy)
5    ensures x↦cell(vy) * y↦cell(vx);
6  { int tmp = x.val;   x.val = y.val;   y.val = tmp; }
7
8  void thread2(thrd t1, cell y)
9    requires t1↦thrd⟨y↦cell(vy)⟩
10   ensures y↦cell(vy + 2) ∧ dead(t1);
11 { // {t1↦thrd⟨y↦cell(vy)⟩}
12   join(t1);
13   // {y↦cell(vy) ∧ dead(t1)}
14   y.val = y.val+2;
15   // {y↦cell(vy + 2) ∧ dead(t1)}
16 }
17
18 void main()
19   requires emp ensures emp;
20 { cell x = new cell(1);   cell y = new cell(2);
21   // {x↦cell(1) * y↦cell(2)}
22   thrd t1 = fork(thread1,x,y);
23   // {t1↦thrd⟨x↦cell(2) * y↦cell(1)⟩}
24   // {t1↦thrd⟨x↦cell(2)⟩ * t1↦thrd⟨y↦cell(1)⟩}
25   thrd t2 = fork(thread2,t1,y);
26   //{t1↦thrd⟨x↦cell(2)⟩ * t2↦thrd⟨y↦cell(3)∧dead(t1)⟩}
27   join(t1);
28   //{x↦cell(2) * t2↦thrd⟨y↦cell(3)∧dead(t1)⟩ ∧ dead(t1)}
29   x.val = x.val+1;
30   //{x↦cell(3) * t2↦thrd⟨y↦cell(3)∧dead(t1)⟩ ∧ dead(t1)}
31   join(t2);
32   // {x↦cell(3) * y↦cell(3) ∧ dead(t1) ∧ dead(t2)}
33   assert(x↦cell(3) * y↦cell(3)); /*valid*/
34   destroy(x); destroy(y);
35   // {emp ∧ dead(t1) ∧ dead(t2)}
36 }
```

Figure 1. A Motivating Example

the program, the main thread executing the procedure `main` (called `main` thread) forks a new thread `t1` executing the procedure `thread1` (line 22). `thread1` will swap the values of the cells `x` and `y`. `main` then forks another thread `t2` executing the procedure `thread2` with `t1` passed as one of its arguments (line 25). Afterward, `t2` will join with `t1` (line 12) and manipulate the cell `y`, while `main` will also join with `t1` (line 27) but manipulate the cell `x`. In separation logic, a heap node $x \mapsto \mathit{cell}(vx)$ represents the ownership of an object of type *cell* pointed to by x and having the field `val` of vx (called ownership of x for short).

The program is challenging to verify because (1) fork and join operations on `t1` are non-lexically scoped (i.e. `t1` is forked in `main` but joined in thread `t2`), and (2) `t1` is shared and joined in both `t2` and `main` (i.e. a multi-join). In this program, the ownerships of `x` and `y` are flexibly transferred across thread boundaries, between `main`, `t1` and `t2`, via fork/join calls. To the best of our knowledge, we are not aware of any existing approaches capable of verifying this program. We propose *"threads as resource"* to verify such programs soundly and modularly. The key points to handle this program are (1) considering `t1` as resource, and (2) allowing it to be split and transferred between `main` and `t2` via fork/join calls.

Our approach is based on the following observation: when a thread (joiner) joins with another thread (joinee), the joiner expects to receive (in order to later read or write) certain resource transferred from the joinee. In the example program, `main` joins with `t1` and expects the ownership of `x` transferred from `t1`, while `t2` joins with `t1` and expects the ownership of `y`. Hence, the verification of the program in Fig. 1 is achieved by introducing the thread ownership $v \mapsto \mathsf{thrd}\langle\Phi\rangle$ indicating that v points to a possibly live thread (as resource) carrying certain resource Φ. A thread having the ownership $v \mapsto \mathsf{thrd}\langle\Phi\rangle$ can perform a `join(`v`)`, and yield the resource Φ and a pure predicate $\mathsf{dead}(v)$ after joining. This special predicate $\mathsf{dead}(v)$ explicitly indicates that thread v is no longer alive. In Fig. 1, when `t1` is forked (line 22), its precondition is consumed and exchanged for the thread's ownership $t1 \mapsto \mathsf{thrd}\langle x \mapsto \mathit{cell}(2) * y \mapsto \mathit{cell}(1)\rangle$ carrying the post-state of `thread1` (i.e. `t1`'s state after it has finished its execution). This is sound and modular as other threads can only observe the post-state of `thread1` when they join with `t1`. Our approach enables the thread's ownership to be split into $t1 \mapsto \mathsf{thrd}\langle x \mapsto \mathit{cell}(2)\rangle$ and $t1 \mapsto \mathsf{thrd}\langle y \mapsto \mathit{cell}(1)\rangle$ (from line 23 to line 24). This allows the latter to be transferred to `t2` while the former remains with `main`. Consequently, having the ownerships of `t1`, both `t2` and `main` can perform `join(t1)` and get the corresponding resource: `t2` obtains the ownership of `y` to write to it, while `main` obtains and writes to `x` (i.e. `t2` and `main` write-share the resource transferred from `t1`). Using our "threads as resource" approach, the program can be verified as both data-race-free and functionally correct.

Our treatment of "threads as resource" allows the ownership of a thread to be flexibly split and transferred. For example, in a program similar to Fig. 1, instead of writing to cells `x` and `y`, both `main` and t2 may want to concurrently read the value of the cells. Using fractional permissions [2], we could now split the ownership of `t1` from $t1 \mapsto \mathsf{thrd}\langle x \mapsto \mathit{cell}(2) * y \mapsto \mathit{cell}(1)\rangle$, into $t1 \mapsto \mathsf{thrd}\langle x \overset{0.6}{\longmapsto} \mathit{cell}(2) * y \overset{0.6}{\longmapsto} \mathit{cell}(1)\rangle$ and $t1 \mapsto \mathsf{thrd}\langle x \overset{0.4}{\longmapsto} \mathit{cell}(2) * y \overset{0.4}{\longmapsto} \mathit{cell}(1)\rangle$, and transfer them into the corresponding codes for `main` and `t2`. This allows `main` and `t2` to be able to read concurrently cells `x` and `y` after joining with the `t1` thread.

In summary, we propose to treat threads as resource, thus allowing threads' ownerships to be soundly split and transferred across procedure and thread boundaries. This supports first-class threads and enables modular reasoning of intricate concurrent programs with non-lexically-scoped fork/join and multi-join.

P	$::=$	$data\_decl^*\ global\_decl^*\ proc\_decl^*$	Program
$data\_decl$	$::=$	$\textbf{data}\ C\ \{\ field\_decl^*\ \}$	Data declaration
$field\_decl$	$::=$	$type\ f;$	Field declaration
$global\_decl$	$::=$	$\textbf{global}\ type\ v$	Global variable declaration
$proc\_decl$	$::=$	$type\ pn(param^*)\ spec^*\ \{\ S\ \}$	Procedure declaration
$spec$	$::=$	$\textbf{requires}\ \Phi_{pr}\ \textbf{ensures}\ \Phi_{po};$	Pre/Post-conditions
$param$	$::=$	$type\ v$	Parameter
$type$	$::=$	$\textbf{void} \mid \textbf{int} \mid \textbf{bool} \mid \textbf{thrd} \mid C$	Type
e	$::=$	$v \mid v.f \mid k \mid e_1{+}e_2 \mid e_1{=}e_2 \mid e_1{\neq}e_2$	Variable/field/constant/expression
S	$::=$	$v = \textbf{new}C(v^*) \mid \textbf{destroy}(v) \mid v = e$ $\mid v = \textbf{fork}(pn, v^*) \mid \textbf{join}(v) \mid pn(v^*)$ $\mid \textbf{if}\ e\ \textbf{then}\ S_1\ \textbf{else}\ S_2 \mid S_1; S_2$ $\mid \ldots$	Statement

Figure 2. Core Programming Language with First-Class Threads

3. Programming and Specification Languages

In this section, we present our core programming language and specification language, with a focus on modeling threads as resource.

3.1 Programming Language

We use the core programming language in Fig. 2 to convey our idea. A program consists of data declarations ($data\_decl^*$), global variable declarations ($global\_decl^*$), and procedure declarations ($proc\_decl^*$). Each procedure declaration is annotated with pairs of pre/post-conditions (Φ_{pr}/Φ_{po}). New objects of type C can be dynamically created and destroyed using **new** and **destroy**. A **fork** receives a procedure name *pn* and a list of parameters v^*, creates a new thread executing the procedure *pn*, and returns an object of **thrd** type representing the newly-created thread. **join**(v) waits for the thread that is pointed to by v to finish its execution. Note that a joinee could be joined in multiple joiners. At run-time, the joiners wait for the joinee to complete its execution. If a joiner waits for an already-completed (or dead) thread, it proceeds immediately without waiting (i.e. the join operation becomes no-op). We do not allow canceling a thread. A thread is dead after it is joined or when the entire program has finished its execution. The semantics of other program statements (such as procedure calls $pn(v^*)$, conditionals, loops, assignments) are standard as can be found in the mainstream languages.

3.2 Specification Language

Comp. formula	Δ	$::=$	$\Phi \mid \Delta_1 \vee \Delta_2 \mid \Delta_1 \wedge \pi \mid \Delta_1 * \Delta_2 \mid \exists v{\cdot}\Delta$
Disj. formula	Φ	$::=$	$\bigvee(\exists v^* \cdot \kappa \wedge \pi)$
Heap formula	κ	$::=$	$\texttt{emp} \mid \iota \mid \kappa_1 * \kappa_2$
Atomic heap	ι	$::=$	$v \overset{\varepsilon}{\mapsto} C(v^*) \mid v \mapsto \texttt{thrd}\langle\Phi\rangle$
Pure formula	π	$::=$	$\alpha \mid \pi_1 \wedge \pi_2 \mid \pi_1 \vee \pi_2 \mid \neg\pi$ $\mid \exists v{\cdot}\pi \mid \forall v{\cdot}\pi \mid \texttt{dead}(v)$
Arith. formula	α	$::=$	$\alpha_1^t{=}\alpha_2^t \mid \alpha_1^t{\neq}\alpha_2^t \mid \alpha_1^t{<}\alpha_2^t \mid \alpha_1^t{\leq}\alpha_2^t$
Arith.term	α^t	$::=$	$k \mid v \mid k \times \alpha^t \mid \alpha_1^t + \alpha_2^t \mid -\alpha^t$

Fractional permission var. $\varepsilon \in (0,1]$ $v \in$ Variables
$k \in$ Integer or fractional constants $C \in$ Data names

Figure 3. Grammar for Core Specification Language

Fig. 3 shows our specification language for concurrent programs manipulating "threads as resource". A classical separation logic formula Φ is in disjunctive normal form. Each disjunct in Φ consists of a heap formula κ and a pure formula π. Furthermore, Δ denotes a composite formula which could always be translated into the Φ form. A pure formula π includes standard equality/inequality, Presburger arithmetic, and a pure predicate $\texttt{dead}(v)$ indicating that the thread v has completed its execution. π could also be extended to include other constraints such as set constraints. A heap formula κ consists of multiple atomic heap formulas ι connected with each other via the separation connective $*$. An atomic heap formula $v \overset{\varepsilon}{\mapsto} C(v^*)$ (or heap node) represents the fact that the current thread has a certain fractional permission ε to access an object of type C pointed to by v. v^* captures a list of variables representing the fields of the object v.

The atomic heap formula $v \mapsto \texttt{thrd}\langle\Phi\rangle$ (or thread node) captures our idea of "threads as resource": v points to a thread carrying certain resource Φ, which is available after the thread is joined. By representing threads as heap resource, we allow them to be flexibly split and transferred in a similar way to other types of resource such as heap nodes. Note that thread nodes themselves are non-fractional, but their resources can already be flexibly split. Furthermore, no resource leakage from threads is possible since we explicitly track when each thread becomes dead.

Our approach allows for expressive reasoning about threads and their liveness. For example, a formula $t \mapsto \texttt{thrd}\langle\Phi\rangle \bigvee \texttt{dead}(t)$ specifies the fact that the thread t could be either alive or dead. On the other hand, a formula with $t \mapsto \texttt{thrd}\langle\Phi\rangle \wedge \texttt{dead}(t)$ indicates the fact that t is already dead and hence the resource Φ can be safely released.

4. Threads as Resource

In this section, we first introduce our forward verification rules. We then present a set of sub-structural rules for manipulating resource, especially threads as resource. Finally, we discuss the soundness of our approach.

4.1 Forward Verification Rules

Our verification system is built on top of entailment checking:

$$\Delta_A \vdash \Delta_C \leadsto \Delta_R$$

This entailment checks if antecedent Δ_A is precise enough to imply consequent Δ_C, and computes the residue Δ_R for the next program state (we write $\Delta_A \vdash \Delta_C$ when ignoring the residue). For example:

$$x \overset{0.6}{\longmapsto} cell(1) * y \overset{0.6}{\longmapsto} cell(2) \vdash x \overset{0.6}{\longmapsto} cell(1) \leadsto y \overset{0.6}{\longmapsto} cell(2)$$

Fig. 4 presents our forward verification rules. Here we only focus on three key constructs affecting threads' resource: procedure call, fork, and join. Forward verification is formalized using Hoare's triple for partial correctness: $\{\Phi_{pr}\}P\{\Phi_{po}\}$. Given a program P starting in a state satisfying the pre-condition Φ_{pr}, if the program terminates, it will do so in a state satisfying the post-condition Φ_{po}. For simplicity, in this paper, we describe the verification rules with one pair of pre/post condition. Muliple pre/post specifications can be handled in the same way as [5].

$$\frac{\begin{array}{c} spec(pn) := pn(w^*) \textbf{ requires } \Phi_{pr} \textbf{ ensures } \Phi_{po}; \{ s \} \\ \Delta \vdash \Phi_{pr} \leadsto \Delta_1 \quad \Delta_2 \stackrel{\text{def}}{=} \Delta_1 * \Phi_{po} \end{array}}{\{\Delta\}\ pn(w^*)\ \{\Delta_2\}} \quad \underline{\textbf{CALL}}$$

$$\frac{\begin{array}{c} spec(pn) := pn(w^*) \textbf{ requires } \Phi_{pr} \textbf{ ensures } \Phi_{po}; \{ s \} \\ \Delta \vdash \Phi_{pr} \leadsto \Delta_1 \quad \Delta_2 \stackrel{\text{def}}{=} \Delta_1 * v \mapsto \mathsf{thrd}\langle \Phi_{po} \rangle \end{array}}{\{\Delta\}\ v := \textbf{fork}(pn, w^*)\ \{\Delta_2\}} \quad \underline{\textbf{FORK}}$$

$$\{\Delta * v \mapsto \mathsf{thrd}\langle \Phi_{po} \rangle\}\ \textbf{join}(v)\ \{\Delta * \Phi_{po} \wedge \mathsf{dead}(v)\} \quad \underline{\textbf{JOIN-1}}$$

$$\{\Delta \wedge \mathsf{dead}(v)\}\ \textbf{join}(v)\ \{\Delta \wedge \mathsf{dead}(v)\} \quad \underline{\textbf{JOIN-2}}$$

Figure 4. Selected Verification Rules

In order to perform a procedure call (CALL), the caller should be in a state Δ that can entail the pre-condition Φ_{pr} of the callee (i.e the procedure pn). $spec(pn)$ denotes the specification of the procedure pn. For conciseness, we omit the substitutions that link actual and formal parameters of the procedure prior to the entailment. After the entailment, the caller subsumes the post-condition Φ_{po} of the callee with the residue Δ_1 to form a new state Δ_2. Ownerships are transferred across procedure boundaries, from the caller to the callee via the entailment of the pre-condition and from the callee to the caller via the spatial conjunction on the post-condition.

Similarly, when performing a fork (FORK), the forker should be in a state Δ that can entail the pre-condition Φ_{pr} of the forkee (i.e the newly-created thread executing the procedure pn). Afterward, a new thread node $v \mapsto \mathsf{thrd}\langle \Phi_{po} \rangle$ carrying the post-condition Φ_{po} of the forkee is created. The thread node is then combined with the residue Δ_1 to form a new state Δ_2. The thread node is considered as resource in Δ_2; hence, it can be flexibly split and transferred in subsequent parts of the program. The FORK rule is sound since other threads can only observe the post-state of the forkee when joining with it. It also ensures modularity as the forker only knows the pre/post-conditions of the forkee.

When joining a thread (JOIN−1), the joiner simply exchanges the thread node, which carries a resource Φ_{po}, with the resource itself. Each joinee could be joined by multiple joiners. Our verification rules are based on the observation that when a joiner joins with a joinee, the joiner is expecting to receive certain resource transferred to it from the joinee. Hence, each joiner will receive the current resource carried by the thread node. After a thread has been joined, it becomes dead (indicated by the pure `dead` predicate). Joining a dead thread is equivalent to a no-op (JOIN−2).

Using our verification rules, a CALL can be modeled as a FORK immediately followed by a JOIN. As threads are considered as resource, fork and join operations can be in different lexical scopes and thread nodes can be transferred across procedure and thread boundaries. Furthermore, if there is a recursive fork call in a procedure (also called nested fork) such as the parallel Fibonacci program[1], the verification proceeds normally: a new thread node corresponding to the newly-created thread executing the procedure is created. Therefore, in our system, a nested fork is handled in the same way as a normal fork.

4.2 Manipulating "Threads as Resource"

The notion of "threads as resource" plays a critical role in our approach as it enables threads to be treated in a similar way to other objects: a thread node can be created, stored, split, and transferred (or shared) among multiple threads, allowing them to join and to receive suitable resource after joining.

Our sub-structural rules for manipulating resource are presented in Fig. 5. The rules rearrange resource in a separation logic formula into equivalent forms. We denote resource equivalence as $\Longleftrightarrow$. By resource equivalence, we mean that the total resource on the left and the right sides of $\Longleftrightarrow$ are the same. Our approach allows resource to be split, combined, and transferred across procedures and threads, while it guarantees that the total resource remains unchanged. The rules R−DISJ, R−CONJ, R−SCONJ, R−COM, and R−EMP are straightforward. With fractional permissions ε, heap nodes can be split and combined in a standard way (R−FRAC). The left-to-right direction indicates permission splitting while the right-to-left indicates permission combining. We also allow thread nodes to be split and combined (R−THRD1). Splitting a thread node (left-to-right) will split the resource carried by the node while combining thread nodes (right-to-left) will combine the resource of the constituent nodes. Finally, when a thread is dead, its carried resource can be safely released (R−THRD2).

4.3 Soundness

This section presents the soundness of our approach. The proof is based on the soundness proof of Gotsman et al. [12], which is tailored towards locks and threads (but not threads as resource). Our proof, on the other hand, is tailored towards threads as resource. We first present the memory model of the specification language presented in Section 3.2. We then introduce the interleaving semantics of the programming language presented in Section 3.1. Finally, we prove the soundness of our approach with respect to the operational semantics.

Memory Model.

Our basic memory model is extended from the model proposed in [12]. As a simplification, we consider objects of type `cell` and `thrd` only. User-defined data types can be supported by extending from `cell` to objects with fields. This, however, unnecessarily complicates the memory model. Instead, we focus on modeling threads as resource. We also impose a restriction whereby thread nodes can only be passed between the caller and callee of the same thread, or between different threads (i.e. from forker to forkee, or from joinee to joiner). Thread nodes, therefore, are not allowed to belong to external environment such as lock invariants. This is to avoid circularity when the two thread nodes of two different threads refer to each other as their carried resource.

In our memory model, formulas are interpreted over program state $\sigma \in \Sigma$, defined as follows:

[1] `http://loris-7.ddns.comp.nus.edu.sg/~project/threadhip/`

$$\frac{\Phi_1 \Longleftrightarrow \Phi_1' \qquad \Phi_2 \Longleftrightarrow \Phi_2'}{\Phi_1 \bigvee \Phi_2 \Longleftrightarrow \Phi_1' \bigvee \Phi_2'} \qquad \text{R-DISJ}$$

$$\frac{\kappa \Longleftrightarrow \kappa'}{\kappa \wedge \pi \Longleftrightarrow \kappa' \wedge \pi} \qquad \text{R-CONJ}$$

$$\frac{\kappa_1 \Longleftrightarrow \kappa_1' \qquad \kappa_2 \Longleftrightarrow \kappa_2'}{\kappa_1 * \kappa_2 \Longleftrightarrow \kappa_1' * \kappa_2'} \qquad \text{R-SCONJ}$$

$$\kappa_1 * \kappa_2 \Longleftrightarrow \kappa_2 * \kappa_1 \qquad \text{R-COM}$$

$$\kappa * \mathsf{emp} \Longleftrightarrow \kappa \qquad \text{R-EMP}$$

$$v \overset{\varepsilon_1+\varepsilon_2}{\longmapsto} C(v^*) \Longleftrightarrow v \overset{\varepsilon_1}{\longmapsto} C(v^*) * v \overset{\varepsilon_2}{\longmapsto} C(v^*) \qquad \text{R-FRAC}$$

$$v \mapsto \mathsf{thrd}\langle \Phi_1 * \Phi_2 \rangle \Longleftrightarrow v \mapsto \mathsf{thrd}\langle \Phi_1 \rangle * v \mapsto \mathsf{thrd}\langle \Phi_2 \rangle \qquad \text{R-THRD1}$$

$$v \mapsto \mathsf{thrd}\langle \Phi \rangle \wedge \mathsf{dead}(v) \Longrightarrow \Phi \qquad \text{R-THRD2}$$

Figure 5. Sub-structural Rules

$$\texttt{Loc} \overset{\text{def}}{=} \{1,2,\ldots\} \qquad \texttt{Perm} \overset{\text{def}}{=} (0,1]$$
$$\texttt{Var} \overset{\text{def}}{=} \{x,y,\ldots\} \qquad \texttt{TIDS} \overset{\text{def}}{=} \{1,2,\ldots\}$$
$$\texttt{Val} \overset{\text{def}}{=} \{\ldots,-1,0,1,\ldots\} \qquad \texttt{TStates} \overset{\text{def}}{=} \{F, D\}$$

$$\Sigma \overset{\text{def}}{=} \texttt{Stack} \times \texttt{Heap} \times \texttt{THRDS}$$
$$\texttt{Heap} \overset{\text{def}}{=} \texttt{Loc} \rightharpoonup \texttt{cell}(\texttt{Val} \times \texttt{Perm})$$
$$\texttt{Stack} \overset{\text{def}}{=} \texttt{Var} \rightharpoonup \texttt{Val}$$
$$\texttt{THRDS} \overset{\text{def}}{=} \texttt{TIDS} \rightharpoonup \texttt{THRD}(\texttt{TStates} \times \Pi)$$

Program state $\sigma = (s,h,t) \in \Sigma$ consists of a stack $s \in \texttt{Stack}$, a heap $h \in \texttt{Heap}$, and a threadpool $t \in \texttt{THRDS}$. Each heap cell is associated with a fractional permission $\varepsilon \in \texttt{Perm}$. THRDS maps a thread identifier $k \in \texttt{TIDS}$ into a thread with a state $\diamond \in \texttt{TStates}$ (F = forked, and D = dead) and a resource $\Phi \in \Pi$. Our memory model is mostly similar to that described in [12]; it additionally captures a threadpool of threads with their states (i.e. their liveness) and their carried resource.

We denote $f(x)\downarrow$ if the function f is defined on x, $f(x)\uparrow$ if the function f is undefined on x. We write $f = []$ if $dom(f)$ is empty. We denote $f[(x,v)]$ (defined only if $f(x)\uparrow$) as a function that has the same value as f everywhere, except for x where it has the value v. We now define $*$ on program states, which interprets the $*$-connective in our logic.

For $s_1, s_2 \in \texttt{Stack}$,

$s_1 \# s_2 \Leftrightarrow \forall x. s_1(x)\downarrow \wedge s_2(x)\downarrow \Rightarrow (\exists v. s_1(x) = v \wedge s_2(x) = v)$

If $s_1 \# s_2$, then

$$s_1 * s_2 \overset{\text{def}}{=} \{(x,v) \mid (s_1(x) = v \wedge s_2(x)\uparrow) \vee s_1(x)\uparrow \wedge (s_2(x) = v)\},$$

otherwise $s_1 * s_2$ is undefined. Note that, for simplicity, we do not consider permissions on program variables which can be separately exented as described in [1].

For $h_1, h_2 \in \texttt{Heap}$,

$$h_1 \# h_2 \Leftrightarrow (\forall l. h_1(l)\downarrow \wedge h_2(l)\downarrow \Rightarrow (\exists v, \varepsilon_1, \varepsilon_2. h_1(l) = \texttt{cell}(v,\varepsilon_1) \wedge h_2(l) = \texttt{cell}(v,\varepsilon_2) \wedge \varepsilon_1 + \varepsilon_2 \leq 1))$$

If $h_1 \# h_2$, then

$$h_1 * h_2 \overset{\text{def}}{=} \{(l, \texttt{cell}(v,\varepsilon) \mid (h_1(l) = \texttt{cell}(v,\varepsilon) \wedge h_2(l)\uparrow) \vee (h_1(l)\uparrow \wedge h_2(l) = \texttt{cell}(v,\varepsilon)) \vee (h_1(l) = \texttt{cell}(v,\varepsilon_1) \wedge h_2(l) = \texttt{cell}(v,\varepsilon_2) \wedge \varepsilon_1 + \varepsilon_2 = \varepsilon)\},$$

otherwise $h_1 * h_2$ is undefined.

For $t_1, t_2 \in \texttt{THRDS}$,

$$t_1 \# t_2 \Leftrightarrow (\forall k. t_1(k)\downarrow \wedge t_2(k)\downarrow \Rightarrow (\exists v, h_1, s_1, h_2, s_2, i. t_1(k) = \texttt{THRD}(\diamond, \Phi_1) \wedge t_2(k) = \texttt{THRD}(\diamond, \Phi_2) \wedge s_1 \# s_2 \wedge h_1 \# h_2 \wedge (h_1, s_1, t_1, i) \models_k \Phi_1 \wedge (h_2, s_2, t_2, i) \models_k \Phi_2))$$

For thread states,

$$F * F = F \qquad D * D = D \qquad F * D = D$$

If $t_1 \# t_2$, then

$$t_1 * t_2 \overset{\text{def}}{=} \{(k, \texttt{THRD}(\diamond, \Phi) \mid (t_1(k) = \texttt{THRD}(\diamond, \Phi) \wedge t_2(k)\uparrow) \vee (t_1(k)\uparrow \wedge t_2(k) = \texttt{THRD}(\diamond, \Phi)) \vee (t_1(k) = \texttt{THRD}(\diamond_1, \Phi_1) \wedge t_2(k) = \texttt{THRD}(\diamond_2, \Phi_2) \wedge \diamond = \diamond_1 * \diamond_2 \wedge \Phi = \Phi_1 * \Phi_2)\},$$

otherwise $t_1 * t_2$ is undefined. We lift $*$ to states and set of states pointwise.

The satisfaction relation for our specification language formulas is presented in Fig 6. One can easily show that the sub-structural rules in Fig. 5 are sound with respect to the satisfaction relation. A formula is interpreted with respect to a thread identifier $k \in \{m\} \cup \texttt{TIDS}$ (m is the identifier of the main thread), a stack s, a heap h, a threadpool t, and an interpretation i mapping logical variables to values. We assume a function $[\![e]\!]_{(s,i)}$ that evaluates an expression e with respect to the stack s and the interpretation i. We write $[\![e]\!]_s$ when s is sufficient to evaluate e. Note that, in our definitions, the predicate $t_1 \# t_2$ refers to the satisfaction relation $\models$, which is defined based on $\#$. However, due to the restriction that two thread nodes of two different threads cannot refer to each other as their carried resource, $\#$, $*$, and $\models$ are simultaneously defined by induction which is guaranteed to terminate. Let $[\![\Phi]\!]_i^k$ denote the set of states in which the formula Φ is valid with respect to a thread identifier k and an interpretation i. We write $[\![\Phi]\!]^k$ when the deno-

Satisfaction Relation: $(s,h,t,i) \models_k \Phi$

$$
\begin{array}{lcl}
(s,h,t,i) \models_k \exists x.\,\Phi & \Leftrightarrow & \exists v.\,(s,h,t,i[(x,v)]) \models_k \Phi \\
(s,h,t,i) \models_k \texttt{emp} & \Leftrightarrow & s=[] \wedge h=[] \wedge t=[] \\
(s,h,t,i) \models_k \Phi_1 * \Phi_2 & \Leftrightarrow & \exists s_1,s_2,h_1,h_2,t_1,t_2.\, s=s_1*s_2 \wedge h=h_1*h_2 \wedge t=t_1*t_2 \wedge \\
 & & \qquad (s_1,h_1,t_1,i) \models_k \Phi_1 \wedge (s_2,h_2,t_2,i) \models_k \Phi_2 \\
(s,h,t,i) \models_k \Phi_1 \bigvee \Phi_2 & \Leftrightarrow & (s,h,t,i) \models_k \Phi_1 \vee (s,h,t,i) \models_k \Phi_2 \\
(s,h,t,i) \models_k \kappa \wedge \pi & \Leftrightarrow & (s,h,t,i) \models_k \kappa \ \wedge\ (s,[],t,i) \models_k \pi \\
(h,s,t,i) \models_k x \overset{\varepsilon}{\mapsto} \texttt{cell}(v) & \Leftrightarrow & \exists l.\, s=[(x,l)] \wedge h=[(l,\texttt{cell}(v,\varepsilon))] \\
(s,h,t,i) \models_k x \mapsto \texttt{thrd}\langle\Phi\rangle & \Leftrightarrow & \exists id,s_1,t_1.\, s=s_1*[(x,id)] \wedge t=t_1*[(id,\texttt{THRD}(F,\Phi))] \wedge (s_1,h,t_1,i) \models_k \Phi \\
(s,h,t,i) \models_k \texttt{dead}(x) & \Leftrightarrow & \exists id.\, s=[(x,id)] \wedge t=[(id,\texttt{THRD}(D,\texttt{emp}))] \\
(s,h,t,i) \models_k \pi_1\ op\ \pi_2 & \Leftrightarrow & (s,h,t,i) \models_k \pi_1\ op\ (s,h,t,i) \models_k \pi_2 \quad \text{, where } op \in \{\wedge,\vee\} \\
(s,h,t,i) \models_k \neg\pi & \Leftrightarrow & \neg((s,h,t,i) \models_k \pi) \\
(s,h,t,i) \models_k \exists x.\,\pi & \Leftrightarrow & \exists v.\,(s,h,t,i[(x,v)]) \models_k \pi \\
(s,h,t,i) \models_k \forall x.\,\pi & \Leftrightarrow & \forall v.\,(s,h,t,i[(x,v)]) \models_k \pi \\
(s,h,t,i) \models_k x_1\ op\ x_2 & \Leftrightarrow & [\![x_1]\!]_{(s,i)}\!\downarrow \wedge [\![x_2]\!]_{(s,i)}\!\downarrow \wedge ([\![x_1]\!]_{(s,i)}\ op\ [\![x_2]\!]_{(s,i)}) \quad \text{, where } op \in \{=,\neq,<,\leq\}
\end{array}
$$

Figure 6. Satisfaction Relation for Specification Language Formulas

tation of Φ is sufficient with respect to a thread identifier k. When the denotation of a formula Φ does not depend on the thread identifier and the interpretation of logical variables, we simply write $[\![\Phi]\!]$. Similar to [12], we say that a predicate $p \subseteq \Sigma$ is *precise* if for any state σ, there exists at most one substate σ_0 that satisfies p.

Operational Semantics.

We consider a well-formed program P with the main procedure $main()\{S_m\}$ and a set of procedures $f^i(v_i^*)\{S_i\}$ $(i = 1..n)$. Let Γ denote the procedure context in the program P, i.e. Γ=$\{\ \{\Phi^i_{pr}\}f^i(v_i^*)\{\Phi^i_{po}\} \mid i = 1..n\}$. The Hoare's triples $\{\Phi_{pr}\}S\{\Phi_{po}\}$ presented in Section 4.1 are implicitly defined under Γ, that is $\Gamma \vdash \{\Phi_{pr}\}S\{\Phi_{po}\}$.

Definition 1 (Well-formedness). *A program is well-formed if the following conditions hold:*

- *In the program text, there exists a procedure called main, which indicates the entry point of the program.*
- *Procedure names are unique within a program. Procedure parameters are unique within a procedure. Free variables in the body of a procedure are the procedure parameters.*
- *A normal procedure call or a fork statement mentions only procedure names defined in the program text. The number of actual parameters and formal parameters are equal.*

The interleaving semantics of the program P is presented in Fig. 7. The semantics is defined by a transition relation $\rightsquigarrow_P$ that transforms pairs of program counters (which map a thread identifier into its corresponding remaining statement, i.e. $pc \in (\texttt{TIDS} \cup \{m\}) \rightharpoonup SS$, where SS is the set of statements), and states (s, h, t). The relation $\rightsquigarrow_P$ is defined as the least one satisfying the rules in Fig. 7. We denote $\rightsquigarrow_P^*$ as the reflexive and transitive closure of $\rightsquigarrow_P$ The initial program counter pc_0 is $[(m, S_m)]$ which contains only the main thread whose identifier is m and whose remaining statement is S_m.

In Fig. 7, *spec*(pn) denotes the specification of the procedure pn in the program, $[v/w]S$ denotes the substitution in S where w is substituted by v. The rules for fork and join are of special interest. In the fork rule, a new thread is spawned and the return value v points to its identifier j. The resource carried by j is captured in t. We explicitly add an `end` statement to signify the end of each newly spawned thread.[2] As a quick observation, a thread identifier corresponds to a thread node in our logic. Any threads (joiners) knowing the identifier can perform a join operation to join with the newly-created thread (joinee). In the join rule, if the joinee has not yet finished its execution (i.e. it is not in a D state), the joiners have to wait for the joinee to finish its execution. Note that when a joinee is joined, it will not be removed from the threadpool. This allows for the multi-join pattern and enables the joiners to immediately proceed without waiting in case the joinee has already finished its execution. There is a direct relation between the D state of a thread during run-time and its `dead` predicate during verification-time.

Definition 2 (Safety). *A program P is safe when running from an initial state σ_0 if it is not the case that $pc_0, \sigma_0 \rightsquigarrow_P^* pc, \top$ for some pc.*

Proof.

The proof is based on the soundness proof of Gotsman et al. [12]. We first present a thread-local semantics based on a thread-local forward predicate transformer $\texttt{Post}^\gamma_k()$, and define the notion of validity of Hoare's triples for program statements with respect to the thread-local semantics (Definition 3). We then prove the soundness of our approach with respect to the thread-local semantics (Lemma 1). Finally, we prove that the thread-location semantics is adequate with respect to the interleaving semantics, which justifies the soundness of our approach (Lemma 2 and 3). Additionally, in a similar way to [12], using the thread-local semantics, we prove that provable programs are race-free (Lemma 4).

For a state σ and a predicate p, define

$$\texttt{rest}(\sigma,p) = \begin{cases} \sigma_1, & \text{if } \sigma = \sigma_1 * \sigma_2 \text{ and } \sigma_2 \in p \\ \top, & \text{otherwise} \end{cases}$$

Let the domain $\mathcal{D}$ be topped powerset of states. Then, we define a thread-local forward predicate transformer $\texttt{Post}^\gamma_k(S) : \mathcal{D} \rightarrow \mathcal{D}$ for every thread k, statement S, and semantical procedure context γ consisting of triples of the form $\{p\}f(v^*)\{q\}$ where $p, q \subseteq \Sigma$ and p is precise. For statement S other than fork, join, and procedure call, $\texttt{Post}^\gamma_k(S) = \texttt{Post}_k(S)$ as defined in [12]. Here, we define those for fork, join, and procedure call. Let

$$\texttt{Post}^\gamma_k(f(v^*),(s,h,t)) = \{(s',h',t')\} * q$$

if $\{p\}f(v^*)\{q\} \in \gamma$, and $\texttt{rest}((s,h,t),p) = \{(s',h',t')\}$, and $\texttt{Post}^\gamma_k(f(v^*),(s,h,t)) = \top$ otherwise. Let

[2] We also add an end statement at the end of the main procedure to signify the end of the main thread.

Transition Relation for Atomic Commands: $S, \sigma \leadsto_k \sigma'$

$$
\begin{array}{lll}
x = \mathbf{new}\ \mathtt{cell}(v), (s[(x, l_1)], h, t) & \leadsto_k & (s[(x, l_2)], h[(l_2, \mathtt{cell}(v, 1))], t), \quad \text{if } h(l_2)\uparrow \\
\mathbf{destroy}(x), (s, h[(\llbracket x \rrbracket_s, \mathtt{cell}(v, 1))], t) & \leadsto_k & (s, h, t) \\
x = e, (s[(x, v)], h, t) & \leadsto_k & (s[(x, \llbracket e \rrbracket_{s[(x,v)]})], h, t) \\
S, (s, h, t) & \leadsto_k & \top, \quad \text{otherwise}
\end{array}
$$

Transition Relation for Programs: $pc, \sigma \leadsto_P pc', \sigma'$

$$
\frac{k \in \mathtt{TIDS} \qquad S_1, (s, h, t) \leadsto_k \sigma}{pc[(k, S_1; S_2)], (s, h, t) \leadsto_P pc[(k, S_2)], \sigma} \quad (S_1 \text{ is an atomic command})
$$

$$
\frac{k \in \mathtt{TIDS}}{pc[(k,\ \mathbf{if}\ \mathit{true}\ \mathbf{then}\ S_1\ \mathbf{else}\ S_2;\ S)], (s, h, t) \leadsto_P pc[(k,\ S_1; S)], (s, h, t)}
$$

$$
\frac{k \in \mathtt{TIDS}}{pc[(k,\ \mathbf{if}\ \mathit{false}\ \mathbf{then}\ S_1\ \mathbf{else}\ S_2;\ S)], (s, h, t) \leadsto_P pc[(k,\ S_2; S)], (s, h, t)}
$$

$$
\frac{k \in \mathtt{TIDS}}{pc[(k,\ \mathbf{if}\ e\ \mathbf{then}\ S_1\ \mathbf{else}\ S_2;\ S)], (s, h, t) \leadsto_P pc[(k,\ \mathbf{if}\ \llbracket e \rrbracket_s\ \mathbf{then}\ S_1\ \mathbf{else}\ S_2;\ S)], (s, h, t)}
$$

$$
\frac{\begin{array}{c} spec(pn) := pn(w_1, \ldots, w_n)\ \mathbf{requires}\ \Phi_{pr}\ \mathbf{ensures}\ \Phi_{po};\ \{\ S_1\ \} \\ k \in \mathtt{TIDS} \quad \forall i. \llbracket v_i \rrbracket_s \downarrow \quad \rho = [v_1/w_1, \ldots, v_n/w_n] \quad S_1' = \rho S_1 \end{array}}{pc[(k,\ pn(v_1, \ldots, v_n); S)], (s, h, t) \leadsto_P pc[(k,\ S_1'; S)], (s, h, t)}
$$

$$
\frac{\begin{array}{c} spec(pn) := pn(w_1, \ldots, w_n)\ \mathbf{requires}\ \Phi_{pr}\ \mathbf{ensures}\ \Phi_{po};\ \{\ S_1\ \} \\ k, j \in \mathtt{TIDS} \quad t(j)\uparrow \quad \llbracket v \rrbracket_s \downarrow \quad \forall i. \llbracket v_i \rrbracket_s \downarrow \quad \rho = [v_1/w_1, \ldots, v_n/w_n] \quad S_1' = \rho S_1 \quad \Phi'_{po} = \rho \Phi_{po} \end{array}}{pc[(k,\ v{=}\mathbf{fork}(pn, v_1, \ldots, v_n); S)], (s, h, t) \leadsto_P pc[(k,\ S), (j,\ S_1'; \mathtt{end})], (s[(v, j)], h, t[(j, \mathtt{THRD}(F, \Phi'_{po}))])}
$$

$$
\frac{k \in \mathtt{TIDS} \qquad \llbracket v \rrbracket_s \downarrow}{pc[(k,\ \mathbf{join}(v); S), (\llbracket v \rrbracket_s, \mathtt{end})], (s, h, t[(\llbracket v \rrbracket_s, \mathtt{THRD}(F, \Phi))]) \leadsto_P pc[(k,\ S)], (s, h, t[(\llbracket v \rrbracket_s, \mathtt{THRD}(D, \mathtt{emp}))])}
$$

$$
\frac{k \in \mathtt{TIDS} \qquad \llbracket v \rrbracket_s \downarrow}{pc[(k,\ \mathbf{join}(v); S)], (s, h, t[(\llbracket v \rrbracket_s, \mathtt{THRD}(D, \mathtt{emp}))]) \leadsto_P pc[(k,\ S)], (s, h, t[(\llbracket v \rrbracket_s, \mathtt{THRD}(D, \mathtt{emp}))])}
$$

Figure 7. Operational Semantics of Well-formed Programs. ($\top$ indicates a fault.)

$$
\begin{array}{l}
\mathtt{Post}_k^{\gamma}(v{=}\mathbf{fork}(f, v^*), (s, h, t)) = \\
\qquad \{(s'[(v, j)], h', t'[(j, \mathtt{THRD}(F, \Phi_{po}))])\}
\end{array}
$$

where $j \in \mathtt{TIDS}$, if $\{p\}f(v^*)\{q\} \in \gamma$, Φ_{po} is the post-condition of $f(v^*)$, and $\mathtt{rest}((s, h, t), p) = \{(s', h', t')\}$, and $\mathtt{Post}_k^{\gamma}(v = \mathbf{fork}(f, v^*), (s, h, t)) = \top$ otherwise. Let

$$
\begin{array}{l}
\mathtt{Post}_k^{\gamma}(\mathbf{join}(v), (s, h, t[(\llbracket v \rrbracket_s, \mathtt{THRD}(F, \Phi))])) = \\
\qquad \{(s, h, t[(\llbracket v \rrbracket_s, \mathtt{THRD}(D, \mathtt{emp}))]\} * \llbracket \Phi \rrbracket, \\
\mathtt{Post}_k^{\gamma}(\mathbf{join}(v), (s, h, t[(\llbracket v \rrbracket_s, \mathtt{THRD}(D, \mathtt{emp}))])) = \\
\qquad \{(s, h, t[(\llbracket v \rrbracket_s, \mathtt{THRD}(D, \mathtt{emp}))]\},
\end{array}
$$

if $\{p\}f(v^*)\{q\} \in \gamma$, $\llbracket v \rrbracket_s \downarrow$, and $\mathtt{Post}_k^{\gamma}(\mathbf{join}(v), (s, h, t)) = \top$ otherwise. The requirement that the preconditions in γ are precise is to ensure the determinism of splitting the state at fork and procedure call. $\mathtt{Post}_k^{\gamma}()$ for other non-atomic commands are defined as in [12] with the help of a function $F_k(\gamma, S, \sigma)$. We first assume a control-flow relation G where $(v, S, v') \in G$ indicates the program points v before and v' after the statement S in the program's control flow graph ($G_{pr}(S) = v$ and $G_{po}(S) = v'$ for short). In addition, let $proc(v)$ denote the name of the procedure to which the program point v belongs ($main$ for the main procedure in the main thread). We sometimes overload $proc(S)$ to denote the name of the procedure to which the statement S belongs. We also assume a function g that takes a program point and returns the corresponding program state at that point. In addition, we assume that a thread executing a procedure f will start and end at the program points $\mathtt{start}_f$ and $\mathtt{stop}_f$ respectively. Then, $F_k(\gamma, S, \sigma)(g) = g'$ where $g'(\mathtt{start}_f) = \sigma$ and for every program point v_2 such that $v_2 \neq \mathtt{start}_f$, $g'(v_2) = \bigsqcup_{(v_1, S, v_2) \in G} \mathtt{Post}_k(S, g(v_1))$. Hence, $\mathtt{Post}_k(S, \sigma) = (\mathtt{lfp}(F_k(\gamma, S, \sigma)))(\mathtt{stop})$. For a procedure context Γ, we denote $\llbracket \Gamma \rrbracket$ as its corresponding semantical procedure context, i.e. $\{\Phi_{pr}\}f(v^*)\{\Phi_{po}\} \in \Gamma$ iff $\{\llbracket \Phi_{pr} \rrbracket\}f(v^*)\{\llbracket \Phi_{po} \rrbracket\} \in \gamma$. We now extend the validity $\models_k$ of Hoare's triples with respect to the thread-local semantics for thread k.

Definition 3. *For a statement S,*

$$
\Gamma \models_k \{\Phi_{pr}\}S\{\Phi_{po}\} \Leftrightarrow \mathtt{Post}_k^{\llbracket \Gamma \rrbracket}(S, \llbracket \Phi_{pr} \rrbracket^k) \sqsubseteq \llbracket \Phi_{po} \rrbracket^k.
$$

Lemma 1 (Soundness with respect to thread-local semantics)**.** *If $\Gamma \vdash \{\Phi_{pr}\}S\{\Phi_{po}\}$, then for all $k \in \mathtt{TIDS}$, $\Gamma \models_k \{\Phi_{pr}\}S\{\Phi_{po}\}$.*

Proof. Standard verification rules (such as those for creating a new object, deallocating an existing object, etc.) have been proven sound with respect to the thread-local semantics in [12]. Here, it is easy to show that the definition of $\mathtt{Post}_k^{\gamma}()$ implies the soundness of CALL, FORK, JOIN−1, and JOIN−2 (presented in Fig. 4) with respect to the thread-local semantics. We can then perform induction on the derivation of $\Gamma \vdash \{\Phi_{pr}\}S\{\Phi_{po}\}$. □

The following lemma states that the thread-local semantics is an over-approximation of the interleaving operational semantics described in Fig. 7.

Lemma 2 (Over-approximating Lemma). *Consider a program P with the main procedure $main()\{S_m\}$ equipped with a precondition $p \in \mathcal{D}$, a set of procedures $f^i(v_i^*)\{S_i\}$ $(i = 1..n)$, and a semantical procedure context $\gamma = \{\{p^i\}f^i(v_i^*)\{q^i\} \mid i = 1..n\}$ such that $\mathtt{Post}_k^{\gamma}(S_i, p_i) \sqsubseteq q_i$ for all $i = 1..n$ and $k \in \mathtt{TIDS}$. Let $g_m(main)=\mathtt{lfp}(F_m(\gamma, S, p))$ and $g_k(f^i)=\mathtt{lfp}(F_k(\gamma, S_i, p^i))$ for all $k \in \mathtt{TIDS}$ and $i = 1..n$. Then for any state $\sigma_0 = (h_0, s_0, [])$ such that*

$$\{\sigma_0\} \sqsubseteq p \tag{1}$$

whenever $pc_0, \sigma_0, \rightsquigarrow_P pc, \sigma_1$, it is the case that

$$\{\sigma_1\} \sqsubseteq \left(\underset{\{k \mid pc(k)\downarrow\}}{\circledast} g_k(G_{pr}(pc(k))) \right). \tag{2}$$

Proof. The proof is done by induction on the length m of the derivation of σ_1. For $m = 0$, it trivially holds. Now, suppose that $pc_0, \sigma_0 \rightsquigarrow_P^* pc[(j, S; S')], \sigma_1 \rightsquigarrow_P pc'[(j, S')], \sigma_2, (v, S, v') \in G$ and

$$\{\sigma_1\} \sqsubseteq \left(\underset{\{k \mid pc(k)\downarrow\}}{\circledast} g_k(G_{pr}(pc(k))) \right) * g_j(v),$$

we have to prove that

$$\{\sigma_2\} \sqsubseteq \left(\underset{\{k \mid pc'(k)\downarrow\}}{\circledast} g_k(G_{pr}(pc'(k))) \right) * g_j(v') \tag{3}$$

The proof for statements other than fork, join, and procedure call has been given in [12]. Here, we focus on those for fork, join, and procedure call.

1. S is v=**fork**$(f^i, v_1, \ldots, v_n)$. Assume that $\sigma_1 = \sigma_1' * \sigma_1''$, where $\sigma_1' \in g_j(v)$, $\sigma_1'' = \circledast_{\{k \mid pc(k)\downarrow\}} g_k(G_{pr}(pc(k)))$, $\sigma_1' = (s, h, t)$, $pc' = pc[j' : S_i]$, $\sigma_2 = (s[(v, j')], h, t[(j', \mathtt{THRD}(F, \Phi_{po}^i))]) * \sigma_1''$, $\mathtt{Post}_k^{\gamma}(S, \sigma_1') \sqsubseteq g_j(v')$; otherwise, the right-hand side of Eq. 3 is $\top$. Now, we have to prove that $\{\sigma_2\} \sqsubseteq g_j(v') * \{\sigma_1''\}$. Let $\sigma_3 = (s[(v, j')], h, t[(j', \mathtt{THRD}(F, \Phi_{po}^i))])$, then $\mathtt{Post}_k^{\gamma}(S, \sigma_1') \sqsubseteq g_j(v')$ implies $\{\sigma_3\} \sqsubseteq g_j(v')$, hence $\{\sigma_2\} = \{\sigma_3\} * \{\sigma_1''\} \sqsubseteq g_j(v') * \{\sigma_1''\}$.

2. S is **join**(v). We consider two cases: v is dead and v is alive. When v is dead, assume that $\sigma_1 = \sigma_3 * \sigma_4$, $\sigma_3 = (s, h, t[(\llbracket v \rrbracket_s, \mathtt{THRD}(D, \mathtt{emp}))])$, $\sigma_3 \in g_j(proc(v))$, $pc' = pc$, and $\sigma_4 = \circledast_{\{k \mid pc(k)\downarrow\}} g_k(G_{pr}(pc(k)))$. Since $\mathtt{Post}_k^{\gamma}(\mathbf{join}(v), \sigma_3) = \{\sigma_3\} \sqsubseteq g_j(v')$, Eq. 3 trivially holds. We now consider the case where v is alive. Assume that $\sigma_1 = \sigma_3 * \sigma_4 * \sigma_5$, $\sigma_3 \in g_j(proc(v))$, $\sigma_3 = (s, h, t[(\llbracket v \rrbracket_s, \mathtt{THRD}(F, \Phi))])$, $t' = t[(\llbracket v \rrbracket_s, \mathtt{THRD}(D, \mathtt{emp}))]$, $\sigma_4 = \circledast_{\{k \mid pc(k)\downarrow\}} g_k(G_{pr}(pc(k)))$, $pc = pc'[(\llbracket v \rrbracket_s, \mathtt{end})]$, $\{\sigma_5\} \sqsubseteq \llbracket \Phi \rrbracket$, and $\sigma_2 = (s, h, t') * \sigma_4 * \sigma_5$; otherwise, either the left-hand side of Eq. 3 is $\{\}$ or the right-hand side of Eq. 3 is $\top$. Now, we have to prove that $\sigma_2 \sqsubseteq g_j(v') * \{\sigma_4\}$. By definition of $\mathtt{Post}()$ for **join**(v), we get $\{(s, h, t')\} * \{\sigma_5\} \sqsubseteq g_j(v')$. Hence, $\{\sigma_2\} = \{(s, h, t')\} * \{\sigma_5\} * \{\sigma_4\} \sqsubseteq g_j(v') * \sigma_4$.

3. S is $f^i(v_1, \ldots, v_n)$. $f^i(v_1, \ldots, v_n)$ can be modeled as v=**fork**$(f^i, v_1, \ldots, v_n)$; **join**(v). Since the cases of fork, join, and sequential composition have been proven sound, the case of procedure call follows. □

The soundness of our approach is now established by the following lemma.

Lemma 3 (Soundness of Threads as Resource). *Consider a program P with the main procedure $main()\{S_m\}$ and a set of procedures $f^i(v_i^*)\{S_i\}$ $(i = 1..n)$ together with their corresponding pre/post-conditions $(\Phi_{pr}^i/\Phi_{po}^i)$ where Φ_{pr}^i is precise. Let $\Gamma = \{\{\Phi_{pr}^i\}f^i(v_i^*)\{\Phi_{po}^i\} \mid i = 1..n\}$. If our verifier derives a proof for P, i.e.*

$$\Gamma \vdash \{\Phi_{pr}^1\}S_1\{\Phi_{po}^1\},\ \ldots,\ \Gamma \vdash \{\Phi_{pr}^n\}S_n\{\Phi_{po}^n\}, \Gamma \vdash \{\Phi_{pr}\}S_m\{\Phi_{po}\},$$

then for any interpretation j and the state $\sigma_0=(s_0, h_0, [])$ such that $\sigma_0 \in \llbracket \Phi_{pr} \rrbracket_j^m$ the program P is safe when running from σ_0 and if $pc_0, \sigma_0 \rightsquigarrow_P pc_1, (s, h, t)$, where $\forall k.pc_1(k)\downarrow \implies pc_1(k)=\mathtt{end}$, then $(s, h, t) \in \llbracket \Phi_{po} \rrbracket_i^m * (\circledast_{\{k \mid t(k)=\mathtt{THRD}(F,\Phi)\}} \llbracket \Phi \rrbracket)$.

Proof. Consider an interpretation j and the state $\sigma_0 = (s_0, h_0, [])$ such that $\sigma_0 \in \llbracket \Phi_{pr} \rrbracket_j^m$. By Lemma 1, for all $k \in \mathtt{TIDS}$, $\Gamma \models_k \{\Phi_{pr}^i\}S_i\{\Phi_{po}^i\}$ and $\Gamma \models_m \{\Phi_{pr}\}S_m\{\Phi_{po}\}$. By Definition 3, we have $\mathtt{Post}_k^{\gamma}(S_i, \llbracket \Phi_{pr}^i \rrbracket) \sqsubseteq \llbracket \Phi_{po}^i \rrbracket$ and $\mathtt{Post}_m^{\gamma}(S, \llbracket \Phi_{pr} \rrbracket_j^m) \sqsubseteq \llbracket \Phi_{po} \rrbracket_j^m$. Since Eq. 1 is fulfilled, we are now able to establish the safety of P. Suppose that $pc_0, \sigma_0, \rightsquigarrow_P pc_1, (s, h, t)$ and $\forall k.pc_1(k)\downarrow \implies pc_1(k)=\mathtt{end}$, then from Eq. 2 we have $\{(s, h, t)\} \sqsubseteq \llbracket \Phi_{po} \rrbracket_i^m * (\circledast_{\{k \mid t(k)=\mathtt{THRD}(F,\Phi)\}} \llbracket \Phi \rrbracket)$ □

In addition to partial correctness, in a similar way to [12], we can prove that, when using our approach, provable programs are race-free, as stated in Lemma 4.

Definition 4 (Data Race). *When running from an initial state σ_0, a program P has a data race if for some pc and a state σ_1 such that $pc_0, \sigma_0 \rightsquigarrow_P pc, \sigma_1$, there exists two atomic statements S_1 in thread k (i.e. $pc(k) = S_1; S_1'$) and S_2 in thread j (i.e. $pc(j) = S_2; S_2'$) $(k \neq j)$ such that $(S_1, \sigma_1 \not\rightarrow_k \top)$, $(S_2, \sigma_1 \not\rightarrow_j \top)$, and $S_1 \bowtie_{\sigma_1} S_2$ (i.e., S_1 and S_2 both access the same memory location in state σ_1 and at least one of the accesses is a write).*

Lemma 4 (Data-race Freedom). *Consider a program P with the main procedure $main()\{S_m\}$ and a set of procedures $f^i(v_i^*)\{S_i\}$ $(i = 1..n)$ together with their corresponding pre/post-conditions $(\Phi_{pr}^i/\Phi_{po}^i)$ where Φ_{pr}^i is precise. Let $\Gamma = \{\{\Phi_{pr}^i\}f^i(v_i^*)\{\Phi_{po}^i\}\}$ $(i = 1..n)$. If our verifier derives a proof for P, i.e.*

$$\Gamma \vdash \{\Phi_{pr}^1\}S_1\{\Phi_{po}^1\},\ \ldots,\ \Gamma \vdash \{\Phi_{pr}^n\}S_n\{\Phi_{po}^n\}, \Gamma \vdash \{\Phi_{pr}\}S_m\{\Phi_{po}\},$$

then the program P has no data race when running from an initial state $\sigma_0 = (s_0, h_0, [])$ such that $\sigma_0 \in \llbracket \Phi_{pr} \rrbracket_j^m$ for any interpretation j.

Proof. It directly follows from Theorem 15 of [12]. Intuitively, one can prove that, for a provable program, given state σ_1, two interfering atomic statements S_1 and S_2, $(S_1, \sigma_1 \not\rightarrow_k \top)$, and $(S_2, \sigma_1 \not\rightarrow_j \top)$, there do not exist σ_2 and σ_3 such that $\sigma_1 = \sigma_2 * \sigma_3 * \sigma_4$, $(S_1, \sigma_2 \not\rightarrow_k \top)$, and $(S_2, \sigma_3 \not\rightarrow_j \top)$. □

5. Applications

5.1 Verifying the Multi-join Pattern

A program with multi-join pattern allows a thread (joinee) to be shared and joined in multiple threads (joiners). During the execution of the program, the joiners wait for the joinee to finish its execution. If joiners wait for an already-completed joinee, they proceed immediately without waiting. By joining with the joinee, the joiners expect to receive certain resource transferred from the joinee. The motivating program in Fig. 1 is an example of such a multi-join pattern. As we have shown in previous sections, our approach handles the multi-join pattern naturally. Our approach allows the ownership of the joinee to be split, shared, and joined by multiple joiners, where each joiner obtains their corresponding part of the joinee's resource upon join.

```
data node { int val; node next; }
data list { node head; }
data count { int val; }
self ↦ ll(n) ≝ self=null ∧ n=0
 ∨ ∃q · self ↦ node(_, q) ∗ q ↦ ll(n−1)
 inv n≥0;

void  countList(list l)
 requires l ↦ list(h) ∗ h ↦ ll(n) ∧ n≥0
 ensures l ↦ list(h) ∗ h ↦ ll(n) ∧ res=n;
  { ...}

list  createList(int n)
 requires n≥0
 ensures res ↦ list(h) ∗ h ↦ ll(n);
  { ...}

list  destroyList(list l)
 requires l ↦ list(h) ∗ h ↦ ll(n)
 ensures emp;
  { ...}

void  mapper(list l, list o, list e)
 requires l ↦ list(h) ∗ h ↦ ll(n) ∗ o ↦ list(null) ∗ e ↦ list(null)
 ensures o ↦ list(oh) ∗ oh ↦ ll(n1) ∗ e ↦ list(eh) ∗
           eh ↦ ll(n2) ∧ n=n1+n2;
  { ...}

void  reducer(thrd m, list l, count c)
 requires m ↦ thrd⟨l ↦ list(h) ∗ h ↦ ll(n) ∧ n≥0⟩ ∗ c ↦ count(_)
 ensures l ↦ list(h) ∗ h ↦ ll(n) ∗ c ↦ count(n) ∧ dead(m);
{ join(m); /*multi-joined by the two reducers*/
  c.val = countList(l); }

void  main()
 requires emp ensures emp;
{ int n = 10000;  list l = createList(n);
  list ol = new list(null); list el = new list(null);
  count c1 = new count(0); count c2 = new count(0);
  /*fork mapper/reducer threads*/
  thrd m = fork(mapper,l,ol,el);
  thrd r1 = fork(reducer,m,ol,c1);
  thrd r2 = fork(reducer,m,el,c2);
  /*wait for them to finish*/
  join(r1);
  join(r2);
  assert(c1.val + c2.val = n); /*valid*/
  destroyList(ol); destroyList(el);
  destroy(c1); destroy(c2);
}
```

Figure 8. Map/Reduce Pattern using Multi-join

We now illustrate another example of multi-join concurrency pattern in Fig. 8, based on the map/reduce paradigm. In this program, the `main` thread concurrently forks three threads: a mapper `m` to produce two lists, and two reducers `r1` and `r2` to process a list each. Both the reducers each take `m` as a parameter and joins it at an appropriate place to recover their respective lists from `m`. The main thread subsequently joins up the two reducers before completing its execution. This multi-join program is challenging to verify because (i) fork and join operations on the mapper `m` are non-lexically scoped (i.e. `m` is forked in `main` but joined in threads `r1` and `r2`), and (2) part of the computed resources from `m` is made available to `r1`, while another part is made available to `r2`. In this program, the ownerships of two lists produced by the mapper must be flexibly transferred across thread boundaries, via fork/join calls. The key points to handle this program are (1) considering the executing thread of `m` as resource, and (2) allowing it to be split and transferred between `main`, `r1` and `r2` via fork/join calls. Using our approach, the program can be verified as both data-race-free and functionally correct.

5.2 Inductive Predicates and Threads as Resource

Modeling threads as resource open opportunities for applying current advances in separation logic, which were originally designed for heap objects, to threads. In this section, we describe how "threads as resource" together with inductive predicates [11, 20] can be used to naturally capture a programming idiom, called threadpool, where threads are stored in data structures.

An example program is presented in Fig. 9. The program receives an input `n`, and then invokes `forkThreads` to create `n` concurrent threads executing the procedure `thread`. For simplicity, we assume each thread will have a read permission of the cell `x` in the pre-condition and will return the read permission in the post-condition. The program will wait for all threads to finish their execution by invoking `joinThreads`. At the end, as threads already

```
data cell { int val; }
data item { thrd t; item next; }

int input() requires emp  ensures res>0;

void thread(cell x,int M)
 requires x ↦^{1/M} cell(_) ∧ M>0  ensures x ↦^{1/M} cell(_);

item forkHelper(cell x, int n, int M)
 case { n = 0 → requires emp ensures emp ∧ res = null;
        n > 0 → requires x ↦^{n/M} cell(_) ∧ M≥n
                 ensures res ↦ pool(x, n, M); }
{ if (n==0){ return null;} else {
    thrd t = fork(thread,x,M);
    item p = forkHelper(x,n-1,M);
    item i = new item(t,p);
    return i; }

item forkThreads(cell x, int n)
 requires x ↦ cell(_) ∧ n>0
 ensures res ↦ pool(x, n, n);
{ return forkHelper(x,n,n); }

void joinHelper(item tp, cell x, int n, int M)
 requires tp ↦ pool(x, n, M) ∧ M≥n ∧ n>=0
 ensures x ↦^{n/M} cell(_) ∧ n>0 ∨ emp ∧ n = 0;
{ if (tp==null){ return;} else {
    joinHelper(tp.next,x,n-1,M);
    join(tp.t); destroy(tp); }

void joinThreads(item tp, cell x, int n)
 requires tp ↦ pool(x, n, n) ∧ n>0;
 ensures x ↦ cell(_);
{ return joinHelper(tp,x,n,n); }

void main()  requires emp ensures emp;
{ cell x = new cell(1);  int n = input();
  item tp = forkThreads(x,n);
  joinThreads(tp,x,n);
  destroy(x); }
```

Figure 9. Verification of a Program with Dynamic Threads using Inductive Predicates

finished, it is safe to destroy the cell `x`. In this program, each item in the threadpool is a data structure of type `item`. Each `item` will store a thread in its field `t` and a pointer `next` to the next item in the pool. The `forkThreads` returns the first item in the pool, while the `joinThreads` receives the item and joins with all threads in the pool. In the program's specifications, "*res*" is used to denote the returned result of a procedure and "_" represents an unknown value.

The key idea to verify this program is to use an inductively defined predicate, called `pool` to abstract the threadpool. As threads are modeled as resource, they can be naturally captured inside the predicate in the same way as other heap resource, as follows:

$$\begin{array}{l} self \mapsto pool(x, n, M) \stackrel{\text{def}}{=} self{=}null \wedge n{=}0 \wedge M{>}0 \\ \quad \bigvee \exists t, p \cdot self \mapsto item(t, p) * t \mapsto \mathsf{thrd}\langle x \xrightarrow{1/M} cell(\_) \rangle * \\ \qquad p \mapsto pool(x, n{-}1, M) \\ \quad \textbf{inv}\ n{\geq}0 \wedge M{>}0; \end{array}$$

The above predicate definition asserts that a `pool` can be empty (the base case $self{=}null$) or consists of a head item (specified by $self \mapsto item(t, p)$), a thread node ($t \mapsto \mathsf{thrd}\langle x \xrightarrow{1/M} cell(\_) \rangle$) and a tail data structure which is also a `pool`. The invariant $n{\geq}0 \wedge M{>}0$ must hold for all instances of the predicate. Using the above definition and case analysis [11], the program can be verified as functionally correct and data-race-free. Although we use linked lists here, our approach easily adapts to other data structures, such as arrays.

5.3 Thread Liveness and Resource Leakage

Using our approach, threads' liveness can be precisely tracked. For example, we could modify the program in Fig. 9 to additionally keep track of already-completed (or dead) threads. In the procedure `joinHelper`, after a thread is joined, instead of destroying the corresponding item (line 29), we could capture all items and their dead threads in a *deadpool* [3], inductively defined as follows:

$$\begin{array}{l} self \mapsto deadpool(n) \stackrel{\text{def}}{=} self{=}null \wedge n{=}0 \\ \quad \bigvee \exists t, p \cdot self \mapsto item(t, p) * p \mapsto deadpool(n{-}1) \wedge \mathsf{dead}(t) \\ \quad \textbf{inv}\ n{\geq}0; \end{array}$$

Our approach is also able to keep track of threads' resource in a precise manner. This is important for avoiding leakages of thread resource. As an example, consider the use of a resource split, prior to a join operation.

```
// {t ↦ thrd⟨Φ1 * Φ2⟩}
// {t ↦ thrd⟨Φ1⟩ * t ↦ thrd⟨Φ2⟩}
join(t);
// {Φ1 * t ↦ thrd⟨Φ2⟩ ∧ dead(t)}
// {Φ1 * Φ2 ∧ dead(t)}  /*R-THRD2 applied*/
```

This split causes the join operation to release only resource Φ_1, whilst Φ_2 remains trapped as resource inside a thread node. This results in a resource leakage if the scenario is not properly considered. However, our verification system handles such scenarios by releasing the trapped resource using the R−THRD2 rule in Fig. 5, thus ours avoids the leakages of thread resource.

6. Implementation and Experimental Results

We demonstrate the feasibility of our "threads as resource" approach by implementing it on top of PARAHIP [18], a current state-of-the-art verifier for fork-join concurrency and mutex locks that is able to verify functional correctness and deadlock-freedom. PARAHIP models threads as separate **and**-conjuncts, and its threads are not allowed to be split and shared. In contrast, besides verifying functional correctness, data-race freedom, deadlock freedom, and non-lexically-scoped fork/join, our implementation (called THREADHIP) is also capable of verifying first-class threads and multi-join.

The expressiveness of "threads as resource" is beyond that of other verification systems for fork/join programs. However, as there is a lack of commonly accepted benchmarks in the literature, we cannot easily compare THREADHIP with other systems. In order to give readers an idea of the applicability of our approach, we did an experimental comparison between PARAHIP and THREADHIP. Experimental programs consist of 16 deadlock/deadlock-freedom programs from PARAHIP's benchmark and other intricate programs inspired by the literature. [4] Besides the theoretical contributions, the empirical questions we investigate are (1) whether the "threads as resource" approach is capable of verifying more challenging programs, and (2) how THREADHIP performs, compared with PARAHIP. All experiments were conducted on a machine with Ubuntu 14.04, 3.20GHz Intel Core i7-960 processor, and 12GB memory.

The experimental results are presented in Table 1. THREADHIP is able to verify all programs of PARAHIP's benchmark and other programs found in the literature. For these programs, PARAHIP and THREADHIP showed comparable verification times (e.g. for PARAHIP's benchmark, the difference is +2.0%). Nonetheless, THREADHIP is more expressive than PARAHIP since THREADHIP is also capable of verifying more complex programs that manipulate the multi-join pattern and/or require expressive treatment of threads' resource such as `mapreduce`, `threadpool`, and `multicast`. We believe that existing verifiers for verifying concurrent programs can easily integrate our "threads as resource" approach into their systems (as we did for PARAHIP) and benefit from its greater expressiveness with negligible performance difference.

7. Related Work

This section discusses related works on reasoning about shared-memory concurrent programs. Our approach currently supports only partial correctness. Proving (non-)termination is an orthogonal issue and could be separately extended.

Traditional works on concurrency verification such as Owicki-Gries [22] and Rely/Guarantee reasoning [16] often focused on simple parallel composition, rather than fork/join. Fork/join concurrency is more general than the parallel composition for two main reasons. First, fork/join supports dynamic thread creation and termination. Second, while threads in a parallel composition are lexically scoped, threads in fork/join programs can be non-lexically scoped. Therefore, fork/join programs are more challenging for verification. Even recent approaches such as CSL [21], RGSep [25], LRG [9], and Views [6], omit fork/join concurrency from their languages. Our "threads as resource" is complementary to the above approaches and could be integrated into them.

There also exist approaches that can handle fork/join operations. Both Hobor [14] and Feng and Shao [10] support fork and omit join with the claim that thread join can be implemented using synchronization. However, without join, the former allows threads to leak resource upon termination while the latter requires global specifications of inter-thread interference. Approaches that can handle both fork and join can be grouped as modeling threads as tokens [12, 15, 19] and modeling threads as **and**-conjuncts [17, 18]. Though syntactically different, they are semantically similar in that the tokens and the **and**-conjuncts are used to represent the post-states of forked threads. However, they offer limited support

[3] We refer interested readers to `deadpool` program in our project webpage for more details.

[4] THREADHIP and all experimental programs are available for both online use and download at `http://loris-7.ddns.comp.nus.edu.sg/~project/threadhip/`.

Program	Properties	Verification Time (s)		
		PARAHIP	THREADHIP	Diff
PARAHIP's benchmark	F/L/(N)	*	*	+2.0%
fibonacci [17]	F	0.076	0.077	+1.3%
parallel-mergesort [17]	F	1.326	1.236	-6.8%
oracle [14]	F/L	1.654	1.646	-0.5%
owicki-gries [15]	F/L	1.227	1.241	+1.1%
multi-join1	F/N/M	-	0.075	-
multi-join2	F/N/M	-	0.216	-
mapreduce	F/N/M	-	0.515	-
threadpool	F/N/P	-	0.199	-
deadpool	F/N/P	-	0.261	-
multicast [12]	F/L/N/P	-	1.057	-
no-deadlock-nonlexical2	F/L/N/M	-	0.122	-

Table 1. Experimental Results. The second column indicates properties of a program, i.e. whether it uses fork/join (F), locks (L), non-lexical fork/join (N), multi-join (M), and inductive predicates (P); verification times are average of the 10 runs (in seconds); the final column is computed as $\frac{\text{THREADHIP}-\text{PARAHIP}}{\text{PARAHIP}}$; ($*$) details of PARAHIP's benchmark are presented in Table 2, here the final column of PARAHIP's benchmark reports the average of its 16 programs.

Program	Properties	Verification Time (s)		
		PARAHIP	THREADHIP	Diff
deadlock1	F/L	0.085	0.085	0.0%
deadlock2	F/L	0.088	0.090	+2.3%
deadlock3	F/L	0.095	0.097	+2.1%
deadlock-nested-forkjoin	F/L	0.150	0.156	+4.0%
disj-deadlock	F/L	0.103	0.102	-1.0%
disj-no-deadlock1	F/L	0.131	0.132	+0.8%
disj-no-deadlock2	F/L	0.136	0.142	+4.4%
double-acquire	F/L	0.760	0.750	-1.3%
fork-join-as-send-recv	F/L	0.176	0.189	+7.4%
no-deadlock1	F/L	0.104	0.099	-4.8%
no-deadlock2	F/L	0.104	0.108	+3.8%
no-deadlock3	F/L	0.137	0.414	+2.9%
ordered-locking	F/L	0.189	0.195	+3.2%
unordered-locking	F/L	0.173	0.180	+4.0%
deadlock-nonlexical	F/L/N	0.098	0.097	+1.0%
no-deadlock-nonlexical	F/L/N	0.116	0.119	+2.6%
Average	-	-	-	+2.0%

Table 2. Experimental Results on PARAHIP's benchmark. 14 out of 16 programs in PARAHIP's benchmark have properties F/L; two programs have properties F/L/N.

for first-class threads: tokens and **and**-conjuncts are not allowed to be split and shared among concurrent threads. As such, they are not expressive enough to verify programs with more intricate fork/join behaviors such as the multi-join pattern where threads are shared and joined in multiple threads. Existing works could encode the multi-join pattern by using synchronization primitives such as channels or locks. However, the encoding requires additional support for the primitives and could complicate reasoning (i.e. we have to reason about channels or locks instead of just focusing on threads). Our approach is more elegant and natural. Inspired by the key notation of resource in separation logic [1, 21], we propose to model threads as resource, thus allow ownerships of threads to be flexibly split and distributed among multiple joiners. This enables verification of the multi-join pattern. In addition, unlike ours, none of related works that we are aware of support explicit reasoning about thread liveness. To the best of our knowledge, only Haack and Hurlin [13] can reason about some multi-join scenarios. In their approach, a thread token can be associated with a fraction and this allows multiple joiners to join with the same joinee in order to read-share the joinee's resource. However, this simple multiplicative treatment of thread tokens is not expressive enough as it is unable to verify programs that require the joiners to write-share the resource of the joinee (e.g. the program in Fig 1). In order to cater to a more flexible treatment of joinees and their resource, modeling threads as resource is essential.

The concept of higher-orderness, where a heap node carries other heap nodes, has been proposed in the literature. Typical examples are lock nodes that carry the locks' resource invariants [12, 14, 15]. However, thread nodes and lock nodes are fundamentally different. First, locks and threads are used differently. While the resource inside a lock node can be repeatedly acquired/released, the resource inside a thread node can be obtained only once when the thread is joined. Second, unlike the resource in a lock node which is exclusively acquired by a single thread, the resource in a thread node can be split and shared among multiple joiners. Our "threads as resource" also shares some similarities with Concurrent Abstract Predicates (CAP) [7, 8, 24]. The basic idea behind CAP is to provide an abstraction of possible interferences from concurrently running threads, by partitioning the state into regions with protocols governing how the state in each region is allowed to evolve. Ours is simpler; a thread node is an abstraction of a thread and can be considered as a placeholder for the resource that it carries. The placeholder is created when forking, split and shared across procedure boundaries, and destroyed when joining. Hence, our approach enables reasoning about first-class threads without resorting to any additional protocols.

8. Conclusion

We proposed to model first-class threads as resource to enable expressive treatment of threads' ownerships. Our approach allows resources of threads to be flexibly split, combined, and transferred across procedure boundaries. This enables verification of multi-join pattern, where multiple joiners can share and join the same joinee in order to manipulate (read or write) the resource of the joinee after join. In addition, we demonstrated how threads as resource is combined with inductive predicates to capture the thread-pool idiom. Using a special `dead` predicate, we showed that thread liveness can be precisely tracked. We have implemented our approach in a tool, called THREADHIP, to verify partial correctness and data-race freedom of concurrent programs with non-lexically-scoped fork/join, first-class threads, and multi-join. Our experiment showed that THREADHIP is more expressive than PARAHIP while achieving comparable verification time.

As future work, we plan to exploit current advances in resource synthesis (such as [3, 4]) to synthesize "threads as resource" specification automatically.

Acknowledgments

We are grateful to the anonymous reviewers and our colleagues for their insightful comments and feedbacks.

References

[1] R. Bornat, C. Calcagno, and H. Yang. Variables as Resource in Separation Logic. *ENTCS*, 155:247–276, 2006.

[2] J. Boyland. Checking Interference with Fractional Permissions. In *SAS*, 2003.

[3] C. Calcagno, D. Distefano, P. W. O'Hearn, and H. Yang. Compositional Shape Analysis by Means of Bi-Abduction. *JACM*, 58(6):26, 2011.

[4] C. Calcagno, D. Distefano, and V. Vafeiadis. Bi-abductive Resource Invariant Synthesis. In *APLAS*, pages 259–274, 2009.

[5] W.N. Chin, C. David, H.H. Nguyen, and S. Qin. Multiple Pre/Post Specifications for Heap-Manipulating Methods. In *HASE*, pages 357–364, 2007.

[6] T. Dinsdale-Young, L. Birkedal, P. Gardner, M. Parkinson, and H. Yang. Views: Compositional Reasoning for Concurrent programs. In *POPL*, 2013.

[7] T. Dinsdale-Young, M. Dodds, P. Gardner, M. J. Parkinson, and V. Vafeiadis. Concurrent abstract predicates. In *ECOOP*, pages 504–528, 2010.

[8] M. Dodds, S. Jagannathan, and M. J. Parkinson. Modular reasoning for deterministic parallelism. In *POPL*, pages 259–270, 2011.

[9] X. Feng. Local Rely-Guarantee Reasoning. In *POPL*, pages 315–327, 2009.

[10] X. Feng and Z. Shao. Modular Verification of Concurrent Assembly Code with Dynamic Thread Creation and Termination. In *ICFP*, pages 254–267, 2005.

[11] C. Gherghina, C. David, S. Qin, and W.N. Chin. Structured Specifications for Better Verification of Heap-Manipulating Programs. In *FM*, pages 386–401, 2011.

[12] A. Gotsman, J. Berdine, B. Cook, N. Rinetzky, and M. Sagiv. Local Reasoning for Storable Locks and Threads. In *APLAS*, pages 19–37, 2007.

[13] C. Haack and C. Hurlin. Separation Logic Contracts for a Java-Like Language with Fork/Join. In *AMAST*, pages 199–215, 2008.

[14] A. Hobor. *Oracle Semantics*. PhD thesis, Princeton University, 2008.

[15] B. Jacobs and F. Piessens. Expressive Modular Fine-grained Concurrency Specification. In *POPL*, pages 271–282, New York, NY, USA, 2011.

[16] Cliff B. Jones. Specification and Design of (Parallel) Programs. In *IFIP Congress*, pages 321–332, 1983.

[17] D.K. Le, W.N. Chin, and Y.M. Teo. Variable Permissions for Concurrency Verification. In *ICFEM*, pages 5–21, 2012.

[18] D.K. Le, W.N. Chin, and Y.M. Teo. An Expressive Framework for Verifying Deadlock Freedom. In *ATVA*, pages 287–302, 2013.

[19] K. R. M. Leino, P. Müller, and J. Smans. Deadlock-Free Channels and Locks. In *ESOP*, pages 407–426, 2010.

[20] H.H. Nguyen, C. David, S. Qin, and W.N. Chin. Automated Verification of Shape and Size Properties via Separation Logic. In *VMCAI*, Nice, France, 2007.

[21] P. W. O'Hearn. Resources, Concurrency and Local Reasoning. In *CONCUR*, 2004.

[22] S. Owicki and D. Gries. Verifying Properties of Parallel Programs: an Axiomatic Approach. *CACM*, pages 279–285, 1976.

[23] J. Reynolds. Separation Logic: A Logic for Shared Mutable Data Structures. In *LICS*, Copenhagen, Denmark, July 2002.

[24] K. Svendsen, L. Birkedal, and M. J. Parkinson. Modular reasoning about separation of concurrent data structures. In *ESOP*, pages 169–188, 2013.

[25] V. Vafeiadis and M. Parkinson. A Marriage of Rely/Guarantee and Separation Logic. In *CONCUR*, pages 256–271. Springer, 2007.

Constraint Specialisation in Horn Clause Verification

Bishoksan Kafle
Roskilde University, Denmark
kafle@ruc.dk

John P. Gallagher
Roskilde University, Denmark and IMDEA Software Institute, Spain
jpg@ruc.dk

Abstract

We present a method for specialising the constraints in constrained Horn clauses with respect to a goal. We use abstract interpretation to compute a model of a query-answer transformation of a given set of clauses and a goal. The effect is to propagate the constraints from the goal top-down and propagate answer constraints bottom-up. Our approach does not unfold the clauses at all; we use the constraints from the model to compute a specialised version of each clause in the program. The approach is independent of the abstract domain and the constraints theory underlying the clauses. Experimental results on verification problems show that this is an effective transformation, both in our own verification tools (convex polyhedra analyser) and as a pre-processor to other Horn clause verification tools.

Categories and Subject Descriptors CR-number [*subcategory*]: third-level

Keywords constraint specialisation; query-answer transformation; Horn clauses; abstract interpretation; convex polyhedral analysis

1. Introduction

In this paper, we present a method for specialising the constraints in constrained Horn clauses with respect to a goal. To this end, we first compute a query-answer transformation of a given set of clauses (also called a constraint logic program) with respect to a goal; the aim of the transformation is to simulate the top-down evaluation of the clauses in a bottom-up framework. Then we use abstract interpretation to compute a model of the query-answer transformed program. The idea is to propagate the constraints from the goal top-down and propagate answer constraints bottom-up. Finally we compute a specialised version of each clause in the original program using the constraints from the model without unfolding the clauses at all.

As a result, each clause is further strengthened or removed altogether, preserving the derivability of the goal. Static analysis of the specialised program becomes easier since the implicit constraints in the original clauses are made explicit in the specialised version. In addition to this, since the specialised clauses are more constrained or more specific than the original ones, more specific information will be available for proving the given goal or a failure to prove the goal may be detected at an early stage.

The approach is independent of the abstract domain and the constraints theory. Query-answer transformations, closely related to so-called "magic set" transformations, have been used for Datalog query processing and logic program analysis since the 1980s [3, 16], but have not, to our knowledge, been applied to verification problems. Experimental results on verification problems show that this is an effective transformation, propagating information both backwards from the statement to be proved, and forwards from the Horn clause theory. We show its effectiveness both in our own verification tools and as a pre-processor to other Horn Clause verification tools. In particular, we run our specialisation procedure as a pre-processor both to our *convex polyhedra analyser* and to QARMC [24, 43], a state of the art verification tool. We make the following contributions in this paper:

- we present a method for specialising the constraints in the clauses using *query-answer transformation* and abstract interpretation (see Section 4); and
- we demonstrate the effectiveness of transformation by applying it to Horn clause verification problems (see Section 6).

2. Preliminaries

A constrained Horn clause (CHC) is a first order predicate logic formula of the form $\forall(\phi \wedge p_1(X_1) \wedge \ldots \wedge p_k(X_k) \rightarrow p(X))$ ($k \geq 0$), where ϕ is a conjunction of constraints with respect to some background theory, X_i, X are (possibly empty) vectors of distinct variables, $p_1, \ldots, p_k, p$ are predicate symbols, $p(X)$ is the head of the clause and $\phi \wedge p_1(X_1) \wedge \ldots \wedge p_k(X_k)$ is the body.

Pure constraint logic programs (CLP) are syntactically and semantically the same as CHC. Unlike CLP, CHCs are not always regarded as executable programs, but rather as specifications or semantic representations of other formalisms. However these are only pragmatic distinctions and the semantic equivalence of CHC and CLP means that techniques developed in one framework are applicable to the other. We follow the syntactic conventions of CLP and write a Horn clause as $p(X) \leftarrow \phi, p_1(X_1), \ldots, p_k(X_k)$. In this paper we take the constraint theory to be linear arithmetic with the relation symbols $\leq, \geq, <, >$ and $=$, but the contributions of the paper are independent of the constraint theory.

2.1 Interpretations and models

An interpretation of a set of CHCs is a truth assignment to each atomic formula $p(a_1, \ldots, a_n)$ where p is a predicate and $a_1, \ldots, a_n$ are constants from the constraint theory. An interpretation is represented as a set of *constrained facts* of the form $A \leftarrow \phi$ where A is an atomic formula $p(Z_1, \ldots, Z_n)$ where $Z_1, \ldots, Z_n$ are distinct variables and ϕ is a constraint over $Z_1, \ldots, Z_n$. If ϕ is true we write $A \leftarrow$ or just A. The constrained fact $A \leftarrow \phi$ is

PEPM '15, January 13–14, 2015, Mumbai, India.

http://dx.doi.org/10.1145/2678015.2682544

shorthand for the set of variable-free facts $A\theta$ such that $\phi\theta$ holds in the constraint theory, and an interpretation M denotes the set of all facts denoted by its elements; M assigns true to exactly those facts. $M_1 \subseteq M_2$ if the set of denoted facts of M_1 is contained in the set of denoted facts of M_2.

Minimal models. A model of a set of CHCs is an interpretation that satisfies each clause. There exists a minimal model with respect to the subset ordering, denoted $M[\![P]\!]$ where P is the set of CHCs. $M[\![P]\!]$ can be computed as the least fixed point (lfp) of an immediate consequences operator (called S_P^D in [28, Section 4]), which is an extension of the standard T_P operator from logic programming, extended to handle the constraint domain D. Furthermore $\mathsf{lfp}(S_P^D)$ can be computed as the limit of the ascending sequence of interpretations $\emptyset, S_P^D(\emptyset), S_P^D(S_P^D(\emptyset)), \ldots$. This sequence provides a basis for abstract interpretation of CHC clauses.

3. Abstract Interpretation

Abstract interpretation [11] is a static program analysis technique which derives sound overapproximations of programs by computing abstract fixed points. Convex polyhedra analysis (CPA) [13] is a program analysis technique based on abstract interpretation [11]. When applied to a set of CHCs P it constructs an over-approximation M' of the minimal model of P, where M' contains at most one constrained fact $p(X) \leftarrow \phi$ for each predicate p. The constraint ϕ is a conjunction of linear inequalities, representing a convex polyhedron.

The first application of convex polyhedra analysis to CHCs was by Benoy and King [4]. We summarise briefly the elements of convex polyhedra analysis for CHC; further details (with application to CHC) can be found in [4, 13]. Let $\mathcal{A}$ be the set of convex polyhedra (for some fixed dimension). Let P be a set of CHCs. Suppose there are n predicates in P, say $p_1, \ldots, p_n$, and assume to simplify the discussion that all predicates have the same arity (the dimension of $\mathcal{A}$). The *abstract domain* for P is the set of n-tuples of convex polyhedra $\mathcal{A}^n$. Let the empty polyhedron be denoted $\perp$. Inclusion of polyhedra is a partial order on $\mathcal{A}$ and the partial order $\sqsubseteq$ on $\mathcal{A}^n$ is its pointwise extension. Given an element $\langle d_1, \ldots, d_n\rangle \in \mathcal{A}^n$, define the *concretisation* function γ such that $\gamma(\langle d_1, \ldots, d_n\rangle) = \{\langle p_1(a_1), \ldots, p_n(a_n)\rangle \mid a_i \text{ is a point in } d_i, 1 \leq i \leq n\}$. Construct an *abstract semantic function* $F : \mathcal{A}^n \to \mathcal{A}^n$ satisfying the *safety condition* $S_P^D \circ \gamma \subseteq \gamma \circ F$ which is monotonic with respect to $\sqsubseteq$, where S_P^D is the immediate consequences operator mentioned above. Let the increasing sequence $Y_0, Y_1, \ldots$ be defined as follows. $Y_0 = \perp^n, Y_{n+1} = F(Y_n)$. These conditions are sufficient to establish that if the limit of the sequence exists, say Y, that $M[\![P]\!] = \mathsf{lfp}(S_P^D) \subseteq \gamma(Y)$ [12].

Since $\mathcal{A}^n$ contains infinite increasing chains, the sequence can be infinite. The use of a *widening* operator for convex polyhedra [11, 13] is needed to ensure convergence of the abstract interpretation. Define the sequence $Z_0 = Y_0$, $Z_{n+1} = Z_n \nabla F(Z_n)$ where ∇ is a widening operator for convex polyhedra [13]. The conditions on ∇ ensure that the sequence stabilises; thus for some finite j, $Z_i = Z_j$ for all $i > j$ and furthermore that Z_j is an upper bound for the sequence $\{Y_i\}$. The value Z_j thus represents, via the concretisation function γ, an over-approximation of the least model of P. Furthermore much research has been done on improving the precision of widening operators. One technique is known as widening-upto, or widening with thresholds [27]. A threshold is an assertion that is combined with a widening operator to improve its precision. Recently, a technique for deriving more effective thresholds was developed [34], which we have adapted and found to be very effective in experimental studies. In brief, the method collects constraints by iterating the concrete immediate consequence function S_P^D three times starting from the "top" interpretation, that is, the interpretation in which all atomic facts are true.

4. Specialisation by constraint propagation

We next present a procedure for specialising CHCs. In contrast to classical specialisation techniques based on partial evaluation with respect to a goal, the specialisation does not unfold the clauses at all; rather, it computes a specialised version of each clause, in which the constraints from the goal are propagated top-down and answers are propagated bottom-up.

We first make precise what is meant by "specialisation" for CHCs. Let P be a set of CHCs and let A be an atomic formula. The specialisation of P with respect to A is a set of clauses P_A such that for every constraint ϕ over the variables of A, $P \models \forall(\phi \to A)$ if and only if $P_A \models \forall(\phi \to A)$. This is a very general definition that allows for many transformations. In practice we are interested in specialisations that eliminate consequences of P that have no relevance to A.

For each clause $H \leftarrow \mathcal{B}$ in P, P_A contains a new clause $H \leftarrow \phi, \mathcal{B}$ where ϕ is a constraint. If the addition of ϕ makes the clause body unsatisfiable, it is the same as removing the clause. Clearly P_A may have fewer consequences than P but our procedure guarantees that it preserves the inferability of (constrained instances of) A. The procedure is summarised as follows: the inputs are a set of CHCs P and an atomic formula A.

1. Compute a *query-answer transformation* of P with respect to A, denoted P^{qa}, containing predicates p^{q} and p^{a} for each predicate p in P.
2. Compute an over-approximation M of the model of P^{qa}.
3. Strengthen the constraints in the clauses in P, by adding constraints from the answer predicates in M.

Next we will explain each step in detail.

4.1 The query-answer transformation

The *query-answer transformation* in CLP was inspired by the magic-set transformation from deductive databases and the language Datalog [3]. Its purpose, both in deductive databases and in subsequent applications in logic program analysis [16] was to simulate goal-directed (*top-down*) computation or deduction in a goal-independent (*bottom-up*) framework.

In the following, for each atom $A = p(t)$, A^{a} and A^{q} represent the atoms $p^{\mathsf{a}}(t)$ and $p^{\mathsf{q}}(t)$ respectively. Given a set of CHCs P and an atom A, the (left-) query-answer clauses for P with respect to A, denoted P_A^{qa} or just P^{qa}, are as follows.

- (Answer clauses). For each clause $H \leftarrow \phi, B_1, \ldots, B_n$ $(n \geq 0)$ in P, P^{qa} contains the clause $H^{\mathsf{a}} \leftarrow \phi, H^{\mathsf{q}}, B_1^{\mathsf{a}}, \ldots, B_n^{\mathsf{a}}$.
- (Query clauses). For each clause $H \leftarrow \phi, B_1, \ldots, B_i, \ldots, B_n$ $(n \geq 0)$ in P, P^{qa} contains the following clauses:

$$
\begin{array}{l}
B_1^{\mathsf{q}} \leftarrow \phi, H^{\mathsf{q}}. \\
\cdots \\
B_i^{\mathsf{q}} \leftarrow \phi, H^{\mathsf{q}}, B_1^{\mathsf{a}}, \ldots, B_{i-1}^{\mathsf{a}}. \\
\cdots \\
B_n^{\mathsf{q}} \leftarrow \phi, H^{\mathsf{q}}, B_1^{\mathsf{a}}, \ldots, B_{n-1}^{\mathsf{a}}.
\end{array}
$$

- (Goal clause). $A^{\mathsf{q}} \leftarrow \mathsf{true}$.

The clauses P^{qa} encodes a left-to-right, depth-first computation of the query $\leftarrow A$ for CHC clauses P (that is, the standard CLP computation rule, SLD extended with constraints). This is a complete proof procedure, assuming that all clauses matching a given call are explored in parallel. (Note: the incompleteness of standard Prolog

CLP proof procedures arises due to the fact that clauses are tried in a fixed order). It is important to generate the queries and answers in a single set of clauses, since in general the predicates p^{q} and p^{a} are mutually recursive. Independent analyses propagating constraints from head to body of the clauses and propagating constraints from body to head would not in general achieve the same specialisation.

The relationship of the model of the clauses P^{qa} to the computation of the goal $\leftarrow A$ in P is expressed by the following property[1]. An SLD-derivation in CLP is a sequence $G_0, G_1, \ldots, G_k$ where each G_i is a goal $\leftarrow \phi, B_1, \ldots, B_m$, where ϕ is a constraint and $B_1, \ldots, B_m$ are atoms. In a left-to-right computation, G_{i+1} is obtained by resolving B_1 with a program clause. The model of P^{qa} captures the set of atoms that are "called" or "queried" during the derivation, together with the answers (if any) for those calls. This is expressed precisely by Property 1.

PROPERTY 1 (Correctness of query-answer transformation). *Let P be a set of CHCs and A be an atom. Let P^{qa} be the query-answer program for P wrt. A. Then*

(i) if there is an SLD-derivation $G_0, \ldots, G_i$ where $G_0 = \leftarrow A$ and $G_i = \leftarrow \phi, B_1, \ldots, B_m$, then $P^{\mathsf{qa}} \models \forall(\phi|_{\mathsf{vars}(B_1)} \rightarrow B_1^{\mathsf{q}})$;

(ii) if there is an SLD-derivation $G_0, \ldots, G_i$ where $G_0 = \leftarrow A$, containing a sub-derivation $G_{j_1}, \ldots, G_{j_k}$, where $G_{j_i} \leftarrow \phi', B_1, \mathcal{B}'$ and $G_{j_k} = \leftarrow \phi, \mathcal{B}'$, then $P^{\mathsf{qa}} \models \forall(\phi|_{\mathsf{vars}(B_1)} \rightarrow B_1^{\mathsf{a}})$. (This means that the atom B_1 in G_{j_i} was successfully answered, with answer constraint $\phi|_{\mathsf{vars}(B_1)}$).

(iii) As a special case of (ii), if there is a successful derivation of the goal $\leftarrow A$ with answer constraint ϕ then $P^{\mathsf{qa}} \models \forall(\phi \rightarrow A^{\mathsf{a}})$.

Variations such as the following have been used.

- (Refined call predicates). Call predicates of the form $p^{\mathsf{q}}_{i,j}$ could be generated representing calls to the ith atom in the body of clause j [20], giving more fine-grained information on calls.
- (Relaxed answer predicates). In this version the answer clauses are the same as the original clauses of p, and every answer predicate p^{a} is just replaced by p. This can be used where the only interest is in the model of the query predicates, and the motivation is to increase efficiency of analysis of P^{qa}, while possibly losing precision [9].
- (Other computation rules). Left-to-right computation could be replaced by right-to-left or any other order. The success or failure of a goal is independent of the computation rule; hence we could generate answers using other computation rules, or combining computation rules [21]. While different computation rules do not affect the model of the answer predicates, more effective propagation of constraints during program analysis, and thus greater precision, can sometimes be achieved by varying the computation rule.

For each such variation a correctness property can be stated relating the model of the query-answer program to the SLD computation of the given program P and goal A.

4.2 Over-approximation of the model of P^{qa}

The query-answer transformation of P with respect to A is computed. It follows from Property 1(iii) that if A is derivable from P then $P^{\mathsf{qa}} \models A^{\mathsf{a}}$. Abstract interpretation of P^{qa} yields an over-approximation of $M[\![P^{\mathsf{qa}}]\!]$, say M', containing constrained facts for the query and answer predicates. These represent the calls and answers generated during all derivations starting from the goal A. In our experiments we use a convex polyhedra approximation of $M[\![P^{\mathsf{qa}}]\!]$, as described in Section 3.

[1] Note that the model of P^{qa} might not correspond exactly to the calls and answers in the SLD-computation, since the CLP computation treats constraints as syntactic entities through decision procedures and the actual constraints could differ.

4.3 Strengthening the constraints in P

We use the information in M' to specialise the original clauses in P. Suppose M' contains constrained facts $p^{\mathsf{q}}(X) \leftarrow \phi^{\mathsf{q}}$ and $p^{\mathsf{a}}(X) \leftarrow \phi^{\mathsf{a}}$. (If there is no constrained fact $p^*(X) \leftarrow \phi^*$ for some p^* then we consider M' to contain $p^*(X) \leftarrow \mathit{false}$).

For each clause

$$p(X) \leftarrow \phi, p_1(X_1), \ldots, p_k(X_k)$$

in P, construct a clause

$$p(X) \leftarrow \phi, \phi_0, \phi_1, \ldots, \phi_n, p_1(X_1), \ldots, p_k(X_k)$$

in P_A, where $p^{\mathsf{a}}(X) \leftarrow \phi_0$, $p_1^{\mathsf{a}}(X) \leftarrow \phi_1, \ldots, p_n^{\mathsf{a}}(X) \leftarrow \phi_n$ are in M'. Here we assume that there is exactly one constrained fact in M' for each predicate $p^a, p_1^a, \ldots, p_n^a$. Disjunctive constraints can be eliminated from the specialised clauses by further transformation and clauses containing the constraint false in the body are eliminated.

Note that wherever M' contains constrained facts $p^{\mathsf{a}}(X) \leftarrow \phi^{\mathsf{a}}$ and $p^{\mathsf{q}}(X) \leftarrow \phi^{\mathsf{q}}$, we have $\phi^{\mathsf{a}} \rightarrow \phi^{\mathsf{q}}$ since the answers for p are always stronger than the calls to p. Thus it suffices to add only the answer constraints to the clauses in P and we can ignore the model of the query predicates. A special case of this is where M' contains a constrained fact $p^{\mathsf{q}}(X) \leftarrow \phi^{\mathsf{q}}$ but there is no constrained fact for $p^{\mathsf{a}}(X)$, or in other words M' contains the constrained fact $p^{\mathsf{a}}(X) \leftarrow \mathit{false}$. This means that all derivations for $p(X)$ fail or loop in P and so adding the answer constraint false for p eliminates looping and failed derivations for p.

Specialisation by strengthening the constraints preserves the answers of the goal with respect to which the query-answer transformation was performed. In particular, we have the following property.

PROPERTY 2. *If P is a set of CHCs and P_A is the set obtained by strengthening the clause constraints as just described, then $P \models A$ if and only if $P_A \models A$.*

The proof of Property 2 is by induction on the length of derivations of A. For each derivation of A using the clauses of P we can construct a derivation of A in P_A and conversely.

The specialisation and analysis are separate in our approach. More complex algorithms intertwining them can be envisaged, though the benefits are not clear. Iteration of our procedure could potentially yield further specialisation.

5. Application to the CHC verification problem

In this section, we discuss the application of our constraint specialisation in Horn clause verification. We assume that there is a distinguished predicate symbol false in P which is always interpreted as false. In practice the predicate false only occurs in the head of clauses; we call clauses whose head is false *integrity constraints*, following the terminology of deductive databases. Thus the formula $\phi_1 \leftarrow \phi_2 \wedge B_1(X_1), \ldots, B_k(X_k)$ is equivalent to the formula $\mathsf{false} \leftarrow \neg\phi_1 \wedge \phi_2 \wedge B_1(X_1), \ldots, B_k(X_k)$. The latter might not be a CHC (e.g. if ϕ_1 contains $=$) but can be converted to an equivalent set of CHCs by transforming the formula $\neg\phi_1$ and distributing any disjunctions that arise over the rest of the body. For example, the formula $X = Y \leftarrow p(X,Y)$ is equivalent to the set of CHCs $\{\mathsf{false} \leftarrow X > Y, p(X,Y),\ \mathsf{false} \leftarrow X < Y, p(X,Y)\}$.

Integrity constraints can be seen as safety properties. For example if a set of CHCs encodes the behaviour of a transition system, the bodies of integrity constraints represent unsafe states. Thus proving safety consists of showing that the bodies of integrity constraints are false in all models of the CHC clauses. Figure 1 shows an example set of CHCs taken from [23].

```
c1. false :- A>0,B=0,C=0,D=0,l(B,C,D,A).
c2. l(A,B,C,D) :- -A+D>0,A-G= -1, l_body(B,C,E,F),
                  l(G,E,F,D).
c3. l(A,B,C,D) :- A-D>=0,B+C-3*D>0.
c4. l(A,B,C,D) :- A-D>=0,-B-C+3*D>0.
c5. l_body(A,B,C,D) :- A-C= -1,B-D= -2.
c6. l_body(A,B,C,D) :- A-C= -2,B-D= -1.
```

Figure 1. Example program *t4.pl* [23]

5.1 The CHC verification problem.

To state this more formally, given a set of CHCs P, the CHC verification problem is to check whether there exists a model of P. If so we say that P is safe. Obviously any model of P assigns false to the bodies of integrity constraints. We restate this property in terms of the logic consequence relation. Let $P \models F$ mean that F is a logical consequence of P, that is, that every interpretation satisfying P also satisfies F.

LEMMA 1. *P has a model if and only if $P \not\models$ false.*

This lemma holds for arbitrary interpretations (only assuming that the predicate false is interpreted as false), uses only the textbook definitions of "interpretation" and "model" and does not depend on the constraint theory.

The verification problem can be formulated deductively rather than model-theoretically. We can exploit proof procedures for constraint logic programming [28] to reason about the satisfiability of a set of CHCs. Let the relation $P \vdash A$ denote that A is derivable from P using some proof procedure. If the proof procedure is sound then $P \vdash A$ implies $P \models A$, which means that $P \vdash$ false is a sufficient condition for P to have no model, by Lemma 1. This corresponds to using a sound proof procedure to find or check a counterexample. On the other hand to show that P does have a model, soundness is not enough since we need to establish $P \not\models$ false. As we will see in Section 5.2 we approach this problem by using *approximations* to reason about the non-provability of false, applying the theory of abstract interpretation [10] to a complete proof procedure for atomic formulas (the "fixed-point semantics" for constraint logic programs [28, Section 4]). In effect, we construct by abstract interpretation a proof procedure that is *complete* (but possibly not sound) for proofs of atomic formulas. With such a procedure, $P \not\vdash$ false implies $P \not\models$ false and thus establishes that P has a model.

5.2 Proof Techniques

Proof by over-approximation of the minimal model. It is a standard theorem of CLP that the minimal model $M[\![P]\!]$ is equivalent to the set of atomic consequences of P. That is, $P \models p(v_1, \ldots, v_n)$ if and only if $p(v_1, \ldots, v_n) \in M[\![P]\!]$. Therefore, the CHC verification problem for P is equivalent to checking that false $\notin M[\![P]\!]$. It is sufficient to find a set of constrained facts M' such that $M[\![P]\!] \subseteq M'$, where false $\notin M'$. This technique is called proof by *over-approximation of the minimal model.*

Proof by specialisation. A specialisation of a set of CHCs P with respect to an atom A is the transformation of P to another set of CHCs P' such that $P \models A$ if and only if $P' \models A$. In our context we use specialisation to focus the verification problem on the formula to be proved. More specifically, we specialise a set of CHCs with respect to a "query" to the atom false; thus the specialised CHCs entail false if and only if the original clauses entailed false. The constraint strengthening procedure described in Section 4 is our method of specialisation.

Consider the application of the procedure in Section 4 to the clauses in Figure 1, where the *query-answer transformation* is performed with respect to the atom false. The result is shown in Figure 2. Note that the constraint in clause c4 is strengthened to `false`, showing that c4 is definitely not used in any derivation of false (and hence can be removed).

```
c1. false :- A>0,B=0,C=0,D=0,l(B,C,D,A).
c2. l(A,B,C,D) :- 2*A-B>=0,-A+D>0,-A+B>=0,3*A-B-C=0,
                  A-G= -1,l_body(B,C,E,F),l(G,E,F,D).
c3. l(A,B,C,D):- A-D>0,D>0,2*A-B>=0,-A+D> -1,
                 -A+B>=0,3*A-B-C=0.
c4. l(A,B,C,D):- false.
c5. l_body(A,B,C,D) :- -A+2*B>=0, 2*A-B>=0,
                       A-C= -1,B-D= -2.
c6. l_body(A,B,C,D) :- -A+2*B>=0,2*A-B>=0,A-C= -2,
                       B-D= -1.
```

Figure 2. Example program *t4.pl* [23] with strengthened constraints

5.3 Analysis of the specialised clauses

Having specialised the clauses with respect to false, it may be that the clauses P_{false} do not contain a clause with head false. In this case safety is proven, since clearly this is a sufficient condition for $P_{\mathsf{false}} \not\models$ false.

If this check fails we still do not know whether P has a model. In this case we can perform the convex polyhedral analysis on the clauses P_{false}. As the experiments later show, safety is often provable by checking the resulting model; if no constrained fact for false is present, then $P_{\mathsf{false}} \not\models$ false. If safety is not proven, there are two possibilities: the approximate model is not precise enough, but P has a model, or there is a proof of false. Refinement techniques could be used to distinguish these, but this is not the topic of this paper.

In summary, our experimental procedure for evaluating the effectiveness of constraint specialisation contains two steps. Given a set of CHCs P with integrity constraints: (1) Compute a specialisation of P with respect to false yielding P_{false}. If P_{false} contains no integrity constraints, then P is safe. (2) If P_{false} does contain integrity constraints, perform a convex polyhedra analysis of P_{false}. If the resulting approximation of the minimal model contains no constrained fact for the predicate false, then P_{false} is safe and hence P is safe. If we find a concrete derivation for false then we conclude that P is unsafe. Otherwise, P is possibly unsafe.

6. Experimental evaluation

Table 1 presents experimental results of applying our constraint specialisation to a number of Horn clause verification benchmarks taken from the repository of Horn clause verification[2] and other sources including [5, 15, 23, 25, 29]. The columns CPA and QARMC present the results of verification using convex polyhedra and QARMC respectively, whereas columns CS + CPA and CS + QARMC show the result of running constraint specialisation followed by CPA or QARMC. The symbol "-" in the table denotes irrelevant. The experiments were carried out on an Intel(R) X5355 quad-core (@ 2.66GHz) computer with 6 GB memory running Debian 5. We set 5 minutes of timeout for each experiment. The specialisation procedure is implemented in 32-bit Ciao Prolog [7] and uses the Parma Polyhedra Library [1].

[2] https://svn.sosy-lab.org/software/sv-benchmarks/trunk/clauses/

The results show that constraint specialisation is effective in practice. We report that 109 out of 218, that is 50%, of the problems are solved by constraint specialisation alone. When used as a pre-processor for other verification tools, the results show improvements on both the number of instances solved and the solution time. Using our tool, we report approximately 47% increase in the number of instances solved and twice as much faster in average. Similarly using QARMC, we report 13% increase in the number of instances solved and 5 times faster in average.

	CPA	CS + CPA	QARMC	CS + QARMC
solved (safe/unsafe)	61 (48/13)	162 (144/18)	178 (141/37)	205 (171/34)
unknown / timeout	144/12	49/7	-/40	-/13
total time (secs)	2317	1303	13367	2613
average time (secs)	10.62	5.97	61.31	11.98
%solved	27.98	74.31	81.65	94.04

Table 1. Experiments on a set of 218 (181 safe and 37 unsafe) CHC verification problems

The (perhaps surprising) effectiveness of this relatively simple combination of specialisation and convex polyhedral analysis is underlined by noting that it can solve problems for which more complex methods have been proposed. For example, apart from the many examples from the Horn clause verification benchmarks that require refinement using CEGAR-based approaches, the technique solves the "rate-limiter" and "Boustrophedon" examples presented by Monniaux and Gonnord [40] (Section 5) (directly encoded as Horn clauses); their approach, also based on convex polyhedra, uses bounded model checking to achieve a partitioning of the approximation, while other approaches to such problems use trace-partitioning and look-ahead widening.

7. Related Work

Techniques for strengthening the constraints of logic programs go back at least to the work of Marriott *et al.* on most specific logic programs [39]. In that work the constraints were just equalities between terms and the strengthening was goal-independent. In [19] the idea was similar but it was extended to strengthen constraints while preserving the answers with respect to a goal.

The partial evaluation of (constraint) logic programs also has a long history [17, 18, 30, 32]. The aim is to specialise a program with respect to a goal, but usually unfolding is the key technique for propagating constraints. Global analysis using abstract interpretation was combined with partial evaluation algorithms to propagate constraints bottom-up as well as top-down [22, 31, 33, 35, 36].

Abstract interpretation over the domain of convex polyhedra was introduced by Cousot and Halbwachs [13] and applied to constraint logic programs by Benoy and King [4]. Abstract interpretation over convex polyhedra was incorporated in a program specialisation algorithm by Peralta and Gallagher [41].

The method of widening with thresholds for increasing the precision of widening convex polyhedra was first presented by Halwachs *et al.* [27]. We applied a technique for generating threshold constraints presented by Lakhdar-Chaouch *et al.* [34].

In summary, the basic specialisation techniques that we apply are well known, though we are not aware of previous work combining them in the same way. Our method is a specialisation with respect to a goal but does not perform partial evaluation by unfolding. The aim of our specialisation is to make constraints explicit and propagate constraints as much as possible, thereby making other tools more effective, rather than to produce a more efficient computation of a goal.

Verification of CLP programs using abstract interpretation and specialisation has been studied for some time. Our aim in this paper is not to demonstrate a verification tool but to identify a transformation that benefits CLP verification tools generally.

The idea of improving analysis by applying it to a specialised program was first expressed by Turchin [44] and it was more recently demonstrated using supercompilation [38]. The use of program transformation to verify properties of logic programs was pioneered by Pettorossi and Proietti [42] and Leuschel [37] and continues in recent work by De Angelis *et al.* [14, 15]. Transformations that preserve the minimal model (or other suitable models) of logic programs are applied systematically to make properties explicit.

Much other work on CLP verification exists, much of it based on property abstraction and refinement using interpolation, for example [2, 6, 8, 24, 26, 43]. Our specialisation technique is not directly comparable to these methods, but as we have shown in experiments with QARMC, constraint specialisation can be used as a pre-processor to such tools, increasing their effectiveness.

8. Conclusion and future Work

We introduced a method for specialising the constraints in constrained Horn clauses with respect to a goal using abstract interpretation and *query-answer transformation*. The approach propagates constraints globally, both forwards and backwards, and makes explicit constraints from the original program. This allows better analysis of the transformed program. Furthermore, our approach is independent of the abstract domain and the constraints theory underlying the clauses. Finally, we showed effectiveness of this transformation in Horn clause verification problems.

In the future, we will continue to evaluate its effectiveness in a larger set of benchmarks and as a pre-processor for other existing tools. We also would like to use the specialised version for other purposes, for instance in program debugging since more specific information may make errors in the original program apparent.

Acknowledgments

The research leading to these results has received funding from the EU 7th Framework 318337, ENTRA-Whole-Systems Energy Transparency and the Danish Natural Science Research Council grant NUSA: Numerical and Symbolic Abstractions for Software Model Checking.

References

[1] R. Bagnara, P. M. Hill, and E. Zaffanella. The Parma Polyhedra Library: Toward a complete set of numerical abstractions for the analysis and verification of hardware and software systems. *Science of Computer Programming*, 72(1–2):3–21, 2008.

[2] T. Ball, V. Levin, and S. K. Rajamani. A decade of software model checking with slam. *Commun. ACM*, 54(7):68–76, 2011.

[3] F. Bancilhon, D. Maier, Y. Sagiv, and J. Ullman. Magic sets and other strange ways to implement logic programs. In *Proceedings of the* 5th *ACM SIGMOD-SIGACT Symposium on Principles of Database Systems*, 1986.

[4] F. Benoy and A. King. Inferring argument size relationships with CLP(R). In J. P. Gallagher, editor, *Logic-Based Program Synthesis and Transformation (LOPSTR'96)*, volume 1207 of *Springer-Verlag LNCS*, pages 204–223, August 1996.

[5] D. Beyer. Second competition on software verification - (summary of sv-comp 2013). In N. Piterman and S. A. Smolka, editors, *TACAS*, volume 7795 of *LNCS*, pages 594–609. Springer, 2013.

[6] N. Bjørner, K. L. McMillan, and A. Rybalchenko. On solving universally quantified horn clauses. In F. Logozzo and M. Fähndrich, editors, *SAS*, volume 7935 of *LNCS*, pages 105–125. Springer, 2013.

[7] F. Bueno, D. Cabeza, M. Carro, M. Hermenegildo, P. López-García, and G. Puebla. The Ciao Prolog system. reference manual. Technical Report CLIP3/97.1, School of Computer Science, Technical University of Madrid (UPM), August 1997. Available from http://www.clip.dia.fi.upm.es/.

[8] E. M. Clarke, O. Grumberg, S. Jha, Y. Lu, and H. Veith. Counterexample-guided abstraction refinement for symbolic model checking. *J. ACM*, 50(5):752–794, 2003.

[9] M. Codish and B. Demoen. Analyzing logic programs using "PROP"-ositional logic programs and a magic wand. *J. Log. Program.*, 25(3): 249–274, 1995. .

[10] P. Cousot and R. Cousot. Abstract interpretation: a unified lattice model for static analysis of programs by construction or approximation of fixpoints. In *Proceedings of the 4th ACM Symposium on Principles of Programming Languages, Los Angeles*, pages 238–252, 1977.

[11] P. Cousot and R. Cousot. Abstract interpretation: A unified lattice model for static analysis of programs by construction or approximation of fixpoints. In R. M. Graham, M. A. Harrison, and R. Sethi, editors, *POPL*, pages 238–252. ACM, 1977.

[12] P. Cousot and R. Cousot. Abstract interpretation frameworks. *Journal of Logic and Computation*, 2(4):511–547, 1992.

[13] P. Cousot and N. Halbwachs. Automatic discovery of linear restraints among variables of a program. In *Proceedings of the 5th Annual ACM Symposium on Principles of Programming Languages*, pages 84–96, 1978.

[14] E. De Angelis, F. Fioravanti, A. Pettorossi, and M. Proietti. Verifying programs via iterated specialization. In E. Albert and S.-C. Mu, editors, *PEPM*, pages 43–52. ACM, 2013.

[15] E. De Angelis, F. Fioravanti, A. Pettorossi, and M. Proietti. Verimap: A tool for verifying programs through transformations. In E. Ábrahám and K. Havelund, editors, *TACAS*, volume 8413 of *LNCS*, pages 568–574. Springer, 2014. ISBN 978-3-642-54861-1.

[16] S. Debray and R. Ramakrishnan. Abstract Interpretation of Logic Programs Using Magic Transformations. *Journal of Logic Programming*, 18:149–176, 1994.

[17] H. Fujita. An algorithm for partial evaluation with constraints. Technical Report TR-258, ICOT, 1987.

[18] J. P. Gallagher. Specialisation of logic programs: A tutorial. In *Proceedings PEPM'93, ACM SIGPLAN Symposium on Partial Evaluation and Semantics-Based Program Manipulation*, pages 88–98, Copenhagen, June 1993. ACM Press.

[19] J. P. Gallagher and M. Bruynooghe. Some low-level source transformations for logic programs. In *Proceedings of Meta90 Workshop on Meta Programming in Logic*. Katholieke Universiteit Leuven, Belgium, 1990.

[20] J. P. Gallagher and D. de Waal. Deletion of redundant unary type predicates from logic programs. In K. Lau and T. Clement, editors, *Logic Program Synthesis and Transformation*, Workshops in Computing, pages 151–167. Springer-Verlag, 1993.

[21] J. P. Gallagher and D. de Waal. Fast and precise regular approximation of logic programs. In P. Van Hentenryck, editor, *Proceedings of the International Conference on Logic Programming (ICLP'94), Santa Margherita Ligure, Italy*. MIT Press, 1994.

[22] J. P. Gallagher, M. Codish, and E. Shapiro. Specialisation of Prolog and FCP programs using abstract interpretation. *New Generation Computing*, 6:159–186, 1988.

[23] G. Gange, J. A. Navas, P. Schachte, H. Søndergaard, and P. J. Stuckey. Failure tabled constraint logic programming by interpolation. *TPLP*, 13(4-5):593–607, 2013.

[24] S. Grebenshchikov, A. Gupta, N. P. Lopes, C. Popeea, and A. Rybalchenko. Hsf(c): A software verifier based on Horn clauses - (competition contribution). In C. Flanagan and B. König, editors, *TACAS*, volume 7214 of *LNCS*, pages 549–551. Springer, 2012.

[25] A. Gupta and A. Rybalchenko. Invgen: An efficient invariant generator. In A. Bouajjani and O. Maler, editors, *CAV*, volume 5643 of *LNCS*, pages 634–640. Springer, 2009. ISBN 978-3-642-02657-7.

[26] A. Gupta, C. Popeea, and A. Rybalchenko. Solving recursion-free horn clauses over li+uif. In H. Yang, editor, *APLAS*, volume 7078 of *LNCS*, pages 188–203. Springer, 2011. ISBN 978-3-642-25317-1.

[27] N. Halbwachs, Y. E. Proy, and P. Raymound. Verification of linear hybrid systems by means of convex approximations. In *Proceedings of the First Symposium on Static Analysis*, volume 864 of *LNCS*, pages 223–237, September 1994.

[28] J. Jaffar and M. Maher. Constraint Logic Programming: A Survey. *Journal of Logic Programming*, 19/20:503–581, 1994.

[29] J. Jaffar, J. A. Navas, and A. E. Santosa. Unbounded symbolic execution for program verification. In S. Khurshid and K. Sen, editors, *RV*, volume 7186 of *LNCS*, pages 396–411. Springer, 2011.

[30] N. Jones, C. Gomard, and P. Sestoft. *Partial Evaluation and Automatic Software Generation*. Prentice Hall, 1993.

[31] N. D. Jones. Combining abstract interpretation and partial evaluation. In P. Van Hentenryck, editor, *Symposium on Static Analysis (SAS'97)*, volume 1302 of *Springer-Verlag LNCS*, pages 396–405, 1997.

[32] H. J. Komorowski. An introduction to partial deduction. In A. Pettorossi, editor, *META*, volume 649 of *LNCS*, pages 49–69. Springer, 1992. ISBN 3-540-56282-6.

[33] L. Lafave and J. P. Gallagher. Partial evaluation of functional logic programs in rewriting-based languages. In N. Fuchs, editor, *Logic Program Synthesis and Transformation (LOPSTR'97)*, Springer-Verlag LNCS, 1998.

[34] L. Lakhdar-Chaouch, B. Jeannet, and A. Girault. Widening with thresholds for programs with complex control graphs. In T. Bultan and P.-A. Hsiung, editors, *ATVA 2011*, volume 6996 of *LNCS*, pages 492–502. Springer, 2011.

[35] M. Leuschel. Advanced logic program specialisation. In J. Hatcliff, T. Æ. Mogensen, and P. Thiemann, editors, *Partial Evaluation - Practice and Theory*, volume 1706 of *LNCS*, pages 271–292. Springer, 1999.

[36] M. Leuschel. A framework for the integration of partial evaluation and abstract interpretation of logic programs. *ACM Trans. Program. Lang. Syst.*, 26(3):413–463, 2004. . URL `http://doi.acm.org/10.1145/982158.982159`.

[37] M. Leuschel and T. Massart. Infinite state model checking by abstract interpretation and program specialisation. In A. Bossi, editor, *LOPSTR'99*, volume 1817 of *LNCS*, pages 62–81. Springer, 1999.

[38] A. Lisitsa and A. P. Nemytykh. Reachability analysis in verification via supercompilation. *Int. J. Found. Comput. Sci.*, 19(4):953–969, 2008. . URL `http://dx.doi.org/10.1142/S0129054108006066`.

[39] K. Marriott, L. Naish, and J.-L. Lassez. Most specific logic programs. In *Proc. Fifth International Conference on Logic programming, Seattle, WA*. MIT Press, 1988.

[40] D. Monniaux and L. Gonnord. Using bounded model checking to focus fixpoint iterations. In E. Yahav, editor, *Static Analysis - 18th International Symposium, SAS 2011, Venice, Italy, September 14-16, 2011. Proceedings*, volume 6887 of *LNCS*, pages 369–385. Springer, 2011. ISBN 978-3-642-23701-0.

[41] J. C. Peralta and J. P. Gallagher. Convex hull abstractions in specialization of CLP programs. In M. Leuschel, editor, *LOPSTR*, volume 2664 of *LNCS*, pages 90–108. Springer, 2002. ISBN 3-540-40438-4.

[42] A. Pettorossi and M. Proietti. Perfect model checking via unfold/fold transformations. In J. W. Lloyd, V. Dahl, U. Furbach, M. Kerber, K.-K. Lau, C. Palamidessi, L. M. Pereira, Y. Sagiv, and P. J. Stuckey, editors, *Computational Logic*, volume 1861 of *LNCS*, pages 613–628. Springer, 2000.

[43] A. Podelski and A. Rybalchenko. ARMC: the logical choice for software model checking with abstraction refinement. In M. Hanus, editor, *Practical Aspects of Declarative Languages, 9th International Symposium, PADL 2007, Nice, France, January 14-15, 2007.*, volume 4354 of *LNCS*, pages 245–259. Springer, 2007. ISBN 978-3-540-69608-7. . URL `http://dx.doi.org/10.1007/978-3-540-69611-7_16`.

[44] V. F. Turchin. The use of metasystem transition in theorem proving and program optimization. In J. W. de Bakker and J. van Leeuwen, editors, *Automata, Languages and Programming, 7th Colloquium, Noordweijkerhout, The Netherland, July 14-18, 1980, Proceedings*, volume 85 of *LNCS*, pages 645–657. Springer, 1980. ISBN 3-540-10003-2. . URL `http://dx.doi.org/10.1007/3-540-10003-2_105`.

SWIN: Towards Type-Safe Java Program Adaptation between APIs *

Jun Li[1,2] Chenglong Wang[1,2] Yingfei Xiong[1,2] Zhenjiang Hu[3,1,2]

[1]Key Laboratory of High Confidence Software Technologies, Ministry of Education
[2]Software Engineering Institute, Peking University, Beijing, 100871, China
[3]National Institute of Informatics, 2-1-2 Hitotsubashi, Chiyoda-ku, Tokyo 101-8430, Japan
{lij, chenglongwang, xiongyf}@pku.edu.cn, hu@nii.ac.jp

Abstract

Java program adaptation between different APIs is a common task in software development. When an old API is upgraded to an incompatible new version, or when we want to migrate an application from one platform to another platform, we need to adapt programs between different APIs. Although different program transformation tools have been developed to automate the program adaptation task, no tool ensures type safety in transforming Java programs: given a transformation program and any well-typed Java program, the transformed result is still well-typed. As a matter of fact, it is often observed that a dedicated adaptation tool turns a working application into a set of incompatible programs.

We address this problem by providing a type-safe transformation language, SWIN, for Java program adaptation between different APIs. SWIN is based on Twinning, a modern transformation language for Java programs. SWIN enhances Twinning with more flexible transformation rules, formal semantics, and, most importantly, full type-safe guarantee. We formally prove the type safety of SWIN on Featherweight Java, a known minimal formal core of Java. Our experience with three case studies shows that SWIN is as expressive as Twinning in specifying useful program transformations in the case studies while guaranteeing the type safety of the transformations.

1. Introduction

Modern programs often depend on different APIs (Application Programming Interfaces), and it is a common task for the developers to adapt programs between alternative APIs. One example is *API update*: when an old API is updated to a new version with incompatible changes, we need to transform client programs with the old API to new programs using the new API. Another example is *API switching*: we often need to migrate programs between different platforms, such as from the Android platform to iOS, or from Java Swing to SWT. In such cases, we need to transform the programs with the API on one platform to new ones with the API on another platform. However, manually adapting programs is not easy: we need to examine every use of the source API and replace them with the suitable target API. Thorough knowledge of the source and target APIs as well as the client program is required.

Given the importance of program migration, it would be helpful and beneficial for tool vendors to provide automated tools to assist application adaptations. When API upgrades, API providers could provide tools to automate the upgrade of client applications, preventing potential loss of users from the incompatibility of the new API. Similarly, platform providers could provide tools to facilitate the migration of application from other platforms to their own platforms, attracting more applications and users on their platform. For example, Microsoft has provided the Visual Basic upgrade wizard tool, to facilitate the transition from Visual Basic to Visual Basic.Net. RIM has provided a tool suite to transform Android applications into blackberry applications. These tools work in the form of program transformation: they take a client program as input, and produce a new program that preserves the behavior of the source program as much as possible while targeting the new API.

However, providing a program transformation tool is not easy. Among the large body of API adaptations performed in practice, only a small portion has transformation tool supports, and it is common for the transformation tools to introduce bugs in the transformed programs. A particular type of bugs we are concerned with in this paper is type error: a well-typed program becomes *not* well-typed after the transformation. For example, Python has provided an official 2to3 script to transform Python programs from Python 2.x to 3.x. However, as discovered in a case study by Pilgrim and Willison [21], the script will introduce a type error in the transformed code whenever the original code contains a call to the "`file()`" method.

To overcome the difficulty of providing transformation tools, a large number of program transformation languages [1, 11–13, 20] have been proposed. These languages provide high-level constructs for specifying transformations between programs, reducing the development cost and preventing certain kinds of errors. For example, a number of program transformation languages prevent the possibility of introducing grammatical errors in transformation, either by specifying the transformation on top of context-free grammars [11, 12] or by designing the transformation language specifically for a programming language [1]. However, as far as we know, no transformation language for mainstream object-oriented programs ensures *type safety*: for any transformation program p and a

* This work is supported by the National Basic Research Program of China (973) under Grant No. 2011CB302604, the High-Tech Research, the Development Program of China under Grant No.2013AA01A605, the National Natural Science Foundation of China under Grant No.61202071, 61121063, U1201252, and the JSPS Grant-in-Aid for Scientific Research (A) Grant Number 25240009.

PEPM '15, January 13–14, 2015, Mumbai, India.

http://dx.doi.org/10.1145/2678015.2682534

well-typed source program s, the transformed program $p(s)$ is still well-typed. As a result, given a program transformation, we have no guarantee that a well-typed program will still be well-typed after the transformation.

It is not easy to ensure type safety in transformation languages. We highlight two challenges here. First, typing is one of the most complex components in modern programming language design, involving many interleaving of issues. The design of a transformation language needs to carefully check each intersection of the issues, which is not an easy job. Second, type safety involves two aspects: correctness and completeness. Correctness means that every transformed piece in the program is well-typed, while completeness means that all unchanged pieces are still well-typed under the new API. It is easy to ignore one aspect in transformation language design. As a matter of fact, Twinning [1], a modern transformation language for Java programs, have introduced strict rules for checking types in the transformation program to prevent the introduction of type errors. However, as our motivation section will show later, these rules still fail to establish full type safety.

In this paper we report our first attempt to design a type-safe transformation language for Java. As the first attempt, we focus on the class of one-to-many mappings between APIs. One-to-many mappings mean one method invocation in the source API will be replaced as one or multiple method invocations in the target API with possible gluing code. We choose this class for two reasons. 1) One-to-many mappings are dominant in the migration between alternative APIs. An empirical study [22] shows that 95.3% of the required changes are one-to-many mapping in the API update of struts, log4j, and jDOM. 2) Studying one-to-many mappings is a necessary step toward more general many-to-many mappings. Since one-to-many mappings are a sub class of many-to-many mappings, type safety in many-to-many mappings requires type safety in one-to-many mappings. As a matter of fact, the language Twinning is designed for one-to-many mappings, and is known for its simplicity and usefulness in many adaptation applications. Our approach is built upon Twinning, where we add extra conditions to ensure type safety.

More concretely, our contributions are summarized as follows.

- We propose a new transformation language, SWIN (Safe tWINning), for Java program adaptation between alternative APIs. The SWIN language is based on Twinning [1], a modern program adaptation language for Java. Compared with Twinning, SWIN includes a set of type checking rules to ensure type safety. These type checking rules enable a cross-checking over the source API, the target API, and the transformation program, and ensure that any well-typed Java program using the source API will be transformed into a well-typed Java program only using the target API, if the transformation program is well-typed under the type checking rules. SWIN also has more flexible replacement rules than Twinning.
- We formalize a core part of SWIN, known as core SWIN. Core SWIN works on Featherweight Java (FJ) [7], a formal model of the core Java language often used to reason typing-related properties of Java. We formally prove the type safety of core SWIN on FJ. We also informally describe the rest of SWIN and discuss the type safety of full SWIN.
- We have implemented SWIN[1] and evaluated SWIN by implementing three real world transformation programs in SWIN. These programs range from web APIs [19] to local APIs, including both API updating and API switching. Our case study shows that SWIN is able to specify a range of useful program transformations in practice. More importantly, compared with Twinning, the additional type checking rules in SWIN does not confine the expressiveness of the language.

The rest of our paper is structured as follows. Section 2 motivates our approach. Section 3 presents core SWIN. Section 4 gives the type system for core SWIN. Section 5 explains how to extend core SWIN to full SWIN. Section 6 evaluates SWIN with three cases. Finally, Section 7 discusses related work and Section 8 concludes the paper.

2. Motivating Examples

Before explaining SWIN, we briefly explain the type safety problem in the existing systems. We shall first briefly describe Twinning [1], a typical API adaptation language. Then, we will give some examples to show why Twinning cannot preserve the type correctness in program transformation. Finally, we will informally present an overview of our work.

Twinning is a rule-based language for adapting programs between alternative APIs. The design goal of Twinning is to be easy to use while allowing a reasonable set of adaptation tasks to be specified. A Twinning program basically consists of a set of replacement rules in the form of

$$
\begin{array}{l}
[\\
\quad \mathtt{T_{10}}(\mathtt{T_{11}}\ \mathtt{x_1}, \ldots, \mathtt{T_{1n}}\ \mathtt{x_n})\ \{\ \mathbf{return}\ \text{javaExp}_1;\ \}\\
\quad \mathtt{T_{20}}(\mathtt{T_{21}}\ \mathtt{y_1}, \ldots, \mathtt{T_{2n}}\ \mathtt{y_n})\ \{\ \mathbf{return}\ \text{javaExp}_2;\ \}\\
]
\end{array}
$$

which means (1) $\mathtt{T_{1i}}$ will be replaced by $\mathtt{T_{2i}}$ for all $\mathtt{i}$ (the set of pairs $[\mathtt{T_{1i}}, \mathtt{T_{2i}}]$ from all replacement rules are called a *type mapping*); (2) $\mathtt{x_i}$ is a meta variable that will match a Java expression of type $\mathtt{T_{1i}}$ in the source code and instantiates $\mathtt{y_i}$ with that expression; (3) javaExp_1, which is a Java expression of type $\mathtt{T_{10}}$ that uses meta variables $\mathtt{x_1} \ldots \mathtt{x_n}$, will be used to match Java expressions, and these expressions will be replaced by javaExp_2 of type $\mathtt{T_{20}}$, where the meta variables $\mathtt{y_i}$ are instantiated with the matched expressions by $\mathtt{x_1} \ldots \mathtt{x_n}$ [2].

As a simple example, consider the following replacement rule

```
[
 Enumeration(Hashtable x)
  {return x.elements();}
 Iterator(HashMap x)
  {return x.values().iterator();}
]
```

which will match any call to `elements` in class `Hashtable`, and replace it by a call to `values().iterator()` in class `HashMap`. For instance, given the following piece of code,

```
void f(Hashtable t) {
  Enumeration e = t.elements():
  ...
}
```

the replacement rule will produce the following piece of code, where the meta variable `x` in the replacement rule matches the expression `t`.

```
void f(HashMap t) {
  Iterator e = t.values().iterator():
  ...
}
```

[1] https://github.com/Mestway/SWIN-Project

[2] Strictly speaking, Twinning also allows replacing a block of statements rather than a single expression. For the ease of presentation, we shall only consider expression replacement in this paper. All discussions apply to statements replacement as well.

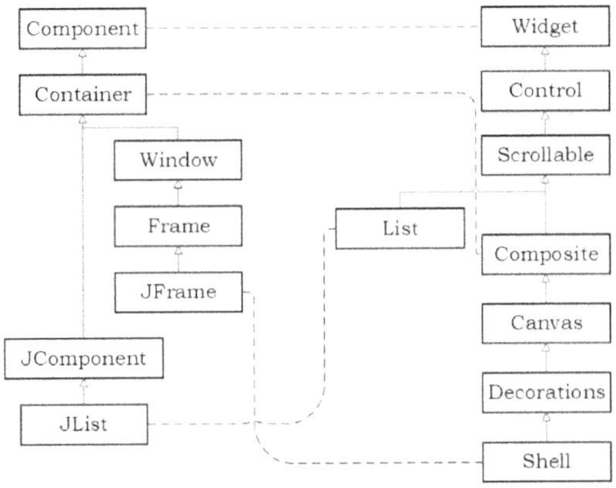

Figure 1. Swing (left) and SWT (right) type mapping: boxes represent classes, arrows indicate the class hierarchy, and dotted lines indicate the type mapping relations.

Twinning mainly checks two conditions to avoid introducing new type errors in the code. First, Twinning requires each replacement must be well-typed under the typing rules of Java. In this way, we can ensure the replacement of expressions does not introduce new type errors. Second, Twinning requires that one type is only mapped to one type in the type mapping (i.e., one type cannot be mapped to different types by replacement rules). This condition ensures that the replacement of types can be correctly performed.

Unfortunately, these two conditions cannot fully ensure type safety. First, type errors may be introduced when subtyping relations are involved. To see this, consider a practical example to adapt programs from Java Swing API to SWT API [2], where the correspondences between types of the two APIs are summarized in Figure 1, and the following presents part of the rules for replacing type constructors to their counterparts.

```
[
 Container () {return new Container();}
 Composite ()
  {return new Composite(new Shell(), 0);}
]

[ JList () { return new JList(); }
  List  () { return new List(); } ]
```

The typing problem happens if we apply the above rules to the following piece of code:

```
Container x = new JList();
```

Clearly, it will yield the code

```
Composite x = new List();
```

which actually contains a type error: JList is a subtype of Container, but List is not a subtype of Composite, so we cannot assign a `List` object to a `Composite` variable. This example shows that, although the two conditions used in Twinning ensure the replacement of expressions and the replacement of types are correct by themselves, the *intersection* of the two replacements would introduce type errors.

Second, Twinning has no guarantee the replacement rules cover all necessary changes. When there are components appearing only in the old API but are not transformed by any transformation rule, type errors may be introduced. For instance, consider the upgrade of Java SDK from v1.0 to v1.2: class `Hashtable` (Figure 2) is replaced by `HashMap` (Figure 3). For this change, we write a set of replacement rules (Figure 4). To be sure that any program using `Hashtable` can be transformed in a type-safe way, we must guarantee that all methods and classes in `Hashtable` have their replacements. However, the method `contains` in class `Hashtable` has no such replacements in the above set of rules.

```
class Hashtable {
    Enumeration elements() { }
    boolean contains(Object v) { }
    ...
}
class Enumeration {
    ...
}
```

Figure 2. Hashtable API

```
class HashMap {
    Collection values() { }
    boolean containsValue(Object v) { }
    ...
}
class Collection {
    Iterator iterator() { }
    ...
}
class Iterator {
    ...
}
```

Figure 3. HashMap API

```
[ Hashtable () { return new Hashtable();}
  HashMap () { return new HashMap(); } ]

[ Enumeration (Hashtable x)
    { return x.elements(); }
  Iterator (HashMap x)
    { return x.values().iterator(); } ]
```

Figure 4. Replacement Rules From Hashtable to HashMap

In summary, the conditions of Twinning are not enough to ensure type-safety of the transformation program. We need additional conditions to prevent the above two problems. For the first case, we need to ensure that the type mapping does not break the subtyping relations. For the second case, we need to ensure the replacements cover the full API changes. Putting them together with the original two conditions from Twinning, we have the following four conditions.

- For each code snippet introduced in a replacement rule, the code snippet itself must be well-typed.
- The type mapping must form a function, i.e., no type in the source API is mapped to two or more types in the target API.
- The type mapping must preserve the subtyping relation. If X is a subtype of Y in the source API and m is the mapping, $m(X)$ must be a subtype of $m(Y)$ in the target API.
- The replacement rules must cover all type changes between the source API and target API.

It will be interesting to see later that these four conditions are sufficient to ensure type safety. However, as Twinning is presented informally in the original publication [1], to reason about type safety, we need to first build a formal model of the Twinning semantics. A particular challenge of presenting this formal model is to understand how the replacement rules can be sequentially applied. For example, to transform the following piece of code

```
new Hashtable().elements()
```

into

```
new HashMap().values().iterator()
```

we need to begin with the second rule in Figure 4 to replace "`elements()`" and then apply the first rule to replace "`new Hashtable()`". If we begin with the first rule, we shall get an expression

```
new HashMap().elements()
```

where the second rule cannot be applied because "`new HashMap()`" has a type `HashMap` that cannot be matched by the meta variable `x` of type `Hashtable`. In other words, the transformation is not *confluent* since applying the rules in different orders gives us different results.

A related issue is that some sequences of rule applications may be infinite. For example, let us consider the following rule.

```
[A (A x) {return x.a();}
 A (A x) {return x.a().a();}]
```

Since the target side of the right also contains the call to `a()`, the rule can be applied again after the transformation, forming a *non-terminating* transformation. A terminating and confluent transformation is called a *convergent* transformation. A well-formed transformation language should always produce convergent transformations. However, the publication on Twinning [1] provides no information how Twinning deals with these issues.

Another usability issue of Twinning is that Twinning allows only exact type matching, i.e., a meta variable of type T matches a Java expression only when the expression has exactly type T but not a subtype of T. This design eases the analysis as we can infer all type changes from the type mapping, but also makes transformation more difficult to write. For example, in Java v1.0 class `Properties` is a sub class of `Hashtable`, and thus any call to `Properties.elements()` should be transformed in the same way as `Hashtable.elements()`. However, the second rule in Figure 4 does not apply to calls to `Properties.elements()` because the meta variable `x` has type `Hashtable`. As a result, for any replacement rule for a class `C`, we need to repeat the rule for each sub class of `C`, which is quite tedious.

To overcome this problem, we design a new language, SWIN (Safe tWINning). SWIN is based on Twinning but with the following differences.

- SWIN has full formal semantics.
- SWIN has more flexible rule application behavior, allowing a meta variable to match an expression of its sub type.
- SWIN is convergent. A well-typed SWIN program can act on any Java program confluently and free from non-terminating problems.
- SWIN includes a set of type checking rules to check the four conditions presented above.

In the following sections we shall introduce SWIN formally and present our proof of type safety.

3. Syntax and Semantics of Core SWIN

Before explaining full SWIN for Java, which will be discussed in Section 5, we start with core SWIN for Featherweight Java [7], a known minimal core of Java. If no confusion will be caused, we shall directly use SWIN to refer core SWIN. We shall briefly review Featherweight Java, and explain the syntax and semantics of our transformation language SWIN for it.

3.1 Background: Featherweight Java

Featherweight Java (FJ for short) is a minimal core calculus for Java [7]. FJ is small enough that a concise proof of the type-safety property is possible while it can be easily extended to full Java.

Class Declaration

$$\mathtt{CL} ::= \mathtt{class\ C\ extends\ C}\{\bar{\mathtt{C}}\ \bar{\mathtt{f}}; \mathtt{K}\ \bar{\mathtt{M}}\}$$

Constructor Declaration

$$\mathtt{K} ::= \mathtt{C}\ (\bar{\mathtt{C}}\ \bar{\mathtt{f}})\ \{\mathtt{super}(\bar{\mathtt{f}}); \mathtt{this}.\bar{\mathtt{f}} = \bar{\mathtt{f}}\}$$

Method Declaration

$$\mathtt{M} ::= \mathtt{C\ m}(\bar{\mathtt{C}}\ \bar{\mathtt{x}})\ \{\mathtt{return\ t};\}$$

Term

$$\mathtt{t} ::= \mathtt{x} \mid \mathtt{t.f} \mid \mathtt{t.m}(\bar{\mathtt{t}}) \mid \mathtt{new\ C}(\bar{\mathtt{t}}) \mid (\mathtt{C})\ \mathtt{t}$$

Figure 5. Syntax of Featherweight Java

Figure 5 shows the syntax of FJ. The class declaration

$$\mathtt{class\ C\ extends\ D}\ \{\bar{\mathtt{C}}\ \bar{\mathtt{f}};\ \mathtt{K}\ \bar{\mathtt{M}}\}$$

introduces a class named `C` with superclass `D`. The class has fields $\bar{\mathtt{f}}$ with types $\bar{\mathtt{C}}$, a single constructor `K`, and a suite of methods $\bar{\mathtt{M}}$.

In the formal notations, we use the bar notation adopted by Pierce [29] for repetitive elements: $\bar{a}$ to indicate a vector a, and all operations defined on single values expand componentwisely to vectors. For example, let x_i be the ith element in $\bar{x}$, we have $\bar{a} < \bar{b}$ is equal to $\forall i.\ a_i < b_i$ and $\bar{a} \in S$ is equal to $\forall i.\ a_i \in S$. Here, we write $\bar{\mathtt{C}}\ \bar{\mathtt{f}}$, for $\mathtt{C}_1\ \mathtt{f}_1, \cdots, \mathtt{C}_n\ \mathtt{f}_n$, where `n` is the length of $\bar{\mathtt{C}}$ and $\bar{\mathtt{f}}$. Similarly, $\bar{\mathtt{M}}$ denotes $\mathtt{M}_1 \cdots \mathtt{M}_n$.

The constructor declaration

$$\mathtt{C}\ (\bar{\mathtt{C}}\ \bar{\mathtt{f}})\{\mathtt{super}(\bar{\mathtt{f}});\ \mathtt{this}.\bar{\mathtt{f}} = \bar{\mathtt{f}};\}$$

defines the way to initialize a Java object, including a call to superclass constructor and assignments to class fields.

The method declaration

$$\mathtt{C\ m}(\bar{\mathtt{C}}\ \bar{\mathtt{x}})\{\ \mathtt{return\ t};\ \}$$

introduces a method named `m` with return type `C` and parameters $\bar{\mathtt{x}}$ of types $\bar{\mathtt{C}}$. The body of the method is just a single term `return t`.

There are only five terms in FJ, variable `x`, field access `t.f`, method invocation $\mathtt{t.m}(\bar{\mathtt{t}})$, object creation $\mathtt{new\ C}(\bar{\mathtt{e}})$, and cast operation `(C)e`. The key simplification in FJ is the omission of assignment. This implies that an object's field is initialized by its constructor and never changed afterwards. This restricts FJ to a "functional" fragment of Java.

The typing rules of FJ are the same as plain Java. One exception is that FJ does not support method overloading. We refer the reader to the original paper [7] and Appendix A for the typing rules.

3.2 Core SWIN

In this subsection we describe the syntax and evaluation rules of SWIN formally. The type checking rules and the proof of the type-safety property will be presented in Section 4 later.

3.2.1 Syntax

The formal definition of SWIN is presented in Figure 6. Similar to Twinning, a SWIN program Π is a set of transformation rules, and each transformation rule ($\pi = (\bar{\mathtt{d}})\ [\mathtt{l} : \mathtt{C}_\mathtt{l} \rightarrow \mathtt{r} : \mathtt{C}_\mathtt{r}]$) consists of three parts: 1) meta variable declarations ($\bar{\mathtt{d}}$), 2) left hand side source code pattern `l` and 3) right hand side target code pattern `r`. The source code pattern `l` will be used to match an expression in an old client program, and the target code pattern `r` is an FJ term

Π	::=	$\{\overline{\pi}\}$	Transformation program
π	::=	$(\overline{\mathtt{d}})\,[\mathtt{l} \rightarrow \mathtt{r}]$	Transformation rule
d	::=	$\mathtt{x} : \mathtt{C}_1 \hookrightarrow \mathtt{C}_2$	Variable declaration
l	::=	$\mathtt{x.f} \mid \mathtt{new\ C}(\overline{\mathtt{x}}) \mid \mathtt{x.m}(\overline{\mathtt{x}})$	Code pattern
r	::=	t	FJ term

Figure 6. Syntax of SWIN

using a new API with meta-variables bounded in d, which is used to generate updated client code. And the variable declaration part ($\mathtt{d} = \mathtt{x} : \mathtt{A} \hookrightarrow \mathtt{B}$) associates a metavariable with its type migration information: x is of type A in l and of type B in r.

An informal explanation of the rule can be seen from its correspondence with the replacement rule in Section 2. For example, the mapping rule

$$\pi = (\mathtt{x} : \mathtt{A} \hookrightarrow \mathtt{L}, \mathtt{y} : \mathtt{B} \hookrightarrow \mathtt{M})\,[\,\mathtt{x.m(y)} : \mathtt{C} \rightarrow \mathtt{x.h(y)} : \mathtt{D}\,]$$

can be seen as the following replacement rule:

```
[
 C (A x, B y) { return x.m(y); }
 D (L x, M y) { return x.h(y); }
]
```

Now if there is a client source code term (new A()).m(new B()), the rule will match the term as x binds to new A(), y binds to new B(), and the method name m matches the method name in the term. It results in that the updated term (new A()).h(new B()) is of type D. Note that this rule does not match the term (new C()).m(new B()), as the type of the variable x (type A) does not match the type of the term new C() (type C).

To ensure convergence, we do not allow the left hand sides of two rules to be the same. If two rules have the same left hand side, they will always match the same term, resulting in possibly divergent results.

3.2.2 Semantics: Evaluation Rules

We assume that an FJ program, which is a set of class declarations, can be divided into two parts: $\{\overline{\mathtt{CL}_{\mathtt{API}}}\}$ and $\{\overline{\mathtt{CL}_{\mathtt{client}}}\}$, where $\{\overline{\mathtt{CL}_{\mathtt{API}}}\}$ is the source API, consisting of class definitions that are type-correct by themselves; $\{\overline{\mathtt{CL}_{\mathtt{client}}}\}$ is the client program to be transformed, consisting of class definitions that depends on $\{\overline{\mathtt{CL}_{\mathtt{API}}}\}$. A transformation on an FJ program is to apply the transformation rules on $\{\overline{\mathtt{CL}_{\mathtt{client}}}\}$ to get $\{\overline{\mathtt{CL}'_{\mathtt{client}}}\}$, and then replace $\{\overline{\mathtt{CL}_{\mathtt{API}}}\}$ with the target API $\{\overline{\mathtt{CL}'_{\mathtt{API}}}\}$, such that $\{\overline{\mathtt{CL}'_{\mathtt{API}}}\}$ and $\{\overline{\mathtt{CL}'_{\mathtt{client}}}\}$ form a type-correct program.

In formal notations, we use API to denote $\{\ \overline{\mathtt{CL}_{\mathtt{API}}}\ \}$, and operations on APIs are naturally set operations (e.g. $\mathtt{API}_1 - \mathtt{API}_2$ is set substraction, which excludes class declarations in $\mathtt{API}_2$ from $\mathtt{API}_1$). In particular, we use the notation $\mathtt{API}_\mathtt{s}$ to denote the source API, $\overline{\mathtt{CL}_{\mathtt{API}}}$, and $\mathtt{API}_\mathtt{d}$ to denote the target API, $\overline{\mathtt{CL}'_{\mathtt{API}}}$, respectively.

Figure 7 summarizes the formal semantics of SWIN. In the rules, A <: B indicates that A is a subtype of B. A transformation program Π is formalized as a transformation from source code to target code on both types and terms. This transformation consists of the following three steps.

1. *Transformation Promotion*: The first three rules (E-DECLARATION, E-CONSTRUCTOR, E-METHOD) are used to promote Π up to types and terms through a class declaration, a construction definition, and a method definition, respectively.
2. *Type Transformation*: The next E-CLASS rule is used to transform source types in the source API to target types in target API based on the type mappings defined in Π. Those types which are not involved in the type mapping of Π will stay the same according to the rule E-ALTER-CLASS. An important components of the two rules is **TypeMapping**, which records how types in $\mathtt{API}_\mathtt{s}$ is mapped to $\mathtt{API}_\mathtt{d}$ by the transformation program, and it is defined in Figure 8.
3. *Term Transformation*: The rest of the rules are used to transform source code terms. As the syntactic definitions in Figure 6 show, an FJ term takes five forms. The form x and (C)t are evaluated by E-T-VAR and E-T-CAST, respectively, which basically further applies Π to sub terms. The other three forms are handled by E-T-FIELD, E-T-NEW, E-T-INVOKE, respectively. The three evaluation rules apply matched SWIN transformation rules to the current term. A term is matched by a rule when the signature of the rule matches the term and there is no rule that more "closely" matches the term. A rule r more closely matches a term than another rule r' when any of the meta variable in r has closer type to the matched term than r'. To deal with client defined classes, evaluation rules E-ALTER-FIELD, E-ALTER-INVOKE, E-ALTER-NEW are designed and they will apply Π to sub terms. In the definitions, we use **Type**(t) to get the type of a term t based on FJ typing rules.

To be concrete, let us see an example. Suppose that we want to switch from the old API ($\mathtt{API}_\mathtt{s}$) to a new one ($\mathtt{API}_\mathtt{d}$)[3]

$$\mathtt{API}_\mathtt{s} = \{\mathtt{class\ A}\ \{\ \mathtt{A}()\{...\};\ \mathtt{A\ h(A\ a)}\{...\};\ \};\}$$
$$\mathtt{API}_\mathtt{d} = \{\mathtt{class\ B}\ \{\ \mathtt{B}()\{...\};\ \mathtt{B\ k(B\ b, B\ c)}\{...\};\ \};\}$$

and we use the following SWIN transformation program

$$\begin{aligned}
&\Pi = [\pi_1, \pi_2] \\
&\textbf{where} \\
&\quad \pi_1 = ()\,[\,\mathtt{new\ A}() : \mathtt{A} \rightarrow \mathtt{new\ B}() : \mathtt{B}\,] \\
&\quad \pi_2 = (\mathtt{x} : \mathtt{A} \hookrightarrow \mathtt{B}, \mathtt{u} : \mathtt{A} \hookrightarrow \mathtt{B}) \\
&\qquad\quad [\,\mathtt{x.h(u)} : \mathtt{A} \rightarrow \mathtt{x.k(u, new\ B())} : \mathtt{B}\,]
\end{aligned}$$

to transform the following source client Java code.

$$(\mathtt{new\ A}()).\mathtt{h}(\mathtt{new\ A}())$$

The transformation is done as follows:

$$\begin{aligned}
& \Pi((\mathtt{new\ A}()).\mathtt{h}(\mathtt{new\ A}()) \\
= &\quad \{\ \text{by E-T-INVOKE with rule } \pi_2\ \} \\
& [\mathtt{x} \rightarrow \Pi(\mathtt{new\ A}()), \mathtt{u} \rightarrow \Pi(\mathtt{new\ A}())](\mathtt{x.k}(\mathtt{u}, \mathtt{new\ B}())) \\
= &\quad \{\ \text{replace x and u in } \mathtt{x.k(u, new\ B())}\ \} \\
& \Pi(\mathtt{new\ A}()).\mathtt{k}(\Pi(\mathtt{new\ A}()), \mathtt{new\ B}()) \\
= &\quad \{\ \text{by E-T-NEW with rule } \pi_1\ \} \\
& [\,](\mathtt{new\ B}()).\mathtt{k}([\,](\mathtt{new\ B}()), \mathtt{new\ B}()) \\
= &\quad \{\ \text{since } [\,](\mathtt{new\ B}()) = \mathtt{new\ B}()\ \} \\
& \mathtt{new\ B}().\mathtt{k}(\mathtt{new\ B}(), \mathtt{new\ B}())
\end{aligned}$$

Thus it results in the target code new B().k(new B(), new B()).

4. Type Checking System for Core SWIN

Now we turn to our type system that is used to check the type safety of transformation programs in SWIN. Given two APIs ($\mathtt{API}_\mathtt{s}$ and $\mathtt{API}_\mathtt{d}$), and a transformation program (Π), mapping from $\mathtt{API}_\mathtt{s}$ to $\mathtt{API}_\mathtt{d}$, if Π passes our type checking, we can guarantee that Π will transform *any* FJ program using $\mathtt{API}_\mathtt{s}$ to a well-typed FJ program using $\mathtt{API}_\mathtt{d}$ instead.

[3] We omit the API method bodies here as it is not necessary to see the details of how an API method is implemented; it is sufficient to show the input types and the return type of each method in API. And this kind of omission is also used in later sections.

$$\frac{\mathtt{CL} = \mathtt{class}\ \mathtt{C}_1\ \mathtt{extends}\ \mathtt{C}_2\ \{\ \bar{\mathtt{C}}\ \bar{\mathtt{f}};\ \mathtt{K}\ \bar{\mathtt{M}}\ \}}{\Pi(\mathtt{CL}) = \mathtt{class}\ \Pi(\mathtt{C}_1)\ \mathtt{extends}\ \Pi(\mathtt{C}_2)\ \{\ \Pi(\bar{\mathtt{C}})\ \bar{\mathtt{f}};\ \Pi(\mathtt{K})\ \overline{\Pi(\mathtt{M})}\ \}}\ \text{(E-DECLARATION)}$$

$$\frac{\mathtt{K} = \mathtt{C}_1\ (\bar{\mathtt{C}}_2\ \bar{\mathtt{f}}_2)\ \{\mathtt{super}(\bar{\mathtt{f}}_3);\ \mathtt{this}.\bar{\mathtt{f}}_i = \bar{\mathtt{f}}_j\}}{\Pi(\mathtt{K}) = \Pi(\mathtt{C}_1)\ (\Pi(\bar{\mathtt{C}}_2)\ \bar{\mathtt{f}}_2)\ \{\mathtt{super}(\bar{\mathtt{f}}_3);\ \mathtt{this}.\bar{\mathtt{f}}_i = \bar{\mathtt{f}}_j\}}\ \text{(E-CONSTRUCTOR)}$$

$$\frac{\mathtt{M} = \mathtt{C}_1\ \mathtt{m}(\bar{\mathtt{C}}\ \bar{\mathtt{x}})\ \{\mathtt{return}\ \mathtt{t};\}}{\Pi(\mathtt{M}) = \Pi(\mathtt{C}_1)\ \mathtt{m}(\Pi(\bar{\mathtt{C}})\ \bar{\mathtt{x}})\ \{\mathtt{return}\ \Pi(\mathtt{t});\}}\ \text{(E-METHOD)} \qquad \frac{\mathtt{C}_0 \hookrightarrow \mathtt{C}_1 \in \mathbf{TypeMapping}(\Pi)}{\Pi(\mathtt{C}_0) = \mathtt{C}_1}\ \text{(E-CLASS)}$$

$$\frac{\forall \mathtt{C}.\ \mathtt{C}_0 \hookrightarrow \mathtt{C} \notin \mathbf{TypeMapping}(\Pi)}{\Pi(\mathtt{C}_0) = \mathtt{C}_0}\ \text{(E-ALTER-CLASS)} \qquad \frac{}{\Pi(\mathtt{x}) = \mathtt{x}}\ \text{(E-T-VAR)}$$

$$\frac{\begin{array}{c}(\mathtt{x} : \mathtt{C}_1 \hookrightarrow \mathtt{C}_2)[\ \mathtt{x.f} : \mathtt{C}\ \rightarrow\ \mathtt{r} : \mathtt{D}\ ] \in \Pi \quad \mathbf{Type}(\mathtt{t}) <: \mathtt{C}_1 \\ \neg\exists\ (\mathtt{x} : \mathtt{C}_3 \hookrightarrow \mathtt{C}_4)[\ \mathtt{x.f} : \mathtt{C}\ \rightarrow\ \mathtt{r} : \mathtt{D}\ ] \in \Pi.(\mathbf{Type}(\mathtt{t}) <: \mathtt{C}_3 <: \mathtt{C}_1 \wedge \mathtt{C}_3 \neq \mathtt{C}_1)\end{array}}{\Pi(\mathtt{t.f}) = [\ \mathtt{x} \mapsto \Pi(\mathtt{t})\ ]\mathtt{r}}\ \text{(E-T-FIELD)}$$

$$\frac{}{\Pi((\mathtt{C})\ \mathtt{t}) = (\Pi(\mathtt{C}))\ \Pi(\mathtt{t})}\ \text{(E-T-CAST)} \qquad \frac{\begin{array}{c}(\bar{\mathtt{d}})[\ \mathtt{new}\ \mathtt{C}_0(\ \bar{\mathtt{x}}\ ) : \mathtt{C}\ \rightarrow\ \mathtt{r} : \mathtt{D}] \in \Pi \\ \{\ \bar{\mathtt{x}} : \overline{\mathtt{C}_1 \hookrightarrow \mathtt{C}_2}\ \} \subseteq \bar{\mathtt{d}} \qquad \mathbf{Type}(\bar{\mathtt{t}}_u) <: \bar{\mathtt{C}}_1\end{array}}{\Pi(\mathtt{new}\ \mathtt{C}_0(\bar{\mathtt{t}}_u)) = [\ \bar{\mathtt{x}} \mapsto \overline{\Pi(\mathtt{t}_u)}\ ](\mathtt{r})}\ \text{(E-T-NEW)}$$

$$\frac{\begin{array}{c}(\bar{\mathtt{y}} : \overline{\mathtt{C}_1 \hookrightarrow \mathtt{C}_2},\ \mathtt{x}_0 : \mathtt{C}_3 \hookrightarrow \mathtt{C}_4)[\ \mathtt{x}_0.\mathtt{m}_0(\ \bar{\mathtt{y}}\ ) : \mathtt{C}\ \rightarrow\ \mathtt{r} : \mathtt{D}] \in \Pi \\ \mathbf{Type}(\mathtt{t}_0) <: \mathtt{C}_3 \qquad \mathbf{Type}(\bar{\mathtt{t}}_u) <: \bar{\mathtt{C}}_1 \\ \neg\exists\ (\bar{\mathtt{y}} : \overline{\mathtt{C}_1 \hookrightarrow \mathtt{C}_2},\ \mathtt{x}_0 : \mathtt{C}_5 \hookrightarrow \mathtt{C}_6)[\ \mathtt{x}_0.\mathtt{m}_0(\ \bar{\mathtt{y}}\ ) : \mathtt{C}\ \rightarrow\ \mathtt{r} : \mathtt{D}] \in \Pi.(\mathbf{Type}(\mathtt{t}_0) <: \mathtt{C}_5 <: \mathtt{C}_3 \wedge \mathtt{C}_5 \neq \mathtt{C}_3)\end{array}}{\Pi(\mathtt{t}_0.\mathtt{m}_0(\bar{\mathtt{t}}_u)) = [\ \mathtt{x}_0 \mapsto \Pi(\mathtt{t}_0),\ \bar{\mathtt{y}} \mapsto \overline{\Pi(\mathtt{t}_u)}\ ](\mathtt{r})}\ \text{(E-T-INVOKE)}$$

$$\frac{\text{no other inference rule can be applied}}{\Pi(\mathtt{new}\ \mathtt{C}_0(\bar{\mathtt{t}}_u)) = \mathtt{new}\ \mathtt{C}_0(\ \overline{\Pi(\mathtt{t}_u)}\ )}\ \text{(E-ALTER-NEW)}$$

$$\frac{\text{no other inference rule can be applied}}{\Pi(\mathtt{t}_0.\mathtt{m}_0(\bar{\mathtt{t}}_u)) = \Pi(\mathtt{t}_0).\mathtt{m}(\ \overline{\Pi(\mathtt{t}_u)}\ )}\ \text{(E-ALTER-INVOKE)}$$

$$\frac{\text{no other inference rule can be applied}}{\Pi(\mathtt{t.f}) = \Pi(\mathtt{t}).\mathtt{f}}\ \text{(E-ALTER-FIELD)}$$

Figure 7. Evaluation Rules of SWIN

$$\mathbf{TypeMapping}((\ \bar{\mathtt{x}} : \overline{\mathtt{C}_1 \hookrightarrow \mathtt{C}_2}\ )[\mathtt{l} : \mathtt{C}\ \rightarrow\ \mathtt{r} : \mathtt{D}]) = \{\mathtt{C} \hookrightarrow \mathtt{D}\} \cup \{\ \overline{\mathtt{C}_1 \hookrightarrow \mathtt{C}_2}\ \}$$

$$\mathbf{TypeMapping}(\{\bar{\pi}\}) = \bigcup_{\pi} (\mathbf{TypeMapping}(\pi)) \qquad \text{(Extract type migration information)}$$

$$\mathbf{Decl}(\mathtt{class}\ \mathtt{C}\ \mathtt{extends}\ \mathtt{D}\ \{...\}) = \mathtt{C} \qquad \text{(Extract the declared class name)}$$

Figure 8. Auxiliary Functions used in Figure 7 and Figure 10

In the following sections, we will define our type-checking rules and prove the type-safety property of SWIN.

4.1 Type Checking Rules

We present the rules in Figure 9 and Figure 10. Figure 9 depicts the rule for checking a single transformation rule π. Figure 10 depicts the rules for checking a transformation program Π.

Checking Rule for π This rule checks whether the types declared in a transformation rule conforms to the actual types inferred using FJ typing rules. In the formal notation, we use $\Gamma \vdash_{\mathtt{FJ}}^{\mathtt{APIs}} \mathtt{t} : \mathtt{C}$ to denote that the term $\mathtt{t}$ has type $\mathtt{C}$ under context Γ by FJ typing rules when considered together with $\mathtt{API_s}$. When checking the left hand sides, we introduce modified type checking rules $*\mathtt{FJ}$, which is used to ensure the exact matching on the parameters, so that our rules are only declared on valid methods.

$$
\begin{aligned}
&\mathbf{RuleOK}(\Pi) = \forall\, \pi.(\pi \in \Pi \Rightarrow \pi\ ok)\\
&\mathbf{ConstrCover}(\Pi, \mathtt{API_s}, \mathtt{API_d}) =\\
&\quad \forall\, \mathtt{C_1}, \bar{\mathtt{C}}.(\mathtt{class}\ \mathtt{C_1}\ \mathtt{extends}\ \_\ \{\mathtt{C_1}(\bar{\mathtt{C}}\ \bar{\_})\ ...\ \} \in (\mathtt{API_s} - \mathtt{API_d})\\
&\qquad \Rightarrow\ \exists\, \mathtt{C_2}, \bar{\mathtt{C}}', \bar{\mathtt{x}}, \mathtt{r}.((\ \bar{\mathtt{x}} : \overline{\mathtt{C} \hookrightarrow \mathtt{C}'}\ )[\mathtt{new}\ \mathtt{C_1}(\bar{\mathtt{x}}) : \mathtt{C_1} \rightarrow \mathtt{r} : \mathtt{C_2}] \in \Pi))\\
&\mathbf{MethCover}(\Pi, \mathtt{API_s}, \mathtt{API_d}) =\\
&\quad \forall\, \mathtt{C_1}, \mathtt{C_2}, \mathtt{m}, \bar{\mathtt{C}}.(\mathtt{class}\ \mathtt{C_1}\ \mathtt{extends}\ \_\ \{\ \mathtt{C_2}\ \mathtt{m}(\ \bar{\mathtt{C}}\ \bar{\_}\ )\{...\}\ ...\ \} \in (\mathtt{API_s} - \mathtt{API_d})\\
&\qquad \Rightarrow\ \exists\, \mathtt{x}, \bar{\mathtt{y}}, \mathtt{C}'_1, \mathtt{C}'_2, \bar{\mathtt{C}}', \mathtt{r}.((\mathtt{x} : \mathtt{C_1} \hookrightarrow \mathtt{C}'_1,\ \ \bar{\mathtt{y}} : \overline{\mathtt{C} \hookrightarrow \mathtt{C}'}\ )[\mathtt{x.m}(\bar{\mathtt{y}}) : \mathtt{C_2} \rightarrow \mathtt{r} : \mathtt{C}'_2] \in \Pi))\\
&\mathbf{FieldCover}(\Pi, \mathtt{API_s}, \mathtt{API_d}) =\\
&\quad \forall\, \mathtt{C_1}, \mathtt{C_2}, \mathtt{f}.(\mathtt{class}\ \mathtt{C_1}\ \mathtt{extends}\ \_\ \{\mathtt{C_2}\ \mathtt{f};...\} \in (\mathtt{API_s} - \mathtt{API_d})\\
&\qquad \Rightarrow\ \exists\, \mathtt{x}, \mathtt{C}'_1, \mathtt{C}'_2.((\mathtt{x} : \mathtt{C_1} \hookrightarrow \mathtt{C}'_1\ )[\mathtt{x.f} : \mathtt{C_2} \rightarrow \mathtt{r} : \mathtt{C}'_2] \in \Pi))\\
&\mathbf{MapChecking}(\Pi, \mathtt{API_s}, \mathtt{API_d}) =\\
&\quad \forall\, \mathtt{C}, \mathtt{D}.(\mathtt{C} \hookrightarrow \mathtt{D} \in \mathbf{TypeMapping}(\Pi)\\
&\qquad \Rightarrow\ (\exists\, \mathtt{CL} \in \mathtt{API_s} \cap \mathtt{API_d}.(\mathbf{Decl}(\mathtt{CL}) = \mathtt{C} \wedge \mathtt{D} = \mathtt{C}))\\
&\qquad\quad \vee(\exists\, \mathtt{CL} \in \mathtt{API_s} - \mathtt{API_d}.(\mathbf{Decl}(\mathtt{CL}) = \mathtt{C})))\\
&\mathbf{Subtyping}(\Pi, \mathtt{API_s}, \mathtt{API_d}) =\\
&\quad \forall\, \mathtt{C_i}, \mathtt{D_i}, \mathtt{C_j}, \mathtt{D_j}.(\mathtt{C_i} \hookrightarrow \mathtt{D_i}, \mathtt{C_j} \hookrightarrow \mathtt{D_j} \in \mathbf{TypeMapping}(\Pi)\ \ \Rightarrow\ \ (\mathtt{C_i} <: \mathtt{C_j} \Rightarrow \mathtt{D_i} <: \mathtt{D_j}))
\end{aligned}
$$

Figure 10. Checking rules (or checking funtions) for Π. A SWIN program Π with specified source API ($\mathtt{API_s}$) and destination API ($\mathtt{API_d}$) should pass these checking rules to maintain type safety. Underscore(_) is a wildcard and apostrophe (...) represents omitted declaration sequences (field declarations or method declarations). And a special use of the notations used in **ConstrCover** etc. is $\bar{\mathtt{C}}\ \bar{\_}$, which represents $\mathtt{C_1}\ \_, \mathtt{C_2}\ \_, ..., \mathtt{C_n}\ \_$, as their types are known while the variable names are not necessary.

$$
\frac{\{\ \bar{\mathtt{x}} : \bar{\mathtt{C}}\ \} \vdash^{\mathtt{API_s}}_{*\mathtt{FJ}} \mathtt{l} : \mathtt{C_1} \qquad \{\ \bar{\mathtt{x}} : \bar{\mathtt{D}}\ \} \vdash^{\mathtt{API_d}}_{\mathtt{FJ}} \mathtt{r} : \mathtt{C_2}}{(\bar{\mathtt{x}} : \overline{\mathtt{C} \hookrightarrow \mathtt{D}})[\mathtt{l} : \mathtt{C_1} \rightarrow \mathtt{r} : \mathtt{C_2}]\ ok} \quad (\text{T-}\pi)
$$

$$
\frac{\Gamma \vdash^{\mathtt{API}}_{\mathtt{FJ}} \mathtt{x} : \mathtt{C_0} \quad \mathtt{mtype}(\mathtt{m}, \mathtt{C_0}) = \bar{\mathtt{D}} \rightarrow \mathtt{C} \quad \Gamma \vdash^{\mathtt{API}}_{\mathtt{FJ}} \bar{\mathtt{y}} : \bar{\mathtt{D}}}{\Gamma \vdash^{\mathtt{API}}_{*\mathtt{FJ}} \mathtt{x.m}(\bar{\mathtt{y}}) : \mathtt{C}} \quad (\text{T-L1})
$$

$$
\frac{\mathtt{fields}(\mathtt{C}) = \bar{\mathtt{D}}\ \bar{\mathtt{f}} \quad \Gamma \vdash^{\mathtt{API}}_{\mathtt{FJ}} \bar{\mathtt{x}} : \bar{\mathtt{D}}}{\Gamma \vdash^{\mathtt{API}}_{*\mathtt{FJ}} \mathtt{new}\ \mathtt{C}(\bar{\mathtt{x}}) : \mathtt{C}} \quad (\text{T-L2})
$$

$$
\frac{\mathtt{fields}(\mathtt{C}) = \bar{\mathtt{D}}\ \bar{\mathtt{f}} \quad \Gamma \vdash^{\mathtt{API}}_{\mathtt{FJ}} \mathtt{x} : \mathtt{C}}{\Gamma \vdash^{\mathtt{API}}_{*\mathtt{FJ}} \mathtt{x.f_i} : \mathtt{D_i}} \quad (\text{T-L3})
$$

Figure 9. The checking rule for π

Please note that this rule also indicates that we can drop the type declarations in the transformation rules, i.e., instead of writing $[\ \mathtt{x.m(y)} : \mathtt{C} \rightarrow \mathtt{x.h(y)} : \mathtt{D}\ ]$, we can write $[\ \mathtt{x.m(y)} \rightarrow \mathtt{x.h(y)}\ ]$ and deduce C and D using FJ typing rules. However, we decide to keep these declarations in the code because with these declarations, **TypeMapping**(Π) becomes more explicit, avoiding subtle bugs on erroneous type mappings.

Checking Rules for Π The main goal of the type checking rules is to check the four conditions presented in Section 2. Next we explain how this is achieved.

1. All rules are well-typed themselves. (Rule **RuleOK**)
2. The class mapping in **TypeMapping**(Π) should be a function, i.e. one class in the old API should be mapped to only one class in new API. In fact, this property is covered by the subtyping relationship check, as type equality can be treated as a bi-directional subtyping relation. (Rule **Subtyping**)
3. The class transformation preserves the subtyping relationship in the old API. (Rule **Subtyping**)
4. The transformation program covers all classes/methods/constructors/fields that only exist in the old API but not the new API (Rules **ConstrCover**, **MethCover**, **FieldCover**), and no unnecessarily type conversion is introduced (Rule **MapChecking**). Note that the above three rules are declared on constructors, methods, and fields directly. The coverage of classes is implied by rule **ConstrCover** and the definition of **TypeMapping**.

We say a SWIN program is *well-typed* iff it satisfies the checking rules presented in Figure 10. As will be proved in Section 4.3, a well-typed transformation program Π is type-safe, guaranteeing the well-typedness of the target code when Π is applied to any client code with old API. Otherwise, there must exist some client code that cannot be transformed to a well-typed target code with this transformation program.

4.2 Convergence Theorem

Our checking rules and evaluation rules ensure the convergence of any SWIN program, which is discussed in the following theorem and its proof sketch.

Theorem 1. *Any SWIN program is convergent.*

Proof sketch. SWIN employs a normal order evaluation semantics. First, the evaluation rules visit a term leftmost and outermost. After performing the transformation on that term, the evaluation rules recursively visit the sub terms of the term, and for each visit, the transformation will be applied on the original sub terms, and produce the transformation result by combining the transformed sub terms. In this way we can ensure each recursive visit will be terminated as the length of the sub terms are always shorter than the term. Also, we can ensure the transformation on a term is confluent, as each program element is transformed by exactly one rule according to the restrictions on π (checking rules for π) and the definitions of the evaluation rules. □

4.3 Type-Safety Theorem

In this subsection, we reason type safety of SWIN formally and outline the key theorems and lemmas here.

Intuitively, SWIN is type-safe if and only if a well-typed SWIN program can transform *any* well-typed FJ program to a well-typed FJ program. The proof needs to bridge the type inference tree on an old API to the new type inference tree on a new API, and we need to generate a derivation tree based on conditions in checking rules and the derivation tree on original client code.

Because of the space limit, we cannot present the full proofs here. Instead, we present four key lemmas that can stepwise lead to the final theorem. The full proofs of lemmas and the theorem can be found in the technical report on the formal definition of SWIN [23].

In our lemmas, $\Gamma = \bar{\mathtt{x}} : \bar{\mathtt{C}}$ represents the typing context of an FJ term t, which designates each variable x in the term with a type C. Specially, given a term t in client code and a transformation program Π, Γ_s represents the variable environment for t (before transformation) and Γ_d represents the environment of the transformed term $\Pi(\mathtt{t})$. The proof also depends on the typing rules of FJ, which is presented in Appendix A.

Lemma 1 (Typing Context). *Suppose the typing context for a term* t *is* $\Gamma_s = \bar{\mathtt{x}} : \bar{\mathtt{C}}$. *Given a SWIN program* Π *acting on* $\mathtt{API_s}$ *to* $\mathtt{API_d}$, *we know that the typing context for* $\Pi(\mathtt{t})$ *is* $\Gamma_d = \bar{\mathtt{x}} : \overline{\Pi(\mathtt{C})}$.

Proof sketch. Note that an FJ typing context Γ will be created in the rule FJ-M-OK and will not change during the type deriving of a term. According to the rule E-DELCARATION and E-METHOD, the types of the method argument and the variable "this" (they are all of the variables binded in Γ) will both be updated to $\Pi(\mathtt{C})$. □

Lemma 2 (Subtyping). *Suppose a well-typed SWIN program* Π *transforms an FJ program* P *with* $\mathtt{API_s}$ *to a new program* P' *with* $\mathtt{API_d}$, *then the following holds.*

$\mathtt{C_1} <: \mathtt{C_2}$ *in* $P \implies \Pi(\mathtt{C_1}) <: \Pi(\mathtt{C_2})$ *in* P'.

Proof sketch. The subtype relation between classes have the following two cases:

- $\mathtt{C_1}$ is declared in client code: E-DECLARATION will guarantee that the subtype relation will be preserved in transformation.
- $\mathtt{C_1}$ is declared in API: the checking rule **Subtyping** guarantees it.

Combining these two cases and the transitivity of subtype relation, we know that the lemma holds. □

Lemma 3 (Variable Substitution). *Suppose that an FJ term* t *is well-typed under context* $\Gamma = \Gamma_1, \{\bar{\mathtt{x}} : \bar{\mathtt{C}}_x\}$, *i.e.* $\Gamma \vdash_{FJ} \mathtt{t} : \mathtt{C_t}$. *After substituting terms* $\bar{\mathtt{t}}_u$ *for variables* $\bar{\mathtt{x}}$, *with the property that* $\Gamma_1 \vdash_{FJ} \bar{\mathtt{t}}_u : \bar{\mathtt{C}}_u$ *and* $\bar{\mathtt{C}}_u <: \bar{\mathtt{C}}_x$, t *can be typed to* $\mathtt{C_t}$ *or a sub-class of* $\mathtt{C_t}$. *Namely,*

$$\Gamma_1, \{\bar{\mathtt{x}} : \bar{\mathtt{C}}_x\} \vdash_{FJ} \mathtt{t} : \mathtt{C_t} \Longrightarrow \Gamma_1 \vdash_{FJ} [\bar{\mathtt{x}} \mapsto \bar{\mathtt{t}}_u]\mathtt{t} : \mathtt{C}'_t,\ \mathtt{C}'_t <: \mathtt{C_t}$$

Proof sketch. By induction on the derivation of a term t, we have fives cases to discuss. (x, (C)t, t.f, new C($\bar{\mathtt{t}}$) and t.m($\bar{\mathtt{t}}$)). The first three cases (x,(C)t and t.f) are obvious according to their evaluation rules.

For case 4 and case 5, the following properties are used in proof:

- The arguments in the method invocation will be substitute by terms whose types are subtypes of the original argument variables (Arguments are compatible).
- The target term (the caller) is of a type that is subtype to the original caller variable (The method can be found in the new caller term).

With subtype relation cleared, the proof is also obvious according to the rule FJ-METHOD and FJ-CONSTRUCTOR. □

Lemma 4 (Term Formation). *Given a well-typed SWIN program* Π, *if a term* t *in the original typing context can be typed to* C, *then after transformation by* Π, *the term is well-typed and its type is a subtype of* $\Pi(\mathtt{C})$. *i.e.*

$$\Gamma_s \vdash_{FJ}^{\mathtt{API_s}} \mathtt{t} : \mathtt{C} \Longrightarrow \Gamma_d \vdash_{FJ}^{\mathtt{API_d}} \Pi(\mathtt{t}) : \mathtt{C}', \text{ where } \mathtt{C}' <: \Pi(\mathtt{C})$$

Proof sketch. Induction on the term derivation. Again we have five cases to prove. (x, (C)t, t.f, new C($\bar{\mathtt{t}}$) and t.m($\bar{\mathtt{t}}$))

The first two cases (x, (C)t) are obvious according to Lemma 1 and their evaluation rules (E-T-VAR, E-T-CAST). The last three cases are not trivial in proof, we simply mention some points for case 5 (method invocation) as an example, and the full proof can be found in the technical report [23].

For case $\mathtt{t} = \mathtt{t_0.m}(\bar{\mathtt{t}}_u)$, we have two subcases to deal with:

- The method is defined in a class which is defined in client code: to prove that arguments and the caller terms are well-formed terms whose types are subtypes of the original ones.
- The method is defined in a class defined in old API: to prove that the rule π to transform the term will finally leads to a well-typed term according to the Substitution Lemma and Subtyping Lemma.

And with these five cases proved, we have the property that a well-typed SWIN program can correctly transform FJ terms. □

Theorem 2 (Type-Safety). *Any FJ program is well-typed after a transformation by a well-typed SWIN program* Π. *i.e. For any* CL,

$$\Pi(\mathtt{CL}) = \mathtt{class}\ \Pi(\mathtt{C_1})\ \mathtt{extends}\ \Pi(\mathtt{C_2})\ \{\ \Pi(\bar{\mathtt{C}}_i)\ \bar{\mathtt{f}}_i;\ \Pi(\mathtt{K})\ \overline{\Pi(\mathtt{M})}\ \}$$

is well-typed with new API if Π *is well-typed.*

Proof sketch. We need to prove that method calls are well formed in the transformed FJ program and the class declarations are well formed.

This can be a direct result from: 1) all terms are well formed after transforamtion (Lemma 4), 2) arguments and super class declarations are well formed (this can be checked through E-METHOD-DECLARATION, E-CLASS-DECLARATION and **TypeMapping**). □

5. From Core SWIN to Full SWIN

In this section, we present the way to extend core SWIN on Featherweight Java to full SWIN on full Java language formally. Generally, the extension is based on the term extension and type extension. By extending source code pattern and target code pattern to a term in full Java and extending types to full Java in variable declaration part of update rules, we are able to match a Java term and then transform it to a term with new API by meta-variable substitution.

Extending SWIN to full SWIN, we need some special treatments of the following key points :

Package Full Java supports the `package` and `import` commands for name organization. Pacakges support modularity naturally and APIs in a full Java program should be stored in different packages. When we transform Java programs with packages, we simply need to transform the client codes and then replace the corresponding API packages without touching other API packages.

To ease the writing of transformation rules, we also support `import` command in SWIN, yet all internal processing is based on fully qualified names.

Field and Assignment FJ has no assignment statements and all fields are read-only. When assignments are introduced, expressions in Java can be distinguished into L-value and R-value. To ensure type safety, we need to ensure the transformation does not change an L-value into an R-value. The most common L-value is field access. For example, given "`a.x = b`", if a transformation rule transforms "`a.x`" into "`new A()`", the new code will fail to compile because "`new A()`" is not a L-value. This check can be implemented by applying the Java rules for distinguishing L-value and R-value on the source patterns and the destination patterns.

Static Method Access In full Java, a method can be defined as a static method, and we can access it by `C.m(a, b, ...)`. We treat the application of full SWIN on static method access as a normal method invokation, except that we need to apply the term directly on the class identifier. As the transformation of a class definition is by class name replacement, type safety can be guaranteed.

Interface In FJ, the subtyping relation is linear and full order. So during pattern matching, there is always a "closest" parent class for each class and this ensure that the term will always match that class to ensure confluent.

In full Java, there may exist multiple parent classes, which will then lead to no single "closest" parent class exists. For example, if class `A` has two super types, class `B` and interface `C`, and all three classes declare a method `m`. If there are two transformation rules declared on `B.m` and `C.m`, respectively, we cannot find a closest rule on `A.m`. In such case, we will report an error when executing the transformation, and the programmers could resolve the error by adding a rule on `A.m`, which is always closer than any other rules.

Overload When method overloading is considered, we need to match a method not only using its name, but also the type of its input parameters. Also, the subtyping relation should be considered in the same way as Java: when there are several overloaded methods that can be matched, we choose the one with the closest subtyping relation on the parameters. For example, if we have a relationship `A` <: `B` <: `C`, and in class `D`, we have methods `f(B x)` and `f(C x)`. Then `(new D()).f(new A())` is a call to the first method as they have a closer subtyping relationship. A pattern matching `f(C x)` should not match this term.

Generics Generics in full Java affects the evaluation rules E-CLASS and E-T-NEW. We have two extending rules to solve this problem.

1. During pattern matching, a rule matches a generic type without considering its type parameters.
2. After performing transformation on a generic type, the rules recursively visit the type parameters.

The type safety is guaranteed because we require the preservation of subtyping relation, and thus the constraints on generic parameters will not be broken. Note that our rules always treat the generic type and its parameters independently, and thus do not allow the change in the number of type parameters from the source API to the target API. This design choice keeps our language simple, but does not affect its expressiveness: we have never observe any change in the number of type parameters in Java in practice.

6. Case Studies

6.1 Research Questions

Since SWIN puts two more conditions on the replacement rules than Twinning, a natural question to ask is whether these two additional conditions confine the expressiveness of the language. In other words, there are programs that can be written in Twinning but not in SWIN, but are these programs useful in practice? Furthermore, beyond Twinning, we also want to understand the expressiveness of SWIN in general. These considerations lead to two research questions.

1. Does the extra conditions confine the expressiveness of SWIN compared with Twinning?
2. In general, how much expressive is SWIN?

6.2 Study Setup

To answer these two research questions, we perform three case studies. To answer the first research question, we need to compare SWIN with Twinning. To do this, we repeat a case study in Twinning that migrate programs from Crimson v1.1.3[4] to dom4j v1.6.1[5]. Crimson and dom4j are both Java libraries for manipulating XML files, but Crimson is no longer supported. Thus, developers may want to migrate programs from Crimson to dom4j.

To answer the second research question, we perform two more case studies, one is about migration from one API to another API, the other one is to upgrade clients for incompatible API upgrade. More concretely, we chose the program migration from Twitter4J v4.0.1[6] to Sina Weibo Java API v2[7], and the client upgrade from Google Calendar API[8] v2 to v3. Twitter4J is a Java wrapper for the RESTful Twitter API. Sina Weibo is the Chinese counterpart of Twitter, and it provides an official Java library for accessing its web API. Google Calendar API is the official Java library for accessing the data in Google Calendar.

The two case studies of program migration (from Crimson to dom4j, from Twitter4J to Sina Weibo API) both involve large APIs, and it is difficult for us to cover the full APIs. In the case study from Crimson to dom4j, the Twinning authors [1] chose a client (log4j v1.2.14[9]) and only wrote transformations for the part of the API covered by the client. We followed the same step as their case study. In the case study from Twitter4J to Sina Weibo API, we consider three example clients on manipulating the timeline provided in the example directory in the Twitter4J source package, and cover only the part of the API used in these examples.

To perform the case studies, we implemented SWIN in Java using the Polyglot compiler framework [25]. Both our implementation and all evaluation data are available at the project web site[10].

6.3 Results

6.3.1 General Expressiveness

In total, we wrote 94 rules for the three case studies, each transforming a method call to the old API into an expression using the new API. Our rules cover 97% of the total API methods that needed to be transformed in the three case studies. This results indicate that, though our approach deals only with one-to-many mappings, it is able to perform a significant portion of program adaptation tasks in practice.

6.3.2 Comparison with Twinning

The only uncovered API changes are three method changes in Google Calendar API, consisting of 3% of the total API methods that needs to be transformed. In the three uncovered method changes, one method splits into several methods, and we need to decide which new method to replace the original one based on the calling context, which is not supported in SWIN.

[4] `http://xml.apache.org/crimson/`

[5] `http://www.dom4j.org/`

[6] `https://github.com/yusuke/twitter4j/`

[7] `https://code.google.com/p/weibo4j/`

[8] `https://developers.google.com/google-apps/calendar/`

[9] `http://logging.apache.org/log4j/1.2/`

[10] `https://github.com/Mestway/SWIN-Project`

More concretely, method "EventWho.getAttendeeType()" in Google Calendar v2 returns a string that may contain either "attendee" or "organizer". Google Calender v3 replaces this method with two methods: "boolean getSelf()" which returns true when "attendee" should be returned and "boolean getOrganizer()" which returns true when "organizer" should be returned. To migrate the client, we may need to transform the code as follows, where "getSelf()" is a client-written method to test whether the argument is equal to "attendee",

```
String attendeeType = attendee.getAttendeeType();
boolean isSelf = isAttendee(attendeeType);
```

into the code as follows.

```
boolean isSelf = attendee.getSelf();
```

This example shows two fundamental limitations of SWIN. First, to perform the above transformation, we need to match a sequence of statements and transform them into one method calls. This requires many-to-one mapping and is not supported by SWIN. Second, we need to perform a semantic analysis on the implementation code of isAttendee to decide whether to transform the code into getSelf() or getOrganizer(). This kind of conditional transformation is not supported by SWIN.

Clearly, Twinning also has these limitations and cannot handle the three split methods in Google Calendar API as well. This result indicates that SWIN is as expressive as Twinning on our three case studies. Please note that many API classes have sub classes, and thus the SWIN programs should be much shorter than Twinning, as in Twinning we need to repeat the rules for the parent class also on each sub class.

6.3.3 Interesting Transformation Patterns

In the implementation of the three case studies, we also found that many transformations are not direct method replacement, but can still be expressed in SWIN by flexible use of the transformation rules. We summarize three patterns below.

Method $\leftrightarrow$ Constructor. We may need to map between class constructors and methods, and in SWIN we can directly specify such a replacement. For example, in the case from Crimson to dom4j, we write the following piece of code. This program is in the text form of SWIN, where we use ->> to denote $\hookrightarrow$ and -> to denote $\rightarrow$.

```
(f : DocumentBuilderFactory ->> DocumentFactory)
[ (f.newDocumentBuilder()):DocumentBuilder ->
    (new SAXReader(f)):SAXReader ]
```

Type Merging. Sometimes a set of classes in the old API become one class in the new API. In class CalendarEvent in Google Calendar v2, there is a method getTitle(). Developers can use this method to acquire the title of a source, but the type of the title is TextConstruct. Class TextConstruct is a wrapper of a string, and there is a method getPlainText() which returns the internal string. In Google Calendar v3, the class CalendarEvent becomes Event, which directly contains a method getSummary() to return the string of title. As a result, we may need to transform a sequence of method invocations "x.getTitle().getPlainText()" into a single invocation "x.getSummary()".

Although such a transformation implies a many-to-many mapping, it can be implemented in SWIN because TextConstruct is only used in the return type of getTitle() in Google Calendar API. We can consider the API upgrade as merging classes CalendarEvent and TextConstruct into Event and merging methods getTitle() and getPlainText() into getSummary(). As a result, we can remove the call to getPlainText() and replace getPlainText() with getSummary(). The rules are as follows.

```
(x : CalendarEvent ->> Event)
    [ (x.getTitle()):TextConstruct -> x:Event ]
(l : TextConstruct ->> Event)
    [ (l.getPlainText()):String
        -> (l.getSummary()):String ]
```

This pattern indicates that though SWIN is design for one-to-many mappings, many-to-many mappings can also be supported in a limited form from the flexibility of the rules.

Type Deletion. A class in the old API may become totally useless in the new API. In twitter4j, a Twitter object can be obtained by first creating a factory TwitterFactory and then invoking the getInstance() method, but in Sina Weibo API class Weibo, the counterpart of Twitter, can be directly created. In other words, the class TwitterFactory is deleted. Similar to the previous case, we may need to merge a sequence of method invocations "new TwitterFactory().getInstance()" into one single invocation "new Weibo()".

To implement this transformation in SWIN, we use the dummy class method [1]. We introduce a dummy class NoF into the client code to represent the deleted TwitterFactory. This dummy class has no class body and can be added to the client code before the transformation. In this way we can delete a class while maintaining the type safety. The transformation rules are as follows.

```
()[ (new TwitterFactory()):TwitterFactory
    -> (new NoF()):NoF ]
(f : TwitterFactory ->> NoF)
    [ (f.getInstance()):Twitter
     -> (new Weibo()):Weibo ]
```

7. Related work

General Transformation Frameworks. A number of general-purpose program transformation languages/frameworks have been proposed. To be independent of any programming languages, most of these languages work on the grammatical level, defining transformations on top of syntax trees. For example, TXL [11] and Stratego/XT [12] are general-purpose and grammar-oriented transformation languages, which allow the definitions of a set of rules to rewrite the abstract syntax trees of a program. Tom [13] is a language extension for Java designed to manipulate tree structures. In Tom, term rewriting and plain Java code can be mixed to write more powerful program transformations. Compared with these general-purpose transformation languages, SWIN mainly focuses on transforming Java programs in the scope of API evolution and API switching. By using Java features, SWIN allows more concise programs to be written for these tasks. Furthermore, none of the general transformation languages guarantees type-safety, for type-safety is difficult to specify in a language-independent way.

Transformation Frameworks for Java. Besides Twinning [1], several transformation languages/frameworks for Java programs are proposed. For example, Spoon [27] is a transformation framework for Java programs, providing the ability to directly read and modify program elements in Java programs. As far as we know, these transformation frameworks for Java do not consider type safety either, and there is no guarantee that the transformation does not introduce compilation errors. Refaster [28] uses compilable before-and-after examples of Java code to specify a Java refactoring. Similarly to our work, this work also mainly focuses on solving the method replacement which is useful in real API migration. Moreover, using direct Java examples to describe the transformation is convenient. However, Refaster cannot assure the well-typedness of the whole program during transformation, as it only requires that each transformed expression is well-typed.

Type-Safe Transformations. Approaches for ensuring type safety also exist. Hula [15] is a rule-based update (or transformation) language for Haskell, ensuring updates are performed in a type-safe manner. The type-safe transformation depends on a core calculus–update calculus [16], which provides type-safe transformation over lambda calculus. This work distinguishes program changes into declaration changes, definition changes, and application changes, and requires the three changes to be consistent. Compared with our work, update calculus allows the dynamic change of type definitions during transformation while our approach focuses on static type mappings as the difference between the old API and the new API are already known during program adaptation for different APIs. On the other hand, update calculus allows only the replacement of a type to a more generic type, while our approach supports more type mapping between independent types, such as Vector to ArrayList, because these type changes are dominant in program adaptation between APIs.

The work of Balaban [14] et al. focuses on a particular problem in the adaptation of program between APIs: when some part of the program cannot be changed, how to change the other parts while preserving well-typedness and other properties. This work extracts the type constraints from the Java program, then solves the constraints using a constraint solver to prevent type incorrect program transformations. Different from this work that considers the well-typedness of a particular client program, our work focuses on the type-safety of the transformation itself, taking into account all possible client programs. The work of Spoon [27] focuses on the well-typedness of a program using API with forthcoming or deprecated methods. This work extends FJ with forthcoming and deprecated methods, and proves the soundness of extended FJ. However, this work only allows update on methods, rather than update on classes.

Semantic-Preserving Transformations. Refactoring-based approaches [3, 4] treat the API changes as a set of refactorings. The API developers records their changes on the API as a set of refactorings, and the later these refactorings can be replayed on the client programs to transform the client programs to the new API. In this way, the adaptation of the client programs is not only type-safe but also semantic-preserving. However, this approach has limitations. First, this approach cannot support API changes that cannot be expressed as refactorings. Second, this approach only applies to API update, and cannot support migrating programs between alternative APIs, which are independently developed. The work of Leather [17] et al. provides an approach to preserve semantics of a program while changing terms involving type A to terms involving type B using type-changing rewrite rules. This work mainly focuses on conversion between isomorphic types, whereas our work focuses on transformation between any two types. Moreover, unlike this work performing transformations on lambda calculus with let-polymorphism, our work performs transformations on Featherweight Java which need to solve problems introduced by object orientation, such as subtyping.

Package templates [18] is an extension to Java to write reusable and adaptable modules. Since the template instantiation process in package templates includes operations like renaming and class merging, it can be considered as a semantics-preserving program transformation process. Different from our work, the program transformation in package templates mainly focuses on the changes on the class level, and does not consider the replacement of method invocations. A key point in package templates is to avoid name collision in transformation. Our approach does not consider this issue because in Java language, the client code and the API are usually in different packages, and the names are almost impossible to collide.

Heuristic-based Transformations. Several approaches try to further reduce the cost of program adaptation between APIs by automatically discovering the transformation program using heuristic rules. The heuristic rules range from comparing API source code [5], analyzing existing client source code [6, 8, 9, 24], and discovering similar code pieces [10]. Since these approaches are heuristic-based, there is no guarantee the discovered transformations are type-safe.

8. Conclusion and Future Work

In this paper, we have proposed a type-safe transformation language SWIN for program adaptation in the scope of API switching and API updating. Different from the existing language Twinning, SWIN provides a full type-safe guarantee, more flexible rule matching, and formal semantics of its core part. The type safety of core SWIN is proved about formally in Featherweight Java, and the case studies show that SWIN is expressive enough to handle many useful transformations in practice and is as expressive as Twinning on the cases.

In future, the inability of SWIN to handle the three method splitting changes as discussed in Section 6.3 needs to be addressed. This could possibly be handled by adding the dataflow information into SWIN to handle many-to-many mapping, adding semantic conditions to allow semantic checking, and loosing the restriction on the type mapping to allow one-to-many type mapping.

Acknowledgments

We are grateful for the fruitful discussions with Prof. Martin Erwig at Oregon State University on update calculus [16] and Prof. James R. Cordy at Queen's University on TXL [11].

References

[1] M. Nita and D. Notkin. Using twinning to adapt programs to alternative APIs, in: *Proc. ICSE*, 2010.

[2] T. Bartolomei, K. Czarnecki, and R. Lämmel. Swing to SWT and Back: patterns for API migration by wrapping, in: *Proc. ICSM*, 2010.

[3] D. Dig, S Negara, and R. Johnson. ReBA: refactoring-aware binary adaptation of evolving libraries, in: *Proc. ICSE*, 2008.

[4] J. Henkel and A. Diwan. CatchUp!: capturing and replaying refactorings to support API evolution, in: *Proc. ICSE*, 2005.

[5] D. Dig, C. Comertoglu, D. Marinov, and R. Johnson. Automated detection of refactorings in evolving components, in: *Proc. ECOOP*, 2006.

[6] H. Nguyen, T. Nguyen, G. Jr, A. Nguyen, M. Kim, and T. N. Nguyen. A graph-based approach to API usage adaptation, in: *Proc. OOPSLA*, 2010.

[7] A. Igarashi, B. C. Pierce, and P. Wadler. Featherweight Java: a minimal core calculus for Java and GJ, *ACM Trans. Program. Lang. Syst*, 2001.

[8] Y. Padioleau, J. Lawall, R. R Hansen, and G. Muller. Documenting and automating collateral evolutions in linux device drivers, in: *Eurosys*, 2008.

[9] J. Andersen and J. L. Lawall. Generic patch inference, in: *Proc. ASE*, 2008.

[10] N. Meng, M. Kim, and K. S. Mckinley. Systematic editing: generating program transformations from an example, in: *Proc. PLDI*, 2011.

[11] J. R. Cordy. The TXL source transformation language, *Science of Computer Programming*, 2006.

[12] E. Visser. Program transformation in stratego/xt: rules, strategies, tools and systems in stratego xt/0.9, *Domain Specific Program Generation*, 2004.

[13] E. Balland, P. Brauner, R. Kopetz, P.-E. Moreau, and A. Reilles. Tom: piggybacking rewriting on Java, in: *Proc. RTA*, 2007.

[14] I. Balaban, F. Tip, and R. Fuhrer. Refactoring support for class library migration, in: *Proc. OOPSLA*, 2005.

[15] M. Erwig and D. Ren. A rule-based language for programming software updates, *SIGPLAN Notices.*, 2002.

[16] M. Erwig and D. Ren. An update calculus for expressing type-safe program update, *Science of Computer Programming*, 2007.

[17] S. Leather, J. Jeuring, A. Löh, and B. Schuur. Type-changing rewriting and semantics-preserving transformation, in: *Proc. PEPM*, 2014.

[18] E. W. Axelsen and S. Krogdahl. Package templates: a definition by semantic-preserving source-to-source transformations to efficient Java code, in: *Proc. GPCE*, 2012.

[19] J. Li, Y. Xiong, X. Liu, and L. Zhang. How does web service API evolution affect clients?, in: *Proc. ICWS*, 2013.

[20] E. Visser. A survey of strategies in rule-based program transformation systems, *Journal of Symbolic Computation*, 2005.

[21] M. Pilgrim. Dive into Python 3, *2nd edition, APress*, 2009.

[22] B. E. Cossette and R. J. Walker. Seeking the ground truth: a retroactive study on the evolution and migration of software libraries, in: *Proc. FSE*, 2012.

[23] C. Wang, J. Li, Y. Xiong, and Z. Hu. Formal Definition of SWIN language, *Technical Note, available at* `https://github.com/Mestway/SWIN-Project/blob/master/docs/pepm-15/TR/TR.pdf`, 2014.

[24] Q. Wu, G. Liang, Q. Wang, and H. Mei. Mining Effective Temporal Specifications from Heterogeneous API Data, *Journal of Computer Science and Technology*, 2011.

[25] N. Nystrom, M. R. Clarkson, and A. C. Myers. Polyglot: an extensible compiler framework for Java, in: *Proc. CC*, 2003.

[26] R. Pawlak, C. Noguera, and N. Petitprez. Spoon: program analysis and transformation in Java, *Technical Report 5901*, INRIA, 2006.

[27] S. A. Spoon. Fined-grained API evolution for method deprecation and anti-deprecation, in: *Proc. FOOL*, 2006.

[28] L. Wasserman. Scalable, example-based refactorings with refaster, in: *Proc. WRT*, 2013.

[29] B. Pierce. Types and Programming Languages, *MIT Press*, 2002.

Appendix

A. Feather Weight Java

A.1 Syntax

This part presents the syntax for FJ.

$$\begin{array}{rcl} \texttt{CL} & ::= & \texttt{class C extends C } \{\bar{\texttt{C}}\ \bar{\texttt{f}};\ \texttt{K}\ \bar{\texttt{M}}\} \\ \texttt{K} & ::= & \texttt{C}(\bar{\texttt{C}}\ \bar{\texttt{f}})\{\texttt{super}(\bar{\texttt{f}});\ \texttt{this}.\bar{\texttt{f}} = \bar{\texttt{f}};\} \\ \texttt{M} & ::= & \texttt{C m}(\bar{\texttt{C}}\ \bar{\texttt{x}})\{\texttt{return t};\} \\ \texttt{t} & ::= & \texttt{x} \mid \texttt{t.f} \mid \texttt{t.m}(\bar{\texttt{t}}) \mid \texttt{new C}(\bar{\texttt{t}}) \mid (\texttt{C})\ \texttt{t} \\ \texttt{v} & ::= & \texttt{new C}(\bar{\texttt{v}}) \end{array}$$

A.2 Subtyping

This part presents the derivation of subtype relation in FJ.

$$\frac{}{\texttt{C} <: \texttt{C}}\ \text{(S-SELF)}$$

$$\frac{\texttt{C} <: \texttt{D} \qquad \texttt{D} <: \texttt{E}}{\texttt{C} <: \texttt{E}}\ \text{(S-TRANS)}$$

$$\frac{\texttt{CL} = \texttt{class C extends D } \{\ldots\}}{\texttt{C} <: \texttt{D}}\ \text{(S-DEF)}$$

A.3 Typing Rules

In this section we present the typing rules for FJ term and FJ class declaration obtained from [29].

Note that CAST rule in FJ type system is divided into three rules. FJ-UCAST and FJ-DCAST are for cast between two classes with subtype relation while FJ-SCAST is the typing rule for cast between two irrelevant classes, which will generate a "stupid warning" in the typing progress.

$$\frac{\texttt{x} : \texttt{C} \in \Gamma}{\Gamma \vdash \texttt{x} : \texttt{C}}\ \text{(FJ-VAR)}$$

$$\frac{\Gamma \vdash \texttt{t}_0 : \texttt{C}_0 \qquad \texttt{fields}(\texttt{C}_0) = \bar{\texttt{C}}\ \bar{\texttt{f}}}{\Gamma \vdash \texttt{t}_0.\texttt{f}_i : \texttt{C}_i}\ \text{(FJ-FIELD)}$$

$$\frac{\Gamma \vdash \texttt{t}_0 : \texttt{C}_0 \qquad \texttt{mtype}(\texttt{m}, \texttt{C}_0) = \bar{\texttt{D}} \to \texttt{C} \qquad \Gamma \vdash \bar{\texttt{t}} : \bar{\texttt{C}} \qquad \bar{\texttt{C}} <: \bar{\texttt{D}}}{\Gamma \vdash \texttt{t}_0.\texttt{m}(\bar{\texttt{t}}) : \texttt{C}}\ \text{(FJ-INVK)}$$

$$\frac{\texttt{fields}(\texttt{C}_0) = \bar{\texttt{D}}\ \bar{\texttt{f}} \qquad \Gamma \vdash \bar{\texttt{t}} : \bar{\texttt{C}} \qquad \bar{\texttt{C}} <: \bar{\texttt{D}}}{\Gamma \vdash \texttt{new C}_0(\bar{\texttt{t}}) : \texttt{C}}\ \text{(FJ-NEW)}$$

$$\frac{\Gamma \vdash \texttt{t}_0 : \texttt{D} \qquad \texttt{D} <: \texttt{C}}{\Gamma \vdash (\texttt{C})\texttt{t}_0 : \texttt{C}}\ \text{(FJ-UCAST)}$$

$$\frac{\Gamma \vdash \texttt{t}_0 : \texttt{D} \qquad \texttt{C} <: \texttt{D} \qquad \texttt{C} \neq \texttt{D}}{\Gamma \vdash (\texttt{C})\texttt{t}_0 : \texttt{C}}\ \text{(FJ-DCAST)}$$

$$\frac{\Gamma \vdash \texttt{t}_0 : \texttt{D} \qquad \texttt{C} \not<: \texttt{D} \qquad \texttt{D} \not<: \texttt{C} \qquad \textit{stupid warning}}{\Gamma \vdash (\texttt{C})\texttt{t}_0 : \texttt{C}}\ \text{(FJ-SCAST)}$$

$$\frac{\bar{\texttt{x}} : \bar{\texttt{C}}, \texttt{this} : \texttt{C} \vdash \texttt{t}_0 : \texttt{E}_0 \qquad \texttt{E}_0 <: \texttt{C}_0 \qquad \texttt{CT}(\texttt{C}) = \texttt{class C extends D } \{\ldots\} \qquad \texttt{override}(\texttt{m}, \texttt{D}, \bar{\texttt{C}} \to \texttt{C}_0)}{\texttt{C}_0\ \texttt{m}\ (\bar{\texttt{C}}\ \bar{\texttt{x}})\ \{\texttt{return t}_0;\}\ \texttt{OK in C}}\ \text{(FJ-M-OK)}$$

$$\frac{\texttt{K} = \texttt{C}\ (\bar{\texttt{C}}\ \bar{\texttt{f}})\{\texttt{super}(\bar{\texttt{f}});\ \texttt{this}.\bar{\texttt{f}} = \bar{\texttt{f}}\} \qquad \texttt{fields}(\texttt{D}) = \bar{\texttt{D}}\ \bar{\texttt{g}} \qquad \bar{\texttt{M}}\ \texttt{OK in C}}{\texttt{class C extends D } \{\bar{\texttt{C}}\ \bar{\texttt{f}}; \texttt{K}\ \bar{\texttt{M}}\}\ \texttt{OK}}\ \text{(FJ-C-OK)}$$

A.4 Auxiliary Definition

This part presents the auxiliary functions used in FJ typing rules.

$$\frac{}{\texttt{fields}(\texttt{Object}) = \{\}}\ \text{(FIELD-OBJECT)}$$

$$\frac{\texttt{CT}(\texttt{C}) = \texttt{class C extends D } \{\bar{\texttt{C}}\ \bar{\texttt{f}};\ \texttt{K}\ \bar{\texttt{M}}\} \qquad \texttt{fields}(\texttt{D}) = \bar{\texttt{D}}\ \bar{\texttt{g}}}{\texttt{fields}(\texttt{C}) = \bar{\texttt{D}}\ \bar{\texttt{g}},\ \bar{\texttt{C}}\ \bar{\texttt{f}}}\ \text{(FIELD-LOOKUP)}$$

$$\frac{\texttt{CT}(\texttt{C}) = \texttt{class C extends D } \{\bar{\texttt{C}}\ \bar{\texttt{f}};\ \texttt{K}\ \bar{\texttt{M}}\} \qquad \texttt{B m}\ (\bar{\texttt{B}}\ \bar{\texttt{x}})\ \{\texttt{return t};\} \in \bar{\texttt{M}}}{\texttt{mtype}(\texttt{m}, \texttt{C}) = \bar{\texttt{B}} \to \texttt{B}}\ \text{(METHOD-LOOKUP1)}$$

$$\frac{\texttt{CT}(\texttt{C}) = \texttt{class C extends D } \{\bar{\texttt{C}}\ \bar{\texttt{f}};\ \texttt{K}\ \bar{\texttt{M}}\} \qquad \texttt{m is not defined in } \bar{\texttt{M}}}{\texttt{mtype}(\texttt{m}, \texttt{C}) = \texttt{mtype}(\texttt{m}, \texttt{D})}\ \text{(METHOD-LOOKUP2)}$$

$$\frac{\texttt{mtype}(\texttt{m}, \texttt{D}) = \bar{\texttt{D}} \to \texttt{D}_0 \texttt{ implies } \bar{\texttt{C}} = \bar{\texttt{D}} \texttt{ and } \texttt{C}_0 = \texttt{D}_0}{\texttt{override}(\texttt{m}, \texttt{D}, \bar{\texttt{C}} \to \texttt{C}_0)}\ \text{(OVERRIDE)}$$

Safe Concurrency Introduction through Slicing

Huiqing Li Simon Thompson
School of Computing, University of Kent, UK
h.li@kent.ac.uk s.j.thompson@kent.ac.uk

Abstract

Traditional refactoring is about modifying the structure of existing code without changing its behaviour, but with the aim of making code easier to understand, modify, or reuse. In this paper, we introduce three novel refactorings for retrofitting concurrency to Erlang applications, and demonstrate how the use of program slicing makes the automation of these refactorings possible.

Categories and Subject Descriptors D. Software [*D.2 SOFTWARE ENGINEERING*]: D.2.3 Coding Tools and Techniques

Keywords refactoring; slicing; Erlang; functional programming; concurrency; parallelisation

1. Introduction

Erlang [3, 7] is a functional programming language with built-in support for concurrency based on share-nothing processes and asynchronous message passing. With Erlang, the world is modelled as sets of parallel processes that can interact by exchanging messages. Erlang concurrency is directly supported in the virtual machine, rather than indirectly by operating system threads. Erlang processes are very lightweight, and as a result a program can be made up of thousands or millions of processes that may run on a single processor, a multicore processor or a many-core system.

The advent of the multicore era and the demise of Moore's Law have persuaded programmers to build more parallelism into their programs. However, for the majority of existing Erlang applications, especially those legacy applications written before Erlang's support for symmetric multi-processing (SMP), despite the fact that a certain amount of concurrency is built into the application, the amount of parallelism exhibited is insufficient to keep all the Erlang schedulers as busy as possible. The performance of these applications could therefore be improved by introducing more parallelism to those parts of the application where multi-core resource utilisation is low. Detecting where more parallelism should be introduced to an Erlang application is supported by profiling tools such as Percept2 [20] and etop [2].

The need to retrofit parallelism to existing Erlang applications has given rise to a collection of new Erlang refactorings. Unlike traditional Erlang refactorings, which are mostly structural transformations aiming to make code easier to understand, modify, or reuse, parallelisation-related refactorings are mostly performance-driven; furthermore, some parallelisation refactorings might well make code harder to understand. Another difference we observed between traditional structural refactorings and parallelisation-related refactorings for Erlang is the program analysis techniques needed in order to carry out refactorings; in particular, the use of program slicing is essential for a number of the refactorings that we have automated.

Program slicing is a general technique of program analysis for extracting a part of a program, also called the *slice*, that influences or is influenced by a given point of interest, i.e. the *slicing criterion*. Static program slicing is generally based on program dependency analyses including both control dependency and data dependency. *Backward intra-function slicing*, which extracts the program slice that influences a particular variable/expression, is the kind of slicing used by the implementation of the refactorings proposed.

While there are a number of refactoring tools available for Erlang programs, such as Wrangler [17, 27] and RefactorErl [21], the number of refactorings for retrofitting concurrency is limited. The major contribution of this paper is a set of parallelisation/process-related refactorings for Erlang programs, through which we demonstrate how the use of program slicing techniques makes the automation of these refactorings possible. All these refactorings have been automated, and are supported through the Erlang refactoring tool **Wrangler** developed by the authors.

It has been observed that the refactorings presented here complicate the code, making it more difficult to read and maintain, and that these transformations should be left to a compiler to perform automatically. While this is possible, we prefer the approach presented here for three reasons.

- First, the refactorings can be seen as one component of the general process of program development, and as such they should be an explicit part of the history held in a repository, to be maintained together with other development steps.
- It may well be that an automated approach would not lift precisely the code that a user would wish, and so that the approach presented here may need some manual assistance to "tune" the transformation.
- Complex compiler transformations are notoriously "fragile", with a small syntactic change to a program changing the transformation radically: this is clearly undesirable when the results of the transformation are not visible to the programmer.

The rest of the paper is organised as follows. In Section 2, we give a brief introduction to Erlang and its support for concurrent programming. In Section 3, we give an overview of the existing refactoring and slicing support for Erlang programs. Our slicing-based concurrency introduction refactorings are presented in Section 4, and the facilities used in their implementation are covered in Section 5. In Section 6, we discuss the handling of side-effects in Erlang, as it relates to the work here. Related work is covered in Section 7, and

PEPM '15, January 13–14, 2015, Mumbai, India.

ACM 978-1-4503-3297-2/15/01... $15.00.
http://dx.doi.org/10.1145/2678015.2682533

finally, Section 8 concludes the paper and briefly discusses future work.

2. Introducing Erlang

Erlang [1] is a strict, dynamically typed, functional programming language with support for higher-order functions, pattern matching, concurrency, distribution, fault-tolerance, and dynamic code reloading. Erlang's data types include atoms, numbers and process identifiers, and the compound data types of tuples and lists.

2.1 Syntax: functions, pattern-matching and assignment

The principal definition form in an Erlang module is the *function*. Each function has a fixed number of arguments, its *arity*, and when we need to denote 'the `foo` function with arity 2', we write `foo/2`. The same name can be used for functions of different arities, and these are seen as completely separate definitions: a typical case is where the definition of a function like `foo/2` has an auxiliary function defined by tail recursion, and this would be named `foo/3`.

A function definition consists of a number of *clauses* where each clause consists of a head and a body, separated by an arrow '`->`'; the `qsort` example in Figure 6 has two such clauses. Clauses are separated by semi-colons, '`;`', and the final clause (and so the definition itself) is terminated with a full stop (period), '`.`'.

The *head* of each clause consists of the function name applied to a *pattern* for each argument, (this may be followed by an optional guard, indicated by the keyword `when`). In the `qsort` (Figure 6) the head of the first clause consists of the function applied to an empty list, '`[]`'. The pattern in the second clause, '`[Pivot|Rest]`' matches any *non-empty* list, with `Pivot` matching the first element (or head) of the list, and `Rest` matching the remainder (or tail). Thus, `[...|...]` is the *cons* operation for lists (following Prolog).

When a function is applied to some actual parameters, the *first* clause that matches the parameters is used. As well as variables, patterns can contain the wild-card '`_`', and indeed any variable of the form '`_Foo`' acts as a wild-card, and cannot be used in the body.

The *body* of a function consists of a sequence of statements, separated by commas, '`,`'. These expressions are evaluated in turn, and the result returned by the function is the value of the final expression in the sequence. Expressions can be assignments of the form `Pat = Expr`, where `Pat` is a pattern.

Erlang binding is *single assignment*, so that each (instance of a) variable has a single value. When there is an attempt to re-bind a variable this becomes an attempt to pattern match against a variable that is already bound: this succeeds if the 'new' value is the same as the 'old' and fails otherwise.

Within a module `foo` the function `bar/1` may be called like this

```
bar(Argument)
```

but within another module it must be called in *fully-qualified form:*

```
foo:bar(Argument)
```

(and indeed it may be called in this way within `foo` itself too). In order to understand some of the finer details of the examples, some other notations are seen in Figures 1, 2, 3 and 6.

- Erlang contains records, and these are signalled by the use of '`#`'. In the fragment
  ```
  #child{pid = Pid, ...}
  ```
  the value of the `pid` field of a `child` record is assigned the value (or indeed has its value matched with) the variable `Pid`.
- In line with a number of languages, Erlang has *list comprehensions* that define lists by a combination of generate, test and transform. This is seen in the example
  ```
  [X || X <- Rest, X<Pivot]
  ```
  from Figure 6: this describes the list built by running through the elements `X` of `Rest` and including only those that meet the test `X<Pivot`.
- Finally, Figures 2 and 3 contain an *anonymous function* introduced by `fun`. The function
  ```
  fun(P1 -> B1; P2 -> B2; ...)
  ```
  has exactly the same behaviour as the function
  ```
  anon(P1) -> B1;
  anon(P2) -> B2;
  ...
  ```
  except that is it unnamed. In these examples it is *mapped* along a list by means of the library function `lists:map/2`.

```
-module(echo).

-export([start/0, loop/0]).

start() ->
   Pid = spawn(echo, loop, []),
   Pid ! {self(), hello},
   receive
      {Pid, Msg} ->
          io:format("~p\n", [Msg])
   end,
   Pid ! stop.

loop() ->
   receive
      {From, Msg} ->
          From ! {self(), Msg},
          loop();
      stop ->
         true
   end.
```

Figure 1. A concurrent Erlang program

2.2 Concurrency: processes and message passing

Processes and message passing are fundamental to Erlang. A process is a self-contained unit of computation which executes concurrently with other processes in the system. The primitives `spawn`, '`!`' (send) and `receive` allow a process to create a new process and to communicate with other processes through asynchronous message passing.

The example code in Figure 1 demonstrates process creation, execution and interaction in Erlang. The function `start` initiates a process whose first action is to `spawn` a child process. This child process starts executing the `loop` function from the module `echo` (with an empty list of parameters, `[]`) and is immediately suspended in the `receive` clause waiting for messages of the right format. The parent process, still executing `start`, uses the identifier of the child process (`Pid`) to send the child a message containing a tuple with the parent's process identifier (given by calling `self()`) and the atom `hello`.

Once the message is sent, the parent suspends in the `receive` clause. The child, upon receiving the message from the parent process, sends the message, tupled with its own process identifier, back to the parent. Once the parent has received the echoed message, it prints the message, sends the `stop` message to the child, and terminates. The child receives the `stop`, returns `true`, and terminates.

The main implementation of Erlang is the Erlang/OTP system [1], an open source implementation supported by Ericsson AB. This was first equipped with symmetric multi-processing (SMP) capabilities in 2006, and this support has been improved continuously since then. In the current release (R17), the Erlang Virtual Machine (VM) detects the CPU topology automatically at startup, and creates a scheduler for each CPU core available. Each scheduler has it own process run-queue, and processes are migrated between run-queues if scheduler loads need to be balanced [22, 24].

2.3 Erlang/OTP

In addition to the language itself, Erlang comes with the OTP (Open Telecom Platform) middleware library. OTP provides a set of generic behaviours, most notably a *generic server* implementation, together with a *supervisor* behaviour that supports robustness through a hierarchical restart model in the face of component failure.

One of the generic design patterns supported by Erlang/OTP is *gen_server*. A *gen_server* implements a client-server model which is characterized by a central server and an arbitrary number of clients. The server is responsible for managing a common resource shared by different clients. This common resource is represented as the internal state held by the server process.

Two kinds of requests can be sent from client processes to a server process: asynchronous requests and synchronous requests. When an asynchronous request is received, the *gen_server* process only needs to process the request and update its internal state accordingly; no reply needs to be sent back to the client process. On the other hand, when a synchronous request is received, the *gen_server* process needs to calculate two things: the reply which should be sent back to the client – for which the client will wait – and the new value for the state of the *gen_server*.

When implementing a client-server model using Erlang's *gen_server* component, the user needs to define a number of interface functions and callback functions. The callback function for handling synchronous requests must have the following signature:

```
handle_call(Request, From, State)->Result
```

where `Result` is an Erlang tuple. This result typically has the format `{reply, Reply, NewState}`, and uses the Erlang convention that an atom in the first field – here `reply` – identifies or 'tags' the data. The field `Reply` is the value to be sent back to the client, and `NewState` the updated value of the state of the server. The `handle_call` function will typically consist of a number of clauses, each matching a different `Request` pattern in its head.

3. Refactoring and Slicing Support for Erlang

There are a number of refactoring tools for Erlang. **Wrangler** [17, 19] (`https://github.com/RefactoringTools/Wrangler`) is an interactive refactoring and code inspection tool for Erlang developed by the authors. It is implemented in Erlang, and integrated with (X)Emacs and with Eclipse. One of the features that distinguish Wrangler from most other refactoring tools is its user-extensibility. Wrangler provides a high-level *template- and rule-based API* [17], so that users can write their own refactorings, or general program transformations, in a concise and intuitive way without having to understand the underlying Abstract Syntax Tree (AST) representation and other implementation details. User-defined refactorings can be invoked via the Emacs interface to Wrangler, in exactly the same way as built-in refactorings, and so their results can be previewed and undone. Wrangler also provides a domain-specific language (DSL) for composing large-scale refactorings from elementary refactorings.

Complementing Wrangler, RefactorErl [21] is another interactive refactoring tool for Erlang. RefactorErl takes a database approach to store the syntactical and semantical information of the application under refactoring. More recent developments to RefactorErl concentrate on its facilities for program analysis rather than transformation [28].

ParTE [5] is a new refactoring tool built on top of Wrangler and RefactorErl. In particular, Wrangler's API and DSL support for scripting is used in ParTE to build refactorings [6], whereas RefactorErl's program analysis support is used to find parallelisable code candidates. The approach used by ParTE to introducing concurrency is to use an abstract skeleton library called Skel (`skel.weebly.com`). Skel is a collection of common patterns of parallelism that hide explicit process manipulation behind the scene.

In the area of program slicing for Erlang programs, M. Tóth *et al.* [4, 29] have investigated the use of data, behaviour and control dependency information to carry out inter-function forward slicing. Their aim was to detect the impact of a change on a certain point of the program so as to reduce the number of regression test cases to be rerun after the change. In [26], J. Silva *et al.* investigated the use of a system dependence graph (SDG) to support inter-function backward slicing of sequential Erlang programs.

Comparing with program slicing for imperative programs, program slicing for functional programs has its own peculiarities. For instance, Erlang does not contain loop commands such as `while`, `for` or `repeat`. All loops are implemented through recursion. In Erlang, variables can only be assigned once, and pattern matching is used to control the execution flow of a function.

Intra-function backward slicing is supported by Wrangler, and used by the implementation of the refactorings to be introduced in this paper. Since the slicing is within the scope of a function clause, only control and data dependency are used. Instead of generating a dependency graph for programming slicing purposes, Wrangler uses the AST annotated with extra semantic and dependency information as the internal program representation. The advantage of using an annotated AST is that we have a single internal representation for both program slicing and refactoring.

4. Slicing-based Concurrency Refactorings

In this section, we propose three slicing-based refactorings for introducing concurrency to Erlang applications. We would like to point out that there are many other ways for introducing concurrency to an Erlang application. For instance, the use of the sequential *map* operation over a list of data can be refactored to use parallel *map* instead; server processes can be replicated to handle client requests, and so on. In this paper, we focus only on those new refactorings in which the use of slicing plays an important role. We explain these refactorings one by one in more detail now.

4.1 Spawning a worker process for `handle_call`

As we noted earlier, one of the generic design patterns supported by Erlang/OTP is *gen_server*, and two kinds of request can be sent from client processes to a server process: asynchronous requests and synchronous requests. In this section we show how synchronous requests can be transformed to asynchronous ones under certain circumstances.

Requests sent to a *gen_server* process are handled sequentially. Depending on the amount of computation a *gen_server* needs to do when handling a request, there can be situations when a *gen_server* process is overloaded with request messages. Hence it is good practice to check the clauses of the `handle_call` function and see whether any of them can be divided into two parts: one that must be executed on the main *gen_server* process because it affects the state, and the another that does not affect the server state and may be executed in a worker process spawned for it. For instance, the `handle_call` clause shown in Figure 2 can be refactored to that in Figure 3 using our tool Wrangler.

In the code after refactoring, a new worker process is spawned, using `spawn_link`, to carry out the computation of `Resp`. The result is then sent back to the client through a different mechanism, namely:

```
handle_call(which_children, _From, State) ->
    Resp = lists:map(fun(#child{pid = ?restarting(_), name = Name,
                               child_type = ChildType, modules = Mods}) ->
                             {Name, restarting, ChildType, Mods};
                        (#child{pid = Pid, name = Name,
                                child_type = ChildType, modules = Mods}) ->
                             {Name, Pid, ChildType, Mods}
                     end,
                     State#state.children),
    {reply, Resp, State};
```

Figure 2. Introduce a worker process to **handle_call** (code before refactoring).

```
handle_call(which_children, From, State) ->
   spawn_link(
     fun () ->
           Resp =
                  lists:map(fun(#child{pid = ?restarting(_), name = Name,
                                        child_type = ChildType, modules = Mods}) ->
                                     {Name, restarting, ChildType, Mods};
                                 (#child{pid = Pid, name = Name,
                                        child_type = ChildType, modules = Mods}) ->
                                     {Name, Pid, ChildType, Mods}
                             end,
                             State#state.children),
           gen_server:reply(From, Resp)
     end),
   {no_reply, State};
```

Figure 3. Introduce a worker process to **handle_call** (code after refactoring).

```
gen_server:reply(From, Res)
```

Note also that the pattern match in the head of the **handle_call** has changed, since in this case the value of this parameter is used in the body of the function, unlike the case before the refactoring.

The *gen_server* process itself does not wait for the child process to finish, instead it returns immediately from this **handle_call** function with the return value of {**no_reply, State**}. Thus it can be seen that that the two components of the {**reply, ..., ...**} are returned by the transformed code, but in this case by two separate mechanisms.

In the particular example showing Figures 2 and 3 the state was not modified by the **handle_call** function; it is possible to perform the refactoring even in the case that the state *is* modified, so long as this calculation can be separated from the calculation of the reply. Once the new state computation is complete, the *gen_server* can process the next message: note that here we're performing parallelisation within the processing of a single message; we are *not* parallelising the implementation of the *gen_server* itself, which would be substantially more of a challenge.

This refactoring makes the assumption that the last expression of the **handle_call** function clause has a particular format, namely {**reply, Reply, NewState**}, where **Reply** and **NewState** are both variables. If that isn't the case, it is straightforward to refactor the code so that it has this format before invoking the transformation.

Slicing is used by this refactoring to decide which part of the computation of a **handle_call** function clause can be moved to a new process. We will use S_R and S_N to represent the program slices regarding the slicing criteria **Reply** and **NewState** respectively. Both S_R and S_N consist of a list of top-level expressions from the function clause body, and those expressions do not have to be contiguous. The expressions that can be computed in a worker process are those included in the set difference $S_R \setminus S_N$. The spawning of the new process is placed just before the last expression of the **handle_call** clause.

4.2 Introduce a new process

The refactoring ***Spawn a worker process for*** **handle_call** handles a special case of introducing concurrency, as it can only be applied to a **handle_call** function defined in a **gen_server** implementation. A more general case is to spawn a new process to execute a task in parallel with its parent process, with the computation result of the new process being sent back to the parent process, which will consume it.

As an example, Figure 4 shows a function that sequentially performs image processing on data from two files; Figure 5 shows the result of refactoring to introduce a new process to calculate the values of $R1$ and $F1$ of the code from Figure 4. The highlighted code in Figure 4 is the program slice of the slicing criterion selected, that is the expression sequence: R_1, F_1. In order not to block the execution of the parent process, the **receive** expression is placed immediately before the point where the result is needed, 'as late as possible' in the computation.

If the task to be executed by the new process consists of a sequence of contiguous expressions, the user could just highlight this block of expressions, and apply the refactoring. However this refactoring process could also be driven by the target of the task, in which case a user may want to move into a new process only those parts of the computation that influence the value of the target. In this case, a backward slice of the target could reveal the code fragments, which may or may not be contiguous, that influence the value of the target expression. In order to move those parts of the slice that only influence the target selected, i.e. have no influence on any other code, a static analysis of the annotated AST presentation of the slice is then carried out to remove those expressions that have influence beyond the slicing criterion selected. We place the **spawn_link** expression right after the last expression on which the

```
readImage(FileName, FileName2) ->
  {ok, #erl_image{format=F1, pixmaps=[PM1]}}
    = erl_img:load(FileName),
  Cols1 =PM1#erl_pixmap.pixels,

  {ok, #erl_image{format=F2, pixmaps=[PM2]}}
    = erl_img:load(FileName2),
  Cols2=PM2#erl_pixmap.pixels,

  R1 = [B1||{_A1, B1}<-Cols1],
  R2 = [B2||{_A2, B2}<-Cols2],

  {R1, F1, R2, F2}.
```

Figure 4. Introduce a new process (before)

```
readImage(FileName, FileName2) ->
  Self = self(),
  Pid = spawn_link(
    fun () ->
      {ok, #erl_image{format=F1,
                      pixmaps=[PM1]}}
          = erl_img:load(FileName),
      Cols1 =PM1#erl_pixmap.pixels,
      R1 =[B1||{_A1, B1}<-Cols],
      Self ! {self(), {R1, F1}}
    end),

  {ok, #erl_image{format=F2, pixmaps=[PM2]}}
    = erl_img:load(FileName2),
  Cols2=PM2#erl_pixmap.pixels,

  R2 = [B2||{_A2, B2}<-Cols2],

  receive {Pid, {R1, F1}} -> {R1, F1} end,

  {R1, F1, R2, F2}.
```

Figure 5. Introduce a New Process (after)

```
qsort([]) -> [];
qsort([Pivot|Rest]) ->
  qsort([X || X <- Rest, X<Pivot]) ++
  [Pivot] ++
  qsort([X||X<-Rest, X>=Pivot]).
```

Figure 6. Quicksort in Erlang

slice has a dependency, and the `receive` expression immediately before the expression where the result slice is used so that there is the maximum computation time for the new process to complete before its result is needed.

4.3 Parallelise tail-recursive functions

Iteration, or looping, in functional languages is in general implemented via *recursion*. Recursive functions invoke themselves, allowing an operation to be performed repeatedly until a *base case* is reached. For example, Fig 6 shows a recursive implementation of *quicksort*. A parallel version of this quicksort function can be implemented as shown in Figure 7. In order to control the granularity of parallelism, a new parameter `P` is added, which specifies the maximum number of processes that can be spawned. The value of `P` is generally decided by the number of cores available on the machine. Granularity control is especially useful for parallel recursive functions, to avoid spawning too many processes. Note that the sequential definition of `qsort` is still needed even with the parallel version.

```
par_qsort(List) -> par_sort(P, List).

par_qsort(0, List) -> qsort(List);
par_qsort(P, []) -> [];
par_qsort(P, [Pivot|Rest]) ->
  Parent = self(),
  spawn_link(fun() ->
    Parent ! par_qsort(P-1, [X || X<-Rest, X>=Pivot])
  end),
  par_qsort(P-1, [X||X<-Rest, X<Pivot]) ++
  [Pivot] ++
  receive Result -> Result end.
```

Figure 7. Parallel Quicksort in Erlang

```
fac(N) -> fac(N, 1).

fac(0, Acc) -> Acc;
fac(N, Acc) when N>0 -> fac(N-1, N*Acc).
```

Figure 8. Tail-recursive `factorial`

```
do_grouping([], _, _, _, Acc) -> {ok, Acc};
do_grouping(Nodes, _Size, 1, Counter, Acc) ->
  {ok,  [make_group(Nodes, Counter)|Acc]};

do_grouping(Nodes, Size, NumGroup, Counter, Acc) ->
  Group = lists:sublist(Nodes, Size),
  Remain = lists:subtract(Nodes, Group),
  NewGroup = make_group(Group, Counter),
  NewAcc = [NewGroup|Acc],
  do_grouping(Remain, Size, NumGroup-1, Counter+1, NewAcc).
```

Figure 9. An example tail-recursive list processing function

The *qsort* example represents one style of writing recursive functions, i.e. *general recursion*, where the recursive call to itself can happen anywhere in the function body. Another style of writing recursive functions is called *tail recursion*. A recursive function is tail-recursive if the recursive call is the last thing the function does (before returning). Tail-recursive functions often use an accumulating parameter to hold the partial results of the calculation. As an example, Figure 8 shows a tail-recursive implementation of the `factorial` function. Two functions are defined in this example, namely `fac` with the arities of 1 and 2, since in Erlang different arities mean different functions. The parameter `Acc` to the second function is the accumulating parameter, which holds the result of the function as it is calculated.

While some tail-recursive list processing functions can be automatically refactored to an explicit *map*, or *map-reduce* operation, many are not straightforward without knowledge of the domain. For instance, the example shown in Figure 9 does a recursion over the list `Nodes` while accumulating results to the accumulator variable `Acc`. Each recursive call processes a number of elements in `Nodes`, and the values of `NumGroup` and `Counter` depend on their values in the previous recursion. The recursion reaches its base case when either the list `Nodes` becomes empty or the value of `NumGroup` becomes 1.

Suppose the computation of `make_group(Group, Counter)` is expensive, and there is a need for performance improvement, then simply spawning a new process to do this computation, as shown in the previous examples in Figure 5 and Figure 7 would not help, as the result returned by this computation is immediately needed by the next expression. Spawning a new process in this case will immediately put the current process into a waiting state. In order to handle this kind of situation, we examined a set of direct tail-recursive functions that meet certain constraints, and developed a new refactoring, ***parallelise tail-recursive function***, for automating the parallelisation of such functions.

The rationale behind this refactoring is to identify the computation component that is independently repeated in every recursion, and delegate the computation task to a worker process so that the main recursion can be run in parallel with a number of worker processes. The pre-condition analysis and transformation of this refactoring are described in more detail in what follows.

This refactoring takes a function definition as input, and carries out a sequence of static analyses to decide whether the function meets the pre-conditions of the automatic parallelisation refactoring. These steps are:

Step 1 is to check whether the function is a direct tail-recursive function with one or more base case clauses, and the only recursive calls appear as the last expression of the function clause body. For simplicity, in this paper we assume the tail-recursive function is of the following form:

```
fun_name(Arg_11, . . ., Arg_1n) -> Body1;
. . .
fun_name(Arg_m1, ...., Arg_mn) ->
   BodyExpr1,
   BodyExpr2,
   . . .
   fun_name(NewArg_m1, ..., NewArg_mn).
```

where the last function clause is the recursive function clause, and all the other function clauses handle base cases. The approach described here can equally well be applied to tail-recursive functions with multiple recursive clauses, and so the assumption here is without loss of generality.

Step 2 is to distinguish accumulating parameters from non-accumulating parameters. In this step, data dependency is used as a heuristic to decide whether or not a parameter is an accumulating parameter. We assume that a parameter is an accumulating parameter if

- its value is influenced by its own value and (possibly) the value of some other parameters,
- the parameter itself does not influence the value of any other parameters, and
- the value of the parameter is not used as a base case condition to terminate the recursion.

Program slicing is used to decide the dependency between parameters in the recursive function clause. In particular, each argument to the recursive function call, i.e. `NewArg_mi`, is selected as a slicing criterion, and its backward slice is calculated. We say that argument `Arg_mi` depends on argument `Arg_mj` if `Arg_mj` is included in the backward slice of `NewArg_mi`.

Taking the `do_grouping` example shown in Figure 9 as an example, the program slices for some of the recursive call arguments are shown in Figure 10. From the slicing result, together with further analysis of the base cases, we are able to conclude that `Acc` is the accumulating parameter of `do_grouping`.

Step 3 is to partition the recursive function clause body. Once the accumulating parameter has been identified, the refactoring needs to decide which part of the computation should be delegated to worker processes, and which part should stay in the main loop. With our approach, the part of the computation that can be moved to a worker process is extracted from the program slice of the

```
do_grouping([], _, _, _, Acc) -> {ok, Acc};
do_grouping(Nodes, _Size, 1, Counter, Acc) ->
  {ok, [make_group(Nodes, Counter)|Acc]};
do_grouping(Nodes, Size, NumGroup, Counter, Acc) ->
  Group = lists:sublist(Nodes, Size),
  Remain = lists:subtract(Nodes, Group),
  NewGroup = make_group(Group, Counter),
  NewAcc = [NewGroup|Acc],
  do_grouping(Remain, Size, NumGroup-1, Counter+1, NewAcc).
```

(a) program slice for `Remain`

```
do_grouping([], _, _, _, Acc) -> {ok, Acc};
do_grouping(Nodes, _Size, 1, Counter, Acc) ->
  {ok, [make_group(Nodes, Counter)|Acc]};
do_grouping(Nodes, Size, NumGroup, Counter, Acc) ->
  Group = lists:sublist(Nodes, Size),
  Remain = lists:subtract(Nodes, Group),
  NewGroup = make_group(Group, Counter),
  NewAcc = [NewGroup|Acc],
  do_grouping(Remain, Size, NumGroup-1, Counter+1, NewAcc).
```

(b) program slice for `NumGroup-1`

```
do_grouping([], _, _, _, Acc) -> {ok, Acc};
do_grouping(Nodes, _Size, 1, Counter, Acc) ->
  {ok, [make_group(Nodes, Counter)|Acc]};
do_grouping(Nodes, Size, NumGroup, Counter, Acc) ->
  Group = lists:sublist(Nodes, Size),
  Remain = lists:subtract(Nodes, Group),
  NewGroup = make_group(Group, Counter),
  NewAcc = [NewGroup|Acc],
  do_grouping(Remain, Size, NumGroup-1, Counter+1, NewAcc).
```

(c) program slice for `NewAcc`

Figure 10. Program slices

accumulating parameter. To be more precise, only the part of the slice that does not depend on the value of the accumulator itself, and does not overlap with the slices of other parameters is to be moved to the worker process.

With the `go_grouping` example, the piece of computation that can be delegated to worker processes is:

```
NewGroup=make_group(Group, Counter).
```

So, up to this point, this refactoring will proceed only if the code fragment that can be moved to a worker process is not empty. Of course, the user could also abort the refactoring process if s/he thinks that the computation to be delegated to worker processes is not the critical part of the computation.

The remaining clause body is further partitioned into two parts. A part for evaluating the new values of recursion control parameters, and a part for evaluating the new value of the accumulating parameter. The former is executed before a task is dispatched to a worker process, and the latter is executed after a result has been received from a worker.

To illustrate how the transformation part of this refactoring works, we continue with the `do_grouping` example. The parallelised version of `do_grouping` resulting from this refactoring is shown in Fig 11. As this example shows, the original tail-recursive function is replaced with a non-recursive function with the same interface. The function `do_grouping` starts by spawning a number of worker processes executing the function `do_grouping_worker_loop/1`. The number of worker processes to be spawned is the same as the number of schedulers available on the Erlang VM. After that, another process is spawned by the entry function `do_grouping_dispatch_and_collect_loop/5`. As its name indicates, this function is in charge of dispatching new tasks to worker processes, collecting results from worker processes in a specific order, and handling the base cases. We refer to this as the *dispatch and collect* process.

```
do_grouping(Nodes, Size, NumGroup,Counter, Acc) ->
  Parent = self(),
  Workers = [spawn(fun() ->
                         do_grouping_worker_loop(Parent)
                     end)
                || _ <- lists:seq(1, erlang:system_info(schedulers))],
  Pid = spawn_link(
          fun() ->
              do_grouping_dispatch_and_collect_loop(Parent, Acc, Workers, 0, 0)
           end),
  Pid ! {Nodes, Size, NumGroup, Counter},
  receive
    {Pid, Acc} ->
        [P ! stop || P <- Workers],
        Acc
  end.

do_grouping_dispatch_and_collect_loop(Parent, Acc, Workers, RecvIndex, CurIndex) ->
   receive
      {[], Size, NumGroup, Counter} when  RecvIndex == CurIndex ->
          Parent ! {self(), {ok, Acc}};
      {[], Size, NumGroup, Counter} when  RecvIndex < CurIndex ->
          self() ! {[], Size, NumGroup, Counter},
          do_grouping_dispatch_and_collect_loop(
             Parent, Acc, Workers, RecvIndex, CurIndex);
      {Nodes,_Size, 1, Counter} when RecvIndex == CurIndex ->
           Parent ! {self(), {ok, [make_group(Nodes, Counter)|Acc]}};
      {Nodes, Size, 1, Counter} when RecvIndex < CurIndex ->
           self() ! {Nodes, Size, 1, Counter},
           do_grouping_dispatch_and_collect_loop(
             Parent, Acc, Workers, RecvIndex, CurIndex);
      {Nodes, Size, NumGroup, Counter} ->
           Group = lists:sublist(Nodes, Size),
           Remain = lists:subtract(Nodes, Group),
           Pid = oneof(Workers),
           Pid ! {self(), Group, Size, Counter},
           self() ! {Remain, Size, NumGroup-1, Counter+1},
           do_grouping_dispatch_and_collect_loop(
              Parent, Acc, Workers, RecvIndex, CurIndex+1);
       {{worker, _Pid}, RecvIndex, NewGroup} ->
           NewAcc = [NewGroup|Acc],
           do_grouping_dispatch_and_collect_loop(
              Parent, NewAcc, Workers, RecvIndex+1, CurIndex)
   end.

do_grouping_worker_loop(Parent) ->
      receive
         {Group, Size, Counter, Index} ->
             NewGroup = make_group(Group, Counter),
             Parent ! {{worker, self()}, Index, NewGroup},
             do_grouping_worker_loop(Parent);
         stop ->
             ok
     end.

oneof(Workers) ->
     ProcInfo = [{Pid, process_info(Pid, message_queue_len)} || Pid <- Workers],
     [{Pid, _}|_] = lists:keysort(2, ProcInfo),
    Pid.
```

Figure 11. A parallel implementation of the do_grouping function

The initial computing task in then sent to the *dispatch and collect* process as shown in line 11, after that the parent process is suspended in a `receive` clause waiting for the final result to come. Once the final result has been received, the parent process sends a `stop` signal to each worker process to terminate them, then terminates itself and returns the final result to its caller.

On the other hand, the *dispatch and collect* process is immediately suspended in a `receive` clause after its creation. The first message it receives represents the initial computation task sent by the parent process in line 11. This message is then pattern-matched in turn with each pattern in the `receive` expression. If the initial task does not match any of the base cases, then it should match the non-base case clause in line 32. The body of this `receive` clause first executes the program slice (lines 33-34) whose result affects the initial value passed onto the worker process, as well as the next iteration, then selects a worker process from the list of available worker process identifiers: `Pids`.

With the current implementation of this refactoring, the process with the shortest message queue is selected, as defined in the function `oneof` (lines 56-59). Once a worker process has been selected, a message containing the initial parameters for the new task is then sent to the worker process. Instead of waiting for the worker process to return the result, the *dispatch and collect* process continues to run in parallel with the worker process. It sends the remaining task to itself, and iterates the process.

Once a worker process has finished the computation of a task, it sends the result back to the *dispatch and collect* process, and waits for the next message to come. This is defined in the function `do_grouping_worker_loop` in lines 46-54. The *dispatch and collect* process uses indices to track each job dispatched and collected. Results from worker processes are received in the expected order, that is the order in which jobs are dispatched. Once an expected result has been received, this process takes the new result and the current value of the accumulator, calculates and updates the accumulator's value accordingly as shown in lines 40-43. Note that in the tail recursive call in line 43 the `RecvIndex` parameter is incremented: stepping this through by single increments ensures that the results are collected in the same order as the sub-tasks are dispatched, which is crucial for preserving the semantics of the computation.

When a base case message has been received, the process first checks if all the expected results have been received by checking if the two indices `RecvIndex` and `CurIndex` have the same value. If the result is `true`, then the final result is calculated and sent back to the parent process, otherwise the process will have to wait until all the results have been collected. To do so, it sends the base case message to itself so that it will eventually be processed.

As this refactoring shows, the transformation process is rather complex and error prone if done manually. With this refactoring support, the user is able to experiment with the parallel version with little effort.

5. Implementation

Wrangler is a mature refactoring tool for Erlang, written in Erlang, and we have used the facilities of Wrangler to implement the refactorings discussed here. We briefly discuss these here, and refer readers to the articles cited for more information about the details.

5.1 Wrangler in a nutshell

Architecture. Wrangler consists of a pipeline of stages:

- parsing, to give an abstract syntax tree (AST);
- semantic analysis, to give an annotated AST (AAST);
- transformation of the AAST, and
- pretty-printing to file.

and as it presents the top-level functions from each of the stages to build refactorings through the `api_interface`. More details of the architecture can be found in the overview [27].

Syntax. Erlang comes with a `syntax_tools` library that encapsulates various aspects of the syntax including macros; we have extended the tokeniser used by `syntax_tools` to include column information and preserve white spaces and comments.

Analysis. Information from the static semantic analysis is stored in the AAST, and this can be accessed directly or through API functions. These include operations to give the free and bound variables in syntactic components, as well as – for example – allowing the generation of 'fresh' identifiers on demand.

The analyses here are also supplemented with the slicing technology described in the previous section.

Wrangler extensibility. Wrangler supports user extension [18] in two complementary ways.

The **API** [17] allows users to define new refactorings 'from the bottom up'. It provides templates that can describe fragments of (A)AST through fragments of Erlang concrete syntax, augmented with meta-variables that range over syntactic elements. On top of these templates it is possible to build rules explaining how code is to be transformed, when the code meets appropriate pre-conditions. In the work presented here, we use templates in the *code synthesis* needed in building transformed programs.

The **DSL** [19] supports complex scripting of refactorings, with control on their transactional nature, their interactivity, tracking of (renamed) names etc. It can be used in this context to present the facilities in a more exploratory way, allowing uses choices between possible variants of parallelisation refactorings, for instance.

Wrangler is written in Erlang. Functional languages – with pattern matching over structured data, and higher-order functions – are particularly well suited as metalanguages for transformation and analysis, and we leverage that here.

5.2 Implementing Refactorings Using Wrangler

The refactorings presented in this paper are implemented using Wrangler's API, in particular these refactorings implement a behaviour, named *gen_refac*, exposed by Wrangler. In Erlang, a behaviour is an application framework that is parameterised by a *call-back* module. The behaviour implements the generic parts of the solution, while the callback module implements the specific parts. A number of pre-defined behaviours are provided through Erlang/OTP. In the same spirit, the *gen_refac* behaviour implements those parts of a refactoring that are generic to all refactorings, such as the generation and annotation of ASTs, the outputting of refactoring results, the collection of change candidates and the workflow of the refactoring processes. To implement a refactoring using *gen_refac*, the user only needs to implement a number of callback functions, of which the two most important are `check_pre_condition` and `transform`.

To illustrate how these refactorings are implemented, we take the transformation part of *introduce a worker process to handle call* as an example. While the implementation of *tail-recursive function parallelisation* is more complex due to the amount of analysis involved, the methodology used is the same.

The implementation of the callback function `transform` of *introduce a worker process to handle call* is as shown in Fig 12. This function applies a transformation rule defined by function `rule1` to the current file under refactoring. The function `rule1` implements a transformation that modifies a `handle_call` clause at a given position to introduce parallelism. `?RULE` is a macro defined

```
transform(_Args=#args{current_file_name=File,
                      cursor_pos=Pos}) ->
    ?STOP_TD_TP([rule1(Pos)], [File]).


rule1(Pos) ->
   ?RULE(?T("handle_call(Args@@) when Guard@@->
                  Body@@,{reply, Res@, State@};"),
          gen_new_handle_call(_This@, Res@, State@,
               {Args@@, Guard@@, Body@@, State@}),
          begin
             {S, E} = api_refac:start_end_loc(_This@),
             S=<Pos andalso E>=Pos
          end).

gen_new_handle_call(C, Res, State,
                         {Args, Guard, Body, State}) ->
    {Slice1, _}=wrangler_slice_new:backward_slice(C, Res),
    {Slice2, _}=wrangler_slice_new:backward_slice(C, State),
    ExprLocs = Slice1 -- Slice2,
    Exprs =[B||B<-Body,
               lists:member(
                 api_refac:start_end_loc(B), ExprLocs)],
    NewBody = Body -- Exprs,
    api_refac:subst(
        ?T("handle_call(Args@@) when Guard@@ ->
                 Body@@,
                 spawn_link(
                       fun()->
                            Resp= begin Exprs@@ end,
                         gen_server:reply(From, Resp)
                        end),
                 {no_reply, State@};"),
           [{'Args@@', Args}, {'Guard@@', Guard},
             {'Body@@', NewBody}, {'State@', State},
             {'Exprs@@', Exprs}]).
```

Figure 12. Transform a handle_call function clause

```
print_list(0) -> ok;
print_list(N) ->
  io:format("*");
  print_list(N-1).

test()->print_list(3).
```

(a) Code before *generalisation*

```
print_list(F, 0) -> ok;
print_list(F, N) ->
  F(),
  print_list(F, N-1).

test() ->
  print_list(fun() ->io:format("*") end, 3).
```

(b) Code after *generalisation*

Figure 13. Generalisation over an expression with side-effects

in Wrangler used to define transformations. It takes three parameters: a template characterising the program fragment to transform, a description of the new program fragment that replaces the old one, and a pre-condition on the application of the rule; the call takes the form `?RULE(Template, NewCode, Cond)`.

The function **`gen_new_handle_call`** is the one that generates the new code. This function first calculates the fragment of code to be executed by the new process as well the part that remains in the main process, then generates the new code using a template as indicated by the macro call `?T`.

6. Side-effect Analysis

Being side-effect free plays an important part in functional programming languages. In a side-effect free language, the same expression always produces the same value when evaluated multiple times. This *referential transparency* feature makes program analysis, comprehension and transformation easier. Unlike other functional programming languages such as Haskell and Clean, which have a substantial pure subset, Erlang has controlled side-effects to support communication amongst other features.

Erlang is pure in having immutable data structures and single assignment variables; it is not pure due to its support for concurrency, Erlang built-in **T**erm **S**torage (ETS), process dictionary, etc. In an Erlang program, both pure functions and impure functions can be used in any context (except function guards).

For refactorings that do not change the execution context of the code under refactoring – i.e. the process in which the code is executed – there are some workarounds when side-effects are a concern. For example, naively generalising a function over an expression that has side-effects could potentially change the behaviour of the function. The solution to this problem is to wrap the side-effecting expression up as a *closure*, as shown in the *generalisation* example in Fig 13, where the function `print_list` is generalised over the expression `io:format("*")`.

Concurrency-related refactorings are vulnerable to side-effects due to the fact that very often a concurrency-related refactoring needs to migrate some computation from one process to another, and this potentially affects those execution-context-aware operations. For instance, the Erlang built-in function `self()` returns the process identifier of the calling process, hence care has to be taken if a refactoring changes the execution context of `self()`, because in a new process the same expression will return a different process identifier. On the other hand, it might be perfectly ok to migrate some code with side-effects into another process.

In order to support safe concurrency introduction refactorings, side-effect analysis of the code affected by a refactoring is a necessity. With the knowledge that side effects in Erlang are due to a small number of known reasons, but *not* to single assignment, we are able to identify an initial set of functions whose side-effects are predefined. This hard-coded information indicates not only that a function has side-effects, but also specifies the kind of side-effects associated with it.

With this pre-defined side-effect information, static AST-based techniques are then used to establish function dependencies, and side-effect information is then propagated over the dependency graph until a fixed point is reached. To improve the efficiency of side-effect analysis, side-effect information about library functions is pre-computed, and stored in a persistent table.

In the case that the code to be migrated to another process does have side-effects, the user is presented with the side-effect information derived, and it is the user's choice whether or not to continue with the refactoring.

7. Related Work

Slicing. A direct application of program slicing in the field of refactorings is *slice extraction*, which has been formally defined by Ettinger [13] as the extraction of the computation of a set of variables from a program as a reusable program entity, and the update of the original program to reuse the extracted slice. Ettinger's study was not concerned about concurrency.

In [10], J. Cheng extends the notion of slicing for sequential programs to concurrent programs and presents a graph-theoretical approach to slicing concurrent programs. In addition to the usual control and data dependencies, J. Cheng introduces three new types of primary program dependences in concurrent programs, named the selection dependence, synchronisation dependence and communication dependence. The techniques developed aim to help the debugging of concurrent programs by finding all the statements that possibly or actually caused the erroneous behaviour of an execution of a concurrent program where an error occurs.

A more precise slicing algorithm is proposed by J. Krinke: in [15] he proposes a context-sensitive approach to slicing concurrent programs. This approach makes use of a new notation for concurrent programs by extending the control flow graph and program dependence graph to their threaded counterparts.

In [14], M. Kamkar *et al.* propose a tracing-based algorithm for distributed dynamic slicing on parallel and distributed message-passing based applications. With this approach, the authors introduce the notion of Distributed Dynamic Dependence Graph (DDDG) which represents control, data and communication dependences in a distributed program. This graph is built at run-time and used to compute slices of the program through graph traversals.

Parallelisation. There is a substantial literature on parallelisation of programs, the vast majority of which addresses parallel programs in the object-oriented (typically Java, C++) and imperative (x10, Fortran) paradigms. In common with our observation for Erlang, Dig notes in [12] that "unlike sequential refactoring, refactoring for parallelism is likely to make the code more complex, more expensive to maintain, and less portable".

Dig's paper [12] exemplifies the main approach for OO languages in targetting thread-safe libraries and data structures within a general-purpose language, which, once achieved, provides further refactoring opportunities. Alternatively, programs can be targeted at specialised hardware, such as GPUs [11] and multicore systems [9]. These approaches typically require pointer analyses to identify access to mutable data structures, a problem which is not evident in Erlang – which features single assignment – and other functional languages. Working within parallel languages such as x10, which embodies the partitioned global address space (PGAS) model, some work has been done in loop parallelisation [23], and, while these are not included in the main release, there have been some experiments in parallelisation in the Fortran refactoring tool Photran [25]. Other work on loop parallelisation [16] notes the importance of user input into the parallelisation process.

Work on parallelisation of functional programs has typically taken two routes. First, *skeletons* have been used to identify potential sites for parallelisation, and this forms the basis of the work of the ParaPhrase project [6]. Secondly, data parallel systems have been developed – including Data Parallel Haskell [8] – but to the best of our knowledge there has been no work on refactoring for data parallelism in a functional context.

8. Conclusions and Future Work

In this paper, we presented three novel slicing-based refactorings for introducing concurrency to Erlang applications, and in that way parallelising the systems. All these refactorings are automated in the Erlang refactoring tool Wrangler. While there are other ways for retrofitting concurrency to existing Erlang applications, such as the use of skeletons/patterns, our refactorings complement the existing ones. The application of program slicing to the refactoring field is not new, but our work demonstrates its usefulness for supporting concurrency introduction refactorings.

As we noted in the introduction, we have chosen to implement these refactorings explicitly as part of the software development process, rather than implicitly – and 'invisibly' – inside a compiler. We have done this to make the transformation a part of the software development process, and also because we see that fully automated transformations often need some modifications in application or scope in order to deliver precisely what is required. In doing this we agree with others working in the field [16] who note that "automatic parallelization of loops is a fragile process" and so include user input in the process, rather than incorporating the transformation within the internals of a compiler.

Our future work lies in a few directions. First, we will investigate other refactorings, and code inspection functionalities, which can benefit from program slicing techniques; second, we will extend Wrangler to support automatic discovery of candidates where concurrency can be introduced; and finally we will connect Wrangler with concurrency profiling tools such as Percept2 [20] to provide feedback on the performance impact after concurrency introduction.

Acknowledgments

This research is supported by EU FP7 project RELEASE, grant number 287510, (`www.release-project.eu`); we thank our funders and colleagues for their support and collaboration.

References

[1] Erlang/OTP. `http://www.erlang.org`.

[2] ETop - The Erlang Top. `http://www.erlang.org/doc/man/etop.html`.

[3] J. Armstrong. *Programming Erlang*. Pragmatic Bookshelf, 2007.

[4] I. Bozó and M. Tóth. Building Dependency graph for slicing Erlang Programs. In *Periodca Politechnica*, pages 372–390. 2010.

[5] I. Bozó, V. Fordós, et al. Discovering Parallel Pattern Candidates in Erlang. In *Proceedings of the Thirteenth ACM SIGPLAN Workshop on Erlang*, Erlang '14, pages 13–23. ACM, 2014.

[6] C. Brown, K. Hammond, M. Danelutto, P. Kilpatrick, H. Schöner, and T. Breddin. Paraphrasing: Generating Parallel Programs Using Refactoring. In *Formal Methods for Components and Objects*, pages 237–256. Springer, 2013.

[7] F. Cesarini and S. Thompson. *Erlang Programming*. O'Reilly Media, Inc., 2009.

[8] M. M. T. Chakravarty, R. Leshchinskiy, S. Peyton Jones, G. Keller, and S. Marlow. Data parallel haskell: A status report. In *Proceedings of the 2007 Workshop on Declarative Aspects of Multicore Programming*, DAMP '07, pages 10–18, New York, NY, USA, 2007. ACM.

[9] F. Chen, H. Yang, W.-C. Chu, and B. Xu. A Program Transformation Framework for Multicore Software Reengineering. In *Quality Software (QSIC), 2012 12th International Conference on*, pages 270–275. IEEE, 2012.

[10] J. Cheng. Slicing Concurrent Programs - A Graph-Theoretical Approach. In *Proceedings of the First International Workshop on Automated and Algorithmic Debugging*, AADEBUG '93, pages 223–240, London, UK, 1993. ISBN 3-540-57417-4.

[11] K. Damevski and M. Muralimanohar. A Refactoring Tool to Extract GPU Kernels. In *Proceedings of the 4th Workshop on Refactoring Tools*, WRT '11, pages 29–32, New York, NY, USA, 2011. ACM.

[12] D. Dig. A Refactoring Approach to Parallelism. *IEEE Software*, 28 (1):17–22, 2011.

[13] R. Ettinger. Refactoring via Program Slicing and Sliding. In *23rd IEEE International Conference on Software Maintenance*, pages 505–506, Paris, France, 2007.

[14] M. Kamkar, P. Krajina, and P. Fritzson. Dynamic Slicing of Parallel Message-Passing Programs. In *PDP*, pages 170–178. IEEE Computer Society, 1996.

[15] J. Krinke. Context-sensitive Slicing of Concurrent Programs. In *Proceedings of the 9th European Software Engineering Conference Held Jointly with 11th ACM SIGSOFT International Symposium on Foundations of Software Engineering*, pages 178–187, New York, NY, USA, 2003.

[16] P. Larsen, R. Ladelsky, J. Lidman, S. McKee, S. Karlsson, and A. Zaks. Parallelizing more Loops with Compiler Guided Refactoring. In *Parallel Processing (ICPP), 2012 41st International Conference on*, pages 410–419. IEEE, 2012.

[17] H. Li and S. Thompson. A User-extensible Refactoring Tool for Erlang Programs. Technical Report 4-11, School of Computing, Univ. of Kent, UK, 2011.

[18] H. Li and S. Thompson. Let's Make Refactoring Tools User-extensible! In *Proceedings of the Fifth Workshop on Refactoring Tools*, WRT '12, pages 32–39. ACM, 2012.

[19] H. Li and S. Thompson. A Domain-Specific Language for Scripting Refactorings in Erlang. In *15th International Conference on Fundamental Approaches to Software Engineering(FASE)*, pages 501–515, 2012.

[20] H. Li and S. Thompson. Multicore profiling for Erlang programs using percept2. In *Proceedings of the twelfth ACM SIGPLAN workshop on Erlang*, pages 33–42. ACM, 2013.

[21] L. Lövei, C. Hoch, H. Köllő, T. Nagy, A. Nagyné-Víg, D. Horpácsi, R. Kitlei, and R. Király. Refactoring Module Structure. In *Proceedings of the 7th ACM SIGPLAN workshop on Erlang*, pages 83–89, Victoria, British Columbia, Canada, Sep 2008.

[22] K. Lundin. About Erlang/OTP and Multi-core Performance in Particular. Erlang Factory London 2009.

[23] S. A. Markstrum, R. M. Fuhrer, and T. D. Millstein. Towards Concurrency Refactoring for x10. *SIGPLAN Not.*, 44(4):303–304, 2009.

[24] P. Nyblom. Erlang SMP Support. Erlang User Conference 2009.

[25] J. Overbey, S. Xanthos, R. Johnson, and B. Foote. Refactorings for Fortran and High-performance Computing. In *Proceedings of the Second International Workshop on Software Engineering for High Performance Computing System Applications*, SE-HPCS '05, pages 37–39, New York, NY, USA, 2005. ACM.

[26] J. Silva, S. Tamarit, and C. Tomas. System Dependence Graphs in Sequential Erlang. In J. de Lara and A. Zisman, editors, *Fundamental Approaches to Software Engineering*, Lecture Notes in Computer Science, pages 486–500. Springer Berlin Heidelberg, 2012.

[27] S. Thompson and H. Li. Refactoring tools for functional languages. *Journal of Functional Programming*, 23(03):293–350, 2013.

[28] M. Tóth and I. Bozó. Static Analysis of Complex Software Systems Implemented in Erlang. In V. Zsák, Z. Horváth, and R. Plasmeijer, editors, *Central European Functional Programming School*, volume 7241, pages 440–498. 2012.

[29] M. Tóth, I. Bozó, et al. Impact Analysis of Erlang Programs Using Behaviour Dependency Graphs. In Z. Horváth et al., editors, *Central European Functional Programming School*, Lecture Notes in Computer Science, pages 372–390. 2013.

Static Backward Demand-Driven Slicing

Björn Lisper   Abu Naser Masud   Husni Khanfar
School of Innovation, Design and Engineering, Mälardalen University, Västerås, Sweden
{bjorn.lisper,masud.abunaser,husni.khanfar}@mdh.se

Abstract

Program slicing identifies the program parts that may affect certain properties of the program, such as the outcomes of conditions affecting the program flow. Ottenstein's Program Dependence Graph (PDG) based algorithm is the state-of-practice for static slicing today: it is well-suited in applications where many slices are computed, since the cost of building the PDG then can be amortized over the slices. But there are applications that require few slices of a given program, and where computing all the dependencies may be unnecessary. We present a light-weight interprocedural algorithm for backward static slicing where the data dependence analysis is done using a variant of the Strongly Live Variables (SLV) analysis. This allows us to avoid building the Data Dependence Graph, and to slice program statements "on-the-fly" during the SLV analysis which is potentially faster for computing few slices. Furthermore we use an abstract interpretation-based value analysis to extend our slicing algorithm to slice low-level code, where data dependencies are not evident due to dynamically calculated addresses. Our algorithm computes slices as sets of Control Flow Graph nodes: we show how to adapt existing techniques to generate *executable slices* that correspond to semantically correct code, where jump statements have been inserted at appropriate places. We have implemented our slicing algorithms, and made an experimental evaluation comparing them with the standard PDG-based algorithm for a number of example programs. We obtain the same accuracy as for PDG-based slicing, sometimes with substantial improvements in performance.

Categories and Subject Descriptors F.3.2 [*Semantics of Programming Languages*]: Program analysis; D.2.6 [*Software Engineering*]: Programming Environments

Keywords Static backward slicing; Unstructured control flow; Data flow equations; Computational complexity; Strongly live variable; Abstract Interpretation

1. Introduction

Program slicing refers to a collection of techniques to identify which parts in a program may affect a so called "slicing criterion" that expresses certain properties of a program. The slicing criterion may be, for instance, the possible values of some program variables in some program points. The result of the slicing is usually a new program, formed by extracting certain statements from the original code. Program slicing was first considered by Weiser [44] in the context of debugging. Other applications of slicing have emerged since then, including program comprehension [20], integration [9], testing [5, 16], parallelization of sequential code [45], software maintenance [15], compiler optimization [30] and many more.

Slicing comes in different dimensions. *Static slicing* computes a safe overapproximation of the code that might affect, or be affected by the slicing criterion, whereas *dynamic slicing* considers the statements that will affect (or be affected by) the criterion in different runs. *Intraprocedural slicing* is performed on a single nonrecursive procedure whereas *interprocedural slicing* considers multiple procedures possibly containing multiple call sites. *Syntax-preserving* slices are the subset of the original program statements whereas *amorphous* slicing transforms program code. *Backward slicing* computes the code-segment that affects the slicing criterion whereas *forward slicing* computes the code-segment that is affected by the slicing criterion.

Today, state of the practice in static slicing are algorithms based on the Program Dependence Graph (PDG) [14, 23, 35]. These algorithms first build the PDG for the whole program, and then compute the slices by a simple linear-time graph traversal. This is good for applications like program understanding, where many slices may be taken using different slicing criteria, since then the cost of building the PDG can be amortized over the different slices taken.

However, there are applications that require to compute only few slices. An example is Worst-Case Execution Time (WCET) analysis [47], where supporting analyses to constrain the WCET program flow can benefit greatly from slicing the analysed program with respect to the conditions, thus removing the parts of the program that surely cannot affect the control flow [13, 31, 40]. For such applications it can be advantageous to compute dependencies on the fly, for the parts of the program that actually produce the slice, rather than for the whole program.

In this paper we present such an algorithm for static backward slicing. We start with an intraprocedural analysis, which is subsequently extended to an interprocedural analysis. These analyses work for a high-level view of memory that consists of distinct program variables. Next we extend the analyses to slice code with a low-level view of memory, where reads and writes are made to addresses that may be dynamically computed rather than to program variables of given type and size. This is interesting for applications such as the aforementioned WCET analysis, which often is performed on linked binaries. Finally we show how to generate executable slices from our computed slices, which are sets of Control-Flow Graph (CFG) nodes. These executable slices can be directly translated into executable (or compilable) textual code.

This paper makes the following contributions:

PEPM '15, January 13–14, 2015, Mumbai, India.

ACM 978-1-4503-3297-2/15/01.
http://dx.doi.org/10.1145/2678015.2682538

1. An interprocedural slicing algorithm is developed for high-level code based on the *Relevant Strongly Live Variables* (SLV) dataflow analysis on the CFG representation of the input program. This analysis is a modification of standard SLV analysis, where the generated SLVs carry a dependency relation with the slicing criterion. This algorithm slices program statements on the fly during the analysis of SLVs.
2. We show how to adapt the SLV-based slicing algorithm to slice code with a low-level memory model, by augmenting it with an abstract interpretation-based value analysis that is used to determine addresses for memory accesses in the dataflow analysis.
3. We show how to convert the slices into executable slices, which can be directly translated into textual code with the same semantics as the original, CFG-based slices.
4. We have implemented the SLV-based algorithm and the standard PDG-based slicing algorithm in the WCET analysis tool SWEET [1, 32], and we have performed a comparative evaluation on a number of example programs. The evaluation shows that our algorithm computes the same slices as the PDG-based algorithm, sometimes with a significantly lower execution time.

The rest of this paper is organized as follows. Section 2 reviews some basic theory of data flow analysis, and introduces some notations used in the rest of the paper. Section 3 presents the SLV-based intraprocedural slicing algorithm and discusses its complexity. Section 4 extends the intraprocedural slicing algorithm to interprocedural slicing. In Section 5 we show how the SLV-based slicing can be extended to slice low-level code, and produce executable slices. Experimental results are given in Section 6, Section 7 gives an account for related work, and Section 8 concludes the paper.

2. Preliminaries

We now introduce some standard concepts and notation for completeness and clarity. A *control-flow graph* (CFG) [34] is defined as a directed graph $(N, Flow)$ where the nodes in N are labeled either with conditions, assignments, a special label $start$, or ditto $stop$, and $Flow \subseteq N \times N$ is a relation describing the possible flows of execution in the graph. Each CFG contains a unique start node and a unique stop node. The start node has no predecessors, and the stop node no successors. An assignment node has exactly one successor, and a condition node has exactly two successors (labeled *true* and *false*, respectively).

We will sometimes write $[c]^n$ for a node n labelled with the condition c, and $[x := a]^n$ for a node n labelled with the assignment $x := a$. This notation makes it easier to define the data flow equations in Sections 2.1 and 3.1.

Conditions, and right-hand sides in assignments, are expressions. We assume that expressions have no side-effects, and that they are simple expressions built from program variables, constants, operators and primitive functions (not user-defined). For simplicity we do not allow pointers and operations on such: all the analyses presented here can however be extended to deal with them. We assume that program variables are unaliased, i.e., an assignment to the program variable x can not affect the value of another program variable $y \neq x$. For an expression e, $FV(e)$ denotes the set of program variables that appear in e.

Note that we label the nodes by single statements, whereas in compiler literature the nodes often are considered to represent basic blocks. This is for two reasons: first, we want to perform the slicing on statements rather than basic blocks, and similarly it is easier to define data flow analyses and other static program analyses by equations over statements.

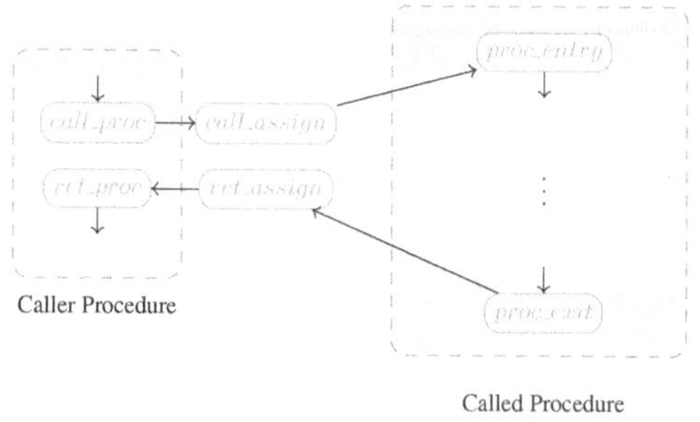

Figure 1: Relations among node types at call site in the CFG

For procedure calls, our CFG representation is based on [34] with some extensions. Some new kinds of nodes are introduced for representing procedure calls and entries: *proc_entry* and *proc_exit* nodes correspond to procedure entry and procedure exit. Without loss of generality, we assume that procedure parameters can be divided into a set of input and a set of output parameters where output parameters may be updated by the procedure. A procedure call is then represented by four types of nodes in the CFG: *call_proc* nodes represent the procedure calls, *call_assign* nodes represent the assignments of actual input parameters to formal input parameters, *ret_assign* nodes represent the assignments of formal output parameters to the actual output parameters, and *ret_proc* nodes represent returns from procedure calls.

There are some rules how procedure call nodes can appear. *call_proc* nodes and *call_assign* nodes always come in pairs, where the *call_assign* node is the unique successor to the *call_proc* and vice versa. The relation is similar for *ret_assign* and *ret_proc* nodes, but the order is reversed. The (unique) successor of a *call_assign* node must be a *proc_entry* node, and every predecessor of a *proc_entry* node must be a *call_assign* node. Similarly the unique predecessor to a *ret_assign* node must be a *proc_exit* node, and every successor of a *proc_exit* node must be a *ret_assign* node. *call_proc* and *ret_proc* nodes belong to the CFG of the caller, *proc_entry* and *proc_exit* nodes belong to the CFG of the callee, and the *call_assign* and *ret_assign* nodes are special nodes which may contain variables (in assignment expressions) that are scoped in both caller and callee procedures. See Fig. 1 and 2 for examples.

Postdominators [36] play an important role in slicing. A node n in a CFG is said to postdominate a node n_0 if and only if every path from n_0 to the stop node goes through n. There are many algorithms to compute postdominators, as well as *postdominator trees* which can be used to efficiently represent sets of postdominators for different nodes. Postdominator relations are used to determine *control dependencies*, see Section 2.2.

2.1 Data Flow Analysis

An important part of slicing is to compute data dependencies. A data flow analysis [34] is often used for this purpose. Data flow analyses are usually defined over CFGs in the following way. For each node n in the CFG, the analyses compute sets $S_{entry}(n)$ and $S_{exit}(n)$ which are present before and after the node, respectively. The sets represent some kind of data flow information. Depending on the direction of the data flow computed, an analysis is a *forward* or *backward* analysis. The sets are related through equations. We restrict our attention to *bit vector analyses*: for a backward bit-

```
void main() {
 int f=1,s=0,sp;
 while(f=<50){
   add(f,s,sp);
   s=sp;
   add(f,2,sp);
   f=sp;
   sp=0;
 }
 print(s);
}

void add(int x,
     int y, int z) {
 int t=x+y;
 z=t;
 t=0;
}
```

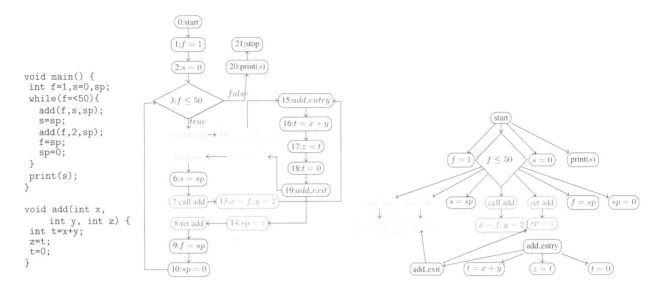

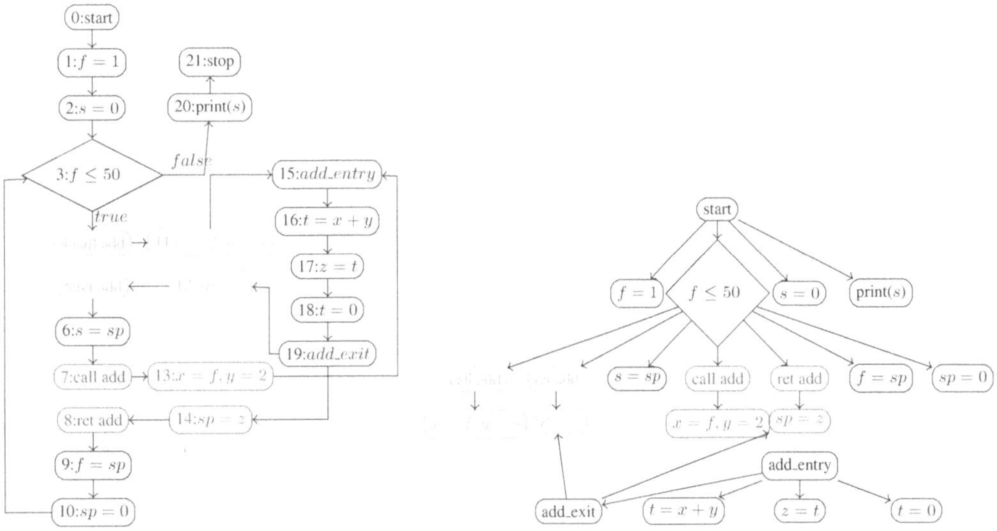

Figure 2: CFG and CDG of the Running Example

vevtor analysis, the form of the equations is as follows:

$$
\begin{array}{lcll}
S_{exit}(stop) & = & S_{init} & \\
S_{entry}(stop) & = & S_{exit}(stop) & \\
S_{entry}(start) & = & S_{exit}(start) & \\
S_{entry}(n) & = & (S_{exit}(n) \setminus kill(n)) \cup gen(n), & (1) \\
 & & \text{where } n \notin \{start, stop\} & \\
S_{exit}(n) & = & \bigcup_{n' \in succ(n)} S_{entry}(n'), & \\
 & & \text{where } n \notin \{start, stop\} &
\end{array}
$$

(The equations for forward bit vector analyses are similar, see [34].) Here, $succ(n)$ is the set of immediate successors to n in the CFG, and S_{init} is some set describing the data flow information that is present at the exit of the program. The equations defining $S_{entry}(n)$ have the form $S_{entry}(n) = f_n(S_{exit}(n))$, where f_n is the *transfer function* of node n. Data flow analyses are further divided into may and must analyses. We will only deal with may analyses here: (1) is valid for these.

A classical data flow analysis is Reaching Definitions (RD). It is a forward may analysis which computes sets of pairs (x, n), where x is a program variable and n is a node in the CFG. If (x, n) belongs to the set associated with node p then the value of x that was assigned at n may still reside in x at p, and then there is a possible data flow from n to p.

RD can be used to compute def-use pairs of variable assignments and possible uses. The def-use pairs for a program constitute its *Data Dependence Graph*, which is used in PDG-based slicing: see Section 2.2.

(1) yields a system of $2 \cdot |N|$ equations, where the unknowns are the sets $S_{entry}(n)$ and $S_{exit}(n)$ for the different nodes n in the CFG. The classical way to solve the system is by *fixed-point iteration*: all unknown sets are initialized to $\emptyset$, and then the system of equations is iterated until no more sets change. The underlying theory of complete lattices [34] ensures that this procedure converges, and always yields the least (most precise) solution. There is a generic worklist (or work set) algorithm to perform fixed-point iteration [34] that handles both forward and backward analyses. It computes an array S of sets, indexed by the nodes in the CFG $(N, Flow)$, where each element $S[n]$ equals $S_{entry}(n)$ for forward analyses, and $S_{exit}(n)$ for backward analyses.

The number of fixed-point iterations can be at most $h \cdot |N|$, where h is the height of the lattice iterated over and $|N|$ is the number of nodes in the CFG. For dataflow analysis, h equals the size of the largest possible set of data flow information. Thus the maximal execution time is $O(t \cdot h \cdot |N|)$, where t is an upper bound for the time needed to perform one fixed-point iteration.

2.2 PDG-based Slicing

The standard algorithms for static backward slicing use the Program Dependence Graph (PDG) [14, 23, 35]. The PDG is the union of two graphs, whose nodes are the same as those in the CFG: the Data Dependence Graph (DDG) and the Control Dependence Graph (CDG). The DDG is usually computed using the aforementioned RD dataflow analysis. The CDG has edges from conditions to CFG nodes, where there is an edge from condition c to node n if the outcome of c possibly can affect whether n is executed or not (i.e., n is *control dependent* on c). This can be formalised through postdominators: we say that n is control dependent on c if there is a path from c to n in the CFG and if n does not postdominate c. The CDG can be computed efficiently using postdominator trees. Fig. 2 shows the CFG and CDG for a given example program.

Once the PDG is built, the backward slicing can be performed by a simple graph search for the nodes in the PDG that are backward reachable from the slicing criterion. This operation is linear in the number of nodes and edges of PDG that are part of the sliced code, and can thus be performed quickly for different slicing criteria.

3. An Intraprocedural Slicing Based on Relevant SLV Analysis

As mentioned in the introduction, we do not want to compute all the data dependencies before the slicing. Rather we want to discover the relevant data dependencies on demand during slicing. In the following, we describe the Relevant Strongly Live Variables analysis which allows us to perform slicing concurrently with the data dependence analysis.

3.1 The Relevant Strongly Live Variables Analysis

The Strongly Live Variables (SLV) analysis (Exercise 2.4 in [34]) is an alternative data flow analysis for computing data dependencies. Given some sets of variables in some different program points, representing "uses" of these variables (like being written to some output device), it computes for each program point a set of "strongly live variables" whose values in that program point might (transitively) reach a use of some variable. It is a backward may analysis, with *kill*, *gen* and S_{init} sets defined as follows:

$$
\begin{array}{rcl}
S_{init} & = & \emptyset \\
kill([x := a]^n) & = & \{x\} \\
gen([x := a]^n) & = & FV(a) \\
kill([c]^n) & = & \emptyset \\
gen([c]^n) & = & FV(c)
\end{array}
\tag{2}
$$

The transfer functions for SLV analysis are set up according to (1), however with the following modification (for n being an assignment or a condition):

$$
S_{entry}(n) = \begin{cases} (S_{exit}(n) \setminus kill(n)) \cup gen(n), \\ \quad \text{if } kill(n) \subseteq S_{exit}(n) \\ S_{exit}(n), \text{ otherwise} \end{cases}
\tag{3}
$$

The above defines the "standard" SLV analysis, as known from the literature. It is based on the following assumptions on variable uses:

- variables are not used at the end of a program,
- variables in conditions are always used, and
- variables are not used in any other program points.

For slicing, a slicing criterion corresponds to a set of variable uses. To allow for a more flexible specification of slicing criteria, not necessarily adhering to the assumptions on variable uses above, we introduce *Relevant SLVs* defined as follows:

Definition 3.1 (Relevant Strongly Live Variables). *The Relevant Strongly Live Variables at any program point are those strongly live variables on which the variables at the slicing criterion have data dependency.*

So, relevant SLVs are a kind of SLVs that can affect some slicing criterion through data dependencies. They are defined through the following, modified equations. Let the slicing criterion be specified by a (possibly empty) set $S_{crit}(n)$ for each node n in the CFG. The *kill*, *gen* and S_{init} sets for Relevant SLV analysis are then defined according to (2) with the following modifications:

$$
\begin{array}{rcl}
S_{init} & = & S_{crit}(stop) \\
gen([x := a]^n) & = & FV(a) \cup S_{crit}(n) \\
gen([c]^n) & = & S_{crit}(n), \quad c \text{ is a condition}
\end{array}
\tag{4}
$$

The second case in (3) is modified accordingly:

$$
S_{entry}(n) = S_{exit}(n) \cup S_{crit}(n), \text{ if } kill(n) \not\subseteq S_{exit}(n)
\tag{5}
$$

For brevity we will refer to Relevant SLVs as SLVs below.

3.2 A Worklist Algorithm for Slicing on the Fly

In each program point, the relevant strongly live variables are the ones that can carry a dependence to some slicing criterion. Thus, for an assignment $x := a$, if x is strongly live at exit then there is a possible data dependence from the assignment to some slicing criterion, and it can be immediately put into the slice. We call this "slicing on-the-fly" as it slices during the SLV analysis, in contrast to data dependence analysis with RD where an explicit data dependence graph has to be built first. We now describe an algorithm to perform static backward slicing based on slicing on-the-fly. The slicing algorithm in Fig. 3 computes data dependencies according to the Relevant SLVs defined in Section 3.1, it traces control dependencies, and it performs slicing-on-the-fly. It is an adaptation of the generic worklist algorithm for data flow analysis [34] modified in the following way:

Algorithm 1: $SLVSlicing(N, F, C, S_{crit}, \langle f_n | n \in N \rangle)$

```
/* Initialization */
```
1   $W := \emptyset$;
2   $N_{slice} := \emptyset$;
3   **forall** $n \in N$ **do**
4      $S[n] := S_{crit}[n]$;
5   **if** $S_{crit}[n] \neq \emptyset$ **then**
6          $N_{slice} := N_{slice} \cup \{n\}$;
7   **forall** n' *where* $(n, n') \in F$ **do**
            $W := W \cup \{(n, n', CFG)\}$;
8   **forall** n' *where* $(n', n) \in C$ **do**
            $W := W \cup \{(n, n', CDG)\}$;
9   **end**
10 **endfor**
```
/* Iteration */
```
11 **while** $W \neq \emptyset$ **do**
12      $(n, n', T) := Select(W)$ /* Pick new element from W */;
13      $W := W \setminus \{(n, n', T)\}$;
14   **if** $T = CFG \wedge f_n(S[n]) \not\subseteq S[n']$ **then**   /* $S[n']$ has changed: add new work item to W */
15   **if** n' *is an assignment* $x := a$ *and* $x \in f_n(S[n])$ **then**
16              $N_{slice} := N_{slice} \cup \{n'\}$;
17   **forall** n'' *where* $(n'', n') \in C$ **do**
                $W := W \cup \{(n', n'', CDG)\}$;
18   **end**
19          $S[n'] := S[n'] \cup f_n(S[n])$;
20   **forall** n'' *where* $(n', n'') \in F$ **do**
            $W := W \cup (n', n'', CFG)$;
21   **end**
22   **if** $T = CDG$ **then**   /* The edge is a control dependence */
23          $S[n'] := S[n'] \cup FV(c(n'))$;
24   **if** $S[n'] \neq S[n'] \setminus FV(c(n'))$ *or* $n' \notin N_{slice}$ **then**
            /* to avoid potential infinite loop */
25              $N_{slice} := N_{slice} \cup \{n'\}$;
26   **forall** n'' *where* $(n', n'') \in F$ **do**
                $W := W \cup (n', n'', CFG)$;
27   **forall** n'' *where* $(n'', n') \in C$ **do**
                $W := W \cup \{(n', n'', CDG)\}$;
28   **end**
29   **end**
30 **end**
```
/* Finalization */
```
31 **return** N_{slice}

Figure 3: Slicing-on-the-fly with SLV analysis

- The worklist W holds two types of edges, which are tagged to keep them apart: (n, n', CFG) for edges in the CFG, and (n, n', CDG) for edges in the CDG.
- The algorithm uses the explicit CDG C to perform slicing due to control dependencies. F is the set of reversed edges $Flow^{-1}$.
- A set N_{slice} of sliced CFG nodes is maintained by the algorithm.
- A node $[x := a]^n$ is included in the slice whenever $x \in S[n]$. This takes care of slicing due to data dependencies.
- If n is included in the slice, and if $(n', n) \in C$ (where n' is a conditional node with condition c), then n' is included in the slice as well, $FV(c)$ is added to $S[n']$, for each edge $(n'', n') \in C$, (n', n'') is added to the worklist W, and if $S[n']$ changes then all edges $(n', n'') \in F$ are added to the worklist as well.
- The array S is initialized to an array S_{crit} containing the slicing criteria (sets of variables in certain program points). Furthermore, N_{slice} is initialized to the set of nodes n where $S_{crit}[n] \neq \emptyset$.
- For any node n, the transfer function f_n is defined according to (4) and (5).

In Algorithm 1 $select(W)$ picks non-deterministically an element from W, and for any conditional nodes n in the CFG $c(n)$ denotes the condition of n.

Each SLV set can contain at most v elements, where v is the number of variables in the program. Thus, the total size of the SLV sets is $O(|N| \cdot v)$, where $|N|$ is the number of nodes in the CFG. The height of the lattice is also v and thus the time to do fixed-point iteration for the standard SLV analysis is $O(t \cdot |N| \cdot v)$ where t is an upper bound to the time required to perform one fixed-point iteration. The complexity for Algorithm 1 is essentially the same, since the termination criterion for the worklist iteration is the same as well as the lattice of SLV sets. The factor t will of course change, but its order should be the same as for the original SLV analysis since the same set operations are used.

3.3 Slicing on the Fly With Respect to all Conditions

As mentioned in Section 1, in the flow analysis phase of WCET analysis it is often interesting to slice with respect to all the conditions in the program. In the SLV slicing algorithm, the slicing criterion will thus consist of all conditions in the program plus their sets of variables. As the conditions thus are contained in the slice from the beginning, the control dependencies can be disregarded. This is since the sole function of computing the control dependencies is to determine which conditions to include in the slice: thus, if all conditions are already included, the control dependencies will have no use and the CDG need not even be generated.

Algorithm 1 can be simplified accordingly, by removing lines 8, 17 and 22-29. Also the worklist elements will not have to be tagged as CFG or CDG edges as no CDG is needed. This is close to the original SLV algorithm as described in Section 3.1. The worst-case complexity will be the same as for the general SLV slicing algorithm, but the real execution time can be expected to be lower since the handling of the CDG is eliminated. As mentioned the CDG does not even have to be generated, which eliminates another phase in the slicing. This results in an algorithm that works directly on the CFG and does not require any other additional data structures than the worklist and the SLV sets.

4. Interprocedural Slicing

Any interprocedural slicing technique needs to deal with two problems. The first one is how to handle context-sensitivity: a very context-sensitive slicing will be precise but can be time-consuming, whereas a less context-sensitive approach will be faster but less precise. The second problem is how to precisely trace the dependencies between the input and output arguments of procedure calls. This is non-trivial since procedure calls may be arbitrarily nested and program variables might be aliased.

For PDG-based slicing, a solution has been developed where the PDG is extended into the *System Dependence Graph* (SDG) that captures also the interprocedural dependencies [23]. The SDG allows to handle both the context-sensitivity and the tracing of dependencies [23, 38]. As we avoid building the PDG (and thus also the SDG), we have developed a solution where these problems instead are handled on-the-fly. Our solution is context-sensitive and works for programs without (direct or indirect) recursive procedures. This may yield a costly algorithm: however, it turns out that we can mitigate this problem in a manner that is similar to how it is handled in the SDG-based algorithm. Note that even though our method works for non-recursive procedures, it is possible to extend it to handle recursive procedures as well by using some of the optimizations discussed in Section 4.1.

It is worth noting that Weiser's interprocedural slicing algorithm [42, 44], which is not SDG-based and has some similarities with our algorithm, does not handle these two problems and thus is less precise.

As mentioned in Section 2, a call site is represented by four distinct nodes in our CFGs: a $call\_proc$, a $call\_assign$, a ret_assign, and a ret_proc node. The call site nodes are connected to a $proc\_entry$ and $proc\_exit$ node representing the entry and exit of the called procedure.

Some control dependencies are added in the interprocedural case. Every node in the CFG of a procedure P including the $proc\_exit$ node is control dependent on its $proc\_entry$ node. So, if any node in P is sliced then its $proc\_entry$ node is sliced as well. The $call\_proc$ and the ret_proc nodes correspond to the same program statement, and the $call\_assign$ and the ret_assign nodes correspond to the assignments of actual arguments into formal arguments. So, the $call\_assign$ and the ret_assign nodes in a procedure call are control dependent on the $call\_proc$ and the ret_proc nodes respectively. Moreover, the ret_assign node is control dependent on the corresponding $proc\_exit$ node. Note that the sole purpose of these control dependencies is to include some relevant call site nodes into the slice. When a procedure containing procedure calls is being sliced by computing the SLV sets for each of its nodes, as soon as any ret_proc node is reached during the backward traversal of the CFG the slicing of the current procedure is postponed, and instead slicing continues to the called procedure (with some exceptions described later in this section). The called procedure is then sliced with respect to the SLV set obtained at the $proc\_exit$ node from the caller. This SLV set can be considered as the slicing criterion for the called procedure. Once the called procedure has been sliced, the slicing continues at the original call site.

Example 4.1. Let us consider the CFG in Fig. 2. Suppose the SLV analysis reaches node 15 (the *add_entry* node). Now the next visited node can be (i) node 11 corresponding to the first call site of procedure *add*, or (ii) node 13 corresponding to the second call site of the same procedure. If node 15 is reached from node 12 during the SLV analysis then the SLV analysis should continue to node 11, otherwise node 13.

We solve the calling-context problem by introducing a unique ghost variable g_n into the set $S[n]$ for the ret_assign node n in each call site. The transfer functions for the call site nodes are defined as follows.

$$S_{entry}(n) = \begin{cases} S_{exit}(n) & n : T \\ \bigcup_i S_{exit}(n)|_{x_i \to FV(e_i)} \cup \{g_n\} & n : ret\_assign \\ \bigcup_i S_{exit}(n)|_{x_i \to FV(e_i)} \setminus \{g_{rasgn(n)}\} & n : call\_assign \\ S_{exit}(n) \cap [vars(proc(n)) \cup G_V] & n : proc\_exit \\ S_{exit}(n) \cup [S_{exit}(retp(n)) \setminus & n : call\_proc \\ \quad kill(rasgn(n))] & \end{cases} \tag{6}$$

Here, $n : X$ represents that node n is of type X, T can be ret_proc or $proc\_entry$, and $proc(n)$ is the procedure containing the node n, $vars(P)$ returns the set of variables in the scope of procedure P, $retp(n)$ and $rasgn(n)$ return the ret_proc and ret_assign nodes respectively of the corresponding node n belonging to the same call site, g_n is the unique ghost variable for the call site containing the ret_assign node n, and G_V is the set of all ghost variables. Furthermore we define

$$S_{exit}(n)|_{x_i \to FV(e_i)} = \begin{cases} S_{exit}(n) \setminus \{x_i\} \cup FV(e_i) & \text{if } x_i \in S_{exit}(n) \\ S_{exit}(n) & \text{otherwise} \end{cases}$$

The $call\_assign$ and ret_assign nodes contain lists of concurrent assignments $x_1 = e_1, \ldots, x_m = e_m$ for some variables x_i and expressions e_i. As mentioned in Section 2, the $call\_assign$ node contains the assignments of actual input parameters into the formal input parameters, and the ret_assign node includes the assignments of formal output parameters into the actual output parameters.

Now suppose $n_1, \ldots, n_k$ are the $call\_assign$ nodes corresponding to k call sites calling any procedure P in the input program. The $proc\_entry$ node n_0 of procedure P is the successor node of each n_i. If the SLV analysis described in Section 3 reaches node n_0, the worklist will be updated by $W = W \cup \{(n, n_j, CFG)\}$ where $g_j \in S[n_j] \cap G_V$ represents the ghost variable corresponding to the call site j. That means the previous slicing of the caller procedure of P is resumed at call site j that has been postponed before. However, if $S[n_j] \cap G_V = \emptyset$, it means that the slicing of the current procedure is not invoked by any of its callers. Since all the caller procedures are backward reachable from the current procedure, they should be sliced as well. In such case, the worklist should be updated by $W = W \cup \{(n, n_i, CFG) \mid 1 \leq i \leq k\}$. These conditions can be included in line 20 of Algorithm 1.

Note that introducing the ghost variable in each call site makes the interprocedural data flow analysis very context sensitive. Different call patterns generate distinguishing sequences of ghost variables representing call strings obtained from the corresponding $proc\_entry$ nodes. Since every call site has a distinguishing ret_assign node, introducing a unique ghost variable at this node distinguishes calls from different call sites. Moreover, since we do not allow recursion, if the $Select$ function in Algorithm 1 picks the most recent element from the worklist, it does not merge data flow from different call sites. This is because even though ghost variables are inserted into the ret_assign nodes, they are discarded from the $call\_assign$ nodes. So, (6) merges contexts where relevant but splits contexts where appropriate.

4.1 Avoiding Unnecessary Multi-Pass Analysis of Procedures

If a procedure is called several times from multiple call sites, it may be required to slice a procedure more than once possibly with different slicing criteria. Here, the slicing criterion for a procedure corresponds to the SLV set of the *proc_exit* node in the CFG of the called procedure. If the *proc_exit* node of any procedure obtains a slicing criterion during the SLV analysis and it has been sliced before with the same slicing criterion, then the called procedure does not need to be analyzed again for slicing. Instead, the SLV set in the corresponding *proc_entry* node of the called procedure can be reused to continue the slicing in the caller procedure. This essentially requires that we save the SLV set at the *proc_exit* and *proc_entry* node of each procedure. If the newly generated slicing criterion is a superset of the previously generated slicing criterion, the previous analysis results can be reused in the extended analysis of the called procedure. This will reduce the negative impact of the context-sensitivity on the performance of the slicing.

Suppose procedure P is already sliced with criterion C_1. If it needs to be sliced again with criterion C_2 such that $C_2 \supset C_1$, then intuitively, it is enough to slice P with the criterion $(C_2 \backslash C_1)$. This may reduce the running time of the slicing, as a smaller slicing criterion on average should yield faster convergence of the fixed-point iteration in Algorithm 1. The intuition behind this optimization is as follows. Suppose a CFG node of the form $[x := e]^n$ is sliced during slicing the procedure P with the slicing criterion C_2. Then either $x \in C_2$, or $x \in S[n']$ and n' already belongs to the slice of P. If $x \in C_2$, then either $x \in C_1$ or $x \in (C_2 \setminus C_1)$ and hence node n should be sliced during slicing the procedure P with criterion either C_1 or $(C_2 \setminus C_1)$. However, when $x \in S[n']$ for some node n' already in the slice during slicing with criterion C_2, it can be proven inductively that n' belongs to the sliced set of P when it is sliced either with C_1 or with $(C_2 \setminus C_1)$. This intuition suggests that if slicing P generates the SLV set $S_{C_1}[k]$ and $S_{C_2 \backslash C_1}[k]$ when slicing P with criterion C_1 and $C_2 \backslash C_1$ at the $proc\_entry$ node k of P, then the SLV set $(S_{C_1}[k] \cup S_{C_2 \backslash C_1}[k])$ should be generated at k when P is sliced with criterion C_2. We leave a formal proof of this intuition as future work.

If $C_2 \subseteq C_1$ then P does not need to be sliced again at all, which definitely saves slicing time. But in order to continue slicing the caller of P without slicing P again, the *call_proc* node at the call site must obtain the right SLV set. This requires to keep the data dependence relation from the output parameters to the input parameters of the already analyzed procedure. During the update of any SLV set $S_{entry}(n)$ for any node n by the transfer function (3), we update the dependence relation $\mathbb{H}_P$, from procedure variables to procedure output parameters of P, which is initially empty. For any node n, suppose $kill(n) \subseteq S_{exit}(n)$. Then for all $v \in gen(n)$, we update first $\mathbb{H}_P[v]$ and then $\mathbb{H}_P[t]$ as follows:

$$\begin{aligned} \mathbb{H}_P[v] = \; & \mathbb{H}_P[v] \cup \{x \mid x \in kill(n), x \in out(proc(n))\} \cup \\ & \{x \mid x \in \mathbb{H}_P[t], t \in kill(n), t \notin out(proc(n))\} \\ \mathbb{H}_P[t] = \; & \emptyset \text{ for all } t \in kill(n), t \notin out(proc(n)) \end{aligned} \tag{7}$$

where $out(P)$ is the set of output arguments of P. Moreover, any set $S[n]$ for the conditional node $[c]^n$ is updated due to the control dependency edge (n, n') in the CDG where node n' is already in the slice. In such case, for all $v \in FV(c(n))$, we update $\mathbb{H}_P[v]$ as follows:

$$\begin{aligned} \mathbb{H}_P[v] = \; & \mathbb{H}_P[v] \cup \{x \mid x \in S_{exit}(n'), x \in out(proc(n'))\} \cup \\ & \{x \mid x \in \mathbb{H}_P[t], t \in S_{exit}(n'), t \notin out(proc(n'))\} \end{aligned} \tag{8}$$

Note that $\mathbb{H}_P$ keeps all the data and control dependences from procedure variables to formal output parameters. In order to obtain the dependences from formal output parameters to formal input parameters, we need an inverse relation. For any $v \in out(proc(n_k))$ at the $proc\_entry$ node n_k, the inverse data dependence relation $\mathbb{H}^{-1}[v]$ is obtained according to the following equation

$$\mathbb{H}_P^{-1}[v] = \{x \mid v \in \mathbb{H}_P[y], x \in rec(\mathbb{H}_P[y])\}$$

where $rec(\mathbb{H}_P[y])$ is defined as follows

$$rec(\mathbb{H}_P[y]) = \begin{cases} y & \text{if } y \in in(proc(n_k)) \\ rec(\mathbb{H}_P[z]) & \text{if } y \notin in(proc(n_k)), y \in \mathbb{H}_P[z] \end{cases}$$

where $in(P)$ is the set of input arguments of procedure P.

Theorem 1. *If the SLV analysis of procedure P with the slicing criterion C generates the SLV set S in the proc_entry node n_k (i.e. $S = S_{entry}(n_k)$), then $S = \{w \mid w \in \mathbb{H}_P^{-1}[v], v \in C\}$*

Proof. "$\Rightarrow$": Suppose $x \in S$. x can be included into S due to (1) data, or (2) control dependences. Case (1): there exists a CFG node $[t = e]^n$ of P where $x \in FV(e)$, there exists a path from n_k to n in the CFG of P and there is no node in between n_k and n in such path which defines x. That means $t \in kill(n)$, $x \in gen(n)$ and $kill(n) \subseteq S_{exit}(n)$ for which x is added to S by the transfer function. Also $x \in in(P)$ as it is not defined before its first use. If $t \in C, t \in \mathbb{H}_P[x]$ and $x \in \mathbb{H}_P^{-1}[t]$ as C contains only formal output variables. If $t \notin C$, suppose $t_1 \in \mathbb{H}_P[x]$ for some variable t_1. Then we have a sequence of updates of $\mathbb{H}_P$ on variables $t_1, t_2, \ldots, t_j = t$ at different iterations of the fixpoint computation such that $t_1 \in C$, and $t_i \in \mathbb{H}_P[t_{i+1}]$ for all $1 \leq i \leq j-1$. This implies that $x \in \mathbb{H}^{-1}[t_1]$. Case (2): there exists a path from n_k to some conditional node $[c]^n$ such that $x \in FV(c(n))$ and x is not defined by any node in this path. Otherwise it would not be the case that $x \in S$. Then according to equation (8), $t \in \mathbb{H}_P[x]$ for some $t \in out(P)$. According to the construction of $\mathbb{H}_P$ in equations (7 and 8), any $t \in out(P)$ can be included in $\mathbb{H}_P$ if $t \in S_{exit}(n')$ for some node n'. Since $C = S_{exit}(n'')$ where n'' is the *proc_exit* node of P, any $t \in out(P)$ and $t \in S_{exit}(n')$ is possible only if $t \in C = S_{exit}(n'')$ is propagated backward to $S_{exit}(n')$ by the iterations in Algorithm 1. So, $t \in C$, and $x \in \mathbb{H}_P^{-1}[t]$.
"$\Leftarrow$": Suppose $w \in \mathbb{H}_P^{-1}[v], v \in C$. This implies that $v \in out(P)$, $w \in in(P)$, and $v \in \mathbb{H}_P[w]$. Case (1): according to the construction of $\mathbb{H}_P$ in (7), there exists a node n in the CFG of P such that $kill(n) \subseteq S_{exit}(n)$, $w \in gen(n)$, and either (1) $v \in kill(n)$ or (2) $v \in \mathbb{H}_P[t]$ for some $t \in kill(n)$. In any case, w is added to $S_{entry}(n)$ by the transfer function. Case (2): according to the construction of $\mathbb{H}_P$ in (8), there exists a conditional node $[c]^n$ such that $w \in FV(c(n))$ and hence $w \in S_{entry}(n)$. We can assume without loss of generality that there exists a path from n_k to n in the CFG of P. If $w \notin kill(n')$ or $kill(n') \not\subseteq S_{exit}(n')$ for any node n' in the path from n_k to n, $w \in S_{entry}(n)$ implies that $w \in S_{entry}(n_k) = S$. However, if $w \in kill(n')$ and $kill(n') \subseteq S_{exit}(n')$, we argue that node n' does not exist with this condition. Let's assume that node n' have the assignment $w = e$. For any $l \in FV(e)$[1], $w \notin \mathbb{H}_P[l]$ as $w \in in(P)$. So, according to equation 7, $\mathbb{H}_P[w]$ is copied into $\mathbb{H}_P[l]$, $v \in \mathbb{H}_P[w]$ implies $v \in \mathbb{H}_P[l]$, and then $\mathbb{H}_P[w]$ is reset to empty set. As $v \notin \mathbb{H}_P[w]$ anymore due to this reset, $v \notin \mathbb{H}_P[w]$ at the *proc_entry* node n_k which is a contradiction. So, no such node n' exists such that $w \in kill(n')$ and $kill(n') \subseteq S_{exit}(n')$. □

Consider the situation where we slice procedure P first with slicing criterion C, and then with C' such that $C' \subseteq C$. As noted above, in this situation P does not need to be sliced again for C' as the slice will be contained in the slice obtained for C. However, the SLV set S for the *proc_entry* node of P must still be generated. Assume that $\mathbb{H}_P^{-1}$ was computed when slicing P with respect to C. According to Theorem 1, S can then be computed directly from $\mathbb{H}_P^{-1}$ as $\{w \mid w \in \mathbb{H}_P^{-1}[v], v \in C'\}$. Thus, the SLV dataflow analysis need not be applied to P anew.

Further improvements of efficiency in slicing are possible by delaying the slicing of any called procedure. Suppose a procedure P receives multiple requests for slicing with the slicing criteria $C_1, \ldots, C_k$. Then instead of slicing P k times, it is possible to slice P just once by combining all the slicing criteria $C = \bigcup_{1 \leq i \leq k} C_i$. This will yield the same slice as slicing with the different C_i. Let $\mathbb{H}^{-1}$ is generated when slicing with respect to C. Then, similarly, Theorem 1 allows us to compute the SLV sets for the respective *proc_entry* nodes for the slicing criteria C_i directly from $\mathbb{H}^{-1}$. The handling of the worklist in Algorithm 1 can be tuned to create opportunities for this optimization.

Example 4.2. Consider the program in Fig. 2. Assume that we wish to slice it on the statement "print(s)". This statement corresponds to node 20 in the CFG and the slicing criterion is $\{s\}$. The CFG is traversed backwards, the sequence of visited nodes are $3, 10, 9, 8, 14, 19$, and the SLV sets are $S[3] = S[10] = S[9] = S[8] = \{s\}$, $S[14] = S[19] = \{g_2\}$ where g_2 is the ghost variable at the second call site of procedure *add*. At node 19, the slicing criterion for procedure *add* is basically empty as $g_2 \notin vars(add)$, and slicing this procedure can be stopped. The *proc_call* node at this call site is node 7 and $S[7] = \{s\}$ according to (6). Next, traversing the CFG, the generated SLV sets are $S[6] = S[5] = \{sp\}$, $S[12] = \{z, g_1\}$, $S[19] = \{z, g_1\}$ and the slice set is $N_{slice} = \{6, 3\}$ where g_1 corresponds to the first call site of procedure *add*. Node 6 is sliced due to data dependency and as it is control dependent on node 3, 3 is also sliced. During slicing the procedure *add*, the SLV sets are $S[18] = \{z, g_1\}$, $S[17] = \{t, g_1\}$, $S[16] = S[15] = \{x, y, g_1\}$, $\mathbb{H}_{add}[x] = \mathbb{H}_{add}[y] = \{z\}$, $\mathbb{H}_{add}^{-1}[z] = \{x, y\}$, and $N_{slice} = \{6, 3, 5, 12, 17, 16, 15, 19\}$. $g_1 \in S[15]$ implies that the next visited node will be 11. This procedure continues until a fixpoint is reached. Note that procedure *add* does not need to be sliced again, instead when the control reaches node 19 and $z \in S[19]$ implies that $S[15]$ will include x and y as $\mathbb{H}_{add}^{-1}[z] = \{x, y\}$. The fixpoint is reached in 2 iterations for this program and the sliced program contains all nodes except nodes 10, 18, and 21.

5. Slicing Low-level Code

The SLV-based slicing algorithm presented so far relies on a high-level model of memory. The data dependence analyses, whether separate or integrated with the slicing, are based on program variables that are distinct and non-overlapping: an assignment to a variable x can thus not affect the value of any other variable $y \neq x$. Even if pointers to program variables are introduced, as long as this assumption holds it is well-known how to modify the data dependence analyses to cope with the possible aliasing that ensues.

However, for low-level code the memory model is different. Here a memory access is typically done to a numerical address, accessing a certain number of bits. Both the addresses and the sizes of accesses may vary dynamically (an example of the latter is block transfer instructions, where whole memory blocks are copied). Thus, it is not entirely straightforward to decide whether two memory accesses may overlap or not. Here we will sketch a way to analyze memory references to decide this. As the data flow analyses under consideration are may analyses, we are interested in approaches that can safely decide when accesses can not overlap: if they surely don't, then they cannot carry a data dependence. On the other hand, if there is a possible overlap then we will assume that there is a possible data dependence. This will yield a safe analysis where all data dependencies surely are included in the result.

5.1 The Memory Model

We will assume the memory model of the language ALF [17, 19], which is the language analyzed by the WCET analysis tool SWEET [1, 32]. ALF is designed to be able to faithfully represent both high- and low-level code, and its memory model,which is similar to the monolithic memory model [37], is chosen accordingly. Memory in ALF is organized into frames. Each frame is a separate memory area. An ALF address consists of a so-called "frameref",

[1] We are ignoring the case that $FV(e) = \emptyset$ for any input parameter w before its first use as this is unusual and it will complicate the proof and the definition of $\mathbb{H}_P$, however it is doable.

which can be seen as a symbolic base pointer to the frame, and a numerical offset. This memory model is close to the one for unlinked code, where base addresses are not yet resolved. It is assumed that memory accesses to different frames never overlap, whereas accesses to the same frame may do. This memory model supports both the high- and low-level view. If a high-level language is translated to ALF, then distinct variables are preferably mapped to single, distinct frames with the same number of bits as the variables they represent. For low-level code larger memory areas might be mapped to frames: e.g., for executable binaries, the data memory may be modeled by a single frame. Memory accesses in ALF use an address as above, and a specified size. Thus an access can be represented by a triple (f, o, s), where f is a symbolic frameref, o is an offset (non-negative, in bits) and s is a size (same). The semantics is that the bits o to $o + s - 1$ are accessed in frame f. Two memory accesses (f, o, s) and (f', o', s') will thus overlap iff $f = f'$, and $[o, o + s - 1] \cap [o', o' + s' - 1] \neq \emptyset$.

5.2 Abstract Domains

Data flow analysis on ALF code must be based on memory access triples rather than program variables. Also, to decide def-use chains, possible overlap of triples must be considered rather than program variables. Thus, the data flow analysis should be preceded by a value analysis that yields safe overapproximations to the memory access triples (f, o, s). Such analyses are standard, and can be developed within the framework of abstract interpretation [12, 34]. The set of possible triples T for a memory access in the code will then be approximated by an "abstract triple" $T^{\#}$ in an abstract domain, where $T^{\#}$ represents a set of triples that surely contains T.

The scenario described above is somewhat simplified. Since not only addresses depend on values, but also values may depend on addresses, it is in general not possible to first perform a value analysis and then an address analysis. Thus, the address and value analyses have to be combined into a joint analysis where approximated addresses and values are computed concurrently. What is needed is a combined abstract domain for these where the analysis can be carried out by a fixed-point iteration using standard methods.

If $\mathbf{F}$ is the set of framerefs in the program under analysis, and $\mathbf{Int}$ is the domain of integer intervals, then two possible abstract domains for memory access triples are $\mathcal{P}(\mathbf{F}) \times \mathbf{Int} \times \mathbf{Int}$ and $\mathcal{P}(\mathbf{F} \times \mathbf{Int} \times \mathbf{Int})$. The first domain represents set of triples by "abstract triples" (F, I_o, I_s) where F is a set of framerefs, and I_o and I_s are intervals surely containing the possible offsets and sizes, respectively. The second domain represents set of triples by finite set of abstract triples $\{(f_1, I_{o1}, I_{s1}), \cdots, (f_n, I_{on}, I_{sn})\}$ where $f_1, \cdots, f_n$ are frame-refs and I_{ok}, I_{sk} are intervals surely containing the possible offsets and sizes for the accesses to frame f_k. The second domain allows for more precise representations than the first, but is also potentially more costly. Both abstract domains are standard within abstract interpretation, and it is well-known how to implement value analyses that compute abstract values in these domains for different memory accesses in a program.

5.3 Abstract Operations

If abstract values are computed for memory accesses by a value analysis, safe tests for overlaps will look as follows. With the domain $\mathcal{P}(\mathbf{F}) \times \mathbf{Int} \times \mathbf{Int}$, $(F, [l_o, u_o], [l_s, u_s])$ and $(F', [l'_o, u'_o], [l'_s, u'_s])$ represent possibly overlapping accesses if $F \cap F' \neq \emptyset$, and $[l_o, u_o + u_s - 1] \cap [l'_o, u'_o + u'_s - 1] \neq \emptyset$. For $\mathcal{P}(\mathbf{F} \times \mathbf{Int} \times \mathbf{Int})$, $\{(f_1, [l_{o1}, u_{o1}], [l_{s1}, u_{s1}]), \cdots, (f_n, [l_{om}, u_{om}], [l_{sm}, u_{sm}])\}$ and $\{(f'_1, [l'_{o1}, u'_{o1}], [l'_{s1}, u'_{s1}]), \cdots, (f'_n, [l'_{on}, u'_{on}], [l'_{sn}, u'_{sn}])\}$ represent possibly overlapping accesses if there exists i, j such that $f_i = f'_j$, and $[l_{oi}, u_{oi} + u_{si} - 1] \cap [l'_{oj}, u'_{oj} + u'_{sj} - 1] \neq \emptyset$. These overlap tests can be used when checking for possible data dependencies in the PDG-based slicing.

if	$\mathbf{M_1 \setminus M_2}$	$\mathbf{M_1 \cup M_2}$	$\mathbf{M_1 \cap M_2}$
$f_1 \neq f_2$	$\{M_1\}$	$\{M_1, M_2\}$	$\emptyset$
$(l_{o2} > sup_1 \vee l_{o1} > sup_2) \wedge f_1 = f_2$	$\{M_1\}$	$\{M_1, M_2\}$	$\emptyset$
$l_{o1} \leq l_{o2} \leq sup_1 \wedge sup_2 \geq sup_1 \wedge f_1 = f_2$	$\{M_3\}$	$\{M_4\}$	$\{M_7\}$
$l_{o1} \leq l_{o2} \leq sup_1 \wedge sup_1 \geq sup_2 \wedge f_1 = f_2$	$\{M_3, M_5\}$	$\{M_4\}$	$\{M_2\}$
$l_{o2} \leq l_{o1} \leq sup_2 \wedge sup_2 \leq sup_1 \wedge f_1 = f_2$	$\{M_5\}$	$\{M_6\}$	$\{M_8\}$
$l_{o2} \leq l_{o1} \leq sup_2 \wedge sup_1 \leq sup_2 \wedge f_1 = f_2$	$\emptyset$	$\{M_6\}$	$\{M_1\}$

Table 1: Abstract operations of two memory accesses $M_1 \equiv (f_1, [l_{o1}, u_{o1}], [l_{s1}, u_{s1}])$ and $M_2 \equiv (f_2, [l_{o2}, u_{o2}], [l_{s2}, u_{s2}])$.
Let
(i) $M_3 \equiv (f_1, [l_{o1}, l_{o1}], [l_{o2} - l_{o1}, l_{o2} - l_{o1}])$
(ii) $M_4 \equiv (f_1, [l_{o1}, max(sup_{max} - s_{max} + 1, l_{o1})], [s_{min}, s_{max}])$
(iii) $M_5 \equiv (f_1, [sup_2 + 1, sup_2 + 1], [sup_{max} - sup_2, sup_{max} - sup_2])$
(iv) $M_6 \equiv (f_1, [l_{o2}, max(sup_{max} - s_{max} + 1, l_{o2})], [s_{min}, s_{max}])$
(vi) $M_7 \equiv (f_1, [l_{o_{max}}, l_{o_{max}}], [sup_{min} - l_{o_{max}}, sup_{min} - l_{o_{max}}])$
(vii) $M_8 \equiv (f_1, [l_{o1}, l_{o1}], [sup_2 - l_{o1}, sup_2 - l_{o1}])$
where $sup_1 = u_{o1} + u_{s1} - 1$, $sup_2 = u_{o2} + u_{s2} - 1$, $l_{o_{max}} = max(l_{o1}, l_{o2})$ $sup_{min} = min(sup_1, sup_2)$, $sup_{max} = max(sup_1, sup_2)$, $s_{min} = min(l_{s1}, l_{s2})$, and $s_{max} = max(u_{s1}, u_{s2})$

Set operations for the abstract domains above can be built on top of the operations on $\mathbf{F} \times \mathbf{Int} \times \mathbf{Int}$ that are defined in Table 1. For instance, if $S_1, S_2 \in \mathcal{P}(\mathbf{F} \times \mathbf{Int} \times \mathbf{Int})$ then $S_1 \setminus S_2 = \bigcup_{M_2 \in S_2} \bigcup_{M_1 \in S_1} M_1 \setminus M_2$. Other set operations can be computed accordingly. However, for $\mathcal{P}(\mathbf{F}) \times \mathbf{Int} \times \mathbf{Int}$, the conditions $f_1 = f_2$ and $f_1 \neq f_2$ should be replaced by $F_1 \cap F_2 \neq \emptyset$ and $F_1 \cap F_2 = \emptyset$, respectively, in the definitions in Table 1.

5.4 Producing Executable Slices

Low-level code often contains *jump* or *goto* statements. The SLV-based slicing algorithm introduced in the previous sections does not include these statements in the slice, as it is based on a CFG model where the nodes are conditions and assignments, and jumps are implicitly represented as edges. Also if explicit *goto* nodes are present in the CFG they will typically not be included by a data-dependence based slicing, since they do not perform any reads or writes.

If *gotos* are not properly included, then that might change the semantics of the slice. Informally the semantics of the slice should be such that the same values are computed for the variables in the slicing criterion, at the respective program points, as in the original program. So, for instance, if the slicing criterion is within a loop then the loop structure will typically have to be preserved even if most of the loop is sliced away.

An example is shown in Fig. 4a, where the slicing criterion is the variable x at `L3` and the boxed statements constitute the slice. In this example, the slicing criterion is located within a loop where `x` is incremented for each iteration. In the computed slice the loop structure is removed, and `x` will only be incremented once. This is clearly not the original semantics for the slicing criterion. To restore this semantics, the statements `goto L1` and `goto L3` must be included to form the loop structure anew.

Fig. 4b gives another example, with slicing criterion `x` at `L2`. Here the order of executing the statements can be garbled if the proper *goto* statements are not preserved in the slice. In the original program `x` will be incremented if `c` is true and decremented if `c` is false, but if no *gotos* are included then `x` will always be incremented.

```
L1: if(c) goto L3;
    else { y := y+1;
           goto L2;}
L2: update(c); goto L1;
L3: x := x+1;
    if(P) goto L1;
```

(a)

```
if(c) goto L1;
y:=-1;
goto L2;
L1: y:=1;
L2: x:=x+y
```

(b)

Figure 4: Illustrating the importance of preserving (a) loop structure, and (b) flow order in the sliced program

Thus, in order to preserve the loop structure and the flow order in the sliced program, it is important to include the relevant *goto* statements and (when relevant) their associated control predicates. Also, at the same time we would like to keep the sliced program minimal. In particular, our assumption is that it is sufficient to include the following nodes from the CFG of the given program into the sliced program that preserves the loop structure and flow order:

- We include all *strongly live goto* nodes according to the definition 5.3 below
- We include all control structures that become live due to strongly live goto nodes.

In order to define *strongly live goto* nodes, we borrow the concept of *lexical successor tree*.

Definition 5.1 (Lexical Successor Tree [2]). *Two statements s and s′ in the program code constitute a parent node and its immediate successor node respectively in the lexical successor tree if during the execution of the program, whenever control reaches s′, then replacing s′ by skip yields a program flow to s.*

Note that in the presence of unstructured code, the CFG representation loses the information of whether two statements in the program code are consecutive or not. We can retrieve such information by using the lexical successor tree which can be constructed in a purely syntax directed manner [2]. Given a set of nodes S in the lexical successor tree T, two nodes n_1, n_k are immediate successors with respect to S if there is a path $n_1, n_2, \cdots, n_k$ in T and $S \cap \{n_2, \cdots, n_{k-1}\} = \emptyset$, and we say that $(n_1, n_k) \in T_S$. If $(n_1, n_k) \notin T_S$, we say that n_1, n_k are non-lexically adjacent.

Given the CFG $(N, Flow)$ and the set of nodes $S \subseteq N$ that does not include any goto nodes, an edge is considered live according to the following definition.

Definition 5.2 (Live Edges [21]). *Given a set of nodes S in the CFG $(N, Flow)$, an edge from a branch node $b \in N$ to its non-syntactic successor (e.g. the first statement in the else block of an if-then-else) is live only if $b \in S$. All other CFG edges are always live.*

A goto node g is considered strongly live with respect to the given set S according to the following definition.

Definition 5.3 (Strongly Live Goto Node). *A goto node $g \in N$ becomes live with respect to S, if (1) there exists a node in S that is reachable from g by traversing live edges containing at least one non-lexically adjacent edge, and (2a) g is reachable from any node in S by traversing live edges or (2b) g is the descendant of a node reachable via live edges that does not have any lexical predecessor.*

The PDG based slicing algorithm can be adapted according to the 'Strong, syntax-preserving, Ottenstein-more" slicing algorithm in [21] in order to preserve the termination behaviour and flow-order. Our SLV-based slicing Algorithm 1 can be extended to produce similar slices as follows:

1. First, two boolean variables $Live[n]$ and $NonLex[n]$ is maintained for each node n in the CFG. These two variables represent whether the node n is reachable and non-lexically adjacent by at least one edge respectively from any node in S by traversing backward live edges. Initially, $Live[n] = yes$ for all $n \in N_{slice}$ and no otherwise, and $NonLex[n] = no$ for all n in the CFG. An auxiliary workset W' is also maintained which is initially empty and the iteration of algorithm 1 terminates when $W \cup W' = \emptyset$. A *lexical successor tree* T is maintained that contains all the successor relations.
2. Next, for each node n in the CFG, a set $G[n]$ is maintained which contains the potential goto nodes to be included in the slice if n is included in the slice as it meets the condition (2a) of Definition 5.3. Initially all $G[n]$ are empty.
3. During the iteration of the algorithm, for any $(n, n', CFG) \in W$, $Live[n']$ is updated according to the following equation:

$$Live[n'] = \begin{cases} yes & \text{if } Live[n] = yes \wedge (n, n') \in F \\ & \text{is live w.r.t } N_{slice} \\ no & \text{otherwise} \end{cases}$$

   $NonLex[n']$ is updated as follows:

$$NonLex[n'] = \begin{cases} yes & \text{if } (NonLex[n] = yes \vee (n', n) \\ & \notin T_{N_{slice}}) \wedge n' \notin N_{slice} \\ no & otherwise \end{cases}$$

4. For any $(n, n', CFG) \in W$, if $Live[n'] \wedge NonLex[n'] = yes$ and n' is a *goto* node, it is a potential *goto* node to be included in the slice as it meets the condition (1) of definition 5.3. So, we update $G[n'] = G[n'] \cup G[n] \cup \{n\}$. If n' is not a *control-predicate* and $(n, n') \in F$ is live w.r.t N_{slice}, $G[n'] = G[n'] \cup G[n]$; $G[n']$ is unchanged in all other cases. If $Live[n'] \wedge NonLex[n'] = no$, W' is updated by $W' = W' \cup \{(n, n', CFG)\}$.
5. During the iteration of Algorithm 1, if $n \in N_{slice}$ and $G[n]$ is not empty, add all the goto nodes in $G[n]$ to the slice as it meets condition (2a) of definition 5.3. Any conditional node n is also included in the slice if $G[n]$ is not empty and there exists $n' \in G[n]$ which is already included in the slice as the conditional structure controls a live goto node included in the slice.
6. At the end of the iteration, check for any node n such that $G[n]$ is not empty and it does not have any lexical predecessor node. Add n and all $n' \in G[n]$ into the slice (as condition (2b) of definition on 5.3 is satisfied).

In order to prove the correctness (as defined in [29]) of the above sketch, it needs to be proved that (i) Definition 5.3 of strongly live goto nodes has *semantic effect* (Definition 0 in [29]) on N_{slice}, and (ii) any goto node other than the strongly live goto nodes in the program does not have any semantic effect on N_{slice}. Intuitively, any strongly live goto node with respect to N_{slice} causes program flow to a node in N_{slice} and thus have a semantic effect on N_{slice} if it is removed from the sliced program. Furthermore, removing lexically adjacent strongly live goto nodes keep N_{slice} minimal. We leave the proof of correctness of the above sketch as future work.

6. Experimental Evaluation

We have implemented the the SLV-based and the PDG-based slicing in SWEET, and run them on a number of benchmark programs

		P_{BV}		P_{PDG}		P_{SLV}	
Benchmarks	N_{CFG}	N_{BV}	T_{BV}	N_{PDG}	T_{PDG}	N_{SLV}	T_{SLV}
loop	39	26	2	26	67	26	35
expint*	139	59	0	51	1	51	1
cnt	145	55	0	21	0	21	0
bmp	161	105	3	40	4	40	4
edn*	639	455	1	56	4	56	3
edn2	1391	1300	19	24	39	24	14
fir	1569	800	1	48	6	48	5
nsichneu	1860	5	6	4	19	4	4
esab_mod	2349	817	2	802	57	802	54
bmp2	3725	3273	348	41	306	41	16
arrayloop	12044	12029	14	33	33	33	27

Table 2: Comparison among three slicing algorithms. N represents number of nodes, and T represents time measured in seconds. Examples marked with $*$ are generated from ARM7 binaries.

obtained mostly from the Mälardalen WCET benchmark suite [18]. The original benchmark programs are written in C, and have been transformed into ALF for subsequent analysis by SWEET. In order to evaluate the effectiveness of our analysis for low-level code we have first compiled some benchmarks into ARM7 binaries (obtained by the GCC ARM7 compiler version 4.6.1), and translated the resulting binaries into ALF. Other benchmarks have been manipulated in order to make the memory model more low-level, by putting several variables into the same struct or array. Since the ALF translator that we have used then generates a single frame for them, the data dependence analysis will have to decide offsets and sizes of memory accesses to resolve the dependencies as described in Section 5.3. All experiments have been performed on a 1.7 GHz Intel Core i7 processor with 8GB RAM.

The current implementation of the SLV-based slicing algorithm is interprocedural, and several of the benchmark codes contain function calls. However, none of the optimization described in Section 4.1 are implemented in the current version. The data dependency analysis is based on abstract operations over the interval domain as described in Section 5. So, each element in the SLV sets as well as the gen and $kill$ sets contains the memory access triples (f, o, s) where o and s are intervals. Two versions of the PDG-based slicing have been implemented in SWEET. They differ in the RD analysis for computing the data dependencies: both use bit vectors to represent the RD sets, but the first implementation only distinguishes frames whereas the second also considers offsets and possible overlaps within frames as described in Section 5.3. The first version is thus less precise but faster, whereas the second should compute the same slices as our SLV-based algorithm. The control dependencies are computed using post-dominators. All the analyses use Steensgard's points-to analysis [41] for checking possible memory aliasing between frames. No further optimizations are implemented in any of the slicing algorithms, and none of them implement the generation of executable code (the computed slices are sets of nodes in the CFG).

Table 2 compares the results of the three slicing algorithms: the PDG-based slicing algorithm that operates on frame level, P_{BV}, the PDG-based slicing that also considers offsets and possible overlaps within frames, P_{PDG}, and the SLV-based slicing algorithm, P_{SLV}. The slicing criteria have in all runs been either the loop conditions or the conditional statements. These are typically the slicing criteria used when slicing is performed in the context of WCET analysis [13, 40], which is our primary client application of slicing. Note that the optimizations described in Section 3.3 have not been applied even though we used loop conditions or conditional statements as slicing criterion. So, our experimental results should not be biased to this kind of slicing criterion.

The algorithms have been run on the example programs several times, with the same slicing criteria, and the running times have been averaged and rounded afterwards. N_{CFG} is the number of nodes in the CFG of the analysed ALF program. N_{BV}, N_{PDG} and N_{SLV} stand for the number of nodes in the sliced programs obtained from the P_{BV}, P_{PDG}, and P_{SLV} slicing algorithms respectively. T_{BV}, T_{PDG}, and T_{SLV} are the running times, measured in seconds, of the corresponding algorithms. Note that there is a small variation in the number of nodes in the slices obtained for P_{SLV} and P_{PDG}. This is due to the fact that the slices computed by P_{SLV} consist of CFG nodes whereas those computed by P_{PDG} consist of PDG nodes. The call site nodes in the CFG and PDG in SWEET have slightly different representations, which yields the difference. When this discrepancy is compensated for, the number of nodes in the slices are the same for the two algorithms for all benchmarks and the slices indeed represent the same code in all cases, as expected. It is the "cleaned" number of nodes that is given in Table 2.

It can be observed from the above table that $N_{BV} \geq N_{PDG}$ and $N_{BV} \geq N_{SLV}$ for all benchmark programs. This illustrates that P_{BV} is much less precise than P_{SLV} for slicing the low-level code. Sometimes, this loss of precision by the P_{BV} algorithm is very significant compared to the other two algorithms. For example, in the *edn2* benchmark, the number of nodes in the slice computed by P_{BV} is 1391 compared to 24 nodes by P_{SLV}. This result is obvious as P_{BV} is loosing a lot of precision in computing the SDG. This is due to the fact that if a statement writes in a frame and another statement reads from the same frame but from another location, P_{BV} considers that they are data dependent which is not necessarily the case.

Regarding the execution time of the slicing algorithms, $T_{SLV} \leq T_{PDG}$ in all examples. Thus, P_{SLV} is faster than P_{PDG} for computing a single slice for these benchmark codes. This is because the construction of the SDG in P_{PDG} is slower compared to running a single SLV analysis. For small examples, the timing difference is not significant. However, for large examples like *bmp2* the difference in execution time is large: for instance, P_{SLV} takes 16 seconds whereas P_{PDG} takes approximately 5 minutes for the *bmp2* program. This indicates that P_{SLV} scales better than P_{PDG} when computing single slices.

P_{BV} is faster than P_{PDG} or P_{SLV} in almost all examples as it does not require the value analysis to resolve data dependencies within frames. But this speed advantage comes at the cost of seriously deteriorated precision in the computed slices.

7. Related Work

Since the seminal work of Weiser [44, 46], there has been much work on different kinds of program slicing. Different approaches to slicing include static [35, 44, 46], quasi-static [43], conditioned [10], dynamic [28], and amorphous [20] slicing, of which static slicing techniques are the ones that are most comparable to our approaches. Solving the dataflow equations, the reachability problem in a dependence graph, and using information-flow relations are the most dominant static slicing approaches found in the literature. Our SLV-based slicing technique is similar to the approach of Weiser [22, 44, 46] and Lyle [33]. The computational complexity of Weiser's approach for the intraprocedural slicing is $O(v \times |(N + Flow)|)$ [42] which is higher than our intraprocedural SLV-based slicing algorithm. Our contemporary work [27] also uses the SLV analysis to do slicing on the fly, but it is based on a different way to solve the data flow equations that works on well-structured intraprocedural code.

Ottenstein and Ottenstein [35] proposed that program slicing can be viewed as a reachability problem on the program dependence graph. Following this work, reachability-based slicing techniques that work on PDGs or variants of them have been used by many researchers [6, 23–25, 39]. The emphasis of these works have been on properties such as precision, complexity, applicability, and scalability. All these approaches compute all the dependencies of the given program before the slicing, which is good when the same code is sliced many times (since the cost for computing the dependencies then can be amortized over the slices). There have been several empirical studies and survey papers [7, 8, 42, 48] that compare the reachability-based slicing techniques. Unstructured program slicing was considered by Ball and Horwitz [4], Choi and Ferrante [11], Agrawal [2], Kumar and Horwitz [29]: all these techniques are based on the PDG or its variants. The approaches of Lyle [33], Gallagher and Lyle [15], and Jiang et al. [26] are based on solving dataflow equations, and the solutions are either conservative or incorrect. We are not aware of many efforts for slicing low-level code except CodeSurfer/x86 [3]. CodeSurfer/x86 implements the PDG-based slicing on x86 executables, and data dependencies among memory accesses are computed using a value-set analysis ("VSA") which is based on congruences and intervals. Our approach to slicing of low-level code uses a simpler value analysis (intervals) but attempts to use information about the ALF frames to increase the precision. This is somewhat comparable to using debug information from a compiler.

8. Conclusion and Future Work

Program slicing extracts the program parts that can possibly affect certain slicing criteria. In this paper, we have developed a lightweight interprocedural slicing technique that performs better when few slices of a given program are required. We perform slicing on-the-fly during a variant of the SLV data flow analysis on the CFG representation, and thus we avoid computing an explicit data dependence graph. Our slicing technique handles low-level code using abstract interpretation based value analysis, and we also show how it can be extended to produce executable slices. Comparing our approach with PDG based slicing, we obtain exactly the same accuracy as in PDG-based slicing on a set of benchmark codes and our algorithm is at least as fast, and sometimes much faster, than the PDG-based algorithm on this set of benchmark codes. Our results indicate that our algorithm scales better since we obtain the largest speedups for larger benchmark codes.

Future works include implementing all the features of SLV-based slicing that have been described here, and make an empirical evaluation in order to compare our approach with other slicing approaches over a set of larger programs. We would like to know about the program patterns for which the SLV-based slicing performs better. For example, when slicing the same code many times, with different slicing criteria then we would like to know the break-even point where SLV-based slicing gets worse than PDG-based slicing. We would also like to implement various optimization techniques in order to improve the performance of SLV-based slicing. For example, the performance of the slicing can most likely be improved by a judicious choice of iteration order [34].

Acknowledgments

The research presented in this paper is supported by the European Commission through the Marie Curie IAPP 251413 APARTS project, by the Swedish Foundation for Strategic Research under the SYNOPSIS project, and by the Knowledge Foundation through the TOCSYC project. We would like to thank Linus Källberg for his help with the SWEET WCET tool, Niklas Holsti for providing us the ALF code generated from ARM7 binaries, and the anonymous reviewers for their comments that helped us to improve the paper.

References

[1] SWEET home page, 2011. URL `http://www.mrtc.mdh.se/projects/wcet/sweet/`.

[2] H. Agrawal. On slicing programs with jump statements. In *Proc. ACM SIGPLAN 1994 Conference on Programming Language Design and Implementation*, PLDI '94, pages 302–312, New York, NY, USA, 1994. ACM.

[3] G. Balakrishnan and T. Reps. WYSINWYX: What you see is not what you execute. *ACM Trans. Program. Lang. Syst.*, 32(6):23:1–23:84, Aug. 2010.

[4] T. Ball and S. Horwitz. Slicing programs with arbitrary control-flow. In *Proc. First International Workshop on Automated and Algorithmic Debugging*, AADEBUG '93, pages 206–222, London, UK, UK, 1993. Springer-Verlag.

[5] S. Bates and S. Horwitz. Incremental program testing using program dependence graphs. In *Proc. 20th ACM SIGPLAN-SIGACT Symposium on Principles of Programming Languages*, POPL '93, pages 384–396, New York, NY, USA, 1993. ACM.

[6] D. Binkley. Precise executable interprocedural slices. *ACM Lett. Program. Lang. Syst.*, 2(1-4):31–45, Mar. 1993.

[7] D. Binkley and M. Harman. A large-scale empirical study of forward and backward static slice size and context sensitivity. In *Proc. International Conference on Software Maintenance*, ICSM '03, pages 44–, Washington, DC, USA, 2003. IEEE Computer Society.

[8] D. Binkley and M. Harman. A survey of empirical results on program slicing. In *Advances in Computers*, volume 62 of *Advances in Computers*, pages 105 – 178. Elsevier, 2004.

[9] D. Binkley, S. Horwitz, and T. Reps. Program integration for languages with procedure calls. *ACM Trans. Softw. Eng. Methodol.*, 4(1): 3–35, Jan. 1995.

[10] G. Canfora. Conditioned program slicing. *Information and Software Technology*, 40(11-12):595–607, Dec. 1998.

[11] J.-D. Choi and J. Ferrante. Static slicing in the presence of goto statements. *ACM Trans. Program. Lang. Syst.*, 16(4):1097–1113, July 1994.

[12] P. Cousot and R. Cousot. Abstract interpretation: A unified lattice model for static analysis of programs by construction or approximation of fixpoints. In *Proc. 4th ACM SIGACT-SIGPLAN Symposium on Principles of Programming Languages*, proc. POPL '77, pages 238–252, New York, NY, USA, 1977. ACM.

[13] A. Ermedahl, C. Sandberg, J. Gustafsson, S. Bygde, and B. Lisper. Loop bound analysis based on a combination of program slicing, abstract interpretation, and invariant analysis. In *Proc. Seventh International Workshop on Worst-Case Execution Time Analysis, (WCET2007)*, July 2007.

[14] J. Ferrante, K. J. Ottenstein, and J. D. Warren. The program dependence graph and its use in optimization. *ACM Trans. Program. Lang. Syst.*, 9(3):319–349, July 1987.

[15] K. B. Gallagher and J. R. Lyle. Using program slicing in software maintenance. *IEEE Trans. Softw. Eng.*, 17(8):751–761, Aug. 1991.

[16] R. Gupta, M. Jean, M. J. Harrold, and M. L. Soffa. An approach to regression testing using slicing. In *Proc. Conference on Software Maintenance*, pages 299–308. IEEE Computer Society Press, 1992.

[17] J. Gustafsson, A. Ermedahl, B. Lisper, C. Sandberg, and L. Källberg. ALF - a language for WCET flow analysis. In N. Holsti, editor, *Proc. 9th International Workshop on Worst-Case Execution Time Analysis (WCET09)*. OCG, June 2009.

[18] J. Gustafsson, A. Betts, A. Ermedahl, and B. Lisper. The Mälardalen WCET benchmarks - past, present and future. In *Proc. 10th International Workshop on Worst-Case Execution Time Analysis*, July 2010. URL `http://www.es.mdh.se/publications/1895-`.

[19] J. Gustafsson, A. Ermedahl, and B. Lisper. ALF (ARTIST2 language for flow analysis) specification. Technical report, Oct. 2011. URL `http://www.es.mdh.se/publications/1138-`.

[20] M. Harman, D. Binkley, and S. Danicic. Amorphous program slicing. In *Software Focus*, pages 70–79. IEEE Computer Society Press, 1997.

[21] M. Harman, A. Lakhotia, and D. Binkley. Theory and algorithms for slicing unstructured programs. *Information and Software Technology*, (7):549–565, 2006.

[22] H. R. H.K.N. Leung. Comments on program slicing. *IEEE Transactions on Software Engineering*, SE-13, 12:1370–1371, 1987.

[23] S. Horwitz, T. Reps, and D. Binkley. Interprocedural slicing using dependence graphs. In *Proc. ACM SIGPLAN 1988 Conference on Programming Language Design and Implementation*, PLDI '88, pages 35–46, New York, NY, USA, 1988. ACM.

[24] C. R. C. J. C. Hawang, M. W. Du. Finding program slices for recursive procedures. In *Proc. 12th Annual International Computer Software and Applications Conference*, COMPSAC '88, pages 220–227, Chicago, 1988.

[25] D. Jackson and E. J. Rollins. A new model of program dependences for reverse engineering. In *Proc. 2Nd ACM SIGSOFT Symposium on Foundations of Software Engineering*, SIGSOFT '94, pages 2–10, New York, NY, USA, 1994. ACM.

[26] J. Jiang, X. Zhou, and D. J. Robson. Program slicing for C — the problems in implementation. In *Proceedings, Conference on Software Maintenance 1991*, pages 182–190, Sorrento, Italy, Oct. 15–17, 1991. IEEE Computer Society Press.

[27] H. Khanfar. Objects-based slicing. Technical Report MDH-MRTC-284/2014-1-SE, School of Innovation, Design and Engineering, Mälardalen University, May 2014.

[28] B. Korel. Dynamic program slicing. In *Information Processing Letters, 29 Oct*, 1988.

[29] S. Kumar and S. Horwitz. Better slicing of programs with jumps and switches. In *Proc. 5th International Conference on Fundamental Approaches to Software Engineering*, FASE '02, pages 96–112, London, UK, UK, 2002. Springer-Verlag.

[30] J. R. Larus, S. Ch, and R. Y. Using tracing and dynamic slicing to tune compilers. Technical report, University of Wisconsin Computer Sciences Department, 1993.

[31] B. Lisper. Fully automatic, parametric worst-case execution time analysis. In J. Gustafsson, editor, *Proc. Third International Workshop on Worst-Case Execution Time (WCET) Analysis*, pages 77–80, July 2003.

[32] B. Lisper. SWEET – a tool for WCET flow analysis. In B. Steffen, editor, *Proc. 6th International Symposium on Leveraging Applications of Formal Methods (ISOLA'14)*, lncs, pages 482–485, Korfu, Greece, oct 2014. Springer-Verlag.

[33] J. R. Lyle. *Evaluating Variations on Program Slicing for Debugging (Data-flow, Ada)*. PhD thesis, College Park, MD, USA, 1984.

[34] F. Nielson, H. R. Nielson, and C. Hankin. *Principles of Program Analysis*. Springer-Verlag New York, Inc., Secaucus, NJ, USA, 1999. ISBN 3540654100.

[35] K. J. Ottenstein and L. M. Ottenstein. The program dependence graph in a software development environment. *SIGSOFT Softw. Eng. Notes*, 9(3):177–184, Apr. 1984.

[36] R. T. Prosser. Applications of boolean matrices to the analysis of flow diagrams. In *Papers Presented at the December 1-3, 1959, Eastern Joint IRE-AIEE-ACM Computer Conference*, IRE-AIEE-ACM '59 (Eastern), pages 133–138, New York, NY, USA, 1959. ACM.

[37] Z. Rakamarić and A. J. Hu. A scalable memory model for low-level code. In N. D. Jones and M. Müller-Olm, editors, *Proc. 10th International Conference on Verification, Model Checking and Abstract Interpretation (VMCAI 2009)*, volume 5403 of *Lecture Notes in Computer Science*, pages 290–304. Springer, Jan. 2009.

[38] T. Reps, S. Horwitz, M. Sagiv, and G. Rosay. Speeding up slicing. In *Proceedings of the 2Nd ACM SIGSOFT Symposium on Foundations of Software Engineering*, SIGSOFT '94, pages 11–20, New York, NY, USA, 1994. ACM.

[39] T. Reps, S. Horwitz, and M. Sagiv. Precise interprocedural dataflow analysis via graph reachability. In *Proc. 22Nd ACM SIGPLAN-SIGACT Symposium on Principles of Programming Languages*, Proc. POPL '95, pages 49–61, New York, NY, USA, 1995. ACM.

[40] C. Sandberg, A. Ermedahl, J. Gustafsson, and B. Lisper. Faster WCET flow analysis by program slicing. In *Proc. ACM SIGPLAN Conference on Languages, Compilers and Tools for Embedded Systems (LCTES2006)*. ACM, June 2006.

[41] B. Steensgaard. Points-to analysis in almost linear time. In *Proceedings of the 23rd ACM SIGPLAN-SIGACT Symposium on Principles of Programming Languages*, POPL '96, pages 32–41, New York, NY, USA, 1996. ACM.

[42] F. Tip. A survey of program slicing techniques. *Journal of Programming Languages*, 3:121–189, 1995.

[43] G. A. Venkatesh. The semantic approach to program slicing. In *Proc. ACM SIGPLAN 1991 Conference on Programming Language Design and Implementation*, PLDI '91, pages 107–119, New York, NY, USA, 1991. ACM.

[44] M. Weiser. Program slicing. In *Proc. 5th International Conference on Software Engineering*, ICSE '81, pages 439–449, Piscataway, NJ, USA, 1981. IEEE Press.

[45] M. Weiser. Reconstructing sequential behavior from parallel behavior projections. *Inf. Process. Lett.*, 17(3):129–135, 1983.

[46] M. Weiser. Program slicing. *IEEE Trans. Software Eng.*, 10(4):352–357, 1984.

[47] R. Wilhelm, J. Engblom, A. Ermedahl, N. Holsti, S. Thesing, D. Whalley, G. Bernat, C. Ferdinand, R. Heckmann, T. Mitra, F. Muller, I. Puaut, P. Puschner, J. Staschulat, and P. Stenström. The worst-case execution-time problem: overview of methods and survey of tools. *ACM Transactions on Embedded Computing Systems (TECS)*, 7(3): 1–53, Apr. 2008.

[48] B. Xu, J. Qian, X. Zhang, Z. Wu, and L. Chen. A brief survey of program slicing. *SIGSOFT Softw. Eng. Notes*, 30(2):1–36, Mar. 2005.

Type-based Exception Analysis for Non-strict Higher-order Functional Languages with Imprecise Exception Semantics

Ruud Koot * Jurriaan Hage

Department of Computing and Information Sciences
Utrecht University
{r.koot,j.hage}@uu.nl

Abstract

Most statically typed functional programming languages allow programmers to write partial functions: functions that are not defined on all the elements of their domain as specified by their type. Applying a partial function to a value on which it is not defined will raise a run-time exception, thus in practice well-typed programs can and *do* still go wrong.

To warn programmers about such errors, contemporary compilers for functional languages employ a local and purely syntactic analysis to detect partial **case**-expressions—those that do not cover all possible patterns of constructors. As programs often maintain invariants on their data, restricting the potential values of the scrutinee to a subtype of its given or inferred type, many of these incomplete **case**-expressions are harmless. Such an analysis does not account for these invariants and will thus report many false positives, overwhelming the programmer.

We develop a constraint-based type system that detects harmful sources of partiality and prove it correct with respect to an imprecise exception semantics. The analysis accurately tracks the flow of both exceptions—the manifestation of partiality gone wrong—and ordinary data through the program, as well as the dependencies between them. The latter is crucial for usable precision, but has been omitted from previously published exception analyses.

Categories and Subject Descriptors D.2.4 [*Software Engineering*]: Software/Program Verification; F.3.1 [*Logics and Meanings of Programs*]: Specifying and Verifying and Reasoning about Programs—Mechanical verification; F.3.2 [*Logics and Meanings of Programs*]: Semantics of Programming Languages—Program analysis

General Terms Languages, Theory, Verification

Keywords type-based program analysis, exception analysis, imprecise exceptions, pattern-matching

* This material is based upon work supported by the Netherlands Organisation for Scientific Research (NWO) under grant number 612.001.120.

PEPM '15, January 13–14, 2015, Mumbai, India.

ACM 978-1-4503-3297-2/15/01... $15.00.
http://dx.doi.org/10.1145/2678015.2682542

1. Introduction

Many modern programming languages come equipped with a type system. Type systems attempt to prevent bad behaviour at run-time by rejecting, at compile-time, programs that may cause such behaviour. As predicting the dynamic behaviour of an arbitrary program is undecidable, type systems—or at least those in languages relying on type inference—will always have to either reject some programs that can never cause bad behaviour, or accept some that do.

A major source of trouble are *partial functions*—functions that are not defined on all the elements of their domain, usually because they cannot be given any sensible definition on those elements. Canonical examples include the division operator, which is undefined when its right-hand argument is zero, and the *head* function (extracting the first element from a list) which is undefined on the empty list. Outright rejecting such functions does not seem like a reasonable course of action, so we are left only with the possibility of accepting them as well-typed at compile-time and having them raise an *exception* at run-time, when invoked on an element of their domain on which they were left undefined.

Still, we would like to warn the programmer when we accept a program as correctly typed that may potentially crash due to an exception at run-time. Most compilers for functional languages will already emit a warning when a function is defined by a non-exhaustive pattern-match, listing the missing patterns. These warnings are generated by a very local and syntactic analysis, however, and generate many false positives, distracting the programmer. For example, they will complain that the *head* function is missing a clause for the empty list, even if *head* is only ever invoked on a syntactically non-empty list, or not at all. Worse still are spurious warnings for non-escaping let-bound functions, for which one can no longer argue the warning is useful, as the function cannot be called from a different context at a future time.

Unlike other exception analyses that have appeared in the literature—which primarily attempt to track uncaught user-thrown or environment-induced exceptions, such as those that could be encountered when reading invalid data from disk—we are first and foremost concerned with accurately tracking the exceptions raised by failed pattern-matches. Therefore, our analysis might equally well be called a *pattern-match analysis*, although it is certainly not strictly limited to one as such. Getting results of usable accuracy—eliminating as many false positives as possible—requires carefully keeping track of the data-flow through the program. This additionally improves the accuracy of reporting potential exceptions not related to pattern matching and opens the way for employing the analysis to perform static contract checking.

1.1 Contributions

Our contributions include the following:

- We develop a type-driven—and thus *modular*—exception analysis that tracks data flow in order to give accurate warnings about exceptions raised due to pattern-match failures.
- Accuracy is achieved through the simultaneous use of *subtyping* (modelling data flow), *conditional constraints* (modelling control flow), *parametric polyvariance* (to achieve context-sensitivity) and *polyvariant recursion* (to avoid poisoning).
- The analysis works for *call-by-name* languages with an *imprecise exception semantics*. Such a semantics is necessary to justify several program transformations applied by optimizing compilers for call-by-name languages with distinguishable exceptions
- We give an operational semantics for imprecise exceptions and prove the analysis sound with respect to this semantics.
- The analysis presented in this paper is implemented as a prototype and, in addition to a pen-and-paper proof, the metatheory has been mostly mechanized in Coq. Both are available from: `http://www.staff.science.uu.nl/~0422819/tbea/`.

2. Motivation

Many algorithms maintain invariants on the data structures they use that cannot easily be encoded into their types. These invariants often ensure that certain incomplete **case**-expressions are guaranteed *not* to cause a pattern-match failure.

2.1 *risers*

An example of such an algorithm is the $risers$ function from Mitchell and Runciman (2008), which computes monotonically increasing subsegments of a list:

$$\begin{array}{ll} risers\ : Ord\ \alpha \Rightarrow [\alpha] \rightarrow [[\alpha]] & \\ risers\ [] & = [] \\ risers\ [x] & = [[x]] \\ risers\ (x_1 :: x_2 :: xs) = & \\ \quad \textbf{if}\ x_1 \leqslant x_2\ \textbf{then}\ (x_1 :: y) :: ys\ \textbf{else}\ [x_1] :: (y :: ys) & \\ \qquad \textbf{where}\ (y :: ys) = risers\ (x_2 :: xs) & \end{array}$$

For example:

$$risers\ [1,3,5,1,2] \longrightarrow^* [[1,3,5],[1,2]].$$

The irrefutable pattern in the **where**-clause in the third alternative of $risers$ expects the recursive call to return a non-empty list. A naive analysis might raise a warning here. If we look a bit longer at the program, however, we see that we also pass the recursive call to $risers$ a non-empty list. This means we will end up in either the second or third alternative inside the recursive call. Both the second alternative and both branches of the **if**-expression in the third alternative produce a non-empty list, satisfying the assumption we made earlier and allowing us to conclude that this function is total and will never raise a pattern-match failure exception. (Raising or propagating an exception because we pattern-match on exceptional values present in the input is still possible, though.)

2.2 *bitstring*

Another example, from Freeman and Pfenning (1991), comprises a collection of mathematical operations working on bitstrings: integers encoded as lists of the binary digits 0 and 1, with the least significant bit first. We model bitstrings as the type

$$\textbf{type}\ Bitstring = [\mathbb{Z}]$$

This type is too lenient in that it does not restrict the elements of the lists to the digits 0 and 1. We can however maintain this property as an implicit invariant.

If we now define an addition operation on bitstrings:

$$\begin{array}{llll} add : Bitstring \rightarrow Bitstring \rightarrow Bitstring &&& \\ add\ [] & y & = y \\ add\ x & [] & = x \\ add\ (0 :: x) & (0 :: y) & = 0 :: add\ x\ y \\ add\ (0 :: x) & (1 :: y) & = 1 :: add\ x\ y \\ add\ (1 :: x) & (0 :: y) & = 1 :: add\ x\ y \\ add\ (1 :: x) & (1 :: y) & = 0 :: add\ (add\ [1]\ x)\ y \end{array}$$

we see that the patterns in add are far from complete. However, if only passed arguments that satisfy the invariant it will neither crash due to a pattern-match failure, nor invalidate the invariant.

2.3 *desugar*

Compilers work with large and complex data types to represent the abstract syntax tree. These data structures must be able to represent all syntactic constructs the parser is able to recognize. This results in an abstract syntax tree that is unnecessarily complex, and too cumbersome for the later stages of the compiler—such as the optimizer—to work with. This problem is resolved by *desugaring* the original abstract syntax tree into a simpler—but semantically equivalent—abstract syntax tree that does not use all of the constructors available in the original abstract syntax tree.

The compiler writer now has a choice between two different options: either write a desugaring stage $desugar : ComplexAST \rightarrow SimpleAST$—duplicating most of the data type representing and functions operating on the abstract syntax tree—or take the easy route $desugar : AST \rightarrow AST$ and assume certain constructors will no longer be present in the abstract syntax tree at stages of the compiler executed after the desugaring phase. The former has all the usual downsides of code duplication—such as having to manually keep multiple data types and the functions operating on them synchronized—while the latter forgoes many of the advantages of strong typing and type safety: if the compiler pipeline is restructured and one of the stages that was originally assumed to run only after desugaring suddenly runs before that point the error might only be detected at run-time by a pattern-match failure. A pattern-match analysis should be able to detect such errors statically.

3. Overview

We formulate our analysis in terms of a constraint-based type and effect system (Talpin and Jouvelot 1994; Nielson et al. 1997; Abadi et al. 1999).

3.1 Data flow

How would we capture the informal reasoning we used in Section 2.1 to convince ourselves that $risers$ does not cause a pattern-match failure using a type system? A reasonable first approach would be to annotate all list types with the kind of list it can be: **N** if it must be an empty list, a list that necessarily has a nil-constructor at the head of its spine; **C** if it must be a non-empty list having a cons-constructor at its head; $\mathbf{N} \sqcup \mathbf{C}$ if it can be either. We can then assign to each of the three individual branches of $risers$ the following types:

$$\begin{array}{ll} risers_1 & : \forall \alpha. Ord\ \alpha \Rightarrow [\alpha]^{\mathbf{N}} \rightarrow [[\alpha]^{\mathbf{N} \sqcup \mathbf{C}}]^{\mathbf{N}} \\ risers_2, risers_3 & : \forall \alpha. Ord\ \alpha \Rightarrow [\alpha]^{\mathbf{C}} \rightarrow [[\alpha]^{\mathbf{N} \sqcup \mathbf{C}}]^{\mathbf{C}} \end{array}$$

From the three individual branches we may infer:

$$risers : \forall \alpha. Ord\ \alpha \Rightarrow [\alpha]^{\mathbf{N} \sqcup \mathbf{C}} \rightarrow [[\alpha]^{\mathbf{N} \sqcup \mathbf{C}}]^{\mathbf{N} \sqcup \mathbf{C}}$$

Assigning this type to $risers$ will unfortunately still let us believe that a pattern-match failure may occur in the irrefutable pattern in the **where**-clause, as this type tells us any invocation of $risers$—including the recursive call in the **where**-clause—may evaluate to an empty list. The problem is that $risers_1$—the branch that can never be reached from the call in the **where**-clause—is *poisoning* the overall result. *Polyvariance* (or *property polymorphism*) can rescue us from this precarious situation, however. We can instead assign to each of the branches, and thereby the overall result, the type:

$$risers : \forall \alpha\beta. Ord\ \alpha \Rightarrow [\alpha]^{\beta} \rightarrow [[\alpha]^{\mathbf{N} \sqcup \mathbf{C}}]^{\beta}$$

In the recursive call to $risers$ we know the argument passed is a non-empty list, so we can instantiate β to **C**, informing us that the result of the recursive call will be a non-empty list as well and guaranteeing that the irrefutable pattern-match will succeed. There is one little subtlety here, though: in a conventional Hindley–Milner type system we are not allowed, or even able, to instantiate β to anything, as the type is kept monomorphic for recursive calls. We, therefore, have to extend our type system with *polyvariant recursion*. While inferring polymorphic recursive types is undecidable in general (Kfoury et al. 1993; Henglein 1993)—and, being an automatic analysis, we do not want to rely on any programmer-supplied annotations—earlier research (Tofte and Talpin 1994; Dussart et al. 1995; Rittri 1995; Leroy and Pessaux 2000) has shown that this special case of polyvariant recursion is often both crucial to obtain adequate precision and feasible to infer automatically.

3.2 Exception flow

The intention of our analysis is to track the exceptions that may be raised during the execution of a program. As with the data flow we express this set of exceptions as an annotation on the type of a program. For example, the program:

$$f\ x = x \div 0$$

should be given the exception type:

$$f : \forall \alpha. \mathbb{Z}^{\alpha} \xrightarrow{\emptyset} \mathbb{Z}^{\alpha \sqcup \textbf{division-by-zero}}$$

This type explains that f is a function accepting an integer as its first and only parameter. As we are working in a call-by-name language, this integer might actually still be a thunk that raises an exception from the set α when evaluated. The program then divides this argument by zero, returning the result. While the result will be of type integer, this operation is almost guaranteed to raise a division-by-zero exception. It is *almost* guaranteed and not completely guaranteed to raise a division-by-zero exception, as the division operator is strict in both of its arguments and might thus force the left-hand side argument to be evaluated before raising the **division-by-zero** exception. This evaluation might then in turn cause an exception from the set α to be raised first. The complete result type is thus an integer with an exception annotation consisting of the union (or *join*) of the exception set α on the argument together with an additional exception **division-by-zero**. Finally, we note that there is an empty exception set annotating the function space constructor, indicating that no exceptions will be raised when evaluating f to a closure.

While this approach seems promising at first, it is not immediately adequate for our purpose: detecting potential pattern-match failures that may occur at run time.

Consider the following program:

$$head\ (x :: xs) = x$$

After an initial desugaring step, a compiler will translate this program into:

$$\begin{aligned} head\ xs = \mathbf{case}\ xs\ \mathbf{of} \\ [\,] \quad &\mapsto \lightning^{\textbf{pattern-match-failure}} \\ y :: ys &\mapsto y \end{aligned}$$

which can be assigned the exception type:

$$head : \forall \tau\alpha\beta. [\tau^{\alpha}]^{\beta} \xrightarrow{\emptyset} \tau^{\alpha \sqcup \beta \sqcup \textbf{pattern-match-failure}}$$

This type tells us that $head$ might always raise a **pattern-match-failure** exception, irrespective of what argument it is applied to. Clearly, we won't be able to outperform a simple syntactic analysis in this manner. What we need is a way to introduce a dependency of the exception flow on the data flow of the program, so we can express that $head$ will only raise a **pattern-match-failure** if it is possible for the argument passed to it to be an empty list. We can do so by introducing conditional constraints into our type system:

$$\begin{aligned} head : \forall \tau\alpha\beta\gamma. [\tau^{\alpha}]^{\beta} \xrightarrow{\emptyset} \tau^{\alpha \sqcup \beta \sqcup \gamma} \\ \mathbf{with}\ \{\mathbf{N} \sqsubseteq \beta \Rightarrow \textbf{pattern-match-failure} \sqsubseteq \gamma\} \end{aligned}$$

This type explains that $head$ will return an element of type τ that might—when inspected—raise any exception present in the elements of the list (α), the spine of the list (β) or from an additional set of exceptions (γ), with the constraint that if the list to which $head$ is applied is empty, then this exception set contains the **pattern-match-failure** exception, and otherwise is taken to be empty. (We apologize for the slight abuse of notation—using the annotation β to hold both data and exception-flow information—this will be remedied in the formal type system.)

4. Formalities

4.1 Language

As our language of discourse we take a call-by-name λ-calculus with booleans, integers, pairs, lists, exceptional values, general recursion, let-bindings, pattern-matching, and a set of primitive operators:

$$v ::= b \mid n \mid \lightning^{\ell} \mid [\,] \mid \mathbf{close}\ e\ \mathbf{in}\ \rho$$

$$\begin{aligned} e ::= &\ x \mid v \mid \lambda x.e \mid \mathbf{fix}\ f.\ e \mid e_1\ e_2 \\ \mid &\ \mathbf{let}\ x = e_1\ \mathbf{in}\ e_2 \mid \mathbf{if}\ e_1\ \mathbf{then}\ e_2\ \mathbf{else}\ e_3 \\ \mid &\ e_1 \oplus e_2 \mid (e_1, e_2) \mid \mathbf{fst}\ e \mid \mathbf{snd}\ e \\ \mid &\ e_1 :: e_2 \mid \mathbf{case}\ e_1\ \mathbf{of}\ \{[\,] \mapsto e_2; x_1 :: x_2 \mapsto e_3\} \\ \mid &\ \mathbf{bind}\ \rho\ \mathbf{in}\ e \end{aligned}$$

$$b \in \mathbb{B} \quad n \in \mathbb{Z} \quad f, x \in \mathbf{Var} \quad \ell \in \mathcal{P}(\mathbf{Lbl})$$

Syntax The values v of the language include an exceptional value $\lightning^{\ell}$ where the annotation ℓ denotes a set of *exception labels*. We leave the exception labels uninterpreted, but an actual implementation will use them to distinguish between distinct exceptions (for example, division-by-zero or a pattern-match failure), as well as to store any additional information necessary to produce informative error messages, such as source locations.

We adopt the following syntactic convention: we denote non-exceptional values by v and possibly exceptional values by v^{ℓ}, where ℓ corresponds to the set of exception labels in case v^{ℓ} is an exceptional value and corresponding to the empty set otherwise.

The **case**-construct in the language is always assumed to be complete. As our primary goal is to detect pattern-match failures produced by incomplete **case**-expressions, we assume any incomplete **case**-expressions written by the programmer has first been appropriately desugared into an equivalent complete **case**-expression by filling out any missing arms in the incomplete **case**-expression with an exceptional value $\lightning^{\textbf{pattern-match-failure}}$ before being passed to the analysis (Augustsson 1985; Maranget 2008).

The **close** and **bind** constructs are only necessary to formalize the small-step operational semantics (Section 4.4) and are assumed to be absent in the source program.

As call-by-name languages model exceptions as exceptional values, instead of exceptional control-flow, we do not need a **throw** or **raise**-construct. As most call-by-name languages omit a **catch**-construct from their pure fragment, we shall do so as well.

Static semantics We assume that the program is well-typed according to the canonical monomorphic type system and the underlying type of each subexpression is available to the analysis. In Section 6.1 we discuss how the analysis can be extended to a language with a polymorphic underlying type system.

4.2 Types

The types $\tau \in \textbf{Ty}$ of the type system are given by:

$$\tau \quad ::= \quad \alpha \quad | \quad \tau_1 \xrightarrow{\alpha} \tau_2 \quad | \quad \tau_1 \times^{\alpha} \tau_2 \quad | \quad [\tau]^{\alpha}$$

Types are *simply annotated types*, comprised of a single base type consisting of an *annotation variable* $\alpha \in \textbf{AnnVar}$ and the compound types for functions, pairs and lists, each having its constructor annotated with an annotation variable. Simply annotated types are given meaning in combination with a mapping or substitution from its free annotation variables to a lattice Λ, forming Λ-annotated types.

The auxiliary function $\lceil \cdot \rceil : \textbf{Ty} \to \textbf{AnnVar}$ extracts the outermost annotation from a simply annotated type τ:

$$\lceil \alpha \rceil = \alpha \qquad \lceil \tau_1 \times^{\alpha} \tau_2 \rceil = \alpha$$
$$\left\lceil \tau_1 \xrightarrow{\alpha} \tau_2 \right\rceil = \alpha \qquad \lceil [\tau]^{\alpha} \rceil = \alpha$$

A type τ can be combined with a constraint set C (Section 4.5) and have some of its free annotation variables quantified over into a type scheme $\sigma \in \textbf{TySch}$:

$$\sigma \quad ::= \quad \forall \overline{\alpha}.\ \tau \textbf{ with } C$$

4.3 Environments

An environment Γ binds variables to type schemes and an environment ρ binds variables to expressions:

$$\Gamma \quad ::= \quad \epsilon \quad | \quad \Gamma, x : \sigma$$
$$\rho \quad ::= \quad \epsilon \quad | \quad \rho, x : e$$

As environments can be permuted, so long as shadowing of variables is not affected, we take the liberty of writing $\Gamma, x : \tau$ and $\rho, x : e$ to match the nearest (most recently bound) variable x in an environment.

4.4 Operational semantics

The operational semantics of the language is given in Figure 1 and models a call-by-name language with an *imprecise exception semantics* (Peyton Jones et al. 1999).

The small-step reduction relation $\rho \vdash e \longrightarrow e'$ has an explicit environment ρ, mapping variables to expressions (not necessarily values). Closures are represented by the operator **close** e **in** ρ, which closes the expression e in the environment ρ. The operator **bind** ρ **in** e binds the free variables in the expression e to expressions in the environment ρ. While similar there is one important distinction between the **close** and the **bind**-construct: a closure **close** e **in** ρ is a value, while a **bind**-expression can still be reduced further.

[E-VAR] reduces a variable by looking up the expression bound to it in the environment. As we do not allow for recursive definitions without a mediating **fix**-construct, the variable x is removed from the scope by binding e to the environment ρ, having the (nearest) binding of x removed. [E-ABS] reduces a lambda-abstraction to a closure, closing over its free variables in the current scope. [E-APP] first reduces e_1 until it has been evaluated to a function closure, after which [E-APPABS] performs the application by binding x to e_2 in the scope of e_1. The scope of e_2 is ρ_1, the scope that was closed over, while e_1 gets bound by the outer scope ρ, as it is not necessarily a value and may thus still have free variables that need to remain bound in the outer scope. In case e_1 does not evaluate to a function closure, but to an exceptional value, [E-APPEXN1] will first continue reducing the argument e_2 to a (possibly exceptional) value. Once this is done, [E-APPEXN2] will reduce the whole application to a single exceptional value with a set of exceptional labels consisting of the union of both the exception labels associated with the applicee as well as the applicant. This behaviour is part of the imprecise exception semantics of our language and will be further motivated in the reduction rules for the **if-then-else** construct. [E-LET] binds x to e_1 in the scope of e_2. [E-FIX] performs a one-step unfolding, binding any recursive occurrences of the binder to the original expression in its original scope. To reduce an **if-then-else** expression, [E-IF] will start by evaluating the conditional e_1. If it evaluates to either the value **true** or the value **false**, [E-IFTRUE] respectively [E-IFFALSE], will reduce the whole expression to the appropriate branch e_2 or e_3. In case the conditional e_1 reduces to an exceptional value $\lightning^{\ell}$, the rules [E-IFEXN1] and [E-IFEXN2] will continue evaluating both branches of the **if-then-else** expression, as dictated by the imprecise exception semantics. Finally, once both arms have been fully evaluated to possibly exceptional values v^{ℓ_2} and v^{ℓ_3}, [E-IFEXN3] will join all the exception labels from the conditional and both arms together—remembering that we by convention associate an empty set of exception labels with non-exceptional values—in an exceptional value $\lightning^{\ell_1 \sqcup \ell_2 \sqcup \ell_3}$. This "imprecision" is necessary to validate program transformations, such as **case**-switching, in the presence of distinguishable exceptions:

$$\begin{array}{l} \forall e_i.\textbf{if } e_1 \textbf{ then} \\ \qquad \textbf{if } e_2 \textbf{ then } e_3 \textbf{ else } e_4 \\ \quad \textbf{else} \\ \qquad \textbf{if } e_2 \textbf{ then } e_5 \textbf{ else } e_6 = \textbf{if } e_2 \textbf{ then} \\ \qquad\qquad\qquad\qquad\qquad\qquad \textbf{if } e_1 \textbf{ then } e_3 \textbf{ else } e_5 \\ \qquad\qquad\qquad\qquad\qquad \textbf{else} \\ \qquad\qquad\qquad\qquad\qquad\qquad \textbf{if } e_1 \textbf{ then } e_4 \textbf{ else } e_6 \end{array}$$

Note that [E-OP1] and [E-OP2] (as well as several other reduction rules) make the reduction relation non-deterministic, instead of enforcing a left-to-right evaluation order for operators by requiring its left-hand argument to already be fully evaluated. Not enforcing an evaluation order for operators will allow the compiler to apply optimizing transformations, such as making use of the associativity or commutativity of the operator. If both the left- and right-hand side of the operator reduce to a numeric value, [E-OPNUM] will reduce the expression to its interpretation $[\![n_1 \oplus n_2]\!]$. If either of, or both, the arguments reduce to an exceptional value, the rules [E-OPEXN1], [E-OPEXN2] and [E-OPEXN3] will propagate the exception labels of all the exceptional values in the expression. The rules [E-PAIR] and [E-CONS] wrap the syntactic pair and cons constructors in a closure to make them into values—in a call-by-name language constructors are only evaluated up to weak head normal form (*whnf*) and can still contain unevaluated subexpressions that

$$\frac{}{\rho, x : e \vdash x \longrightarrow \mathbf{bind}\ \rho\ \mathbf{in}\ e}\ [\text{E-VAR}] \qquad \frac{}{\rho \vdash \lambda x.e \longrightarrow \mathbf{close}\ \lambda x.e\ \mathbf{in}\ \rho}\ [\text{E-ABS}]$$

$$\frac{\rho \vdash e_1 \longrightarrow e_1'}{\rho \vdash e_1\ e_2 \longrightarrow e_1'\ e_2}\ [\text{E-APP}] \qquad \frac{}{\rho \vdash (\mathbf{close}\ \lambda x.e_1\ \mathbf{in}\ \rho_1)\ e_2 \longrightarrow \mathbf{bind}\ (\rho_1, x : \mathbf{bind}\ \rho\ \mathbf{in}\ e_2)\ \mathbf{in}\ e_1}\ [\text{E-APPABS}]$$

$$\frac{\rho \vdash e_2 \longrightarrow e_2'}{\rho \vdash \lightning^{\ell_1}\ e_2 \longrightarrow \lightning^{\ell_1}\ e_2'}\ [\text{E-APPEXN1}] \qquad \frac{}{\rho \vdash \lightning^{\ell_1}\ v_2^{\ell_2} \longrightarrow \lightning^{\ell_1 \sqcup \ell_2}}\ [\text{E-APPEXN2}]$$

$$\frac{}{\rho \vdash \mathbf{let}\ x = e_1\ \mathbf{in}\ e_2 \longrightarrow \mathbf{bind}\ (\rho, x : \mathbf{bind}\ \rho\ \mathbf{in}\ e_1)\ \mathbf{in}\ e_2}\ [\text{E-LET}] \qquad \frac{}{\rho \vdash \mathbf{fix}\ f.\ e \longrightarrow \mathbf{bind}\ (\rho, f : \mathbf{bind}\ \rho\ \mathbf{in}\ \mathbf{fix}\ f.\ e)\ \mathbf{in}\ e}\ [\text{E-FIX}]$$

$$\frac{\rho \vdash e_1 \longrightarrow e_1'}{\rho \vdash \mathbf{if}\ e_1\ \mathbf{then}\ e_2\ \mathbf{else}\ e_3 \longrightarrow \mathbf{if}\ e_1'\ \mathbf{then}\ e_2\ \mathbf{else}\ e_3}\ [\text{E-IF}] \qquad \frac{}{\rho \vdash \mathbf{if}\ \mathbf{true}\ \mathbf{then}\ e_2\ \mathbf{else}\ e_3 \longrightarrow e_2}\ [\text{E-IFTRUE}]$$

$$\frac{}{\rho \vdash \mathbf{if}\ \mathbf{false}\ \mathbf{then}\ e_2\ \mathbf{else}\ e_3 \longrightarrow e_3}\ [\text{E-IFFALSE}] \qquad \frac{\rho \vdash e_2 \longrightarrow e_2'}{\rho \vdash \mathbf{if}\ \lightning^{\ell_1}\ \mathbf{then}\ e_2\ \mathbf{else}\ e_3 \longrightarrow \mathbf{if}\ \lightning^{\ell_1}\ \mathbf{then}\ e_2'\ \mathbf{else}\ e_3}\ [\text{E-IFEXN1}]$$

$$\frac{\rho \vdash e_3 \longrightarrow e_3'}{\rho \vdash \mathbf{if}\ \lightning^{\ell_1}\ \mathbf{then}\ e_2\ \mathbf{else}\ e_3 \longrightarrow \mathbf{if}\ \lightning^{\ell_1}\ \mathbf{then}\ e_2\ \mathbf{else}\ e_3'}\ [\text{E-IFEXN2}] \qquad \frac{}{\rho \vdash \mathbf{if}\ \lightning^{\ell_1}\ \mathbf{then}\ v_2^{\ell_2}\ \mathbf{else}\ v_3^{\ell_3} \longrightarrow \lightning^{\ell_1 \sqcup \ell_2 \sqcup \ell_3}}\ [\text{E-IFEXN3}]$$

$$\frac{\rho \vdash e_1 \longrightarrow e_1'}{\rho \vdash e_1 \oplus e_2 \longrightarrow e_1' \oplus e_2}\ [\text{E-OP1}] \qquad \frac{\rho \vdash e_2 \longrightarrow e_2'}{\rho \vdash e_1 \oplus e_2 \longrightarrow e_1 \oplus e_2'}\ [\text{E-OP2}] \qquad \frac{}{\rho \vdash n_1 \oplus n_2 \longrightarrow [\![n_1 \oplus n_2]\!]}\ [\text{E-OPNUM}]$$

$$\frac{}{\rho \vdash \lightning^{\ell_1} \oplus n_2 \longrightarrow \lightning^{\ell_1}}\ [\text{E-OPEXN1}] \qquad \frac{}{\rho \vdash n_1 \oplus \lightning^{\ell_2} \longrightarrow \lightning^{\ell_2}}\ [\text{E-OPEXN2}] \qquad \frac{}{\rho \vdash \lightning^{\ell_1} \oplus \lightning^{\ell_2} \longrightarrow \lightning^{\ell_1 \sqcup \ell_2}}\ [\text{E-OPEXN3}]$$

$$\frac{}{\rho \vdash (e_1, e_2) \longrightarrow \mathbf{close}\ (e_1, e_2)\ \mathbf{in}\ \rho}\ [\text{E-PAIR}] \qquad \frac{\rho \vdash e \longrightarrow e'}{\rho \vdash \mathbf{fst}\ e \longrightarrow \mathbf{fst}\ e'}\ [\text{E-FST}] \qquad \frac{\rho \vdash e \longrightarrow e'}{\rho \vdash \mathbf{snd}\ e \longrightarrow \mathbf{snd}\ e'}\ [\text{E-SND}]$$

$$\frac{}{\rho \vdash \mathbf{fst}\ (\mathbf{close}\ (e_1, e_2)\ \mathbf{in}\ \rho_1) \longrightarrow \mathbf{bind}\ \rho_1\ \mathbf{in}\ e_1}\ [\text{E-FSTPAIR}] \qquad \frac{}{\rho \vdash \mathbf{snd}\ (\mathbf{close}\ (e_1, e_2)\ \mathbf{in}\ \rho_1) \longrightarrow \mathbf{bind}\ \rho_1\ \mathbf{in}\ e_2}\ [\text{E-SNDPAIR}]$$

$$\frac{}{\rho \vdash \mathbf{fst}\ \lightning^{\ell} \longrightarrow \lightning^{\ell}}\ [\text{E-FSTEXN}] \qquad \frac{}{\rho \vdash \mathbf{snd}\ \lightning^{\ell} \longrightarrow \lightning^{\ell}}\ [\text{E-SNDEXN}] \qquad \frac{}{\rho \vdash e_1 :: e_2 \longrightarrow \mathbf{close}\ e_1 :: e_2\ \mathbf{in}\ \rho}\ [\text{E-CONS}]$$

$$\frac{\rho \vdash e_1 \longrightarrow e_1'}{\rho \vdash \mathbf{case}\ e_1\ \mathbf{of}\ \{[] \mapsto e_2; x_1 :: x_2 \mapsto e_3\} \longrightarrow \mathbf{case}\ e_1'\ \mathbf{of}\ \{[] \mapsto e_2; x_1 :: x_2 \mapsto e_3\}}\ [\text{E-CASE}]$$

$$\frac{}{\rho \vdash \mathbf{case}\ []\ \mathbf{of}\ \{[] \mapsto e_2; x_1 :: x_2 \mapsto e_3\} \longrightarrow e_2}\ [\text{E-CASENIL}]$$

$$\frac{}{\rho \vdash \mathbf{case}\ (\mathbf{close}\ e_1 :: e_1'\ \mathbf{in}\ \rho_1)\ \mathbf{of}\ \{[] \mapsto e_2; x_1 :: x_2 \mapsto e_3\} \longrightarrow \mathbf{bind}\ (\rho, x_1 : \mathbf{bind}\ \rho_1\ \mathbf{in}\ e_1, x_2 : \mathbf{bind}\ \rho_1\ \mathbf{in}\ e_1')\ \mathbf{in}\ e_3}\ [\text{E-CASECONS}]$$

$$\frac{\rho \vdash e_2 \longrightarrow e_2'}{\rho \vdash \mathbf{case}\ \lightning^{\ell_1}\ \mathbf{of}\ \{[] \mapsto e_2; x_1 :: x_2 \mapsto e_3\} \longrightarrow \mathbf{case}\ \lightning^{\ell_1}\ \mathbf{of}\ \{[] \mapsto e_2'; x_1 :: x_2 \mapsto e_3\}}\ [\text{E-CASEEXN1}]$$

$$\frac{\rho, x_1 : \lightning^{\emptyset}, x_2 : \lightning^{\emptyset} \vdash e_3 \longrightarrow e_3'}{\rho \vdash \mathbf{case}\ \lightning^{\ell_1}\ \mathbf{of}\ \{[] \mapsto e_2; x_1 :: x_2 \mapsto e_3\} \longrightarrow \mathbf{case}\ \lightning^{\ell_1}\ \mathbf{of}\ \{[] \mapsto e_2; x_1 :: x_2 \mapsto e_3'\}}\ [\text{E-CASEEXN2}]$$

$$\frac{}{\rho \vdash \mathbf{case}\ \lightning^{\ell_1}\ \mathbf{of}\ \left\{[] \mapsto v_2^{\ell_2}; x_1 :: x_2 \mapsto v_3^{\ell_3}\right\} \longrightarrow \lightning^{\ell_1 \sqcup \ell_2 \sqcup \ell_3}}\ [\text{E-CASEEXN3}]$$

$$\frac{\rho_1 \vdash e_1 \longrightarrow e_1'}{\rho \vdash \mathbf{bind}\ \rho_1\ \mathbf{in}\ e_1 \longrightarrow \mathbf{bind}\ \rho_1\ \mathbf{in}\ e_1'}\ [\text{E-BIND1}] \qquad \frac{}{\rho \vdash \mathbf{bind}\ \rho_1\ \mathbf{in}\ v_1^{\ell_1} \longrightarrow v_1^{\ell_1}}\ [\text{E-BIND2}]$$

Figure 1. Operational semantics ($\rho \vdash e_1 \longrightarrow e_2$)

need to have their free variables closed over in their original scope. [E-FST] evaluates the argument passed to **fst** to a normal form. If it is an exceptional value, [E-FSTEXN] will propagate it; if it is a closed pair constructor, [E-FSTPAIR] will project the first argument and bind its free variables in the environment it has been closed over. Accordingly for [E-SND], [E-SNDEXN] and [E-SNDPAIR]. [E-CASE] will evaluate the scrutinee of a **case**-expression to a normal form. If it evaluates to a nil-constructor, [E-CASENIL] will select the first arm. If it evaluates to a closed cons-constructor, [E-CASECONS] will select the second arm, binding x_1 and x_2 to respectively the first and second component of the constructor in the environment the constructor was closed over. In case the scrutinee evaluates to an exceptional value [E-CASEEXN1], [E-CASEEXN2] and [E-CASEEXN3] will continue evaluating both arms and gather and propagate all exception labels encountered. In the reduction rule [E-CASEEXN2] we still need to bind x_1 and x_2 to some expression in ρ. As this expression we take $\lightning^{\emptyset}$ in both cases, as it is the least committing value in our system: it is associated with both an empty set of exceptional values, as well as with an empty set of non-exceptional values. [E-BIND1] and [E-BIND2] will continue evaluating any expression e in the given environment ρ_1 until it has been fully reduced to a value, which either contains no free variables, or has them explicitly closed over by a **close**-construct.

Diverging expressions Note that diverging expressions, such as $\lightning$ (**fix** $f.\ f$) will not raise an exception in this operational semantics. This is not consistent with Haskell's imprecise exception semantics, where this is possible. Resolving this discrepancy without sacrificing precision would involve adding a termination analysis (*cf.* Vazou et al. 2014). While we believe this can be accommodated with minor changes to the analysis, we shall not further address this issue in remainder of the paper.

4.5 Constraints

A constraint c restricts the Λ-substitutions that may be applied to a simply annotated type to turn it into an Λ-annotated type. A constraint c is a conditional, consisting of a left-hand side g and a right-hand side r:

$$\begin{array}{lcl} c & ::= & g \Rightarrow r \\ g & ::= & \Lambda_\iota \sqsubseteq_\iota \alpha \mid \exists_\iota \alpha \mid g_1 \vee g_2 \mid \mathbf{true} \\ r & ::= & \Lambda_\iota \sqsubseteq_\iota \alpha \mid \alpha_1 \sqsubseteq_\iota \alpha_2 \mid \tau_1 \leqslant_\iota \tau_2 \end{array}$$

The left-hand side g of a conditional constraint, its *guard*, consists of a disjunction of *atomic guards* $\Lambda_\iota \sqsubseteq_\iota \alpha$, relating an element of the lattice Λ_ι to an annotation variable α, and *non-emptiness guards* $\exists_\iota \alpha$, a predicate on the annotation variable α.

The right-hand side r of a conditional or unconditional constraint can either be an *atomic constraint* $\Lambda_\iota \sqsubseteq_\iota \alpha$, relating an element of the lattice Λ_ι to an annotation variable α, or an atomic constraint $\alpha_1 \sqsubseteq_\iota \alpha_2$, relating two annotation variables, or it can be a *structural constraint* $\tau_1 \leqslant_\iota \tau_2$, relating two simply annotated types.

The asymmetry between the allowed forms of the antecedent g and consequent r of the conditional constraints is intentional: they allow constraints to be formed that are expressive enough to build an accurate analysis, but limited enough so as to allow tractable constraint solving. Both allowing constraints of the form $g_1 \vee g_2$ on the right-hand side of a conditional, or allowing constraints of the form $\alpha_1 \sqsubseteq_\iota \alpha_2$ on the left-hand side of a conditional make constraint solving notoriously difficult: the former because it cannot be trivially decomposed into a set of simpler constraints and the latter because it does not behave monotonically under a fixed-point iteration.

The atomic and structural constraint relations are qualified by an index ι, which for the purpose of our analysis can be one of two constants:

$$\iota \quad ::= \quad \delta \mid \chi$$

Here δ is used to indicate data-flow, while χ indicates exception-flow.

To ease the syntactic burden we freely write constraint expressions indexed by the two constraint indices $\delta\chi$ simultaneously. Formally these should always be read as standing for two separate constraint expressions: one indexed by δ and the other indexed by χ. As none of the constraint expressions in this paper contain more than one such paired index, no ambiguities should arise. Furthermore,

$$\tilde{c} \quad ::= \quad c \mid g$$

and constraints $\mathbf{true} \Rightarrow r$ shall be written simply as r.

Constraints are given meaning by the *constraint satisfaction* predicate $\theta \vDash \tilde{c}$, which relates a constraint c, g or r to the meaning of its free variables, which are in turn given by a pair of ground substitutions $\theta = \langle \theta_\delta, \theta_\chi \rangle$:

$$\frac{\theta_\iota\alpha_1 \sqsubseteq_\iota \theta_\iota\alpha_2}{\theta \vDash \alpha_1 \sqsubseteq_\iota \alpha_2}\,[\text{CM-VAR}] \qquad \frac{\ell_\iota \sqsubseteq_\iota \theta_\iota\alpha}{\theta \vDash \ell_\iota \sqsubseteq_\iota \alpha}\,[\text{CM-CON}]$$

$$\frac{\ell_\iota \sqsubseteq_\iota \theta_\iota\alpha \quad \ell_\iota \neq \bot_\iota}{\theta \vDash \exists_\iota\alpha}\,[\text{CM-EXISTS}] \qquad \frac{}{\theta \vDash \mathbf{true}}\,[\text{CM-TRUE}]$$

$$\frac{\theta \vDash g_1}{\theta \vDash g_1 \vee g_2}\,[\text{CM-LEFT}] \qquad \frac{\theta \vDash g_2}{\theta \vDash g_1 \vee g_2}\,[\text{CM-RIGHT}]$$

$$\frac{\theta \vDash g \Rightarrow \theta \vDash r}{\theta \vDash g \Rightarrow r}\,[\text{CM-IMPL}] \qquad \frac{\theta_\iota\tau_1 \leqslant_\iota \theta_\iota\tau_2}{\theta \vDash \tau_1 \leqslant_\iota \tau_2}\,[\text{CM-SUB}]$$

Working with constraints in terms of the constraint satisfaction predicate is rather tedious, so we prefer to work with a *constraint entailment* relation $C \Vdash \tilde{c}$ and an associated constraint logic:

$$\frac{}{C \Vdash \bot_\iota \sqsubseteq_\iota \alpha}\,[\text{CL-}\bot] \qquad \frac{}{C \Vdash \alpha \sqsubseteq_\iota \top_\iota}\,[\text{CL-}\top]$$

$$\frac{C, g \Vdash r}{C \Vdash g \Rightarrow r}\,[\text{CL-}{\Rightarrow}\text{I}] \qquad \frac{C \Vdash g \Rightarrow r}{C, g \Vdash r}\,[\text{CL-}{\Rightarrow}\text{E}]$$

$$\frac{C \Vdash g_1}{C \Vdash g_1 \vee g_2}\,[\text{CL-}\vee\text{I}] \qquad \frac{C \Vdash g_1 \vee g_2}{C \Vdash g_2 \vee g_1}\,[\text{CL-}\vee\text{C}]$$

$$\frac{C \Vdash \Lambda_\iota \sqsubseteq_\iota \alpha}{C \Vdash \exists_\iota\alpha}\,[\text{CL-}\exists\text{I}] \qquad \frac{C_1 \Vdash \tilde{c}}{C_1, C_2 \Vdash \tilde{c}}\,[\text{CL-WEAK}]$$

$$\frac{C \Vdash \tilde{c}_1 \quad C, \tilde{c}_1 \Vdash \tilde{c}_2}{C \Vdash \tilde{c}_2}\,[\text{CL-MP}]$$

We lift the constraint entailment relation to work on constraint sets $C_1 \Vdash C_2$ in the obvious way.

Theorem 1 (Soundness of constraint logic)**.** *If $\theta \vDash C$ and $C \Vdash D$ then $\theta \vDash D$.*

The subtyping relation is as usual for a type and effect system, thus note the subeffecting of the annotations:

$$\frac{C \Vdash \tau_1 \leqslant_\iota \tau_2 \quad C \Vdash \tau_2 \leqslant_\iota \tau_3}{C \Vdash \tau_1 \leqslant_\iota \tau_3}\,[\text{S-TRANS}]$$

$$\frac{}{C \Vdash \tau \leqslant_\iota \tau}\,[\text{S-REFL}] \qquad \frac{C \Vdash \alpha_1 \sqsubseteq_\iota \alpha_2}{C \Vdash \alpha_1 \leqslant_\iota \alpha_2}\,[\text{SA-BASE}]$$

$$\frac{C \Vdash \tau_3 \leqslant_\iota \tau_1 \quad C \Vdash \tau_2 \leqslant_\iota \tau_4 \quad C \Vdash \alpha_1 \sqsubseteq_\iota \alpha_2}{C \Vdash \tau_1 \xrightarrow{\alpha_1} \tau_2 \leqslant_\iota \tau_3 \xrightarrow{\alpha_2} \tau_4}\,[\text{SA-FUN}]$$

$$\frac{C \Vdash \tau_1 \leqslant_\iota \tau_3 \quad C \Vdash \tau_2 \leqslant_\iota \tau_4 \quad C \Vdash \alpha_1 \sqsubseteq_\iota \alpha_2}{C \Vdash \tau_1 \times^{\alpha_1} \tau_2 \leqslant_\iota \tau_3 \times^{\alpha_2} \tau_4}\,[\text{SA-PAIR}]$$

$$\frac{C \Vdash \tau_1 \leqslant_\iota \tau_2 \quad C \Vdash \alpha_1 \sqsubseteq_\iota \alpha_2}{C \Vdash [\tau_1]^{\alpha_1} \leqslant_\iota [\tau_2]^{\alpha_2}}\,[\text{SA-LIST}]$$

4.6 Type system

A syntax-directed type system for exception analysis is given in Figure 2.

[T-VAR] combines a lookup in the type environment with instantiation of variables quantified over in the type scheme. [T-CON] and [T-EXN] make sure that any constants and exception literals flow into the top-level annotations of their type. Constants will have to be abstracted into an element of the lattice Λ_δ, using the auxiliary function i, first. [T-APP] incorporates a subtyping check between the formal and the actual parameter and flows all exceptions than can be caused by evaluating the function abstraction—as represented by the annotation on the function-space constructor—into the top-level annotation of the resulting type. The final premise flows any exceptions that can be raised by evaluating the argument to weak head normal form to the top-level annotation on the result type if it is possible for the function that the argument is applied to, to evaluate to an exceptional value. This is necessary to soundly model the imprecise exception semantics. [T-ABS] is standard, with only an additional annotation present on the function-space constructor. [T-FIX] and [T-LET] are the conventional rules for polymorphic recursion and polymorphic let-bindings with constrained types and are the only rules with a non-trivial algorithmic interpretation (see Section 5). [T-IF] uses subtyping to ensure that the exceptional and non-exceptional values of both branches,

$$\frac{C \Vdash D\left[\overline{\beta}/\overline{\alpha}\right]}{C;\Gamma, x : \forall\overline{\alpha}.\,\tau\ \textbf{with}\ D \vdash x : \tau\left[\overline{\beta}/\overline{\alpha}\right]}\ [\text{T-VAR}] \quad \frac{C \Vdash i(c) \sqsubseteq_\delta \alpha}{C;\Gamma \vdash c : \alpha}\ [\text{T-CON}] \quad \frac{C \Vdash \ell \sqsubseteq_\chi \lceil\tau\rceil}{C;\Gamma \vdash \lightning^{\ell} : \tau}\ [\text{T-EXN}]$$

$$\frac{C;\Gamma \vdash e_1 : \tau_1 \xrightarrow{\alpha} \tau_2 \quad C;\Gamma \vdash e_2 : \tau_3 \quad C \Vdash \tau_3 \leqslant_{\delta\chi} \tau_1 \quad C \Vdash \tau_2 \leqslant_{\delta\chi} \tau_4 \quad C \Vdash \alpha \sqsubseteq_\chi \lceil\tau_4\rceil \quad C \Vdash \exists_\chi\alpha \Rightarrow \lceil\tau_3\rceil \sqsubseteq_\chi \lceil\tau_4\rceil}{C;\Gamma \vdash e_1\, e_2 : \tau_4}\ [\text{T-APP}]$$

$$\frac{C;\Gamma, x : \tau_1 \vdash e : \tau_2}{C;\Gamma \vdash \lambda x.e : \tau_1 \xrightarrow{\alpha} \tau_2}\ [\text{T-ABS}] \quad \frac{D;\Gamma \vdash e_1 : \tau_1 \quad C;\Gamma, x : \forall\overline{\alpha}.\,\tau_1\ \textbf{with}\ D \vdash e_2 : \tau_2 \quad \overline{\alpha} \cap fv(\Gamma) = \emptyset}{C;\Gamma \vdash \textbf{let}\ x = e_1\ \textbf{in}\ e_2 : \tau_2}\ [\text{T-LET}]$$

$$\frac{C \Vdash D\left[\overline{\beta}/\overline{\alpha}\right] \quad D;\Gamma, f : \forall\overline{\alpha}.\,\tau_1\ \textbf{with}\ D \vdash e : \tau_2 \quad D \Vdash \tau_2 \leqslant_{\delta\chi} \tau_1 \quad \overline{\alpha} \cap fv(\Gamma) = \emptyset}{C;\Gamma \vdash \textbf{fix}\ f.\, e : \tau_1\left[\overline{\beta}/\overline{\alpha}\right]}\ [\text{T-FIX}]$$

$$\frac{\begin{array}{c} C;\Gamma \vdash e_1 : \alpha_1 \quad C;\Gamma \vdash e_2 : \tau_2 \quad C;\Gamma \vdash e_3 : \tau_3 \\ C \Vdash \mathbf{T} \sqsubseteq_\delta \alpha_1 \vee \exists_\chi\alpha_1 \Rightarrow \tau_2 \leqslant_{\delta\chi} \tau \quad C \Vdash \mathbf{F} \sqsubseteq_\delta \alpha_1 \vee \exists_\chi\alpha_1 \Rightarrow \tau_3 \leqslant_{\delta\chi} \tau \quad C \Vdash \alpha_1 \sqsubseteq_\chi \lceil\tau\rceil \end{array}}{C;\Gamma \vdash \textbf{if}\ e_1\ \textbf{then}\ e_2\ \textbf{else}\ e_3 : \tau}\ [\text{T-IF}]$$

$$\frac{C;\Gamma \vdash e_1 : \alpha_1 \quad C;\Gamma \vdash e_2 : \alpha_2 \quad C \Vdash \alpha_1 \sqsubseteq_\chi \alpha \quad C \Vdash \alpha_2 \sqsubseteq_\chi \alpha \quad C \Vdash \omega_\oplus(\alpha_1, \alpha_2, \alpha)}{C;\Gamma \vdash e_1 \oplus e_2 : \alpha}\ [\text{T-OP}]$$

$$\frac{C;\Gamma \vdash e_1 : \tau_1 \quad C;\Gamma \vdash e_2 : \tau_2}{C;\Gamma \vdash (e_1, e_2) : \tau_1 \times^\alpha \tau_2}\ [\text{T-PAIR}]$$

$$\frac{C;\Gamma \vdash e : \tau_1 \times^\alpha \tau_2 \quad C \Vdash \tau_1 \leqslant_{\delta\chi} \tau \quad C \Vdash \alpha \sqsubseteq_\chi \lceil\tau\rceil}{C;\Gamma \vdash \textbf{fst}\ e : \tau}\ [\text{T-FST}] \quad \frac{C;\Gamma \vdash e : \tau_1 \times^\alpha \tau_2 \quad C \Vdash \tau_2 \leqslant_{\delta\chi} \tau \quad C \Vdash \alpha \sqsubseteq_\chi \lceil\tau\rceil}{C;\Gamma \vdash \textbf{snd}\ e : \tau}\ [\text{T-SND}]$$

$$\frac{C \Vdash \mathbf{N} \sqsubseteq_\delta \alpha}{C;\Gamma \vdash [] : [\tau]^\alpha}\ [\text{T-NIL}] \quad \frac{\begin{array}{c} C;\Gamma \vdash e_1 : \tau_1 \quad C;\Gamma \vdash e_2 : [\tau_2]^{\alpha_2} \\ C \Vdash \tau_1 \leqslant_{\delta\chi} \tau \quad C \Vdash \tau_2 \leqslant_{\delta\chi} \tau \quad C \Vdash \mathbf{C} \sqsubseteq_\delta \alpha \quad C \Vdash \alpha_2 \sqsubseteq_\chi \alpha \end{array}}{C;\Gamma \vdash e_1 :: e_2 : [\tau]^\alpha}\ [\text{T-CONS}]$$

$$\frac{\begin{array}{c} C;\Gamma \vdash e_1 : [\tau_1]^{\alpha_1} \quad C;\Gamma \vdash e_2 : \tau_2 \quad C;\Gamma, x_1 : \tau_1, x_2 : [\tau_1]^\beta \vdash e_3 : \tau_3 \\ C \Vdash \mathbf{N} \sqsubseteq_\delta \alpha_1 \vee \exists_\chi\alpha_1 \Rightarrow \tau_2 \leqslant_{\delta\chi} \tau \quad C \Vdash \mathbf{C} \sqsubseteq_\delta \alpha_1 \vee \exists_\chi\alpha_1 \Rightarrow \tau_3 \leqslant_{\delta\chi} \tau \quad C \Vdash \alpha_1 \sqsubseteq_\chi \lceil\tau\rceil \\ C \Vdash \mathbf{N} \sqcup \mathbf{C} \sqsubseteq_\delta \beta \quad C \Vdash \alpha_1 \sqsubseteq_\chi \beta \end{array}}{C;\Gamma \vdash \textbf{case}\ e_1\ \textbf{of}\ \{[] \mapsto e_2; x_1 :: x_2 \mapsto e_3\} : \tau}\ [\text{T-CASE}]$$

$$\frac{C;\Delta \vdash e : \sigma \quad C \vdash \Delta \bowtie \rho}{C;\Gamma \vdash \textbf{close}\ e\ \textbf{in}\ \rho : \sigma}\ [\text{T-CLOSE}] \quad \frac{C;\Delta \vdash e : \sigma \quad C \vdash \Delta \bowtie \rho}{C;\Gamma \vdash \textbf{bind}\ \rho\ \textbf{in}\ e : \sigma}\ [\text{T-BIND}]$$

Figure 2. Syntax-directed type system ($C;\Gamma \vdash e : \sigma$)

as well as any exceptions that can occur while evaluating the conditional are propagated to the resulting type. Additionally, conditional constraints are used to ensure that only reachable branches will contribute to the resulting type. A branch is considered reachable if either the conditional can evaluate to **true** respectively **false**, or because evaluating the conditional can cause an exception and we have to consider both branches as being reachable to validate the **case**-switching transformation. The typing rule [T-OP] for primitive operators will be discussed in Section 4.7. [T-PAIR] is the standard type rule for pairs, except that we add an unconstrained annotation to the pair constructor. [T-FST] and [T-SND] are standard type rules for projections from a pair. As they implicitly perform a pattern-match, they have to propagate any exceptions that can occur when evaluating the pair-constructor to the resulting type. [T-NIL] gives the nil-constructor the type list of τ, with τ unconstrained, and an annotation α indicating the head of the spine of the list can at least contain a nil-constructor. [T-CONS] merges data-flow and exception-flow of the head and elements in the tail of the list, annotates the resulting type with an α indicating the head of the spine of the list can at least contain a cons-constructor, and propagates the exceptions that can occur in the tail of the spine of the list to the resulting type. [T-CASE] is similar to [T-IF]. The additional complication lies in the fact that the pattern for a cons-constructor must also bring its two fields into scope and give them an appropriate type. Note how in [T-CONS] and [T-CASE] exceptional and non-exceptional values are treated asymmetrically. In the rule [T-CONS] exceptional values in the spine of the tail of the list flow into the result, while we only remember **C** as the non-exceptional value than can occur at the head of the spine of the resulting list. This choice means that in [T-CASE], while we have more precise information about the head of the list, we have to be *pessimistic* about the shape of the list that gets bound to x_2. Conversely, for exceptional values we have less precise information about the head of the spine of the list. We can, however, be *optimistic* about the exceptional values occuring in the spine of the list that gets bound to x_2. Not being able to do so would be disasterous for the precision of the analysis. Any further pattern-matching on the spine of x_2, whether directly or through applying operations such as *map* or *reverse* to it, would cause the—likely spurious—exceptions to propagate. Finally, [T-CLOSE] and [T-BIND] type the expression e they close over or bind in an expression environment ρ, under a type environment Δ that types the expression environment ρ. These rules relate the type environments Γ with the expression environments ρ using an *environmental consistency* relation $C \vdash \Gamma \bowtie \rho$:

$$\frac{}{C \vdash \epsilon \bowtie \epsilon} \text{ [EC-EMPTY]}$$

$$\frac{C \vdash \Gamma \bowtie \rho \quad C; \Gamma \vdash e : \sigma}{C \vdash \Gamma, x : \sigma \bowtie \rho, x : e} \text{ [EC-EXTEND]}$$

4.7 Primitive operators

The typing rule [T-OP] for primitive operators relies on an auxiliary function ω that assigns a constraint set for each operator, giving its abstract interpretation. For an addition operator $+$ one can take the constraint set:

$$\omega_+(\alpha_1, \alpha_2, \alpha) \stackrel{\text{def}}{=} \{\top_{\mathbb{Z}} \sqsubseteq_\delta \alpha\}$$

or the more precise:

$$\omega_+(\alpha_1, \alpha_2, \alpha) \stackrel{\text{def}}{=} \left\{ \begin{array}{c} \mathbf{-} \sqsubseteq_\delta \alpha_1 \Rightarrow \mathbf{-} \sqsubseteq_\delta \alpha \\ \mathbf{-} \sqsubseteq_\delta \alpha_2 \Rightarrow \mathbf{-} \sqsubseteq_\delta \alpha \\ \mathbf{0} \sqsubseteq_\delta \alpha \\ \mathbf{+} \sqsubseteq_\delta \alpha_1 \Rightarrow \mathbf{+} \sqsubseteq_\delta \alpha \\ \mathbf{+} \sqsubseteq_\delta \alpha_2 \Rightarrow \mathbf{+} \sqsubseteq_\delta \alpha \end{array} \right\}$$

If we would extend our constraints to allow conjunctions on the left-hand side of conditionals we can even get rid of the spurious **0**'s:

$$\omega_+(\alpha_1, \alpha_2, \alpha) \stackrel{\text{def}}{=} \left\{ \begin{array}{c} \mathbf{-} \sqsubseteq_\delta \alpha_1 \Rightarrow \mathbf{-} \sqsubseteq_\delta \alpha \\ \mathbf{-} \sqsubseteq_\delta \alpha_2 \Rightarrow \mathbf{-} \sqsubseteq_\delta \alpha \\ \mathbf{-} \sqsubseteq_\delta \alpha_1 \wedge \mathbf{+} \sqsubseteq_\delta \alpha_2 \Rightarrow \mathbf{0} \sqsubseteq_\delta \alpha \\ \mathbf{0} \sqsubseteq_\delta \alpha_1 \wedge \mathbf{0} \sqsubseteq_\delta \alpha_2 \Rightarrow \mathbf{0} \sqsubseteq_\delta \alpha \\ \mathbf{+} \sqsubseteq_\delta \alpha_1 \wedge \mathbf{-} \sqsubseteq_\delta \alpha_2 \Rightarrow \mathbf{0} \sqsubseteq_\delta \alpha \\ \mathbf{+} \sqsubseteq_\delta \alpha_1 \Rightarrow \mathbf{+} \sqsubseteq_\delta \alpha \\ \mathbf{+} \sqsubseteq_\delta \alpha_2 \Rightarrow \mathbf{+} \sqsubseteq_\delta \alpha \end{array} \right\}$$

Similarly, we are able to detect division-by-zero exceptions caused by an integer division operator $\div$:

$$\omega_\div(\alpha_1, \alpha_2, \alpha) \stackrel{\text{def}}{=} \left\{ \begin{array}{c} \mathbf{0} \sqsubseteq_\delta \alpha_2 \Rightarrow \{\textbf{div-by-0}\} \sqsubseteq_\chi \alpha \\ \mathbf{-} \sqsubseteq_\delta \alpha_1 \wedge \mathbf{-} \sqsubseteq_\delta \alpha_2 \Rightarrow \mathbf{+} \sqsubseteq_\delta \alpha \\ \mathbf{-} \sqsubseteq_\delta \alpha_1 \wedge \mathbf{+} \sqsubseteq_\delta \alpha_2 \Rightarrow \mathbf{-} \sqsubseteq_\delta \alpha \\ \mathbf{+} \sqsubseteq_\delta \alpha_1 \wedge \mathbf{-} \sqsubseteq_\delta \alpha_2 \Rightarrow \mathbf{-} \sqsubseteq_\delta \alpha \\ \mathbf{+} \sqsubseteq_\delta \alpha_1 \wedge \mathbf{+} \sqsubseteq_\delta \alpha_2 \Rightarrow \mathbf{+} \sqsubseteq_\delta \alpha \\ \mathbf{0} \sqsubseteq_\delta \alpha \end{array} \right\}$$

We do impose two restrictions on the operator constraint sets; they need to be *consistent* and *monotonic*:

Definition 1. An operator constraint set $\omega_\oplus$ is said to be *consistent* with respect to an operator interpretation $[\![\cdot \oplus \cdot]\!]$ if, whenever $C; \Gamma \vdash n_1 : \alpha_1$, $C; \Gamma \vdash n_2 : \alpha_2$, and $C \Vdash \omega_\oplus(\alpha_1, \alpha_2, \alpha)$ then $C; \Gamma \vdash [\![n_1 \oplus n_2]\!] : \alpha'$ with $C \Vdash \alpha' \leqslant_{\delta\chi} \alpha$ for some α'.

This restriction states that the interpretation of an operator and its abstract interpretation by the operator constraint set should coincide. We need one slightly more technical restriction to be able to prove our system sound:

Definition 2. An operator constraint set $\omega_\oplus$ is *monotonic* if, whenever $C \Vdash \omega_\oplus(\alpha_1, \alpha_2, \alpha)$ and $C \Vdash \alpha_1' \sqsubseteq_{\delta\chi} \alpha_1$, $C \Vdash \alpha_2' \sqsubseteq_{\delta\chi} \alpha_2$, $C \Vdash \alpha \sqsubseteq_{\delta\chi} \alpha'$ then $C \Vdash \omega_\oplus(\alpha_1', \alpha_2', \alpha')$.

Informally this means that operator constraint sets can only let the result of evaluating an operator and its operands depend on the values of those operands and not the other way around: the operator constraint sets must respect the fact that we are defining a *forwards* analysis.

4.8 Declarative rules

While we have formulated the analysis directly as a syntax-directed type system, we do need to appeal to the three logical rules that have been folded into the non-logical ones—in order to make the system syntax-directed—in the metatheoretic proofs. Their formulation should hold no surprises:

$$\frac{C; \Gamma \vdash e : \forall \overline{\alpha}.\, \tau \textbf{ with } D \quad C \Vdash D\,[\overline{\beta}/\overline{\alpha}]}{C; \Gamma \vdash e : \tau\,[\overline{\beta}/\overline{\alpha}]} \text{ [T-INST]}$$

$$\frac{C, D; \Gamma \vdash e : \tau \quad \overline{\alpha} \cap fv(\Gamma; C) = \emptyset}{C; \Gamma \vdash e : \forall \overline{\alpha}.\, \tau \textbf{ with } D} \text{ [T-GEN]}$$

$$\frac{C; \Gamma \vdash e : \tau \quad C \Vdash \tau \leqslant_{\delta\chi} \tau'}{C; \Gamma \vdash e : \tau'} \text{ [T-SUB]}$$

4.9 Metatheory

Three theorems imply the correctness of the analysis:

Theorem 2 (Conservative extension)**.** *If e is well-typed in the underlying type system, then it can be given a type in the annotated type system.*

Theorem 3 (Progress)**.** *If $C; \Gamma \vdash e : \sigma$ then either e is a value or there exist an e', such that for any ρ with $C \vdash \Gamma \bowtie \rho$ we have $\rho \vdash e \longrightarrow e'$.*

Theorem 4 (Preservation)**.** *If $C; \Gamma \vdash e : \sigma_1$, $\rho \vdash e \longrightarrow e'$ and $C \vdash \Gamma \bowtie \rho$ then $C; \Gamma \vdash e' : \sigma_2$ with $C \Vdash \sigma_2 \leqslant_{\delta\chi} \sigma_1$.*

5. Algorithm

The analysis can be implemented as a three-stage type inference process. In the first stage we invoke a standard Hindley–Milner type inference algorithm to make sure the input program is well-typed and to give the second stage access to the underlying types of all subexpressions. The second stage generates a set of constraints and the third stage solves those constraints.

5.1 Constraint generation

The constraint inference algorithm $\mathcal{W}$ is given in Figure 3. The case for **fix** is discussed in Section 5.3. As the **close** and **bind**-constructs are included for metatheoretic purposes only and assumed not to be present in the initial unevaluated program text, we do not need to include any cases for them in the algorithm.

The auxiliary function *freshFrom* creates a type with the same type-constructor shape as the given underlying type v, with all annotation variables fresh; gen quantifies over all annotation variables free in τ but not free in Γ; $inst$ instantiates all quantified annotation variables in τ and C with fresh ones.

5.2 Constraint solving

The constraint solver $\mathcal{S}$ takes a constraint set C and produces a substitution θ that solves it. The solver assumes that all structural constaints ($\leqslant_\iota$) have been decomposed into atomic constraints ($\sqsubseteq_\iota$) using the syntax-directed part of the subtyping relation (SA-) as a decomposition algorithm.

The constraint solver $\mathcal{S}$ relies on the function dv that determines the *dependent variables* of a constraint c: the variables that if updated may require the constraint to be reevaluated during the fixpoint iteration.

$$
\begin{array}{lll}
\mathcal{W} & : & \mathbf{Env} \times \mathbf{Expr} \to \mathbf{Ty} \times \mathcal{P}\,\mathbf{Constr} \\
\mathcal{W}\,\Gamma\,x & = & \mathit{inst}\ \Gamma_x \\
\mathcal{W}\,\Gamma\,c & = & \mathit{typeOf}\ c \\
\mathcal{W}\,\Gamma\,(\lightning^{\ell} : \upsilon) & = & \mathbf{do}\ \tau \leftarrow \mathit{freshFrom}\ \upsilon \\
 & & \quad \mathbf{return}\ \langle \tau, \{\ell \sqsubseteq_{\chi} \lceil\tau\rceil\}\rangle \\
\mathcal{W}\,\Gamma\,(\lambda x : \upsilon.e) & = & \mathbf{do}\ \tau_1 \leftarrow \mathit{freshFrom}\ \upsilon \\
 & & \quad \langle \tau_2, C_2\rangle \leftarrow \mathcal{W}\,(\Gamma, x : \tau_1)\ e \\
 & & \quad \alpha \leftarrow \mathit{fresh} \\
 & & \quad \mathbf{return}\ \left\langle \tau_1 \xrightarrow{\alpha} \tau_2, C_2\right\rangle \\
\mathcal{W}\,\Gamma\,(e_1\ e_2 : \upsilon) & = & \mathbf{do}\ \left\langle \tau_1 \xrightarrow{\alpha} \tau_2, C_1\right\rangle \leftarrow \mathcal{W}\,\Gamma\,e_1 \\
 & & \quad \langle \tau_3, C_2\rangle \leftarrow \mathcal{W}\,\Gamma\,e_2 \\
 & & \quad \tau_4 \leftarrow \mathit{freshFrom}\ \upsilon \\
 & & \quad C_3 \leftarrow \left\{ \begin{array}{c} \tau_3 \leqslant_{\delta\chi} \tau_1, \tau_2 \leqslant_{\delta\chi} \tau_4, \alpha \sqsubseteq_{\chi} \lceil\tau_4\rceil \\ \exists_{\chi}\ \alpha \Rightarrow \lceil\tau_3\rceil \sqsubseteq_{\chi} \lceil\tau_4\rceil \end{array} \right\} \\
 & & \quad \mathbf{return}\ \langle \tau_4, C_1 \cup C_2 \cup C_3\rangle \\
\mathcal{W}\,\Gamma\,(\mathbf{let}\ x = e_1\ \mathbf{in}\ e_2) & & \\
 & = & \mathbf{do}\ \langle \tau_1, C_1\rangle \leftarrow \mathcal{W}\,\Gamma\,e_1 \\
 & & \quad \sigma_1 \leftarrow \mathit{gen}\ \Gamma\ \tau_1\ C_1 \\
 & & \quad \langle \tau_2, C_2\rangle \leftarrow \mathcal{W}\,(\Gamma, x : \sigma_1)\ e_2 \\
 & & \quad \mathbf{return}\ \langle \tau_2, C_1 \cup C_2\rangle \\
\mathcal{W}\,\Gamma\,(\mathbf{if}\ e_1\ \mathbf{then}\ e_2\ \mathbf{else}\ e_3 : \upsilon) & & \\
 & = & \mathbf{do}\ \langle \alpha_1, C_1\rangle \leftarrow \mathcal{W}\,\Gamma\,e_1 \\
 & & \quad \langle \tau_2, C_2\rangle \leftarrow \mathcal{W}\,\Gamma\,e_2 \\
 & & \quad \langle \tau_3, C_3\rangle \leftarrow \mathcal{W}\,\Gamma\,e_3 \\
 & & \quad \tau \leftarrow \mathit{freshFrom}\ \upsilon \\
 & & \quad C_4 \leftarrow \left\{ \begin{array}{c} \alpha_1 \sqsubseteq_{\chi} \lceil\tau\rceil \\ \mathbf{T} \sqsubseteq_{\delta} \alpha_1 \vee \exists_{\chi}\ \alpha_1 \Rightarrow \tau_2 \leqslant_{\delta\chi} \tau \\ \mathbf{F} \sqsubseteq_{\delta} \alpha_1 \vee \exists_{\chi}\ \alpha_1 \Rightarrow \tau_3 \leqslant_{\delta\chi} \tau \end{array} \right\} \\
 & & \quad \mathbf{return}\ \langle \tau, C_1 \cup C_2 \cup C_3 \cup C_4\rangle \\
\mathcal{W}\,\Gamma\,(e_1 \oplus e_2) & = & \mathbf{do}\ \langle \alpha_1, C_1\rangle \leftarrow \mathcal{W}\,\Gamma\,e_1 \\
 & & \quad \langle \alpha_2, C_2\rangle \leftarrow \mathcal{W}\,\Gamma\,e_2 \\
 & & \quad \alpha \leftarrow \mathit{fresh} \\
 & & \quad C_3 \leftarrow \{\alpha_1 \sqsubseteq_{\chi} \alpha, \alpha_2 \sqsubseteq_{\chi} \alpha\} \\
 & & \quad C_4 \leftarrow \omega_{\oplus}(\alpha_1, \alpha_2, \alpha) \\
 & & \quad \mathbf{return}\ \langle \alpha, C_1 \cup C_2 \cup C_3 \cup C_4\rangle
\end{array}
$$

$$
\begin{array}{lll}
\mathcal{W}\,\Gamma\,(e_1, e_2) & = & \mathbf{do}\ \langle \tau_1, C_1\rangle \leftarrow \mathcal{W}\,\Gamma\,e_1 \\
 & & \quad \langle \tau_2, C_2\rangle \leftarrow \mathcal{W}\,\Gamma\,e_2 \\
 & & \quad \alpha \leftarrow \mathit{fresh} \\
 & & \quad \mathbf{return}\ \langle \tau_1 \times^{\alpha} \tau_2, C_1 \cup C_2\rangle \\
\mathcal{W}\,\Gamma\,(\mathbf{fst}\ e : \upsilon) & = & \mathbf{do}\ \langle \tau_1 \times^{\alpha} \tau_2, C_1\rangle \leftarrow \mathcal{W}\,\Gamma\,e \\
 & & \quad \tau \leftarrow \mathit{freshFrom}\ \upsilon \\
 & & \quad C_2 \leftarrow \{\tau_1 \leqslant_{\delta\chi} \tau, \alpha \sqsubseteq_{\chi} \lceil\tau\rceil\} \\
 & & \quad \mathbf{return}\ \langle \tau, C_1 \cup C_2\rangle \\
\mathcal{W}\,\Gamma\,(\mathbf{snd}\ e : \upsilon) & = & \mathbf{do}\ \langle \tau_1 \times^{\alpha} \tau_2, C_1\rangle \leftarrow \mathcal{W}\,\Gamma\,e \\
 & & \quad \tau \leftarrow \mathit{freshFrom}\ \upsilon \\
 & & \quad C_2 \leftarrow \{\tau_2 \leqslant_{\delta\chi} \tau, \alpha \sqsubseteq_{\chi} \lceil\tau\rceil\} \\
 & & \quad \mathbf{return}\ \langle \tau, C_1 \cup C_2\rangle \\
\mathcal{W}\,\Gamma\,([\,] : \upsilon) & = & \mathbf{do}\ \tau \leftarrow \mathit{freshFrom}\ \upsilon \\
 & & \quad \alpha \leftarrow \mathit{fresh} \\
 & & \quad \mathbf{return}\ \langle [\tau]^{\alpha}, \{\mathbf{N} \sqsubseteq_{\delta} \alpha\}\rangle \\
\mathcal{W}\,\Gamma\,(e_1 :: e_2) & = & \mathbf{do}\ \langle \tau_1, C_1\rangle \leftarrow \mathcal{W}\,\Gamma\,e_1 \\
 & & \quad \langle [\tau_2]^{\alpha_2}, C_2\rangle \leftarrow \mathcal{W}\,\Gamma\,e_2 \\
 & & \quad \tau \leftarrow \mathit{fresh} \\
 & & \quad \alpha \leftarrow \mathit{fresh} \\
 & & \quad C_3 \leftarrow \left\{ \begin{array}{c} \tau_1 \leqslant_{\delta\chi} \tau, \tau_2 \leqslant_{\delta\chi} \tau \\ \mathbf{C} \sqsubseteq_{\delta} \alpha, \alpha_2 \sqsubseteq_{\chi} \alpha \end{array} \right\} \\
 & & \quad \mathbf{return}\ \langle [\tau]^{\alpha}, C_1 \cup C_2 \cup C_3\rangle \\
\mathcal{W}\,\Gamma\,(\mathbf{case}\ e_1\ \mathbf{of}\ \{[\,] \mapsto e_2; x_1 :: x_2 \mapsto e_3\} : \upsilon) & & \\
 & = & \mathbf{do}\ \langle [\tau_1]^{\alpha_1}, C_1\rangle \leftarrow \mathcal{W}\,\Gamma\,e_1 \\
 & & \quad \langle \tau_2, C_2\rangle \leftarrow \mathcal{W}\,\Gamma\,e_2 \\
 & & \quad \beta \leftarrow \mathit{fresh} \\
 & & \quad \langle \tau_3, C_3\rangle \leftarrow \mathcal{W}\,(\Gamma, x_1 : \tau_1, x_2 : [\tau_1]^{\beta})\ e_3 \\
 & & \quad \tau \leftarrow \mathit{freshFrom}\ \upsilon \\
 & & \quad C_4 \leftarrow \left\{ \begin{array}{c} \alpha_1 \sqsubseteq_{\chi} \lceil\tau\rceil \\ \mathbf{N} \sqsubseteq_{\delta} \alpha_1 \vee \exists_{\chi}\ \alpha_1 \Rightarrow \tau_2 \leqslant_{\delta\chi} \tau \\ \mathbf{C} \sqsubseteq_{\delta} \alpha_1 \vee \exists_{\chi}\ \alpha_1 \Rightarrow \tau_3 \leqslant_{\delta\chi} \tau \\ \mathbf{N} \sqcup \mathbf{C} \sqsubseteq_{\delta} \beta, \alpha_1 \sqsubseteq_{\chi} \beta \end{array} \right\} \\
 & & \quad \mathbf{return}\ \langle \tau, C_1 \cup C_2 \cup C_3 \cup C_4\rangle
\end{array}
$$

Figure 3. Constraint inference algorithm

5.3 Knowing when to stop

So far we have omitted the algorithmic rule for **fix**. It performs a Kleene–Mycroft fixed-point iteration:

$$
\begin{array}{l}
\mathcal{W}\,\Gamma\,(\mathbf{fix}\,f : \upsilon.\ e) = \mathbf{do}\ \sigma \leftarrow \bot_{\upsilon} \\
\qquad \mathbf{repeat} \\
\qquad\quad \sigma' \leftarrow \sigma \\
\qquad\quad \langle \tau, C\rangle \leftarrow \mathcal{W}\,(\Gamma, f : \sigma)\ e \\
\qquad\quad \sigma \leftarrow \mathit{gen}\ \Gamma\ \tau\ C \\
\qquad \mathbf{until}\ \sigma \preceq \sigma' \\
\qquad \langle \tau_2, C_2\rangle \leftarrow \mathit{inst}\ \sigma \\
\qquad \mathbf{return}\ \langle \tau_2, C_2\rangle
\end{array}
$$

Problematically, it is not guaranteed that σ' will ever become a generic instance of σ. Dussart et al. (1995) show that this is the case for a simpler type of constraints (subtyping only) by noting that any variable that does not occur free in σ or Γ can be eliminated (e.g., the constraint set $\{\alpha_1 \sqsubseteq \alpha_2, \alpha_2 \sqsubseteq \alpha_3\}$ with α_2 not free in σ and Γ can be reduced to $\{\alpha_1 \sqsubseteq \alpha_3\}$). The result then follows from the fact that only a finite (quadratic) number of subtype constraints can be formed over the finite set of remaining variables.

However, we also have conditional constraints and variables occurring in their left-hand side cannot easily be eliminated. If we want to maintain soundness and termination of the analysis we will have to introduce an additional layer of approximation.

The constraint set

$$\{\Lambda_{\iota} \sqsubseteq_{\iota} \alpha \Rightarrow r, g_1 \Rightarrow \beta_1 \sqsubseteq_{\iota} \alpha, g_2 \Rightarrow \beta_2 \sqsubseteq_{\iota} \alpha\}$$

with α not free in σ or Γ, can—after having suitably extended the allowed syntax of constraints to allow for nested implications—be rewritten into:

$$\{\Lambda_{\iota} \sqsubseteq_{\iota} (g_1 \Rightarrow \beta_1 \sqcup g_2 \Rightarrow \beta_2) \Rightarrow r\}$$

As g_1 and g_2 may again contain variables that need to be eliminated, and we want to keep the size of the individual constraints bounded, we may eventually need to approximate constraints $g \Rightarrow \alpha$ by setting their guard g to **true**.

Alternatively, during the first k Kleene–Mycroft iterations we can neglect to eliminate variables that occur on the left-hand side of a constraint, building an additional finite set I of ineliminable variables. During the later iterations we intentionally introduce poisoning by instead of generating a fresh variable that will end up in the left-hand side of constraint, reusing a variable from I. The trick would then be in picking variables in such a way that would not disturb a fixed-point that may already have been reached after k iterations.

```
𝒮     : 𝒫 Constr → Subst
𝒮 C = do — initialization
          for each α ∈ fv C do
              θ_δ[α] ← ∅
              θ_χ[α] ← ∅
              D[α]  ← ∅
          — dependency analysis of constraints
          for each c ∈ C do
              for each α ∈ dv c do
                  D[tv c] ← D[α] ∪ {c}
          — fix-point iteration using worklist
          W ← C
          while W ≢ ∅ do
              {g ⇒ r} ∪ W ← W
              if ⟨θ_δ, θ_χ⟩ ⊨ g then
                  case r of
                      Λ_ι ⊑_ι α   ↦ if θ_ι[α] ≢ θ_ι[α] ⊔ Λ_ι then
                                         θ_ι[α] ← θ_ι[α] ⊔ Λ_ι
                                         W ← W ∪ D[α]
                      α₁ ⊑_ι α₂ ↦ if θ_ι[α₂] ≢ θ_ι[α₁] ⊔ θ_ι[α₂] then
                                         θ_ι[α₂] ← θ_ι[α₁] ⊔ θ_ι[α₂]
                                         W ← W ∪ D[α₂]
          return ⟨θ_δ, θ_χ⟩
dv    : Constr → 𝒫 Var
dv c = do V ← ∅
            case c of
                g ⇒ α₁ ⊑_ι α₂ ↦ V ← V ∪ {α₁}
            case c of
                Λ_ι ⊑_ι α ⇒ r   ↦ V ← V ∪ {α}
                ∃_ι α ⇒ r        ↦ V ← V ∪ {α}
                g₁ ∨ g₂ ⇒ r      ↦ V ← V ∪ dv g₁ ∪ dv g₂
            return V
tv    : Constr → Var
tv c  = do case c of
                r ⇒ Λ_ι ⊑_ι α   ↦ return α
                r ⇒ α₁ ⊑_ι α₂   ↦ return α₂
```

Figure 4. Constraint solver

6. Extensions

To handle the motivating examples from Section 2 a number of extensions to the language and analysis are necessary. (These are not supported by the prototype mentioned in Section 1.1, but are being implemented in an improved prototype.)

6.1 Polymorphism

Consider the polymorphic function *apply*:

$$\begin{aligned} &\mathit{apply} : \forall \alpha\beta.(\alpha \to \beta) \to \alpha \to \beta \\ &\mathit{apply}\ f\ x = f\ x \end{aligned}$$

As we cannot inspect an expression with a polymorphic type other than by the exceptions that it may raise when forced to weak head normal form, it is sufficient to treat them as any other base type.

Thus, the function *apply* will be given the following type by our analysis:

$$\forall \alpha\beta\gamma\delta\epsilon\zeta.\ \left(\alpha \xrightarrow{\delta} \beta\right) \xrightarrow{\epsilon} \gamma \xrightarrow{\zeta} \beta$$
$$\textbf{with } \{\gamma \leqslant_{\delta\chi} \alpha, \delta \sqsubseteq_{\chi} \beta, \exists_{\chi}\delta \Rightarrow \gamma \sqsubseteq_{\chi} \beta\}$$

Care needs to be taken when we instantiate the polymorphic variables of a polymorphic type in the underlying type system. When doing so we must also simultaneously update the corresponding polyvariant type used by the analysis.

For example, instantiating the polymorphic underlying type of *apply* with $[\alpha \mapsto \mathbb{Z} \times \mathbb{Z}, \beta \mapsto \mathbb{B} \times \mathbb{B}]$ will give rise to the instantiation $\left[\alpha \mapsto \eta \times^{\alpha} \theta, \beta \mapsto \iota \times^{\beta} \kappa, \gamma \mapsto \lambda \times^{\gamma} \mu\right]$ of the polyvariant type used in the analysis:

$$\forall \alpha\beta\gamma\delta\epsilon\zeta\eta\theta\iota\kappa\lambda\mu.\ \left(\eta \times^{\alpha} \theta \xrightarrow{\delta} \iota \times^{\beta} \kappa\right) \xrightarrow{\epsilon} \lambda \times^{\gamma} \mu \xrightarrow{\zeta} \iota \times^{\beta} \kappa$$
$$\textbf{with } \{\lambda \times^{\gamma} \mu \leqslant_{\delta\chi} \eta \times^{\alpha} \theta, \delta \sqsubseteq_{\chi} \beta, \exists_{\chi}\delta \Rightarrow \gamma \sqsubseteq_{\chi} \beta\}$$

In the general case we need to:

1. Generate an *almost* fresh linear type for each of the polyvariant variables positionally corresponding to a polymorphic variable that has been instantiated in the underlying type. This type is almost, but not entirely, fresh as we do need to preserve the original variable as the top-level annotation on the new fresh type. Thus, for a type substitution $\alpha \mapsto \tau$, we need $\lceil \tau \rceil = \alpha$.

   Note that multiple polyvariant type variables in the type inferred by the analysis might correspond to a single polymorphic type variable that is being instantiated in the underlying type. In the example given above both the polyvariant variables α and γ correspond positionally to the polymorphic type variable α.
2. We need to quantify over all the fresh variables introduced.
3. We need to apply the type substitution to the constraint set, but only to the structural constraints ($\leqslant_{\iota}$) and not the atomic constraints ($\sqsubseteq_{\iota}$), as the latter were generated solely to relate top-level annotations to each other.

Due to structural constraints being treated differently from atomic constraints, the analysis now must also be careful not to decompose the structural constraints into atomic constraints too early. While an implementation will already want to postpone this until right before sending all the gathered constraints to the constraint solver for performance reasons, this now also becomes important for correctness.

6.2 Algebraic data types

We admit that "non-strict higher-order functional languages with imprecise exception semantics" is something of a euphemism for Haskell. The biggest remaining piece of the puzzle to scaling this analysis to work on the full Haskell language is the support for pattern-matching on arbitrary user-defined algebraic data types.

While the construction and destruction rules we defined for lists—keeping track of the constructors that can occur at the head of the spine, assuming the constructors occurring in the tail can always be both a nil and a cons-constructor—work adequately for functions operating on nil-terminated lists, this approach will not give useful results when extended to other algebraic data types and applied to the desugaring example from Section 2.3, even if extended to keep track of the constructors that can occur in the first k positions of the spine. We critically rely on knowing which of the constructors can occur throughout the *whole* spine of the abstract syntax tree.

We would need to combine both approaches for an accurate analysis: we need to know which constructor can occur at the head of a data structure and which constructors can occur throughout the rest of the spine or, formulated differently, at the recursive positions of the data type. This approach is reminiscent of Catch's *multipatterns* (Mitchell and Runciman 2008).

The most straightforward implementation splits the data flow into two separate flows δ_1 and δ_2: one to track the constructors occurring at the head of a spine and one to keep track of the constructors occuring in the tail of the spine.

$$\iota, \kappa \quad ::= \quad \delta_1 \quad | \quad \delta_2 \quad | \quad \chi$$

While technically simple, the required modifications to the type system are notationally heavy as—unlike between the data flow and the exception flow—values can flow directly between δ_1 and δ_2 and it therefore is no longer sufficient to attach a single flow index ι to atomic constraints between variables:

$$r \quad ::= \quad \ldots \quad | \quad \alpha_1 \; {}_{\iota}{\sqsubseteq_{\kappa}} \; \alpha_2 \quad | \quad \ldots$$

The updated typing rules involving lists would read:

$$\frac{C \Vdash \mathbf{N} \sqsubseteq_{\delta_{12}} \alpha}{C; \Gamma \vdash [] : [\tau]^{\alpha}} \text{[T-NIL]}$$

$$\frac{\begin{array}{c} C; \Gamma \vdash e_1 : \tau_1 \quad C; \Gamma \vdash e_2 : [\tau_2]^{\alpha_2} \\ C \Vdash \tau_1 \leqslant_{\delta_{12}\chi} \tau \quad C \Vdash \tau_2 \leqslant_{\delta_{12}\chi} \tau \\ C \Vdash \mathbf{C} \sqsubseteq_{\delta_1} \alpha \quad C \Vdash \alpha_2 \; {}_{\chi}{\sqsubseteq_{\chi}} \; \alpha \quad C \Vdash \alpha_2 \; {}_{\delta_{12}}{\sqsubseteq_{\delta_2}} \; \alpha \end{array}}{C; \Gamma \vdash e_1 :: e_2 : [\tau]^{\alpha}} \text{[T-CONS]}$$

$$\frac{\begin{array}{c} C; \Gamma \vdash e_1 : [\tau_1]^{\alpha_1} \quad C; \Gamma \vdash e_2 : \tau_2 \\ C; \Gamma, x_1 : \tau_1, x_2 : [\tau_1]^{\beta} \vdash e_3 : \tau_3 \\ C \Vdash \mathbf{N} \sqsubseteq_{\delta_1} \alpha_1 \vee \exists_{\chi}\alpha_1 \Rightarrow \tau_2 \leqslant_{\delta_{12}\chi} \tau \\ C \Vdash \mathbf{C} \sqsubseteq_{\delta_1} \alpha_1 \vee \exists_{\chi}\alpha_1 \Rightarrow \tau_3 \leqslant_{\delta_{12}\chi} \tau \\ C \Vdash \alpha_1 \; {}_{\delta_2}{\sqsubseteq_{\delta_{12}}} \; \beta \quad C \Vdash \alpha_1 \; {}_{\chi}{\sqsubseteq_{\chi}} \; \beta \quad C \Vdash \alpha_1 \; {}_{\chi}{\sqsubseteq_{\chi}} \; \lceil \tau \rceil \end{array}}{C; \Gamma \vdash \mathbf{case}\; e_1 \;\mathbf{of}\; \{[] \mapsto e_2; x_1 :: x_2 \mapsto e_3\} : \tau} \text{[T-CASE]}$$

Some additional issues need to be resolved to generalize to arbitrary algebraic data types. In general polyvariance in the analysis should not be directly related to polymorphism in the underlying type system, so all fields in a data type can or should be polyvariantly parameterized, irrespective of whether the field is polymorphically parameterized in the underlying system (Wansbrough 2002). Since we are making use of subtyping, the variance (co-, contra-, in- or non-) of fields should be propagated to the polyvariant parameters.

6.3 Static contract checking

Our analysis can also be used for static contract checking. A contract can be desugared into a Findler–Felleisen wrapper (Findler and Felleisen 2002), raising a contract violation exception (together with some additional information on who to blame for the violation) when a contract violation is detected. The data flow-dependence of the analysis should be able to statically determine some contract can never be violated and prevent the contract violation exception from being propagated.

7. Related Work

Catch and Dialyzer The Catch case totality checker (Mitchell and Runciman 2008) employs a first-order backwards analysis, inferring preconditions on functions under which it is guaranteed that no exceptions will be raised or pattern-match failures will occur. To analyze Haskell programs, a specially crafted and incomplete defunctionalization step is required. In contrast, our forwards analysis is type-driven and will naturally work on higher-order programs. Furthermore, Catch assumes functions are strict in all their arguments, while our analysis tries to model the call-by-name semantics more accurately.

The Dialyzer discrepancy analyzer for Erlang (Lindahl and Sagonas 2006) works in a similar spirit to our analysis, except that it has a dual notion of soundness: Dialyzer will only warn about function applications that are guaranteed to generate an exception.

Exception analyses Several exception analyses have been described in the literature, primarily targeting the detection of uncaught exceptions in ML. The exception analysis in Yi (1994) is based on abstract interpretation. Guzmán and Suárez (1994) and Fahndrich et al. (1998) describe type-based exception analyses, neither are very precise. The row-based type system for exception analysis described in Leroy and Pessaux (2000) does containing a data-flow analysis component, although one that is specialized towards tracking value-carrying exceptions instead of value-dependent exceptions and thus employs a less precise unification method instead of subtyping. Glynn et al. (2002) developed the first exception analysis for non-strict languages. It is a type-based analysis using Boolean constraints and, although it does not take data flow into account, has a similar flavour to our system.

Conditional constraints The use of conditional constraints in program analysis can be traced back to Reynolds (1968). Heintze (1994) uses conditional constraints to model branches in **case**-expressions for a dead-code analysis. Constraint-based k-CFA analyses (Shivers 1988), although traditionally not formulated as a type system, can use conditional constraints to let the control flow depend on the data flow. Aiken et al. (1994) uses conditional constraints to formulate a soft-typing system for dynamic languages. Pottier (2000) developed an expressive constraint-based type system incorporating subtyping, conditional constraints and rows and applied it to several inference problems, including accurate pattern-matchings.

Refinement types (à la dependent types) and contract checking There has been a long line of work exploring various approaches of *refinement types* in the sense of using *dependent types* to specify contracts (also termed *contract types* or *refinement predicates*). A refinement type expressing all natural numbers greater than or equal to five would be written as:

$$\{x : \mathbb{N} \mid x \geqslant 5\}$$

Dependent ML (Xi 2007) purposely limits the expressiveness of contracts, so contract checking—although not inference—remains decidable. Xu et al. (2009) uses symbolic evaluation to check contracts on Haskell programs. Knowles and Flanagan (2010) developed a framework for *hybrid type checking*, where the checking of contracts that could not be proven to either always hold or be violated at compile-time are deferred until run-time. The work on *liquid types* by Rondon et al. (2008) attempts to automatically infer such refinements using the technique of predicate abstraction. MoCHi (Kobayashi et al. 2011) employs higher-order model checking. HALO (Vytiniotis et al. 2013) is a static contract checker that works by translating a Haskell program and its contracts into first-order logic, which can then be proven using an SMT solver.

Refinement types (à la intersection types) The refinement type system in Freeman and Pfenning (1991) attempts to assign more accurate, refined types to already well-typed ML programs using *union* and *intersection types* (Pierce 1991) with the detection of potential pattern-match failures and reduction of warnings about incomplete patterns as one of its goals. In addition to allowing the programmer to define algebraic data types, e.g.:

$$\mathbf{data}\ [\alpha] = [] \mid \alpha :: [\alpha]$$

it also allows the programmer to specify a finite number of "interesting" recursive types that refine those algebraic types:

$$\begin{array}{lcl} \mathbf{rectype}\ [\alpha]^{\mathbf{0}} & = & [] \\ \mathbf{rectype}\ [\alpha]^{\mathbf{1}} & = & \alpha :: [] \end{array}$$

The refinements $[\alpha]^0$ and $[\alpha]^1$ respectively select the subtypes of empty and singleton lists from the complete list type. From these recursive types, and using a type union operator, a finite type lattice can be computed automatically:

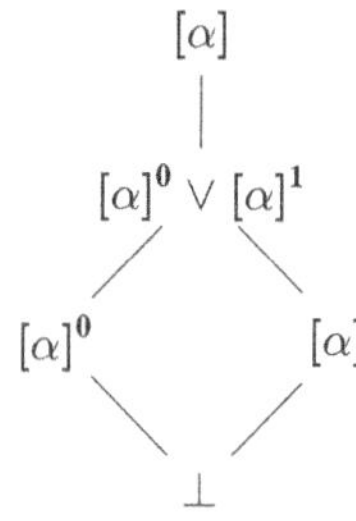

The constructors of the algebraic data type in question can then be more accurately typed in terms of intersection types over this lattice:

$$\begin{array}{ll} [] & : \forall\alpha.\,[\alpha]^0 \\ \_ :: \_ & : \forall\alpha.\alpha \to [\alpha]^0 \to [\alpha]^1 \\ & \quad\wedge\ \alpha \to [\alpha]^1 \to [\alpha] \\ & \quad\wedge\ \alpha \to [\alpha] \quad \to [\alpha] \end{array}$$

Finally, the **case**-construct, interpreted as a higher-order function and specialized to lists, can be given the intersection type:

$$\begin{array}{lllll} \forall\alpha\,\beta_1\,\beta_2. & [\alpha]^0 & \to \beta_1 \to (\alpha \to [\alpha] & \to \bot\,) \to \beta_1 \\ \wedge & [\alpha]^1 & \to \beta_1 \to (\alpha \to [\alpha]^0 & \to \beta_2) \to \beta_1 \vee \beta_2 \\ \wedge & [\alpha] & \to \beta_1 \to (\alpha \to [\alpha] & \to \beta_2) \to \beta_1 \vee \beta_2 \end{array}$$

Compared to our analysis the inference of intersection types would make this a *relational analysis*, while our use of subtyping and conditional constraints only define a *functional* relation between input and output variables. This would seem to imply our analysis is less precise. As the system by Freeman put some restrictions on recursive definitions of recursive types, it is unclear to us if *risers* could be given a suitable refinement type that precludes the occurrence of pattern-match failures. Additionally, the use of intersection types leads to a superexponential blowup of the size of types in the number of **rectype**-definitions.

Acknowledgments

We would like to thank Stefan Holdermans for his contributions in the earlier stages of this research, Matthijs Steen for implementing an improved version of the prototype, and Neil Mitchell for answering several questions related to Catch. Lastly we would like to thank the anonymous reviewers for providing valuable feedback and criticisms over various iterations of this paper.

References

M. Abadi, A. Banerjee, N. Heintze, and J. G. Riecke. A core calculus of dependency. POPL '99, pages 147–160, 1999.

A. Aiken, E. L. Wimmers, and T. K. Lakshman. Soft typing with conditional types. POPL '94, pages 163–173, 1994.

L. Augustsson. Compiling pattern matching. FPCA '85, pages 368–381, 1985.

D. Dussart, F. Henglein, and C. Mossin. Polymorphic recursion and subtype qualifications: Polymorphic binding-time analysis in polynomial time. SAS '95, pages 118–135, 1995.

M. Fahndrich, J. Foster, J. Cu, and A. Aiken. Tracking down exceptions in Standard ML programs. Technical report, 1998.

R. B. Findler and M. Felleisen. Contracts for higher-order functions. ICFP '02, pages 48–59, 2002.

T. Freeman and F. Pfenning. Refinement types for ML. PLDI '91, pages 268–277, 1991.

K. Glynn, P. J. Stuckey, M. Sulzmann, and H. Søndergaard. Exception analysis for non-strict languages. ICFP '02, pages 98–109, 2002.

J. C. Guzmán and A. Suárez. An extended type system for exceptions. ML '94, pages 127–135, 1994.

N. Heintze. Set-based analysis of ML programs. LFP '94, pages 306–317, 1994.

F. Henglein. Type inference with polymorphic recursion. *ACM Trans. Program. Lang. Syst.*, 15(2):253–289, Apr. 1993.

A. J. Kfoury, J. Tiuryn, and P. Urzyczyn. Type reconstruction in the presence of polymorphic recursion. *ACM Trans. Program. Lang. Syst.*, 15(2):290–311, Apr. 1993.

K. Knowles and C. Flanagan. Hybrid type checking. *ACM Trans. Program. Lang. Syst.*, 32(2):6:1–6:34, Feb. 2010.

N. Kobayashi, R. Sato, and H. Unno. Predicate abstraction and CEGAR for higher-order model checking. PLDI '11, pages 222–233, 2011.

X. Leroy and F. Pessaux. Type-based analysis of uncaught exceptions. *ACM Trans. Program. Lang. Syst.*, 22(2):340–377, Mar. 2000.

T. Lindahl and K. Sagonas. Practical type inference based on success typings. PPDP '06, pages 167–178, 2006.

L. Maranget. Compiling pattern matching to good decision trees. ML '08, pages 35–46, 2008.

N. Mitchell and C. Runciman. Not all patterns, but enough: an automatic verifier for partial but sufficient pattern matching. Haskell '08, pages 49–60, 2008.

H. R. Nielson, F. Nielson, and T. Amtoft. Polymorphic subtyping for effect analysis: The static semantics. In *Analysis and Verification of Multiple-Agent Languages*, volume 1192 of *LNCS*, pages 141–171. 1997.

S. Peyton Jones, A. Reid, F. Henderson, T. Hoare, and S. Marlow. A semantics for imprecise exceptions. PLDI '99, pages 25–36, 1999.

B. C. Pierce. Programming with intersection types, union types, and polymorphism. Technical report, 1991.

F. Pottier. A versatile constraint-based type inference system. *Nordic J. of Computing*, 7(4):312–347, Dec. 2000.

J. C. Reynolds. Automatic computation of data set definitions. In *IFIP Congress (1)*, pages 456–461, 1968.

M. Rittri. Dimension inference under polymorphic recursion. FPCA '95, pages 147–159, 1995.

P. M. Rondon, M. Kawaguci, and R. Jhala. Liquid types. PLDI '08, pages 159–169, 2008.

O. Shivers. Control flow analysis in Scheme. PLDI '88, pages 164–174, 1988.

J.-P. Talpin and P. Jouvelot. The type and effect discipline. *Inf. Comput.*, 111(2):245–296, June 1994.

M. Tofte and J.-P. Talpin. Implementation of the typed call-by-value λ-calculus using a stack of regions. POPL '94, pages 188–201, 1994.

N. Vazou, E. L. Seidel, R. Jhala, D. Vytiniotis, and S. Peyton-Jones. Refinement types for Haskell. ICFP '14, pages 269–282, 2014.

D. Vytiniotis, S. Peyton Jones, K. Claessen, and D. Rosén. HALO: Haskell to logic through denotational semantics. POPL '13, pages 431–442, 2013.

K. Wansbrough. Simple polymorphic usage analysis. Technical report, 2002.

H. Xi. Dependent ML: An approach to practical programming with dependent types. *J. Funct. Program.*, 17(2):215–286, Mar. 2007.

D. N. Xu, S. Peyton Jones, and K. Claessen. Static contract checking for Haskell. POPL '09, pages 41–52, 2009.

K. Yi. Compile-time detection of uncaught exceptions in Standard ML programs. In *Static Analysis*, volume 864 of *LNCS*, pages 238–254. 1994.

Polyvariant Cardinality Analysis for Non-strict Higher-order Functional Languages

Brief Announcement

Hidde Verstoep Jurriaan Hage

Department of Computing and Information Sciences
Utrecht University
hiddeverstoep@gmail.com,J.Hage@uu.nl

Abstract

In this brief announcement we outline work we have done on defining a polyvariant cardinality analysis for a non-strict higher-order language equipped with user defined datatypes and explicit strictness that includes sharing analysis, absence analysis, strictness analysis and uniqueness typing as a special case. It aims to be the basis of an analysis framework in a compiler for a Haskell-like language, that does not have access to an aggressive inliner such as the one present in GHC.

Categories and Subject Descriptors D.3 [*Software*]: Applicative (functional) languages; F.3.2 [*Logics and Meanings of Programs*]: Semantics of Programming Languages—Program analysis; D.3.3 [*Programming Languages*]: Language Constructs and Features—Polymorphism

General Terms Languages, Theory, Verification

Keywords type-based program analysis, cardinality analysis, uniqueness typing, polyvariance, absence analysis, sharing analysis, usage analysis

1. Introduction

In this paper we motivate and shortly describe a type system for cardinality analysis for a non-strict, higher-order functional language: an analysis that counts how often a value may be used. Cardinality analysis is an analysis that generalizes uniqueness typing (unique values are never used more than once), sharing analysis (which values are used at most once), strictness analysis (which values are used at least once) and absence analysis (which values are not needed at all). In combining multiple analyses, our work has a similarity in spirit with work by Hage et al. [6] and Sergey et al. [10].

In the former, a usage analysis is defined, that can be instantiated to uniqueness typing and sharing analysis, making precise in which way the two differ. In this case, genericity is restricted to the *specification* of the analysis: if you want to compute both uniqueness and sharing information, two different instantiations of the generic analysis have to be run in separation. The analysis we consider in this paper is run once, and afterwards strictness, sharing and absence information can be read off (uniqueness information can also be read off, but this is more subtle). Moreover, [6] does not include absence and strictness analysis. Absence information in particular can be useful to improve also the precision for uniqueness typing and sharing analysis. Consider the following function:

$$\begin{aligned}g\ xs = {}&\mathbf{let}\\ &\quad len = length\ xs\\ &\mathbf{in}\\ &\quad map\ (\lambda x \to x + len)\ xs\end{aligned}$$

To discover that the elements xs are accessed exactly once, we need to determine that $length$ uses the spine of xs once, but does not access the elements of xs at all. Having derived for map that it uses the spine and elements of xs exactly once, we can then derive a type for g that specifies that the spine of its first argument xs is used more than once, but elements of the list are used only once.

Sergey et al. [10] integrates sharing analysis, strictness analysis and absence analysis for a higher-order language in a single analysis. Their work is tailored to the back-end of GHC, and is more akin to abstract interpretation than a type and effect system. Their analysis is not polyvariant. The rationale for a monovariant analysis is that due to GHC's aggressive inliner, not much is to be gained from complicating the analysis by introducing polyvariance. Our motivation is to help those without access to such an inliner achieve good precision; the Utrecht Haskell Compiler (UHC) [3] and Mozilla's Rust language (`www.rust-lang.org`) are typical examples.

It makes sense to want to combine analyses into a single specification, since specifications, implementations, and meta-theory can be shared. On the other hand, since our analysis is polyvariant, and includes subtyping, running it does not come cheap. But since we need to run the analysis only once to obtain the results of what otherwise would be four different analyses that are run in separation, we may hope to recoup some of this additional cost, and gain some precision as well, as our example above shows.

In the remainder of the paper we sketch the ideas behind our analysis, leaving a description of the exact details of the analysis and the solver, and an empirical evaluation of the cost and benefits of the analysis within the UHC compiler for later. For more details, the interested reader is directed to [11]. A prototype implementation of the algorithm that implements the analysis (written in Haskell), and a partial proof of the soundness of the full type system can be downloaded from `http://www.cs.uu.nl/wiki/Hage/Downloads`.

PEPM '15, January 13-14 2015, Mumbai, India.
Copyright © 2015 ACM 978-1-4503-3297-2/15/01... $15.00.
http://dx.doi.org/10.1145/2678015.2682536

2. Approach

Sharing analysis [4, 6, 9] is an analysis that determines whether or not an expression is used at most once. Consider the expression $(\lambda x \to x + x)\ (1+1)$. In a lazy setting, the value of the expression $(1 + 1)$ is needed twice, but only evaluated once. After it has been evaluated, the thunk that represents the expression is "updated", overwriting the thunk by the computed value, 2, for immediate access later on. But in $(\lambda x \to x)\ (1 + 1)$ the value of $(1 + 1)$ is only used once, and the thunk update could have been omitted. To avoid the update we need to find out which values are used at most once.

In type and effect systems sharing analysis is often formulated using the lattice $1 \sqsubset \omega$. The annotation 1 says that the expression is guaranteed to be used at most once, while ω says that an expression can be used more than once. A subeffecting rule will allow the value of an expression $\mathbf{e}$ for which we have inferred annotation ω to be considered as a value that is used at most once:

$$\frac{\vdash \mathbf{e} : \tau^{\varphi'} \qquad \vdash \varphi \sqsubseteq \varphi'}{\vdash \mathbf{e} : \tau^{\varphi}}$$

The thunk created for $\mathbf{e}$ may then superfluously perform an update, but that is not unsound (it won't crash the program).

Uniqueness Uniqueness analysis [1, 2, 6] determines whether values are used at most once, or more than once, just like sharing analysis. The purpose of uniqueness typing is however quite different.

Consider the function: $\mathit{writeFile} :: \mathit{String} \to \mathit{File} \to \mathit{File}$ that writes data to a file, thereby exhibiting a side effect. Then

$$\lambda f \to (\mathit{writeFile}\ \texttt{"O"}\ f, \mathit{writeFile}\ \texttt{"K"}\ f) \qquad (1)$$

can be evaluated in two ways when applied: the file may contain either "OK" or "KO", depending on the order in which the writeFile functions are evaluated; it is obviously not a pure function.

Uniqueness typing provides us with a safe way to use functions with side effects. With uniqueness analysis, we can give *writeFile* a type such that the uniqueness type system guarantees that it has access to an unduplicated *File*. Under that regime, expression (1) would be rejected. Uniqueness analysis can automatically annotate expressions with 1 and ω and will reject a program when this is not possible. A 1 annotation indicates that an expression must be unique. A ω annotation indicates that an expression is not necessarily unique. The subeffecting rule that should then be used is:

$$\frac{\vdash \mathbf{e} : \tau^{\varphi'} \qquad \vdash \varphi' \sqsubseteq \varphi}{\vdash \mathbf{e} : \tau^{\varphi}}$$

Note that the condition on the annotation is swapped with respect to the rule for sharing analysis. The result is that an expression which is marked unique can still be used as a parameter to a function which accepts non-unique parameters.

A valid annotated type for the *writeFile* function:

$$\mathit{writeFile} :: (\mathit{String}^{\omega} \to (\mathit{File}^{1} \to \mathit{File}^{1})^{\omega})^{\omega}$$

The ω annotations mean that the first parameter, the entire function and its partial applications may be shared. However, the second parameter, a *File*, must be unique, and the resulting *File*, may also not be duplicated. That is clearly not the case in expression (1). A valid expression, in which the file is used uniquely, would be:

$$\lambda f \to \mathit{writeFile}\ \texttt{"2"}\ (\mathit{writeFile}\ \texttt{"1"}\ f)$$

Uniqueness analysis is tricky. Consider the function

$$\mathit{writeFile}' :: (\mathit{File}^{1} \to (\mathit{String}^{\omega} \to \mathit{File}^{1})^{1})^{\omega}$$

which is like *writeFile* but with its parameters swapped. A consequence is that the partial application may no longer be shared. If allowed, the following expression (2) would become typeable, but its behavior would be like that of expression (1).

$$\lambda f \to (\lambda w \to (w\ \texttt{"1"}, w\ \texttt{"2"}))\ (\mathit{writeFile}'\ f) \qquad (2)$$

So, any partial application that has access to unique values must also be unique. Although this might seem to solve the problem, when the type and effect system includes subeffecting it is possible to change the annotation on $(\mathit{writeFile}'\ f)$ from 1 to ω. This makes expression (2) type correct, something that we do not want.

Strictness Strictness analysis [7, 12] is an analysis that determines whether expressions are used at least once. If a parameter to a function is guaranteed to be used at least once, its value could be calculated immediately instead of passing an unevaluated thunk. This leads to performance benefits: passing a value on the stack is more efficient than creating a thunk – which might even refer to more thunks – on the heap.

A possible lattice to use with strictness is: $S \sqsubset L$. The meaning of the elements is: (i) an expression is used at least once, or evaluated strictly, for S; and (ii) an expression is used any number of times, or possibly evaluated lazily, for L. Even if a function has a parameter annotated S, we want to accept an argument annotated L. The subeffecting rule that that implies is exactly the same as the one for sharing analysis.

Absence Absence analysis is an analysis that determines whether expressions are used or not. It is similar to dead or unreachable code elimination. For the standard Haskell function $\mathit{const}\ x\ y = x$, it is easy to see that its second argument is not used.

In human-written code, there are typically not many functions that do not use their arguments. There are however many frequently used functions that use only a part of their argument, e.g., *length*, *fst* and *snd*. So absence analysis does make sense, particularly when (user defined) datatypes are present. Other code that might benefit from this analysis is computer generated code. Computer generated code is often less "smart" and might contain a lot of dead code this analysis can detect.

2.1 Similarities

The questions that these analyses try to answer are very similar, and involve counting in some way how often values are used: (i) sharing and uniqueness analysis ask which values are used at most once, (ii) strictness analysis asks which value is used at least once, and (iii) absence analysis asks which values are not used at all.

The analyses differ only in the way subeffecting is achieved, and the difficulties that arise when uniqueness is considered in the presence of partial application. Also, uniqueness is different from all the other analyses in that it can lead to the rejection of programs; the other analyses provide information about the program for the purpose of optimization.

Our aim in the following, where we make our ideas more precise, is to compute an approximation of how often a value is used, or demanded. Essentially, the abstract values in our domain are sets over $0, 1$ and ∞. In that case, a set like $\{0\}$, describes a value that is not used, and $\{0, 1\}$ a value that can be used zero times, or once. Because language constructs differ in the way they place demands on their subexpressions, we introduce a number of abstract operators to cover the variety of ways in which they behave. For example, if in application $f\ \mathbf{e}$, both f and $\mathbf{e}$ use a given value, then $f\ \mathbf{e}$ uses the value at least twice, adding them together as it were. But if the uses of the value are found in the then-part and the else-part of a single conditional, then we should not add them together, but combine them in some other way. We shall also need additional operators to deal with partial application, and with conditional use.

3. The analysis lattice

In annotated type systems, types have annotations attached to them. The (concrete) annotations in our annotated type system are

$$\begin{array}{rcl} \varpi & ::= & \emptyset \mid \{\pi\} \mid \varpi_1 \cup \varpi_2 \\ \pi & ::= & 0 \mid 1 \mid \infty \end{array}$$

In other words, annotations are (isomorphic to) the powerset of $\{0, 1, \infty\}$. In the following we write $\bot$ for $\emptyset$, the bottom of the lattice, $\mathbf{0}$ for $\{0\}$, $\mathbf{1}$ for $\{1\}$, ω for $\{\infty\}$ and $\top$ for $\{0, 1, \infty\}$.

Since we aim for a polyvariant analysis, we add annotation variables to the mix:

$$\varphi \; ::= \; \beta \mid \varpi$$

For clarity, we shall distinguish between *use annotation* ν that tells us how often a value is used, and *demand annotations* δ that tell us how often a variable is demanded.

$$\begin{array}{rcl} \nu & ::= & \varphi \\ \delta & ::= & \varphi \end{array}$$

Note that even though the definitions are the same they describe different things ("use" and "demand" respectively) and are used differently in the type system.

A *type* can be a type variable α, a fully applied datatype, or a function type; as usual, we write $\overline{\varphi_l}$ for a sequence of l φs:

$$\begin{array}{rcl} \tau & ::= & \alpha \mid T\,\overline{\varphi_l}\,\overline{\tau_k} \mid \rho_\tau \to \eta_\tau \\ \eta_\mu & ::= & \mu^\nu \;\; \text{where } \mu \in \{\tau, \sigma\} \\ \rho_\mu & ::= & \mu^{\nu,\delta} \;\; \text{where } \mu \in \{\tau, \sigma\} \end{array}$$

Definitions η_μ and ρ_μ are indexed by μ, which can be either the symbol τ, or (defined below) the symbol σ. Since a function produces a value, we use η_τ to attach a use annotation to its result type. Because the argument is available to the body of the function as a variable we attach both use and demand annotations to the argument, and use ρ_τ for the argument. The slogan: η for use only, ρ for use and demand both. Datatypes will be explained in more detail later on.

With types now defined, we can provide the usual definitions for annotation and type polymorphic type schemes σ, and environments Γ, in which we store not only the type scheme associated with each variable, but also its use and demand. Constraints C will be defined later on.

$$\begin{array}{rcl} \sigma & ::= & \gamma \mid \forall \overline{v} \,.\, C \Rightarrow \tau \\ v & ::= & \alpha \mid \beta \\ \Gamma & ::= & \epsilon \mid \Gamma, x : \rho_\sigma \end{array}$$

We now define the explicitly annotated term language for our analysis. Before analysis, annotations are still unavailable; we use annotation variables to make terms valid. Terms consist of (in that order) variables, functions, applications, mutually recursive lets, *seq* $\mathbf{e_1}$ $\mathbf{e_2}$ expressions to force evaluation of $\mathbf{e_1}$ before returning the value of $\mathbf{e_2}$, constructor expressions, and case expressions:

$$\begin{array}{rcl} \mathbf{e} & ::= & x \mid \lambda^\nu\, x \to \mathbf{e} \mid \mathbf{e}\; x \\ & \mid & \mathbf{let}\; \overline{x_i =^{\nu,\delta} \mathbf{e_i}}\; \mathbf{in}\; \mathbf{e} \mid \mathit{seq}\; \mathbf{e_1}\; \mathbf{e_2} \\ & \mid & K^\nu\, \overline{x_i} \mid \mathbf{case}\; \mathbf{e}\; \mathbf{of}\; \overline{K_i\, \overline{x_{ij}} \to \mathbf{e_i}} \end{array}$$

To simplify analysis, and without loss of generality, function and constructor application can only take variables as arguments; constructors must always be fully applied.

Constraints

Many type systems encode operations on annotations in the type rules. Since our annotations are quite complex, we first define some operations on annotations using annotation operators and introduce some additional notation. This will simplify the type rules significantly.

We start out by motivating the (four) operations we shall need:

1. To perform the addition of two numbers $\mathbf{e_1} + \mathbf{e_2}$, it is clear that both expressions are needed to calculate a result. Suppose a variable x occurs in both $\mathbf{e_1}$ and $\mathbf{e_2}$, then we need a way to combine the uses of x in both branches to find the use of x in the expression $\mathbf{e_1} + \mathbf{e_2}$. The way the uses are combined must reflect that *both* expressions are used.
2. Given the expression **if** $\mathbf{e}$ **then** $\mathbf{e_1}$ **else** $\mathbf{e_2}$ it is clear that either $\mathbf{e_1}$ or $\mathbf{e_2}$ will be evaluated depending on $\mathbf{e}$, but certainly not both. We need a way to combine the uses associated with variables in the expressions $\mathbf{e_1}$ and $\mathbf{e_2}$ that reflects that only one of the branches will be evaluated.
3. A function $\lambda x \to \mathbf{e}$ can be applied multiple times. However, all variables occurring in $\mathbf{e}$ that are defined outside of the function are used repeatedly for every application of the function. It might even be the case that one of these variables is never used at all if the function is never applied. So, we need to be able to express repeated use.
4. Consider the expression **let** $b = 0; a = b$ **in** $f\ a$. The value of b is only used if a is used, and a is used only if f uses its argument. So, we need to be able to express conditional use.

Now that we have a basic understanding of the operations we will be needing, we can define them as operators (Figure 1). The operator $\oplus$ expresses the combination of branches that are both used (case 1). The operator $\sqcup$ expresses the combination of branches of which only one is used (case 2). The operator $\cdot$ expresses repeated use (case 3). The formula that defines the operator can be explained as follows: for every element m in ϖ_1, for all combinations of m elements from ϖ_2, take the sum of the m elements. For example, suppose a function (which is applied twice) uses a value at most once, then the value is used: $\{\omega\} \cdot \{\mathbf{0}, \mathbf{1}\} = \{\mathbf{0}+\mathbf{0}, \mathbf{0}+\mathbf{1}, \mathbf{1}+\mathbf{0}, \mathbf{1}+\mathbf{1}\} = \{\mathbf{0}, \mathbf{1}, \omega\}$. This is as it should be: neither call may use the value ($\mathbf{0}$), one call uses it, but the other does not ($\mathbf{1}$), or both may use it (ω). The operator $\triangleright$ expresses conditional use (case 4). The result of this operator is equal to ϖ_2 unless ϖ_1 includes 0.

$$\begin{array}{rcl} \varpi_1 \oplus \varpi_2 & ::= & \{m + n \mid m \in \varpi_1, n \in \varpi_2\} \\ \varpi_1 \sqcup \varpi_2 & ::= & \varpi_1 \cup \varpi_2 \\ \varpi_1 \cdot \varpi_2 & ::= & \{\sum_{i=1}^{min(m,2)} n_i \mid m \in \varpi_1, \forall i. n_i \in \varpi_2\} \\ \varpi_1 \triangleright \varpi_2 & ::= & \bigcup_{m \in \varpi_1} (m \equiv 0\, ?\, \mathbf{0} : \varpi_2) \end{array}$$

Figure 1. Annotation value operators

Defining the operators for annotation values ϖ is relatively easy since they do not include variables. However, we want to lift the operators to annotations, types, type schemes and environments and these can include annotation variables. An operator requires two concrete annotation values to directly calculate a result. Since we might encounter annotation variables we cannot assume this is always the case. The usual solution, and one we also use, is to employ constraints to keep track of the relations between annotations (whether they are variables or values).

Figure 3 contains an overview of all different kinds of constraints. A constraint C can be an equality, $\oplus$, $\sqcup$, $\cdot$ or $\triangleright$ constraint for annotations, types and type schemes. We also need instantiation and generalization constraints to deal with polyvariance and polymorphism. We forego the definitions that rephrase our operators in terms of constraints, for annotations, types, type schemes, and type environments.

$$\frac{\Gamma_1 \vdash_{\sqsubseteq} \mathbf{e} : ({\eta_2}^{\delta_2} \to \eta_3)^{\mathbf{1}} \leadsto C_1 \qquad x : {\eta_4}^{\mathbf{1}} \vdash_{\diamond} x : \eta_2 \leadsto C_2 \qquad \Gamma_1 \oplus x : {\eta_4}^{\delta_2} = \Gamma_2 \leadsto C_3}{\Gamma_2 \vdash \mathbf{e}\ x : \eta_3 \leadsto C_1 \cup C_2 \cup C_3}\ \textsc{App}$$

$$\frac{\begin{array}{c}\overline{\mathbf{data}\ T\ \overline{u_l}\ \overline{\alpha_k} = \overline{K_i\ \overline{\rho_{ij}}} \qquad {\tau_{ij}}^{\nu_{ij},\delta_{ij}} = \rho_{ij}\ [\overline{\varphi_l}/\overline{u_l}, \overline{\tau_k}/\overline{\alpha_k}]} \\ \Gamma_0 \vdash_{\sqsubseteq} \mathbf{e} : (T\ \overline{\varphi_l}\ \overline{\tau_k})^{\mathbf{1}} \leadsto C_1 \qquad \Gamma_i, x_{ij} : (\forall \emptyset\,.\ \emptyset \Rightarrow \tau_{ij})^{\nu_{ij},\delta_{ij}} \vdash \mathbf{e_i} : \eta \leadsto C_2 \qquad \Gamma_0 \oplus (\bigsqcup_i \Gamma_i) = \Gamma \leadsto C_3\end{array}}{\Gamma \vdash \mathbf{case}\ \mathbf{e}\ \mathbf{of}\ \overline{K_i\ \overline{x_{ij}} \to \mathbf{e_i}} : \eta \leadsto C_1 \cup C_2 \cup C_3}\ \textsc{Case}$$

Figure 2. A few rules of the static semantics

$$\begin{array}{rcl} C & ::= & \emptyset \mid \varphi_1 \equiv \varphi_2 \mid \varphi \equiv \varphi_1 \oplus \varphi_2 \mid \varphi \equiv \varphi_1 \sqcup \varphi_2 \\ & \mid & \varphi \equiv \varphi_1 \cdot \varphi_2 \mid \varphi \equiv \varphi_1 \rhd \varphi_2 \mid \tau_1 \equiv \tau_2 \\ & \mid & \tau \equiv \tau_1 \oplus \tau_2 \mid \tau \equiv \tau_1 \sqcup \tau_2 \mid \tau \equiv \varphi_1 \cdot \tau_2 \\ & \mid & \tau \equiv \varphi_1 \rhd \tau_2 \mid \sigma_1 \equiv \sigma_2 \mid \sigma \equiv \sigma_1 \oplus \sigma_2 \\ & \mid & \sigma \equiv \sigma_1 \sqcup \sigma_2 \mid \sigma \equiv \varphi_1 \cdot \sigma_2 \mid \sigma \equiv \varphi_1 \rhd \sigma_2 \\ & \mid & \mathit{inst}\ (\sigma) \equiv \tau \mid \mathit{gen}\ (\rho_\tau, C, \Gamma) \equiv \rho_\sigma \mid C_1 \cup C_2 \end{array}$$

Figure 3. Constraints

Usually, algebraic datatypes are defined like so:

$$\mathbf{data}\ T\ \overline{\alpha} = \overline{K_i\ \overline{\tau_{ij}}},$$

where T is the name of the datatype, $\overline{\alpha}$ is a sequence of mutually distinct type parameters, $\overline{K_i}$ are the constructors and each τ_{ij} refers to the unannotated type of a field of a constructor. To be able to express for the example in the introduction that the spine of the list can be used at most once, while the elements are not used at all, we have to annotate the elements and the spine of the list in separation. This leads to reserving extra space for annotation variables in datatype definitions: $\mathbf{data}\ T\ \overline{\beta}\ \overline{\alpha} = \overline{K_i\ \overline{\tau_{ij}}}$ The problem of deciding what to annotate and to which extent is a hard one; [12] provides a detailed account.

4. A fragment of the type system

In this section we discuss a few of the type rules that make up our type system. The main judgement is $\Gamma \vdash \mathbf{e} : \eta_\tau \leadsto C$, under environment Γ, $\mathbf{e}$ has demand η_τ, subjected to the constraints that remain in C.

The remaining rules, and the constraint solver to solve the generated constraints can be found in [11].

The APP-rule ensures the function and argument are type correct. The function is used exactly once due to the application. However, since the function may be shared it is important to apply subeffecting here. Since the use should include one, we fix the way of subeffecting to $\sqsubseteq$. When typing the argument, which is a variable by definition, the variable will be found to be demanded exactly once. However, the function specifies (using δ_2) how often it demands an argument, so we set the demand to δ_2 when creating the result environment. This is also the only place where it is necessary to use the analysis dependent subeffecting parameter $\diamond$.

The CASE-rule starts with creating a fresh instance of the annotated datatype, similar to the CON-rule. We make sure to type the expression we match on with use $\mathbf{1}$ and subeffecting set to $\sqsubseteq$, similar to the function expression in the APP-rule. The result type is the same as that of each of the case-arms. The result environment is built by adding Γ_0 to the combined environment of all the arms, Γ_i. Since only one of the case-arms will be executed combining is done using the $\sqcup$ operator.

5. Conclusion and Future Work

We have sketched a polyvariant cardinality analysis for a non-strict higher-order functional language, that includes as a special case absence analysis, sharing analysis, strictness analysis and uniqueness typing.

In the short term, we shall build the analysis into the UHC compiler so that we can experiment with its effectiveness [3]. This also paves the way for introducing the heap-recycling directives of [5] for writing in-place algorithms in a pure setting; these heavily depend on a uniqueness type system. Other tasks for the future are to complete our soundness proof in Coq, and to experiment with formulation that supports higher-ranked polyvariance [8].

References

[1] E. Barendsen, S. Smetsers, et al. Uniqueness typing for functional languages with graph rewriting semantics. *Mathematical Structures in Computer Science*, 6(6):579–612, 1996.

[2] E. De Vries, R. Plasmeijer, and D. Abrahamson. Uniqueness typing simplified. *Implementation and Application of Functional Languages*, pages 201–218, 2008.

[3] A. Dijkstra, J. Fokker, and S. D. Swierstra. The architecture of the Utrecht Haskell Compiler. In *Haskell '09: Proceedings of the 2nd ACM SIGPLAN Symposium on Haskell*, pages 93–104, New York, NY, USA, 2009. ACM.

[4] J. Gustavsson. *A type based sharing analysis for update avoidance and optimisation*, volume 34. ACM, 1998.

[5] J. Hage and S. Holdermans. Heap recycling for lazy languages. In *Proceedings of the 2008 ACM SIGPLAN symposium on Partial evaluation and semantics-based program manipulation*, pages 189–197. ACM, 2008.

[6] J. Hage, S. Holdermans, and A. Middelkoop. A generic usage analysis with subeffect qualifiers. In *ACM SIGPLAN Notices*, volume 42, pages 235–246. ACM, 2007.

[7] S. Holdermans and J. Hage. Making stricterness more relevant. In *Proceedings of the 2010 ACM SIGPLAN workshop on Partial evaluation and program manipulation*, pages 121–130. ACM, 2010.

[8] S. Holdermans and J. Hage. Polyvariant flow analysis with higher-ranked polymorphic types and higher-order effect operators. In *Proceedings of the 15th ACM SIGPLAN 2010 International Conference on Functional Programming (ICFP '10)*, pages 63–74. ACM Press, 2010.

[9] J. Launchbury, A. Gill, J. Hughes, S. Marlow, S. Jones, and P. Wadler. Avoiding unnecessary updates. *Functional Programming, Glasgow*, pages 144–153, 1992.

[10] I. Sergey, D. Vytiniotis, and S. Peyton Jones. Modular, higher-order cardinality analysis in theory and practice. In *Proceedings of the 41st ACM SIGPLAN-SIGACT Symposium on Principles of Programming Languages*, POPL '14, pages 335–347, New York, NY, USA, 2014. ACM.

[11] H. Verstoep. Counting analyses, 2013. MSc thesis, `http://www.cs.uu.nl/wiki/Hage/CountingAnalyses`.

[12] K. Wansbrough. *Simple polymorphic usage analysis*. PhD thesis, University of Cambridge, 2002.

Author Index

www.ingramcontent.com/pod-product-compliance
Lightning Source LLC
LaVergne TN
LVHW060143070326
832902LV00018B/2919
* 9 7 8 1 4 5 0 3 3 2 9 7 2 *